P9-ECU-162

Kurt Weill in Europe

Studies in Musicology, No. 14

Other Titles in This Series

Kurt Weill in Europe

by
Kim H. Kowalke

umi
RESEARCH PRESS

Produced and distributed by
University Microfilms International
Ann Arbor, Michigan 48106

Library of Congress Cataloging in Publication Data

Kowalke, Kim H   1948-
  Kurt Weill in Europe.

   (Studies in musicology ; no. 14)
   "Catalogue of Weill's compositions, 1900-1935": p.
   Bibliography: p.
   Includes indexes.
   1. Weill, Kurt, 1900-1950. Works.   I. Title. II. Series.

ML410.W395K7   780'.92'4   79-23221
ISBN 0-8357-1076-9

CONTENTS

ACKNOWLEDGMENTS

Miss Lotte Lenya, the foremost interpreter of her late husband's works and executrix of the Weill-Estate, answered many questions and graciously expedited my research by granting access to unpublished material. I am also most indebted to David Drew, the former general administrator of the European office of the Weill-Estate, for his efforts on my behalf. He encouraged my entry into the field, guided my inquiry, and answered numerous documentary questions. His editions and essays provide the foundation for any study of Weill's music. Other associates of Weill—Lys Symonette, Maurice Abravanel, Ernst Wolff, Eric Simon, Lehman Engel—provided valuable personal insights and information. Mr. John G. Peck, Jr. permitted me to use unpublished manuscripts in the possession of the library of Westminster Choir College, Princeton, New Jersey.

The criticism, encouragement, and advice of Professor Allen Forte and Professor Robert Bailey contributed immeasurably to the accomplishment of this study. I am also grateful to Professors William Waite, Maury Yeston, and Craig Wright for their careful readings of the dissertation. Bradley Smith's editorial assistance in preparing the original dissertation for this publication is much appreciated. My research was supported by grants from Yale University, the Martha Baird Rockefeller Fund for Music, the Mrs. Giles Whiting Foundation, and Occidental College.

Finally, I am thankful for the personal and financial support of my wife, Elizabeth, my parents, and my family, to whom this book is dedicated with love and appreciation.

Kim H. Kowalke
Los Angeles, California
August 1979

INTRODUCTION

INTRODUCTION

Kurt Weill . . .

A composer of unmistakable originality and irrepressible genius. One of the few essential forces in the music of this century.

        — Hans Redlich —

His is the only music in the world in which I can find no quality at all.

        — Arnold Schoenberg —

Everything he wrote became in one way or another historic. He was probably the most original single workman in the whole musical theatre, internationally considered, during the last quarter century.

        — Virgil Thomson —

Kurt Weill wrote skillfully but he wrote in a way that appealed to the most uninformed tastes. His music is vulgar . . .

        — Paul Collaer —

Broadway's greatest composer . . .

        — Clive Barnes —

A phony Richard Strauss . . .

        — Bertolt Brecht —

Just as there is a Debussy-style, a Stravinsky-style, a Schoenberg-style, one can also rightfully speak of a Weill-style.

        — Herbert Fleischer —

We need say no more about the nature and aims of operatic Jewry, because the energy with which . . . the smutty cabaret talent of a Weill was made out to be strong enough to create a style is still fresh enough in everyone's memory.

        — Walter Abendroth —[1]

The preceding collection of conflicting evaluations of a composer whose career represents an almost unprecedented dichotomy itself and whose music claims as its most distinguishing stylistic feature a paradoxical duality is illustrative of the diverse critical reactions to Kurt Weill's output. Cited by many contemporaries in Germany as the outstanding composer for the theater of his generation, Weill won similar acclaim from an entirely different audience in an alien cultural milieu following his emigration to the United States in 1935. The primary thread linking the two distinct periods of his career was a lifelong commitment to the theater: "My entire life has been devoted to the theater, and I have dedicated it to combining the theater of our time with a higher form of music toward the formation of a permanent musical theater."[2] But even with this connection, it is a perplexing task to reconcile the esoteric self-consciously "difficult" compositions of the Busoni-disciple with the gold-record "September Song" of the popular American composer. Today, more than twenty-five years after his death, Weill is still not easily assigned a defensible yet compensatory position in the history of music. Donald J. Grout evidently considered him superfluous to *A History of Western Music,* as the composer's name does not appear in the text of the second edition.[3] While that omission might be excused by the scope and nature of the book, when Arthur Cohn in *Twentieth-Century Music in Western Europe*[4] deems Arthur Bliss, André Jolivet, Ernst Toch, and Joaquín Turina worthy of discussion—but not Weill—one is prompted to investigate the reasons for the critical neglect of Weill's music.

After Weill's emigration to the United States in 1935, it soon became apparent to him that he could not expect an American audience to understand or accept his earlier works. Therefore, he did not encourage (and often, in fact, discouraged) attempts to perform his German works in the United States. Because Hitler's ban against performance of Weill's music in Germany was gradually expanded to include most of the continent (in direct proportion to the success of Nazi armies), until the mid-1950s critics and scholars could know Weill only through his works for the Broadway stage or through vague and painful recollections of a pre-Hitler Europe.[5] Like many of his central-European colleagues in exile, Weill was confronted with the disruptive crisis an artist faces when transplanted onto foreign soil.[6] Harboring no inclination to accept the sheltered security of an academic post and maintaining his commitment to opera in a country which had no tradition of support for the genre, Weill attempted to continue along a course toward the creation of a viable modern musical theater—but with numerous adjustments in approach:

I do not believe that America can simply take up this music theatre development right where Europe left off. The prerequisites for artistic construction here are quite different. But I do believe that a movement has already begun which runs parallel to the European, and which will come closer to the goal we set in Europe. . . .

All the signs indicate that the soil is favorable for development. What will grow on it is hard to say, for there is no sort of tradition. The general public, outside of the large cities, knows little or nothing about opera. . . . Whether the growth will be opera in the European sense or music theatre in a broader sense, a new amalgam of word and tone bearing a new idea, it is certain that it will be an active, vital part of the modern theatre, that dramatists and composers will cooperate in its creation, that from the plentiful supply of young singers a generation of singer-performers will emerge.[7]

Ten years after writing those words and with a series of Broadway successes to his credit, Weill introduced his "American opera," *Street Scene*. He had become convinced that the Broadway stage was to the American public what the opera and concert halls were to the European and that the American audience was ready to accept its own form of grand opera.[8] But by this time, music critics had long since relinquished responsibility for reviewing Weill's works for the musical stage to their theatrical counterparts, who even in their highest praise often did the composer a disservice in misinterpreting both the intention and musical content of his scores. Eventually in the collective eyes of the so-called "world of serious music," Weill was categorized among the best of craftsmen within an inferior genre and, therefore, worthy of only superficial consideration. If the widespread scholarly prejudice against his American works (that persists yet today) had arisen from objections to Weill's miscalculation of his American audience, overestimation of the capabilities of Broadway theater, and resultant failure to create an authentic American operatic tradition, such a judgment would have been understandable if not entirely accurate. But in reality, Weill's American scores were rejected by many music critics and scholars *a priori* in that they had to be performed in a commercial theater rather than in the Metropolitan Opera, which did not include a work by Weill in its repertory until 1979. In a curiously ironic twist, Weill was generally dismissed not for his failure to accomplish aesthetic or musical goals, but for an embarrassing success—his music was popularized in a manner and to an extent that precluded his continued consideration as a "serious" composer. Many critical prelates in the United States somberly lamented Weill's disappointing abdication of early promise, his sacrifice of artistic integrity on the altar of American commercialism.

After the war ended, even Weill's most enthusiastic admirers in Europe who had managed to survive the debacle were neither disposed toward nor capable of reinstating his pre-war rank.[9] The chain of theatrical institutions which had nurtured his output in Germany were no longer extant. The same cultural barriers that had prevented transference of his European output to the United States before the war now served to hinder any flow in the opposite direction. Those of Weill's manuscripts which had been surreptitiously protected from purposeful destruction or systematic suppression lay scattered across the continent. With no assurance of a market, Universal-Edition was reluctant to reprint Weill's all but forgotten pre-War publications. Weill himself had lost his original points of contact with the "new music" and displayed no desire to renew them. The emerging generation of European composers who had reached maturity during the almost fifteen-year ban of Weill's music were already unilaterally committed to a single visionary model, Anton Webern. If, in terms of influence, Schoenberg was now dead for them, Weill was so irrelevant or ill-known as to be practically non-existent.[10] At the time of Weill's sudden death in 1950, it appeared that the music of the composer who once stated that he "didn't give a damn about writing for posterity"[11] would be forever entombed with its creator.

The first hint that Weill's historical role might be larger than that of a miscast, spear-carrying Broadway tunesmith or a picturesque but dated musical caricaturist of the Weimar Republic surfaced in the mid-1950s. This reassessment of his talent was somewhat artificially kindled as the by-product of an overdue recognition of Bertolt Brecht's genius. Fueled by Lotte Lenya's performances and recordings, the Weill flamelet, barely kept glimmering by a few enthusiasts, flared into a blaze with the revival of *Threepenny Opera* in New York during 1954. Achieving 2611 performances in New York alone—more than the combined total of his works originally intended for the American stage—*Die Dreigroschenoper* (in Marc Blitzstein's American version) successfully sparked interest in Weill's legacy. But any renewed concern with Weill's music *per se* was rapidly subordinated to the more encompassing Brecht-renaissance. Indeed, the rediscovery of *Aufstieg und Fall der Stadt Mahagonny, Happy End,* and *Die sieben Todsünden* led to the emergence of a new pseudo-entity, "Brecht-Weill." When the extent and nature of that collaboration was recognized, Weill had to be promoted posthumously and erroneously to the token position of valet-*Musikant* to Brecht. It was tacitly assumed that Weill's works outside his association with the towering dramatist would be of little interest and of the same mold. With no evidence or arguments to the contrary forthcoming from the musical realm, theatrical scholars accepted at face value Brecht's few published statements implying that he was responsible for the overall bearing (if not also the particulars) of Weill's music. As a result, there was insufficient stimulus for independent studies of Weill's music composed outside the collaboration on which his rejuvenated reputation depended.

Quite understandably, Brecht's musical collaborators were of interest to his biographers and critics only in their circumscribed relationship to the dramatist. The numerous translations, editions, and critical studies of Brecht's literary works and apologetic writings only peripherally shed any light on Weill's career and by sheer volume inadvertently shoved Weill's non-Brechtian compositions farther back into the shadows. But in tracing the course of Weill scholarship, one must begin with the Brecht-literature. Starting with Ernst Schumacher's *Die dramatischen Versuche Bertolt Brechts 1918-1933,*[12] a lengthy series of books, focused on Brecht but relevant to a study of Weill's German career, were issued. These included standard biographies of Brecht by Martin Esslin, Frederic Ewen, and Reinhold Grimm; critical studies by John Willett, Peter Demetz, and Werner Hecht; several editions of Brecht's complete works and documentary collections such as *Bertolt Brechts Dreigroschenbuch* and *Bertolt Brechts Der Jasager und Der Neinsager: Vorlagen, Fassungen, Materialen.*[13] When discussing the Brecht-Weill products, theatrical and literary critics as a whole have hesitated to undertake a detailed discussion of Weill's music, and this collective benign neglect has tended to veil Weill's contribution to the collaboration.

Those who have taken the plunge from neighboring disciplines into the treacherous waters of musical criticism have usually done so from the viewpoint of the theatrical or socio-political function of Weill's music. Often the consequent observations are enlightening on their own terms, but one seldom finds specific musical treatments—when one does, they are usually neither rigorous nor convincing. Obvious errors about Weill's career have been perpetuated in the Brecht-literature: Robert Marx has Weill studying with Busoni in 1927, three years after Busoni's death; John Willett asserts that Weill's reputation was made with a string quartet performed at the Donaueschingen Festival in 1922, even though none of Weill's works was ever performed there and the festival in question occurred a year before the quartet was composed.[14] Such mistakes are easily corrected, but certain underlying assumptions which permeate the Brecht-literature are not as quickly dispelled. The most fallacious and persistent of them is that Brecht was always the dominant partner, retaining full authority in his collaboration with Weill. Robert Marx even goes so far as to state as self-evident that Brecht was "the guiding force in matters of musical tone and expression."[15] Based on the uncorroborated testimony of Brecht alone, such statements are only beginning to be seen as nonsense, now that Weill's other compositions and his own enormous literary output are surfacing from the morass left by the Nazi deluge.

In the late 1950s musical scholarship initiated its own belated inquiry into Weill's career. The Berlin Academy of Arts commissioned British musicologist David Drew to compile a catalogue of Weill's works and to write a critical biography of the composer. Now, more than twenty years later, since neither of these projects has reached publication, such basic musicological foundations as a chronology of works, thematic catalogue, collected edition, and an accurate biography still do not exist. Fortunately, Weill-scholarship has enjoyed the interim benefits of Drew's exhaustive research through the publication of his numerous editions, essays, and translations. In addition, as general administrator of the European office of the Weill-Estate, Drew encouraged the first post-war performances of a number of Weill's compositions. His most extensive contribution to date has been the edition of two collections of essays, *Ueber Kurt Weill* and *Kurt Weill: Ausgewählte Schriften,* published in 1975 as a commemorative tribute marking the seventy-fifth anniversary of Weill's birth.[16] *Ueber Kurt Weill* is an anthology of fifty-one reviews, biographical sketches, and stylistic discussions, for the most part written and published elsewhere during Weill's lifetime. Drew's lengthy preface, published in English as "Kurt Weill and His Critics," is by far the most astute treatment of Weill's career in its historical context that has yet appeared. *Ausgewählte Schriften* comprises ninety-three essays (or excerpts thereof) by Weill that represent only a fraction of his voluminous literary output.

A brief bibliographic survey of other existing resources reveals the infancy of musical scholarship concerning Weill's music. The only published biography is Helmut Kotschenreuther's *Kurt Weill* (Berlin: Max Hesse Verlag, 1962), a 100-page "popular biography" in German that makes no claim of comprehensiveness and no pretense of scholarly intent. Apparently written without reference to primary source material, it is an undocumented compilation of information focusing principally on the Brecht-Weill collaboration and secondarily on the American stage works. Its inaccurate and incomplete chronology of works is indicative of its limited value as an introduction to Weill's career. There is only the most meager attempt at musical analysis, and there is no mention of Weill's literary output in *Der deutsche Rundfunk.* In all fairness, however, it must be stated that a number of Weill's compositions that had been presumed lost were not rediscovered until after Kotschenreuther's monograph had been published. The short biographical essays by Weill's associates in Germany and Austria, H. H. Stuckenschmidt,

Hans Heinsheimer, Heinrich Strobel, Rudolph Kastner, and Hans Curjel, are generally more reliable than Kotschenreuther.[17]

When the present author began this study in 1973, the only completed dissertations dealing specifically with Weill's music were studies of the Brecht-Weill collaborations. The one thesis in English, Susan Clydette Harden's "The Music for the Stage Collaborations of Weill and Brecht,"[18] is, charitably stated, beset by problems, of which the absence of any musical examples is the least disconcerting. Since 1973, two additional dissertations concerning the Brecht-Weill works have been completed: Thomas R. Nadar, "The Music of Kurt Weill, Hans Eisler and Paul Dessau in the Dramatic Works of Bertolt Brecht,"[19] and Gottfried Wagner, "Die musikalische Verfremdung in den Bühnenwerken von Kurt Weill und Bertolt Brecht."[20] Nadar's comparative study of selected librettos by Brecht and their musical settings by Weill, Eisler, and Dessau is of wider scope and significantly more accurate than Harden's dissertation.[21] Unfortunately, Nadar's dramaturgical insights and commanding knowledge of the Brecht literature are not matched by comparable musical expertise.[22] In the grand tradition of Brecht scholarship, Nadar comes dangerously close to crediting Brecht with the composition of the music. Although one can take exception to some of his unsupported conclusions (for example, he states that Eisler was the "greatest" composer to collaborate with Brecht), Nadar's work takes advantage of several recently published books which shed considerable light on the actual nature of the collaboration,[23] and it represents a valuable contribution to Weill-scholarship. Gottfried Wagner's detailed study of *Verfremdungseffekt* in the works of Brecht and Weill was published as *Weill und Brecht: Das musikalische Zeittheater.*[24] A brief excerpt from his dissertation was translated in the commemorative book *Weill-Lenya*, edited by Henry Marx for the Goethe House in 1976 in conjunction with an exhibit of memorabilia and documents at the New York Public Library. The value of *Weill-Lenya* lies in its fascinating collection of photographs, drawings, and facsimiles; its chronology of works is hampered by an inordinate number of errors.

The most striking feature of the entire body of literature concerning Weill's music is the virtual non-existence of studies that might properly be considered analytic in nature. Weill's contemporaneous critics in Germany almost universally restricted their discussions to the more general musical, theatrical, or aesthetic aspects of his compositions. Modern studies, most of which again proceed from an essentially non-analytic viewpoint, are no less single-minded in avoiding a thorough exploration of his musical language.[25] This dearth of investigation into the subterranean levels of Weill's music is undoubtedly symptomatic of the difficulties that his approach to composition, more intuitive than systematic, presents to would-be analysts. Without an understanding of the internal musical procedures of the scores themselves, any previous attempts to establish stylistic relationships between Weill and his predecessors, contemporaries, and successors must be viewed with some suspicion.

Although the present study was originally conceived primarily as an "analytic" inquiry, it became apparent that without the basis of an accurate biography or chronology of works a number of documentary issues also had to be considered. Therefore, Chapters 1 and 2 comprise a chronicle of Weill's works dating from 1900 to 1935. This does not represent a comprehensive biography, but rather only a summary of historical information directly relevant to the music composed during Weill's European career. Whenever possible, I have allowed representative contemporary critics to describe the compositions as well as to voice their own reactions to the music. In so doing, a composite view of Weill's career in the eyes of his contemporaries is reflected in the chronicle—an image which clashes conspicuously with the present general appraisal of his output. The chronicle is supplemented by Appendix I, a catalogue of works which may serve as a convenient bibliographical and documentary reference until Drew's more complete catalogue is published.

Chapter 3 is devoted to a discussion of Weill's literary works, twenty-seven of which have been translated into English in their entirety for the first time in Appendix II.[26] Because a number of the essays are apologetic or explanatory in nature, those of his own compositions discussed by Weill are analyzed in the context of his theoretical and aesthetic statements about them. Although the products of the Brecht-Weill collaboration have received close attention in previous studies and are not emphasized in my treatment of Weill's music, in Chapter 3 they are viewed in terms of Weill's—rather than Brecht's—related commentary. The third chapter also includes a sampling of Weill's criticism of compositions by his musical predecessors and contemporaries.

The third part of the book is an investigation of the evolution of Weill's musical style. The early unpublished works are stressed in this attempt to trace the development of Weill's musical language and compositional procedures. Chapter 4 embraces the instrumental works dating from 1919 to 1921; Chapter 5 roughly corresponds to Weill's period of study with Busoni; Chapter 6 considers the synthesis and characteristics of Weill's mature style. Because of the substantial volume and diversified scope of his European output—two symphonies, two string quartets, three cantatas, three orchestral compositions, thirteen works for the musical stage, a song cycle, numerous songs, choral pieces, and incidental music have survived—choices based on significance of works within Weill's output and their previous treatment in other studies had to be made regarding emphases in my own discussion. I have taken the following suggestion of David Drew as the guideline for my study of Weill's career in Europe:

> If there is to be a new approach to Weill, it could not more profitably differ from the old ones than by starting with strictly musical problems, and remaining close to them.[27]

CHAPTER 1

CHRONICLE: WEILL'S CAREER, 1900-1927

I think he had more to give his age than any other man I knew.[1]

— *Maxwell Anderson* —

I

The year 1900 witnessed the chronological eclipse of the nineteenth century, symbolized by the deaths of Friedrich Nietzsche, Oscar Wilde, Queen Victoria (22 January 1901), and the dawn of the twentieth century, represented by the births of composers Aaron Copland, Ernst Krenek, and George Antheil. During the first year of this century of scientific "miracles," magnetic recording of sound was devised, the first Zeppelin had its trial flight, and Max Planck elaborated upon his new quantum theory. As the cakewalk pranced across the United States, in Germany Kaiser Wilhelm II maneuvered passage of the Second Naval Act, which portentously called for a fleet of thirty-eight battle ships by 1920. The influential Exposition Universelle in Paris, which featured the dance and music of the Far East, curiously paralleled the Boxer Rebellion against European presence in China. Monet unveiled *Harmony in Rose* and Renoir *Nude in the Sun* during this year of the premieres of Debussy's "Nuages" and "Fêtes." As Elgar completed *The Dream of Gerontius,* Arnold Schoenberg began work on *Gurrelieder.* Such disparate compositions as Sibelius' *Finlandia,* Puccini's *Tosca,* and Rimsky-Korsakov's *Tale of the Tsar Sultan* premiered in this year of Breitkopf & Härtel's publication of the first volume of Berlioz' collected works and the last volume of the Bach-Gesellschaft edition. In retrospect, however, perhaps none of these incidents was more premonitory of the era than the birth of a composer whose lifetime precisely spanned the first fifty years of the century and whose distinctly personal art was both saturated with and reflective of the manifestations of the period. On 2 March 1900 Emma Ackermann Weill gave birth to her and Albert Weill's fourth child, Kurt.

The musical interests of both Albert and Emma Weill, who was an amateur pianist herself, greatly affected Kurt's early development. As cantor of the synagogue in Dessau, located sixty miles southwest of Berlin, Kurt's father was a professional singer and published composer of liturgical music. A collection of his arrangements of chants for cantor and male chorus appeared in 1893.[2] These four-part responsorial settings of Psalm 118 were intended to "assist the formation of a progressive and valuable public worship" and were motivated by the "tangible scarcity of suitable compositions for Hebraic male chorus."[3] Thus, these pieces were not meant for concert performance; their harmonic and rhythmic simplicity is indicative of a utilitarian, liturgical function. The final section of this eighteen-page collection, which is to my knowledge the only publication of his compositions preserved in libraries in the United States, presents the most complex of the arrangements. Here (Example 1.1) imitation replaces the homophonic texture that characterizes the remainder of the settings. The range of the elder Weill's compositional output and talent cannot be ascertained from this one collection, but the sphere of his musical activity appears to have been primarily liturgical in scope.

Without concrete documentary evidence it is often difficult and sometimes misleading to evaluate the role of cultural environment, family heritage, personal experiences and religious orientation in the evolution of a composer's style—especially in so cosmopolitan a period as the twentieth century. Even when such factors can be documented, their relevance and significance for actual musical composition tends to be exaggerated; but in the case of Kurt Weill it is essential to note at the outset of this chronicle that the course and nature of his career is inextricably linked to his German-Jewish heritage, which his father could proudly trace back to the fourteenth century. Although in early adulthood Kurt abandoned his parents' orthodox faith, the explicit religious preoccupation evident in his works dating from 1920 to 1925 and the subsequent commitment in his music to social and moral activism must stem from his early familial and cultural environment. There is, in any case, no doubt that Weill's ethnic and religious background was more decisive for his inclusion on Goebbel's blacklist and for his forced exodus from Germany than any accusations of "artistic decadence" or "cultural-Bolshevism."

In 1935 Weill's collaboration in Max Reinhardt's production of Franz Werfel's biblical pageant, *The Eternal Road*, based on historical events of the Old Testament, provided the stimulus for his emigration to the United States.[4] Weill stated that his task was "to bind speech and music into perfect fusion, to have the score an integral part of the play, so that the action would be more perfectly communicated and dramatically heightened by the power of the music."[5] In order to accomplish the desired fusion of subject matter and music, Weill tapped the subliminal storehouse of his Hebraic heritage for musical material:

> I set to work in the fall of 1934, putting to paper all the Hebraic melodies I had learned from childhood. I had an abundance of material. For my father, who is a cantor and composer, had set great store upon my learning this heritage. In several days' memory seeking, I had written about two hundred songs, and then I began work at the Bibliothèque Nationale to trace their sources as far as possible. Many I discovered had been composed in the eighteenth and nineteenth centuries,

Example 1.1   Albert Weill: *Synagogen Gesänge*

a. Opening

b. Conclusion

some borrowed from the most surprising sources, from opera, "hit-songs" of the time, street tunes, concert music, and symphonies. Those I dismissed, retaining only the old music, and with that as my guide, I attempted to create music of the same mood that would communicate naturally and inevitably the stories of the Old Testament.[6]

Weill's oratorio-like score for Reinhardt's spectacular production of *The Eternal Road* signaled the beginning of Weill's new path to success on the Broadway stage and finalized the permanent renunciation of the homeland that had forced him into exile.

During this second career as a naturalized citizen of the United States and composer of a lengthy list of works for the American musical theater, Weill was an ardent supporter of the Zionist movement. He contributed the score to Ben Hecht's *A Flag is Born*, a production sponsored by the American League for a Free Palestine.[7] In 1947, the Boston Symphony Orchestra presented the first performance of Weill's orchestration of "Hatikva," the national anthem of Israel, to which his parents had emigrated. He was also asked to contribute a composition to an evening of Jewish service music by contemporary composers, sponsored by the Park Avenue Synagogue. Among the contributors to the concert on 10 May 1946 were Roy Harris, William Grant Still, Arthur Berger, Alexander Tansman, and Paul Pisk. Weill's response to the invitation was a responsorial setting of the "Kiddush" (Prayer of Sanctification) for cantor and mixed chorus with organ accompaniment. Certainly this ingenious and poignant mixture of "blues" and traditional chant styles (Example 1.2) seems far removed from the analogous arrangements of synagogue chants by Albert Weill that had been published seven years before Kurt's birth.[8] Yet Kurt recognized and communicated the intrinsic affinity of intent and affirmed the continuity of his heritage in dedicating the score, published posthumously in 1951, "to my father."[9]

Kurt's precocious musical talent was evident by the age of eight when his parents arranged for him to study piano. Within two years, without any formal guidance other than that of his father, Kurt was filling notebooks with attempts at composition.[10] His first operatic endeavor, undertaken at age 11, was based on a play by Karl Theodor Körner (1791-1813). A few years later, Weill wrote a second opera and adapted his own libretto from Hermann Sudermann's *Das Hohe lied* (1903).[11] A number of small piano pieces, songs, and a song cycle, *Schilflieder*, also originated before he began formal lessons in music theory and composition in 1915 with Albert Bing, the conductor of the Dessau Opera.[12] Having studied piano in Coburg during his adolescence, Weill became one of the official accompanists of the Dessau opera and

Example 1.2   Kurt Weill: "Kiddush"; mm. 1 - 5

traveled with some of the singers on their concert tours to smaller cities.[13] By the age of fifteen, Weill was already employed in the theater— learning the standard repertory and absorbing basic fundamentals of stagecraft.

He remained in Dessau until 1918, the year of his public debut as a composer of two duets, one of which was entitled "Maikäferlied."[14] Since only a few of Weill's songs and several fragments of his other

Jugendwerke (composed before 1918) have survived, titles and descriptions of the early compositions must be gleaned from Weill's own recollections, which date from decades later, and biographical essays that were written during the 1920s.[15] Although Weill usually referred to the ballet-pantomime, *Die Zaubernacht* (1922), as his first mature work and never mentioned his earlier compositions by name in his own writings, he briefly discussed his musical activities at school in an interview dating from 1930:

> Dr. Fischer: What was the nature of your musical activity in school?
>
> Kurt Weill: Even though the singing instruction was bad, the director of my Dessau Gymnasium and the professor of the upper classes showed the greatest interest in music. Already at that time they strongly encouraged me. I composed for the school orchestra and wrote (amazingly enough, considering who I am today) even war choruses.[16]

Having passed the entrance examination of the Berlin Hochschule für Musik in April 1918 and having attended classes both there and at the University during the spring of that year, Weill matriculated as a full-time student at the Hochschule in September.[17] He studied composition with Humperdinck (1854-1921), whom he assisted in orchestrating *Gaudeamus: Szenen aus dem deutschen Studentenleben,* counterpoint with Friedrich E. Koch (1862-1927), and conducting with Rudolf Krasselt (1879-1954).[18] Apparently Weill found the rigid academic atmosphere stifling, for he left after completing only one semester despite the fact that he had been awarded a grant-in-aid of three hundred marks from the Felix Mendelssohn Bartholdy Foundation.[19] But before he departed, the Hochschule Orchestra performed his symphonic poem based on Rilke's *Die Weise von Liebe und Tod des Cornets Christoph Rilke.*[20] Neither it nor a choral fantasy entitled *Sulamith*, which dated from this period, has survived, but Heinrich Strobel briefly described them:

> If one looks at one of the manuscript compositions of this period, one notices that the musical sphere in which he [Weill] had lived scarcely twenty years extended up to Debussy and early Schoenberg. Impressionistic sound and an expansive, expressive melodic style flow together in a choral fantasy, *Sulamith.* But only temporarily do the clearer contours emerge from the dramatically surging movement. Of even more significance are the precipitous voice-leading that bursts open the tonal regions and the attempt to articulate clearly and distinctly the poem that is divided between women's chorus and soprano. A symphonic poem based on Rilke's *Weise von Liebe und Tod* strove for stronger concentration of tensely-expressive melodic style (like that of Schoenberg's *Pelleas und Melisande*) in the superimposition of lines that are at the same time chord-bearers [*Klangträger*]. Here one first perceives a developmental value: a cautious

departure from the superficial pathos of late romantic decadence in art. Significantly enough, the glitter of Straussian instrumentation no longer covers these first works.[21]

After leaving Berlin early in 1919, Weill returned to Dessau as a *Repetiteur* (coach and chorus master) at the Friedrichstheater under Hans Knappertsbusch (1888-1965), who served as music director of the Dessau Opera from 1919 to 1922.[22] In December Weill, at the age of 19, advanced to the position of Kapellmeister of the small municipal theater in Lüdenscheid, a city of approximately thirty thousand people located in Westphalia, about two hundred miles west of Dessau. As musical director of a small provincial theater that necessarily included operas, operettas, plays, and revues in its repertory, Weill received broad practical theatrical experience, which later proved to be invaluable.[23] He himself considered his tenure at Dessau and Lüdenscheid the most instructive period of his life in that "it represented a specific, theatrical participation and training as distinguished from deadly abstract study."[24] Because of the Lüdenscheid theater's limited budget and staff, Weill not only coached the singers and conducted the performances, but also frequently directed scenes of dialogue, reduced instrumentation and re-orchestrated passages to fit the constitution of the theater's orchestra, and even wrote incidental music. In spite of the heavy work load, Weill said that it was precisely at this time that he chose the musical theater as his field of special activity.[25]

During this period Weill composed a one-act opera based on the drama *Ninon von Lenclos* by Ernst Hardt.[26] Since it was never performed and is now assumed lost, no description of the opera is available. Two other compositions dating from 1919-20 have survived in manuscript: a String Quartet in B minor and a Sonata for cello and piano.[27] The Quartet, consisting of four movements, was never published and probably was not performed publicly until 1975.[28] The Cello Sonata of 1920 is dedicated to Weill's teacher, Albert Bing, and to Fritz Rupprecht (b. 1885), the principal cellist of the Dessau Friedrichstheater Orchestra from 1913 to 1921. It comprises three movements; again there is no documentary evidence of a public performance during Weill's lifetime.[29]

To conquer Berlin was to conquer the world.[30]

— *Carl Zuckmayer* —

II

   In September 1920 Weill returned to Berlin and in so doing joined
the massive influx into one of the most receptive and energized artistic
climates of modern times.[31] By 1920 Berlin was no longer the provincial
capital of militaristic Prussia with a population of less than two million
people that it had been at the turn of the century under the
Hohenzollerns, but instead a sprawling metropolis of four million and the
capital of the Weimar Republic.   Struggling to recover from the
devastation of the First World War and grappling with the problems of a
newly-instituted democracy without the aid of a tradition of self-
government or even a pro-democratic majority in the Reichstag, Berlin
was also assembling an explosive critical mass of artistic and intellectual
talent.   "Opening its arms wide to everything that was new, young,
daring, different,"[32] the city imported the raw materials necessary for
both physical and spiritual reconstruction in its golden decade.
   Nothing is more symbolic of Berlin's renewal than the
reconstruction of the Staatsoper (*Unter den Linden*) at a cost to the
Prussian state of nearly thirteen million marks.   Not to be out-glittered,
the city itself established its own competitive theater in Charlottenburg,
the Städtische Oper (Municipal Opera).   In 1927 the Staatsoper (State
Opera) expanded its operations to include another theater—"Staatsoper
am Platz der Republik," more commonly known as the Krolloper. As a
result, from 1927 to 1931 (when the Krolloper was sacrificed to the
National Socialists) Berlin supported three major opera houses, each with
a ten-month season.   Government subsidy alone amounted to more than
seven million marks per season and thereby provided the financial
security which encouraged the vital productions and experimentation that
beckoned a new generation of operatic talent under the leadership of
Carl Ebert, Otto Klemperer, Bruno Walter, Erich Kleiber, and Leo Blech.[33]
   The artistic boom was not limited to opera.   Max Reinhardt,
Leopold Jessner, and Erwin Piscator managed only the most famous of
over eighty 'live' theaters in Berlin, which competed with more than two
hundred and fifty motion picture theaters, not to mention the numerous
cabarets featuring the biting political satire of Brecht, Wedekind, and
Tucholsky.   In addition to operatic productions, Klemperer and Walter
conducted series of orchestral concerts which rivaled Furtwängler's
Philharmonic performances.   Young virtuosos such as Horowitz, Serkin,

Arrau, Piatigorsky, and Menuhin infused Berlin's concert life with even more vitality, and the succession of composition teachers at the Hochschule für Musik (Humperdinck, Schreker, Hindemith) and the Prussian Academy of Arts (Busoni, Schoenberg) attracted the most promising young composers. Indeed, Kurt Weill's move was motivated by his intent to study with Ferruccio Busoni (1866-1924), whose own return in 1920 ended five years of voluntary exile.

In autumn 1919 Busoni had received an invitation from Leo Kestenberg, his former piano pupil and newly-appointed official in the Prussian Ministry of Education, to teach a class in advanced composition at the Academy of Arts.[34] Appealing to Busoni's long-standing desire to teach a composition class, Kestenberg persuaded Busoni to return from Zürich to his apartment on Viktoria-Luise-Platz.[35] Busoni's contract allowed him to travel six months of the year and limited the size of the class to six pupils, who were to be chosen only on the basis of talent and were to pay no tuition.[36] After receiving an honorary doctorate from the University of Zürich in July (in response he dedicated the libretto of *Doktor Faust* to the faculty), Busoni arrived in Berlin during September 1920. The following month he gave two concerts in Philharmonic Hall and negotiated with the Staatsoper for productions of *Turandot* and *Arlecchino*.[37] In December, on the basis of a portfolio of compositions he had submitted, Weill was admitted to the class, which also included Luc Balmer (b. 1898), Robert Blum (b. 1900), Walter Geiser (b. 1897) and Vladimir Vogel (b. 1896).[38] Even though he paid no tuition, Weill was compelled to support himself by playing piano in a rather obscure *Bierkeller,* described by Hans Heinsheimer:

> His earnings depended upon the generosity of the patrons, who were expected to drop their contributions on a plate conspicuously displayed on the piano. To encourage donations Weill would break into an exorcising crescendo whenever he perceived a prosperous-looking party preparing to depart.[39]

At least twice a week Weill and the other students went to Busoni's apartment for a class, for which Busoni admitted a less than enthusiastic predilection in a letter to his wife dated 30 July 1921: "The young men come on Mondays and Thursdays, but I can send them away after an hour or an hour and a half."[40] The focus of the class was undoubtedly not the technical aspect of composition, for Weill eventually felt compelled to supplement his course of study with Busoni with counterpoint lessons from Phillip Jarnach (b. 1892).[41] Ernst Krenek described Busoni's daily afternoon meetings as sessions "where musicians were in a minority and painters, writers, poets, architects, scientists, and a large number of miscellaneous intellectuals were all attracted by the fireworks of his fascinating soliloquy which would go on for an hour or more, before he retired ceremoniously to the inner sanctum, obviously to attend to his creative work proper."[42] Like these informal gatherings, the composition classes followed the generalized aesthetic and vaguely theoretical approach that characterized Busoni's writings, in which he extolled clarity and conciseness of musical form, freedom from literary dependence, renewed commitment to chamber music, revival of opera (as opposed to music drama), avoidance of the tortuously expressive pathos of late Romantic and Expressionist composers, and expansion of musical materials. He advocated transparency of form and structure within the greatest freedom of expression: a "new classicism."[43] Quite clearly Busoni did not encourage his students to imitate his own musical style; the majority of his pupils developed their own highly-individual idioms. The members of his class brought their compositions to class to be performed, discussed, and criticized. Weill described the sessions:

> He called us disciples and there were no actual lessons, but he allowed us to breathe his aura, which emanated in every sphere, but eventually manifested itself in music. . . . It was a mutual exchange of ideas in the very best sense, with no attempt to force an opinion, no autocracy, and not the slightest sign of envy or malice; and any piece of work that revealed talent and ability was immediately recognized and enthusiastically received.[44]

Weill's admiration for his teacher, whom he called "the invisible leader of European musical life," is evident in his essays, most particularly "Busoni und die neue Musik," "Ferruccio Busoni: Zu seinem 60. Geburtstag," and "Busonis Faust und die Erneuerung der Opernform."[45] According to Kastner, the bond of affection was a mutual one:

> One afternoon Busoni introduced to me a small, quiet man, maybe twenty years old. Two pupils beamed and flickered behind spectacles. In conversation an uncommonly serious, resolute man of strong character was revealed. In his absence, Busoni spoke of him with exceptional warmth. In fact, he "cultivated" him like a fatherly, loving gardener who bestowed all his love on one flower, one tree. Kurt Weill was allowed to experience the painful happiness of the approaching end, in that he stayed with Busoni in the sad period of misfortune and separation. In addition to Phillip Jarnach, he was allowed to see every page of the evolving *Faust*, and each of Weill's own works received the benefit of the reciprocal effect. Now that Busoni is gone, Jarnach and Weill remain his most genuine "pupils" in the intellectual or technical sense.[46]

Busoni entrusted the piano reduction of his Divertimento for Flute and Orchestra, op. 52 (1920), to Weill and in a reciprocal gesture made the piano-vocal arrangement of one movement of Weill's song cycle,

Frauentanz, op. 10.[47]   Furthermore, it was on the recommendation of
Busoni that Dr. Hertzka of Universal-Edition offered Weill a contract.

Weill's first major composition after joining Busoni's master class
was a one-movement orchestral work, now entitled Symphony no. 1, but
variously known as "Berliner Sinfonie" or "Sinfonie in einem Satz."[48]
On its title page the Symphony carried a motto from Johannes R.
Becher's *Arbeiter, Bauern, Soldaten: Der Aufbruch eines Volks zu Gott,*
an Expressionist play with a socialist and pacifist world view.[49] *Workers,
Peasants, Soldiers: A Community's Awakening to God* was labelled a
"Festspiel" and was to have been produced by Max Reinhardt.   The
production did not materialize, but the play was published in 1921 by
Insel Verlag, Leipzig.[50]   Three years later, Becher rewrote the entire play
and excised the ecstatic mystical and religious aspects in favor of a more
doctrinaire Communist slant.[51]   Weill's Symphony is probably more aptly
described as a multi-sectional symphonic poem, for its outlines can be
interpreted as roughly paralleling those of Becher's play.

A prolific poet and author, Becher (1891-1958) was one of the most
vociferous advocates of revolutionary social and economic reform in
Germany during the twenties.   *Arbeiter, Bauern, Soldaten* is typical of his
Expressionist visions of a new social order.   In 1918 he joined the
Communist Party and was elected to the Reichstag in 1933, but was
almost immediately forced into exile.   He lived out the war in Moscow,
returned to Germany in 1945, and was appointed Minister of Culture by
the East German government in 1954.[52]   Weill met Becher in Berlin in
1920 and later wrote of him: "It appears that this prodigious talent is on
the way to transforming the political ideals of a young generation into a
new artistic form."[53]   Considering Weill's own religious preoccupation
evident in his works dating from 1920 to 1924, it is not surprising that
Becher's visionary play evoked a musical response from Weill.   Becher
and Bertolt Brecht met in 1922 and initiated a lifelong personal and
political alliance that culminated in Becher's oratory at the memorial
celebration following Brecht's death in 1956.[54]

Symphony no. 1 was never performed publicly during Weill's
lifetime.   In 1929 the autograph orchestral score, along with a number of
Weill's other early works, was entrusted by the composer to a Professor
Fleischer, who was writing a biography of Weill.   When the Nazi regime
came to power in 1933, Professor Fleischer sent the manuscripts to
Universal-Edition in Vienna.[55]   Somehow the score of the Symphony was
included by mistake in a shipment of Fleischer's personal possessions
that eventually weathered the war in an Italian convent where the
caretakers removed the title page of the score to prevent confiscation.   It
remained in this anonymity until 1955, when Weill's widow, Lotte Lenya,

returned to Berlin and placed an advertisement in the newspaper requesting information concerning the fate of Weill's manuscripts. In response, Fleischer remembered the score and returned it to Lenya.[56] More than thirty-six years after its composition, the Symphony was premiered in Hamburg under Wilhelm Schüchter in 1957.

Although composed during Weill's first year of participation in the master class, Symphony no. 1 was not written under Busoni's supervision. However, Weill did present the work to Busoni's class in a four-hand piano arrangement, which has survived in part. In view of the extra-musical associations and Expressionist idiom of the score, it is hardly surprising that only the fugal and chorale sections met with Busoni's approval.[57] The autograph of the Symphony, which is scored for 2 flutes (piccolo), oboe, 2 clarinets, 2 bassoons, 2 horns, trumpet, trombone, percussion, and strings, contains a number of corrections and one passage that has been re-orchestrated.[58]

In the only critique of the work written during Weill's lifetime, Heinrich Strobel provided a valuable evaluation of the Symphony in the context of Weill's earlier compositions, many of which are now lost:

> The reduction of orchestral forces was a first step toward the present. Weill still used the stylistic means of Romanticism and allowed himself to be stimulated by literary ideas, but the ties had been loosened. He wanted the themes in which he stylized the intellectual ideas to develop independently. The "Symphonie für Streicher mit einigen Bläsern" still sounds pathetic. But this pathos is to communicate something new, like that signified by the inscribed prefatory motto from Becher's *Arbeiter, Soldaten und Bauern* [sic]: a socialistic, pacifistic world view. For the first time a reference to the tendencies of the time is revealed; this becomes decisive for later works. Already the new musical inclination heralds a melodically-suspended tension. Rhythmic elements, which until now had been lost in the chaos of sound and musico-dramatic intensifications, advance forward eruptively. The structure is significantly more compact. A theme such as:

is still pure Strauss, but the viola melody:

signifies a change. The line is consolidated as if the expansive harmony had exploded.[59]

Only when I discovered that my music contains the tension of scenic events did I turn to the stage.

— Kurt Weill —

III

The first of Weill's compositions for the theater to be performed was a ballet-pantomime entitled *Die Zaubernacht* [*The Magic Night*]. Commissioned by a Russian ballet troupe in the summer of 1922 and intended as children's theater, it was based on a scenario by Vladimir Boritsch that dealt with a fairy who brings toys to life. It was premiered at the Theater am Kurfürstendamm in Berlin on 18 November 1922 in a production by Franz-Ludwig Hörth and shared the program with Stravinsky's *Petrushka.* As children's theater, *Die Zaubernacht* received only matinee performances and attracted little or no attention from musical circles. However, Weill himself considered it his first mature score; in 1930 he referred to *Die Zaubernacht* as "the first work in which the simple style can be recognized."[60] Earlier, in the program notes for the premiere of *Der Protagonist* in Dresden, Weill had commented on the significance of his ballet-pantomime:

> I wrote the pantomime *Die Zaubernacht* for a Russian troupe at the Theater am Kurfürstendamm. I learned two things from the concentrated intensity of Russian theatrical art: that the stage has its own musical form whose conformation grows organically from the flow of the action and that significant events can be expressed scenically only by the simplest, most inconspicuous means. An orchestra of nine men, a singer, two dancers, and a number of children—that was the apparatus of this danced dream.[61]

The score for the complete ballet was never published, but fortunately a piano-vocal reduction has survived in manuscript. Again Strobel provided a description of the work:

> Already in 1922 Weill had written a piece for the theater: music for a pantomime, *Die Zaubernacht,* extraordinarily free-flowing, lively, delicate in its treatment of timbre in the small orchestra. . . . This work, certainly not weighty or dramatic, is of the highest significance for its developmental value. For here the transformed attitude toward the theater is documented for the first time. For Busoni's students, the connection between scene and music could occur only on the basis of the play. The specific development was the liberation from the coloristic and intellectual elements that ultimately made absolute musical composition impossible in the late-Romantic period. It was a liberation from any ties to music drama, which had gradually destroyed every spontaneous outgrowth

of music in the theater and which had brought music into total bondage to the texts that were sketched according to purely literary principles.[62]

In 1923 Weill extracted a suite from the score of *Die Zaubernacht* and arranged it for a larger orchestra. Entitled simply "Orchestersuite aus dem Pantomime *Zaubernacht*," it received its premiere in the fifth subscription concert of the Kapelle des Friedrichstheater on 15 June 1923 with Weill's former teacher, Albert Bing, conducting. Ernst Hamann reviewed this performance in *Die Musik:*

> The young composer has constructed a four-movement suite, which proves to be a thoroughly modern work, out of themes from his children's pantomime *Die Zaubernacht,* which has already been successfully performed in Berlin. Most remarkable is the virtuosic orchestral technique over which Kurt Weill already has supreme command. When this artist can say more with regard to content than he has in this Suite, he will one day certainly cause a great stir. Albert Bing launched the work with his orchestra in as masterly a performance as possible.[63]

In October 1925, after already publishing two of Weill's compositions, Universal-Edition announced the publication of *Quodlibet: Eine Unterhaltungsmusik. Vier Stücke aus einem Kindertheater für grosses Orchester.*[64] This published version of the Suite transmitted about twenty-three minutes of the original seventy-five minute ballet-pantomime.[65] References in a number of reviews indicate that the earlier "Orchestersuite" and *Quodlibet* differed only in title. *Quodlibet* was dedicated to Bing, who conducted the first performance under the new title at Coburg on 6 February 1926. The instrumentation includes flutes, oboes, clarinets, bassoons, horns, trumpets, and trombones in pairs; percussion; strings; and the indispensable 'magical' glockenspiel.

From 1926 to 1929, *Quodlibet* enjoyed a number of performances under such prestigious conductors as Felix Weingartner, who played it at a Vienna Philharmonic concert to the following critical reception:

> Kurt Weill's *Quodlibet,* op. 9, which correctly calls itself entertainment music, is a very fine orchestral suite. Taken from a dance-pantomime *Die Zaubernacht,* a children's fable, these four unpretentious, lively, resonant, first-rate orchestral pieces also delighted the audience of the Philharmonic.[66]

Schoenberg's brother-in-law, Alexander Zemlinsky, conducted the suite in Prague during 1927, and it was selected for presentation at the Krefelder Tonkünstlerfest, 15-17 July 1927.[67] Rudolf Krasselt, Weill's former conducting teacher, performed *Quodlibet* in Hannover, and Jascha Horenstein presented its Berlin premiere in 1929.[68]

Besides its strategic position in Weill's stylistic development, *Die Zaubernacht* proved to be a momentous event in his career because the work came to the attention of Georg Kaiser, the foremost German Expressionist playwright. Kaiser was impressed by Weill's score and ultimately agreed to a collaboration.[69] Furthermore, Lotte Lenya recalls that when she came to Berlin in 1922 as a struggling young actress-dancer:

> My first audition was for a children's ballet, *Die Zaubernacht,* and though I was hired, my teacher, who had applied as director was not. Out of loyalty I refused the part. Incidentally the composer of that work was Kurt Weill. He was in the orchestra pit and saw me—I did not see him. . . . Our meeting was to come some years later.[70]

Weill composed two other orchestral works in 1922: Divertimento für Kleines Orchester mit Männerchor, op. 4 and *Sinfonia sacra* ("Fantasie, Passacaglia, und Hymnus"), op. 6. Neither was published, nor has either been preserved intact. The Divertimento, consisting of six movements, has been partially reconstructed from extant manuscript sources by David Drew. This version, consisting of four movements, received its premiere at the 1971 Holland Festival; its only performance during Weill's lifetime occurred at a private evening session of Busoni's master class, where it proved especially valuable for discussion.[71] Like Symphony no. 1, the Divertimento and *Sinfonia sacra* employ movements that are best described as highly-complex chorale fantasies. Strobel noted the influence of Busoni in that respect also:

> With the progressive mastery of form, Weill achieved the most facile handling of compositional technique. That can be deduced from the fantasy-like movements of the various instrumental works. To be arranged organically is the formal task. Therefore, a chorale theme is introduced in the finales of the Divertimento and the Quartet. In the Divertimento, it puts the finishing touch in a very impressive way to the thoroughly expressive material performed by the male chorus—Busoni's piano concerto comes to mind.[72]

The religious allusions expressed in the First Symphony are again apparent in the Divertimento, most explicitly in the chorale text of the finale:

> Herr Gott dein Zorn tu'von uns wenden,
> Dein blutig Zuchtruth an allen Enden,
> Uns plaget redlich und uns tat schinden,
> Die weil wir voll Sünden.
>
> Denn wolltest nach unser Sünd und gebrechen,
> Uns strafen und uns Urteil sprechen.
> Müsst alles gehen zu Grund und Falle,
> Ja — alle.

Shortly after the Divertimento was performed in Busoni's class, *Sinfonia sacra,* op. 6, received its premiere during April 1923 in a concert of the Berlin Philharmonic with Alexander Selo conducting.[73]   In reviewing the performance, Adolf Weissmann compared Weill with Webern:

> But cannot even Ethos be exaggerated? Kurt Weill has done so. He adheres to the highest standard, but in doing so perhaps he suppresses his best. For his Passacaglia, which conductor Alexander Selo presented with fluency and devotion, arises from the most profound seriousness. Whether a sensuality exists beyond this logically-developed spirituality can hardly be judged. We would like to hope so. To be sure, compared with Anton Webern, Kurt Weill is still a voluptuary of music.[74]

Only fragments of the work have survived, but Kastner noted "its voice-crossing technique based on the new Busoni style (*Berceuse, Nocturne symphonique, Faust-Skizzen*)," its "still harsh melody," its "fundamentally dark" texture, and its "somewhat colorless instrumentation."[75] Strobel is more specific and undoubtedly more accurate in citing Reger's music as the model for Weill's early music:

> Stylistically opus 6 depends upon the Symphony. The pathos of the Hymnus intimates that the symbolic is also to be expressed here. But both principal themes of this movement show how the tightening of melodic material has further progressed.

First Principal Theme:

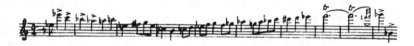

Second Principal Theme:

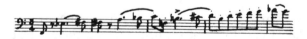

> That the organic link of the Passacaglia variations to the original did not succeed was to be expected. Polyphony, which gained its strength from Reger, is still unable to develop. Virtuosic elan, which generates small figures, always counteracts the plastic pictorial quality of individual episodes. But how clearly all of this is arranged! That will be useful to the dramatist.[76]

I hardly know a piece by a 23-year-old of the present day that is so attractive and worthwhile.

— *Ferruccio Busoni* —

IV

Weill's first exposure to an international public occurred with the premiere of his String Quartet, op. 8, at the penultimate concert of Frankfurt's "Kammermusikwoche" on 24 June 1923.[77]   Sharing the morning program with Stefan Wolpe's *Klavierstücke*, op. 5a, Weill's Quartet was performed by the Hindemith-Amar Quartet (Hindemith had assisted with the organization of the festival). The critical reception for the Quartet was decidedly mixed. Karl Holl compared the compositions of Wolpe and Weill in the *Frankfurter Zeitung*:

> Certainly in Weill there is a more serious, straightforward intention; an inclination toward the melodic, toward the rhythmic, toward organic form in the wider sense. Yet for the present it remains a groping through [*Durchtasten*] the musical expanse toward these possibilities. . . . The beginnings [of creativity] are most likely to be pursued further in the development of the Mahlerian fantasy-like march rhythms and a few distinguished cello fragments of the chorale fantasy.[78]

Even if the Quartet had been one of Weill's better compositions, it is unlikely that it could have made a mark in a festival that included performances of Hindemith's *Das Marienleben* and *Kleine Kammermusik für fünf Bläser*, op. 24 no. 2; Busoni's *Fantasia contrappuntistica;* Bartók's Suite, op. 14; Schoenberg's *Lieder aus dem Buch der Hängenden Gärten*; and Stravinsky's *L'Histoire du Soldat*. Hans Curjel described the impact of the German premiere of *Soldier's Tale*:

> Weill's name had become familiar to me when I read a basically very positive description of his string quartet in a performance report of the *Frankfurter Zeitung* about a modern chamber music festival in Frankfurt. Shortly before that, in the Frankfurter Schauspielhaus we had seen a matinee of the German-language premiere of Stravinsky's *Geschichte vom Soldaten* in the translation of poet Hans Reinhart of Winterthur [Switzerland]. Scherchen conducted, Hindemith played the solo violin, Carl Ebert was the narrator. It was one of the most striking impressions of my early musical life. . . . People discussed it—Scherchen and his wife Gustel, Reinhart, Horenstein—the talented people continued until the next morning at breakfast—they had forgotten to go to bed. The conversation also came to Busoni and with him to Weill, whom Scherchen at that time considered the most talented of Busoni's students.[79]

If Weill did not see the Frankfurt production of *Soldier's Tale,* he definitely attended a performance later in the summer at the Bauhaus Festival in Weimar where Scherchen again conducted it. Busoni, whose piano works were to be played by Egon Petri, and two students—Weill and Vogel—were in the audience.[80] Stravinsky described the event most vividly:

> In August of that same year I made a short visit to Weimar, at the invitation of the organizers of a very fine exhibition of modern architecture (Bauhaus), in the course of which there was a series of musical performances, including, among other things, the presentation of my *Histoire du Soldat.* . . . I made the acquaintance of Ferruccio Busoni, whom I had never met before and who had always been described to me as an irreconcilable opponent of my music. I was therefore very much impressed by the sincere emotion which I saw that he was feeling while my music was being played, which was confirmed by him the same evening. I was all the more touched by this appreciation, since it came from a very great musician, whose work and mentality were fundamentally opposed to my art. It was my first and last sight of him; he died a year later.[81]

Although Stravinsky did not recall meeting Weill until a performance of *Die Dreigroschenoper* and did not "develop an acquaintance with him until later, in Paris, at the time of *Mahagonny* and *Der Jasager*" (both of which Stravinsky admired), the impact of *Soldier's Tale* is recognizable in many of Weill's compositions and acknowledged in his aesthetic statements.[82] In 1926 Weill wrote:

> What Stravinsky attempted in his *Soldier's Tale* undoubtedly can be appraised as the intermediary genre with the most certain future. Standing on the boundary between play, pantomime, and opera, this piece still displays such a strong predominance of operatic elements that it perhaps can become the foundation for a certain course of new opera.[83]

The first performance in Berlin of Weill's Quartet occurred on 22 January 1924 at a concert in the Vox-Haus sponsored by the "Novembergruppe" (November Group). The program also included the premiere of Stefan Wolpe's *Studien für Klavier,* op. 16 (played by the composer himself), five songs of Phillip Jarnach, and Martino Kessel reading his own poetry. Listed on the program as the "first performance from the manuscript," the Quartet was performed by the Roth Quartet.[84] Although this was the first appearance of one of his compositions in a public November Group concert, Weill had become an associate of the Group, which did not officially admit musicians until 1922, soon after his arrival in Berlin in 1920.[85]

Taking its name from the month of the Weimar Revolution (November 1918), the November Group consisted of a number of

Expressionist artists in Berlin organized by Max Pechstein and César Klein. Hoping to achieve unification of the arts and closer contact with the working masses, in 1919 the organization established Workers' Councils for Art and instituted public art exhibitions, lectures, film presentations, and concerts of new music.[86]   Although Scherchen organized a number of musical events related to the November Group, he left Berlin before musicians were admitted to official membership.[87] The first members of the musical branch were Heinz Tiessen (1887-1971) and Max Butting (1888-1976).   A short time later Phillip Jarnach, Vladimir Vogel, Weill, Hanns Eisler, Felix Petyrek, Jascha Horenstein, George Antheil, Stefan Wolpe, and H. H. Stuckenschmidt were offered membership.[88]   From 1923 to 1926, Butting directed the series of concerts, which varied in number from two to five per year.   The programs included works by Berg, Webern, Schoenberg, Hindemith, Bartók, Stravinsky, Krenek, Ravel, Kodály, Satie, Lendvai, as well as compositions of official members.

Busoni's master class was well represented with Jarnach, Vogel, and Weill, who supported the teacher's aesthetic views in many discussions, which encompassed not only musical topics, but literature, art, architecture, politics, and the problems of a new social order.[89]   It is obvious from just these three composers, whose music diverged so far in style and intent, that the November Group musicians were far from unanimous in musical expression.   They did share a common ideal of communication with a wider audience and a desire to educate. Stuckenschmidt, who replaced Butting as co-ordinator of the concerts, described Weill's particular role as follows:

> Weill, the most successful of his generation, distinguished himself as the leader of musical activism: that what is expressed in music is just as important as the music itself.[90]

The religious and social concerns of Weill's music composed during his association with the November Group (Symphony no. 1, Divertimento, *Sinfonia sacra*, String Quartet no. 1) gradually became less prominent in the absolute music written under Busoni's tutelage. Eventually Weill's commitment to the theater, itself one of the most viable vehicles for social commentary, and his collaboration with Brecht, himself an associate of the November Group, drew him away from active participation in the activities of the Group.[91]   However, the social criticism and behavioral ethics of *Mahagonny* and *Die Dreigroschenoper,* the political activism of *Happy End,* the didactic intent of *Der Jasager,* and the moralistic fable of *Die Bürgschaft* are all reflections of the idealistic aims that Weill shared with the intellectuals who comprised

Berlin's November Group. Perhaps more than any of its other members, Weill articulated musically the humanitarian ideals of the Group without falling victim to simplistic slogans or partisan manifestoes which proved to be pitfalls for others.

Weill's Quartet consists of three movements played without pause: Introduktion, Scherzo, Choralphantasie.[92] Kastner cited the Quartet's "conciseness of form and brilliant flow of movement," Strobel the "surprising elegance and motor-rhythm," and Fleischer saw in this early work evidence of the "gestic accent of the march embedded in the Scherzo that was later developed in Weill's parodistic marches."[93] Even Busoni considered the Quartet Weill's best composition to date, and it was on the basis of its quality that he recommended Weill to the powerful head of Universal-Edition, Emil Hertzka (1869-1932), in a letter dating from July 1923:

> I have given my pupil *Kurt Weill* a letter addressed to you, which you ought to receive in a short time. It concerned Weill's string quartet, a work of splendid qualities with power and invention. I hardly know a piece by ,a 23-year-old of the present day that is so attractive and worthwhile.—It is thoroughly "modern," without any ugly features. I emphasized in the letter that you should promptly grab this talent. Incidentally (and yet it is so important), Weill is a man who thinks and is well-read, a man of the most upstanding character.[94]

Hertzka evidently took Busoni's advice in that before the end of the year he offered Weill a contract. Hans Heinsheimer, who joined the staff of Universal in 1923 and eventually headed its opera division, described the less than optimal terms of Weill's contract:

> Kurt Weill's contract with us—as were most composers' contracts—was a ten-year, first-refusal deal. It imposed on the composer the strict obligation to submit every manuscript written during these ten years to the publisher before showing it to anybody else and if he did not submit a carefully stipulated minimum of works during his term of servitude, the contract extended itself automatically until he had done so, which might be forever. The publisher, on the other hand, had only one very strictly spelled out obligation: to prepay the postage on any manuscript he rejected and returned, unpublished, to the composer.[95]

When Weill signed the agreement, Universal accepted the String Quartet for publication, but the first of his compositions to be published was not the Quartet, but rather *Frauentanz: Sieben Gedichte des Mittelalters,* op. 10.[96]

Composed in Heide during a summer holiday in July 1923, *Frauentanz*, a song cycle for soprano and flute, viola, clarinet, bassoon, and horn, was premiered in Berlin during February 1924 with Nora Pisling-Boas as vocalist and Fritz Stiedry conducting.[97] A few months later the work "excited a stir" at the International Society for Contemporary Music (hereafter ISCM) chamber music festival in Salzburg.[98] This performance in August 1924, conducted by Jarnach, was "perhaps still more impressive than the premiere in Berlin, for Lotte Leonard elevated these songs with the beauty of her voice and sensitive delivery."[99] Kastner described the performance in more detail:

> The cycle *Frauentanz*, . . . wonderfully interpreted by Lotte Leonard, made Kurt Weill's name famous at the Salzburg International Chamber Music Festival, 1924. Here with the most reduced musical means, the most extremely fluid expression is found in the most compressed form. With particular power Weill avoided any opulence of harmony, the reef of Schönbergian interval-reproduction, on which so much runs aground. Weill has coined his own melodic arch and impregnated the poetic content with his music.[100]

After its presentation in Salzburg, *Frauentanz* was added to the repertoire of several sopranos who performed it throughout Europe.[101]

The seven poems of the cycle are modern adaptations of texts of *Minnelieder* dating from the twelfth and thirteenth centuries. Three of the poets were identified in Weill's score: Dietmar von Aiste (I); Der von Kürenburg (IV); Herzog Johann von Brabant (V).[102] Only two of the seven movements utilize the entire ensemble; the remaining songs call for smaller combinations of instruments—the fifth is for soprano and viola alone. In addition to the full score and parts, which had been published in 1924, the following year Universal brought out a piano-vocal edition of the cycle. The third movement of this edition bears the superscription: "The piano arrangement of this number is the last work of Ferruccio Busoni."[103] It cannot be determined whether or not Busoni had intended to make the transcription of the entire work; he died on 27 July 1924.

Before terminating his three years of study at the Prussian Academy of Arts in December 1923, Weill completed one other composition: *Recordare: Klagelieder Jeremiae V. Kapitel*, op. 11. Written for four-part *a cappella* mixed chorus and two part boys' chorus in September 1923, *Recordare* was never performed during Weill's lifetime.[104] A virtual compendium of polyphonic techniques dating back to the Renaissance, *Recordare* demanded performers who could negotiate angular part-writing more appropriate for performance by instruments. Weill's admirer, Hermann Scherchen, when offered the score in 1923, told Weill that even with unlimited rehearsals the work was technically so difficult as to be practically unperformable. The score was not published and was assumed to have been lost until 1970, when Oliver Neighbour of the British Museum rediscovered a copyist's manuscript in Paris.[105] The premiere of the twenty-four-minute work occurred in Utrecht as part of the 1971 Holland Festival. Dedicated to his brother Hans Weill and based on the Latin text of the fifth chapter of the Lamentations of Jeremiah, the multi-sectional but single-movement composition awaits an American performance.

In the following years, artistic experiments characterized by struggles for new harmonic and melodic means of expression overpowered my work.[106]

— *Kurt Weill* —

V

Immediately after his return from a trip to Italy, Weill composed a Concerto for Violin and Wind Orchestra, op. 12, in April and May 1924.[107]   Although it was composed for Joseph Szigeti (1892-1973), violinist Marcel Darrieux premiered the concerto at an ISCM concert in Paris on 11 June 1925 with Walter Straram conducting.[108]   It "was widely noticed" and "extraordinarily well-received by Parisian critics."[109]   In October 1925 Dessau served as host for a "home-town" peformance with Stephan Frenkel (b. 1902) as soloist, a virtuoso who possessed the heroic technique demanded by the Concerto.   In reviewing the performance, Peter Bing described the work and noted its parallels with Stravinsky's Piano Concerto (1923-24):

> A new Concerto for Violin and Wind Orchestra by Kurt Weill was heard in the third subscription concert of the Kapelle des Friedrichtheaters as a German premiere—with Bela Bartók's *Dance Suite* in its first local performance.   The work, which was completed already in May 1924, assumes the instrumentation of Stravinsky's Piano Concerto: winds, contrabass, and percussion. . . . What this score particularly exhibits is an abundance of serious ideas, which are contained in the three movements of the Concerto, as well as a tendency toward deeper emotion and a genuinely striking gift for formal construction. . . . Despite its extreme difficulty, the violin part is not ungrateful; without ever being covered by the orchestra, the soloist can unfold a blossoming tone in wide cantilenas.   But then in the runs, chains of trills, double-stops, and sonorous pizzicati he can display his technical bravura and ultimately prove his musicality in the musical shaping.   Stefan Frenkel played the work excellently in all the cited details; he was especially successful with the Cadenza.[110]

Despite excellent notices from these first performances, the Concerto did not receive widespread attention until its appearance at the ISCM Festival in Zürich, 18-23 June 1926.   Frenkel played it with Fritz Busch on the podium in a concert that included Webern's *Five Pieces for Orchestra*, op. 10.[111]   Adolf Weissmann, obviously no fan of Webern, declared the Concerto to be the outstanding composition of the evening:

> Generally speaking, the fourth concert signified a respite for the ear from the hardship of orchestral gluttony.   I regard Kurt Weill's Concerto for Violin and Wind Orchestra as the most noteworthy work of the evening, because here the unusualness of sound is suitably presented by the peculiarity of the conception.

One might point to Stravinsky's example for the exclusion of the strings. But I still believe that Kurt Weill stands absolutely on his own ground in his contrast of violinist and orchestra, admitting the contrabass as the only string instrument. . . . The future development of Kurt Weill, this highly-talented young artist, will show if he can shake off all spasmodic elements. His instinctive certainty is not to be doubted.[112]

Alfred Einstein wrote that Weill had "irritated many people with his violin concerto."[113] One of them obviously was the twenty-six year-old Aaron Copland, who wrote:

Last and probably least, was a Concerto for violin and wood wind [sic] orchestra by Kurt Weill, a young German. The less said about this very dull work, the better, particularly since there seems to be a certain tendency to regard his more recent one-act opera, *Der Protagonist*, as quite important.[114]

Stefan Frenkel continued to play the Concerto throughout Europe; in fact his success and identification with the work was so considerable that his concert management placed a full-page advertisement in *Anbruch*, which cited excerpts from reviews.[115] Although there were a few performances by other soloists, including Kulenkampf (Magdeburg, December 1928), the Concerto remained almost exclusively a showpiece for Frenkel, who played it as late as 1930 under Ansermet.[116] An edition for violin and piano was published in 1925, but the orchestral score, announced in the same year, did not appear until 1965.[117]

Weill's interest in the poetry of Rainer Maria Rilke did not end in 1919 with the composition of his symphonic poem based on *Die Weise von Liebe und Tod des Cornets Christoph Rilke*. In 1922 Weill had begun work on a set of songs for voice and piano on texts of Rilke.[118] He did not finish the cycle at this point, but in 1925 he did complete two sets of three songs each for voice and orchestra: *Stundenbuch, Orchesterlieder nach Texten von Rilke*, op. 13 & 14. In the context of Weill's other works dating from this period, his affinity with the mystical and religious poetry of Rilke's *Book of Hours* is not surprising. In 1926 Weill testified to his continuing admiration for this collection of poetry:

[Rilke] is probably the most sensitive and intense among the previous generation, which may possibly be best compared with the Impressionist course in painting. Yet Rilke's art did not remain merely atmospheric painting; rather it is unusually deepened by its mystical-religious contemplation of God, as it is particularly articulated in his uniquely poetic and extraordinarily rich work, *Das Stundenbuch*.[119]

First published in 1905, *Das Stundenbuch* consisted of three parts: I "Das Buch vom menschischen Leben" (1899), II "Das Buch von der Pilgerschaft" (1901), III "Das Buch von der Armut und vom Tode"

(1903).[120] The subject of this early work, if such a simplistic construction can be applied to this labyrinth of religious reveries and ecstasies, is the salvation of the world through art.

The premiere of the six songs which comprised Weill's op. 13 and 14 occurred in Berlin during 1925.[121] No other performances have been recorded; neither set was published; and there are only peripheral references to the work in contemporary criticism.[122] The manuscript was presumed lost until recently when two songs, one from each set, were found among articles in a bequest to the Library of Westminster Choir College in Princeton, New Jersey.[123] The extant material consists of a piano-vocal reduction, an orchestral score, and a full set of parts for each song.[124] The songs are marked "I" and "VI," but neither composer nor title is indicated. Undoubtedly the songs are the first song of Set I, opus 13 and the last song of Set II, opus 14. The only explicit and conclusive identification is "Kurt Weill" in blue crayon which appears on the bass drum part of "I." The manuscript carries the stamp of Weill's copyist, Dr. Wohlauer.

The text of "I" is the first poem of Rilke's Book III of *Das Stundenbuch*: "Vielleicht, dass ich durch schwere Berge gehe." It is labeled "Grave, un poco largo" and is scored for a large orchestra:

3 flutes	4 horns	tympani
2 oboes	2 trumpets in A	percussion
2 clarinets in A	3 trombones	strings
2 bassoons		voice

"VI" is the eighteenth poem of Rilke's Book II: "In diesem Dorfe steht das letzte Haus." Its tempo marking is "Andante con lento" and the instrumentation is significantly different:

2 flutes	2 horns	tympani
2 oboes	2 trumpets in C	strings
2 clarinets in B♭	3 trombones	voice
2 bassoons		

It is curious that the two sets evidently were numbered consecutively from I to VI and were obviously textually related, but the variation in instrumentation would tend to make performance of the two sets as a unit rather awkward.

Ever since I made up my mind, at the age of 19, that my field of special activity would be the theatre, I have tried continuously to solve, in my own way, the form-problems of the musical theatre, and through the years I have approached these problems from all angles. One of the first decisions I made was to get leading dramatists of our time interested in the problems of the musical theatre.[125]

— *Kurt Weill* —

VI

Weill was not unique among young German composers in his commitment to the theater as a medium for musical expression. The more than eighty major opera houses in Germany, nearly all of which were beneficiaries of government subsidy, could regularly mount productions of new operas without risking financial stability. Such potential for production encouraged composers to write for the theater. In the early twenties, in a conscious break with the previous century's lengthy operas and music dramas, most newly-composed operas were relatively short one-act works—modest in scope, Expressionist or Surrealist in content, often performed several times and then forgotten.[126] The first genuine, sustained operatic success of this younger generation in Germany was that of Weill's *Der Protagonist* [*The Protagonist*].

Weill's collaborator for *Der Protagonist* was Georg Kaiser (1878-1945), the most distinguished, prolific, and frequently performed of German Expressionist dramatists. As one of the most controversial literary figures of the time, Kaiser once had seven plays premiered during a single season, and for a time critics suspected that "Kaiser" might be the pseudonym for a group of playwrights.[127] After the ban in 1933 which prohibited further performances of his works, Kaiser's fifty-nine full-length plays, seven one-act dramas, two novels, and one hundred thirty poems were relegated to virtual obscurity and today remain relatively unknown. Already in 1922, however, Ashley Duke's introduction to his English translation of *From Morn to Midnight* labeled Kaiser as "the founder of a new dramatic school" and cited his "singular economy of words."[128] Indeed, Kaiser's conscious attempt to abandon old syntactical structures in favor of a new language for the modern theater was applauded by Bertolt Brecht, who admired a number of Kaiser's plays, once called him the reigning monarch of German theater, and on the occasion of Kaiser's fiftieth birthday stated that without a knowledge of his innovations all efforts in behalf of drama must remain fruitless.[129]   In the context of Brecht's later formulation of *Verfrem-*

dungseffekt ("distancing effect") in epic theater, it is revealing that Kaiser described his own plays as "a device for keeping reality at a distance."[130]

Kaiser's personal life, marred by private scandals, was much less successful than his artistic endeavors. Seeking solution to his financial problems (despite a considerable income from royalties) by illegally selling furnishings and art objects from houses that he rented, in 1920 he was arrested, tried, and sentenced to six months in prison. "His utterances during the trial build up a picture of a man so completely obsessed by his literary production, by a belief in the supreme value of his work, as to be divorced from the most palpable realities of the world around him."[131] Indeed, the conflict of physical and mental reality is the central theme of many of Kaiser's plays, including *Der Protagonist*:

> He is constantly concerned to observe how these two independent realities come into conflict, how the one merges into the other and the tension between them is finally resolved by the triumph of one or the other—either of the mind or of the body. This problem of the nature of reality is presented at its most acute in the figure of the artist, who must necessarily live vicariously, at least to some extent. The writer, the actor, the sculptor, the musician—in all of these Kaiser examines his own problem of reconciling the ideal with the real world, or shows the vanity of attempting this reconciliation.[132]

Although Kaiser was already familiar with Weill's *Die Zaubernacht,* the two were finally brought together by the conductor Fritz Busch (1890-1951), whom Weill had met at a performance of Busoni's *Arlecchino* at the Dresden State Opera.[133] The actual collaboration between Kaiser and Weill began in January 1924 when they sketched the outlines of a three-act pantomime. Weill described the evolution of *Der Protagonist*:

> I was very happy and delighted when Georg Kaiser offered to write a full-length ballet plot for me. We approached the work together. In ten weeks, almost three-quarters of the work had been completed. The score of the prologue and the first two acts were finished. It stopped there. We had outgrown the subject matter; the silence of these figures tormented us. We had to burst the fetters of this pantomime: it had to become an opera. Georg Kaiser reached back for an older play—the one-act *Der Protagonist*—which in his own mind he had already envisioned as an opera. Here we had what we were looking for: an unconventional, adventitious intermingling of opera and pantomime.[134]

Kaiser's one-act drama, written in 1920 and published the following year, had been premiered in Breslau at the Lobettheater on 16 March 1922.[135] Adaptation of the play as a libretto occupied Kaiser and Weill throughout 1924, when Weill was a frequent house guest of the Kaisers in their country home at Grünheide. During one of his trips he met a young Viennese dancer-actress, Karoline Blamauer (b. 1898). This young actress, whose stage name was Lotte Lenya, later recalled:

> The first time I saw him was at the end of a lake on the outskirts of Berlin. I was staying at the summer house of Georg Kaiser, the playwright; he asked me to row across the lake and pick up a young composer waiting at the station who wanted Kaiser to write a libretto for him. There he was: five feet, three and a half inches tall—an inch taller than I—with his hairline already receding, and thick, thick glasses. But the face was gentle, poetic, warm. That is how I first remember Kurt Weill.[136]

Kaiser finished the libretto in December 1924; in July 1925 Universal-Edition announced that the score, which Weill had completed in April, was being prepared for publication.[137] The piano-vocal score of the opera, dedicated to Lotte Lenya, appeared in October 1925, and Weill and Lenya were married three months later on 28 January 1926. Because Universal's publication predated the premiere of *Der Protagonist* by six months, before it had yet been seen on stage, Kastner wrote:

> It is an old Shakespearean motive that Kaiser treated in this youthful work: *commedia dell'arte* is blended at the request of the host (just as with Molière's *Bourgeois gentilhomme* and Strauss' *Ariadne*) with tragedy. . . . In the plot there are two pantomimes, the comic and the tragic. This gives Weill the desired occasion to employ two orchestras. In the pit with the strings and percussion there are only two oboes and bass clarinets, three horns and trombones—on stage there is a wind octet of two flutes, clarinets, trumpets, and bassoons. The orchestras play alternately, rarely in combination. . . . It is predominantly instrumental, "hollowed-out," dramatized chamber music, and it is strikingly in accord with Berg's *Wozzeck*, which was unknown to Weill, or with Stravinsky's *Soldier's Tale*, but only in the means.[138]

Because Busch had asked to be notified when the opera was finished, Weill kept him informed of the work's progress. Upon its completion, Weill sent him a telegram and in return received a railroad ticket to Dresden. The score met with the approval of Busch, one of the most daring champions of new music, and arrangements were made for the premiere.[139] Directed by Joseph Gielen, *Der Protagonist* opened on 27 March 1926 with Kurt Taucher in the title role and Elisa Stünzer as his sister. A twenty-minute ovation, more than forty curtain calls, and reviews nearly unanimous in their praise greeted the first performance.[140] Oskar Bie, one of the most powerful critics, called it "an almost perfect blending of music and drama," and pointed out the irony of this success of a twenty-five year-old pupil of Busoni—a success which had consistently eluded Busoni himself. "All of the philosophical theories of the teacher Busoni have been swept aside by the reality of Weill's score."[141] Heinrich Strobel perceived *Der Protagonist* as the beginning of a development which "clearly and purposefully leads to a new type of opera."[142] Another critic hailed it as a colossal success, rivaled only by *Wozzeck*.[143]

The most perceptive of the critics was Maurice Abravanel, who studied composition with Weill from 1925 to 1927 and later became one of the foremost interpreters of Weill's music in Germany, France, England, and the United States. His review of *Der Protagonist* for *La Revue musicale* reveals the overwhelming effect of Weill's opera on a musical community seeking to free itself from the domination of Wagnerian music drama and attempting to incorporate the techniques of modern theater in opera. Abravanel described the effect of detachment from the audience that Weill achieved in *Der Protagonist*:

> Weill, whose symphonies and chamber music have made him known along with Hindemith and Krenek as one of the representatives of new German music, does not share the fashionable skepticism of opera. . . . This work not only reveals Weill's extraordinary sense of theater, it crystallizes his talent and clarifies the obscurities of his earlier works. . . . The music does not illustrate the action: it *is* the action. The text conveys the external, visible drama. On a more profound plane, the music explains the psychological action, which is inaccessible through language. In union with his collaborator, Weill carefully avoids anything which could alter the clarity of the drama and lower its value. He neither weeps for the murder of the sister nor does he ask us to empathize with the despair of the hero. He is satisfied only to show them, but with such exactness that the audience is overcome.
>
> This is what gives the work its particular value. *Der Protagonist* is, as far as I know, the first successful attempt in opera at moving an audience without enlisting its sympathy. . . . We have only once seen a German audience (like that at the performance of *Der Protagonist*) completely overwhelmed by the immediate power of a work whose musical essence it could understand: the performance of *Sacre* in Berlin by Ansermet. Isn't it really this immediate impact which is the object of theater? How many operas since Wagner can be said to have attained this objective? The intense success of this creation is reaffirmed at each performance; that bothers the passionate German music-lover who respects only boredom, but this places Kurt Weill in the first rank of contemporary dramatic composers.[144]

After its premiere in Dresden, *Der Protagonist* entered the repertory with productions in Erfurt, Barmen, Danzig, Gotha, and Nürnberg during the 1927-28 season.[145] The following year brought the opera to Berlin, Frankfurt, Hannover, Leipzig, Stuttgart. From 1930 to 1933 its continued production was limited by the economic crises of the opera houses and the less than subtle censorship which preceded the wholesale replacement of artistic leadership in many houses. After 1933, of course, performances of *Der Protagonist*, like those of Weill's other compositions, were prohibited by the new regime's guardians of culture.

Despite its success, *Der Protagonist* did little to help Weill's financial situation. Lenya recalled that "we were so poor that he [Kurt] had to rent a tuxedo to appear at the opening of his first big success."[146] Since Weill's contract with Universal-Edition offered no guarantees, no advances, and no monthly payments, he was dependent upon the meager royalties from his compositions, few of which sold enough to recover their printing cost.[147] In order to improve his economic status, Weill, who was only twenty-five at the time, accepted a number of private composition students, including Maurice Abravanel (b. 1903), Claudio Arrau (b. 1903), and Nikos Skalkottas (1904-49). In addition, he was employed as music and theater critic (Berlin correspondent) of *Der deutsche Rundfunk,* a weekly journal devoted to technical, social, and programmatic aspects of radio. Established in 1923 and edited by Hans S. von Heister, the periodical listed the programs of major German radio stations for the approaching week, printed articles about the role of radio in society and art, and published criticism of musical and theatrical presentations. From 12 April 1925 to 17 May 1929, Weill regularly contributed two or three essays to the weekly.

Undoubtedly Weill's initial motivation in writing for the German radio industry was to bolster his income, but the four-year tenure and the extent of his contributions indicate a genuine enthusiasm for radio as a medium for wider communication of music and theater. The advent of radio, phonograph recordings, and sound-film initiated a general and sustained interest in the relationship of the arts and the new technology. Issues of music journals were devoted to "Musik und Maschine," and sundry essays with titles such as "Die Musikalische Welt in Maschinenzeitalter" and "Rundfunk und musikalische Kultur" explored the possible effects of the new inventions.[148] Like many of the musicians associated with the November Group, Weill was concerned with building a wider, more "democratic" audience. In addition to his regular contributions to *Der deutsche Rundfunk,* Weill wrote several essays that specifically dealt with the relationship of music and radio: "Der Rundfunk und die Umschichtung des Musiklebens," "Ueber die Möglichkeiten einer Rundfunkversuchsstelle," and "Der Rundfunk und die neue Musik."[149] Composers viewed the orchestras, theaters, and choruses that were affiliated with radio stations as instruments capable of reaching a larger audience, since weekly programs included broadcasts of plays, operas, new music, dance music, and jazz. Weill presented a number of lectures on the Berlin radio, among them a formal analysis of Bartók's String Quartet no. 1 and a discussion of Busoni's career and music.[150]

The Berlin Radio Station commissioned Weill to write incidental music for Christian Dietrich Grabbe's five-act tragedy, *Herzog Theodor von Gothland,* adapted as a *Hörspiel* by Klabund and Alfred Braun.[151] Grabbe (1801-36), a German playwright contemporary with Georg Büchner and Heinrich Heine, completed *Herzog Theodor von Gothland* in 1822, and it is his earliest extant work.[152] Weill wrote the score, which calls for a large orchestra and chorus, for this radio drama during July and August 1926. It was broadcast on 1 September 1926 with Bruno Seidler-Winkler conducting.[153] The score was not published and is presumed lost. It was the first of Weill's compositions utilizing saxophones to be performed.[154] Of more significance, however, was the epic nature of Weill's music and its role in the presentation of the drama:

> Kurt Weill's music breaks essentially a new path, dominated completely by the melodic element. His score aims at neither programmatic depiction nor characterization through use of leitmotives; it is entirely devoted to the provisos of the larger issues of the drama. In its textless singing, the chorus, like that of ancient tragedy, provides a somber "pedal point" which flows from the very depths; in comparison the drama appears to be lively ornamentation. All individual effects are subordinated to this basic tone of tragic inevitability that reaches its shattering climax in the beautiful song [*Lied*] of the outcast woman. She speaks the verses while the saxophone carries the melody. In this hermetical work of profound expressive power, the music does not try to accompany the plot in its details. The drama and music meet in the only possible way on the magical level of essential content. The result is a synthesis of lasting significance for both play and music.[155]

Even before *Der Protagonist* and *Herzog Theodor von Gothland* had been performed, Weill was at work on two compositions with texts by Iwan Goll.[156] Goll (1891-1950), also known as Isaac Lang, was a poet, novelist, and dramatist of Jewish Alsace-Lorraine parentage, who wrote with comparable facility in both French and German.[157] Weill and Goll probably met through their mutual friend Kaiser; Stuckenschmidt recalled that they met in the Romanisches Café, the intellectual "watering hole" of Berlin.[158] The first product of their association was *Der neue Orpheus,* op. 16, a cantata for soprano, violin, and orchestra, composed in September 1925. In June 1926 Universal-Edition announced publication of the orchestral score and an arrangement for piano, violin, and voice edited by Arthur Willner.[159] The score was dedicated to Lotte Leonard, the soprano who had sung Weill's *Frauentanz* at the ISCM festival in 1924. *Der neue Orpheus* was premiered as a prelude to the Weill-Goll opera, *Royal Palace,* in the Berlin Staatsoper under Erich Kleiber on Weill's twenty-seventh birthday, 2 March 1927.[160] Like *Royal Palace,* the cantata received mixed reactions from the critics, although despite his negative opinion of the opera which followed it, Paul Stefan wrote that *Der neue Orpheus* "proves that Weill is one of the strongest hopes of today."[161] A more characteristic response was that of Hugo Leichtentritt:

> The opera was preceded by Weill's cantata, *Der neue Orpheus*, for soprano solo (Delia Reinhardt), violin solo (Rudolf Deman) and orchestra. Here Ivan Goll has parodized [sic], not without a certain humor, the struggle of the artist against the world. Weill has taken this cabaret number rather too seriously and has made of it a complicated piece of symphonic writing, with an orchestra à la Stravinsky, a toilsome and not very amusing affair, which passed by without noticeable effect.[162]

Heinrich Strobel also noted the "clear imitation of Stravinsky's language of the cabaret chanson" and described *Der neue Orpheus* as a "scenic cantata," which would indicate that it may have been staged.[163]

The Associated Press news release describing the premiere of *Royal Palace* began:

> Auto horns, moving pictures and a jazz band made their operatic debut at the State Opera House here tonight with the world premiere of Kurt Weill's ultra-modern opera, *The Royal Palace* [sic]. The innovations brought wild applause and a few scattering hisses. . . . The opera, which might be described as a blend of revue and classical opera, consisted of thirty-eight scenes. The performance lasted less than an hour.[164]

Composed between October 1925 and January 1926, *Royal Palace* had the misfortune to be premiered only a few weeks after Krenek's *Jonny spielt auf,* which had stunned the operatic world with its novel jazz sections and obvious topicality. Even though Weill's *Royal Palace* was composed concurrently with Krenek's *Jonny*, critics assumed that Weill's was the duplicate. No one noticed that Weill's integration of popular dance idioms, functioning as social commentary at the behest of the drama, served a purpose different from Krenek's use of jazz.[165] Again Leichtentritt's review is representative:

> *Royal Palace* was intended as a rival to Krenek's *Johnny* [sic], which was given with such success a few weeks ago in Leipsic; and while in positive attainments and shortcomings Krenek and Weill are about equal, the former had the advantage of an insolent but amusing and effective libretto, whereas Ivan Goll's libretto for *Royal Palace* confounds effect with affectation, and stands a good chance of winning first prize for the dullest opera book in existence. It is strange that Weill, a pupil of Busoni and up to now so serious-minded, should have accepted such a book. . . . It is patently impossible to write worthwhile music to the ridiculous dialogue of this action. Moreover, the variety show on the stage is so dazzling that one almost forgets the music, though Weill has taken all possible pains to make his score interesting. Mahler, Schoenberg, Stravinsky and the French school are entirely familiar to him, and he makes liberal use of their

attainments. His talent is noticeable in the facility with which he treats the complicated apparatus, in the brilliancy and rhythmical vivacity of his dance music, and in moments of real expressiveness, alas, too short and too few to give the impression of soulful music. For the most part Weill's score is a cold, glittering, technically interesting but nearly expressionless combination of sounds— the product of a clever intellect.[166]

It is not surprising that Leichtentritt found Goll's libretto rather dull, for Goll considered opera and drama to be complete opposites. As a combination of revue, ballet, pantomime, film, and opera, *Royal Palace* attempted to recount the tale of the heroine's life through flashbacks in lyric poetry rather than through dramatic dialogue. Goll stated his good intentions in an essay, itself rather confusing, entitled "Flucht in die Oper." Like the libretto of *Royal Palace*, it reads as a surrealist stream of consciousness and posits a most eccentric view of opera:

> The greatest fortune that a lyric poet can wish for is to hear his work transformed into music. For does he not write it, in the final sense, for the sound, that heavenly x-ray which illuminates the soul? A sisterly warmth brings music to the poet, who stands freezing in this cold Stone Age. . . . Opera is the most consummate form of lyric poetry. By no means does it belong in the dramatic genre just because it is played on a stage. Opera and drama are complete opposites. The soul of drama is the plot, that of opera is rhythm. In drama it is thought, in opera it is felt. The substance of drama is logic, that of opera is the dream. Drama is life, opera a fairy tale. . . . *Royal Palace* was written directly for music and for an exceptional artist of our time. In it, effects have been calculated which only serve the music and unselfishly neglect brilliant decoration. . . . The text of an opera does not depend on verses or sentences, but rather words. . . . And from the one word "Dejanira," what hasn't Kurt Weill created! More than the magic of the woman is the magic of her name. This word plays the principal role in this opera. . . . *Royal Palace* is the fairy tale of life that is first perceived in death.[167]

Weill certainly did create a great deal from the heroine's name, Dejanira: the final seventeen pages of the piano-vocal score (more than 20% of its total length), a gigantic tango-finale, utilize only the four syllables of "Dejanira" in various permutations, such as "Ja-ni-ra-de," "Ra-je-di-na," and "Ni-ra-ja-de."

Goll's concept of opera and its realization in the libretto of *Royal Palace* now seems too ludicrous for serious discussion. The most striking aspects of the opera are those "brilliant decorations" that Goll said he would unselfishly omit—particularly the film scene, in which the major events in Dejanira's life are recalled. This scene, which prompted Paul Stefan to call *Royal Palace* the first film-opera, depicted an airplane trip around the world.[168] It elicited from Weill an attempt to duplicate the sounds of a metropolis.[169]   For the most part, however, Weill's music comments on the scenic events rather than illustrates them.

Although *Royal Palace* played only seven performances in Berlin, it should not be dismissed as an insignificant score.[170]   It represents a critical transition in Weill's career.   He adopted not only popular dance idioms and instrumentation derived from jazz, but also elements of the revue and innovative theatrical effects that figure prominently in his later music.   One can easily refute Brecht's claim that he was responsible for Weill's conversion from "relatively complicated music of a mainly psychological sort" to the novel, simpler style.[171]   The simplification of Weill's densely contrapuntal and boldly experimental harmonic vocabulary was a gradual one, achieved over a lengthy period of time with deliberate and self-conscious efforts toward that goal.   In a letter to his parents dating from the time of the composition of *Royal Palace*, Weill wrote:

> But this year now I have reached the point where an artist sits on a powder keg, where unused energies must erupt explosively, where a heightened sensitivity engenders a constant state of excitement and stimulation. . . . Now it's exciting for me again.   I am buried in this new opera.   I only go out of the house to settle the most important external matters.   I must master an expression that is still new to me.   And to my satisfaction, I have determined—what I already discovered with *Der neue Orpheus*—that gradually I am forging ahead to "me," that my music is much surer, freer, looser, and—simpler.[172]

In 1926, Universal-Edition published the libretto and piano-vocal score of *Royal Palace* as op. 17.   The orchestral score was never published; the manuscript full score and the only set of orchestral parts were somehow lost even before Weill fled Germany in 1933.   Because the published vocal score, now long out of print, listed the instrumentation and was unusually detailed in its cues, in 1968 Gunther Schuller and Noam Sheriff attempted a reconstruction of the orchestral score as a dance-drama with singing.[173]   Although *Royal Palace* may never achieve success in the theater, its place in Weill's development was succinctly summarized by Strobel:

> *Royal Palace* signifies a definite turning away from traditional subject matter of opera.   Therein lies its significance if one ignores the musical value of the score entirely.   Weill took off from the pantomime music of *Der Protagonist.*   At the same time a new stylistic impulse appears: jazz is introduced into the musical language as the typical musical expression of the era. . . .   The Tango-Finale foreshadows the style of the next encompassing work, *Mahagonny.*   As a whole, *Royal Palace* can be taken only as a transition, an attempt at an artistic configuration of the era, which had to run aground on Iwan Goll's aesthetic world of letters.[174]

Kurt Weill is a great talent, but the danger of being devoured by his intellect threatens him.[175]

— *Karl Holl* —

VII

If *Royal Palace* ran aground on the reef of its libretto, Weill's next opera, *Na und?*, never moved out of dry dock, again primarily because of its faulty libretto, the first attempt of Felix Joachimson, a young music critic. The first reference to this two-act comic opera, Weill's first attempt at a full evening's opera, appeared in January 1926, when Weill was completing *Royal Palace*:

> Kurt Weill, whose *Der Protagonist* (text by Georg Kaiser) will be premiered at the Dresden Staatsoper in March, has completed a new one-act opera, *Royal Palace* (text by Iwan Goll), and has been working for a time on a full-length stage work of comic character.[176]

In the June 1926 issue of *Die Musik* the work was labeled as a "musiquette in two acts" and identified by title as *Na und?*[177] Although *Anbruch* chronicled its completion in September 1926,[178] a reference in the issue of *Blätter der Staatsoper* devoted to *Royal Palace* indicated that *Na und?* was still unfinished in February 1927:

> In Weill's still unfinished latest stage work, the musiquette *Na und?*, the expressive means of *Der Protagonist* and *Royal Palace* (especially the soloistic treatment of the piano in opera) will be further developed.[179]

Up to this point, Weill had been very successful in obtaining performances and publication of his works; however, he was not so fortunate with *Na und?* Although Universal-Edition had already advertised the score as being in preparation,[180] when Weill went to Vienna to play the score for Hertzka and Heinsheimer, their negative response killed any hope that the score would be printed:

> We did not like anything about the work. We did not like the libretto. . . We loathed the title of the opera which seemed to reflect the asphalt cynicism of Berlin . . . We expressed our fears that this work would, at this point in his career, be a dangerous setback.[181]

Weill sought a second opinion from Hans Curjel, the dramaturg of the Kroll Opera, who concurred with the evaluation of Weill's publishers:

He brought me the completed score of the opera *Na und?* whose text Felix
Joachimson had written for him. Weill allowed me to take the score for study,
which took many weeks of my time. Then he came into my office to receive the
verdict. I explained to him that I considered the work unsuccessful, both textually
and musically. He received my judgment with great equanimity. I conceded that
I might be wrong and we resolved to lock the score in my desk for a month; I
had the only key. In order to view his own work from some distance, Weill was
to pick up the score again after four weeks. That's what happened. After a few
days, Weill telephoned me. He had arrived at a similar impression and had
decided never to allow the opera to be performed. The score was then lost in the
course of intervening years. Perhaps it will surface again like the score of Weill's
First Symphony of 1921.[182]

Only an incomplete folder of sketches, which include a number of
musical ideas that eventually found their way into *Aufstieg und Fall der
Stadt Mahagonny,* has survived.[183] *Na und?* was Weill's only completed
stage work composed after the age of twenty that was not performed
during his lifetime. His remarkable record of securing production for his
later operas is at least partially due to very careful choice and supervision
of librettists after the unfortunate experience with Joachimson.

Acceding to the request of producers for a companion piece to *Der
Protagonist,* Weill resumed his collaboration with his trusted friend and
librettist, Georg Kaiser.[184] Their work on a one-act *opera buffa*
commenced in March 1927, approximately the same time that Weill and
Brecht initiated their first artistic association.[185] The six-month gestation
period of *Der Zar lässt sich photographieren* (*The Czar Has His
Photograph Taken,* hereafter *Zar*) witnessed several changes in the
opera's title. The July 1927 issue of *Die Musik* referred to Weill's new
one-act opera as "Photographie und Liebe"; in announcing its
completion in its August-September issue, *Anbruch* called it "Der Zar
lässt sich . . ."; by the time of its premiere on 18 February 1928, the
opera assumed its final ironic but less ambiguous title.[186] The first
performance in Leipzig under Gustav Brecher (1879-1940) was not paired
with *Der Protagonist* but with Nicola Spinelli's *A Basso Porto.*[187]

Critical reception was preponderantly favorable. In a critique of
the premiere, Adolf Aber noted two striking inventions of *Zar:* the use
of a male chorus, bearded and dressed in top hats and formal wear and
positioned in the orchestra pit, to comment on the on-stage events and
the utilization of a phonograph recording of a tango to accompany an
aria. He wrote:

> When Kurt Weill's *Der Protagonist* was staged a few years ago in Dresden
> with absolutely extraordinary success, one knew that impressive things were still to
> be expected from this young music dramatist. And one also recognized that only
> very seldom could so fortunate a collaboration between a librettist and composer

be recorded as the alliance of Kurt Weill with the refined theatrical technician, Georg Kaiser. Now this combination has proven itself for the second time. In an attempt to add a comic companion piece to *Der Protagonist*, the two artists have come together again, and the product of their union is the extremely effective, entertaining, and witty piece that the Leipzig Opera produced in an exceptionally brilliant performance.[188]

Theodor W. Adorno called the male chorus "schizophrenic" in that it prevented events of the plot from achieving the unwanted pathos of a romantic music drama and re-emphasized the overall comic nature of the opera both visually and musically. He also called attention to elements of *Zar* that have been associated with Weill's mature style, namely the "motor-rhythm" and gestic function of his music.[189] Adolf Weissmann, previously one of Weill's most favorable reviewers, however, did not share the enthusiasm for the action-filled, almost Feydeau-like farce:

> Although "new classicism" seems to be the catchword of the day, there are young composers who apparently are of quite a different opinion concerning the musical stage. The visitors to the International Festivals know Kurt Weill, a Busoni pupil, as one of the representatives of modernity in the Busonian sense of the word. . . . He is a child of his age in demanding the most interesting plots from the most interesting dramatists. . . . The libretto is so full of action that I wondered how the composer would keep pace with the dramatist. For the tempo of music, however unemotional, is not equal to that of a sketch developing at such speed. Poor Weill! He worked very hard, but not hard enough, for his music, though striding with hasty paces, remains behind the libretto, as far as the exciting effect of the plot is concerned.[190]

Soon after its premiere, *Zar* was produced in Düsseldorf, paired with Stravinsky's *Oedipus rex*, which had received its first staged performance in Vienna five days before the premiere of *Zar* in Leipzig. The coupling of these two works became the most frequent other than that of *Zar* with *Der Protagonist*, and this juxtaposition elicited a number of discussions about the direction of new opera as indicated by these works of Weill and Stravinsky.[191] During the 1928-29 season, *Zar* was produced by twenty-six houses in Germany and thus ranked as one of the most often performed contemporary operas.[192] Its popularity was not short-lived; even after *Die Dreigroschenoper* and *Aufstieg und Fall der Stadt Mahagonny* had been produced, *Zar* remained fixed in the repertory and achieved productions in more than eighty German theaters before 1933. In 1927 Universal published the libretto and piano-vocal score, edited by Erwin Stein. A year later, in response to popular demand, an orchestral score was issued. The "Tango Angèle," which in the production emanated from a gramophone on stage, was published separately for piano solo and commercially recorded by Parlophon-Beka—it became the first of Weill's succession of "hits."

Before continuing the chronicle of Weill's career with a discussion of the Weill-Brecht collaboration, at this juncture it is instructive to glance backward to note the situation at the time of the initiation of the famous partnership for the *Mahagonny-Songspiel* in March 1927. Barely twenty-seven years old, Weill had completed two string quartets, a cello sonata, at least five orchestral works, a violin concerto, several choral works, a ballet-pantomime, two song cycles, a cantata, incidental music for a radio play, and three operas.[193] His music had been performed throughout Europe and had achieved notable successes at international music festivals. Critics referred to Weill as one of the leaders of "new music," and music journals minutely chronicled his career.[194] Hailed as the outstanding composer for the theater of his generation, Weill had achieved the first sustained operatic success of the younger generation with *Der Protagonist*, which discouraged empathy of the audience for its characters and attempted to influence only through the clarity of the drama. *Royal Palace* had exhibited the aesthetic distance of a film in its revue-like juxtaposition of pictures from the heroine's life. The cabaret song had penetrated the opera house in *Der neue Orpheus*. With Kaiser, Weill explored the "epic nature" of the operatic stage with the commentator-chorus in *Zar* while he began to seek other solutions with Brecht.[195] Under Busoni's tutelage, Weill had attempted to free himself from literary dependence by writing "absolute" music. The simplification of his musical style had been gradual, and his adoption of popular dance idioms and jazz-influenced instrumentation meshed with this quest for clarity and simplicity. He had abandoned the overt religious overtones of his early Expressionist compositions in favor of a more generalized social and moral activism. His activity as a teacher and critic provided both financial stability and additional opportunities for expression of his musical and theatrical ideas.

Weill's stature as a composer had been affirmed, both by public response and his own personal reflection. To be sure, he had yet to carry the aesthetic and musical implications of the works dating from 1918 to 1927 to their most consummate fruition. Klaus Prigsheim described Weill as "one of the most mentioned among composers of the younger generation, advancing more quickly and farther into the world than any productive musician from post-War Germany."[196] Yet even he concluded such a description with the question, "Who is Kurt Weill?" An authoritative answer to that question could arise only from future works in collaboration with an equally talented and visionary representative of the new generation of dramatists—Bertolt Brecht.

CHAPTER 2

CHRONICLE: WEILL'S CAREER, 1927-1935

I have found in my present close collaboration with Brecht the feasibility of constructing a libretto whose total plan and scenario have been worked out together in all details, word for word, according to musical considerations.[1]

— *Kurt Weill* —

I

Although Weill dated his initial artistic association with Brecht as Spring 1927,[2] they probably were at least socially acquainted earlier, since they shared a number of mutual friends and both were connected with the avant-garde theatrical circle of Berlin. Martin Esslin claimed that Brecht had known Weill since the early twenties and cited as evidence Nicolas Nabokov's recollection of how Weill, Brecht, Isadora Duncan, and he had "sniggered indecently" at Stanislavsky's production of Chekhov's *The Three Sisters* by the Moscow Art Theater in Berlin during 1922 or 1923.[3] Soon after Weill assumed his duties as critic for *Der deutsche Rundfunk* in 1925, he had occasion to comment on Brecht's ballads and specifically expressed admiration for the individuality and wealth of language and content, but considered the significance of Brecht's poetry to lie more in drama than in music.[4] At that time such praise from Weill paled before his evaluation of his esteemed collaborator, Georg Kaiser, whom he described as "the most highly-regarded dramatist of the new generation" and "the most successful dramatist of the German theater."[5]

The artistic collaboration between Weill and Brecht may have been synthesized as a by-product of the Berlin Radio's broadcast of Brecht's *Mann ist Mann* on 18 March 1927.[6] In his weekly theater column in *Der deutsche Rundfunk*, Weill previewed and reviewed the production which included music by Edmund Meisel. In his preview, Weill related the plot, testified of his admiration for the playwright, and presented the following appraisal of the play:

> The comedy *Mann ist Mann* by Bertolt Brecht, which one can designate as perhaps the most novel and powerful theatrical work of our time, has not as yet been performed by a Berlin theater following its successful premiere in Darmstadt—characteristic of the current management of Berlin's theatrical life. Now the Berlin Radio is giving the play its first performance in Berlin and thereby attracting the attention of the widest circles.[7]

Following the radio broadcast, Weill not only praised Brecht and his play but also criticized the opera division of the Berlin Radio for its reactionary tendencies:

Again the great superiority of the literary radio play as opposed to the opera division of the Berlin Radio is noticeable. While in the opera division people still speak of the long-appreciated Pfitzner as the boldest thrust into the musical frontier, the drama division is once again moving one of the leading young dramatists into the center of a radio-play evening. That is to say, this radio performance of Brecht's comedy *Mann ist Mann* far surpasses in immediate and lasting effect all that the Berlin Radio has undertaken in this area. This time it was not an approach from some technical aspect of the problem; instead a poet, a genuine poet, has proffered his solution to an essential portion of questions relating to radio drama with a bold grasp and wonderful empathetic power.[8]

In March 1927 Weill was also beginning work with Kaiser on *Zar* and had been invited to contribute a one-act chamber opera to an evening of the Baden-Baden Chamber Music Festival.[9] Since *Zar* was intended as a companion piece for *Der Protagonist* and was in no sense planned as a chamber opera, Weill was searching for another libretto to fulfill his commission. He considered adaptations of scenes from *King Lear* and *Antigone* as possible sources.[10] But Weill had been impressed by Brecht's *Mann ist Mann* and had just recently read his collection of poems, *Die Hauspostille*, which included the five Mahagonny-Songs. Lenya has provided the following colorful account of the early days of the Brecht-Weill collaboration, which appears to have been initiated by Weill:

It was Kurt who first had gone to see Brecht early in 1927 (as I remember). He had read poems by Brecht that had stirred him deeply, and which said in words what he felt increasingly drawn to say in music. He also knew Brecht had written one explosively controversial play, *Mann ist Mann*, produced in Darmstadt, that sounded close to his own ideas of theatre. Kurt had written three operas which had been applauded by the most austere music critics. Weill, Krenek, Hindemith were rated as the three most gifted young opera composers in Germany. But Kurt felt strongly that serious composers had withdrawn into too rarefied an atmosphere. He insisted that the widening gap between them and the great public must be bridged at all costs. "What do you want to become, a Verdi of the poor?" scoffingly asked his teacher Busoni. "Is that so bad?" Kurt had replied, deceptively mild. Now, at his first meeting with Brecht, Kurt discovered that Brecht seemed genuinely excited by the idea of writing something that required music.[11]

In his notes for the full-length *Aufstieg und Fall der Stadt Mahagonny* (hereafter *Aufstieg*), Weill described this initial meeting with Brecht:

As early as my first meeting with Brecht in Spring 1927 the word "Mahagonny" emerged in a conversation about the possibilities of opera and with it the conception of a "Paradise City." In order to pursue further this idea, which had seized me immediately, and to test the musical style that I envisioned for it, I first composed the five Mahagonny-Songs from Brecht's *Die Hauspostille* and linked them into a small dramatic form, a "Songspiel," which was performed in Baden-Baden during the summer of 1927.[12]

Die Hauspostille [*Domestic Breviary*] is a collection of poems, most of which had been written prior to 1922, arranged satirically as a book of prayers, hymns, sermons, and other devotional forms for use by "the pious in the home." In 1926 the collection was printed in a private edition of twenty-five copies by Gustav Kiepenheuer as *Die Taschenpostille*, and a year later the poems received wide circulation in the Propyläen-Verlag publication entitled *Die Hauspostille*. It featured a frontispiece drawing by Caspar Neher depicting a monster with rosary and derby hat and an appendix of melodies for fourteen of the poems. Presumably composed by Brecht himself, these "tunes" included one for each of the five Mahagonny-Songs, which comprised the Fourth Lesson of the collection.[13] Weill called Brecht's melodies "nothing more than an inventory of the speech-rhythm" and asserted that they "cannot be used as music at all."[14]

Two of the Mahagonny-Songs ("Alabama Song" and "Benares Song") were written in pidgin English, which Brecht once predicted would become the first world language; they implied that the geographical location of Mahagonny was America.[15] However, the American location for the mythical city, situated on the Gold-Coast near Florida and Alaska, was intentionally vague. Weill wrote that "the name 'Mahagonny' denotes only the concept of a city; it was chosen on a phonetic basis and the geographic location is unimportant."[16] After he had become a citizen of the United States, he explained the rationale for the American setting:

> For every age and part of the world, there is a place about which fantasies are written. In Mozart's time it was Turkey. For Shakespeare, it was Italy. For us in Germany, it was always America. We had read Jack London and knew absolutely all about your Chicago gangsters, and that was the end. So of course when we did a fantasy, it was about America.[17]

Attempts to reconcile the proximity of Mahagonny (on the Gold Coast) and Pensacola, another city prominent in the libretto, are fruitless, since Weill chose the name 'Pensacola' merely because it was "a marvelous name for a city to be hit by a hurricane."[18] The word 'Mahagonny' was invented, rather than borrowed from an existing city, in order to assure the allegorical universality of its social history. Weill specifically cautioned against producing the *Songspiel* as a local-color play: "Any tendency toward Wild-West or Cowboy romanticism and any emphasis on a typically American milieu are to be avoided."[19]   To discourage inference of an exclusively American setting for the full-length *Aufstieg*, Weill prefaced the orchestral score with a note stating that since the relevance of Mahagonny is international in the widest sense, names of the principal characters should be changed to local idiomatic forms.[20]

Arnolt Bronnen (1895-1959), a close friend of Brecht in the early twenties and a playwright who collaborated with Weill on *Katalaunische Schlacht* in 1928, recalled that Brecht first coined the term 'Mahagonny' in 1923 as he watched the massed brown shirts of marching storm troopers in Munich.[21]   In a letter to Bronnen in the same year, Brecht referred to Berlin as 'Mahagonny', so it is clear that the symbolic city is not limited to an American setting.[22]   Brecht probably derived the name from the German word *Mahagoni* meaning mahogony:

> The wood, the dark brown color of which was associated by Brecht with frontier crudity, with barrenness, and with the banal hunt for pleasure that seemed to him the focus of pathetic petty-bourgeois existence, the color of barroom tables and brothel walls.[23]

When Brecht quipped to Bronnen that "wenn Mahagonny kommt, geh' ich," he could not have suspected that within ten years his prophecy would be fulfilled.[24]   Mahagonny would no longer be "only a made-up word."[25]

In response to Weill's request, during May 1927 Brecht scrambled the original order of the Mahagonny-Songs and supplied a new explanatory text as a finale.[26]   Weill set the six poems and cemented the songs into a new structure, a "Songspiel," with brief orchestral interludes. The *Mahagonny-Songspiel* was scheduled for premiere at the Festival for New Music in Baden-Baden on 17 July 1927 along with Toch's *Die Prinzessin auf der Erbse*, Milhaud's *L'Enlevement d'Europe*, and Hindemith's *Hin und zurück*.[27]   Not only was the form of Weill's contribution, which resembled a scenic cantata more than a chamber opera, rather novel, but the production itself was also far from traditional.   The cast of operatically trained singers included one exception—Lotte Lenya was (to Brecht's delight) vocally untrained and provided a unique contrast to the other female vocalist, Irene Eden. The production staff included Walter Brügmann as co-director (with Brecht) and Ernst Mehlich as conductor of the varicolored orchestra.[28]   Caspar Neher (1897-1962), the "third-among-equals" of the artistic triumvirate of Weill-Brecht-Neher, designed the scenery which consisted of a stark boxing ring in front of a number of projection screens.[29]   The grotesque juxtaposition of an American bar inside the boxing ring completed the unique set.[30]

Whether the festival's administrators anticipated the tumultuous reaction to *Mahagonny* that was to occur or merely wished to expedite the erection of the unusual set, the *Songspiel* was scheduled to conclude the program of chamber operas.[31]   The pistol shot with which the *Songspiel* began could not compare to the clamor of the audience at its conclusion.   Eyewitness Heinrich Strobel reported that "the philistines greeted the aggressive songs of this highly anti-bourgeois piece with hoots, whistles, and rotten apples."[32]   Hans Heinsheimer described the work's impact on a gathering of Europe's musical elite:

> [*Mahagonny*] was played against the background of a festival devoted to atonal cello sonatas and settings of Petrarchian sonnets for string trio, voice, and solo oboe.   Most of the assembled musicians were shocked beyond belief.   The public in the audience, who didn't know that they weren't supposed to, clapped and shouted their approval.   Some left the hall happily humming the tunes.   Nothing like it had ever marred a modern music festival.   It was a terrible disappointment. What had happened to Kurt Weill?[33]

The critical reception was as vociferously divided as the audience, although no one denied that *Mahagonny* had been a genuinely novel "event."   Writing for the *New York Times*, Olin Downes found the economic and social thrust of the *Songspiel's* content objectionable to his political sensibilities, but nevertheless noted the power of Weill's new operatic ideal:

> A piece done at Baden-Baden, a fifteen-minute chamber opera, or "songspiel," by a bold and bad young man, Kurt Weill of Berlin, should properly have been given in Vienna.   It was a little out of the frame in a fashionable watering place, having something to do, to paraphrase a line in "The Mikado," with that kind of modern dissatisfaction which recently culminated in the cutting up of policemen by the proletariat.
>
> This piece is "Mahagonny," a clever and savage skit on the degeneration of society, the triumph of sensualism, the decay of art.   It is done by a young composer who knows his business.   They say that Weill, a pupil of Busoni, born in 1900, has had a hard time of it and that his life has unfortunately colored his social and artistic ideas.   Be that as it may, his was the triumph of the festival, and it is a pity that others could not be as witty, as accomplished in the manipulation of material, and even, save for some offensive and insurrectionary placards shown on the stage, as cognizant of the line between farce and satire.[34]

Perhaps only German critics could understand Weill's rationale for filtering radical intellectual themes through the lens of an American milieu of stylized dance idioms.   Adolf Weissmann, Max Marschalk, and Alfred Baresel hailed it as a bold formulation of the new musical theater,[35] and Strobel perceptively recognized the continuity between Weill's earlier works and *Mahagonny*:

The lyricism of *Royal Palace* and the dramatic intensity of *Der Protagonist* are blended anew in music of the strongest melodic power and gripping currency. It is not a superficial reflection of outward appearances like Krenek's *Jonny spielt auf*, whose gigantic success was purchased only with compromise in the music. Instead this is a work of entirely definite bearing, which seeks to give epic shape to the content of today's life through its completely novel artistic utilization of jazz.[36]

"Das kleine Mahagonny," as the *Songspiel* was later labeled to distinguish it from the three-act opera, *Aufstieg*, was not staged in its original form after its premiere for over thirty years.[37] Although in 1927 Universal advertised a piano-vocal edition of the *Mahagonny-Songspiel* in *Anbruch*, it never materialized during Weill's lifetime.[38] Weill's own neglect of the *Songspiel* is understandable, for in 1930 he wrote that the "Baden-Baden *Mahagonny* is nothing more than a stylistic study for the opera, which, once begun, was continued only after the style had been tested."[39] In early May 1927, even before the *Songspiel* had been completed, Weill wrote to his publisher informing him that a subject for a full-length opera had already been worked out.[40] In response to the stimulus of the tumultuous reception for their "stylistic test" at Baden-Baden, Weill and Brecht continued work on *Aufstieg*, "whose total plan and scenario were worked out together in all details, word for word, according to musical considerations."[41] As early as September 1927, Hans Curjel, dramaturgist of the Krolloper, began making preparations for the premiere of *Aufstieg* under Klemperer,[42] but the opera (Brecht's first) was not completed until April 1929—the composition of *Die Dreigroschenoper* serving as the primary interruption.

Even after completion, the score and libretto underwent frequent revision in response to objections raised by Hertzka and the artistic directors of several theaters who had agreed to mount productions of the opera. Weill added the "Crane Duet" in October 1929, and there were numerous changes in the libretto prior to the premiere in Leipzig. After its first performance, it continued to undergo transformations for productions in other cities; the most radical changes were adopted for the first production in Berlin in 1931.[43] Because the piano-vocal score was published already in 1929, it presents a version which was never performed.[44] After the Berlin production, a definitive edition incorporating the various revisions that Weill and Brecht wished to retain was to have been published, but the decaying political climate prevented the completion of such a project. David Drew's edition, published by Universal-Edition in 1969, includes all of the verifiable revisions and reinstates a few passages of text which had been suppressed in the 1929 edition.

Of all Weill's works composed in Germany, only *Die Dreigroschenoper* has received more critical commentary and enjoyed more numerous revivals than *Aufstieg*. Therefore, only a brief chronicle and critical profile will be included here.[45] The response to the *Songspiel* at Baden-Baden was subdued compared to that which greeted the premiere of the three-act opera in Leipzig with Gustav Brecher conducting and Walter Brügmann again directing.[46] One observer described it as the "liveliest riot which has taken place in a German theater within the memory of the most veteran critics of the land!"[47] H. H. Stuckenschmidt provided a vivid narrative of the premiere:

> It is a long time since a dramatic work has met with such passionate opposition; a long time too, probably, since the first performance of a new work has been awaited with such tense excitement. . . . We have come to the point of decision: the decision that there must be a new form of opera, a radically different way for the theatre. Kurt Weill, now aged 30, has been aiming at this new form ever since his music-dramatic beginnings. In *Die Dreigroschenoper* he achieved it for the first time. These are its characteristics: a total and uninhibited revolution in theme; a complete avoidance of pomposity and false heroics; a ruthless excision of all 'narcotic' elements; and a thoroughgoing adoption of the techniques of film and cabaret.
>
> The work forms a climax in the operatic history of the present age. For all its occasional beery humour, its adolescent romanticism, it strikes a powerful blow for the New Theatre, and for this very reason has aroused passionate hostilities. The whistling of the enemy partisans began even during the first act. Towards the end open tumult broke out. Brecher just managed to bring the performance to an end. And thereupon started a quarter of an hour of the most violent disputation, such as has not been heard for many, many years.[48]

In this case, the turbulence which marred the premiere was motivated more by carefully calculated political planning than by any spontaneous artistic indignation. Rather than launching the new work with a healthy (for the box-office) dosage of controversy, the demonstration in Leipzig prompted several theaters to cancel plans for production of the opera. After just five performances in Leipzig, the opera was again revised and produced with more success in Kassel (seven performances) and Braunschweig (two performances).[49] George Szell then conducted two performances of the opera in Prague during July 1930; during October 1930 it was produced as the concluding event of the fiftieth-anniversary celebration of the Frankfurt Opera. This production, conducted by Wilhelm Steinberg and directed by Herbert Graf, precipitated the most overt political demonstration against the opera that was to occur.[50] Indeed, the second performance was halted when hundreds of storm troopers forced their way into the auditorium and hurled stink bombs.[51] Weill lamented the "senseless anxiety-psychosis of those in authority" of the German opera houses, but praised the city officials of Frankfurt for their refusal to be intimidated:

> The Frankfurt city officials did not permit themselves to be shoved into a corner by a horde of illiterates (led by a long-pursued railroad thief who was apprehended on this occasion) who demonstrated against the epic opera. Since the second performance, which was disrupted, ten additional performances have taken place without disturbance. However, other theaters tried to hide their anxiety behind all kinds of excuses. They voluntarily submitted to censorship which in reality does not yet exist and which, if it should really come, will be attributable primarily to this anxiety in a time of transition like the present.[52]

The long-awaited production in one of Berlin's opera houses never materialized.[53] After Klemperer had lost interest, the rights were acquired by Max Reinhardt in 1930, but again no production was forthcoming.[54] Finally Ernst Aufricht, the producer of *Die Dreigroschenoper* and *Happy End*, leased from Reinhardt the Theater am Kurfürstendamm, where Weill's first completed stage work, *Die Zaubernacht*, had been staged nine years earlier. Weill and Brecht again revised the opera while vacationing together in Le Lavandou during May and June 1931.[55] After a month of rehearsal, the production, directed and designed by Caspar Neher and conducted by Alexander von Zemlinsky, opened on 21 December 1931 with Lotte Lenya, Harald Paulsen, and Trude Hesterberg (who had suggested to Aufricht that he produce the opera) in the principal roles.[56] Although the production was immensely successful and *Aufstieg* became one of the first contemporary operas to achieve a continuous run in a commercial theater—more than fifty consecutive performances—the rehearsal period was marred by controversy. The tensions between librettist and composer over the question of supremacy of text or music and the inherent, longstanding discrepancies between Weill's and Brecht's artistic, aesthetic, and political views finally erupted explosively. Aufricht managed to facilitate continuation of rehearsals of *Aufstieg* by persuading Brecht to stage *Die Mutter* in the Theater am Schiffbauerdamm; as a result, Neher and Weill, who had just completed their own opera, *Die Bürgschaft*, gained control of the Berlin production of *Aufstieg*, which opened on 17 January 1932. Although this solved the immediate problem, the rift between Weill and his librettist was never again breached, with the exception of their brief collaboration in exile for *Die sieben Todsünden*.[57]

    Aufstieg received a few other scattered performances, including one in Vienna (April 1932) and those of the "Paris version," but as the actual political situation in Germany approached that of the mythological Mahagonny, production of the opera was out of the question. The first production of the authentic version after the ban of Weill's works in 1933 by the Nazis occurred in Darmstadt during 1957. Since that time, it has achieved notable success throughout Europe and America.

Shortly after Weill composed the *Mahagonny-Songspiel* (May 1927), he set another of Brecht's ballads from *Die Hauspostille*, "Vom Tod im Wald." The poem had been written in 1918 and first published in *Der Erzähler* during March 1918. Brecht then included it in *Baal* and eventually revised the fifth, sixth, and seventh strophes before it was published as the third poem of the Third Lesson of *Die Hauspostille*.[58] Reproducing the poem exactly as it appeared in *Die Hauspostille* and utilizing no textual repetition, Weill set "Vom Tod im Wald" ("Of Death in the Forest") for bass voice and ten wind instruments. In maintaining a dark texture throughout the ten-minute composition, Weill undoubtedly hoped to capture the poem's atmosphere of death amid the black fir branches of the Hathboury forest near the Mississippi River. The composition was premiered as opus 23 on 23 November 1927 by the Berlin Philharmonic under Eugen Lang.[59] In 1929 Weill published his "Notiz zum *Berliner Requiem*," in which he described the *Requiem* as opening with a ballad, *Vom Tod im Wald*.[60] *Das Berliner Requiem* was never performed in this version, however, because Weill realized that the opening ballad was stylistically incompatible with the other sections of the *Requiem*.[61] *Vom Tod im Wald* was not performed again during Weill's lifetime nor has it been published, although it was revived at the 1971 Holland Festival and the 1975 Berlin Festival.

The only other known compositions by Weill dating from 1927 are incidental music for Victor Barnowsky's production of August Strindberg's *Gustav III*[62] and a setting of the "Klopslied." Early in 1928, Weill contributed incidental music for two plays that were directed by two of Berlin's most imaginative and influential theatrical personalities: Erwin Piscator (1893-1966) and Leopold Jessner (1878-1945). As producer and director of the Volksbühne (a theater in Berlin established and maintained by workers' unions) and later the Piscator-Theater am Nollendorfplatz, Piscator is widely acknowledged as the originator of many techniques of epic theater.[63] At his Nollendorftheater he directed a production of *Konjunktur*, a play dealing with a struggle between Standard Oil Company and Royal Dutch Shell over petroleum in Albania. Premiered on 10 April 1928, it was written by Leo Lania, the pseudonym for Lazar Herrmann (1896-1961).[64] Weill's incidental music included a song entitled "Die Muschel von Margate: Petroleum Song," with lyrics by Felix Gasbarra.[65] Neither Alfred Kerr nor Herbert Jhering mentioned Weill's music in their reviews of the play, but Kerr does note that Tilla Durieux performed "Die Muschel von Margate."[66] Portions of Weill's score have survived in manuscript; it received its first revival at the 1975 Berlin Festival.

Lania described the Piscator 'collective,' of which Weill was a member, as follows:

> With the other members of this dramatic bureau I collaborated on nearly every play he (Piscator) produced. For the first time there arose a close community between authors, painters (George Grosz), composers (Kurt Weill and Hanns Eisler), directors and actors—all in basic agreement, all working directly for the stage. . . . This literary 'collective' made enormous demands on all the collaborators: discipline, subordination of the individual to the general task.[67]

Konjunktur and *Aufstieg* display a number of striking similarities. Weill considered the main character of *Aufstieg* to be the city itself, while Lania called oil the protagonist of his drama. *Aufstieg* explored the repercussions of the rise and fall of a city on its inhabitants, whereas *Konjunktur* traced the effects of the discovery of oil on the hitherto peaceful residents of Albania. The stamp of Piscator's concepts for staging epic theater can be discerned in both works.[68]

Two weeks after the premiere of *Konjunktur*, Jessner opened a production of Arnolt Bronnen's *Katalaunische Schlacht* (1924), again with incidental music by Weill.[69] Kerr ignored the music, although he quoted the lyrics of one song. Jhering, however, wrote:

> Kurt Weill, who took his great talent too lightly in *Konjunktur*, here has written masterful theater music, which provides an exemplary model of bustling diffusion and melodic command with the simplest of means.[70]

The score was not published nor was it performed again.

It seems to me after just one hearing that Die Dreigroschenoper is the most important event of musical theater since Berg's Wozzeck: *perhaps the restitution of opera is actually beginning.*[71]

— Theodor W. Adorno —

II

To devote a section in this chronicle to *Die Dreigroschenoper* may be superfluous since it has won a permanent place in the repertory, its origins have been documented and already mythologized, and it has inspired numerous studies from both dramatic and musical points of view. Because Lotte Lenya and Ernst Joseph Aufricht have published such vivid eyewitness accounts of the events surrounding the premiere of *Die Dreigroschenoper*, here only the most basic skeleton will be included.[72] It is ironic that of all the theatrical collaborations of Brecht and Weill *Die Dreigroschenoper* should have become the most popular, durable, and influential, for it was the most hastily conceived. Yet it has become their classic, despite the fact that it still defies classification; perhaps Weill described it most accurately when he called it the *Urform* or prototype of opera.[73] It is a paradox: a derivative work indebted literarily to Gay, Kipling, and Villon, and musically to cabaret, dance halls, and Baroque opera, and yet the most original of the Brecht-Weill compositions—a work without any notable formal models. It is a topical play but its plot and characters are borrowed from two hundred years earlier (*Beggar's Opera*, 28 January 1728). At the same time, its universality was immediately recognizable—it was translated into eighteen languages for more than ten thousand performances within five years of its premiere. Brecht finally achieved his first popular success, and Weill found a way to intrude upon the "splendid isolation" of opera.

In 1928 Ernst Josef Aufricht, a young actor-turned-producer, leased the Theater am Schiffbauerdamm for his first venture as a producer. Seeking a play suitable for a splashy debut, Aufricht polled various playwrights about their current endeavors. In a chance meeting with Brecht at Schlichter's, he learned that Brecht had completed six of the projected seven scenes of an adaptation of Gay's *Beggar's Opera*. Brecht's secretary and collaborator since November 1924, Elisabeth Hauptmann, had read about the revival of the *Beggar's Opera* in London and had embarked upon a rough translation, which she gave to Brecht a scene at a time.[74] After reading the completed portions, which Brecht had tentatively entitled "Gesindel," and after conferring with his director Erich Engel, Aufricht commissioned Brecht to finish the play for a fall production.[75]   Aufricht was none too pleased that Brecht had already enlisted Kurt Weill, who was known to Aufricht only as a composer of 'atonal' operas, to compose a new score for "Gesindel."[76]   Taking no chances, he secretly commissioned his musical director and friend, Theo Mackeben, to arrange the original Pepusch score for a small orchestra. Weill himself must have had access to Pepusch's score, because the first number of Act I, "Morgenchoral des Peachum," is merely a realization of the first air of Act I of *Beggar's Opera*. Since only a few rhythmic values of the original were altered in Weill's setting (to accommodate Brecht's text), it is clear that Weill and Brecht intended that the first musical number should give the impression that what would follow would be merely an 'arrangement' of *Beggar's Opera*.[77]

Confronted with a late-August deadline, on 1 June 1928 Brecht and Weill secluded themselves at a resort in Le Lavandou on the French Riviera to devote full-time to the play, then called *Die Bettler-Oper*. When they returned to Berlin to begin a month of rehearsal, the script and score had been virtually completed.[78]   Caspar Neher designed the production, and Theo Mackeben engaged the Lewis Ruth Band as the "pit" orchestra. The doubling capabilities of the eight-member band dictated the limitations and possibilities of Weill's orchestration, which included:

> alto saxophone, doubling on flute, clarinet, and baritone saxophone
> tenor saxophone, doubling on soprano saxophone, bassoon, bass clarinet
> 2 trumpets in B♭ (in the Overture, trumpets in C)
> trombone, doubling on double bass
> banjo, doubling on cello, guitar, Hawaiian-guitar, mandolin, bandoneon[79]
> tympani and percussion
> harmonium and celeste
> piano—conductor

In capitalizing upon the versatility of eight musicians who played twenty-one different instruments, Weill created a constantly varied instrumental texture.

The original cast included Erich Ponto as Peachum, Rosa Valetti as Frau Peachum, Carola Neher as Polly (when her husband, Klabund, became critically ill and died on 14 August 1928, Roma Bahn replaced her with only four days remaining before opening night), Helene Weigel as the brothel madam (the role was eliminated when she succumbed to appendicitis), Harald Paulsen as Macheath, Kurt Gerron as Brown/ Streetsinger, Kate Kühl as Lucy, and Lotte Lenya as Jenny.[80]   During the four-week rehearsal period, the play underwent considerable revision to accommodate the cast changes and Brecht's objections to Engel's staging.[81]   The first of Weill's musical numbers to be cut was the third-act "Arie der Lucy."   An actress "with considerable vocal talent" had been considered for the role of Lucy, but when she was not cast, the aria was eliminated because it was too difficult for Kate Kühl, whom Aufricht described as a "ballad-singer with a deep, penetrating voice."[82]   Weill never orchestrated the song, which implies that the orchestrations were probably not begun until after rehearsals were underway.[83]   Jenny's "Salomon-Song" was deleted to shorten the length of the third àct. Upon Paulsen's demand for another song, Brecht wrote the "Moritat vom Mackie Messer," and Weill set it to music overnight.   Zucco Maggio, a hand-organ manufacturer, created a cylinder for the instrument so that the Streetsinger, to whom the song was eventually assigned, could accompany his own ballad.[84]   Finally, even the name of the play was changed, at the suggestion of Lion Feuchtwanger, to *Die Dreigroschenoper*.

The dress rehearsal, which lasted until five a.m., gave no encouragement to the staff that the play might be successful.   But despite the tension of last-minute revisions, the omission of Lenya's name from the program (which enraged Weill), and even a suggestion of cancelling the production, *Die Dreigroschenoper* opened to a capacity audience on 31 August 1928.[85]   It is not an exaggeration to say that the play swept across Europe—within one year *Die Dreigroschenoper* had been per-formed more than 4200 times.   Within a month of its premiere in Berlin, productions were announced for Vienna, Budapest, Munich, Frankfurt, Leipzig, and Hamburg.   The caption of Universal's advertisement, "Der Triumph eines neuen Stils," applied to fifty cities in Italy, France, Russia, Switzerland, Czechslovakia, Austria, and Scandinavia, as well as Germany.[86]   Phonograph recordings of Weill's music were issued by no fewer than seven companies; Brecht himself sang the "Moritat" on one recording.[87]   A *Dreigroschen*-Bar, in which only music from the opera was played, opened in 1929; even wallpaper companies manufactured *Dreigroschen* products in order to capitalize on the sensation.[88]   George Antheil noted that the Weill-Brecht opera had penetrated every level of society: "All over the continent one can hear almost every shop-girl singing its melodies."[89]

Universal-Edition, in the words of Hans Heinsheimer, was hard-pressed to accommodate Weill's newly-won fame:

> We had witnessed the greatest of nature's miracles: the transformation of the drab larva of a prestige composer into the golden-winged beauty of a commercial butterfly. . . . One of the slaves in the arranging department was assigned to make a vocal score of the *Dreigroschenoper*. . . . Mr. Gingold lost seven pounds during

his solitary confinement, but finished the task within four days and nights. . . .
The vocal score of *The Three Penny Opera* sold many more copies in the first few
months of its existence than all other works by Weill combined had sold.[90]

In addition to Norbert Gingold's piano-vocal edition which omitted
Frau Peachum's "Ballade von der sexuellen Hörigkeit," Universal issued
seven of the songs individually, as well as arrangements of "Kanonensong," "Moritat," "Tango-Ballade," a "Blues-Potpourri," and a "Foxtrot-
Potpourri" for jazz orchestra.[91] In 1930 Stefan Frenkel, with Weill's
approval, arranged "Seven Pieces from *Die Dreigroschenoper*" for violin
and piano, which Universal published in both "original" and "simplified"
versions.

Several controversies that were followed with great interest in
newspapers also kept *Die Dreigroschenoper* in the public eye. At the
height of the Alfred Kerr-Brecht plagiarism battle in 1929,[92] Weill and
Brecht sold the film rights for the opera to the Nero-Film Gesellschaft.
But when the company refused to accept Brecht's screenplay, *Die
Beule—Ein Dreigroschenfilm*, which emphasized his growing Marxist
political orientation, Brecht sued for an injunction to prohibit filming.
Weill filed a parallel suit to obtain musical supervision of his score.
Weill won his case, Brecht lost his, and the film was premiered in
Berlin's Atrium Cinema on 19 February 1931.[93] Brecht published his
own script in 1931, along with an essay entitled "Der Dreigroschen-
prozess—Ein soziologisches Experiment." His final reworking of the
material is found in *Der Dreigroschenroman*, a novel completed and
published in 1934.[94]

Weill   also   reworked   his   'threepenny'   material   as   *Kleine
Dreigroschenmusik für Blasorchester*.[95] Consisting of seven movements, it
manages to incorporate ten numbers of the opera by combining the
"Lied von der Unzulänglichkeit menschlichen Strebens" and "Moritat
vom Mackie Messer" in Movement II and linking "Ruf aus der Gruft,"
and "Grabschrift," with the chorale of the third "Dreigroschenfinale" in
Movement VII. *Kleine Dreigroschenmusik* expands the orchestra utilized
in the opera to a large wind ensemble.[96] As a result of the augmented
instrumentation, there are notable changes in scoring from that of the
opera, as well as an entirely new and extensive interlude in Movement
VI: "Kanonen Song." Commissioned by Otto Klemperer, it received its
premiere at a concert of the Berlin Staatsoper Orchestra on 7 February
1929. After its immense success in Berlin, Klemperer conducted it in
Leningrad and Moscow, where the "Kanonensong" was so stormily
applauded that it had to be repeated.[97] It was quickly taken up by other
conductors and broadcast by the Stockholm, Berlin, Königsberg, Prague,

Brussels, and Leipzig radio stations.   Having achieved what Universal advertised as "sensational success in sixty cities," it even received a staged production in Erfurt.[98]

Weill had not yet exhausted the possibilities: in 1938 he adapted music from *Die Dreigroschenoper* for Anthony Tudor's and Hugh Laing's one-act ballet, *Judgment of Paris*.   Premiered on 15 June 1938 at London's Westminster Theater with Agnes de Mille in the role of Venus, the ballet is a nineteenth-century updating of the legend of Paris and his judgment of the beauty contest of Venus, Juno, and Minerva.[99]   In his review, Walter Terry described the ballet:

> The Ballet Theatre let down its hair, accented the human form's posterior and indulged in a rowdy satire that brought down the house. . . . The setting was a cafe, a customer was Paris and three tired but business-like cafe hostesses represented the three goddesses.   Each of these gaudy ladies performed a dance routine, aimed at attracting the customer, who eventually succumbed to their charms and liquor, and was robbed of all he possessed.[100]

Although Weill's music for the ballet is not merely a rescoring of *Kleine Dreigroschenmusik* for an orchestra that includes strings, there are many parallel sections and *Kleine Dreigroschenmusik* obviously served as the skeleton of the ballet score.[101]   However, *Judgment of Paris* contains some music that did not appear in the earlier suite and omits some that did appear there.   The score was not published, but a full score is available at the Library of Congress.

In 1933, when the Nazis banned all performances of Weill's works and requested foreign organizations to return all full scores for immediate destruction, the popularity of *Die Dreigroschenoper* still could not be extinguished.[102]   The Ministry of Culture opened a Museum of Degenerate Art, where songs from *Die Dreigroschenoper* were played continuously in one room to illustrate the archetype of artistic decadence. However, so many spectators crowded into the room each day that it became obvious that the intended effect was not being achieved; the music was discontinued.[103]

Kurt Weill was a prophet of that wonderful, unique cosmopolitan city of
Berlin before Hitler that will never come back—indeed, in many aspects he
was its very incarnation.[104]

— *Heinrich Strobel* —

III

After Weill had captured Berlin's imagination with the implicit
topicality of *Die Dreigroschenoper*, his next two compositions were
explicitly dedicated to the metropolis: the "Berlin im Licht-Song" and
Das Berliner Requiem. The "Berlin im Licht-Song" was commissioned
for performance at a Promenade Concert of the "Berlin im Licht"
festival, 13-16 October 1928.[105] The celebration, modeled on the "ville
lumière" concept, was organized as a demonstration to show that Berlin
had been cloaked in a shroud, both figuratively and literally, but was
now emerging as a new "city of light." Under the leadership of a
committee headed by Hans Wrede, the event attempted to prove that
Berlin could compete with Paris and New York in brilliance. The
festival featured illumination of Berlin's architectural landmarks, historic
avenues, stores, and factories. It drew two million residents into the
streets and prompted twenty special trainloads of visitors from other
German cities to view the spectacle. The show of lights, displays of
fireworks, and contests for window decorations were complemented by
exhibits at museums, concerts, and other cultural events. The climactic
affair was a "Lichtball" at the Krolloper where Richard Tauber, Maria
Müller, and Trude Hesterberg performed.[106]

Weill's slow fox-trot was written for presentation in a revue which
followed the first "Lichtball." It also appeared in a purely instrumental
arrangement on a military band concert in Wittenberg Platz conducted
by Hermann Scherchen. The text of the song was written by Weill
himself, although, according to David Drew, Brecht had a hand in its
final draft.[107] Weill's "Berlin im Licht-Song" proved so popular that
Universal-Edition published the original version for voice and piano, as
well as an arrangement for jazz orchestra.[108]

Weill composed *Das Berliner Requiem: Kleine Kantate für Tenor,*
Bariton, Männerchor und Blasorchester during November and December
1928. The first reference to the work appeared in *Die Musik*:

The Frankfurt Broadcasting Station has commissioned Bert Brecht to write a
cantata. It will be entitled "Gedenktafeln, Grabschriften und Totenlieder" and
will deal with the deaths of French aviators Nungesser and Coli, as well as

famous sports figures. The music, which will be arranged for four singers and small orchestra, will be executed by Kurt Weill.[109]

Such a cantata never materialized, although the jumbled description above represents a conflation of ideas which later surface in *Das Berliner Requiem*, *Der Lindberghflug*, and *Der Badener Lehrstück vom Einverständnis*. In January 1929 *Melos* reported that Weill had composed a small cantata on epitaphs, entitled *Das Berliner Requiem* and commissioned by the Frankfurter Rundfunk.[110] Indeed, it was Weill who had received a commission from the Reichs-Rundfunk-Gesellschaft to write a radio cantata, the fifth in a series of compositions by modern composers, including Hindemith, Schreker, and Hauer.[111] Brecht's texts for *Das Berliner Requiem* were almost all pre-existent; the "Grosser Dankchoral" and "Vom ertrunkenen Mädchen" had appeared in *Die Hauspostille*.[112] The first broadcast of the work was initially scheduled for 22 February 1929, but censors delayed the premiere for three months.[113] Weill published his "Notiz zum *Berliner Requiem*" five days before the cantata was finally broadcast by the Frankfurt station. He wrote:

> The content of *Das Berliner Requiem* unquestionably corresponds to the sentiments and perceptions of the broadest levels of population. We attempted to express what urban man of our time has to say about the phenomenon of death. Some especially stringent censors of the radio have felt it necessary to question this. That attitude gives evidence of an alarming ignorance of the artistic requirements of those classes which in terms of the radio audience occupy the broadest scope. Perhaps later something will be said about the peculiar events behind the scenes of this performance. The overall impression of the performance must show, if we were correct in our statement, that we are dealing here with a serious, non-ironic work, with a type of secular Requiem, with an expression about death in the form of memorial tablets, epitaphs, and funeral dirges.[114]

In the same essay Weill listed the contents of the cantata:

> Eine Ballade "Vom Tod im Wald" für eine Bassstimme und zehn Bläser, ein Lied "Können einem toten Mann nicht helfen," das dem Finale der Mahagonny-Oper entnommen ist, ein Gesang "Vom ertrunkenen Mädchen" und ein "Materl" für den Grabstein dieses Mädchens, zwei Gesänge über den unbekannten Soldaten unter dem Triumphbogen, der erste für mehrere Stimmen und Orchester, der zweite für Bariton und Orgel, und zum Schluss ein Dankchoral für Männerchor und Orchester.[115]

However, before the premiere Weill deleted "Vom Tod im Wald," added "Zu Potsdam unter den Eichen," and rearranged the order of the numbers.[116] The premiere on 22 May 1929 under Ludwig Rottenberg with Hans Grahl, Johannes Willy, Jean Stern, and the orchestra of the

Frankfurt Radio was poorly advertised, and its broadcast was restricted to the Southwest and West-German broadcasting groups.[117]   Therefore, Berlin did not hear its requiem.   In an essay that chastised the radio industry for its failure to honor the agreement for wider transmission because of the pressure of certain censors, Felix Stiemer wrote:

> If the *Berliner Requiem* is still not to be heard at least over German radio stations, after all the previous incidents we must fear that it may still become a Requiem in another sense.   "Können einem toten Mann nicht helfen."[118]

Although in 1929 Universal announced publication of a piano-vocal score, it did not appear during Weill's lifetime.   "Materl" and "Zu Potsdam unter den Eichen" were published separately in Weill's *Song-Album*.   He also arranged "Zu Potsdam unter den Eichen" for four-part *a cappella* male chorus; this version was published by Universal in 1930 and premiered by the Berliner Schubertchor in December 1929 under Karl Rankl, the chorus master of the Krolloper.   Appearing on the same program was Weill's "Die Legende vom toten Soldaten," composed in 1929 for four-part *a cappella* mixed chorus.[119]   In 1930 Weill sent Universal a revised table of contents for *Das Berliner Requiem* which indicated that "Können einem toten Mann nicht helfen" was to be replaced by "Die Legende vom toten Soldaten."   Again no publication appeared.   Two years later a note in *Anbruch* stated that Weill was revising *Das Berliner Requiem* for performance by amateur groups, but no score was issued.   In 1967 David Drew published a 'performing edition' that attempts to reconcile the various versions by including only the movements which remained constant throughout all revisions.   It was in this form that the Cincinnati Symphony presented the American premiere in May 1970.

In the days when humanity began to know itself, we made ourselves carriages of iron and wood and glass, and we flew through the air with great speed.[120]

— Bertolt Brecht —

IV

Charles Lindbergh's transatlantic flight in May 1927, widely acclaimed as the heroic deed of the era, provided the impetus and subject matter for the next project of Brecht and Weill—a cantata, *Der Lindberghflug*. Brecht's treatment of Lindbergh's flight was set to music jointly by Hindemith and Weill in yet another extrapolation of the concept of *Gemeinschaftsmusik*, the theme of the 1929 Baden-Baden Festival.[121]   A review of this performance on 28 July 1929 in the *Christian Science Monitor* described the radio cantata:

> This is music for the wireless; and no more suitable subject could have been chosen. The theater of the air, after all, is alone capable of producing the noise of propellers, the murmur of ocean waves, the ovation of the crowd on Lindbergh's arrival in Paris. We heard this "radio cantata" twice, once through loudspeakers and again in public performance, when all those mighty noises that had thrilled us via wireless were revealed as the product of a modest gramophone. And yet, to this writer at least, the impression of public performance was infinitely stronger. . . .
>
> Weill gives his best, and reveals himself once more as one of the most gifted of Germany's young composers, especially in the lyrical portions—Lindbergh's dialogue with his motor while in full flight, for example. . . . On the whole, this radio cantata is one of the few important choral works produced by contemporary music, and surely one of the finest; and particularly welcome as a refutation of the general notion that the young guard of modern music lack feeling and heart. Weill and Hindemith have it. What they lack is merely false pathos; but pathos would have been amiss in the portrayal of Lindbergh as a twentieth century hero.[122]

It is clear from the circumstances of the premiere that this joint version was specifically designed as a radio cantata. Weill himself wrote that it "was expressly intended for the use of radio broadcasting stations."[123] Of course, both the cantata and the above statement of intention had been completed before Weill's dissatisfaction with the medium of radio had been pushed to its limit by circumstances surrounding the broadcast of *Das Berliner Requiem*. After the festival, both Hindemith and Weill withdrew their portions of the score; the original version was not performed again nor was it ever published.

Reflecting his disillusionment with the radio, Weill completed his own setting of the entire cantata—but now the work was intended for performance in schools.[124] His forty-minute, fifteen-movement "didactic cantata" (as opposed to the earlier "radio cantata") received its premiere under Otto Klemperer at an orchestral concert of the Staatsoper on 5 December 1929. Tenor Eric Wirl sang the part of Lindbergh, Fritz Krenn and Martin Abendroth appeared as the baritone and bass soloists, and the Krolloper furnished the four-part mixed chorus. The work was received favorably, but its appeal was based largely on its topical content. In his review of the premiere of this second version, Alfred Einstein wrote that "in the last analysis the performance of the work is not so important as the fact that it was composed."[125]   Nevertheless, *Der Lindberghflug* enjoyed widespread performance, but primarily in concert halls rather than the designated schools, since the significant demands of the score prohibited its performance by students themselves. Within three months of its premiere in Berlin, the cantata had been performed in Prague, Munich, Dresden, London, Moscow; it had been staged in Breslau and broadcast with Scherchen conducting by the Berlin Radio and relayed to Brussels and London. Ironically *Der Lindberghflug* achieved more performances on radio as a "didactic cantata" than any of Weill's "radio compositions" had received. In April 1931 the Philadelphia Orchestra under Leopold Stokowski performed *Der Lindberghflug* in a translation by George Antheil. It was broadcast over the American radio network on 5 April 1931.

Brecht's poem, which was written in irregular, unrhymed verse and which extolled man's power to overcome nature, was published in *Uhu* before the premiere of the Weill/Hindemith version. The second section of Weill's score, "Vorstellung des Fliegers Lindbergh," was published after the festival as part of his *Song-Album*. The following year, Universal published both a piano-vocal score and an orchestral score of Weill's complete setting.[126] Weill sent Lindbergh an autographed copy of the piano-vocal score in 1930; it was inscribed: "Dedicated to Charles Lindbergh with great admiration by Kurt Weill."[127] Brecht revised the text for inclusion in *Versuche* I (1930) as a didactic play for students entitled "Der Flug des Lindberghs." In an unpublished letter dated 2 January 1950, Brecht directed that in view of what he considered to be Lindbergh's pre-war non-interventionist sentiments the title was to be changed to *Der Ozeanflug*, a prologue added, and all references to Lindbergh deleted.[128]

Who wrote that piece? It's by Bertolt Brecht. Well, who wrote that piece?[129]

— *Kurt Tucholsky* —

V

A year after the premiere of *Die Dreigroschenoper*, its producer, hoping to capitalize on its phenomenal success, persuaded Brecht and Weill to write another musical play for the Theater am Schiffbauerdamm. Aufricht assembled the same staff of Engel, Neher, and Mackeben, as well as the Lewis Ruth Band. All that was missing was a suitable play. In response to Aufricht's request, Elisabeth Hauptmann suggested to Brecht that a short story which she had read in an American magazine might serve as a skeleton for the script.[130] Whatever its actual origin, the story about a Salvation Army girl and her gangster lover underwent elaborate embellishment as Brecht attempted to expand the slim material into a three-act structure.[131] Unfortunately *Happy End*, which took its name from a phrase that was in vogue in Berlin at the time, was not based on so durable a pre-existent work as *Die Dreigroschenoper* had been. From the outset *Happy End* was a misnomer.

Rehearsals began with a cast that was a virtual replica of that for *Die Dreigroschenoper*, and *Happy End* assumed the air of a sequel to its illustrious predecessor.[132] As it became clear that *Happy End* would be no more than a two-dimensional shadow of its model (even with the infusion of wholesale transplants from the nearly-completed *Aufstieg*), Brecht and Hauptmann viewed the play as an opportunity to insert Marxist ideology into the already doomed and improbable plot. But finally Brecht became so dissatisfied with his own efforts that he withdrew his name from the script and assigned authorship to a fictitious "Dorothy Lane." However, Weill insisted that Brecht assume credit for the lyrics. The premiere on 2 September 1929 was a pleasant surprise to Aufricht—up to the intermission before the third act the audience reaction was as favorable as it had been for *Die Dreigroschenoper*.[133] Lenya remembers Weill telephoning her backstage at the Deutsches Theater during intermission to tell her that *Happy End* was a sure hit. However, a fatal incident marred the third act:

Instead of giving her climactic speech, as written, Weigel pulled a well-known Communist Party pamphlet from the pocket of her costume, and began to harangue the audience with excerpts from it. To a politically conscious German audience of the time, it was as a red flag to a bull: the conservatives shouted back, the leftists tried to shout down the conservatives, fights broke out in the aisles, and a near-riot was precipitated. The critics, barely escaping with their dignity intact, assumed this act of provocation had been written into the script, and poured out their anger at Brecht in the next day's papers. The middle-class theatregoers, fearful of being caught in any such stormy event, shunned the play, and *Happy End* closed two days later, an ignominious failure.[134]

After its demise, Brecht repudiated the work entirely; it was not published until an actor's script was found in 1958, after Brecht's death. Universal-Edition, however, did print three of Weill's songs ("Bilbao-Song," "Matrosen-Song" and "Surabaya-Johnny") in both piano-vocal and jazz-orchestra arrangements in 1929.[135] After the libretto had been published in 1958, Universal brought out the entire piano-vocal score, with an English translation by Michael Geliot.[136] The play was first revived in Munich in 1958 and enjoyed a very successful American premiere in an adaptation by Michael Feingold at the Yale Repertory Theater in 1972.

Besides completing the score of *Aufstieg* in 1929, Weill also contributed music for a production of *Die Petroleuminseln* (*The Petroleum Islands*) by Lion Feuchtwanger (1884-1958). Written in 1923 and first staged in October 1927 in Hamburg, *Die Petroleuminseln* is set in a vaguely American locale, and oil supplies the background for the play, as it did in Lania's *Konjunktur*.[137] Lotte Lenya played the leading role in the Berlin production at the Staatstheater in 1929, for which Weill wrote his score. The music included a "Slow-Fox," "Das Lied von der braunen Inseln," which was published in the *Song-Album* of 1929. During this same year, Weill also wrote a number of individual songs, including "Das blinde Mädchen" (text by Günther Weisenborn), and contributed music for the Volksbühne production of *Lied von Hoboken*, in which Lenya again played a principal role.

Pursuing the goals of the didactic cantata to a logical sequel, Weill next composed a "*Schuloper*," *Der Jasager*, which explored educational institutions as viable means for expanding the audience for contemporary music. *Der Jasager* is the first twentieth-century composition to be labeled a *Schuloper*. The term *Schuloper* is probably best translated as "didactic opera" because Weill considered "school-opera" to be only one of several possibilities for combining *Schulung* (training) with opera.[138] In writing an opera that was intended specifically for students, Weill hoped to train a future generation of both performers and listeners:

I aim precisely at youth as the audience of the future. . . . When the present generation of school children has grown up, *the* audience I'm counting on will exist. . . . When I write for students, above all, I submit myself to an intensified self-control. That is, I must reach the utmost degree of simplicity if I want to write for students and wish to be comprehensible to them. But despite all such simplicity, I must give my best and highest. . . . Simple works are not minor works, but major works.[139]

Again it was Brecht's secretary, Elisabeth Hauptmann, who had provided the grist for Brecht's literary mill. In 1929 she translated into German four classical Japanese Noh-plays which had been adapted into English by Arthur Waley. Included among the four was *Taniko* ("The Valley-Hurling" in Waley's adaptation) by Zenchiku (1405-1468).[140] Brecht freely altered Hauptmann's translation to introduce the didactic element of *Einverständnis*, that is, acquiescence: a person must "take upon himself all the consequences for the sake of a community or for an idea to which he has attached himself."[141]

This "Lehrstück vom Ja-Sager," as the *Schuloper* was originally entitled, was intended for premiere at the 1930 Festival of New Music in Berlin, which was to be devoted to music for students, along with Hindemith's *Sabinchen* and *Wir bauen eine Stadt*, Toch's *Das Wasser*, and Eisler's *Die Massnahme*.[142] However, the organizers of the festival, Heinrich Burkhard, Paul Hindemith, and Georg Schünemann, declined to assume responsibility for the Brecht-Eisler sketch of *Die Massnahme* and requested the authors to submit the full text to a committee for approval. When Brecht and Eisler refused, the directorate rejected the work on the basis of the "artistic mediocrity of the text."[143] The controversy, which involved an exchange of "open letters" between Brecht-Eisler and the festival committee during May 1930, prompted the editors of *Melos* to invite Weill to state his position on the matter. In his response, "Musikfest oder Musikstudio?", which condemned the superficiality of much *Gebrauchskunst* and warned of the dangers of censorship, Weill wrote:

> As is well-known, difficulties no one had anticipated concerning the compilation of the program for "Neue Musik 1930" have set in recently. Although in this case they primarily concern only a specific work, the difficulties have gained fundamental significance in their consequences. . . .
> The attempts at stabilization which are undertaken in artistic production today (just as in the most diverse areas of public life) involve a grave danger: the danger of superficiality. . . . Great art of all eras achieved quality in that it relied on great, far-reaching ideas of its time. That which stands behind an art work determines its qualities; for the shaping of an artwork receives its value in that the means of expression are constantly measured against the magnitude, purity, and power of the idea. . . .
> The prerequisite condition of any artistic institution is *complete independence.*[144]

Although the acceptability of *Der Jasager* was never questioned by the committee, in protest Weill and Brecht withdrew the work from the auspices of "Neue Musik 1930." Instead, it was premiered in a radio broadcast on 23 June 1930, with a public performance at the Zentral-institut für Erziehung und Unterricht the following day. Weill and Brecht served as co-directors of the production which featured singers and instrumentalists of the Staatliche Akademie für Kirchen- und Schulmusik.[145] Because the premiere was intentionally scheduled to coincide with the festival (a cause for some embarrassment to the committee), *Der Jasager* was included in most reviews of the 1930 festival.[146]

The *Schuloper* rapidly became Weill's and Brecht's most popular work, with the exception of *Die Dreigroschenoper*. With the endorsement of Leo Kestenberg in the Ministry of Education *Der Jasager* was produced in more than three hundred German schools by 1932.[147] Weill had designed the score so that its performance could be adjusted to suit local capabilities:

> I have arranged *Der Jasager* in such a way that it can be performed by students in all parts (chorus, orchestra, and soloists), and I can even envision students designing the scenery and costumes for this play. The score has been arranged appropriately for the instrumentation-possibilities of a student orchestra: a basic orchestra of strings (without violas) and two pianos, with three woodwinds (flute, clarinet, saxophone), percussion, and plucked instruments added *ad libitum.*[148]
> All occurring vocal parts must be sung by students. I think the boy should be sung by a 10-12 year-old, the teacher by a 16-18 year-old, the mother by a 14-16 year-old girl. Similarly the three students who participate in the journey should be sung by pupils. And finally the entire school chorus should also participate.[149]

Brecht was appalled by the faulty interpretation of *Der Jasager* by many critics who, although nearly unanimous in their praise, were puzzled by his improbable endorsement of reactionary political tendencies which they thought had been extolled in *Der Jasager*. To test the effect of the opera on its intended consumers, Brecht arranged for a performance by the students of the Karl Marx Schule of Neuköln.[150] On the basis of the general confusion of the young performers as to the message of the play, Brecht revised the text according to their suggestions.[151] He also wrote a companion piece, *Der Neinsager*, and asserted that neither should be performed individually. Weill, however, never modified his score, which Universal had published in both piano-vocal and full orchestral editions in 1930. Nor did he ever compose music for *Der Neinsager*, that Brecht could assume that the same music would do for both texts is perhaps indicative of the role to which he wished to relegate music in his works.[152]

Although Weill and Brecht intended the work for performance in schools, they did authorize a number of concert performances. In July

1932, Klaus Prigsheim conducted the Japanese premiere of *Der Jasager* in Tokyo.[153] The following December, Weill was invited to bring *Der Jasager* and *Mahagonny* to Paris.[154] Hans Curjel directed and Maurice Abravanel conducted a cast that included Lenya in *Mahagonny* and thirty members of the Staatliche Akademie für Kirchen- und Schulmusik, which had premiered *Der Jasager* in Berlin. The distinguished audience for the first performance included Stravinsky, Cocteau, Picasso, Milhaud, Auric, Honegger, Gide, Ernst, and Léger.[155] Maurice Abravanel described the occasion as a "turning point in Weill's career":

> The ovation in Paris and the reactions of the musicians and the public were incredibly enthusiastic, leading to commissions to write a ballet for Balanchine's May 1933 season and also a symphony. Andre Gide wanted Weill to write *Amphytrion* with him. Stravinsky, who was at the preview given by the Vicomtesse de Noailles, praised *Mahagonny* to the skies and wanted it to be the companion piece to *L'Histoire du soldat* on a projected tour.[156]

In April 1933 *Der Jasager* received its American premiere at the Grand Street Playhouse in New York in a production sponsored by the Music School of the Henry Street Settlement.[157] One of the final performances of the opera in Europe before the war occurred at the Accademia di Santa Cecilia in Rome during December 1933, again led by Abravanel and staged by Curjel. Ironically the Fascist press, above all *Lavoro fascista*, celebrated the already-exiled Weill and his opera enthusiastically.[158] After his emigration to the United States, Weill stated that he considered *Der Jasager* his most significant composition.[159]

As Brecht's and Weill's ideological and aesthetic paths diverged and the omnipresent tension between composer and librettist exceeded the tensile strength of the relationship—finally breaking apart during the Berlin production of *Aufstieg*—several projects were left unfinished. The comic *Schuloper* that Weill had indicated would follow *Der Jasager* never appeared.[160] A one-act opera, *Der Moabiter Pferdehandel*, was abandoned in the planning stage, as was a musical version of Hasek's fable of the soldier *Schwejk*.[161] After *Der Jasager*, the only score which Weill completed for Brecht in Germany other than the revisions of *Aufstieg* was incidental music for the revival of *Mann ist Mann* in Berlin during February 1931—the same play which had provided the stimulus for their association four years earlier.[162] Unfortunately Weill's score, which included pieces entitled "Nachtmusik," "Schlachtmusik," "Marschmusik," and the "Mann-ist-Mann Song" has not been preserved.[163] Reaffirming his commitment to opera (which Brecht apparently did not share), Weill turned to Caspar Neher for the libretto of his most ambitious score *Die Bürgschaft*.

> *Today Weill is probably the only real opera composer in Germany, a fact*
> *which is generally accepted and which explains the great interest that awaits*
> *all his further development.*[164]
>
> — *Jerzy Fitelberg* —

VI

In 1931 the "situation of opera," as one of Weill's commentaries was entitled, was rapidly decaying in Germany. The number of productions of new operas had declined from a peak of sixty during the 1927/28 season to only sixteen in 1931/32. Because of its commercial appeal and harmless escapism, operetta had virtually wrested the opera houses away from opera proper.[165] Critics lamented the general decline in the quality of operatic productions; the Krolloper was closed.[166] Economic pressures that influenced choice of repertory and production values were compounded by thinly-veiled political censorship, occasional terrorist attacks, and wholesale replacement of artistic leadership in many theaters. Weill recognized the approaching crisis and in several essays cautioned against the reactionary trend.[167] He lamented the demotion of opera's function from a cultural and intellectual institution to superficial entertainment:

> There is a crisis in opera which befalls operatic theaters and naturally also operatic producers correlatively to a considerable degree. . . . I am not inclined to blame the public for this general theatrical crisis. . . . I am enough of an optimist to assume that we in Germany today have not yet come to so barbaric a cultural situation that replaces opera—always a significant component of German culture— with the most superficial type of theater. Rather, I believe that full responsibility for this situation falls on those whose constant pressure nowadays makes German theatrical administrators into timid, overly-cautious businessman.[168]

Weill's next opera was a culmination and summation of his previous experiments with cantata, epic theater, didactic and traditional opera.

Composed during August-October 1931 (that is, before the production of *Aufstieg* in Berlin), *Die Bürgschaft* is based on a parable by Johann Gottfried Herder (1744-1803), "Der africanische Rechtspruch."[169] Caspar Neher transformed this simple fable about trust within a society and the consequences of its betrayal into a libretto that comprises nineteen scenes and is divided into a prologue and three acts. The opera is Weill's longest work—the first performance lasted nearly four hours.[170] The score calls for two choruses, one active on the stage and the other narrative in function and located on a small platform to the left of the orchestra pit. Originally scheduled for production at the Berlin Staatsoper, the premiere of *Die Bürgschaft* was eventually shifted to the Städtische Oper. Its *Intendant* Carl Ebert directed, Fritz Stiedry (1883-1968) conducted, and Neher designed the production of his own opera.[171] *Die Bürgschaft*, which deals with government's misuse of its citizens' trust, was premiered on 10 March 1932—three days before the presidential election in which Hitler polled more than eleven million votes.[172]

Although unusually long and musically uneven, the opera was generally praised by critics. One wrote that it was "the first operatic work of distinctly modern hue that has met with approval from all quarters of the local musical camp."[173] Writing in the *New York Times*, Herbert Peyser described the opera:

> For good or ill the first eight scenes of *Die Bürgschaft* may be said to epitomize the music of Kurt Weill. . . . The pseudo-jazz of the *Dreigroschenoper* and *Mahagonny* virtually disappears from the scheme of *Die Bürgschaft*. But Weill is not yet ready to abandon the cabaret or the "revue." . . . On the other hand, there is counterpoint in abundance. Over and over again the chorus does its narrating and its commenting in strict canonic imitation. Weill writes ensembles that struggle to play the sedulous ape to the severely polyphonic canticles in the oratorios of Handel. It is Stravinsky's *Oedipus rex* and Honegger's *King David* with differences   Taken as a whole, *Die Bürgschaft* was easily Berlin's most imposing modern operatic adventure of the season to date.[174]

Ernst Bloch also noted the parallels with Stravinsky's *Oedipus rex* and pointed out (no doubt to Weill's satisfaction) that *Die Bürgschaft* also "has a piece of Jewish-Verdi in it."[175] The comparison with operas of Handel and Verdi surfaced in many of the reviews and reflected the general renewed interest in both composers that characterized the 'Handel-renaissance' and 'Verdi-renaissance' of the late twenties.[176] Despite such external influences, *Die Bürgschaft* is quite clearly a natural development and extension of certain aspects of *Der Jasager, Der Lindberghflug, Aufstieg,* and *Zar.*[177] But Weill's first major work following an almost exclusive four-year collaboration with Brecht was viewed as a fork in Weill's path in one respect: "*Die Bürgschaft* is a return to large-scale opera, a return to singing, and a return to music as the dominating factor."[178] Weill certainly "returned to music" in the sense that the supremacy of the composer is no longer in doubt: *Die Bürgschaft* is an opera, not a play with music. Brecht did not share the positive reaction to the work; he felt that it catered to the bourgeois taste for "culinary" opera. He was entirely correct in that Weill consciously attempted to emphasize operatic as opposed to didactic elements:

Die Bürgschaft is not a didactic play, but an opera. It was written for the theater. Its purpose is not to demonstrate doctrines, but rather, corresponding to the function of theater, to fashion human events against the background of a timeless idea. . . . In a time when some occupy themselves with artistic games, while others prefer to produce nothing so as not to give offense to anyone, *Die Bürgschaft* attempts to take a position on things which concern all of us.[179]

The position which *Die Bürgschaft* took—against totalitarianism—was not considered an artistic game by the National Socialists. After its premiere in Berlin, productions of *Die Bürgschaft* were scheduled for Basel, Düsseldorf, Wiesbaden, Hamburg, Königsberg, Duisburg, Stettin, Zürich, and Leipzig. That most of the announced productions never materialized was no accident; the opera was the victim of an overt political campaign led by the Kampfbund für Deutsche Kultur and supported by the Goebbels press.[180] Carl Ebert's identification with the opera was reason enough for his dismissal as *Intendant* on the charge of "political subversion."[181] Universal-Edition could still safely publish a piano-vocal score, which Weill dedicated to Walter Steinthal, but eventually the Nazis, who correctly recognized themselves in the tyrannical Commissar of *Die Bürgschaft*, attempted to destroy all orchestral scores.[182] It was believed that they had succeeded; there were no performances after 1933 until a copy of the score was rediscovered after Weill's death. Ebert and Neher revived the opera in a revised version in 1957 at its birthplace, the Berlin Städtische Oper.[183] It awaits an American premiere.

Although I was born in Germany, I do not consider myself a "German composer." The Nazis obviously did not consider me as such either, and I left their country (an arrangement which suited both me and my rulers admirably) in 1933.[184]

— *Kurt Weill* —

VII

Weill's last composition to be both composed and premiered in Germany was based on a play by his first collaborator, Georg Kaiser. In 1930 Kiepenheuer Verlag published Kaiser's *Der Silbersee: Ein Wintermärchen,* and during July-October 1932 Weill composed a score for the play, whose premiere was scheduled for January 1933 at the Deutsches Theater in Berlin.[185] In constructing *Der Silbersee* as a three-act play with an extensive musical score, Weill and Kaiser attempted to circumvent any dependence on government-subsidized opera houses, which had already cancelled scheduled productions of *Die Bürgschaft* and which were increasingly reluctant to produce Weill's operas. Consisting of sixteen musical numbers, including solo songs, ensembles, choral numbers and instrumental movements, *Der Silbersee* was composed for singing actors and demands an exceptionally large orchestra for a work that was not intended for the opera house. Because his score is a virtual compendium of the features and gestures which define his inimitable musical style and also the most explicit statement of his concern for a humane social order, it may be the single work most representative of Weill's German career.

When the production at the Deutsches Theater was halted during rehearsal by political pressure, Kaiser and Weill, anticipating the rapidly deteriorating political climate that would preclude any lengthy production run, took advantage of their combined reputations and arranged for a simultaneous premiere in Leipzig, Magdeburg, and Erfurt on 18 February 1933.[186] During rehearsals, on 30 January 1933, Hitler became Chancellor of Germany, but the play opened as scheduled. At the Altes Theater in Leipzig, the production was designed by Neher, directed by Detlef Sierck, and conducted by Gustav Brecher, who had conducted the premieres of *Aufstieg* and *Zar,* which had opened precisely five years earlier at Leipzig's Neues Theater. Although the performance was extremely well-received by the audience, those newspapers which had already become mouthpieces for propaganda condemned *Der Silbersee* as subversive to the German people and their "Führer." For example, the "critic" of the *Völkischer Beobachter* wrote:

As is well-known, Kurt Weill is responsible for the music of Bert Brecht's *Die Dreigroschenoper* and the opera *Aufstieg und Fall der Stadt Mahagonny*, which experienced a properly unambiguous rejection in March 1930. An "artist" who concerns himself with such subject matter, who writes "music" for licentious texts that consciously undermine art and the sense of genuine art, who lowers himself to the quality of the libretto, must be treated with mistrust since, in addition, as a Jew he has taken the liberty of using the German operatic stage for his own "anti-national" (*unvölkischen*) purposes![187]

The productions in Erfurt and Magdeburg, where the Nazis provoked a riot at the second performance, did not fare any better. A few critics still dared to speak their own minds; Erich Bürger, writing in the *Berliner Tageblatt*, whose editorial policies had not yet been ethnically purified, congratulated those theaters which had done their duty in producing the powerful work.[188] But in the face of political events, any play that included a song entitled "Cäsars Tod," a thinly-disguised indictment of a tyrannical dictator, would not be allowed to continue very long. On 27 February the Reichstag was burned; the following day Brecht emigrated to Prague; on 4 March 1933 *Der Silbersee* was performed for the last time during Weill's lifetime.[189] All performances of his music in Germany were prohibited until 1945. Although Universal-Edition still published the piano-vocal score in 1933, as well as "Six Pieces from *Der Silbersee*,"[190] the Nazis began a systematic attempt to suppress any vestigial residue of such a "cultural Bolshevist."

Like too many of his colleagues, Weill had become accustomed to Nazi protests against his works and had not taken the threats too seriously before *Der Silbersee*. In 1942 he recalled that during a visit to Augsburg in 1930 he had attended a Nazi mass meeting at which Hitler spoke of the alien influences rampant in Germany. The "Führer" had singled out in his speech such dire forces as Albert Einstein, Thomas Mann, and Kurt Weill, but Weill's only fear at the time was that the howling mob would attack him then and there.[191] Now, three years later, Weill was warned by a well-placed friend that Lenya and he were high on the blacklist of Jewish intelligentsia and that arrest was imminent. The danger could no longer be ignored; on 21 March 1933 they fled to Paris by automobile. Having gained some friends and a measure of success with the performance of *Mahagonny* and *Der Jasager* in Paris a few months before, Weill rented one of Madame du Barry's servant-houses in Luveciennes near St. Germain.

Almost immediately after his arrival, Weill received a commission for a ballet from "Les Ballets 1933," which was produced by Diaghilev's secretary, Boris Kochno. In response, Weill invited Brecht to write the scenario for *Die sieben Todsünden.*[192] During April and May 1933, Brecht and Weill restructured the medieval morality-play concept of the seven deadly sins into a critique of the evils of capitalism, comprising seven scenes with prologue and epilogue. It was not to be an ordinary ballet, but a "Ballet mit Gesang," a "Ballet Chanté," or as one reviewer described it, "a sort of mimed cantata."[193] Georges Balanchine choreographed the production which premiered at the Théâtre des Champs Elysées on 7 June 1933. Of course, Caspar Neher designed the sets and costumes, and Maurice Abravanel conducted the orchestra which called for instrumentation virtually identical to that of *Der Silbersee.*[194] Lotte Lenya and Tilly Losch played the two "sisters," Anna I and Anna II, who were actually the visual representation of one personality torn apart by the inhumane demands of society. Anna's family, who sends her to the big cities to earn money for a little house, is portrayed by a male quartet, dominated by a mustachioed mother, a bass.[195]

The ballet was greeted with an exceptionally enthusiastic response. Virgil Thomson, in comparing *Die sieben Todsünden* to Milhaud's *Les Songes* and Sauguet's *Fastes,* which shared the program, wrote:

> Musically the scandal was Weill. Milhaud's ballet is good Milhaud, no more. Sauguet's contains delicious music, rich and gay, but unfortunately it is orchestrated for the chamber rather than for the theater. . . . The Weill, of course, was completely striking, especially to the general public that had never heard any.[196]

Betraying his distaste for such a retrogression from his more clear-cut ideological works, Brecht, however, wrote to his wife Helene Weigel that "the ballet went quite nicely, but (it is) really not so significant."[197] He never permitted his text to be published independently.

After its production in Paris, the ballet was performed in London at the Savoy Theatre (1-15 July 1933) with the same cast and choreography under the title of *Anna-Anna.* In 1936, the Royal Danish Ballet produced it in Copenhagen, but the King, finding the subject matter offensive, ordered that the performance be stopped and muttered "this is not a ballet for royalty."[198] The score of the ballet was not published until five years after Weill's death, nor was it performed again during his lifetime.[199] In 1958 it received its American premiere with the New York City Ballet in an English translation by W. H. Auden and Chester Kallman; the production was again directed by Balanchine. Frankfurt hosted the German premiere in 1960.

Before his hasty departure from Germany, Weill had begun work on an orchestral work that had been commissioned by the Princess

Edmond de Polignac (1865-1943).[200] After completing *Die sieben Todsünden*, Weill resumed composition of the symphony. Its completion was announced in *Die Musik*:

> Kurt Weill, the composer of *Die Dreigroschenoper*, who resides in Paris, recently completed his first symphony. Now Weill will compose a musical comedy, which will differ essentially from *Die Dreigroschenoper* in its comic subject. The book is by an anonymous English author.[201]

Bruno Walter conducted the premiere of what is now labeled Symphony no. 2 in Amsterdam on 11 October 1934 with the Concertgebouw Orchestra. Although Weill considered the work to be non-programmatic, Walter encouraged him to supply a descriptive title, so Weill consented to "Symphonische Fantasie."[202] In a letter to Lenya, Weill described a rehearsal for the first performance:

> The rehearsal was wonderful. Walter does it magnificently, and everyone is genuinely enthusiastic, especially the *whole orchestra*. It's a good piece, and sounds marvelous.[203]

Unfortunately few critics shared Walter's or Weill's enthusiasm for the "Symphonische Fantasie." Herbert Antcliffe wrote of the premiere:

> What promised to be an event of unusual interest petered out as the production of a work that, while pleasant and well-written so far as the orchestration is concerned, proved to be of no great consequence. This was a 'Symphonische Fantasie' (or, as he also describes it, a First Symphony) by Kurt Weill, the composer of 'Mahagonny' and the musical editor of the 'Drei Groschen Oper' [*sic*]. . . . His themes have the same song-like character as those of Mahler, but he has by no means the mastery of development of this Viennese-Bohemian. In fact, in the first movement of his work, which he describes as 'in pure sonata form,' he begs the question of development by writing a *Durchführung* of which the material has no connection whatever with the principal or side-themes of the main subject. The best part of the work is the following slow movement, a 'Cortege,' which has richness of·texture with something of the sentimentality of the Chopin Funeral March. The third and last movement is an attempt at original form, though labelled 'Rondo.' The second theme is a pleasant March for wind instruments, and after the statement of the two main themes, the first develops into a Tarantella. . . . The Concertgebouw Orchestra under Bruno Walter made the best of the work, and the composer was called several times to the platform to acknowledge a very friendly reception.[204]

Walter did not abandon the work; he subsequently conducted it at The Hague and in Rotterdam. In December 1934 he brought the three-movement work (Sonata-Largo-Rondo) to the subscription concerts of the New York Philharmonic.[205] The Symphony had acquired another

new title: "Three Night Scenes: A Symphonic Fantasy." The following
explanatory note appeared in the program:

> It was written without any programmatic intention; but Mr. Walter, hearing it, was
> impressed by "its nocturnal, uncanny, mysterious atmosphere," and he suggested to
> the composer the title *Three Night-Scenes*, which Weill adopted with approval.[206]

American critics were even less kind than their European counterparts
had been. Lawrence Gilman dismissed it: "We need not dwell upon the
Symphonic Fantasy of Mr. Kurt Weill, which, indeed can be most easily
forgotten."[207] Lazare Saminsky called it a "protracted and tearful
midinette elegy, reeking of shrewd obviousness."[208] Olin Downes took
the work more seriously, but wrote no more favorably:

> The Weill pieces, however, are disappointing—the more disappointing because
> Kurt Weill has long been reckoned one of the smartest young men of modern
> Germany. The "Three Night Pieces" are disappointing, first, in the complete
> banality and lack of originality of the musical material; second, in the prolixity
> and dullness and absolute lack of distinction in the development. . . . They are
> dreary, dull, and witless. They end with speed and noise, and some accept these
> qualities today as wit and esprit.[209]

Walter conducted the Symphony again in Vienna in 1937, but thereafter
it was completely neglected until it was finally published in 1966.[210] In
1935 Weill stated that he wrote "absolute music in order to control my
own style" and that "you must turn away from your own habitual way
occasionally, so then I write symphonic works,"[211] but he never again
composed purely instrumental works for the concert hall.

The program notes for the American premiere of Weill's Symphony
no. 2 reveal the remarkably provincial and confused view of Weill's
career that he would encounter a year later when he emigrated to the
United States. Although American newspapers had consistently
published reviews of Weill's major German works, there is no evidence
of comprehension of his aesthetic or musical goals. That Lawrence
Gilman could write that "Kurt Weill is most widely known by his cantata
Lindbergh's Flight" is indicative of the barrier Weill had to overcome
upon arrival in the United States.[212] Even so distinguished a critic as
Virgil Thomson wrote:

> Kurt Weill had done for Berlin what Charpentier did for Paris. . . . He has
> almost created style. One can be indifferent to the subject matter. . . . The stories
> of his little cantatas are very moral. The *Yes-Sayer* is a little boy whose mother
> is about to die for lack of certain medicines. . . . "Les Sept Péchés Capitaux" is
> about a young girl who leaves home to make money for her parents. . . . It is a
> story of filial devotion like *Der Jasager*.[213]

In the context of such naive interpretation of Weill's operatic works, it is easy to understand why the first American production of *The Threepenny Opera* in 1933 was neither appreciated nor welcomed. It also explains why Weill never attempted to revive his German operas for an American audience after he became a citizen of the United States and why his American works form such an abrupt contrast to their German predecessors.

After he had completed Symphony no. 2 in February 1934, Weill collaborated with Jacques Deval (b. 1895) on a "Pièce en 2 Actes et 10 Tableaux" based on Deval's novel, *Marie galante*. The play, which featured Weill's songs and incidental music, was premiered on 22 December 1934 at the Théâtre de Paris with "Florelle" in the title role.[214] Marc Blitzstein reviewed Weill's music in *Modern Music*:

> Kurt Weill's *Marie galante* music got very little hearing; since the piece itself was taken off the boards of the Théâtre de Paris within a week. The tunes "J'Attends un Navire" and "Les Filles de Bordeaux" may pick up and have a career of their own in the music-halls; Margo Lion is at the moment singing the old *Dreigroschenoper* ballads at the Noctambules, and she could do with a change of repertoire. Weill is at present at work upon his next "grosse wurf," a huge oratorio-spectacle, *The Road to Promise*, to a text by Franz Werfel, and scheduled for New York under Reinhardt's direction in the fall. A private piano-performance of this work indicates to me that it is Weill's best score.[215]

"J'Attends un Navire" did indeed have a career of its own, as it was informally adopted by the French underground during the war. Sung in *Marie galante* by a prostitute marooned in Panama who longed to return to Bordeaux, it later symbolized anticipation of ships of a different kind—Allied invasion carriers. Seven songs from *Marie galante* were published by Heugel in 1934.

Weill worked steadily during his two-year stay in Paris. He composed a number of individual songs, including "Complainte de la Seine" and "Je ne t'aime pas" with texts by Maurice Magre,[216] in addition to four theatrical works. But with the exception of *Die sieben Todsünden*, he enjoyed no sustained success. Nor had he been successful in escaping blatant anti-Semitic propaganda in Paris. That German music journals systematically attempted to denigrate such "smutty cabaret talents as Weill" is not surprising, but even in France at a performance of Weill's "Ballade de César," Florent Schmitt "arose and shouted: 'We have enough bad musicians in France already, without having to import German-Jewish ones.'"[217]

Weill described the last work that he composed for a European theater, *A Kingdom for a Cow*, as the biggest failure of his career. Against the advice of a number of friends, including Hans Curjel, Weill collaborated on this operetta with Robert Vambery, who had been Aufricht's dramaturgist at the time of *Die Dreigroschenoper.*[218] Composed during January-July 1934, *A Kingdom for a Cow* opened at the Savoy Theater in London on 28 June 1935 with Muir Matheson conducting. It was withdrawn immediately and never published.[219] In September 1935 Weill sailed for New York to assist with the production of *The Eternal Road* and to begin an unexpected second career in America. His first introduction to American concert life occurred in December 1935 when the League of Composers sponsored a program of excerpts from his operas performed by Lotte Lenya, a chorus of ten singers, and two pianos.[220] One of the pianists, Ernst Wolff, recalls that the illustrious audience of American composers and supporters of contemporary music numbering about one hundred and fifty people at the outset dwindled to not more than thirty before the conclusion of the event.

The roaring cheers of today were no guarantee against the oblivion of tomorrow.[221]

— *Carl Zuckmayer* —

CHAPTER 3

WEILL'S ESSAYS:
A CONTEXT FOR HIS MUSIC

The duties of criticism of contemporary creative works are first to inform the newspaper-reading public of the value and significance of a new composition and to acquaint the public with the related events in the total production of our time, and secondly to give the creative musician himself an opinion concerning his work either from the standpoint of the public or from that of the technical consultant.[1]

— *Kurt Weill* —

I

Although Weill's literary career is one of the least known facets of his output, it provides a critical context for his contemporaneous musical production from 1925 to 1933. Conservatively estimated at more than a million words, Weill's essays may be divided conveniently into two categories. The first group of articles resulted from his position as critic of the journal of the German radio industry, *Der deutsche Rundfunk.* With the exception of a few hiatuses, each issue of the weekly periodical during the four-year period 1925-1929 contained at least one and occasionally as many as four contributions by Weill. Restricted by the format and requirements of the journal, this literary output reflects his opinions on musical and theatrical presentations of the German radio. While dealing specifically with actual programing and its social, cultural, and technical ramifications, Weill has bequeathed a legacy of commentary ranging from Paul Whiteman to Arnold Schoenberg, from Shakespeare to Shaw, and from Palestrina to Pfitzner. The second expediential category comprises those essays written in explanation of Weill's own works or his own theories pertaining to music and theater. Published in musical journals, theatrical periodicals, and newspapers, these articles are especially relevant to any discussion of Weill's music.

The first licensed German broadcasting station, the Funk-Stunde Berlin AG, was established in October 1923, and in the same month its journal, *Der deutsche Rundfunk: Rundshau und Programm für alle Funkteilnehmer. Zeitschrift der am deutschen Rundfunk beteiligten Kreise,* was inaugurated. Edited by Hans S. von Heister and issued weekly on Sundays, the journal became the official bulletin of the Reichs-Rundfunk-Gesellschaft, which during 1923 and 1924 expanded to include nine regional stations. Each issue of the periodical contained a section devoted to the technical and scientific aspects of the radio medium, as well as complete program listings for each broadcasting station in Germany. General discussions about appropriate radio programing complemented previews and reviews of specific broadcast events. In

1924, since the nascent music recording industry could by no means meet the needs of the radio stations, a dramatic and operatic division (*Sendespielbühne*) was added to the already extant musical division, which included its own orchestra, to fulfill the demands of the expanding scope of radio programs.[2] In doing so, the radio station became one of the most advanced and daring centers for production of contemporary musical and theatrical works.

The date of Weill's initial association with *Der deutsche Rundfunk*, undoubtedly initially prompted by financial hardship, cannot be precisely determined. As early as 30 November 1924, musical examples in Weill's script appeared in the journal. However, as a result of the editorial policy that authors of articles were identified only by initials and the coincidence that Weill's predecessor as Berlin correspondent, Karl Wiener, signed his essays "K.W.", the authorship of a number of entries published in the first quarter of 1925 (some of which are unsigned) in which Weill's musical examples appear is open to question.[3] To avoid the confusion between himself and his predecessor, Weill ultimately adopted "Wll." as his signature; the first entry to be so identified appeared in the issue dated 12 April 1925. From this date until 26 December 1926, Weill usually wrote two essays per week.[4] The first, frequently entitled "Vom Berliner Sender: Rück- und Vorschau," was devoted to the musical programs of the Berlin station.[5] Weill usually introduced this feature with commentary of a general nature concerning aspects of the radio as a medium for music, and then proceeded to highlight the upcoming week's musical programs. Often his essay included historical background and brief descriptive analyses, as well as critical commentary on the previous week's musical events. The second regular feature written by Weill was a report of events which occurred in the Sendespielbühne-division of the Berlin radio. Operas, operettas, and plays were previewed and reviewed, with one production singled out for more detailed examination. Thus, Weill functioned as both music and theater critic for the Berlin radio station.

In January 1927 Weill appended an additional essay to his weekly contributions—a panorama of the most significant occurrences on radio programs throughout Germany. This "Allgemeine Sendesbericht" or "Rundschau" effectively resulted in adding the duties of chief critic for the German radio to Weill's position as Berlin correspondent. He continued writing these three weekly essays, which constituted the bulk of the critical section of each issue, until October 1927, when the format of the programing section of *Der deutsche Rundfunk* was again altered. In the new arrangement, Weill's weekly burden was reduced to only one article, the "Allgemeine Sendesbericht," and a new writer, Ascoltante,

assumed some of Weill's former assignments as Berlin correspondent. A
logical shift in the content of Weill's contributions accompanied this
division of labor: plot synopses and cast information for the approximately twenty stage works broadcast each week were presented in a
special section of the journal so that neither Weill, in his role as chief
critic, nor Ascoltante was saddled with the mechanical communication of
that data.

Weill's one weekly essay appeared routinely until 18 May 1928,
about the time that he and Brecht began intensive work on *Die
Dreigroschenoper.* After an absence from four consecutive issues (Weill
was in Le Lavandou on the French Riviera with Brecht), Weill's regular
essay reappeared and a new feature entitled "Kritik" usually opened with
a short paragraph by Weill, the chief critic.   Thereafter, with the
exception of one issue in which he is not represented, each week he
produced the one panoramic article, penned .a paragraph for "Kritik,"
and occasionally submitted a leading article under the by-line "Kurt
Weill" or "K. Wll." This routine came to an abrupt conclusion with the
17 May 1929 issue, which contained Weill's "Notiz zum *Berliner
Requiem,*" wherein his dissatisfaction with the radio industry's treatment
of his cantata is apparent.   The financial stability won with *Die
Dreigroschenoper* allowed Weill to register his protest by resigning his
post with *Der deutsche Rundfunk.* He wrote no more articles for the
journal of the German radio industry, although in following years there
were occasional reviews of his own musical works in its pages. During
his four-year tenure Weill had had occasion to comment upon virtually
every major contemporary composer and dramatist, a number of musical
and theatrical figures of the past, and their foremost performers and
interpreters.[6]

Weill's journalistic career was by no means restricted to discussion
of others' artistic endeavors. From 1925 to 1933 he frequently explained
or defended his own compositions or aesthetic positions in musical and
theatrical journals, as well as newspapers. These "apologetic" essays
appeared in the following publications:

    Music Periodicals: *Melos* (Mainz)
                          Die Musik (Berlin)
                          Anbruch (Vienna)
                          Die Musikpflege (Leipzig)
                          Blätter der Staatsoper (Berlin)
                          Das Tagebuch (Berlin)

    Theater Journals: *Die Scene: Blätter für Bühnenkunst* (Berlin)
                          Der Scheinwerfer (Essen)
                          Die neue Weg (Berlin)

Newspapers: *Berliner Tageblatt*
                     Berliner Börsen-Courier
                     Deutsche Allgemeine Zeitung (Berlin)
                     Vossische Zeitung (Berlin)
                     Frankfurter Zeitung
                     Leipziger neueste Nachtrichten
                     Magdeburgische Zeitung

Others: *Die literarische Welt* (Berlin)
                     Sozialistische Monatshefte (Berlin)
                     Jahrbuch der Universal-Edition (Vienna)

Nor were the subjects of his published literary efforts restricted only to music; as one of Berlin's young intellectuals, Weill ventured to express his opinions on a variety of artistic and cultural topics. However, the twenty-seven essays that have been translated into English in Appendix II all directly address musical or theatrical topics. This collection of essays, all but one of which appears in its entirety in English for the first time in the present study, can also be subdivided conveniently into two groups:

Essays Regarding Particular Works by Weill:

Die Dreigroschenoper. "Korrespondenz über *Dreigroschenoper*" (1929)

Aufstieg: "Vorwort zum Regiebuch der Oper *Aufstieg und Fall der Stadt Mahagonny*" (1930)
               "Anmerkungen zu meiner Oper *Mahagonny*" (1930)
               "Zur Uraufführung der Oper *Mahagonny*" (1930)

Der Jasager. "Aktuelles Zwiegespräch über die Schuloper zwischen Kurt Weill und Dr. Hans Fischer" (1930)
               "Ueber meine Schuloper *Der Jasager*" (1930)

Die Bürgschaft: "Kurt Weill antwortet" (1932)

Essays on Opera and Music:

Opera: "Bekenntnis zur Oper" (1925)
               "Die neue Oper" (1926)
               "Busonis *Faust* und die Erneuerung der Opernform" (1926)
               "Gesellschaftsbildende Oper" (1929)
               "Ueber den gestischen Charakter der Musik" (1929)
               "Entwicklungstendenzen der Oper" (1929)
               "Situation der Oper: Gespräch mit Kurt Weill" (1931)
               "Das Formproblem der modernen Oper" (1932)
               "Wirklich eine Opernkrise?" (1932)

Topicality and Zeittheater: "Zeitoper" (1928)
"Aktuelles Theater" (1929)

Jazz and Dance Music: "Tanzmusik" (1926)
"Notiz zum Jazz" (1929)

Musical Criticism: "Kritik am zeitgenössischen Schaffen" (1929)
"Vom Wesen der Musikzeitschrift—Diskussion über *Melos*"
(1932)

Music and Musical Institutions: "Verschiebungen in der musikalische Produktion"
(1927)
"Gebrauchsmusik und ihre Grenzen" (1929)
"Musikfest oder Musikstudio?" (1930)

Of course, these categories are not mutually exclusive, because in writing essays that dealt with the general musical and operatic situation Weill usually prefaced his remarks with a statement such as: "If I am to reply to a question regarding the current musical situation from the standpoint of a creative musician, I must restrict myself to reflection upon the situation from the position of the development of my own production."[7] Thus, even in his more comprehensive aesthetic statements Weill frequently referred to and commented on his own works and compositional procedures.

The remainder of the present chapter will be devoted to consideration of the content of Weill's literary output as it relates to his own musical compositions. Since the major essays under discussion have been included in English translation in Appendix II, the need for précis of the articles has been eliminated. Documentary data and explanatory notes occasioned by specific passages of the essays have been included in the appendix at the end of each item. Therefore, here only the most provocative aspects of Weill's prose will be examined.

We cannot approach opera with the snobbism of indifferent renunciation. We cannot write operas and at the same time lament the shortcomings of this genre. We cannot view operatic composition as the fulfillment of a purely superficial obligation while we expend our true substance in other forms. . . . Without reservation, we must commit ourselves to opera.[8]

— Kurt Weill —

II

That the majority of Weill's essays written for journals other than *Der deutsche Rundfunk* pertain to opera and that his first essay to receive international circulation was entitled "Commitment to Opera" is not surprising in light of his youthful decision to make musical theater his field of special activity and his subsequent lifelong devotion to its cultivation. Weill's essays dating from 1925 and 1926 exhibit his efforts to reinstate what he deemed to be the only genuine aesthetic basis for opera: music was again to be the solitary goal.[9] Clearly influenced by the neo-classic ideals of Busoni, Weill called for a renunciation of the music drama of the nineteenth century, which he believed to have been burdened by a literary wrapper, a materialistic orientation, verbosity, unnaturalness, and false pathos. In particular, Weill voiced his conviction that composers had to free themselves from Richard Wagner's sphere of influence in order to return to opera that could be constructed according to purely musical precepts.[10] Eschewing music that depicted "floating atmosphere" or expressed "nervously exaggerated sentiments," Weill rejected the illustrative or psychological role of music in opera. Instead he asserted that music must furnish a commentary for the incidents on the stage, which function only as an optical animation of the music. This approach posited two goals for operatic music: clarity of expression and construction of "absolute" musical forms.

A return to absolute music was as central to Weill's theory of opera as it was to the neo-classic tendencies of the entire generation of young composers who reached maturity during the post-World War I era. Weill summarized this development as follows:

An energetic purification process initially eliminated all extra-musical influences, especially the literary points of congruence. Absolute music became the goal of young composers. Complete renunciation of any external or inner "program," intentional avoidance of large orchestral forces, limitation of the means of expression in favor of an intensification of the inner powers of expression, instinctive ties to the style of the masters of *a cappella* music—these were the characteristics of this development. People looked on opera somewhat scornfully as an inferior genre, for they thought only of music drama, from which they wanted to escape. But soon they noticed that absolute music was directly in a position to pave the way for genuine opera. For the musical elements of opera are no different from those of absolute music. In both it is only a question of the musical ideas unfolding in a form that corresponds with the emotional content. The tempo of the stage, which always demands an exceptional response from the operatic composer, is by no means a new, special component of opera, but must be clearly recognizable in our chamber and orchestral music before we approach opera.[11]

Thus Weill clearly stated the rationale for his own compositional output from 1921 to 1924. With the exception of the ballet-pantomime *Die Zaubernacht*, during this period he composed exclusively non-theatrical music. The orchestral works (Symphony no. 1, *Sinfonia sacra*, Divertimento, the "Rilke-Lieder") and smaller instrumental and vocal compositions (String Quartet no. 1, *Frauentanz*, *Recordare*, Violin Concerto) testify to Weill's own attempts to perfect his musical language in non-operatic pieces. The wide range of media and the varied experiments in treatment of harmonic and contrapuntal resources which these compositions exhibit bear witness to the exploratory nature of this period of his career. It is not difficult to suggest models for the compositions in which Weill hoped to achieve "an intensification of musical experience stemming from a pre-occupation with Bach and the pre-Classics."[12] That in some of these works he was not successful at freeing himself from certain extra-musical influences underscores their function as preliminary studies for operatic composition and demonstrates Weill's innate and irrepressible affinity for the theater. In fact, his endeavors are least fruitful in the purely instrumental compositions where dramatic gestures (such as the recitatives in String Quartet no. 1) seem inappropriate and insufficiently integrated into the overall structure. If Weill erred by incorporating theatrical effects in his absolute music, he astutely recognized that the elements of absolute music could not merely be transferred into opera ("that is the path to cantata and oratorio"). He wrote that Mozart, the operatic composer he most admired, had taught him that:

> He [Mozart] is no different in opera than in the symphony or string quartet. He always possesses the pacing of the stage. . . . This reaches the point where with the addition of a text one can convert any movement from his chamber music or orchestral works into a dramatically-animated operatic aria or even into a finale which advances the plot. . . . Mozart certainly does not achieve this by extra-musical means; on the contrary, it is achieved by the most fundamental expression of music. For ultimately what moves us in the theater is the same as what affects us in all art: the heightened experience—the refined expression of an emotion— the human condition.[13]

Weill especially esteemed the crystalline clarity of emotional and musical expression of Mozart, of "all the masters who stem from Mozart: Weber, Berlioz, Bizet, Strauss, Busoni," and of "the great Italians from Pergolesi to Puccini."[14]   For Weill, a restoration of opera depended on the rebirth of music-dominated opera (*Musizieroper*, like that of the eighteenth century), toward which the first decisive step in Germany had been taken, in his opinion, by Richard Strauss in *Ariadne auf Naxos*.

Weill characterized himself as one of those young German musicians, who, after the revolution in Germany were "filled with new ideals" and "swollen with new hopes" but were unable to find the proper musical form.[15]   Describing their almost frantic search for expressive means within their newly-acquired freedom as a "spasm of excess," Weill credited Busoni as the prophet who guided the younger generation to a "new classicism"—a synthesis of all new achievements with the useful material of previous generations.   Busoni's *Doktor Faust* was to be the starting point for the formation of a new golden age of opera.[16]   Weill made such high claims for Busoni's final opera because it exhibited an ideal union of idea and form and a perfect fusion of musical and theatrical impulse; in it Weill found a solution to the problem of formal organization:

> The formal idea—just as the melodic or harmonic—is subject to no other laws than that of the total idea, that of the intellectual material. This material creates the stimulus for formal construction in the first place. The symphonic idea must find itself completely fulfilled in the form of the symphony. Similarly, both the tangible and concealed content of the operatic scene must be in absolute agreement with its musical form.[17]

Specifically Weill noted that Busoni's dense polyphonic style was not an end in itself, but rather the only feasible constructive form for the Faustian subject matter.

Undoubtedly it was the belief that an opera's content must determine its form which accounts for the remarkable variety of works for the musical stage that Weill produced. Even a cursory glance at the external shapes of his theatrical works composed from 1924 to 1934 indicates how each composition represents an individual resolution of formal issues:

Der Protagonist: one-act opera with two scenes in pantomime
Royal Palace: one-act opera with ballet and film
Na und?: two-act comic opera
Mahagonny-Songspiel: song-play in three parts
Der Zar lässt sich photographieren: one-act opera buffa
Die Dreigroschenoper: three-act "Urform" of opera; play in three acts with music

Happy End: comedy in three acts with music
Aufstieg und Fall der Stadt Mahagonny: epic opera in three acts
Der Jasager: Schuloper in two acts
Die Bürgschaft: opera in three acts with *Vorspiel*
Der Silbersee: "a winter's tale" in three acts with music
Die sieben Todsünden: ballet with singing
Marie galante: play in two acts with music
A Kingdom for a Cow: operetta in two acts

In each case, the overall structure of the composition corresponds to Weill's interpretation of the work's content. In certain instances, his solution is an obvious one: for example, *Die sieben Todsünden* comprises seven movements, one for each of the capital sins, with a prologue and epilogue. Less apparent is the fact that in setting Brecht's text as a ballet with singing, Weill created the basis for the differentiation of the two Annas: one sings, the other dances. Furthermore, by casting the family as a male quartet, headed by a bass as the monstrous mother, the composer translated the dramatic function of the family into its musical analogue.[18] In addition to the overall form, even the musical personnel of *Die sieben Todsünden* were dictated by the work's content. In *Aufstieg* the content is a sequence of separate situations in the chronicle of the city, and Weill's twenty-one closed musical "scenes" capture this discrete, stepwise essence of epic opera, which he called "the purest form of musical theater." Even his most derivative work, *Happy End*, which superficially resembles *Die Dreigroschenoper* in outline, received its own unique formulation because the operatic elements of *Die Dreigroschenoper* (finales, recitatives, arias) were replaced by "Salvation Army" anthems. The comic subject matter of *Happy End* was incapable of supporting operatic treatment.[19]

Within each of his stage works, the internal scenic structure is also determined by its content. Consider the first pantomime of *Der Protagonist:* the itinerant troupe's rehearsal of a complicated and licentious comic sketch that exploits the varied possibilities for "love-play" between combinations of husband, wife, mistress, and monk. Weill clarified the dichotomy of the opera's nested structure (two plays, a comedy and a tragedy, occur as scenes in pantomime within the opera) by accompanying the pantomimes with an on-stage wind octet and by writing in an intentionally grotesque style which contrasts with the musical style of the rest of the opera. He also captured the content of the first pantomime in a "theme-and-nine-variations-with-finale" musical structure. Similar examples of such correspondence between musical form and subject matter abound. Yet, Weill made a definite distinction between the correlation of musical form and content and the mere illustration or accompaniment of dramatic incidents with music.[20] He never permitted music to be relegated to a subsidiary role in opera; throughout his career, Weill insisted that music be the determining factor in the overall structure of an operatic work. Even in his collaborations with Brecht, where the reciprocal saturation of music and content is most complete, Weill demanded that the total plan and scenario be constructed according to musical considerations.

Weill's insistence that restoration of music to its predominant role in opera was the only viable aesthetic basis for a renewal of the genre and his aversion to the literary dependence that he felt had crippled music drama did not discourage him from seeking the foremost representatives of spoken drama as his collaborators. Weill recognized a clear distinction between the threat of *literary* dependence and the potential of *dramatic* excellence within musical theater:

> Without a doubt, this treatment in opera of great ideas of our time can result initially only from a collaboration of a musician with one of the representatives of literature who is at least equivalent in standard. The repeatedly expressed apprehension that such a collaboration with valuable literary figures could bring music into a dependent, subservient, or only equal relationship to the text is completely unfounded. For the more powerful the writer, the more he is able to adapt himself to music, and so much the more he is stimulated to create genuine poetry for music.[21]

In his notes to *Street Scene* (1947), Weill wrote that one of the first decisions he made was to interest leading dramatists in the problems of musical theater. He correctly pointed out that the list of his collaborators reads like a good selection of playwrights of different countries: Georg Kaiser, Iwan Goll, Bertolt Brecht, Jacques Deval, Franz Werfel, Paul Green, Maxwell Anderson, Moss Hart, Langston Hughes, Elmer Rice, and Ogden Nash. The fact that the majority of Weill's librettos were written expressly for his musical treatment (under his direct supervision) allowed him to shape the overall structure of works from their outset.

It was no coincidence that in *Die Zaubernacht* Weill first approached musical theater through ballet. He recognized that dance not only required the same clarity of form and vitality of rhythm as opera but also that it was constructed according to the precepts of music alone—the optical proceedings of ballet merely enriched or reinforced the musical effect. Although Weill praised the genre compounded from ballet and opera exemplified by Stravinsky's *Soldier's Tale* as the foundation for a new operatic course, he recognized that it could serve only as an intermediary genre on the path to authentic modern opera. Similarly, Weill was attracted to pantomime as a less-choreographed theatrical medium than ballet, yet one which also demanded and profited from musical accompaniment while maintaining its own independence. In both pantomime and ballet, Weill could circumvent any obligation to illustrate the dramatic events.   His operatic ideal that music should furnish only a commentary for the incidents and that the action on stage should function as an optical extension of musical events could be accomplished in ballet and pantomime without confronting the hurdles raised by the addition of language.[22]   It was only after Weill's successful incorporation of ballet and pantomime in his one-act operas *Der Protagonist* and *Royal Palace* that he extended these principles to include the entire structure of an opera.   However, dance had served as a powerful constructive element already in his earliest stage works.

The use of traditional ballet and older dance idioms in *Die Zaubernacht* paved the way for Weill's embracing American jazz, because for him jazz meant modern dance music. It was from touring American dance bands and their European imitators that Weill learned of the music which expressed "the rhythm of our time."[23]   The primary differences between utilizing popular dance idioms instead of waltzes or minuets in modern music were social rather than musical in nature:

> The Americanization of our whole external life, which is happening slowly but surely, finds its most peculiar outcome here.   Unlike art music, dance music does not reflect the sense of towering personalities who stand above time, but rather it reflects the instinct of the masses.   And a glance into the dance halls of all continents demonstrates that jazz is just as precisely the outward expression of our time as the waltz was of the outgoing nineteenth century.[24]

Weill saw the modern jazz idiom as a means to reach a broader audience, because its musical style was accepted and understood throughout every class of the population. He was well aware of the historical precedent for such an influx into "art music" from the realm of folk or dance music:

> In all times the dance has had an effect on music.   It was so with Bach, Beethoven, Schumann, and others. They took the popular dance music of their or other days and lifted it into the region of art.[25]

Weill perceived jazz to be not only popular dance music but also a fresh storehouse of musical expression that corresponded to the folk song, which during the nineteenth century had provided the literary and musical models for the *Lied*. In fact, not unlike the early Romantics who considered the folk song the most natural expression of man, Weill called jazz an international folk music and described it as a "piece of nature":

Modern music has been reproached because its composers allowed themselves to be influenced more strongly by jazz through its dance forms than by art music of earlier times. In so doing one forgets that jazz, being more than a social dance, includes elements which vastly exceed the influential capabilities of the waltz. In the midst of a time of heightened artistry, jazz appeared as a piece of nature—as the healthiest, most vigorous expression of art, which has arisen immediately from its popular origins to an international folk music of the broadest consequence.[26]

However, Weill carefully stated that talented modern composers "did not go to jazz to borrow its idiom. It was not the actual taking of material. It was an influence you did not feel. Freedom, directness, simplicity, that's what jazz had."[27] He perceptively noted that those composers who were not secure enough in their own style to resist wholesale borrowing of melodic and harmonic elements of jazz were guilty of imitation rather than transformation of the material:

It depended on the strengths of the individual talents who allowed themselves to embrace jazz whether or not they could resist that influence. For the serious European musician the question of wanting to imitate American dance music or even of wanting to ennoble it could never arise. But it is obvious that jazz has played a significant role in the rhythmic, harmonic, and formal relaxation that we have now attained and, above all, in the constantly increasing simplicity and comprehensibility of our music.[28]

As early as 1925, which Copland designated as the peak of European interest in the American dance band,[29] Weill himself was inspired to adopt and transform rhythmic, formal, and orchestral characteristics of modern dance music without yielding to the temptation to borrow specific melodic or harmonic formulas. Despite prevalent misconceptions to the contrary, Weill's melodic and harmonic vocabulary was well-established by the time he embraced jazz, and throughout his German career his music bears an indelible and unmistakable personal stamp. Certainly incorporation of features of jazz-band instrumentation and orchestration, specifically the rhythm section (banjo, piano, percussion), muted trumpets, and saxophones, is the most blatant and enduring effect of jazz on Weill's music. However, it was not the first aspect to appear in his scores. Although *Royal Palace* is the first of his scores to utilize a saxophone, the use of an entire dance-band complement of instruments did not occur until *Die Dreigroschenoper*. It was the characteristic syncopated rhythms of modern dance music that were already assimilated in *Royal Palace*. Moreover, dance idioms were invoked as the bases of large-scale formal constructions in *Royal Palace* and *Zar*. Just as the simple binary form of the minuet grew to sonata proportions in classical symphonies and string quartets, the fox-trot and tango were enlarged to constitute entire scenes in these operas.[30]

It must be pointed out that such usage is very different from Weill's later gestic employment of dance idioms in the songs of his epic operas. In *Royal Palace* and *Zar* the dance idioms were thoroughly integrated into the continuous musical fabric of these one-act operas. Weill did not yet exploit fully the social connotations of the dances as commentary upon the text or dramatic situation. Instead the dances occurred either as a straightforward extension of plot (as in *Royal Palace*, where a fox-trot accompanies the dancing of the hotel guests or where a tango is summoned as the "Tanz der Wasserfrau") or as the result of ingenious theatrical devices (as in *Zar*, where the "Tango-Angèle" emanating from an on-stage gramophone accompanies the singing). It appears that Weill was still self-conscious about justifying the introduction of modern dance idioms in his operas. Therefore, he carefully ensured that their entrances were directly related to a dramatic event and were properly incorporated into the overall structure. For example, the fox-trot which accompanies the film scene in *Royal Palace* (pp. 41-47 of the piano-vocal score) was foreshadowed in the music of the mystical bells and invisible chorus at the beginning of the opera. The transformation of the opening passages (Example 3.1 a, b) into their unmistakable echoes in the fox-trot (Example 3.2 a, b) gives audible yet subtle unity to the two scenes which differ so widely in musical style and dramatic function. Such sophisticated thematic transformation is also evident in Symphony no. 1. However, in later works such as *Die Dreigroschenoper, Aufstieg*, and *Der Silbersee* there is no such preparation for the introduction of dance idioms; the abrupt appearance of a specific dance is itself a powerful commentary about the dramatic situation. Of course, this was more easily achieved in the discrete musical units of dialogue-opera or plays-with-music than in the continuous musical structure of *Royal Palace* and *Zar*.

In summary, Weill's essays from 1925 and 1926 are concerned with new aesthetic bases for opera, founded on the principles of clarity of expression and form which he recognized in such diverse models as eighteenth-century opera, Busoni's *Doktor Faust*, and modern dance music. His operas that survive from this period demonstrate his attempts to incorporate aspects of this new aesthetic foundation within the format of one-act operas wherein music is continuous and predominant. That all three one-act operas are rather short is indicative of the gravity of the formal and structural problems that Weill faced. Each of them represents a different approach to music's role in opera; that the three works display such diversity reflects Weill's conviction that content must determine both musical style and form. In *Der Protagonist* his music shunned the pathos and psychological characterization of nineteenth-century music drama which Weill abhorred and instead attempted to convey the drama with such exactness and power that the audience would be overcome without emotional appeal to its sympathy. In *Royal Palace* Iwan Goll provided Weill a revue-like sketch wherein music could reign supreme and wherein there were a multitude of opportunities to introduce modern dance idioms in such a way that they would not seem incongruous interpolations. Its film and ballet sequences presented the composer with additional occasions for accompanying stage events with music that could not be relegated to illustrative or descriptive effect. In *Zar*, composed concurrently with Weill's initial association with Brecht for the *Mahagonny-Songspiel*, one finds the termination of Weill's predominantly aesthetic approach to opera. The rudimentary gestic function of the "Tango-Angèle" and the novel use of the male chorus in the pit indicated that Weill had arrived at a point where the leap to an epic form of opera was no longer out of reach. What was needed was a collaborator who shared the ideal of clarity and simplicity, who could match Weill's musical strides to that goal with a compatible dramatic instinct and comparable power of language. In 1927 Weill summarized the concerns of his first essays, as well as his earlier compositional output, in an essay entitled "Verschiebungen in der musikalischen Produktion":

> Recently the development of music has been primarily an aesthetic one: liberation from the nineteenth century; struggle against extra-musical influences (program music, symbolism, realism); return to absolute music; achievement of a new means of expression (enrichment of harmony, production of a new linearity) or extension of the old—those were the ideas that claimed the attention of the musician.[31]

The past tense was appropriate, because in his next group of essays and musical works Weill abandoned the aesthetic approach toward a renewal of opera in favor of a sociological one, although many innovations of his one-act operas were preserved and expanded in this new context.

Example 3.1   *Royal Palace*

a. mm. 8-15

b. mm. 21-26

Example 3.2   *Royal Palace*

a. 8 m. after 64

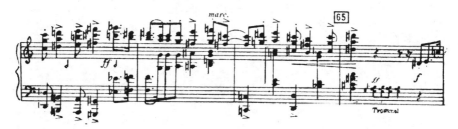

b. 5 m. before 75

Copyright 1926 by Universal Edition. Reproduced by permission of European American Music Distributors Corp.

Beyond the artistic, there is a general human consciousness that springs from a social feeling of some kind and this must be determinant for the formation of an art work.[32]

— *Kurt Weill* —

III

Weill's essays written between 1927 and 1933 reflect a clear-cut shift in his approach to musical composition in general and to musical theater in particular—a displacement of emphasis from aesthetic considerations to sociological concerns. The new stance does not imply disavowal of his earlier goals of clarity and simplicity which had served as the rationale for his diverse output from 1921 to 1926. On the contrary, in 1927 Weill wrote that "the clarity of language, precision of expression, and simplicity of feeling, which the new music has regained following a rectilinear development, form the reliable bases for a broader ramification of this art."[33] As the new path to a larger community emerged from the *Mahagonny-Songspiel* in May 1927, Weill continued his previous course with Kaiser in *Zar*, and eventually both currents merged in mature formulation in *Aufstieg* and *Die Bürgschaft*. As he began his collaboration with the leading representative of the younger generation of German dramatists who were committed to socially-critical theater, Weill deemed the question of the proper role of musical theater in contemporary society to be more urgent than purely aesthetic issues of opera. This new orientation prompted him to seek methods of enlarging the limited audience for opera and to investigate new topics for operatic treatment that could transcend individual concerns in favor of more universal validity.

What Weill termed the "splendid isolation of opera" had to be shattered. He was no longer content to work within the confines of an aristocratic genre, limited in its appeal to a narrowly-prescribed special-interest group:

In Germany it is most clearly shown that musical production must win a new justification for existence. *An unmistakable regrouping of the public* is also to be observed here. The socially-exclusive arts, originating from a different era and from a different artistic attitude, are losing more and more ground. Today new orchestral and chamber music, for which a regular public demand prevailed earlier, is almost exclusively directed toward musical societies and organizations devoted to the cultivation of new music, whose sphere of listeners is composed primarily of musicians. Therefore, music seeks an approach to the sphere of interest of a broader audience, since only thus can it maintain its viability.[34]

Weill was unable to identify with those musicians who, "filled with disdain for the audience, continue to work toward the solution of aesthetic problems as if behind closed doors."[35]   Although he sympathized with the goals of those composers associated with *Gebrauchsmusik*, "musician guilds," the youth movement, mechanical and film music, and the workers' choral movement, Weill himself was more interested in attracting a wider audience for musical theater. He suggested that such expansion could be successful only if musical theater abandoned its socially-exclusive [*gesellschaftlichen*] character for a community-engendering [*gemeinschaftsbildenden*] posture. He stated that this could be accomplished only in close collaboration with equal representatives of other arts who shared the desire to create musical stage works that would conclusively capture the overriding issues of the time in timeless form with universal validity; opera had to evolve into a new epic form.[36]

In order to rescue opera from its state of solemn seclusion, Weill claimed that opera first had to be brought closer to the theater of the era. In his essay "Korrespondenz über *Dreigroschenoper*," he wrote:

> The operatic audience still represents a closed group of people that seemingly stands apart from the larger theatrical audience.   "Opera" and "theater" are still treated as two entirely distinct concepts.   In new operas a dramatic technique is still employed, a language is spoken, and subjects are treated that would be completely unthinkable in the contemporary theater.   Again and again, one must hear: "Maybe that is possible in theater, but not in opera!"[37]

But in his search for a less-restricted community as an audience for music and musical theater, Weill set certain boundaries. In no way were his attempts to be construed as a submission to the tastes of any audience or as capitulation to the temptation to gratify the public's desire for entertainment. He categorically rejected filling a gap among composers of operetta: "under no circumstances should the impression be created that we want to renounce the intellectual bearing of the serious musician in order to be able to compete fully with the producers of lighter market wares."[38]   In endeavoring to create music that was capable of satisfying the musical needs of broader population levels, Weill cautioned against diluting its artistic substance. For that reason, he shunned association with such catchwords as *Gebrauchsmusik* and *Zeitoper*.

Although Weill approved of those composers who put aside aesthetic appraisal in order to eliminate the boundaries between "art music" and "music for use," he voiced reservations that the purveyors of *Gebrauchsmusik* were directing their products at a different, yet still too restricted a community. Furthermore, he sensed that composers were making severe concessions to public taste:

We must not imitate the "hit" (and it has been proven that we are not really able to do that); we may only change our music so far that we can carry on our intellectual tasks, the duties of the artist in his time, in an entirely perceptible, entirely understandable language.[39]

Especially in an art designed for use, the concept of quality must again be emphasized more strongly, since otherwise the danger of confusion with that utilitarian art which was always there as "daily merchandise" emerges again and again.[40]

Certainly Weill's concern for communication with a broader segment of the population led him to investigate radio, film, workers' choruses, and schools as institutions that could reach the masses. However, he refused to "write down" to his audience or sacrifice intellectual content for popularity—one recalls his resistance to censors' attempts to revise the contents of *Das Berliner Requiem*. His objection stemmed not from the indignant outrage of an "art-for-art's-sake" standpoint, but from the view that the *Requiem*, if stripped of the "offensive" social and political connotations, would no longer be "useful" to a general public. Although Weill's music has been frequently categorized as *Gebrauchsmusik* in music histories, such association, in consideration of his writings and the nature of his compositions, obfuscates rather than clarifies this facet of Weill's output.[41]

Similarly, a number of his works have been saddled with the label "*Zeitoper*" or topical opera. First applied to *Royal Palace* because of its use of modern dance idioms, film, and sounds of daily urban life, the term continued to be associated with his later works for the musical stage. *Die Dreigroschenoper, Aufstieg*, and *Die Bürgschaft* were lumped together with Krenek's *Jonny spielt auf* and Hindemith's *Neues vom Tage* despite the extreme differences of intent and format. Weill resented the label because its application to certain works by other composers had led to the denotation that superficial elements of daily life were merely patched into opera for sensational effect. Because he aimed at a thorough renewal of opera rather than a camouflage of the old in a cheap wrapper, Weill wrote two substantial essays in which he attempted to clarify this "incorrectly understood slogan." He noted that the original intention of *Zeittheater* had been to elevate subject matter that treated modern events and mankind to an enduring, timeless formulation. Weill asserted that its purpose was not to photograph the era as a period-piece, but to reflect a world view in a convex or concave mirror. He lamented that the means of *Zeitoper* were quickly made into an end in themselves: "No other factor of modern theater has been snatched up so hastily by the representatives of conservative commercial theater and assimilated in the most superficial manner than the call for topicality."[42]   Quality and intention must be more decisive than any external stimulus of topicality:

> The "*Zeitstück*," as we have come to know it in recent years, moved the superficial manifestations of life in our time into center stage.   People took the "tempo of the twentieth century," combined it with the much praised "rhythm of our time" and, for the rest, limited themselves to the representation of sentiments of past generations. . . . Man in our time looks different, and what drives him outwardly and motivates him inwardly should not be so portrayed for the mere purpose of being current at any price or in the interest of topicality which holds validity only for the narrowest time span of its creation.[43]

Weill disliked that misunderstood topicality which sees the function of modern theater as the dramatization of semi-important, subsidiary problems of everyday life. He considered the jargon of the "rhythm of machines," the "tempo of the large city," and the "melody of the skyscraper" to be ill-used and poorly-constructed bridges to instant success. Again he turned to historical precedents for defense of topical theater which, transcending representation of private emotions and specific questions "that are already forgotten a year later," pictured larger relationships and transmitted enduring treatments of such themes as war, capitalism, inflation, and revolution:

> The influence of contemporary events on dramatic productions was clearly noticeable in all theater epochs. To be sure, almost everywhere it was the great ideas of the period, the intellectual or political currents that were treated in the theater, often in a transformed manner. Rarely were the incidents of the plot drawn from the events of reality, yet there are even examples of that. Even in the operatic theater there are *Zeitstücke* (*Figaro, Fidelio*). But it was always a matter of presenting ideas or themes that could claim to be treated in a more enduring, more significant form than the newspaper would probably be capable of offering. And with regard to the characteristics that kept those works alive, their artistic form stands at least equal to the subject matter.
>
> I am convinced that great art of all periods was topical in the sense that it was not intended for eternity, but rather for the time in which it originated, or at least for the near future, to whose formation it was intended to contribute.[44]

Because the topical aspects of Weill's works are still misinterpreted and exaggerated in both production and discussion, their more notable epic nature has been obscured. Weill was not content to install a few requisite items or figures of modern life in an antiquated form of musical theater. He was convinced that "on the basis of the newly-acquired inner and outer simplicity of content and means of expression, a branch of opera is evolving into a new epic form."[45]

In opera great subjects demand a great form for their representation. The broader and more significant the occasions for making music become, the greater the possibilities for the development of music in opera. The new operatic theater that is being generated today has epic character.[46]

— *Kurt Weill* —

IV

The collaborations of Weill and Brecht represent a synthesis of each of their own earlier experiences, as well as those of colleagues, most especially Erwin Piscator. Both Brecht and Weill had previously approached the problems of contemporary theater but from entirely different directions. Brecht had recognized that certain stylistic elements of the new drama could only be accomplished musically; Weill had sought in modern drama the technical innovations, the everyday language, and the treatment of contemporary issues which he considered prerequisite for a renewal of opera. Their fortunate association permitted a collective assault on the obstacles that neither had completely hurdled individually. The breakthrough came with the *Mahagonny-Songspiel*.[47] In setting six discrete poems, Weill was freed from the onus of musical illustration, psychological characterization, or atmospheric depiction. He found a "loose" form, as he described it, which allowed music its independent and predominant structural role. Brecht encountered a *Mitarbeiter* who could give artistic articulation to his poetry which he himself had conceived for musical realization. After the success of the *Songspiel*, which embodied components of epic opera in rudimentary organization, in their continuing work on *Aufstieg* Brecht and Weill refined and embellished the procedures and principles that would ultimately define the epic style. By March 1929, Weill could already give the following definition of the new operatic genre which incorporated his aesthetic and sociological goals:

The new operatic theater that is being generated today has epic character. It does not want to describe, but to report. It no longer wants to form its plot according to moments of suspenseful tension, but to tell about man, his actions and what impels him to commit them. Music in the operatic theater renounces pumping up the action from within, glazing over the transitions, supplying the background for events, and stirring up passions. It goes its own vast, peaceful way; it begins only at static moments of the plot, and it can, therefore, preserve its absolute, *concertante* character (if it hits upon the right subject matter). Since the narrative form never permits the spectator to be in suspense or uncertainty over the stage events, the music can reserve for itself its own independent, purely musical effect. The sole prerequisite for such an uninhibited musical realization in opera is that music must be, of course, "theater music" (in the Mozartean sense) in its innermost essence in order to be able to achieve a complete liberation from the stresses of the stage.[48]

The extension of the primitive epic structure of the plotless *Mahagonny-Songspiel* to a full-length work was accomplished in *Die Dreigroschenoper*. Weill was able to preserve the independent freedom for his music by adopting the form of "dialogue-opera," which he described as a mixed genre of play and opera and which he designated the "loosest" form of operatic theater.[49] Again it was the subject matter that suggested this formal solution, for *Die Dreigroschenoper* was an adaptation of an eighteenth-century ballad-opera (a type of dialogue-opera), which was itself a parody of eighteenth-century *opera seria*. Therefore, it provided a perfectly suited vehicle for Weill's application of constructive and aesthetic principles which he claimed had been originally inspired by eighteenth-century models. With the Handel-revival at its peak in Germany, *Die Dreigroschenoper* served a function similar to that of Gay's ballad opera, written two hundred years earlier: it commented upon the contemporary operatic situation by means of opera itself. In Weill's own words, "this piece offered us the opportunity to posit the concept of 'opera' as the theme of a theatrical evening. Therefore, it had to be constructed in its purest, most fundamental form. What we wished to make was the prototype of opera."[50] In the number-opera format of *Die Dreigroschenoper*, because the plot was advanced in spoken dialogue and music entered only at static points in the action, music was absolved from "the ungrateful duty of supplying the background for the incidents of the stage and of sustaining the plot."[51]

Weill denied that *Die Dreigroschenoper* was intended as a parody. In contrast to the *Beggar's Opera, Die Dreigroschenoper* adopted eighteenth-century *opera seria* as one of its models, not its object of satire. Although *opera seria* originated from and preserved an aristocratic posture that was alien to the aim of *Die Dreigroschenoper*, their aesthetic correspondences overshadow their sociological divergences. On the most superficial level, *Die Dreigroschenoper* shared the three-act structure of *opera seria* and began with an overture in the ABA form which characterized the *da capo* aria. The poets of *opera seria* envisioned their librettos as schools of virtue, which taught devotion to the higher impulses of man.[52] Brecht aspired to the same purpose but substituted the negative example for Metastasio's positive one. Brecht presented the lowest impulses of man with the expectation that the spectator would be repelled and thereby motivated to loftier behavior. He called for a theatrical audience who took up the attitude of people who attended sports events, watched at ease, and smoked—not unlike the spectators of *opera seria* who sat in their boxes and interrupted their eating, drinking, and chess games only when the main event occurred, that is, when their favorite vocal gymnast began singing an aria.[53]   Even the six principal characters of the typical Metastasian libretto found their counterparts in Jonathon Peachum-Celia Peachum, Macheath-Jenny, and Polly-Lucy of *Die Dreigroschenoper*.   Just as the sparse ensembles of *opera seria* were invoked to conclude the acts, in *Die Dreigroschenoper* the only genuine ensembles occur as the three finales, the last of which embodies the *lieto fine* in conspicuous Handelian garb.[54]   The most striking similarities are formal; in both *opera seria* and epic opera the looseness of structure as a whole allowed free development of both drama and music within the mold.   In *opera seria* the order of musical numbers could be changed, new numbers added, others omitted or reassigned without doing violence to the overall musical plan.[55]   In *Die Dreigroschenoper*, too, Lucy's aria was cut and in various revivals songs were reassigned and reordered without damage to either dramatic or musical structure.[56]

Such "looseness" of structure was possible in both *opera seria* and epic opera because the central position in each was held respectively by the aria and its twentieth-century equivalent, the song.   Thus, the composer's responsibility for formal unity was limited to each closed musical number; the aria or song in both served as a lyrical interruption of the plot.   In *opera seria* the aria was separated from the preceding recitative by the elaborate conventions and abuses of the genre: the singer was expected to bow to the spectators in the loges, smile at the orchestra and the other players, walk about the stage, complain to his friends that he was not in voice, and usually exit after the completion of the aria.[57]   The aria, which communicated the character's state of mind or conveyed a reflection appropriate to the current situation, was directed not to his colleagues on stage but to the audience.[58]   The conventions of epic opera, as described by Brecht and Weill, accomplished the same abrupt separation of song from the preceding dialogue.   "Nothing is more detestable than when an actor gives the impression of not having noticed that he has left the ground of plain speech and is already singing."[59]   In his "Notes to the *Threepenny Opera*," Brecht stated that the singer must address himself directly to the spectator—"the actor must not only sing but show a man who is singing."[60]   The songs were further isolated by abrupt changes in lighting and blocking, as well as projection or announcement of the song's title.   In both *opera seria* and epic opera the mannered performance style resulted in an anti-realistic effect.   Just as eighteenth-century virtuoso singers were expected to take liberties with the written score in their elaborate embellishments, Brecht advised the performers of epic opera that "so far as the melody is concerned, the singer need not follow it blindly."[61]   Thus, in both types of opera, the performer was permitted to intensify the expressive moment through personal departures from the score.

The parallelism between *opera seria* and epic opera extends beyond performance practice: stylized dances such as the siciliano, saraband, minuet, bouree, allemande, courante, and gavotte often served as the framework for certain aria-types within the stock *da capo* aria format of *opera seria*. Weill's incorporation in his songs of contemporary dance idioms such as the fox-trot, tango, and Boston (waltz) had definite eighteenth-century precedents, especially in Handel's extensive and integral inclusion of dance types in his operatic arias.[62]   Although epic opera has not been subjected to the same cataloguing enterprise as that expended by Mattheson on eighteenth-century music, its songs exhibit a comparable degree of stylization and could be as easily categorized. One can identify counterparts in Weill's operas for the "aria parlante," "aria agitata," "aria cantabile," and other standard eighteenth-century categories. For example, "Seeräuberjenny" (No. 6 of *Die Dreigroschenoper*), "Ruf aus der Gruft" (No. 19 of *Die Dreigroschenoper*), and "Die Ballade von der Höllenlili" (No. 12 of *Happy End*) could each be considered to be an "aria agitata." Such comparisons can be made because the aesthetic basis for the aria and song was the same: both presented (rather than expressed) generalized, static, non-psychological attitudes. In *opera seria* the aria was to convey the "affection," in epic opera the song was to present the "*gestus*."[63]

The representation in music of the affections or passions has been characterized as the most determinant feature of Baroque music. Bukofzer has written that "the maintenance of a single affection throughout a composition began tentatively in the middle baroque and became increasingly more rigid toward the end of the period."[64]   The affections were not personal emotions of individuals, but rather mental states (caused, according to Lorenzo Giacomini, by an imbalance of the animal spirits and vapors that flow continually throughout the body) or stereotyped attitudes which could be presented by music and thereby arouse the same affection in the listener.[65] The "simile aria" in which the affection of the singer was compared to a state of nature is one of the most transparent means of communicating an abstract affection in concrete form. That arias expressing the same affection could be and actually were substituted for one another in operas of the period testifies to their generalized, non-individual nature. The manner in which the affections were captured by music was catalogued in the doctrine of figures.

In epic opera, the twentieth-century analogue to *Affekt* was *gestus*. Like the term affection, *gestus* has no concise definition, nor does it have an English equivalent. Martin Esslin defined it as "the clear and stylized expression of the social behavior of human beings towards each other."[66] Brecht at one point referred to *gestus* simply as the attitude adopted by characters toward one another.[67] The crucial aspect of *gestus* was the translation of dramatic emotion and individual characterization into a typical, reproducible physical realization. Weill referred to the "representation of types of human behavior," which forged beyond the private individual emotion to common validity.[68] If one takes into account the advances of modern psychology (emotions could no longer be an imbalance of the vapors) and the sociological thrust of epic theater, one can view *gestus*, itself an eighteenth-century term used by Lessing, as a modern reflection of affection.[69] Both were to be communicated through music in highly stylized presentations. Such a correlation is not just the present author's contrivance; Weill specifically acknowledged pre-classic and classic models for epic opera. He cited the recitatives in Bach's passions and Mozart's music, even his non-operatic compositions, as examples of gestic music. In "Ueber den gestischen Charakter der Musik," Weill called attention to the historical precedents for gestic music:

> In my attempts to arrive at a prototype for works of musical theater, I have made a few observations which at first seemed to me to be completely new perceptions, but with closer consideration can be classified as being thoroughly within the historical continuum.[70]

The abstract relationship between text and music in baroque aesthetic thought was usually discussed in terms of figures derived from rhetoric. The underlying assumption was that the linguistic figures of speech could be applied to music because it too was a "language" capable of expressing affections. Therefore, if music's expressive capabilities were properly exploited by the composer, even compositions that did not involve texts could present the affections convincingly. Although Weill also wrote that "gestic music is in no way bound to a text," he admitted a linguistic foundation for its existence:

> What are the gestic means of music? First of all, the *gestus* is expressed in a rhythmic fixing of the text. Music has the capacity to notate the accents of language, the distribution of short and long syllables, and above all, pauses. Thereby, the sources of the most serious errors in the treatment of the text are eliminated from the stage. Furthermore, one can interpret rhythmically one phrase in the most diverse ways, and the same *gestus* may be expressed in various rhythms; the critical factor is only whether the proper *gestus* is found. This rhythmic fixing which is obtained from the text in this way forms the basis for gestic music. The specific creative work of the composer occurs when he utilizes the remaining means of musical expression to establish contact between the text and what it is trying to express. Even the melody is stamped by the *gestus* of the

action that is to be represented, but, since the stage action is already absorbed rhythmically, much wider latitude exists for the essential means of musical expression—the formal, melodic, and harmonic construction—than in purely descriptive music or in music which parallels the action under constant danger of being concealed.[71]

Weill stated that musical spans must conform to the gestic proceeding; therefore, "a coloratura-type dwelling on a single syllable may be completely suitable if it is based on a gestic lingering at the same spot."[72] Mattheson had expressed a similar position about indecent ornaments (*Coloratur*): "We do not hold ornaments in contempt. . . . We do disapprove of their abuse, however, and of the singers and players who, lacking in taste and sense, use them excessively without moderation, and in the wrong places."[73]

That rhythm, according to Weill, is the key to gestic music explains its decisive and constructive force in his theatrical and non-theatrical music. The vitality of rhythmic figures is perhaps the most recognizable feature of Weill's mature style. His use of modern dance idioms must be construed as one of his most powerful applications of the gestic capability of rhythm, for he seldom borrowed the actual form of a specific dance; instead he isolated its identifying rhythmic kernel and built from it a musical structure that is saturated with this characteristic rhythmic figure. Therefore, the tango can serve as the basis for two songs as different in structure as the "Zuhälterballade" (No. 13 of *Die Dreigroschenoper*) and "Der Matrosen-Song" (No. 4 of *Happy End*). Both are permeated by the characteristic tango rhythm ($\frac{4}{4}$ ♪♩♪♩♩) and its numerous variations, yet the overall forms of the two numbers contrast markedly:[74]

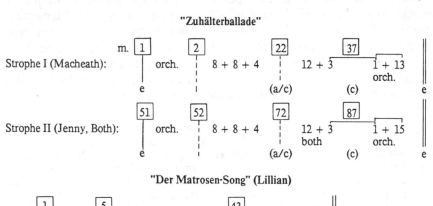

"Zuhälterballade"

	m. 1	2	22	37	
Strophe I (Macheath):	orch.	8 + 8 + 4	12 + 3	1 + 13 orch.	
	e		(a/c)	(c)	e

	51	52	72	87	
Strophe II (Jenny, Both):	orch.	8 + 8 + 4	12 + 3 both	1 + 15 orch.	
	e		(a/c)	(c)	e

"Der Matrosen-Song" (Lillian)

1	5	43	
orch.	Verse I 12 + 9 + 8 + 9	Refrain 8 + 12	
(a/c)	(f♯) b (e)	a	c

"Der Matrosen-Song" (Lillian) (continued)

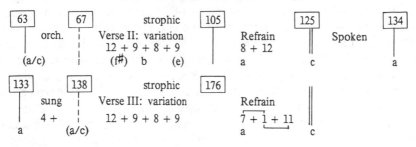

Although Weill labels both as "Tango-Tempo," the two songs have little in common formally, except that in both the regular phrase structure of an actual tango is altered and blurred. Yet, despite the formal differences, the two songs are closely related by an underlying gestic similarity. In each the principal male and female protagonists are alone on stage and are presenting their attitudes toward one another. In "Zuhälterballade," both Macheath and Jenny sing, whereas in "Der Matrosen-Song" only Lillian sings, but in direct interaction with Bill Cracker. In these two tangos, the *gestus* expressed by Weill's music is the relationship between a man and a woman who are at the same time both attracted and repelled by the fascination of a love-hate relationship. Weill undoubtedly chose the tango for both songs because of its original tawdry and immoral associations and its manner of performance as a partner dance.[75] The brutal-erotic duality of the tango commented on the dramatic situation and presented the *gestus* of the moment through a pervasive rhythmic figure. Having thus captured the proper *gestus* rhythmically, Weill was then free to explore other aspects of the text in the remaining elements of his music, most especially melody. Each of the two songs incorporates several types of melodic declamation to articulate the text, which (like the *opera seria* aria's text) had been conceived in musical terms. Having thus fulfilled his responsibility to the drama, the composer retained freedom to structure his music according to purely musical decisions. With the simple choice of the tango-rhythm, Weill made a powerful comment on the text, the dramatic situation, and the attitudes of the characters while still preserving the absolute independence of musical structure.

Such gestic function of dance rhythms is apparent in virtually all of Weill's scores composed between 1927 and 1934. One can readily extract "families" of musical numbers which, although unrelated to one another in form, reproduce the same or a very similar *gestus* through the use of standard and readily recognizable rhythmic gestures derived from dance idioms. These "figures" could be catalogued in the same way that rhetorical devices were during the eighteenth century. At the risk of falling short of the comprehensiveness of Mattheson, an attempt will be made to enumerate the members of these gestic families. The following lists are divided into two categories: (A) dance idioms labeled explicitly as such by Weill and (B) those which display the same features but were not designated as dance types in the scores. I have not included the numerous musical numbers where rhythmic gestures were derived from dance idioms but have been so "digested," transformed, and elaborated that their gestic function has been obscured.[76] Included in this catalogue are the tango and the related habanera; the fox-trot and its derivatives, shimmy and Charleston; the waltz, including the Boston and English varieties; the blues; and finally the march (even though it is not a modern dance idiom, Weill gives it gestic treatment).[77]

Modern Dance Idioms in Weill's Works 1927-34

TANGO

A: *Royal Palace* at 124   (p. 67 of P-V score) "Tanz der Wasserfrau"   2/4
      Zar at 131   (p. 102 of P-V score) "Tango Angèle"   4/4
      Die Dreigroschenoper, No. 13 "Zuhälterballade"   ♩ = 58,   2/4
      Happy End, No. 4 "Der Matrosen-Song"   4/4
      Der Silbersee, No. 6 "Hast du Geld"   ♩ = 56,   ¢

B: *Royal Palace* at 41   Moderato assai,   2/4
      Die Bürgschaft, No. 4 at 30   "Wie in jedem Frühjahr"   ♩ = 52,   ¢
      Die Bürgschaft, No. 13 at 466   "Das ist ein Zustand"   ♩ = 58,   ¢ (Habanera)
      Die Bürgschaft, No. 23 "Langsamer Tanz"   ♩ = 44,   ¢

FOX-TROT

A: *Die Dreigroschenoper*, No. 7 "Kanonensong"   ♩ = 92,   2/2
      Kleine Dreigroschenmusik, No. 6 "Kanonensong" (Charleston Tempo)   ♩ = 92,   ¢
      Die Dreigroschenoper, No. 14 "Ballade von Angenehmen Leben" (Shimmy Tempo)
        ♩ = 96,   4/4
      Kleine Dreigroschenmusik, No. 4 "Ballade von Angenehmen Leben" (Fox-trot)
        ♩ = 96,   4/4
      "Berlin im Licht-Song"   Slow-Fox   ¢
      Happy End, No. 11 "Das Lied von der harten Nuss"   ¢
      Die Petroleuminseln, "Das Lied von der braunen Inseln"   Slow-Fox   ¢
      Marie galante, "Les filles de Bordeaux"   Slow-Fox   ¢
      Marie galante, "Scène au dancing"   ¢

B: *Royal Palace* at 64   Allegro un poco tenuto   ¢ (Shimmy)
      Zar at 46   and 69   Allegro moderato   ¢
      Mahagonny-Songspiel, No. 1 "Prolog" Allegro non troppo   4/4

Happy End, No. 1 "Bilbao Song" ♩ = 72 ¢ (Slow-Fox)
Aufstieg, No. 4 "Auf nach Mahagonny" ♩ = 88 ¢
Der Jasager, No. 2 "Ich bin der Lehrer" ♩ = 92 ¢
Die Bürgschaft, No. 22 "Da kam der Hunger" Allegro molto ♩ = 100 ¢
Der Silbersee, No. 10 Allegro moderato ♩ = 88 ¢
Die sieben Todsünden, No. 3 "Zorn" at ⌐7⌐ Molto agitato 2/4

BLUES

A: *Die Dreigroschenoper*, No. 2 "Moritat vom Mackie Messer" ♩ = 66 2/2
    Kleine Dreigroschenmusik, No. 2 Moderato assai ♩ = 66 ¢
    Aufstieg, No. 16 "Denn wie man sich bettet" (Jenny) ♩ = 86 4/4
    Happy End, No. 10 "Surabaya-Johnny" Sehr Ruhig 4/4
    Der Lindberghflug, No. 2 "Vorstellung des Fliegers Charles Lindbergh" Moderato ¢

B: *Mahagonny-Songspiel*, No. 2 "Alabama-Song" Moderato ♩ = 120 2/4
    Aufstieg, No. 2 "Alabama-Song" Moderato assai ♩ = 69 ¢
    Aufstieg, No. 11 "Denn wie man sich bettet" (Jim) ♩ = 48 ¢

WALTZ

A: *Mahagonny-Songspiel*, No. 5 "Gott in Mahagonny" Walzer: Lento 3/4
    Die Dreigroschenoper, No. 8 "Liebeslied" Boston-Tempo ♩ = 88 3/4
    Aufstieg, No. 13 at ⌐11⌐ "Jetzt hab' Ich gegessen zwei Kälber" Valse Lento
       ♩ = 100 3/4
    Aufstieg, No. 20 at ⌐84⌐ "An einem grauen Mittag" ♩ = 116 3/4
    Das Berliner Requiem, No. 3 "Materl" Tempo di Boston ♩ = 82 3/4
    Happy End, No. 6 Heilsarmeelied III: "Fürchte dich nicht" 3/4
    Der Silbersee, No. 4 "Wir sind zwei Mädchen" Flotter Walzer ♩ = 80 3/4
    Die sieben Todsünden, No. 2 "Stolz" Schneller Walzer 3/8
    Marie galante "Le Roi d'Aquitaine" English Waltz 3/4

B: *Royal Palace* at ⌐10⌐ Allegro molto 3/4
    Zar at ⌐61⌐ Allegro molto 3/4
    Happy End, No. 7 Heilsarmeelied IV: "In der Jugend goldenem Shimmer"
       Tranquillo 3/4
    Die Bürgschaft, No. 5 "Auch im Lande Urb" Moderato ♩ = 88 3/4
    Der Silbersee, No. 16 at ⌐461⌐ Allegretto ♪ = 96 3/8
    Die sieben Todsünden, No. 6 "Habsucht" Allegro giusto 3/4

MARCH

A: *Mahagonny-Songspiel*, No. 1 (Interlude) Kleiner Marsch 4/4
    Zar at ⌐73⌐ Gemessener Marsch 4/4
    Zar at ⌐142⌐ Alla marcia 2/4
    Incidental Music for *Gustav III*, Alla marcia 2/4
    Zu Potsdam unter den Eichen Langsamer Marsch ♩ = 74 4/4
    Happy End, No. 2 "Der kleine Leutnant des lieben Gottes" Mässiges
       Marsch-tempo 4/4

Aufstieg, No. 14 Flotter Marsch ♩ = 138 ¢
Die Bürgschaft, No. 13 Kleiner Marsch ♩ = 116 4/4
Die Bürgschaft, No. 18 Barbarischer Marsch ♩ = 106 2/4
Incidental Music for *Mann ist Mann*, "Marschmusik" (Lost)
Der Silbersee, No. 2 Alla marcia funebre ♩ = 76 4/4
Die sieben Todsünden, No. 7 "Neid" Allegro non troppo 4/4
Symphony no. 2, Mvt. III Alla marcia 2/4
Marie galante "Marche de l'armée panaméenne" 4/4

B: *Mahagonny-Songspiel*, No. 6 Finale: "Aber diese Mahagonny" Largo 4/4
      Happy End, No. 3 Heilsarmeelied I: "Geht hinein in die Schlacht" Allegro molto 2/4
      Aufstieg, No. 5 at ⬚84⬚ ♩ = 72 ¢
      Aufstieg, No. 9 at ⬚33⬚ "Ach mit eurem ganzen Mahagonny" Largo ♩ = 60 4/4
      Aufstieg, No. 18 "Haben alle Zuschauer Billette" Allegro molto ♩. = 140 6/8
      Aufstieg, No. 20 "Können einem toten Mann nicht helfen" Largo ♩ = 56 4/4
      Das Berliner Requiem, No. 4 "Soldaten unter dem Triumphbogen" Moderato assai
          ♩ = 70 4/4
      Der Jasager, No. 4 ♩ = 88 4/4
      Der Silbersee, No. 8 "Cäsars Tod" Larghetto ♩. = 50 6/8
      Symphony no. 2, Mvt. II Largo ♩ = 56 4/4

Within each gestic family of dance idioms there are stylistic affinities which go far beyond similarity of rhythmic figures and comparable gestic function. For example, the melodic style, declamation of text, and accompaniment patterns are so consistent within the Blues-group that the songs almost take on the character of a set of variations. The most striking correspondence is between the "Moritat vom Mackie Messer" (No. 2 of *Die Dreigroschenoper*) and "Surabaya-Johnny" (No. 10 of *Happy End*):

Example 3.3

a) "Moritat vom Mackie Messer" mm. 1-5

b) "Surabaya-Johnny" mm. 27-31

Weill's gestic vocabulary of rhythmic figures was not confined to those specifically associated with modern dance idioms. Many musical numbers from his theatrical works are based on rhythmic cells which have overt gestic function but cannot be ascribed to any dance model. These musical numbers usually depend on a single, readily identifiable rhythmic kernel, although occasionally several contrasting figures are employed within a single unit of musical structure. That Weill's mature style is so consistent from work to work across various genres can be at least partially explained by the utilization of a number of vividly defined rhythmic gestures. Because the other elements of his musical style retain complete freedom, he manages to avoid cliché or actual quotation (with the exception of those instances where he has actually transferred sections from earlier compositions to later works). The individual stamp which unmistakably identifies Weill's mature style as uniquely his own (not unlike the unique character of Mozart's late style) can be traced at least as much to rhythm as to melodic or harmonic mannerisms. Again it is possible to catalogue families of musical numbers according to rhythmic figures that have gestic function; Weill made such a task less formidable by including flagposts such as uniform metric and tempo indications within gestic families.[78] While the following directory is far from exhaustive, it does demonstrate gestic correspondences of rhythmic features among Weill's works. Rather than give an abstract reduction of characteristic rhythmic figures, a representative passage from one of the works in each family has been chosen to illustrate the device.

(An asterisk indicates the source of the musical example.)

FAMILIES OF RHYTHMIC FIGURES

1. *Die Dreigroschenoper*, No. 10 "I. Dreigroschenfinale" Allegro animato ♩ = 132   4/4
    Die Bürgschaft, No. 23 at ⎡896⎤ Allegro molto   ♩ = 132   ¢
    *Der Silbersee, No. 3 Allegro giusto   ♩ = 132   4/4
    Der Silbersee, No. 6b   ♩ = 132   4/4

Example 3.4a

Copyright 1933 by Universal Edition. Reproduced by permission of European American Music Distributors Corp.

2. **Die Dreigroschenoper*, No. 16 "II. Dreigroschenfinale" Moderato assai   ♩ = 70   4/4
    Aufstieg, No. 8 at ⎡109⎤ Moderato assai   ♩ = 90   4/4
    Der Jasager, No. 6   ♩ = 74   4/4
    Die Bürgschaft, No. 10 "I. Finale" Comodo   ♩ = 72   4/4

Example 3.4b

Copyright 1928 by Universal Edition.   Copyright renewed 1956 by Mrs. Karoline Weill-Davis, New York, and Universal Edition A.G., Vienna.   Reproduced by permission of European American Music Distributors Corp.

3. *Die Dreigroschenoper*, No. 4 "Anstatt-dass-Song" Moderato   ♩ = 100   4/4
    Aufstieg, No. 13   ♩ = 100   3/4
    Die Bürgschaft, No. 10 at ⎡1066⎤ ♩ = 92   4/4
    Der Silbersee, No. 7 Allegretto   ♩ = 92   2/4
    Der Silbersee, No. 10 Allegro moderato   ♩ = 88   ¢
    *Die sieben Todsünden, No. 3 "Zorn" Molto agitato   2/4

Example 3.4c

4.   **Die Dreigroschenoper*, No. 11 "Melodram" Andante con moto   ♩ = 70   3/4
       Die Bürgschaft, No. 14 at 895   Larghetto   ♩ = 66   3/4
       Der Silbersee, No. 16 "Melodram" Andantino   ♩ = 69   4/4

Example 3.4d

5.   **Der Jasager*, No. 5   ♩ = 138   4/4
       Die Bürgschaft, No. 10 at 1240   Tempo giusto   ♩ = 138   4/4

Example 3.4e

6.   *Aufstieg*, No. 18 at [26] Allegro molto ♩. = 140   6/8
      Die Bürgschaft, No. 8 at [659] Vivace ♩ = 152   4/4

Example 3.4f

7.   *Die Bürgschaft*, No. 10 at [1346] Larghetto ♩. = 60   9/8
      Der Silbersee, No. 8 Larghetto ♩. = 50   6/8

Example 3.4g

8.   *Der Lindberghflug*, No. 7 "In der Nacht kam ein Schneesturm" ♩ = 168   3/4
      Die Bürgschaft, No. 20 at [380] Vivace ♩ = 164   3/4
      Die sieben Todsünden, No. 6 "Habsucht" Allegro giusto   3/4

Example 3.4h

9. *Die Dreigroschenoper*, No. 20 "Grabschrift" Sostenuto ♩ = 50 4/4
    *Marie galante "Le train du Ciel" Lento 4/4

Example 3.4i

10. *Die Dreigroschenoper*, No. 18 "Salomonsong" Andantino ♩. = 46 3/8
     (harmonium solo)
     **Happy End, No. 8 "Das Lied vom Branntweinhändler" Allegretto ♩. = 66
     3/8 (bandoneon solo)[79]

Example 3.4j

11.   *Die Dreigroschenoper*, No. 19 "Ruf aus der Gruft" Molto agitato ♩.= 66   3/4[80]
      Aufstieg, No. 9 at ⌷119⌷ ♩. = 58   3/4
      Der Silbersee, no. 14 Allegro un poco agitato   ♩ = 112   3/4

Example 3.4k

12.   *Die Dreigroschenoper*, No. 15 "Eifersuchtsduett" Molto agitato   ♩ = 112   3/4
      Die Bürgschaft, No. 23 at ⌷1294⌷   ♩ = 116   4/4

Example 3.4l

13.   *Die sieben Todsünden*, "Prolog" Andante sostenuto   4/4
      Marie galante, "Le grand Lustucru" Andante non troppo   4/4

Example 3.4m

By no means does such a cursory correlation do justice to the infinite subtlety with which Weill manipulates rhythmic elements within a musical number to illuminate or comment upon aspects of the dramatic situation. Once he has established the fundamental *gestus* (*Grundgestus*) in a song through the rhythmic fixing of the text and the choice of an appropriate accompaniment, Weill invariably introduces other musical gestures which either intensify the fundamental *gestus* or inject a new perspective of interpretation. Thereby, Weill's music almost supplies its own subtext. The "Zuhälterballade" of *Die Dreigroschenoper* serves as a lucid illustration. Here the haunting lyricism of the melody has been balanced by the driving tango-rhythm of the accompaniment. Until m. 73 there is no hint from Weill's setting that the sleazy, sentimental nostalgia of the "love-duet" is to be interpreted as anything more than a straightforward expression of Macheath's and Jenny's social attitude toward one another. At the precise point where Jenny becomes most animated and bitter, Weill adds a muted trumpet playing

as a commentary on her utterance; it is as if Weill built the warning "Nicht sentimental" into the musical fabric. This playful and sardonically jaunty figure gives an ironic twist to the entire ballad and thus adds a new, more revealing layer of meaning to the fundamental *gestus* of the text. Note that Weill withheld this figure from Macheath's strophe and the first orchestral interlude so that its entrance is a decisive event used to distinguish Jenny's attitude toward Macheath from its converse. Such a rhythmic figure that embodies satirical or ironic

corrosive commentary is one of Weill's most characteristic signatures.
Often orchestrated for muted trumpet, these double-edged devices lift
Weill's musical settings far above simple accompaniment or indifferent
presentation. On a purely musical level, the animated rhythmic figures,
cited by contemporary critics as the source of the peculiar motor-
rhythmic quality [*Motorik*] of Weill's music, activate the texture of a
musical unit while transmitting the *gestus* of the scene.

Because Weill "absorbed" the *gestus* of the text rhythmically, he
was free to compose in a musical style that often projected an attitude
opposite of that expressed by the text. In this way his music created a
layer of meaning absent from the words. One of the most straightforward examples occurs in "III. Dreigroschenfinale," when Polly rejoices
that Macheath has been saved. The text ("Gerettet! Gerettet! Mein
lieber Macheath ist gerettet! Ich bin sehr glücklich.") would indicate a
fundamental *gestus* of joy and relief. However, Weill reverses the
meaning of Polly's "Ich bin sehr glücklich" by a sudden wrench to minor
inflection at that point. Although the precise meaning of this musical
event is open to several interpretations (Polly's insincerity, Macheath's
salvation may not be a fortunate occurrence for Polly, or a more
generalized example of man's inhumanity to man), the passage no longer
can be construed as a candid utterance.

Example 3.5

Die Dreigroschenoper, No. 21: mm. 111-116.

Weill further intensifies the gesture by recalling four measures of Polly's "Barbarasong" in the instrumental codetta to the section. In performances of such musical numbers, many of which exhibit more subtle and sophisticated mechanisms for illuminating a subtext (non-verbalized dimensions of the text), the separate and dissimilar elements of text and music are engaged in a dynamic dialectic—a perpetual tango between music and words. Mechanisms which Weill frequently utilized include quotation, sudden shifts in tempo, unprepared dissonance, changes in orchestration, parody, alteration of mode and tonality, varied styles of declamation, and abrupt juxtaposition of contrasting musical styles. It is the resulting ambivalence and duality which raises Weill's songs far above the commonplace and accounts for their haunting irony.[81]

If Weill's formulation of gestic music in epic theater is viewed in its historical context and analyzed in detail, it can be perceived not as a totally new phenomenon of modern theater, but rather as the logical and most extensively developed and transformed example of neo-classic operatic ideals. What had been hinted at in Busoni's writings and Stravinsky's *Soldier's Tale* is fully worked out in the epic theater of Brecht and Weill. The song, which presents the *gestus* of a scene primarily through rhythmic figures, is the twentieth-century equivalent of the aria in *opera seria* which conveyed the affection of the situation by means of rhetorical figures. Such an interpretation does not diminish the creativity of Weill and Brecht; it accounts for the powerful impact of both drama and music in epic theater, and it makes the inevitable progression in Weill's career seem entirely consistent. In epic opera Weill united the neo-classic aesthetic principles of his earlier works with the sociological goals that he had embraced. Rather than approaching his operatic works as topical fads of the twenties (*Zeitoper*), one would be better advised to consider Weill's theatrical works to be the ultimate realization of the neo-classic trends of the early twentieth century in an operatic mold which represents "a synthesis of all new achievements with the useful material of earlier generations."[82]

The genre of "Song" which originated in the Baden-Baden piece and was further developed in later works (Die Dreigroschenoper, Das Berliner Requiem, and Happy End) was naturally unable to support a full-length opera by itself. Other larger forms had to be added. But the simple ballad-like style always had to be preserved.[83]

— *Kurt Weill* —

V

The *Song* is one of the units of musical structure most central to Weill's compositions dating from 1927 to 1934. Just as his comments concerning the theoretical bases for his music in general are very sparse and indicate an approach to composition that was more intuitive than systematic in nature, Weill's remarks about the *Song* are, for the most part, limited to discussion of its gestic function within epic theater. The term itself was an innovation, for Weill and Brecht adopted it as a German word to describe a particular type of vocal composition. In 1935 after his emigration to the United States, Weill described its origin and characteristics:

> Bert Brecht, who did several librettos for me, and I coined the German word, "Song." The term became very popular and was used extensively throughout Germany. It was quite different from "Lied." It corresponded, I suppose, to the better type American popular song. And while it consisted of four or five verses and a refrain, it did not conform to a specific number of measures as your popular songs do here.[84]

Although both Brecht and Weill had used the term *Song* prior to their artistic association, it received its first conclusive realization in the *Mahagonny-Songspiel* in 1927.[85] For Weill and Brecht *Song* was not synonymous with the generic category of *Gesang*; the *Song* carried its own specific connotations that distinguished it from the *Lied, Arie* and *Ballade*. Brecht almost always labeled his lyrics as *Song, Lied, Arie,* or *Ballade* according to their content, structure, dramatic function, and the manner of performance he envisioned for them. Although in setting such texts to music Weill frequently ignored the stylistic suggestion implicit in Brecht's titles (in fact, Weill sometimes set a poem in a musical style or form opposite of that implied by its title to extraordinary parodistic or ironic effect), he too acknowledged rather clear-cut distinctions among the categories.[86]

As an art song, the *Lied,* for example, suggested an intimate, personal, and usually psychological expression which required an artful and sophisticated musical setting. The *Arie* implied operatic treatment, whereas the *Ballade*, usually narrative in content and the most "primitive" of Brecht's types of *Gesang*, received the simplest and most direct musical handling by Weill. The *Song* embodied the most overt gestic function. Weill wrote that all songs in *Aufstieg* are "an expression of the masses, even where they are performed by the individual as spokesman of the masses."[87]   This accounts for the *Song's* "popular" characteristics, as well as its use of modern dance idioms.   The distinctions among the four categories are well-defined in the *Mahagonny-Songspiel, Die Dreigroschenoper*, and *Happy End*.   In these works the *Song* is the predominant type of musical composition. Undoubtedly Weill found the format of a *Songspiel*, dialogue-opera, or play-with-music more conducive to a structure based on the interruption of plot by *Songs* than was the case with operas such as *Aufstieg, Der Jasager*, and *Die Bürgschaft*.   In these later works, as well as *Der Lindberghflug, Der Silbersee*, and *Die sieben Todsünden*, the *Song* alone could not support the musical structure of the entire work. Furthermore, Weill had developed means of incorporating *Songs* into a complex musical web, divided into "musical scenes" in which ensembles, arias, choruses, recitatives, spoken dialogue, and instrumental pieces, as well as *Songs*, contributed to a "closed musical form." Since Brecht and Weill explicitly labeled the musical numbers of *Die Dreigroschenoper* and *Happy End* according to their "*Gesang*-classification" (musical numbers in their other collaborations are not consistently labeled or even titled), Weill's musical treatment of *Song, Ballade, Arie*, and *Lied* is most easily studied in these two plays-with-music.[88]

The basis of Weill's *Song*-form and *Ballade*-form is strophic structure; that is, every stanza of text is sung to the same melody with a few modifications to accommodate minor changes in the textual declamation. If one considers the folk song and the hymn, where each stanza is sung to the same melody and accompanied by exactly the same music, as "pure" strophic structure, then Weill seldom employs this straightforward type of setting.[89] He does so only where the musical number functions like a hymn, as in the "Heilsarmeelieder" of *Happy End*. Instead, for the most part, Weill's musical settings of *Songs* and *Balladen* are strophic variations—successive stanzas of poetry set to music which preserves the melodic, harmonic, and phrase structure of the first strophe but which varies or embellishes the "tune" or accompaniment or both. Although Weill's techniques for his strophic variations are almost as numerous and diverse as the *Songs* and *Balladen* themselves, a number of procedures recur frequently:

1) Alteration of accompaniment with melody remaining unchanged.

  Ex.   "Moritat vom Mackie Messer" (No. 2 of *Die Dreigroschenoper*)
         "Salomonsong" (No. 18 of *Die Dreigroschenoper*)

2) Embellishment or alteration of melody; Addition of countermelody.

  Ex.   "Alabama Song" (No. 2 of *Mahagonny-Songspiel, Aufstieg*)

3) Change of tempo or dynamics for one or more strophes.

  Ex.   "Seeräuberjenny" (No. 6 of *Die Dreigroschenoper*)
         "Kanonensong" (No. 7 of *Die Dreigroschenoper*)

4) Addition or Change of Performer.

  Ex.   "Zuhälterballade" (No. 13 of *Die Dreigroschenoper*)
         "II. Dreigroschenfinale" (No. 16 of *Die Dreigroschenoper*)
         "Anstatt-dass-Song" (No. 4 of *Die Dreigroschenoper*)
         "Das kleine Leutnant des lieben Gottes" (No. 2 of *Happy End*)

The manner in which Weill accomplishes these strophic variations is so diversified that, despite the similarity of underlying strophic structure of his *Songs* and *Balladen*, each achieves its own unique formal identity. The technique of variation ranges from that of the "Salomonsong," where the only change occurs in the slightly more animated harmonium accompaniment for the third stanza, to that of "Das Lied vom Branntweinhändler" (No. 8 of *Happy End*), where numerous ingenious devices are invoked. In one of Weill's most famous *Balladen*, the simple sixteen-measure melody of the "Moritat vom Mackie Messer" is repeated verbatim five times, but each stanza after the first two is clothed in new musical attire pieced together from altered instrumentation, rhythmic patterns, countermelodies, and dynamics.

In *Die Dreigroschenoper* fifteen of its twenty-one musical numbers are strophic variations.[90] Of the remaining six, the "Liebeslied," "Morgenchorale," and "Hochzeitslied" take the form of a single stanza. The first "Dreigroschenfinale" is based on three interlocking strophic substructures. Only the Overture and the third "Dreigroschen-finale"— the framing pieces for the work derived from baroque operatic models— stand entirely apart from the strophic mold. (See Chart 3.1.) In *Happy End* the saturation of strophic structure is even more pronounced—all multi-stanza texts are set as strophic variations.[91] (See Chart 3.2.)

CHART 3.1

DIE DREIGROSCHENOPER

1.	Overture		ABA$'$
2.	Moritat vom Mackie Messer	(Ballade)	Strophic, 6 stanzas without refrain
3.	Morgenchorale	Hymn	Chorale, 1 stanza
4.	Anstatt-dass-Song	Song	Strophic, 2 stanzas with refrain
5.	Hochzeitslied	Lied	AA$'$BA$''$, 1 stanza
6.	Seeräuberjenny	(Song)	Strophic, 3 stanzas with refrain
7.	Kanonensong	Song	Strophic, 3 stanzas with refrain
8.	Liebeslied	Lied	Durchkomponiert
9.	Barbarasong	Song	Strophic, 3 stanzas with refrain .
10.	I. Dreigroschenfinale	Finale	Interlocking strophic:

$$A_1A_2B_1C_1C_2C_3B_2C_4$$

--- --- --- --- --- --- --- --- --- ---

11.	Melodram		Strophic (I Melodram
11a.	Polly's Lied	Lied	II Polly's Lied)
12.	Ballade von der Sexuellen Hörigkeit	Ballade	Strophic, 2 stanzas without refrain
13.	Zuhälterballade	Ballade	Strophic, 2 stanzas, orch. refrain
14.	Ballade von angenehmen Leben	Ballade	Strophic, 3 stanzas, without refrain
15.	Eifersuchtsduett	(Song)	Strophic, 2 stanzas with refrain[92]
16.	II. Dreigroschenfinale	Finale	Strophic, 2 stanzas with refrain

--- --- --- --- --- --- --- --- --- ---

17.	Lied von der Unzulänglichkeit menschlichen Strebens	Lied	Strophic, 3 stanzas without refrain
18.	Salomonsong	Song	Strophic, 3 stanzas with 1-verse refrain
19.	Ruf aus der Gruft		Strophic, 2 stanzas without refrain
20.	Grabschrift		2 successive strophic sub-structures
21.	III. Dreigroschenfinale	Finale	Durchkomponiert

CHART 3.2

HAPPY END

1.	Bilbao-Song	Song	Strophic, 3 stanzas with refrain
2.	Der kleine Leutnant des lieben Gottes	(Song)	Strophic, 2 stanzas with refrain
3.	Geht hinein in die Schlacht	Anthem	1 stanza
4.	Der Matrosen-Song	Song	Strophic, 3 stanzas with refrain

— — — — — — — — — — — —

5.	Bruder, gib dir einen Stoss	Anthem	1 stanza
6.	Fürchte dich nicht	Anthem	1 stanza
7.	In der Jugend goldenem Schimmer	Anthem	Strophic, 2 stanzas without refrain
8.	Das Lied vom Branntweinhändler	Lied	Strophic, 3 stanzas with refrain

— — — — — — — — — — — —

9.	Mandalay-Song	Song	Strophic, 2 stanzas with refrain
10.	Surabaya-Johnny	(Song)	Strophic, 3 stanzas with refrain
11.	Das Lied von der harten Nuss	Lied	1 stanza with refrain
12.	Die Ballade von der Höllenlili	Ballade	3 stanzas with refrain

In view of Weill's statement that jazz (and at the time its derivatives of dance music and popular song) had become an international folk music capable of communicating to all classes, his use of strophic structure is a logical reflection of his aesthetic and sociological goals.

The five *Balladen* identified as such in *Die Dreigroschenoper* and *Happy End* were all set strophically by Weill.[93]   In each case only the accompaniment is varied for successive stanzas of text.   Only one of them, "Die Ballade von der Höllenlili," has a refrain, which is more typical of the *Song* than of the narrative *Ballade*.   However, in this number Weill blurs the distinction between stanza and refrain by introducing a major musical division (with a new pattern of declamation and a different meter) which precedes the textual refrain.   Since there is no tempo change between the two sections of Weill's musical strophe, the listener is apt to perceive the number as a straightforward strophic, three-stanza form without refrain.   Conversely, in "Zuhälterballade," where there is no textual or vocal refrain, the orchestral tango, which serves as interlude and postlude, functions like a refrain to give this *Ballade* a *Song*-like presentation.   As a result the "Zuhälterballade" is raised to a more personal, less "historical" level than Weill's other *Balladen*.   The number of strophes in the *Balladen* of *Die Dreigroschenoper* and *Happy End* range from two to six.

All of the *Songs* of *Die Dreigroschenoper* and *Happy End* are strophic structures with refrains, as are the "Alabama Song" and "Benares Song" of the *Mahagonny-Songspiel*.   That within this common format of two or three stanzas with refrain (not the four or five stanzas that he later referred to as being characteristic of his *Songs*) Weill could create such a varied array of musical numbers differing so greatly in dramatic function and musical style is evidence of his remarkable musical imagination.   He wisely avoided the stereotyped harmonic progressions and regular phraseology of the American popular song and instead let the content of each number determine the framework of its musical setting.   The fact that Weill's *Songs* were such specific responses to individual dramatic situations can be cited as the primary reason why so few of them were lifted from their original context and exploited as popular "hits."

Often the overall strophic structure of his *Songs* masks an internal organization which is also masterfully developed.   "Der Song von Mandelay" (No. 9 of *Happy End*) is a representative illustration.   Within the two stanzas of the strophic structure, Weill created a rondo-like substructure:

```
   2 | 4   4 | 4   4 | 4   4 | 8   8 | 4    4  | 4    4
orch.| a   a | b₁  b₂| a   a | c   c | b'₁  b'₂| a'   a'    ℞
vamp |
     |   8       8       8        16       8        8
     A       B       A        C        B'       A'
```

Such musical sophistication is matched by a keen dramatic instinct that revealed itself in such gems as the "Bilbao-Song," where within a straightforward three-stanza strophic structure Weill captured a nostalgia filtered through a gangster's faulty memory in a phrase structure that perfectly accommodates the performer's inability to recall the lyrics. In *Die Dreigroschenoper* and *Happy End* the *Song* was developed to the point that it could serve as the focus of expansion into the "closed musical forms" of epic opera.

In *Aufstieg* and the other works for the musical stage in which Weill could not rely solely upon *Songs* and *Balladen* as musical units, he had to find means to enlarge the scope of such forms to encompass a full-length opera. Of course, he had dealt with similar problems in the one-act operas *Der Protagonist, Royal Palace,* and *Zar,* but now he wanted to preserve the new *Song*-style while ensuring a cohesive musical flow between the "closed musical forms" of *Aufstieg.* Although only two musical numbers of *Aufstieg* (Nos. 2 and 3) are entirely strophic structures, many others incorporate strophic forms within a larger framework. In a work composed of twenty-one separate musical units, most of which are themselves multi-sectional, the problems of continuity, unity, and overall plan claimed the attention of the composer.[94] Weill's solution was multi-faceted; he used several constructive mechanisms to bind *Aufstieg* into a unified whole.

The most apparent device is repetition of certain musical events throughout the opera. For example, "Aber dieses ganze Mahagonny," first sung by Begbick and then repeated immediately by Fatty, Moses and Begbick in Number 1, recurs in three other musical numbers, always at critical points in the chronicle of the city. Such repetition not only relates musical units to one another but also directly comments on the dramatic structure—in each recurrence the passage acquires additional meaning in its new context and brings to that particular situation the connotations accrued in earlier appearances. Similarly, the "Alabama-Song" reappears in the Finale to Act I and the Finale to Act III, each time with greater despair. While such musical repetition functions primarily as dramatic recall, on another level the "refrains" link scattered sections of the opera.[95] Numbers 13-16 of Act II are linked to one another within a gigantic superstructure based on the returns of the instrumental "ritornello" which opens Number 13. Within individual musical numbers, repetition of sections (without correspondence to any stereotyped forms) allows Weill to "close" his musical forms.   Such constructive repetition within a scene is particularly operative in Numbers 3, 14, and 17.

Repetition is a rather static and limited constructive device, however, so Weill used other means which are more dynamic and flexible. One is the careful differentiation of levels of musical expression. In *Aufstieg* the composer employed spoken dialogue, purely instrumental sections, segments where dialogue is spoken over orchestral accompaniment, passages of recitative, arioso and *Sprechstimme*, arias, *Songs*, ensembles, and choral movements in such a way that the invocation of a certain manner of presentation assumed structural importance.   This is particularly true of choral passages, for the chorus is called upon to fulfill several dramatic functions: narrate events, comment on the situation, and actively participate in the chronicle.   Weill distinguished these functions from one another through the musical texture assigned to the choral passages: strictly homophonic four-part chorales, unison *Song*-like passages, and complex contrapuntal sections.   The two choruses of *Die Bürgschaft* play an even more prominent role in its overall structure: Weill separated the active chorus from the commenting chorus by placing the latter on one side of the orchestra pit.

Thematic transformation, evident already in some of Weill's earliest works, is one of the most affective unifying devices in *Aufstieg*.   More subtle and less limited than literal repetition, motivic development of short passages and melodic cells is a purely musical (as opposed to textual) means of organizing large-scale structures.   Elaine Padmore has noted and documented in some detail how the first measure of *Aufstieg* presents a thematic germ that becomes the catalyst for much of the musical material of Act I.[96]   Of even more significance is Weill's manipulation of rhythmic cells which relate diverse thematic groups to one another through a common rhythmic foundation.   This technique is closely interrelated with the gestic function of rhythm, for scenes related in content can be associated through rhythmic identity while other musical elements maintain their independence.

As someone who considered the musical structure of Mozart's operas and Weber's *Der Freischütz* as supreme models, Weill did not overlook the primary device for formal construction: tonal organization. Although *Aufstieg* consists of separate musical numbers, the overall tonal plan was the most powerful means that Weill employed in binding them together.   Because he frequently avoided using key signatures (few of his surviving works composed between 1920 and 1927 utilize key signatures) and because his tonal procedures are so complex, this aspect of the formal plan of *Aufstieg* has not been properly acknowledged.[97]   Weill's harmonic procedures are examined in greater detail in other sections of this study, but a glance at the tonal layout of *Aufstieg* here will illustrate his use of tonal relationships as a constructive mechanism.

While such tonal organization across the boundaries of separate musical numbers was less important in *Die Dreigroschenoper* and *Happy End* because dialogue usually intervened and because Weill readily acquiesced to transposition and re-ordering of the numbers within the play-with-music format, even in these works the well-considered tonal framework organizes into larger units those musical numbers which follow one another without interruption.   In *Die Dreigroschenoper* the sequence of Overture, "Moritat," and "Morgenchorale" is a prime example.   Originally the first vocal number of the work, the "Morgen-chorale" is clearly in g minor; it is no coincidence that Act I concludes in G major.   The Overture in C (it is often irrelevant to distinguish between minor and major because the crux of Weill's harmonic vocabulary is constant vacillation between the two through shifts of a semitone both melodically and harmonically) functions as a logical preparation for the opening of Act I.   When the decision was made late in the rehearsal period to add the "Moritat," Weill had to find a way to preserve the tonal relationship between the Overture and the "Morgenchorale." Rather than simply repeating the tonic of the Overture in the "Moritat," Weill employed a "double-mode" tonic sonority, derived from two inter-locking perfect fifths and encompassing a major (C) and minor triad (A).

(Incidentally this sonority is the concluding chord of Mahler's *Das Lied von der Erde* and one of the hallmarks of Weill's early style.)[98]   The tension and ambiguity of this harmonic axis is "resolved" by Peachum's "Morgenchorale," where the suspended A of the preceding "Moritat" is heard as upper neighbor to G.   Another such chain concludes *Die Dreigroschenoper.*   "Ruf aus der Gruft" is clearly in A; the "Grabschrift" leaves an F♯ suspended as V of B, resolved only in the *deus ex machina* of the "III. Dreigroschenfinale" where by an expressive use of long-range tonal resolution the F♯ is resolved to F to parallel the dramatic resolution precisely.   In *Happy End* only five tonal centers are used for the twelve musical numbers, and all are interlocked in a chain of thirds with C as the focal point: A - C - E♭/E - G.

The tonal organization of *Aufstieg* represents a much more complicated musical web, but one which meshed precisely with the dramatic events in the chronicle of the city:

1.	Founding of Mahagonny	Begbick, Fatty, Moses	(C) - E - A
2.	"Alabama Song"	Jenny & Girls	G
3.	Recruiting Inhabitants	Fatty, Moses, Men	(C) - G♭ - d (A)[99]
4.	"Auf nach Mahagonny"	Lumberjacks	D - E - (D)
5.	Arrival of Lumberjacks	Lumberjacks, Begbick, Jenny, Girls	A - D - A - E
6.	Jenny solicits Jim	Jenny, Jim	A
7.	Crisis: Inhabitants are dissatisfied	Begbick, Fatty, Moses	C - G - E - F - C
8.	Jim wants to leave	Lumberjacks	A
9.	Life in Mahagonny: Eternal Art	All	E♭ - E - C - E - E♭
10.	Crisis: A hurricane	All	B♭ - E (A)
11.	Mahagonny is spared	All	B♭ - G - E - A - D - B

— — — — — — — — — — — — — — —

12.	Rejoicing	All	D (A)
13.	Eating	Men	D - G (C)
14.	Loving	Begbick, Moses, Men	F - G
15.	Boxing	Joe, Fatty, Bill, Jim, Men	C - D - E - F
16.	Drinking, Jim cannot pay	All (who are still alive)	D-A-D-E-B-D-A-B♭

— — — — — — — — — — — — — — —

17.	Jim awaits trial	Jim	D (A)
18.	The trial	All	E - C - E♭ - G - F (B♭)
19.	"Crane Duet," Execution	Jenny, Fatty (All)	E - E♭ - E - C - A
20.	"Gott in Mahagonny"	Jenny, Fatty, Moses, Toby, Bill	D - E - G
21.	Destruction	All	D - G - B

In looking at Weill's tonal plan, one notes that Acts I and III conclude in B while Act II ends in B♭. This illustrates Weill's "expressive" use of tonality (a shift up or down usually by semitone for expressive or intensifying effect) across the entire structure of the opera.[100] In this case the device mirrors the dramatic relaxation of Act II as the city is spared from the hurricane and its inhabitants indulge themselves under the new law that "everything is permitted." Weill uses this "expressive" capability of tonal progressions throughout the opera both within scenes and between musical units. An example of the former occurs in Number 11 when the city's salvation from the hurricane is reflected in the movement from B♭ to B. The progression from E♭ to E between Numbers 17 and 18 reflects the increase in tension from Jim's wait for the trial ("Nur die Nacht") and the trial itself.

Although B emerges as the tonal goal of the entire opera, it plays a relatively insignificant role in the construction of individual numbers. The first act is almost entirely based on the axis A—C, and it is only in the final number of the act that B emerges as the central tone and "mediator" between the poles of A and C. Within the first act, with the exception of two structural units, the relationship between successive musical numbers follows an upward cycle of fifths. The exceptions occur in Numbers 6-8, where the A—C axis is given its most explicit realization, and between Numbers 8 and 9 and Numbers 10 and 11, where the interval of the tritone is effectively used to reflect the dramatic disjunction at these points. The tonality of G receives special treatment in the opera: it is associated with the insatiable sensual needs of man which bring Jenny and the girls to Mahagonny in Number 2, which Begbick recalls she enjoyed satisfying in her youth in Number 7, which are recalled in the reprise of the "Alabama Song" in Number 11, which cause a man to eat himself to death in Number 13, and which drive him to the brothel again and again in Number 14. Unlike Act I, Act II is one continuous musical structure, dominated by the re-entries of the orchestral ritornello (in D) and the male chorus, "Erstens, vergesst nicht." In much the same way as B served as the goal of Act I, B♭ finally emerges as the center of the axis G—D which dominates the structure of Act II. Finally in the third act, all of the strategic tonal areas are recalled along with the reprise of some of the most memorable thematic material of the opera.

The relationships explored in Weill's tonal organization of *Aufstieg* might be summarized in the following diagram:

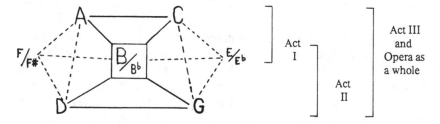

The diagram indicates that the four primary tonal centers for the opera are successive entries in a cycle of fifths, C - G - D - A. B and B♭ serve as the goals of the acts and thereby relate the pairs A—C and D—G to each other. The subsidiary tonalities of E, E♭, F, and F♯, related to C—G and D—A by a third-relationship and to B—B♭ by a fifth-relationship complete the tonal framework.

That Weill was able to preserve the *Song*-style within the mammoth structure of *Aufstieg*, which included so many other modes of expression, is one of his greatest achievements. Those critics who have noticed only the pastiche aspects of this opera have missed the masterful ingenuity Weill displayed in guaranteeing continuity of formal structure. Weill was acutely aware of the formal responsibility and capability of music in opera: "Musical form is more than a mere collection of individual segments; it is one of the remaining effective powers of expression completely appropriate to music."[101] *Aufstieg* represents the realization of the theories which Weill set forth in his numerous essays concerning a renewal of opera.

It was a collaboration that could hardly have survived long enough to produce a single work, let alone six in the space of three years, but for a high degree of self-deception and mutual incomprehension.[102]

— *David Drew* —

VI

Although the phrase "Brecht-Weill" was originally coined by journalists in the twenties as a handy abbreviation to denote the artistic marriage of Brecht and Weill, in the absence of informed scholarship dealing with the actual nature of their relationship this shorthand appellation has now come to imply a single pseudo-entity. The resultant faulty image of identical Siamese twins has obscured the more accurate description of the collaboration as a tenuous and temporary "nuptial" bond. Although the offspring of this fertile union still carry the name of both parents, their births and inherited characteristics have been primarily attributed to the labor of Brecht alone. Because Brecht today has been awarded an overdue and well-deserved stature, viewing his output anachronistically in the context of his current critical aegis is a constant danger. Brecht's voluminous and vigorous writings in defense or explanation of his dramatic ideas have received such wide circulation that the contributions of his numerous collaborators have been eclipsed in darkness by a somewhat artifically-manufactured halo which now surrounds the brilliant dramatist. In contrast, because Weill and his essays about theater in general and the Brecht-Weill works in particular were, with few exceptions, summarily ignored by musical scholars during the period of Brecht's ascension to his rightful reputation, the notion that Weill's ideas were merely reverberations of Brecht's has gained credence. "It is as if some form of osmotic pressure had allowed popular conceptions of 'Brecht' to absorb and completely diffuse those of 'Weill.'"[103]

One cannot hold literary or theatrical scholars culpable for overlooking the possibility that a composer whom few of their musical counterparts took seriously might have been more than a subsidiary appendage to the collective development of epic theater. After all, Brecht had "stacked the deck" against Weill in two assessments of his "*Mitarbeiter*," neither of which were published during Brecht's or Weill's lifetimes. The first appeared in an essay "Ueber die Verwendung von Musik für ein episches Theater," published posthumously in 1957, in which Brecht claims credit not only for the commission of the *Mahagonny-Songspiel* (it was Weill's) and the initiation of the collaboration (again, it was Weill's), but also for a stylistic shift in Weill's music:

> This type of *song* was created on the occasion of the Baden-Baden Music Festival of 1927, where one-act operas were to be performed, when I asked Weill simply to write new settings for half-a-dozen already existing *songs*. Up to that time Weill had written relatively complicated music of a mainly psychological sort, and when he agreed to set a series of more or less banal *song* texts, he was making a courageous break with a prejudice which the solid bulk of serious composers stubbornly held.[104]

The second reference occurs in Brecht's *Arbeitsjournal*, published in 1972. Brecht's stylized and idiomatic German is presented in my approximate English version:

> 16. 10. 40
> a musician, to whom i had given the texts of COURAGE to compose, along with a few guidelines, produced three compositions, he played them for his friends, he overheard someone say that he copied WEILL, so he quit. in vain i explained to him that only the principle had to be preserved, a principle which weill had not invented. (i told him how i had come across weill at a time when he was a student of busoni and schreker and a composer of atonal psychological operas, and how i had whistled for him measure by measure and especially demonstrated performance, etc.)[105]

Both evaluations were written after the collaboration had dissolved on less than amiable terms. With no evidence to the contrary forthcoming from the musical sphere, many literary scholars accepted Brecht's account at face value. Since Weill apparently served as a mere musical amanuensis who transferred Brecht's dictation into musical symbols, there was no reason that Weill should be treated in studies like Werner Hecht's *Brechts Weg zum epischen Theater: Beitrag zur Entwicklung des epischen Theaters 1918-1933* as anything more than a peripheral figure.[106] When Martin Esslin ventured to write that "Brecht and Weill mutually influenced each other" and that "Brecht's theory of the function of opera and of the 'epic theatre' in general owes a great deal to Weill's ideas" without supporting evidence, such an assertion was all too easily ignored by colleagues.[107] In the only American dissertation dealing with Weill's music in any detail, Susan Clydette Harden then proceeded from the assumption that, since Brecht and Weill were of a single mind, one could safely conclude that they spoke through a common mouthpiece—Brecht's.[108]

In fact, Weill's writings about theater, opera, and music often contrast markedly with Brecht's. Weill never abandoned his commitment to a renewal of opera—never an issue of central concern to Brecht. Their differing approaches did share enough aesthetic and sociological goals to constitute a basis for a complementary but not identical assault on the problems of musical theater. The common admiration for the advances of modern theater (especially those of Kaiser) and the jointly-held conviction that musical theater could communicate to a wider audience without abdication of its intellectual seriousness provided a foundation for the initiation of the relationship. However, within this mutual territory the inevitable disputes quickly arose over the proper development of the various resources of music and theater. In retrospect, the differences of opinion were not the crippling handicap that they might seem, for the contrasting backgrounds and viewpoints of the collaborators encouraged reciprocal impregnation of ideas which expanded the conceptions of both. Weill's personal experience with Busoni's *junge Klassizität*, Stravinsky's "epic" endeavors, and the historical models of Mozart, Weber, and Beethoven clearly enriched Brecht's unfolding design for epic theater.[109] On the other hand, Brecht's innovative theatricality and power of language furnished a resolution to the formal and technical impasse which had confronted Weill. But in the end the divergence of the underlying expectations of one another corroded the natural affinity which had cemented the unstable artistic relationship. As the partnership drifted further from the egalitarian pact with which it had begun, Weill saw that his music would be forced to accept an essentially incidental function; such a compromise of his primary purpose was out of the question.

While a detailed comparison of Weill's and Brecht's essays written during the period of their association is beyond the scope of this study, a number of observations seem especially relevant. Although the collaboration between Brecht and Weill added new dimensions to the works and aesthetic statements of both, neither Brecht nor Weill could be said to have altered course from the destinations they had plotted before their encounter. Weill's attitudes toward music's role in musical theater had already crystallized and were no longer in fluid state. Long before Brecht had labeled the effect of alienation as "*Verfremdungseffekt*,"[110] Weill had discussed music's ability to reveal different aspects of a dramatic situation in its alienation from the text in "Busonis *Faust* und die Erneuerung der Opernform" (1926). Furthermore, the most sophisticated examples of the "distancing" capability of music are to be found in Weill's scores of the late twenties. Similarly, although Brecht may have introduced the term "*Gestus*" to Weill, it was the composer who gave the concept its first extensive theoretical formulation and concrete realization of its application to music.[111]

Now that Weill's essays have surfaced, longstanding hypotheses concerning the nature of the collaboration must be re-examined. The persistent and now untenable view that Brecht was always the dominant partner, retaining full authority and serving as "the guiding force in matters of musical tone and expression"[112] is easily dismissed. The predominance of music in musical theater was fundamental to Weill's entire career. Again and again he warned that music must never play a subsidiary role in the structure of opera, and he used his own experience in his collaborations with Brecht to demonstrate that it need not do so. Not that Brecht did not attempt to relegate music to that position or did not try to dictate his own musical concepts to Weill. One of Brecht's friends, Carl Zuckmayer, described Brecht's quest for authority as follows:

> He did not want admirers or disciples; but he did want collaborators who could co-operate with him and therefore subordinate themselves to him. . . . I once said to him: "For you the collective is a group of intelligent people who contribute to what one person wants—that is, what you want." He admitted, with his particular sly smile, that I might not be far wrong at that.[113]

Lenya recalls that Weill at least pretended to be "co-operative" in that sense:

> Brecht and Kurt had the most enormous respect for each other's opinions, though the relationship never deepened into a strong friendship (as it did between Kurt and Georg Kaiser, and later between Kurt and Maxwell Anderson). Sometimes Brecht impressed on Kurt his own ideas for a song, picking out chords on his guitar. Kurt noted these ideas with his grave little smile and invariably said yes, he would try to work them in when he got back to Hassforth's.[114]

The agreeable nature of the shy and self-effacing Weill should not mislead one into believing that he was easily dissuaded from his own musical ideas. Those eyewitnesses to the relationship between Brecht and Weill whom this author has interviewed recall an iron will beneath Weill's amiable exterior. His own statement that Brecht's primitive attempts at composition "cannot be used as music at all" probably is relevant to more than just the context of the *Mahagonny-Songspiel*.[115] Undoubtedly Weill had anticipated that Brecht would serve as a malleable librettist, and Brecht had envisioned Weill as a complaisant song-writer.[116] Therefore, when neither revealed any inclination to fulfill the other's expectations, the resulting tension increased as they worked out the libretto of *Aufstieg* together "in all details, word for word, according to musical considerations."[117]

One needs only to compare Weill's three essays concerning *Aufstieg* that appeared in 1930 with Brecht's "Anmerkungen zur Oper *Aufstieg und Fall der Stadt Mahagonny*" to see how wide a gulf had opened between composer and librettist before their first major work had even been produced.[118]   Although Weill at least conceptually shared Brecht's contempt for "culinary" opera, he used the term *"Geniessende"* to characterize theatrical fodder which catered to the audience's appetite for pleasure.   Like Brecht, Weill had difficulty in transferring abstract aesthetic principles into concrete artistic form without compromise or distortion. It was Weill's inability to excise all culinary elements from his music (no matter how hard he tried to camouflage its "romantic" qualities with ironic or ambiguous understatement) that called forth Brecht's objections to the score of *Aufstieg*. Paradoxically, it is precisely the purely "operatic" elements of *Aufstieg* which lift it above the didactic plane to an intensely personal human relevance. When Brecht called Weill a "phony Richard Strauss" during the rehearsals for the Berlin production of *Aufstieg* in 1931, it was not so much a personal attack as a strike against Weill's commitment to opera, which in Brecht's opinion was symptomatic of an antiquated bourgeois attitude.[119] Weill could not accept the subsidiary space allotted to music within Brecht's epic model, nor could the radical separation of text, music, and production satisfy Weill's demand that music must take part in the execution of the most minute details of a work for the musical stage.[120]   After *Aufstieg* had been completed, Weill did attempt for a time to defer to Brecht's more didactic approach (*Der Lindberghflug, Der Jasager*).   However, soon Weill yearned for a return to genuine opera and a chance "to make real music again"; to that end he recruited Caspar Neher as librettist for *Die Bürgschaft*.

Perhaps the most telltale clues to the nature of the collaboration are to be found in the manner in which it ended. Aufricht's vivid account of the rehearsals of *Aufstieg* in Berlin indicates that the underlying tension between Brecht and Weill, which for all practical purposes had already ended the creative association after the composition of *Der Jasager* and the incidental music for *Mann ist Mann*, manifested itself in the rivalry for supremacy between text and music—a controversy as old as opera itself. However, it was not simply a question of Weill's music masking the intelligibility of words or failing to convey the drama without appealing to the audience's sympathy.   Lenya has stated that "it disconcerted Brecht to discover that the political implications of his drama had been made to seem subsidiary."[121]   By 1931 Brecht had actively embraced Marxism and the goals of the Communist Party. Weill never shared this shift from a moral system of humane, non-political socialism to an overt political identification. Just as Brecht did not want his message diluted by the distraction of Weill's music, Weill had no desire to provide a wrapper for Brecht's ideological positions. Of course, by 1931 Brecht had already found a more like-minded comrade in Hanns Eisler, who was willing to devote himself to the service of a political mission.   Eisler and Brecht quickly established a friendship that had eluded Weill and Brecht. The harmonious nature of the Brecht-Eisler collaboration offers insights into the reasons for the split between Brecht and Weill:

> Once it is recognized that the collaboration of Eisler and Brecht was distinguished by an unprecedented intellectual rapport between writer and musician that embraced every level of the creative relationship and extended as far as the dialectical-materialist method could carry it, then it becomes possible to grasp that the distinguishing features of the earlier collaboration were the exact opposite: the purely instinctive nature of the rapport, and the comprehensiveness of the tension that underlay it.[122]

In this regard, a parallel between Goethe and Brecht comes to mind. Music played a similar integral role in the works of these two outstanding German literary figures.   Just as Goethe preferred the simple, straight-forward musical settings of his musical advisor, Carl Friedrich Zelter (1758-1832), to Schubert's "interpretations" which diluted the linguistic effect, Brecht preferred Eisler's more direct musical treatment over Weill's often ambiguous settings.   In each case, the passage of time has brought about a critical consensus which conflicts with the author's own verdict.

The common misfortune of exile did not bring Weill and Brecht any closer, except for a brief alliance for *Die sieben Todsünden*, which Brecht dismissed as "not so significant." At some point Brecht evidently realized his loss, however, for in 1939 he wrote Weill from Denmark:

> what a pity that through the emigration we have been scattered. we should indeed keep more contacts with each other. i am presently working on the parable "the good woman of sezuan" about which i told you in new york. . . . i am very happy about your success in new york.[123]

Weill was apparently more interested in pursuing his new endeavors on Broadway than in renewing his relationship with Brecht, because in 1942 Brecht asked Theodor W. Adorno to intervene on his behalf. According to Brecht's entry in his *Arbeitsjournal*, Weill's response to Adorno was "an ill-tempered letter full of charges against me and a song of praise for broadway."[124]   By March 1943 Aufricht had succeeded in bringing the two together for a week of negotiations involving several projects. Brecht wrote: "weill wants to produce the setzuan play, and we plan a schwejk. . . . he also wants to compose the 'kinderkreuzzug'."[125]   The entry for 28

June 1943 suggested warmer relations: "weill has good dramaturgical judgment."[126] Finally in March 1944 Brecht signed a contract with Weill for the Setzuan play, "which is to be half opera," but the project (like "Schwejk" and "Kinderkreuzzug") was never completed. The earlier rocky but fruitful collaboration could not be revived, for both artists had a clearer picture of their individual paths that for a time had run parallel to one another but had inevitably led to different destinations.

The struggle of the old against the new, which always is connected with a decisive change in course, will be fought out in the musical sphere with particular vehemence, because here the concepts of tradition, piety, and sacredness, which have always been detrimental to the development of art, are thrown about more than in other artistic areas.[127]

— *Kurt Weill* —

VII

Weill's commentary on the music of his predecessors and contemporaries, found primarily in his critical essays for *Der deutsche Rundfunk*, reveals a discriminating intellect, receptive to such diverse composers as Schoenberg and Gershwin and sensitive to the historical context of individual works of art. That Weill could recognize merit in a vast array of works that were fundamentally alien to his own aesthetic positions is indicative of not only his cosmopolitan musical tastes but also his ability to set aside personal biases in his role as critic. Because excerpts from Weill's most perceptive and colorful reviews of others' endeavors have been included in the recently-published *Kurt Weill: Ausgewählte Schriften*, discussion will be restricted here to his comments on those composers who figured most prominently in the development of his own principles through influence that Weill either openly embraced or actively resisted.

Although Weill's usage of chorales and chorale-fantasies in his early instrumental works could trace its lineage to baroque ancestors, the polyphonic techniques he employed shared more in common with late nineteenth-century derivatives than with the original eighteenth-century models. At the very core of neo-classicism as expressed by Busoni was a return to the music of Bach. The tangible relevance of Bach to Weill's music remained of the filtered variety (primarily through Reger) until the late twenties. But in *Der Lindberghflug, Der Jasager*, and *Die Bürgschaft* (and also sections of *Aufstieg*), the inspiration is no longer indirect; one can find definite models for Weill's inventions, canons, fugues, and other polyphonic procedures in Bach's music. The clarity of form and transparency of contrapuntal texture evident in these works dating from 1928-1931 contrast markedly with the turgid linear expansiveness of Weill's earlier works. In an admission of indebtedness, Weill wrote a brief "Bekenntnis zu Bach" which appeared at the peak of the saturation of his musical thought by Bach's models:

Today when we say that "art must be useful, but it must maintain its quality," Bach is the most persuasive proof of the correctness of this claim. In his case both of these concepts are inseparable. His work is of the highest practicality. For that reason (not in spite of it), its unique standard is preserved.[128]

Although Bach composed no operas, Weill found his music "dramatic" in the best sense and cited passages from the *St. Matthew Passion* as striking examples of gestic music. Bach provided not only musical models but also reinforcement of Weill's aesthetic and sociological goals.

Only Mozart surpassed Bach in rank among Weill's musical idols. In Mozart Weill recognized a composer for the theater who was without equal; Weill found his symphonies, concertos, and string quartets to be as dramatic as his operatic music because his music "is always filled with the passionate breath of the theater" and it "never abandons its gestic function."[129] Mozart was so decisive a figure for Weill that he tended to judge all later composers by their relationship to the classic master. "Among those who go back to Mozart in fundamental questions of compositional style, emotion, and instrumentation, Weber stands—next to Mendelssohn and Berlioz—in first place."[130]

In a lengthy essay commemorating the centenary of Weber's death, Weill called him "one of the greatest musicians of the world, one of the most significant intellects." In the composer of *Der Freischütz*, always a decisive work for Weill, he recognized the direct successor to Mozart:

He [Weber] was able to become the creator of a new musical style only because in realizing his new ideas he in no way renounced the most valuable expressive means of the classic masters (who even then were already 'classic' to him), since he only expanded the technical and intellectual materials of his predecessors toward new possibilities. What Weber created has been stamped with the catchword that he was the progenitor of romantic music. Perhaps we can best define this expression if we compare a scenic situation of Mozart with a similar one of Weber, for example, the Movement through Fire and Water in *Die Zauberflöte* and the Wolf's Glen scene in *Der Freischütz*. With Mozart the scene is nothing more than a high point of the exterior occurrences; the event completely suffices for the designation of what is meant in a higher sense, and the figures involved go through this incident indifferently with fateful necessity. In contrast, the Wolf's Glen scene is viewed entirely from the gloomy point of view of Max and Agathe. The dreadful release of the supernatural forces of nature is intensified by the terror with which simple man faces it. The classic composer maintains distance between man and the powers surrounding him. The romantic places man in the midst of natural occurrences and seeks to grasp the universe through the subjective perception of the creator or his heroes.[131]

Weill's attempt to combine the aesthetic distance of the classic ideal with the theatrical power and personal conviction inherent in *Der Freischütz* was a preoccupation throughout his career.[132] It seems that Weill recognized that his generation was facing a stylistic and aesthetic crisis analogous to that which Weber confronted.

Like Weber, Beethoven was also forced to deal with problems inherent in a period of artistic and social upheaval. But in Weill's opinion, "if one considers the enormous development of opera from *Fidelio* to *Der Freischütz*, it seems hard to believe that Weber died a year before Beethoven; Weber's career represents something fundamentally new when compared with Beethoven's works."[133]   Although Weill considered *Fidelio* one of "the most beautiful of operas," and praised the gestic function of Rocco's and Leonora's duet "Nur hurtig fort," he always maintained an ambivalent and paradoxical attitude toward Beethoven's music as a whole.[134]   During 1927, the one-hundredth anniversary of Beethoven's death, Weill wrote three short essays about Beethoven's relevance to modern music. In "Beethoven und die Jungen," he stated that "the connection lies in the fact that we also live amidst revolutions, and the freedom which characterized the great ideas of Beethoven's time can also serve as subject matter of our art if we can express it through timeless means."[135]   In reacting violently to the prevailing musical aesthetic of the late nineteenth century (which claimed Beethoven as its progenitor), Weill found himself in the awkward dilemma of admiring his compositions but objecting to the effect they had had on later composers. In "Beethoven im Urteil der jungen Komponisten," Weill summarized his position:

> The direct influence of a classic master on the creative endeavors of successive generations is subject to continual fluctuation, which originates from the modification of fundamental aesthetic concepts in the different eras. If the musical attitude of a certain period pushes Beethoven's art more vigorously into the foreground, it arises from a necessity whose fulfillment proclaims the end of that period and the beginning of a new one. With the young generation of composers today one *cannot speak of any such influence by Beethoven.* Through a mistaken Beethoven-exegesis, music of the nineteenth century pushed the human-ethical notions so far into the foreground, while neither recognizing nor seeking the origin of its emotional content, that there was hardly room for free music-making. Since we are withdrawing from that nineteenth-century view, we must neglect or renounce much of what we love and revere in Beethoven. But the clarity and conviction of our opposition to the work of this master will lead to a more powerful bond with him than if we had deliberately and methodically fallen in line as his followers.[136]

Another centenary, that commemorating Schubert's death, stimulated Weill to write about a master of song who in many respects is the predecessor closest to Weill's own spirit. The earlier comparison between Goethe-Schubert and Brecht-Weill has a concrete basis in that several of Weill's earliest surviving compositions ("Reiterlied," "Das schöne Kind," and "Im Volkston,") can be perceived as studies in song composition in the style of Schubert. In the songs of Weill's mature works, procedures (such as immediate repetition of phrases at a pitch level a third higher) that are the hallmarks of Schubert's song style are readily recognizable. Furthermore, in Schubert Weill noted a kindred intention to unite the sentiments common to all people (presented in their most natural expression in folk songs) with the originality of artistic presentation. In his commemorative essay, Weill wrote:

> In Schubert's art the loftiest expression that is within man's reach has been accomplished. The fusion of genuine popularity [*Volkstümlichkeit*] with the highest artistic perfection has seldom been achieved to the same degree as with Schubert. His melodies are of noble, almost philosophical character, but they have found a passageway into the heart of the people because, without a doubt, they still arise from folk-like experience. Perhaps this is the highest that an artist can achieve.[137]

Naturally Wagner, who acknowledged Weber and Beethoven among his musical ancestors, was a problematic figure for Weill.[138] On the one hand, Weill rejected music drama and the *Gesamtkunstwerk* as a debasement of opera; on the other, he greatly admired Wagner's music— his harmonic and tonal procedures, melodic imagination, orchestral technique, and formal organization. This dichotomy was expressed in objection to Wagner the librettist, aesthetician, and sociologist, but approval of Wagner the composer. During his four years with *Der deutsche Rundfunk* Weill had occasion to write about *Tannhäuser, Die Meistersinger von Nürnberg, Tristan und Isolde, Der Ring des Nibelungen*, and *Parsifal*. In view of Weill's opinion that opera must present universal themes of interest to all, it is not surprising that his favorite opera by the "Bayreuth master," as he called Wagner, was *Die Meistersinger*. In a review of a performance of the opera broadcast on radio during 1925, Weill wrote:

> Real human beings, not gods and heroes, stand on stage; they speak a human language, they accomplish human deeds. . . . The human quality of this libretto communicates itself self-evidently in the music. Here we hear affecting tones, full of the purest sentiment, as we find it again in no other work of the master— except in the congenial *Tristan and Isolde*. A blossoming melodic style, an ingenious grasp of theatrical pacing, and a facile transparency of the orchestra mark this serious, powerful work of comic opera.[139]

The general post-war anti-Wagnerian reaction and Brecht's theatrical ideas undoubtedly reinforced Weill's antipathy toward the mythological aspects of music drama, but he always found himself attracted to Wagner's music.

Weill believed that a renewal of genuine opera depended upon a withdrawal from Wagner's sphere of influence; "obviously we must preserve the best of preceding epochs, but one cannot pursue that path any further."[140]   He regarded Berg's *Wozzeck* ("a masterpiece of the greatest power") as the climax of the Wagnerian tradition:

> [*Wozzeck*] certainly cannot be considered to be fruitful for the future; nevertheless, it is the magnificent conclusion of a development leading in a direct line from *Tristan* through Debussy's *Pelléas et Mélisande* and Strauss' *Elektra* to this entirely negative art.   Whatever one's position with regard to the music, the unbiased listener must be left with the impression of a musical personality of unusually rich inspiration and unprecedented ability.[141]

Similarly, Weill dismissed a number of Richard Strauss' operas as being derived from music drama but admired the musical innovations of *Elektra* and the decisive "attempt in *Ariadne auf Naxos* to conform to an eighteenth-century perception of an opera for music-making."[142]   Like most of the young generation of German composers, Weill viewed Strauss with great respect and little current interest:

> Even though his music is far removed from that of the younger generation, it plays as lively a part as ever in our musical life.   Every contemporary musician recognizes him as a master who at the start of the twentieth century created something important for the further development of music.[143]

Neither Mahler nor Reger was open to criticism on dramaturgical grounds, and both offered Weill purely musical inspiration.   In Weill's scores dating from 1918 to 1923, echoes of Mahler and Reger can be distinguished quite clearly by a perceptive listener.   Weill summarized his attraction to Mahler in a review of the Ninth Symphony:

> This powerful work assumes an exceptional position in the development of the symphony.   One could perhaps characterize Mahler's Eighth as the colossal climax of the symphony of the nineteenth century.   In contrast, the Ninth projects farther into our own age.   It already anticipated most of what the musical development of recent years has achieved.   The marvelous interweaving of the most expressive melodic lines, the freedom of harmonic procedure which occasionally is carried out to its final consequence, the soloistic, almost chamber music-like treatment of the orchestra, the other-worldly sounds magically emerging from never suspected beauty, and in addition, the completely new formal construction growing out of a clear presentation of the most profound content—all of these have become the basis of today's music.[144]

Weill found similar command of contrapuntal texture, freedom of harmonic vocabulary, and mastery of form in Reger's chamber music.   In his critique of the String Quartet in E♭, opus 109, Weill wrote:

> It is clear that Reger's chamber music is winning a lasting place in our concert halls. He is shown to be a master not only in an exceptional control of form and structure of chamber music but also in his unique melodic and harmonic language, which represents a significant expansion of the expressive possibilities of the preceding decades.[145]

Weill was reluctant to project his particular view of predecessors' roles within the history of music into the future in his commentary on his contemporaries. "The remarks of a creative artist about his art can have informative character only retrospectively. We can sift the material to see where we stand. We know very little of what tomorrow will bring."[146] Yet he was remarkably accurate in his "sifting," for he cited Schoenberg, Stravinsky, Bartók, Busoni, and Hindemith as the most forceful figures of contemporary music. One of Weill's most often quoted statements has been used as evidence that he despised Schoenberg's music:

> I am convinced that many composers have a feeling of superiority toward their audiences. Schoenberg, for example, has said he is writing for a time fifty years after his death. But the great 'classic' composers wrote for their contemporary audiences. They wanted those who heard their music to understand it and they did. As for myself, I write for today. I don't give a damn about writing for posterity.[147]

In fact, Weill was only presenting a defense of his own aesthetic viewpoint which had been subjected to scorn because several critics viewed his Broadway success as a sacrifice of artistic integrity on the altar of American commercialism. In his numerous comments about Schoenberg's music in *Der deutsche Rundfunk*, Weill enthusiastically campaigned for wider acceptance of "the leader of the boldest movement of modern music." As early as 1925, he noted that Schoenberg "has had to struggle against universal misunderstanding and animosity" because he "renounced tonality, common chords, symmetrical melody, rhythmic and formal constraint and substituted a wonderful interweaving of long melodies, a free polyphony that is sustained with prodigious skill, rich in inspiration, and unquestionable honesty."[148] The following excerpts from Weill's essays show how appreciatively he embraced Schoenberg's music while himself pursuing an entirely different course dictated by the demands of the theater:

> Wide circles of the public still consider Arnold Schoenberg to be a frightening phenomenon, the execrable perpetrator of today's "corruption" in music. This wretched notion is due to the misunderstandings of the fanatical opposition of his numerous opponents. Actually Schoenberg's work is an entirely organic outgrowth of the music of the nineteenth century. It only represents the final result of the style of Wagnerian chromaticism, which he raised to its most acute differentiation;

thus, it attains a "*Farbmelodie*," which renders the progression of a mood in the most sensitive shadings. He carries out everything with the uncompromising imperturbability of a fanatic who considers success within his lifetime almost a retrogression of his art. But even his opponents must recognize in him the purest, most noble artistic personality and the most powerful intellect of today's musical life.[149]

This master can be considered the path-breaker of new music. He was the first to carry the dissociation from the triad, the linear voice-leading of a far-ranging melodic style, and a liberation from the chains of classical form to their logical consequence, and still today, when young musicians have abandoned the Expressionism of recent years in favor of a definite clarification, Schoenberg is unique, unflinching in his steadfast goals. His full significance for the musical public will probably be first recognized after many decades.[150]

It was Schoenberg who could not value Weill's music in the least: "Franz Lehár, yes; Weill, no. His is the only music in the world in which I find no quality at all."[151]

Naturally Weill's music shares more in common with that of Stravinsky, Hindemith, and Busoni than with that of Schoenberg. The direct effect on Weill's own works of Stravinsky's *Soldier's Tale* and *Oedipus rex* has been discussed previously in this study. The latter opera, which received its Berlin premiere on the same bill as Weill's *Zar*, was especially relevant to Weill's own struggles with the role of music in epic opera:

A musical event of particular significance is the broadcast of Stravinsky's *Oedipus rex* from the Staatsoper am Platz der Republik. Without a doubt this work forms a cornerstone in the development of new opera. More clearly than all previous works it shows the unequivocal renunciation of the form of music drama and the adoption of a purely vocal operatic style in which the plot, drama, and visual element is completely repressed in favor of a purely musical construction. The role of music in this work is further amplified in that the text is in Latin and therefore the listener is directed solely to the powerful effect of the music, which is certainly of such power and of such clarity of expression that it cannot fail to have its effect on the listener.[152]

The careers of Weill and Hindemith, whom Weill called the leader of the young generation of German composers, have many points of congruence.[153] However, the superficial points of correspondence are more indicative of a healthy rivalry within a common cultural context than any direct musical influence on one another. Weill's primary involvement in musical theater was shared only peripherally and intermittently by Hindemith. Weill's essays dealing with the other "cornerstones" of modern music, Busoni and Bartók, have been translated in Appendix II.

This documentation of Weill's attitudes toward his predecessors and colleagues should not be construed as reinforcement of any notion that his art was essentially a derivative one—it was not. "Influence" is a nebulous term that is difficult to apply to particular works by composers of Weill's individuality and stature. It is sufficient to note that Weill, as a well-informed and perceptive musical intellect, was especially interested in historical models and precedents. His was a cultivated taste which carefully differentiated between those works that he found relevant to his own compositional problems and those that he deemed irrelevant. In his own words, "stylistic observation can have significance only as a clear backward glance,"[154] and its goal must be "a synthesis of all new achievements with the useful material of earlier generations."[155]

CHAPTER 4

WEILL'S MUSIC, 1919-1921:
ROOTS

The ear of the contemporary musician and music lover is no longer disturbed by far-reaching deviations from diatonic harmonies. This was an obstacle to the contemporaries of Mozart, who called his C-major String Quartet the "Dissonance" Quartet. It was again an obstacle to the contemporaries of Wagner, Mahler, and Strauss and will remain so for some time to come.[1]

— Arnold Schoenberg —

I

Although Weill's String Quartet in B minor (1919), Sonata for Cello and Piano (1920), and Symphony no. 1 (1921) were not publicly performed until years after his death, they constitute the foundation for any study of the composer's musical style. Each of these purely instrumental works, composed before a neo-classic aesthetic had taken root in Weill's scores, indicates how fluently he composed in an idiom solidly based on that of late nineteenth-century German music. Despite his later call for a general renunciation of the aesthetic tenets of Romanticism, Weill's own clarification of form and simplification of musical language did not represent a total reversal of compositional approach but rather a gradual distillation and condensation process in which only the most essential components were extracted from the musical language of these early works. Many elements of Weill's mature style can be discerned in the tonal procedures, harmonic vocabulary, contrapuntal techniques, thematic manipulation, rhythmic gestures, and melodic construction employed in these compositions. Weill attempted not only to assimilate the achievements of his immediate predecessors but also to extend their advances even further, especially in the realm of harmonic materials. An appreciation of the stylistic evolution within this group of instrumental works and cognizance of their bonds with later compositions is crucial to an understanding of the actual nature of Weill's career in Germany.

The String Quartet in B minor, the first composition known to have been completed after Weill left the Berlin Hochschule für Musik, consists of four movements:

I   Mässig 6/8 (3/4)

II   Allegro ma non troppo (In heimlich erzählenden Ton) 2/4

III   Langsam und innig 3/4

IV   Lustig und wild 12/8

The third and fourth movements are played without intermediary pause, and part of the former is recalled in the manner of a reminiscence midway through the lengthy fugal finale (cf. Beethoven's Symphony no. 5). The cyclical nature of the Quartet is also apparent in the recall of motives from the first two movements in the final movement. In addition, the opening theme of the third movement is a slightly transformed version of the second theme of the opening movement. (Example 4.1)[2]   The overall format of "sonata-form"[3] movement—"scherzo"—slow movement—finale is certainly conventional, as is the tonal plan of the work: i—iv—VI—I. The traditional aspects of the Quartet are further reinforced by stylistic affinities with works by predecessors in the Austro-German musical sphere. For example, the character, tempo, and rhythm of the opening theme of the first movement brings to mind Mozart's Piano Sonata in A major, K. 331, and the metric ambiguity of a combination of 3/4 and 6/8 in the second movement recalls similar hemiola-like gestures of Brahms. One supposes that the references to the F major second subject ("Alma" theme) of Mahler's Symphony no. 6 in the first movement of the Quartet were intentional. The Quartet's fugal finale finds its counterpart in many of Reger's chamber works.

Such relationships that place the Quartet in the historical continuum are only a superficial reflection of a more profound reliance upon structural principles and compositional procedures evident in late nineteenth-century German music in general. Although the Quartet is by no means as derivative or tentative as Weill's earliest surviving studies in song composition and its craftsmanship is rather surprising for a nineteen-year-old composer, the work still assumes the character of a compositional etude for one who wished to master the musical language of his immediate predecessors and who hoped to make their advances his own. At the very core of such an effort is an attempt to control chromatic harmony and employ the "expanded" tonal procedures utilized by the post-Wagnerian generations. That Reger and Mahler should be among the apparent models is not surprising; Arnold Schoenberg, in a chapter of *Structural Functions of Harmony* entitled "Extended Tonality," summarized Reger's role as a link between Weill's generation and the preceding one:

> The music of Max Reger, like that of Bruckner and Mahler, is little known outside Germany.   But his music is rich and new, through his application to "absolute" music of Wagner's achievements in the realm of harmony. Because these were invented for dramatic expression, the application of these procedures in this way provoked an almost "revolutionary" movement among Wagner's successors.[4]

This "revolutionary" movement carried chromatic harmony to its tonal limits, affirmed what Schoenberg called the "interchangeability of major and minor"[5] that was implicit in many of Wagner's scores, expanded large-scale musical structure to include the mediant and submediant as alternatives to the dominant for areas of tonal contrast within a ternary "sonata-form," and in its vigorous polyphony reemphasized the linear aspects of musical composition.

Schoenberg discussed "the chromatic scale as a basis of tonality"[6] in his *Harmonielehre* (1911) in which most of the harmonic progressions that Weill used in the Quartet find a theoretical basis. It is the interchangeability of major and minor modes and the application to the major mode of procedures previously associated with the minor mode that accounts for many new possibilities within an extended tonal system. For example, in numerous late nineteenth-century sonata movements, composers transferred the tonal axis of minor tonic—relative major characteristic of movements in the minor mode to movements in the major. Thus, the mediant often complemented or substituted for the dominant in the tonal organization of expositions. It was a logical extrapolation to include the third below the tonic, the submediant, as an additional alternative.[7]   Post-Wagnerian composers found models for expansion of traditional tonal procedures in the music of Wagner; Robert Bailey has noted the ramifications implicit in the interchangeability of mode:

> The first act of *Tristan* is the first example in Wagner's career in which an unchanging tonic base prevails from beginning to the end of an act. In this particular instance, that unchanging tonic is actually a pair of keys—A and C— rather than a single key. The keys of A minor and C major bear an obvious and traditional relationship to each other, and Wagner's extension of the traditional approach to tonality consists not only in the fact that he associates the two related keys together, but also in the fact that he employs both the major and minor modes of each. It is the chromaticism implicit in the use of both the major and minor modes of a given key that accounts for the chromatic foreground details of many passages.[8]

That within a predominantly polyphonic texture, voice-leading considerations often took precedence over harmonic aspects and resulted in numerous "altered" sonorities was emphasized by Schoenberg:

> Good part leading will always be of great assistance. This refers especially to the main voices, the outer voices—soprano and bass. . . . Chromatic and quasi-diatonic progressions can soften many a harsh connection by their melodious qualities. The outer voices are also helpful in introducing substitutes—transformations and vagrant chords—if their directional tendencies are carefully observed.[9]

These features of post-Wagnerian instrumental music can be discerned as the basis for procedures inherent in Weill's String Quartet in B minor.

The exposition of the first movement of the Quartet presents three principal subjects (Example 4.2) in a rondo-like format where the first theme returns at its original pitch level after presentation of each of the other thematic groups. In functioning as an "economical" transition between sections of the exposition, each return of the first theme (T_1) occurs in a new harmonic context. The two areas of tonal contrast within the exposition are those of the submediant, G, and mediant, D. The introduction of the second (T_2) and third (T_3) themes coincides with the moves toward harmonic goals a major third below and minor third above the tonic respectively. Because these secondary key areas are implied by directional tonal procedures and are not confirmed by conclusive cadences, the metric shift from 6/8 to 3/4 which occurs with the arrival of both the second and third themes achieves increased structural significance. The "development" section begins by successive treatment of T_2 and T_3 in symmetrical twelve-measure phrases. A condensed recall of the exposition's sequence $T_1T_2T_1T_3T_1$, in which the first statement of T_1 is presented in augmentation, leads to a decisive recapitulation of the first theme in its original harmonic and metric setting. The restatement of the exposition is in no way literal, and the intervening transitional recurrences of T_1 have been omitted. A brief coda which combines T_1 in augmentation with T_3 concludes the movement. The final V—i cadence is the only authentic, clear-cut cadence in the entire movement.

Even though the thematic treatment of the Quartet's first movement corresponds to that of a late nineteenth-century interpretation of sonata-form, labeling the structure as ternary sonata-form may be misleading because Weill does not "resolve" the non-tonic material of the exposition by restatement in the tonic in the recapitulation. The movement is one continuous unit characterized by alternating statements of themes, and sections are delineated more by metric contrast than by juxtaposition of distinct harmonic plateaus. Phrases dissolve into one another by chromatic slide (Example 4.3), and harmonic progressions involving bass movement by fifth or fourth are almost universally avoided until the final cadence. The absence of traditional internal cadences also blurs any audible subdivisions, and the symmetry of thematic restatement evident in mm. 1-97 and mm. 98-152 (Example 4.2d) makes an overall two-part form a viable alternative reading.

Linearly determined progressions in which each voice moves by semitone (less often by whole tone) or remains constant permeate the Quartet. The result is often a series of simultaneities related to one another by chromatic "sidestep." This allows Weill to extend the chromaticism from the melodic domain to its harmonic analogue, and movement to remote tonal areas is easily accomplished. Conversely, the succession of sonorities influenced by linear movement by semitone saturates each voice with chromatic melodic configurations. Harmonic simultaneities seem to be determined more by the coincidence of linear progressions than by functional root relationships. This accounts for a harmonic vocabulary in which four-note configurations occur more frequently than pure triads.

Within the four voices in the opening four measures of the movement, no less than twenty-eight linear intervals of a minor second occur. (Example 4.4a) Although the framework of the phrase is an embellished arpeggiation of the tonic triad, the foreground melodic events are dominated by semitone inflections. In m. 4, the cello presents an explicit outline of the concealed structure of the four-bar melody, (Example 4.4b, c) Similarly, the chromatic embellishments of the second and third themes mask arpeggiations of the G and D triads, respectively. (Example 4.5) The constant local movement by semitone in all voices camouflages the movement's underlying diatonic organization. Manifestations of the pervasive chromaticism range from simple melodic sequences to extremely complex long-range harmonic progressions. Example 4.6 illustrates the former, where a chromatic sequence merely embellishes a progression between two sonorities differing by only a semitone in two voices. A more extended and tortuous episode appears in Example 4.7, where a chromatically descending chain of parallel tritones (a Weill mannerism) accomplishes an analogous movement between two four-note chords, related by linear intervals of a semitone. A reduction of the progression is found in Example 4.7b. One of the most complex passages involving a similar progression appears as Example 4.8. That a logical and organic overall structure emerges so forcefully from the continuous chromatic flow of the first movement testifies to the teenage composer's mastery of the chromatic idiom, unerring voice-leading, and already remarkable sensitivity to musical form.

The second movement of the Quartet, to be played "in secretive, narrative tone," is also in ternary form, but again without the tonal implications of conventional sonata-form. For the most part the chromaticism and blurred phrase structure of the first movement have been replaced by diatonic melodic and harmonic configurations and musical periods closed by firm cadences. Instead, a different aspect of the "interchangeability of minor and major" is emphasized; E minor and E major are juxtaposed as the primary tonal areas, with G and B functioning in intermediate and transitory roles. The wrenching, unexpected tritone in the first theme (Example 4.9a) becomes the primary motivic cell for development. Example 4.9b, c, d illustrate how the tritone serves as the basis for extended passages of the second movement. The lyrical second theme (Example 4.10a) serves as a distinctive foil for the fragmented opening theme and is constructed to allow simultaneous presentation of both within the "development" section. (Example 4.11) Weill also inverts portions of both themes during the course of the movement. (Example 4.12) Motivic elements from this scherzo-like movement reappear in Weill's Symphony no. 1, where the chorale tune (Example 4.10b) resembles the second theme of this movement of the Quartet too closely to be mere coincidence. In addition, the melodic pattern of interlocking descending fifths and fourths which appears in the Quartet is similar to the cyclic theme which opens the Symphony. (Example 4.13) David Drew has described this configuration as a "Weillian *ur-Motiv*," which recurs in many of his works, including the Sonata for Cello and Piano and *Die Dreigroschenoper*.[10] The passage quoted in Example 4.14a, in which the rhythmic figure ♩♫ presented by the viola on a single pitch animates the texture, displays another gesture which remains in Weill's repertoire throughout his German career. The chromatic passages of the second movement occur either as direct outgrowths of the tritone motive or as foreground embellishments. (Example 4.14b) While the harmonic vocabulary is primarily diatonic, the semitone is the critical interval in delineating the modal contrast of E minor and E major.

The terpsichorean characteristics of the third movement, "Langsam und innig," are almost disguised by its slow tempo. Here the minor-major tension occurs between E minor and G major. In an overall ABA' form, with none of the motivic fragmentation or development which characterized the previous movements, the lyricism of Weill, the song composer, is given free rein. The relationship of E minor and G major is ingeniously exploited in the A (mm. 1-22) and A' (mm. 38-61) sections where the theme presented by the viola takes on a different harmonic color in its repetition by substitution of a different "countermelody." Because the two "countermelodies" predominate by virtue of their placement in the upper voice, it is only in the recall that the *sehr ausdrucksvoll* viola-theme is perceived as primary melodic material. Derived from the second theme of the first movement, the melodic material presented by the first violin in the A section, played over a G—D drone on the open strings of the cello, masks the E-minor orientation of the viola line. (Example 4.15a) The ambiguity between E minor and G major is easily recognized in the cello part. (Example 4.15b) In the A' section a new melody stated in parallel thirds by the violins tilts the balance more toward E minor, although the persistent drone still asserts a G-major orientation. (Example 4.15c) It is hardly surprising that the middle section, which follows a clear cadence on E, is almost entirely chromatic as the semitone inflection central to the minor-major contrast of mode permeates the florid, soloistic texture. (Example 4.15d) The movement ends with a i—V cadence in E minor, but a five-note sonority combining a C major triad with F♯ and A♯ acts as a dramatic gesture linking the third movement to the finale in B major. (Example 4.15e) The strident chord combining pitches of C major and B major and featuring root movement from the preceding sonority of B to C is not arbitrary. It foreshadows the recall of part of the third movement within the finale; there the interval B—C is elevated to structural significance as the recall occurs in C, surrounded by fugal sections in B.

The fugal subject that emerges from the dissonant chordal bridge in successive statement-answer format in the four voices is typical of Weill's themes intended for imitative treatment. (Example 4.16) These subjects are often long, chromatic melodies which exhibit an increase in rhythmic animation toward the close. Although the endpoints of the themes outline tonally stable intervals (unison, octave, fifth, or fourth), the subjects are fashioned from large (ten, eleven, or twelve-note) pitch collections indicative of a chromatic mode that includes pitches common to both major and minor. In all cases the countersubject includes only those pitches found in the subject. Each of Weill's fugue themes contains at least one distinctive rhythmic cell which predominates and imparts an easily recognizable identity to the subject. Usually the theme features a segment in which large leaps are symptomatic of compound melodic structure (denoted by x in Example 4.16). His subjects often conclude with a descending scale passage encompassing at least one octave (denoted by y in Example 4.16), which provides an unambiguous tonal grounding.

The final movement of the Quartet again falls into an ABA' format in which the two imitative sections in B major are separated by an altered recall and expansion of the final portion of the third movement. The effect of this interruption, with Weill's instructions that the tempo is to be a little slower than before and the strings are to be muted, is that of a melancholy, non-literal recollection of a languorous and memory-filtered waltz. The reminiscence of the third movement is introduced by a chromatic passage which concludes with the interval B—C, emphasized both by a trill in Violin I and by an explicit progression in the cello line, which was prepared by the dissonant pivot between the third and fourth movements. (Example 4.17) The recalled portion of the previous movement is extended by a clever combination of motivic units from the two melodies which characterized the A and A' sections. (Example 4.18) In the fugal section of the finale Weill prepared for the recall in a striking bi-metric synthesis of 4/4 and 12/8. (Example 4.19a) The theme presented in duplets by the first violin undergoes a further transformation, increasing its resemblance to the melodic material of the middle section. (Example 4.19b) The motor-rhythms which accompany this passage are a sure presentiment of Weill's later song-style. With the subtle but unmistakable thematic relationships, the recall of the third movement grows out of the preceding fugal section while serving a cyclic function linking the first, third, and fourth movements. Since motives from the second movement appear in the fugal sections, the finale reiterates material from all preceding movements. The A' section of the last movement opens with an altered version of the fugue subject which thinly veils the Weillian "*ur-Motiv*." (Example 4.20)

Harmonic progressions, melodic formations, and rhythmic gestures which carry Weill's identifying mark make the Quartet uniquely his own despite its roots in the post-Wagnerian idiom. In looking at the overall structure of the Quartet (Example 4.21), one notes the unity achieved through thematic, metric, and tonal relationships. Its chromatic harmonic vocabulary is only a superficial manifestation of the underlying contrast and combination of major and minor modes; in this sense the title "String Quartet in B minor" is something of a misnomer. As the work progresses, the orientation gradually shifts from minor to major. Each movement explores a different aspect of modal inflection and in so doing the semitone becomes the most critical interval. The constant vacillation between major and minor, already in 1919 a Weill trademark, is only one stylistic feature of the Quartet that recurs as a component of his music throughout his German career. Composed two years before Weill began study with Busoni, the B-minor Quartet might be considered a demonstration of the accuracy of Busoni's theoretical formulation of the fundamental unity of major and minor:

> We are tyrannized by Major and Minor—by the bifurcated garment. Strange, that one should feel major and minor as opposites. They both present the same face, now more joyous, now more serious; a mere touch of the brush suffices to turn the one into the other. The passage from either to the other is easy and imperceptible; when it occurs frequently and swiftly, the two begin to shimmer and coalesce indistinguishably.—But when we recognize that major and minor form one Whole with a double meaning, and that the "four-and-twenty keys" are simply an elevenfold transposition of the original twain, we arrive unconstrainedly at a perception of the UNITY *of our system of keys* [tonality].[11]

Example 4.1   String Quartet in B minor.

This and all following examples from the String Quartet in B minor are reprinted by permission of the Kurt Weill Estate, Karoline Weill Detwiler (Lotte Lenya), executrix.

a. Movement III, mm. 1 - 4

b. Movement I, mm. 20 - 23

Example 4.2   String Quartet in B minor

a. Movement I, mm. 1 - 4 (T$_1$)

b. Movement I, mm. 20 - 23 (T$_2$)

c. Movement I, mm. 35 - 41 (T$_3$)

d. Formal Chart of Movement I

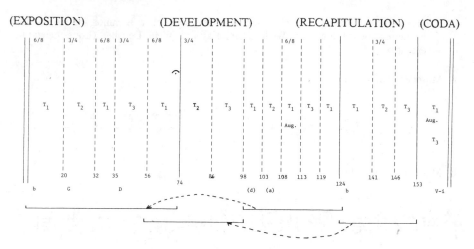

(EXPOSITION)   (DEVELOPMENT)   (RECAPITULATION)   (CODA)

Example 4.3   String Quartet in B minor: Reduction of mm. 86 - 90, Mvt. I

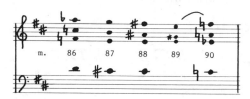

Example 4.4   String Quartet in B minor, Mvt. I, mm. 1 - 4

a.

b. Reduction

c. Abstraction

Example 4.5   String Quartet in B minor

a. Mvt. I, mm. 20 - 23 (T$_2$)

b. Mvt. I, mm. 35 - 41 (T$_3$)

Example 4.6   String Quartet in B minor, Mvt. I, mm. 16 - 19

a.

b. Abstraction of the harmonic progression

Example 4.7   String Quartet in B minor, Mvt. I, mm. 72 - 77

a.

b. Reduction

c. Abstraction

Example 4.8   String Quartet in B minor, Mvt. I, mm. 63 - 72

Example 4.9   String Quartet in B minor, Mvt. II

a. mm. 1 - 2: First Theme

b. mm. 71 - 76

c. mm. 86 - 90

d. mm. 110 - 115

Example 4.10

a. String Quartet in B minor, Mvt. II, mm. 36 - 39

b. Symphony no. 1, mm. 302 - 305

Example 4.11   String Quartet in B minor, Mvt. II, mm. 79 - 84

Example 4.12 String Quartet in B minor, Mvt. II, mm. 91 - 96

Example 4.13

a. String Quartet in B minor Mvt. II, mm. 130 - 131

b. Symphony no. 1, mm. 1 - 2

c. *Die Dreigroschenoper*, No. 20 "Grabschrift"

Example 4.14   String Quartet in B minor, Mvt. II

a. mm. 65 - 71

b. mm. 77 - 78

Example 4.15   String Quartet in B minor, Mvt. III

a. mm. 1 - 4

b. mm. 1 - 8

c. mm. 38 - 42

d. mm. 26 - 30

Example 4.15 continued

e.   mm. 60 - 64 (Transition to Movement IV)

Example 4.16   Weill's Contrapuntal Themes

a.   String Quartet in B minor, Mvt. IV (Subject)

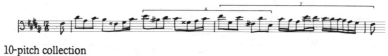

10-pitch collection

b.   Symphony no. 1 (Subject)   Also String Quartet no. 1, Mvt. III

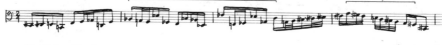

12-pitch collection

c.   Symphony no. 1 (Countersubject)

12-pitch collection

d. String Quartet no. 1, Mvt. III Choralphantasie (Countersubject)

12-pitch collection

e. Divertimento, Mvt. IV Choral (Subject)

11-pitch collection

f. Divertimento, Mvt. IV Choral (Subject)

11-pitch collection

Example 4.17   String Quartet in B minor, Mvt. IV, mm. 115 - 122

Example 4.18   String Quartet in B minor

a. Mvt. IV, mm. 137 - 141

b. Mvt. III, mm. 1 - 4

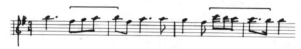

c. Mvt. III, mm. 38 - 46

Example 4.19   String Quartet in B minor, Mvt. IV

a. mm. 91 - 93

b. mm. 102 - 104

Example 4.20   String Quartet in B minor, Mvt. IV, mm. 188 - 191

Example 4.21   Unifying Relationships in String Quartet in B minor

a. Thematic

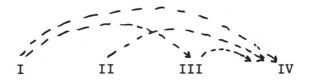

b. Metric

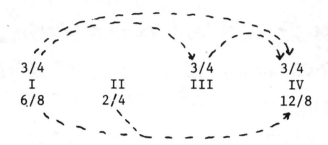

$$
\begin{array}{cccc}
3/4 & & 3/4 & 3/4 \\
\text{I} & \text{II} & \text{III} & \text{IV} \\
6/8 & 2/4 & & 12/8
\end{array}
$$

c. Tonal

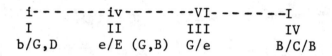

$$
\begin{array}{cccc}
\text{i} - - - - - - \text{iv} - - - - - - \text{VI} - - - - - - \text{I} \\
\text{I} & \text{II} & \text{III} & \text{IV} \\
\text{b/G,D} & \text{e/E (G,B)} & \text{G/e} & \text{B/C/B}
\end{array}
$$

A few years ago when nearly all so-called "modern" music sounded disagreeably the same to most listeners, a few clear terms pointed out to them differences not at first perceived without intellectual aid. Even now it is difficult to indicate very fine distinctions by means of modern terminology since the best known labels refer for the most part to general systems rather than to particular instances.[12]

— *Henry Cowell* —

II

After the post-Wagnerian generation of composers had explored the "interchangeability of major and minor mode" (implicit in Wagner's late works) and often in practice worked with twelve "chromatic keys" rather than twenty-four distinct major and minor ones,[13] models of the Bayreuth master stimulated additional extensions of the tonal system. For example, the traditional close relationship between a major key and its relative minor had been expanded in the first act of *Tristan* to allow simultaneous rather than only successive treatment—a direct corollary to the premise that parallel minor and major could be merged into a single chromatic mode. In certain respects, the combination of a major mode and its relative minor is less problematic because they share the same key signature, their scalar contents differ by only the leading tone of the harmonic minor scale, and the tonic triads include two mutual pitches, scale degrees 1 and 3 of the major mode. Although no satisfactory comprehensive theoretical system that classifies the harmonic and tonal procedures of the post-Wagnerian German composers has been published (a formidable task because each composer self-consciously and intuitively sought individual solutions which varied even within his own compositional output), there are numerous examples of this extension of the tonal system in compositions dating from the final decade of the nineteenth and the first decades of the twentieth century.[14]

The ultimate result of the annexation of the relative minor was substitution for the tonic triad of a four-note sonority comprising the pitches of the tonic triads of the major and its relative minor. One of the most arresting post-Wagnerian examples of such treatment is Mahler's *Das Lied von der Erde* (1908), where the tonic complex is

the combination of A and C (as in *Tristan*, Act I). This sonority accounts not only for large-scale tonal organization but also for many foreground melodic and harmonic constructions (the pentatonic scale, C-D-E-G-A, is implicit in the complex). The four-note sonority is unambiguously stated as the tonic chord in its appearance at the conclusion of the work. Such attempts to extend the tonic sonority beyond the triad were by no means restricted to the German tradition.   Earlier and less complicated than Mahler's *Das Lied von der Erde*, Ravel's *Jeux d'eau* (1901) is based on the tonic sonority

Although the complex resembles that of *Das Lied von der Erde*, the composition's structure does not depend on the E/g♯ polarity, but rather the major/relative minor relationship of E and c♯. The final cadence brings all three elements together as the C♯ "resolves" to the D♯ of the tonic sonority. (Example 4.22) Since there was no "common practice" for such expanded tonal procedures, various composers formulated their own methodology.   Schoenberg wrote that "extended tonality is also characteristic of my first period (1896-1906)."[15]   In his analysis of his song "Lockung," op. 6, no. 7, he noted the pervasive intermixture of E♭ and its relative minor, C minor, which dominates the structure:

> Perhaps the most interesting feature of this song, as mentioned in my *Harmonielehre*, is that the tonic, E♭, does not appear throughout the whole piece; I call this "schwebende Tonalität" (suspended tonality). Many parts of the song must be analyzed in submediant minor.[16]

In that Weill admired Mahler's scores immensely and extolled Schoenberg's orchestral songs as marking a transition to a new method of construction, he was undoubtedly aware of the precedents for expansion of a tonic complex to include the minor third below the tonic triad. The Sonata for Cello and Piano, composed during 1920, represents an effort to assimilate these procedures in his own music.

  In undertaking a discussion of the harmonic vocabulary of the Cello Sonata, one is immediately confronted with the problem of applicable terminology.   Analytic methodology and harmonic labels derived primarily from eighteenth-century tonal relationships are not sufficient. Terms such as "polytonality" and "bitonality" which denote the employment of two or more distinct keys simultaneously are entirely misleading when applied to extensions of the tonal system previously discussed. The whole point of such expansion was not to compose in two keys at once, but to augment the options within a given tonality by treating major, parallel minor, relative minor (and by extension its parallel major) as a composite tonal unit. Therefore, the four-note tonic sonority of the Cello Sonata is not bitonal at all. It is as much a mono-tonal unit as the triad, but the composer has the additional choice of treating it in a manner that temporarily emphasizes one of its two tonal centers.   Perhaps a reasonable compromise in terminology which avoids the connotations of bitonality and yet accurately describes function is "double-mode" tonality and a "double-tonic" sonority.[17]

Such general nomenclature does not solve the more practical problem of specific terminology for local harmonic configurations. The unfortunate tag, "added-sixth chord," has been affixed to the above four-note sonority despite the fact that its function in the music in question is quite different from its earlier usage as a "color modification of the triad."[18]   Furthermore, the term "added sixth" is so overused in the jargon of popular music and jazz (the "Blues-chord") that its application to music unrelated to that tradition creates grave misunderstandings. A handy terminology might be that of pitch-class sets, which has been widely accepted as a useful designation for atonal configurations. However, extension of set names to tonal constructions might imply an irrelevant analytic bias. Also, the prime-form nomenclature defined in Allen Forte's *The Structure of Atonal Music*[19] is based on the equivalence of pitch collections related by transposition and inversion. In a tonal context the actual pitch level is often more important than an abstraction of the sonority's interval content. Since the Sonata's tonic sonority is only one of many forms of the set 4-26, it is not completely described by that designation, but often a structural abstraction is all that is required. Perhaps one could resort to cumbersome numerical or alphabetical spelling of chords or to the even less desirable alternative of lengthy verbal descriptions. When applied to sonorities of more than four notes, however, both of these alternatives seem too unwieldy.

A combination of several nomenclatures will provide a reasonable and workable compromise. Set names will suffice to describe abstract harmonic complexes, even though the label does not describe the particular arrangement.[20] When more precise information concerning the actual pitches of a given sonority and its tonal function is desired, symbols such as Bb/g (denoting a sonority composed of the pitches of the Bb-major and G-minor triads) will be utilized. The reader is cautioned not to infer either atonality or bitonality. In the absence of a more accurate descriptive system, this dual approach will meet the abstract and particular analytical demands.

One could now proceed to a discussion of the Cello Sonata on this basis, but a glance toward later works indicates that double-mode tonality is insufficient in itself to deal with procedures which have their origin in the Sonata and Symphony no. 1. Therefore, it is advisable to digress yet another time to consider the next expansion of harmonic materials represented in Weill's music. We have noted that the tonic sonority of the Cello Sonata resulted from the addition of the submediant to the tonic triad. Historically it stemmed from an attempt to exploit the close relationships between relative and parallel minor and the major mode to the fullest by treating them as a single tonal complex. Implicit in such treatment is the chromaticism produced by a combination of major and minor modes. However, this procedure also embodies diatonic implications. The pentatonic scale, so prominent in Mahler's *Das Lied von der Erde*, is yet another possibility. If the Sonata's four-note tonic sonority is viewed as an abstract configuration, it comprises two interlocking perfect fifths. Taking the fifth as an interval of generation instead of the third leads to a number of other diatonic "sets" which are integral to Weill's harmonic vocabulary. In the same way that the pitches of a major scale can be generated by a seven-note ascending cycle of fifths (for example, starting with E♭ yields the notes of a B♭ major scale), non-triadic but entirely diatonic structures can be derived using the perfect fifth as the only determinant.[21] Example 4.23a illustrates a number of such diatonic chords, all of which appear in Weill's music. A number of other sonorities based on the interval of the fifth, but not generated as successive entries in a cycle of fifths, are presented in Example 4.24b. Just as the major scale is only one ordering of the abstract set 7-35, each of the sonorities in Example 4.23 can be rearranged to disguise the generating interval of the fifth. For example, because the perfect fifth inverts to a perfect fourth, the pitches of set 4-23 may be manipulated to form a pure "fourth-chord." Similarly, 4-20 and 4-26 may be voiced to emphasize the adjacent minor and major triads included in each. (Example 4.24)

Such non-triadic constructions allowed Weill to utilize the diatonic materials of the familiar major or minor scale in new ways—a technique shared with numerous twentieth-century colleagues.[22] While these diatonic sets initially appear in Weill's music in a tonal context (Cello Sonata, Symphony no. 1) and usually can be related to traditional scalar patterns, eventually they are also put to essentially non-tonal uses in the Violin Concerto and *Der Protagonist*. The fact that such fifth-generated structures often retain a central, controlling tone allows them to function in a tonal piece alongside traditional diatonic and chromatic materials. But even in the earliest occurrences in Weill's music, the crucial feature of these diatonic structures is the abandonment of the third (and therefore the triad) as the primary melodic and harmonic interval in a given passage. It is this avoidance of the familiar triad that prompted certain critics during the twenties to classify Weill among the atonalists.[23]

It is quite possible to differentiate the various stylistic periods of Weill's career in Germany by the frequency of occurrence and function of the triad in his scores.

Weill's contemporaries were well aware of non-triadic passages in such seemingly "simple" works as *Die Dreigroschenoper*. In an essay written in 1929, Otto Beer cited a passage from "Zuhälterballade" (Example 4.25), along with excerpts from Schoenberg's Chamber Symphony, opus 9, and Berg's *Wozzeck*, as an example of quartal harmony functioning within a tonal context.[24] Actually the pitches involved in the excerpt from "Zuhälterballade" are successive entries in a cycle of fifths beginning on C, the local tonic. Such constructions allowed Weill to compose melodies dominated by familiar, easily sung intervals without abdicating harmonic complexity and ambiguity in his non-triadic accompaniment. It may be precisely the fifth-generated harmonic material of passages like Example 4.25 which accounts for the "decadent" and slightly distorted quality so characteristic of Weill's mature style. Because traditional bass progressions by powerfully constructive fourths and fifths are easily preserved within this vocabulary, the listener is never allowed to forget completely a familiar triadic prototype. When the expectations of the consequences and continuations characteristic of that prototype are avoided or negated, the music achieves that surprising ironic twist and inimitable sense of detachment which eventually become Weill's personal trademark. Whether such fifth-generated simultaneities, linear progressions, and accompaniment figures resulted from a purely intuitive or strictly systematic process (most likely the former), they recur in Weill's music throughout his career in Germany. A limited selection of sample passages in Example 4.26 illustrates the frequency of their occurence. Even the Weill "*ur-Motiv*"

is only a linear presentation of a fifth-generated sonority. By no means, however, should it be inferred that such constructions account for Weill's entire harmonic vocabulary. On the contrary, they provide only another option for the composer—one which can be employed within an expanded tonal system or as a basis for non-tonal configurations.

The Sonata for Cello and Piano consists of three movements:

    I. Allegro ma non troppo (4/4)
    II. Andante espressivo (7/8)
    III. Allegro assai. Wild bewegt grotesk vorzutragen (3/8).

It is a pivotal work within Weill's output in that the second and third movements do not employ key signatures, and from this point until 1927, Weill rarely resorts to their use. Evidently he found it more convenient to notate music whose harmonic vocabulary is so chromatic and whose tonal makeup is in such a state of flux without recourse to key signatures, which did not represent the nature of extended tonality anyway. The first movement may again be considered a three-part sonata-form movement, with a tonal organization dictated by the double-mode tonic complex bb/g (4-26). The first phrase (Example 4.27a) illustrates the synthesis of G minor and Bb major. Although the opening theme in the cello part is clearly in G minor, it avoids any reference to a leading tone F or F#. The piano's reiteration of the Bb—F open fifth throughout the first eleven measures complements the linear unfolding of the G—D fifth of the melody—the tonic complex is thus stated as the combination of two interlocking fifths. Neither G minor nor Bb major appears alone in its "pure" form until the final cadence, but even here the G-chord lacks the third and the cadence is an inconclusive ii—I. The balance between the two centers of the tonal complex constantly varies with emphasis temporarily shifted from one to the other, but one never unequivocally prevails. For example, the opening section of the exposition, which tilted the Bb/g axis toward g, is offset in the concluding portion of the exposition (mm. 46-65) where Bb assumes control—but still within the context of the complete four-note tonic complex. (Example 4.27c)

The interval of the perfect fifth, so prominent on the foreground level, also controls the large-scale structure of the movement. (Example 4.27f) In this sonata-form movement, the intervallic relationship between tonic and dominant, namely that of the fifth, has been abstracted, extended, and applied to the interlocking fifths of the tonic complex. Therefore, the two areas of tonal contrast to b/Bb are the respective fifths, D (V of g) and F (V of Bb), which are also paired with each other in a secondary complex, F/d. The missing link in the cycle of fifths, Bb-F-G-D, is C, and not surprisingly, it serves as the key of transition between sections of the movement. (Example 4.27f) Since D minor and F major are related in the same way as G minor and Bb major, Weill devotes approximately one-half of the movement to this reflection of the primary tonal pair. The d/F relationship is made explicit in the recapitulation where material originally presented in Bb/g is repeated with the harmonic complex transposed up a fifth. The structure of the movement, with the notes of the non-triadic tonic complex accounting for the primary tonal areas, is remarkably similar (in that respect) to the

Wolf's Glen Scene of *Der Freischütz*, a musical structure which fascinated Weill from his youth. There, too, a four-note sonority, the "Samiel Chord" consisting of two interlocking tritones (A—E♭, F♯—C), controls the overall tonal organization.

Although the Cello Sonata represents a breakthrough for Weill in his use of a non-triadic tonic complex and his abandonment of key signatures, many stylistic features present in the String Quartet in B minor persist. Thematic transformation is again apparent in the first movement as one melodic motif appears in several rhythmic settings to account for the similarity of T_2, T_3, and T_5. (Example 4.28) The chromatic harmonic idiom so predominant in the Quartet is still functional in the Cello Sonata, especially in transitional passages (Example 4.27b,d). Progressions between successive harmonies by chromatic sidestep are omnipresent in the Sonata. (Example 4.29) Rhythmically animated pedal tones (mm. 86-92 and 106-110) and passages built on ostinato figures (mm. 174-181) are constructive techniques (perhaps traceable to Mahler) which reappear in many of Weill's later works. (Example 4.30) The ostinato figure in Example 4.30b serves as the bass line of all but six measures of the coda and confirms for the last time the polarity and synthesis of B♭ and g. The auditory effect of certain passages is somehow reminiscent of Ravel's String Quartet, and other hints of Impressionistic influence are reinforced by coloristic parallel chords in mm. 65-69 (Example 4.27d) and the arpeggiated figures of Example 4.27e.

The second movement opens with a short six-measure span which derives its thematic and harmonic material from the opening movement. (Example 4.31) Here, the G—D fifth is elaborated melodically over a dense piano texture that concludes with the tonic sonority of the Sonata. Four and five-note configurations predominate throughout this movement which unfolds in short spans, each developing a different facet of the thematic material. The tonal balance is shifted from g/B♭ to C, which acts as a fulcrum between the first movement's tonal center and the d/F complex of the finale. The somewhat eclectic patchwork of short phrases, often clearly separated by fermatas or caesuras, produces a rather unconvincing formal structure. The only literal repetition (mm. 18-20 in mm. 60-62) emphasizes the central role of C in the tonal organization. (Example 4.32) Fifth-generated sonorities related linearly by semitone-movement again account for much of the harmonic vocabulary. The coda is based on a striking four-note melodic cell which includes two tritones. That interval becomes the determinant interval of root movement in this section. (Example 4.33) In transposing the G—B♭ third of the opening phrase down a whole tone to a chromatic unfolding of the interval F—A♭, the final cadence (vii^7—i in F minor) prepares for the opening of the third movement—apparently in F.

The final movement departs from the fugal finale that is the norm for Weill's early instrumental works. Undoubtedly the composer realized that the medium of cello and piano was not conducive to four-part imitative texture. Instead the finale here is a rhythmically-animated rondo in 3/8—a welcome contrast to the viscous slow movement in 7/8. It takes its responsibility as a finale seriously in that it grounds the cyclic elements of the Sonata by invoking transformations of themes from the preceding movements. Furthermore, its tonal structure completes the unfolding of the tonic sonority and finally renounces it in a typical Weillian gesture of chromatic sidestep. The main theme (T$_1$ in Example 4.34) reifies the abstract relationship between F and D in the Sonata's tonic sonority, much as the first movement exploited the B♭—G axis. Beginning with a gesture that would indicate a tonal center of F, the "grotesque" main theme immediately negates that assumption with a jagged melody embodying two sets of interlocking tritones which confuse the tonal definition of the phrase. The twelve-bar theme ends with a decisive v—i cadence in D minor, emphasizing the other member of the D—F alliance. The piano's interjections are nearly all fifth-generated chords related to one another by semitonal slide. The main theme admirably illustrates Weill's use of a non-triadic, "enriched" (the term is Weill's) harmonic vocabulary within an entirely tonal framework.

   The five-part rondo format consists of three statements of the opening three-part exposition separated by two episodes, both of which introduce new material as well as rework and transform the recurrent rondo-material. The first episode (mm. 41-127) recalls melodic material from the slow movement and touches upon the other key areas of the fifth-chain, namely B♭, C, and G. The second episode (mm. 179-256) includes a short imitative section with the cello playing pizzicato and the piano relegated to a two-part staccato texture. This is preceded and followed by homophonic sections based on new material (T$_4$). It would be difficult to locate a passage in Weill's works composed before 1926 that is so prefigurative of the later song composer. Here a single rhythmic cell ♩♩♩♩ is repeated in every measure of the accompaniment while the cello "sings" a suspended melody in duplets. The section also illustrates the tonal function of Weill's non-triadic harmony. (Example 4.35a) Each of the twenty-three measures presents a new harmony, with C remaining a constant pitch throughout. This suspended pedal tone is thereby prolonged over a bass line descending chromatically from B♭ to C. Although C is the goal of the progression, it is perceived as such only in retrospect. The non-triadic harmonies give way to a pure C-minor triad, followed immediately by a shift to the major form in a typical Weillian gesture of modal juxtaposition. The inner voices move almost exclusively by semitones, and therefore, in one sense, the vertical simultaneities are determined primarily by voice-leading considerations.

The final restatement of the opening section includes brief recapitulations of the new material from each of the episodes. The coda presents a recognizable transformation of T_5 of the first movement, with the accompaniment derived from m. 33 of the second movement. (Example 4.36) The cadential gesture of mm. 380-383 (Example 4.37a) specifically recalls those of both preceding movements. The final chord of the Sonata resolves the D—F axis of the last movement and intensifies the tonic sonority of the piece by an upward semitonal shift. (Example 4.37b)

In an essay entitled "Weill's Debt to Busoni," John Waterhouse observed:

> A cursory glance at Weill's scores will reveal that one of the most persistent characteristics of his harmony is what could be called 'semitonal instability', whereby one chord or harmonic complex dissolves into the next through the chromatic shift of a semitone by one or more of its notes. The result is a continual hovering between major and minor keys, and a constant threat to tonality itself which is, however, usually maintained by a clear focus in the melodic line and by such devices as pedal points and ostinato basses.[25]

This is essentially an accurate description, but Waterhouse then argued that this 'semitonal instability' is "the single most important thing that Weill inherited from his teacher; for semitonal instability is also one of the commonest features of Busoni's mature music."[26] We have seen that foreground progressions between adjacent sonorities by semitone-slide are integral to both the String Quartet in B minor and the Cello Sonata. Since these works predate Weill's association with Busoni, one must take exception to Waterhouse's conclusion that Weill "inherited" this stylistic element from his mentor. It was an integral component of Weill's earliest scores, and the fact that his music shared this feature with Busoni's may have been one of the motivations which prompted Weill to join Busoni's master class in the first place. In any case, Waterhouse's assertion concerning the origin of this gesture is patently false. Judgments concerning 'influence' cannot be made on the basis of stylistic affinities alone, especially when such conclusions stem from an incomplete knowledge of a composer's output. There are a number of changes in Weill's musical language dating from his period of study with

Busoni, but harmonic progressions which are characterized by semitone-slide are a consistent feature of Weill's music throughout his entire career in Germany.

The Sonata demonstrates Weill's remarkable control of his new diatonic, non-triadic harmonic materials while preserving the most characteristic elements of the String Quartet in B minor. In the Sonata a fifth-generated tonic sonority accounts for the overall tonal organization of the work which complements its cyclic thematic construction. While such procedures have precedents, Weill's attempt to make them his own resulted in a very personal response. Elements of the Cello Sonata remain firmly rooted in Weill's music throughout much of his career and are further explored in his next surviving instrumental work, Symphony no. 1.

Example 4.22   Ravel: *Jeux d'eau*, conclusion

Example 4.23   Fifth-generated chords

a.

b.

Example 4.24

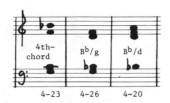

4-23   4-26   4-20

Example 4.25   "Zuhälterballade"

(C)

(D)

5-35

Example 4.26   Fifth-generated constructions in Weill's music

a. Sonata for Cello and Piano, Mvt. I, mm. 1 - 2

6 - 32

b. Symphony no. 1, mm. 1 - 2

6-32   7-35   6-32   7-13   8-22   6-31

c. Divertimento, Mvt. I, mm. 1 - 5[27]

d. String Quartet no. 1, op. 8, Mvt. III

  1. m. 1

6-32

2. 1 measure after ⟨51⟩

3. 1 measure after ⟨52⟩

e. *Quodlibet*, op. 9, Conclusion of Mvt. I

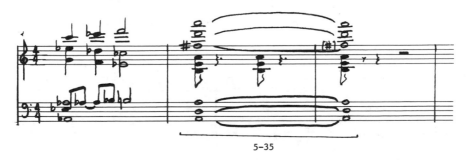

f. *Frauentanz*, op. 10

  1. Conclusion of Mvt. VI

  2. Mvt. IV, mm. 1 - 4

Copyright 1924 by Universal Edition. Reproduced by permission of European American Music Distributors Corp.

g. *Recordare*, op. 11, mm. 55 - 61

h. Violin Concerto, op. 12, mm. 197 - 201

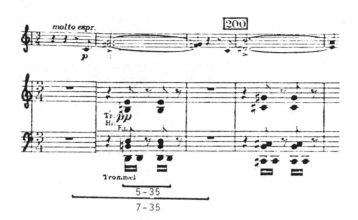

i. "In diesem Dorfe steht das letzte Haus," *Rilke-Lieder* VI, mm. 1 - 3

j. *Der Protagonist*, op. 15

1. 1 measure after 102

2.

3.   8 measures before   83

k. *Der neue Orpheus*, op. 16

1.   6 measures after   4

2.

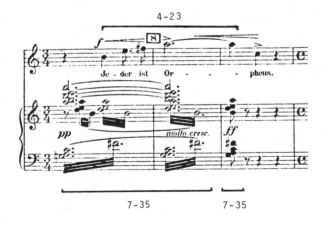

3.

4. 4 measures after [32]

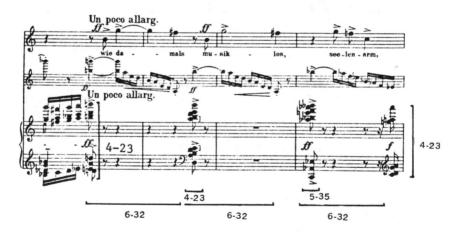

1. *Royal Palace*, op. 17

1.

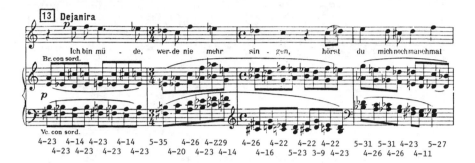

2. 121

3. 3 measures after 50

m. *Der Zar lässt sich photographieren*, op. 21

1. mm. 1 - 2

2. 9 measures after  140

n. *Die sieben Todsünden*, Mvt. V, "Unzucht," mm. 1 - 2

Example 4.27   Sonata for Cello and Piano, Mvt. I

a. T_1 mm. 1 - 5

b. T₂ mm. 12 - 19

c. T₃ mm. 46 - 51

d. T$_4$ mm. 65 - 68

e. T$_5$ mm. 95 - 96

f. Diagram of Movement I

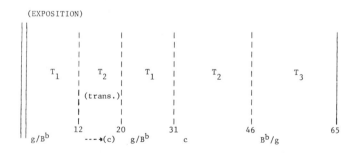

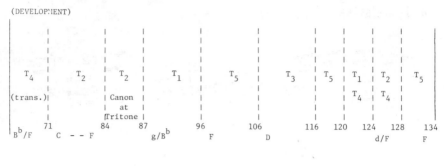

(DEVELOPMENT)

T₄ (trans.)　T₂　T₂ Canon at Tritone　T₁　T₅　T₃　T₅　T₁ T₄　T₂ T₄　T₅

B♭/F 71　C - - F 84 87　g/B♭ 96　F 106　D 116　120　d/F 124 128　F 134

(RECAPITULATION)　　　　　　　　　(CODA)

≅46-51 ≅51-55　≅56-64　≅96-105

T₃　T₃　T₃　T₅　trans.　T₁　T₁

F/d 139　F 148　F/d 159　d 162　b♭ 169 g/B♭ 174 B♭/g　g

Sonata for Cello and Piano copyright 1973 by David Drew. All examples quoted by permission of the Weill Estate, Karoline Weill Detwiler (Lotte Lenya), executrix.

Example 4.28　Cello Sonata, Mvt. I: Thematic Relationships

a.　mm. 12 - 13 (T₂)

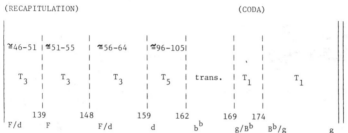

b.　mm. 40 - 42

c.　mm. 46 - 47 (T₃)

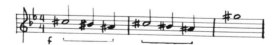

d. mm. 95 - 96 (T$_5$)

Example 4.29   Cello Sonata, Mvt. I

a. mm. 40 - 41 (piano)

b. mm. 52 - 56 (piano)

c. mm. 27 - 30 (piano)

d. mm. 68 - 70

Example 4.30   Cello Sonata, Mvt. I

a. mm. 106 - 110

b. Ostinato, mm. 174 - 181, 186 - 188

Example 4.31   Cello Sonata, Mvt. II, mm. 1 - 7

Example 4.32   Cello Sonata, Mvt. II, mm. 18 - 21

Example 4.33   Cello Sonata, Mvt. II, mm. 68 - 70

Example 4.34   Cello Sonata, Mvt. III

a. T_1 mm. 1 - 12

b. T_2 mm. 13 - 22

c. T3 mm. 77 - 81

(X) mm. 108 - 111

d. mm. 179 - 187

Example 4.34 continued

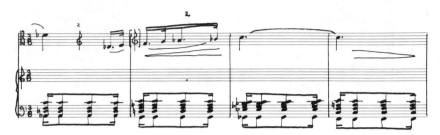

e. Diagram of Movement III

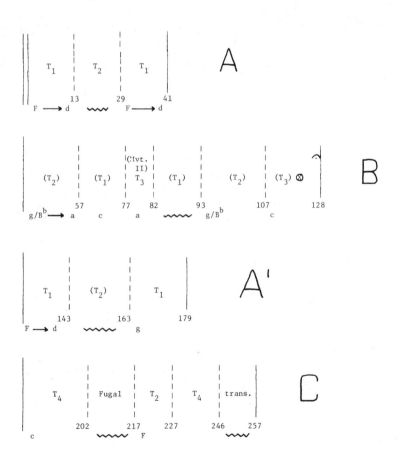

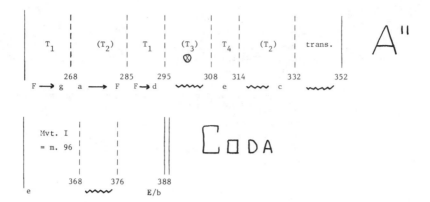

Example 4.35   Cello Sonata, Mvt. III: Harmonic Reduction

Example 4.36   Cello Sonata

a. Mvt. III, mm. 352 - 357

b. Mvt. I, mm. 96 - 97

c. Mvt. III, mm. 371 - 374

d. Mvt. II, m. 33

Example 4.37   Cello Sonata

a. Mvt. III, mm. 380 - 382

b.

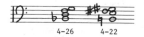

Beginning with Beethoven there exists no modern music which does not have its inner program. . . . But no music is worth anything when the listener has to be instructed as to what is experienced in it.[28]

— *Gustav Mahler* —

III

The *Sinfonie in einem Satz* or Symphony no. 1, as it has come to be known, was the first work Weill completed after joining Busoni's master class in December 1920. That the Symphony was not written under Busoni's guidance is evident from its musical language which represents only an extension of that found in the String Quartet in B minor and the Sonata for Cello and Piano. The work is solidly based in the German symphonic tradition of Mahler and Strauss, and critics have noted its kinship with Schoenberg's Chamber Symphony, op. 9 (1906), and Schreker's one-movement Chamber Symphony (1916). The extra-musical aspects of Weill's Symphony, whose autograph originally bore an inscription from an Expressionist play by Johannes R. Becher, have been treated by David Drew in his notes to the first recording of the work.[29] Because the Symphony is programmatic only in the sense that it expresses the religious and revolutionary preoccupations of Becher's play, the present discussion will concentrate on the musical construction of the work, which parallels that of the play only in the broadest outlines and overall Expressionist character.

The Symphony is scored for a rather small orchestra (compared with Weill's other orchestral works and the Symphony's predecessors— the symphonic poems of Liszt and Strauss), but it cannot be considered a work for chamber orchestra. The elaborate *divisi* string passages demand a full symphonic complement of players. The woodwind group of two flutes (second doubling on piccolo), one oboe, two clarinets (second doubling on bass clarinet), and two bassoons is similar to that of Weill's Violin Concerto, op. 12. As noted previously, Weill often utilized only one oboe or omitted the instrument altogether in many of his "double-wind" orchestrations. (See the instrumentation chart in Example 4.38.) The four-part brass choir consists of two horns, one trumpet, and one trombone.[30] The prevailing string texture in the Symphony is violins I and II *à*3, violas *à*2, cellos *à*2, and double basses *à*2. Each of the string sections is further subdivided in passages which call for solo instruments in addition to the regular *divisi* groupings. Such subdivision of the string section allowed the composer to contrast dense *tutti* passages with transparent solo combinations more typical of chamber music (and Wagner's late scores) than of the symphony or symphonic poem.

Although composed of numerous segments, the Symphony is highly integrated by continual thematic transformation which links widely separated sections of diverse character into a unified cyclic structure. The resulting formal organization defies accurate verbal description because any artificial subdivisions obscure the organic unity of the whole. Example 4.39 illustrates the tonal outline and non-literal repetition of sections within the structure. Despite the continuous thematic and tonal fabric, it is possible to divide the Symphony into three main sections with an introduction and coda. The slow introduction announces the two primary cyclic themes and foreshadows the overall tonal organization. The first large span (mm. 31-226) of the body corresponds to an opening movement of a three-movement symphonic format. Part II (mm. 227-288) can be interpreted as a slow movement preceding the finale (mm. 289-392), which is comprised of chorale-like homophonic sections alternating with imitative passages. The coda (mm. 393-420) reiterates the material of the introduction while conclusively confirming C as tonic. Each of the sections recalls portions of preceding spans so that clear-cut divisions are blurred.

The tonal procedures are extremely complex in that harmonic goals are often not explicitly delineated or function only as temporary oases of stability in the constantly evolving tonal flux. However, C serves as tonic of the whole structure, with the other pitches of the C chromatic mode invoked as secondary tonal centers. Intermixture of major and minor accounts for the pervasive chromaticism, but in the coda pure C major (mm. 403-406 "Jubelnd") precedes a characteristic Weillian modal juxtaposition as the Symphony ends unambiguously in C minor. Although C can be perceived as the central pitch of the tonal complex, the harmonic vocabulary consisting primarily of non-triadic diatonic chords often camouflages its tonal implications. For example, the opening sonority of the Symphony is a simultaneous presentation of the first six notes of the C-major scale (6-32), but it is only in the coda that the passage is distilled to a purely triadic resolution. Fifth-generated harmonic configurations (and inversions to fourth-chords) account for many progressions, and the thematic material mirrors this dependence on fourths and fifths. The semitone and tritone, often arising from linear movement within each voice, are prominent intervals in many thematic units and complement fourths and fifths in displacing the third as primary interval. The Symphony alternates homophonic sections characterized by block sonorities with polyphonic answers which Heinrich Strobel aptly described in 1927 as "explosions of the expansive harmony."[31]   Often these polyphonic passages are multi-layered combinations of linear strands of divergent harmonic implications which coalesce into a single tonality only at widely separated cadential points. Open-fifth drones (mm. 141-160), ostinato bass lines (mm. 161-170), consecutive parallel fifths in the bass line (mm. 232-237), and accompaniments derived from goal-oriented but non-diatonic scales (mm. 247-258) are constructive devices Weill employs to maintain tonal coherence among the various strata of the texture.

The thirty-bar introduction presents four principal thematic ideas (Example 4.40), all of which reappear in transformations throughout the Symphony. In fact, the last one might be considered only a derivative of the opening motive of descending fourths and fifths. This initial six-note melodic cell—a form of the Weill "ur-Motiv"—is symmetric about its midpoint; the second half is a retrograde inversion of the first. Inversion, perhaps suggested by the war-peace dichotomy in Becher's play, is the primary technique of thematic transformation in the work as a whole. A large family of derivatives could be assembled for each cyclic theme. Only the closest relatives of the opening theme are represented in Example 4.41. The original presentation of this melodic cell is accompanied by block sonorities, most of which are large diatonic sets. Movement between chords by semitones within voices veils the diatonic harmonic construction with a linearly determined chromatic overlay which dominates foreground events. The opening passage returns three times in the course of the Symphony. In its first recurrence (mm. 18-21), Weill added a chromatically descending line in the double bass and trombone which emphasizes the chromatic aspect of the progression, yet the diatonic harmonic sets remain unchanged. The implicit tonal function of this dissonant phrase is not clarified until near the end of the piece (mm. 407-410) where the passage is harmonized predominantly with triads. The C-major resolution substitutes for the three-note, fifth-generated sonority (G-D-A, 3-9) which concluded earlier presentations. This is an entirely straightforward example of Weill's manipulation of seemingly non-tonal elements within the large-scale tonal framework of the Symphony.

Part I of the main body (mm. 31-226) begins with an *Allegro vivace* that reworks the thematic material of the introduction. The presentation of new material (mm. 71-125) is abruptly interrupted by ominous recall of the first two sections of the introduction in reverse order. The final section of Part I begins with a metric combination of 4/4 and 3/8; while the solo strings in 3/8 are engaged in imitation, the isolated muted horn in 4/4 foreshadows the chorale theme of Part III. (Example 4.42a) The ensuing *Ländler*-like section in 6/8 is violently disturbed by a restatement of the material which opened Part I. A return of the "concertino" strings and suspended horn solo leads directly into Part II. This "Andante religioso" in 12/8 begins tranquilly with the distinctive principal theme introduced by the cello. However, the contemplative gentility is disrupted by reappearance of the cyclic themes of the introduction as well as elements from Part I.

The chorale of Part III is obviously symbolic of the "community's awakening to God" in Becher's play. It opens with an abortive fugal exercise which leads into a section marked "Wie ein Choral," played by oboe, clarinet, and two bassoons in four-part homophonic texture. The chorale (Example 4.42b) represents the purest example of Weill's expanded harmonic vocabulary. Four-note sonorities which represent the "double-mode" tonal language found in the Cello Sonata resolve into pure triads only at cadence points. The overall progression from B♭/g to C is colored by semitone movement in the inner voices. The fugal section after this symbolic acceptance of God is more successful than the first attempt, and the chorale returns two more times to conclude Part III. The call to a new era of peace and justice in Becher's play is paralleled by the fanfare-like summons which opens the coda of the Symphony. (Example 4.43) Again the block sonorities stated by the winds and brass are almost all fifth-generated. Set 4-26 predominates and the complete melodic configuration represents its complement 8-26. The jubilant C-major section of the coda is dominated by the first appearance in the score of bells. It is tempered by a recall of material from both the introduction and Part I; this triadic recall of earlier struggles is no longer ominous or tonally ambiguous, however. The Symphony concludes in C minor as Weill chose to leave the listener with the subdued closing section of the introduction. David Drew has observed that analogues in Becher's *Festspiel* can be found for the major musical events in the Symphony, but Weill's organization makes perfect musical sense even without extra-musical connotations.

Symphony no. 1 is an impressive achievement for a composer barely twenty-one years of age. Weill not only demonstrated masterful control of his expanded harmonic vocabulary and tonal procedures, but convincingly sustained the musical flow in a unified, twenty-five minute, single-movement structure. That this was not his first orchestral attempt is evident in Weill's confident handling of the orchestral medium—unfortunately the Symphony's predecessors have not survived. Passages revealing acute sensitivity to the sound-possibilities of the orchestra abound, but none is so striking as the passage in Example 4.44. The attention to detail evident in the differentiation of layers of sonority is especially noteworthy: double bass playing pizzicato, *arco* tremolos in the violas and cellos, solo strings playing harmonics, muffled bassoons and horns, woodwinds instructed to play with piercing tone, and each group's dynamics carefully calculated to allow each stratum to sound. Equally remarkable is the rhythmic vitality and intricate metric contrasts which blur the symmetry of many thematic units. The unity imposed by thematic transformation seems entirely natural, and the dense polyphonic texture, often comprised of seemingly aimless individual lines is always cogently controlled—a marked advance over the more academic, less "relaxed" fugal finale of the String Quartet in B minor.

Although none of the three instrumental works considered in this chapter was published during Weill's lifetime and all went virtually unnoticed until after his death, they represent a crucial episode in his development.   The innovations of the post-Wagnerian generation of German composers were gradually assimilated in these works. Although in this sense these instrumental pieces are derivative, Weill succeeded in making the stylistic elements his own to such an extent that many remained firmly entrenched in his musical language. The adoption of classic and pre-classic models which characterized the next period of his career would have produced drastically different results had not Weill already thoroughly digested the musical style of his predecessors. No amount of irony or self-conscious denial can camouflage the fundamentally romantic premise that Weill embraced throughout his career: "Music can only express human emotions." Certainly if Webern had been familiar with the String Quartet in B minor, the Cello Sonata, or Symphony no. 1, he could never have asked Dallapiccola: "Where in Weill can you find anything of our great Austro-German tradition expressed by the names of Schubert, Brahms, Mahler, Schoenberg, Berg—and myself?"[32]

Example 4.38   Instrumentation of Weill's Major Compositions

	pc.	fl.	oboe	cl.	bass cl.	alto sax	tenor sax	sop./bar. sax	bassoon	ctr.bassoon	horn	trumpet	trombone	tuba	piano	harmonium	bandoneon	guitar	banjo	harp	tympani	percussion	violin	viola	cello	bass
Protagonist		2	2	2	2				2		3	2	3								X	X	X	X	X	X
Royal Palace	1	2	2	2			1		2	1	4	2	2	1	1					1	X	X	X	X	X	X
Gustav III	2			2							2	2	1				1	1			X		1			
kl. Mahagonny				2	1	1					2	1			1						X	2				
Konjunktur		1		1	1						2	1			1							1				
Zar		2	2	2					2		3	2	2		1						X	X	X	**X**	X	X
Dreigroschenoper		1		1	1	1	1	1	1			2	1		1	1	1	1	1		X	X			1	1
Happy End		1		2		1	1	1				2	1		1	1	1	1	1		X	X				
Aufstieg (Pit)		2	1	1		1	1		2	1	2	3	2	1	1	1				1	X	X	X	X	X	X
(stage)	2			2		3			2	2	2	2	2	1	1		1			1				X	X	X
Jasager		(1)		(1)	(1)										2			X	X				X	X	X	X
Bürgschaft		2	2	2					2		3	2	1		2						X	X	X	X	X	X
Silbersee		2	1	2					1			2	2		1					1	X	X	X	X	X	X
7 Todsünden	1	2	1	2					1		2	2	1	1	1			1	1	1	X	X	X	X	X	X
Symphony no. 1	1	2	1	2	1				2		2	1	1								X	X	X	X	X	X
Quodlibet		2	2	2					2		2	2	2	2							X	X	X	X	X	X
Frauentanz		1		1					1		1													1		
Vln. Concerto	1	2	1	2					2		2	1									X	X	1			4
Rilke-Lieder I		3	2	2					2		4	2	2								X	X	X	X	X	X
VI		2	2	2					2		2	2	3								X		X	X	X	X
neue Orpheus		2	2	2					2			2	2							1	X	X	1	X	X	X
Vom Tod im Wald				2	.				1	1	2	2	2													
Berliner Requiem				2		2	1		2		2	2	2	1	1	1		1	1		X	X				
kl. Dreigroschenmusik	1	2		2		1	1	1	2			2	1	1	1		1	1	1		X	X				
Lindberghflug		2		2					2		2	2	1								X	X	X	X	X	X
Symphony no. 2	1	2	2	2					2		2	2	2								X		X	X	X	X

Example 4.39   Outline of the Structure of Symphony no. 1

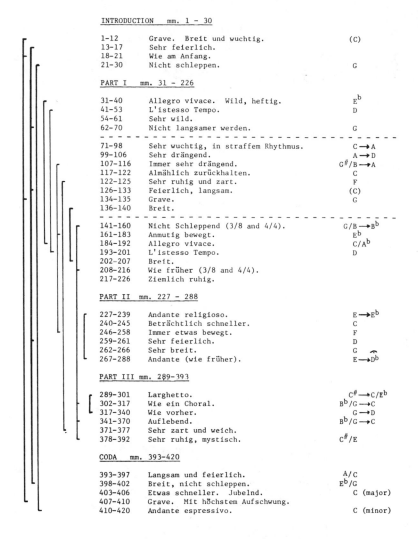

```
INTRODUCTION    mm. 1 - 30

1-12        Grave. Breit und wuchtig.                         (C)
13-17       Sehr feierlich.
18-21       Wie am Anfang.
21-30       Nicht schleppen.                                   G

PART I    mm. 31 - 226

31-40       Allegro vivace. Wild, heftig.                      Eb
41-53       L'istesso Tempo.                                   D
54-61       Sehr wild.
62-70       Nicht langsamer werden.                            G
- - - - - - - - - - - - - - - - - - - - - - - - - - - - - - - -
71-98       Sehr wuchtig, in straffem Rhythmus.                C→A
99-106      Sehr drängend.                                     A→D
107-116     Immer sehr drängend.                               G#/B→A
117-122     Almählich zurückhalten.                            C
122-125     Sehr ruhig und zart.                               F
126-133     Feierlich, langsam.                                (C)
134-135     Grave.                                             G
136-140     Breit.
- - - - - - - - - - - - - - - - - - - - - - - - - - - - - - - -
141-160     Nicht Schleppend (3/8 and 4/4).                    G/B→Bb
161-183     Anmutig bewegt.                                    Eb
184-192     Allegro vivace.                                    C/Ab
193-201     L'istesso Tempo.                                   D
202-207     Breit.
208-216     Wie früher (3/8 and 4/4).
217-226     Ziemlich ruhig.

PART II   mm. 227 - 288

227-239     Andante religioso.                                 E→Eb
240-245     Beträchtlich schneller.                            C
246-258     Immer etwas bewegt.                                F
259-261     Sehr feierlich.                                    D
262-266     Sehr breit.                                        G
267-288     Andante (wie früher).                              E→Db

PART III  mm. 289-393

289-301     Larghetto.                                         C#→C/Eb
302-317     Wie ein Choral.                                    Bb/G→C
317-340     Wie vorher.                                        G→D
341-370     Auflebend.                                         Bb/G→C
371-377     Sehr zart und weich.
378-392     Sehr ruhig, mystisch.                              C#/E

CODA    mm. 393-420

393-397     Langsam und feierlich.                             A/C
398-402     Breit, nicht schleppen.                            Eb/G
403-406     Etwas schneller. Jubelnd.                          C (major)
407-410     Grave. Mit höchstem Aufschwung.
410-420     Andante espressivo.                                C (minor)
```

Tonal Complex:

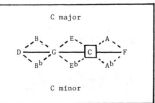

Example 4.40   Symphony no. 1

a. mm. 1 - 4

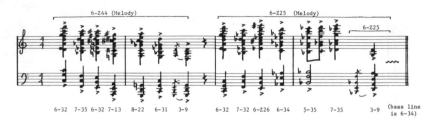

b. mm. 7 - 8

c. mm. 13 - 16

d. mm. 22 - 27

Example 4.41   Symphony no. 1: Thematic Family of First Cyclic Motive

Example 4.41 continued

Example 4.42   Symphony no. 1

a. mm. 141 - 147

b. mm. 302 - 317

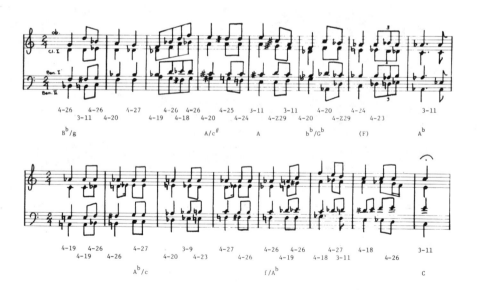

Example 4.43   Symphony no. 1, mm. 393 - 397

Example 4.44   Symphony no. 1, mm. 263 - 266

CHAPTER 5

WEILL'S MUSIC, 1922-1925:
EXPERIMENTATION

Audiences and critics are impatient with musical talents. It takes time to develop a creative style. I find it so in myself.[1]

— Kurt Weill —

I

The religious symbolism of Symphony no. 1 is still very much in evidence in Weill's next two orchestral compositions from 1922: Divertimento and *Sinfonia sacra* ("Fantasia, Passacaglia, and Hymnus"). Although neither work has survived intact, the close stylistic parallels with the Symphony are apparent from the extant material and descriptions by contemporary critics. Both works take the chorale fantasy as their point of departure for elaborate contrapuntal movements. In the finale of the Divertimento (originally Mvt. VI; Mvt. IV in Drew's reconstruction), which *has* been preserved in its entirety, religious allusions are made very explicit. Entitled "Choral," it calls for a male chorus to intone a chorale text which implores God to withhold His judgment of man's sinfulness and to substitute mercy for wrath. The chorale melody is Weill's own and differs markedly from any Lutheran prototype in construction, but not in character. (Example 5.1)

Unlike the Symphony where the untexted "Wie ein Choral" section is presented in a four-part homophonic setting and is preceded and followed by fugal passages, the finale of the Divertimento is contrapuntal throughout. The two strophes of the chorale emerge from the texture much as the chorale does in certain movements of Bach's chorale cantatas. The Bachian model for the finale is emphasized by a striking melodic resemblance between Weill's principal contrapuntal theme and that of the fourth movement of Bach's Cantata no. 140, *Wachet auf.* (Example 5.2) Of course, the extremely elaborate orchestral texture and expanded harmonic vocabulary of Weill's chorale fantasy have more in common with Reger's idiom than with Bach's. After 1925 when straightforward religious symbolism disappeared from Weill's works, the chorale remained a recurring component, but its function was shifted to the ironic or pseudo-religious. The mock-chorales of *Aufstieg, Die Dreigroschenoper, Das Berliner Requiem,* and *Die sieben Todsünden* have little in common with the fervent religiosity of the chorales in Weill's early works.[2] The "Scherzo" of the Divertimento has survived only in piano score. It reveals the first evidence of Stravinsky's influence on Weill's music. In Drew's reconstruction, this movement's light-hearted, jagged themes are set in relief against a pointillistic accompaniment that invites comparison with similar gestures of modern French composers (Ibert, Françaix). (Example 5.3)[3]

Baroque forms served as models for all three movements of *Sinfonia sacra:* chorale fantasy, passacaglia, and fugue. The musical style, however, is still Expressionist as opposed to the neo-Baroque clarity and triadic simplicity which characterize the contrapuntal movements of *Der Jasager, Die Bürgschaft,* and *Der Lindberghflug.* In these later works, musical language as well as outward form are closely related to historical models. The cool detachment of the canonic opening chorus of *Der Jasager,* for example, has none of the overt pathetic quality of the Divertimento or *Sinfonia sacra.* Through his association with the November Group and with the aid of Busoni's considerable influence, Weill was able to obtain performances of these orchestral works, even though in retrospect they were far less worthy of such than the unperformed Symphony no. 1.

Contemporary critics, most notably Strobel and Kastner, noted a gradual change in the bearing of Weill's music at this time, which they credited to Busoni's teaching. Certainly Weill's recurring use of the chorale fantasy, a favorite device of his mentor, is one manifestation of that influence. More striking is an overall "intellectual" and self-consciously "philosophical" bearing absent from the String Quartet in B minor and the Cello Sonata. On the technical side, contrapuntal lines which introduce unexpected accidentals and "deformed" scalar passages corresponding to neither chromatic nor diatonic patterns dominate melodic configurations of the Divertimento and *Sinfonia sacra.* No doubt Busoni's attempts "to exhaust the possibilities of the arrangement of degrees within the seven-tone scale"[4] found audible echoes in these scores composed under his tutelage. Although Weill's application of Busoni's one hundred and thirteen scales was far from systematic or exhaustive, it did allow additional expansion of musical language in compositions saturated with linearly-determined constructions. Passages such as those from the finale of the Divertimento in Example 5.4, in which various unorthodox scales swivel throughout the texture and dissolve into one another, allowed extension of the melodic and harmonic domain without redefinition of tonal boundaries.

Weill's String Quartet no. 1, op. 8, is even more closely related to Symphony no. 1 than the Divertimento or *Sinfonia sacra* are. Like the Symphony, the Quartet is played without pause between its three main parts: "Introduktion," "Scherzo," and "Choralphantasie." The final movement is a reworking of material from the Symphony's chorale fantasy, and several sections are little more than literal transcriptions for the reduced forces of the quartet medium. As mentioned in Chapter 1,

Two Movements for String Quartet, "Allegro deciso" and "Andantino," have survived in manuscript. Because the "Introduktion" of op. 8 borrows much of its material from the "Allegro deciso," it is possible that the Quartet was originally conceived in four movements: "Allegro deciso," "Andantino," "Scherzo," "Choralphantasie." At some point Weill may have substituted the "Introduktion" for the first two movements.

If David Drew's conjecture that the two movements which survive in manuscript were drawn from the Divertimento (as the final movement of the Quartet is based on the chorale fantasy of the Symphony) is correct, then only the "Scherzo" of the published version would be completely original to the Quartet. Drew's reconstruction of the first two movements of the Divertimento is based on this assumption. He expanded the "Allegro deciso" for *concerto grosso* treatment in an otherwise literal transcription of the quartet version. The "Andantino" of the Divertimento as it now stands is to be played by the "concertino" solo string quartet in an unaltered presentation of the version from *Two Movements for String Quartet.* In the absence of conclusive documentary evidence supplementing internal stylistic evidence to prove that the two movements in manuscript were originally part of the Divertimento and then reworked for inclusion in String Quartet no. 1, the relationship of op. 8 to the Divertimento must remain something of an unsolved puzzle. However, the connections of the published version of the Quartet with the movements in manuscript and with Symphony no. 1 are not in dispute. The relationships are summarized in Example 5.5.

Although many composers have reused material and indulged in extensive self-borrowing within their own outputs, Weill was particularly prone to this practice. Throughout his career he raided his earlier works, especially those which were unpublished or had received few if any performances. This involved not only those works written as studies or sketches for later compositions (for example, *Mahagonny-Songspiel* and *Aufstieg*), but also pieces unrelated by subject matter or medium. For example, the incomplete folder of sketches for the lost opera *Na und?* indicates that several musical ideas found their way into *Aufstieg.*[5] Similarly, *Vom Tod im Wald,* unsuccessful in its only performance as an independent composition during Weill's lifetime, was incorporated into the first version of *Das Berliner Requiem*—a version that was never performed. "Können einen toten Mann nicht helfen," originally part of the *Requiem,* was expanded into the finale of the third act of *Aufstieg.* "Der Song von Mandelay" of *Happy End* is closely related both textually and musically to the brothel scene of Act II of *Aufstieg.* Several numbers from *Happy End* turn up again in new settings in *Marie galante.* For example, the Salvation Army anthem, "In dem Jugend goldenem Schimmer," reappears in *Marie galante* as a rather bawdy fox-trot, "Les Filles de Bordeaux." This *contrafactum* is far from literal—the meter, rhythm, and character of the original "sacred" setting are altered considerably in the "secular" version. (Example 5.6a) "Das Lied von der harten Nuss," a fox-trot in *Happy End*, was incorporated without its text into the "Scène au dancing" of *Marie galante*; here the reuse borders on literal quotation. (Example 5.6c) *Der Silbersee*, whose run was cut short in Germany by Hitler's ban against performance of Weill's music, served as a source for material used in Symphony no. 2 and *Die sieben Todsünden*. In these instances and numerous others, Weill seldom borrowed pre-existent material without extensively altering and adapting it to suit the needs dictated by the new musical and textual context. It should be noted that Brecht shared this predilection for recycling "wasted" material from earlier endeavors.

Weill's practice of reworking pre-existent material is not always successful. This is particularly evident in String Quartet no. 1 where the sections based on the chorale fantasy of Symphony no. 1 are unconvincing as presented by the reduced forces of a quartet. The dense well-developed contrapuntal sections of the Symphony, in which the composer could maintain many independent lines engaged in free imitation, are reduced in Quartet no. 1 to a mere shadow of the original. Since the sparse texture of the quartet cannot support the complex interwoven fabric of the Symphony's contrapuntal resources, the fugal sections are not completely developed in the Quartet and hence seem decorative and abortive interpolations rather than logical expansions of the chorale fantasy's material. Weill found it necessary to introduce new material in the finale of the Quartet (Example 5.7) to substitute for development of the primary material. Here the strands of the polyphonic web have been reduced to three: melodic material in the two outer voices supported by busy arpeggiations in the inner voices, which mesh into a single "harmonic" background for the first violin and cello. The introduction of new material unrelated to the kernel of the movement, the chorale, is an unconvincing solution to the formal problem caused by the medium's inability to handle the pre-existent contrapuntal material.

Religious symbolism that was so integrated in Symphony no. 1 is neither prepared nor motivated in the Quartet. In the Symphony, the appearance of the homophonic setting of the chorale is already foreshadowed in the second span (the "disembodied" horn solo), so that the chorale fantasy represents a logical outgrowth and continuation of earlier events. In the Quartet, on the other hand, the chorale seems a contrived constructive device. Similarly, the instrumental recitatives

(Example 5.8) of the Quartet are novel inventions and welcome changes of texture, but nevertheless unprepared interruptions. One wonders what Busoni found in the Quartet to convince him that it was Weill's best work. Ironically, it was this derivative composition which led to Weill's contract with Universal and first brought his name to the attention of the European musical community at the Frankfurt Chamber Music Festival.

One of the most intriguing aspects of the relationship between Symphony no. 1 and Quartet no. 1 is the handling of harmonic material. Certain simultaneities found in the Symphony which included as many as eight different pitches could be played by a quartet only with numerous multiple stops. Even this solution is unsatisfactory because Weill's large diatonic, non-triadic configurations demand the stronger presentation of orchestral sonority. In the Symphony certain voices were doubled in order to emphasize particular pitches of the chord; the four parts of a quartet do not allow such subtle differentiation. Therefore, the passages borrowed in the Quartet are primarily those of the Symphony where four-note configurations predominate. Even in these cases, Weill made changes in voice-leading and altered the harmonic content. The parallel passages in Example 5.9 (the chorale and the "summons") demonstrate changes made in the Quartet. The discrepancies in the harmonization of the chorale can be attributed to voice-leading considerations,[6] but the extensive alterations in the second passage (the "summons") are indicative of Weill's effort to expand his harmonic vocabulary beyond the "double tonic" sonorities which saturated the parallel section in Symphony no. 1. The tonal outline of the chorale itself mirrored those of the entire structure of the Symphony, which opened in G and concluded in C. Because the Quartet ends unequivocally in G, the Chorale does not function as a condensation of its tonal plan.

String Quartet no. 1, of course, does not employ key signatures. Like its predecessors, its tonal structure is of the directional type where pure triads occur as goals of long spans in which continual transition from one implied tonal center to another is the rule. The endpoints of the three movements are respectively F, E, and G. Each of the movements (played as one) is multi-sectional. The contrapuntal complexity of Weill's earlier works has been simplified somewhat, and sections dominated by a lyrical melody with predominantly homophonic accompaniments alternate with polyphonic passages. The opening phrase of the "Introduktion" illustrates how far Weill's harmonic vocabulary had diverged from conventional triadic progressions. (Example 5.10) The semitone-saturated melody, which touches all twelve tones of the chromatic scale, centers on F only by nature of its endpoints and F's role as "center of gravity." The accompanying chords are predominantly fifth-generated sonorities; when triads do occur they do so in passing or "out-of-phase" with the harmonic implications of the melody. Repeated rhythmic patterns animating a homophonic accompaniment occur more frequently in the Quartet than in previous works—a parallel of the increased emphasis on accompanied melody within a transparent texture. (Example 5.11) Non-traditional scale patterns account for many decorative linear configurations. (Example 5.12)

The "Scherzo" is the most original of the movements and the most appropriate to the medium. It consists of five parts: "Vivace" in 3/8, "Alla marcia" in 4/4, "Un poco tranquillo" in 3/8, "Tempo I," and "Piu animato, quasi presto." The march, which assumes the role of Trio, is the earliest occurrence in Weill's non-theatrical scores of this idiom which already might be said to have gestic function. The "Scherzo" is open-ended in that it concludes with a suspended 22-measure ostinato figure which merely fades into the opening of the chorale fantasy. (Example 5.13) This sonority is precisely that which concludes Ravel's *Jeux d'eau.* The "Scherzo" is the most "progressive" movement in the Quartet; it represents Weill's temporary withdrawal from the extra-musical symbolism of the preceding instrumental works and foreshadows the taut angular melodic style of the Violin Concerto.

String Quartet no. 1 is obviously a pivotal work in Weill's output. It is closely tied to Symphony no. 1 and the Expressionist idiom of the Divertimento and *Sinfonia sacra.* Busoni's admonition that Weill should write "absolute" music characterized by formal conciseness and clarity of texture resulted in a new emphasis on pure melody and a reduction of contrapuntal complexity. However, the synthesis of the conflicting stylistic trends is a curious mixture which on the whole is tentative and incomplete. Religious symbolism is neither motivated nor well-developed in the Quartet, and theatrical devices such as the recitative seem to be extraneous interpolations by a frustrated composer for the theater. Weill's disposition toward vocal composition, so evident in the new emphasis on accompanied melody, is barely disguised. Two of Weill's other compositions dating from 1923—*Quodlibet* and *Frauentanz*—are more assured and successful attempts at perfecting a musical language derived from earlier works, but tempered by neo-classic ideals and an irrepressible affinity for the theater and the human voice.

Example 5.1   Divertimento, Mvt. IV, mm. 50 - 69: Chorale

Example 5.2

a. Divertimento, Mvt. IV, mm. 5 - 7

b. Bach's Cantata no. 140, *Wachet auf,* Mvt. IV, 1 - 2

Example 5.3   Divertimento, Mvt. III, mm. 1 - 10

Example 5.4   Divertimento, Mvt. IV

a. mm. 108 - 112

b. mm. 125 - 129

Example 5.5   Correspondences with String Quartet no. 1, op. 8

String Quartet no. 1, Mvt. I	"Allegro deciso" from Two Movements for String Quartet and Divertimento Wieder-Herstellung
mm. 11 - 18	mm. 50 - 55, 68 - 71
23 - 31	72 - 80
33 - 36	149 - 152
37 - 41	84 - 88

String Quartet no. 1, Mvt. III	Symphony no. 1
mm. 3 - 12	mm. 289 - 298
13 - 20	341 - 348
20 - 27	317 - 322, 348 - 356
58 - 64	382 - 390
65 - 78	323 - 340
84 - 99	302 - 317
100 - 110	357 - 366
111 - 118	393 - 399

Example 5.6

a. *Happy End*, No. 7 "In der Jugend goldenem Schimmer"

Example 5.6 continued

Marie galante, "Les filles de Bordeaux"

b. *Marie galante*, "Scène au dancing"

Happy End, No. 11 "Das Lied von der harten Nuss"

Example 5.7   String Quartet no. 1, Mvt. III, mm. 33 - 36

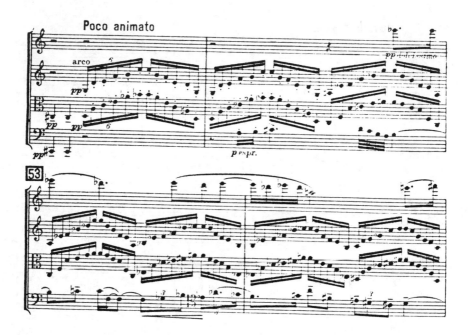

Example 5.8   String Quartet no. 1, Mvt. III

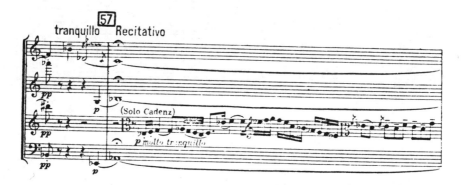

Example 5.9

a. Version of Chorale in String Quartet

b. Version of Chorale in Symphony no. 1

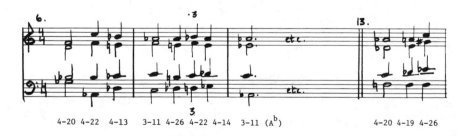

Example 5.9 continued

c. "Summons" in String Quartet, Mvt. III, mm. 111 - 115

4-20   4-18 4-12 4-6 4-26 4-23 4-14   4-20   4-16   4-27 4-26   4-23   4-16

d. "Summons" in Symphony no. 1, mm. 393 - 397

4-23   4-26   4-20 4-26   ---   4-Z15 4-26   4-26   4-26   4-26 4-20   4-26 4-26

Example 5.10   String Quartet no. 1, Mvt. I, mm. 1 - 6

Example 5.11   String Quartet no. 1, Mvt. I, mm. 10 - 12

Copyright 1924 by Universal Edition. Reproduced by permission of European American Music Distributors Corp.

Example 5.12   String Quartet no. 1, Mvt. I, mm. 31 - 32

Example 5.12 continued

Example 5.13   String Quartet no. 1, Conclusion of Scherzo

attacca

My style is melodious. People say they can recognize my music when they hear only three measures of it.[7]

— *Kurt Weill* —

II

The self-consciously "difficult" Expressionist idiom of Symphony no. 1, Divertimento, and *Sinfonia sacra*, which was tempered somewhat in the String Quartet, op. 8 by an increasing emphasis on melody, is temporarily set aside in two compositions dating from 1923: *Quodlibet*, op. 9, and *Frauentanz*, op. 10. *Quodlibet*, subtitled "entertainment music," was based on Weill's ballet-pantomime, *Die Zaubernacht* (1922), and thus represents the first of Weill's compositions originally conceived for the theater to have survived intact. Undoubtedly the nature and scenario of *Die Zaubernacht*, intended for performance as children's theater, prompted the response from Weill that differs so markedly from the instrumental works of 1921-22. Scored for wind and brass instruments in pairs with a full string section, *Quodlibet* ("Suite aus dem Pantomime *Zaubernacht*") was described by various contemporary critics as "lively, delicate, lightly-flowing, and transparent"—adjectives which could not be applied to Weill's earlier orchestral works. In discussing his youthful compositions, Weill categorized *Die Zaubernacht's* predecessors as "immature and lacking stylistic impulse." He cited the ballet as "the first work in which the simple style can be recognized."[8]

In writing for the *theater* and an audience of *children*, Weill felt doubly compelled to simplify his music: "In the theater I can still display 'artistic' simplicity to a certain extent, but with children I must remain totally stringent in my simplicity."[9] This goal is revealed on virtually every page of *Quodlibet*. The dense contrapuntal texture that characterized the earlier orchestral works is consistently avoided, with only a few faint echoes, such as the passage in Example 5.14. Melody supported by an active but predominantly homophonic texture is the rule, and there are a surprising number of passages in orchestral unison. Traditional dance idioms appropriate for the magical scenario of the ballet follow one another throughout the multi-sectional suite. Various episodes in each movement differ in tempo, thematic material, and character, but because of the underlying theatrical impulse, the composer did not feel compelled to introduce artificial unifying devices. Ever-present, sharply-defined rhythmic gestures animate the melody-dominated texture, and ostinato "motor-rhythms" substitute for imitation and polyphony as the foremost constructive feature. Passages involving a slow-moving lyrical theme presented over one or two repeated rhythmic figures within a predominantly homophonic texture occur throughout *Quodlibet*. The excerpts in Example 5.15 might easily be mistaken for sections of works dating from 1927-35, when the "simple" style was conclusively and permanently adopted in Weill's compositions.

With the avoidance of contrapuntal or even genuine polyphonic texture, linear constructions play a diminished role in *Quodlibet* in comparison with earlier works. As a result, the harmonic vocabulary is more triadic and the overall tonal organization rather conventional, although fifth-generated configurations are still frequently employed, and the chromaticism inherent in the combination of major and minor modes is omnipresent. Most indicative of the new quest for clarity are regular phrase structures, closed by rhythmically well-defined cadences. Instrumental recitatives for flute, clarinet, bassoon, and cello are only the most overt demonstration of Weill's emerging preference for primary colors in his orchestration. Generally avoiding the mixed sonority that resulted from frequent inter-choir doubling in his earlier orchestral works, Weill carefully delineated his melodic lines and accompaniment in *Quodlibet* with an orchestrational technique derived from classical models. In fact, *Die Zaubernacht* and its derivative suite are Weill's first genuine neo-classic compositions. He does not merely borrow older forms in the service of an antithetical musical idiom (as in the *Sinfonia sacra*), but rather adapts fundamental traits of classical musical style for his own purposes. The exaggerated pathos of his Expressionist pieces has been excised in favor of concision and clarity of expression.

If one were charged with arranging Weill's German works in chronological order on the basis of stylistic evidence alone without recourse to external data, a strong case could be made for Symphony no. 2 as the immediate successor to *Quodlibet*. Scored for precisely the same orchestra (but in its final version, without *Quodlibet*'s elaborate percussion part), Symphony no. 2 displays the same clarity of form, transparency of melody-dominated texture, rhythmic vitality, and theatrical impetus as *Quodlibet*. The Symphony also includes a movement based on a funeral march, just as the third movement of *Quodlibet* does. Both compositions conclude with frenetic movements based on dance idioms. In actuality, the two works are separated by ten years, 1923-1933. These closely related and stylistically similar orchestral works must be seen in retrospect as the endpoints of Weill's neo-classic period in Germany, but the path between them is far from direct. Weill followed several trails which proved to be dead ends before determining his ultimate destination. The diversions were necessary expeditions into uncharted territory where he explored the boundaries of his musical language.   While such excursions did not lead to the anticipated terminus, they expanded the scope of his means of expression and eventually allowed him to regain his original course with renewed confidence in its validity.

The immediate successor to *Quodlibet* was *Frauentanz*, op. 10, a song cycle for soprano, accompanied by flute, clarinet, bassoon, horn, and viola, which substituted for the ill-favored oboe in the standard woodwind quintet.[10]   A setting of seven modernized adaptations of *Minnesinger* poems, *Frauentanz* takes its starting point from the style of the only vocal number in *Die Zaubernacht*, the "Arie der Fee."   A piano-vocal reduction of this aria, which has survived in manuscript, illustrates the vocal origin of Weill's new emphasis on accompanied melody.   A rhythmically animated homophonic texture accompanies the soprano line, which is characteristically chromatic and modally ambiguous. (Example 5.16) The text is set to music without repetition of words or phrases; clear declamation and straightforward presentation of the poem preclude extensive polyphony. Similarly, in *Frauentanz* the integrity of the seven poems is respected.   The small instrumental ensemble is subdivided still further so that only the first and fourth songs utilize the entire group. *Frauentanz* comprises the following movements:

I   "Wir haben die winterlange Nacht" (Dietmar von Aiste)

     Andantino, quasi Tempo di Menuetto
     soprano, flute, viola, clarinet, bassoon, horn
     38 measures

II   "Wo zwei Herzen-liebe an einem Tanze gan" (Anonymous)

     Allegro non troppo
     soprano, clarinet, bassoon, horn
     48 measures

III   "Ach wär' mein Lieb ein Brünnlein kalt" (Anonymous)

     Molto agitato
     soprano, flute, clarinet, viola, bassoon
     27 measures

IV   "Dieser Stern im Dunkeln, sieh" (Der von Kürenberg)

     Tranquillo e molto piano
     soprano, flute, viola, clarinet, bassoon, horn
     28 measures

V   "Eines Maienmorgens schön tat ich früh aufstehn" (Herzog Johann von
                                                             Brabant)
    Allegro leggiero e scherzando
    soprano, viola
    78 measures

VI   "Ich will Trauern lassen stehen" (Anonymous)

    Allegretto giocoso
    soprano, flute, clarinet, bassoon, horn
    36 measures

VII   "Ich schlaf, Ich wach, Ich geh, Ich steh" (Anonymous)

    Tranquillo dolente
    soprano, flute, clarinet
    52 measures

The title's allusion to dance is made musically explicit in the first song, marked "Andantino, quasi Tempo di Menuetto." Although this is the only movement specifically identified with a particular dance idiom, the rhythmic vitality so evident in the preceding ballet score infuses the entire cycle with a dance-like quality. All of the movements except the final one involve changes of meter. In the second and fourth songs, metric juxtapositions approach Stravinskian complexity as measures in 2/8, 3/8, 4/8, 5/8, and 3/4 alternate with one another. Metric freedom allowed Weill not only to capture precisely the linguistic rhythm of the poem, but also to employ extremely complex rhythms in the accompaniment.

Each of the songs is a compact miniature, ranging in length from 27 to 78 measures; the duration of the entire cycle is only eight minutes. None of the songs is set strophically, nor is the textural refrain of No. VI paralleled by a corresponding musical refrain.[11] All of the songs are *durchkomponiert* in that there is minimal large-scale repetition of musical segments. The music is content to "present" the poem without illustrative effects—unlike Weill's early songs such as "Reiterlied," where musical depiction is of central concern. In *Frauentanz*, however, the overall mood of each poem is only generally mirrored in the tempo, instrumentation, and accompaniment of the musical setting. Weill does not attempt psychological characterization, even though a number of the texts are conducive to such treatment, so integral to the nineteenth-century song cycle. The resulting emotional detachment of the music of *Frauentanz* awards the text greater importance.

With its lack of textual repetition and its accompanying ensemble that varies from one to five instruments, the cycle is one of the most condensed and "economical" of Weill's works. Its musical structure is dictated by the form rather than the content of the poem; in this sense, *Frauentanz* represents Weill's return to "absolute" music. The clarity, balance, and limited means of expression indicate how enthusiastically Weill had embraced Busoni's call for a "new classicism." Although one can discern Weill's personal signature in each of the songs, *Frauentanz* has close ties with the chamber music of Hindemith and Stravinsky. In fact, the fifth movement of the cycle for solo viola and voice could just as well be subtitled "Homage to Stravinsky." Its model is apparent—Weill composed *Frauentanz* during the summer of 1923, when *L'Histoire du Soldat* received its German premiere.

There is no other composition in Weill's output that is so dependent upon fifth-generated constructions. While the vocal part is highly chromatic, usually touching all twelve pitches of the scale within a short span, harmonic configurations are often entirely diatonic. Pure triads occur infrequently, and when they do occur, their tonal function is ambiguous. The conclusion of the first song is a prime example. (Example 5.17) The vocal part cadences in what would be unambiguous F major were it not for the accompaniment, which is out of phase with the voice. When the instruments finally reach F three measures later, it is F minor, and it occurs only in passing. The instruments cadence with the outer voices (bassoon and clarinet) presenting a linear progression of V−I in F major, but the inner voices render any conclusive tonal implications ambiguous by a characteristic semitone-sidestep to D minor. As a result, the final chord is a D-minor triad, which in no way can be construed as tonic. In fact, one is hard-pressed to identify a tonic *triad* for a single movement of *Frauentanz*.

This is not to say that the work is atonal, for each song is tonal in the broadest sense of the term—loyalty to a tonic pitch rather than to a key or triad. A central pitch emerges as tonic in each song (or in some cases a different pitch for each strophe or section) by virtue of its restatement and its position as the "center of gravity" of melodic and harmonic configurations. This expanded concept of tonal structure has more in common with medieval modality than with a tonal system based on functional harmonic relationships. It is probably not mere coincidence that Weill chose to invoke such musical organization in his setting of medieval texts. Because the bass line is saturated with movement by fourths and fifths which no longer have dominant—tonic implications in Weill's harmonic context, familiar progressions are stripped of their conventional tonal relationships and the listener's expectations are not fulfilled. Fifth-generated linear and harmonic configurations (especially ostinato patterns) further contribute to the tonal ambiguity. The principal sonority is 4-23 (generated by successive fifths); Example 5.18 presents only a few of the most apparent occurrences of this sonority and its close relatives.

It is not surprising that *Quodlibet* and *Frauentanz* were two of Weill's most widely performed works composed before 1927. Both are accessible, assured, well-crafted compositions in which the ideals of a new classicism are achieved: economy of means, clarity and conciseness of form, avoidance of extra-musical effects, renunciation of false pathos. Weill accomplished the shift from "the spasms of excess" of Expressionism to the restraint of "the new music" without constricting his expanding harmonic vocabulary. For the most part, *Frauentanz* avoids the triad and traditional tonal progressions while it preserves the coherence of a controlling tonal center within a diatonic harmonic vocabulary. Perhaps correlatively, the lyricism of the song composer finally takes precedence over the polyphony of the instrumental composer. Having reached his Busoni-inspired goals with apparent ease, Weill was not content with this intermediate position. He immediately set out to expand the materials of his musical language still further in the works dating from 1923 to 1925.

Example 5.14　　　*Quodlibet*, Mvt. I, 5 measures before 13

Example 5.15   *Quodlibet*

a. Mvt. I

b. Mvt. III

Example 5.16   *Die Zaubernacht,* "Arie der Fee"

Example 5.17   *Frauentanz,* Mvt. I

(Dietmar von Aiste)

Example 5.18   Frauentanz

a. Mvt. IV, mm. 1 - 4

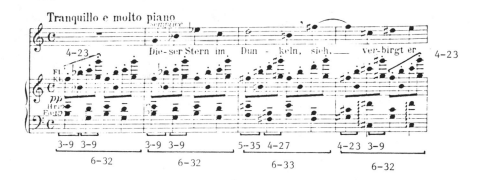

b. Mvt. I

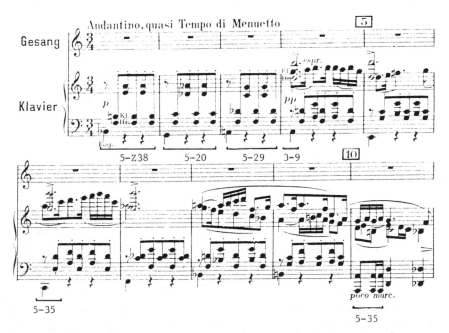

Example 5.18 continued

c. Mvt. II

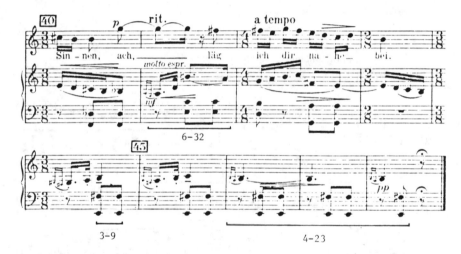

d. Mvt. III

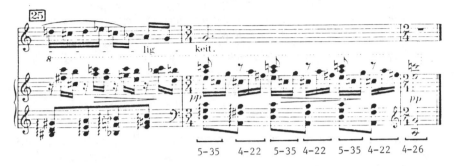

e. Mvt. V.

If someone has something to say, it is not important what means he uses so long as he knows how to use them.[12]

— *Kurt Weill* —

III

There is no more accurate description of Weill's compositions dating from 1923 to 1925 than his own: "Artistic experiments characterized by struggles for new harmonic and melodic means of expression overpowered my work."[13]   The four works which survive from this period—*Recordare*, op. 11; Concerto for Violin and Wind Orchestra, op. 12; two movements of the *Rilke-Lieder*, op. 13 & 14; *Der Protagonist*, op. 15—represent Weill's musical language at its most complex.   The originality of form and content in each of these works is indicative of their wide-ranging experimentation.   The juxtaposition and intermixture of tonal and non-tonal elements and procedures again renders existing terminology inadequate to describe structural organization.   Various vague labels such as "free atonality," "free dissonance," "quasi-tonality," and "quasi-atonality" have been invoked by critics to describe the musical language of these works which in fact lie on the often indistinct boundary between tonality and atonality—terms whose definitions are themselves open to some controversy.   It is a difficult task to describe precisely a predominantly non-triadic musical language which encompasses non-tonal constructions in tonal contexts and traditional tonal gestures in non-tonal structures.   The analytic dilemma is particularly acute because of the deliberately experimental posture of the works—there is no continuity of approach even within this limited group of compositions.   Because each of the "studies" represents an intuitive rather than systematic attempt to expand harmonic, melodic, and formal resources, each must be considered individually on its own terms.   While a detailed analysis of each is beyond the scope of this study, some observations concerning the range, nature, and outcome of Weill's experimentation are in order.   Ultimately Weill retraced his steps back to a simpler style, but he carried with him a new sense of freedom and technical expertise won in his struggle with non-tonal materials.

The group of compositions as a whole reflects Weill's effort to come to grips not only with new expressive means, but also with his own role as an artist in the morally and financially bankrupt society of the Weimar Republic.   All four works are suggestive of a vehement quest for identity—personal, religious, aesthetic, social, and, most important, musical.   Composed when Weill had abandoned the orthodox religion of his parents (at least in practice), *Recordare* and the *Rilke-Lieder* intensify the overt religious symbolism of the Divertimento and *Sinfonia sacra*, which had been temporarily set aside in *Quodlibet* and *Frauentanz*. The appeal for mercy in the chorale text of the finale of the Divertimento is far less desperate and personal than the impassioned yearning of Rilke's mystical-religious poems that Weill selected from *Das Stundenbuch*:

> But misery's lore I've not fully learned,—
> and that's why this great darkness makes me small;
> it's You? grow heavy then, break down the wall;
> and so shall your whole hand to me befall
> and I to you with my whole piteous cry.[14]

The text of *Recordare*, the fifth chapter of Lamentations of Jeremiah, also must have been laden with symbolic associations for post-war Germany;

> 1   Remember, O Lord, what has befallen us;
>   behold, and see our disgrace!
>
> 2   Our inheritance has been turned over to strangers,
>   our homes to aliens.
>
> 3   We have become orphans, fatherless;
>   our mothers are like widows.
>
>   . . .
>
> 14   The old men have quit the city gate,
>   the young men their music.
>
>   . . .
>
> 21   Restore us to thyself, O Lord, that we may be restored;
>   Renew our days as of old!
>
> 22   Or hast thou utterly rejected us?
>   Art thou exceedingly angry with us?

Even the Violin Concerto embodies fragments of the "Dies irae" in its first movement. It seems that no matter how hard Weill tried to write "absolute" music, elements with extra-musical associations could not be excised without relinquishing his fundamental premise that music must express a universal theme. Although an interpretation of *Der Protagonist* as an autobiographical work would be presumptive, its alternative search for identity—the actor's unsuccessful retreat into art for ultimate reality— suggests Weill's own abdication of religious concerns in favor of the social and moral activism of his theatrical compositions.

Although composed just two months after *Frauentanz, Recordare* has little in common with the almost carefree clarity and lucidity of its immediate predecessor. Scored for *a cappella* mixed chorus and boys' choir, *Recordare* assumes the form of a long one-movement, multi-sectional motet, incorporating Renaissance and Baroque polyphonic techniques within a modern melodic and harmonic vocabulary. The formidable demands of its part-writing, more conducive to performance by instruments than by voices (Example 5.19), and its intentionally austere features account for the fact that it was not performed during Weill's lifetime. As in its formal models, Renaissance and Baroque motets, the Latin text of *Recordare* is treated very freely. Often several verses are presented simultaneously in various voices, and certain textual phrases are repeated both within sections and throughout the work. In particular, the opening entreaty, "Recordare, Domine" ("Remember, O Lord"), is continually reiterated—as counterpoint to another verse, as an omnipresent ostinato in some passages, as the text of the "*cantus firmus,*" or as a homphonic motto introducing or concluding the presentation of other verses. (Example 5.20) The musical material associated with "Recordare, Domine" comprises the primary thematic web of the entire structure and constitutes a closely related motivic family, whose members are related by augmentation, diminution, and inversion, as well as less rigorous procedures of thematic transformation. (Example 5.21)

The five principal constructive devices in various sections of the motet-like setting are free imitation in all voices, imitative polyphony with a *cantus firmus*-like slow-moving theme in one voice, recitative, ostinato, and syllabic declamation in a homophonic texture. Although the choral fabric is thereby continually varied and the entrance of the boys' choir midway through the twenty-three minute work opens additional possibilities for variation of color, *Recordare* maintains a consistently somber mood throughout in mirroring the general content of the text. An overall heaviness results from the almost unrelieved 4/4 meter, whose ponderous tempo (Grave—Largo—Sostenuto—Molto tranquillo—Largo) is only infrequently quickened. The rhythmic vocabulary, usually so animated in Weill's works, is surprisingly stagnant, and there is an unsettling lack of forward propulsion—a weariness that may not have been altogether intentional. The limited variation of tempo, rhythm, meter, and mood is counteracted by a number of exquisite passages which testify to Weill's sensitivity and imagination in handling his choral forces. The "Molto tranquillo" section in which the two-part boys' choir is engaged in animated polyphonic exchanges over a homophonic sustained accompaniment by the mixed chorus is one of the most hauntingly beautiful passages in any of Weill's works. (Example 5.22)

Unlike *Frauentanz* and *Quodlibet*, in *Recordare* confluence of independent contrapuntal lines is responsible for the majority of harmonic constructions. The predominance of the perfect fourth, minor second, and their composite—the tritone—as melodic intervals is reinforced by the replacement of the third by the fourth in many harmonic configurations. The interval of the fourth is often presented simultaneously in both melodic and harmonic statements. In Example 4.26g of the preceding chapter, the perfect fourth is the basis of the harmonic progression which includes several occurrences of 4-23 (as the pure fourth-chord) and a non-diatonic linearization of the Db—Ab tetrachord which interrupts the harmonic progression. Non-triadic structures generally take precedence over triads, except in those sections where the simplification of harmonic language parallels a reduction in contrapuntal complexity for dramatic effect. The "Converte nos, Domine" section (mm. 220-236), for example, is entirely homophonic and tonally unambiguous as phrases begin and end with triads. However, in most cases, triads serve more as temporary points of rest from contrapuntal motion than genuine harmonic goals—coincidental products of voice-leading that are favored no more than other sonorities. Even when sections conclude with a minor triad (the major form seldom occurs), its function is that of "final" rather than tonic. Of course, any modal relationships are submerged in the pervasive chromaticism, but one does not readily perceive a tonal framework for *Recordare*. Although many melodic configurations center on D, conclusive cadences confirming D as tonic are not to be found. A glance at the concluding sonorities of various sections in Example 5.20 indicates that triads account for only six of eighteen. Often conflicting harmonic implications of individual voices result in an ambiguity which is nowhere more apparent than in the final phrase. (Example 5.23) It concludes on 3-9 (D — A — E) with A predominating only by virtue of doubling and the powerful D — A bass progression.

One might invoke Stravinsky's "pole of attraction" as an analytic concept to describe Weill's harmonic procedures in the compositions dating from 1923 to 1925:

> We find ourselves confronted with a new logic of music that would have appeared unthinkable to the masters of the past. And this new logic has opened our eyes to riches whose existence we never suspected. Having reached this point, it is no less indispensable to obey, not new idols, but the internal necessity of affirming the axis of our music and to recognize the existence of certain poles of attraction. Diatonic tonality is only one means of orienting music toward these

poles.   The function of tonality is completely subordinated to the force of attraction of the pole of sonority.   All music is nothing more than a succession of impulses that converge toward a definite point of repose.   This is as true of Gregorian chant as of a Bach fugue, as true of Brahms's music as Debussy's. . . .

In view of the fact that our poles of attraction are no longer within the closed system which was the diatonic system, we can bring the poles together without being compelled to conform to the exigencies of tonality.[15]

In retrospect, one can perhaps view Weill's expanded harmonic vocabulary and procedures of organization as extensions of directional tonality to a type of polar control.   In so doing, what Stravinsky called the "exigencies of tonality" could be avoided entirely or at other times utilized to reinforce a polar goal.

This analytic approach is particularly applicable to Weill's Concerto for Violin and Wind Orchestra, op. 12.   Composed during April-May 1924, it consists of three movements:

I   Andante con moto

II   a   Notturno
      b   Kadenza
      c   Serenata

III   Allegro molto un poco agitato.

Although its tripartite second movement finds its formal predecessor in Mahler's Symphony no. 7 (1904-05), the Concerto has far more in common with the musical language of Stravinsky's *Soldier's Tale* (1918), *Symphonies of Wind Instruments* (1921), and the *Octet* (1923).   Scored for ten wind instruments, tympani, percussion, and four double basses, the Concerto was performed at the 1926 ISCM Festival in Zürich, which also included Stravinsky's *Octet* on its program.   Contemporary critics such as Heinrich Strobel and Theodor W. Adorno were quick to point out the influence of Stravinsky in the Concerto's instrumentation, rhythmic ostinatos, and harmonic vocabulary.   In addition, the pervasive rhythmic figure of the Serenata bears a striking resemblance to the ostinato in the third movement of Hindemith's *Kleine Kammermusik für fünf Bläser*, op. 24, no. 2. (Example 5.24)   Despite these associations, the Concerto is by no means derivative; its unique combination of Busoni-inspired lucidity and clarity of sound within an overall polyphonic texture is entirely Weill's own.

The Concerto stands somewhat isolated among Weill's works; it was the last purely instrumental work that he composed for the concert hall until Symphony no. 2 (1933).   *Kleine Dreigroschenmusik*, a derivative from a theatrical work, is the only intervening instrumental work. The Concerto's closest stylistic relative is not its chronological neighbors, *Recordare* or *Der Protagonist*, but *Vom Tod im Wald* (1927). Also scored for ten wind instruments, *Vom Tod im Wald* opens with a duet for trombones that parallels the clarinet duet with which the Concerto begins. (Example 5.25) But there are premonitions of gestures and mannerisms characteristic of Weill's later scores—particularly in the dance-like Notturno. Its repeated dotted rhythmic figures, so prevalent in *Die Dreigroschenoper*, *Aufstieg*, and *Die sieben Todsünden*, and the solo xylophone part are unmistakably "Weillian." (Example 5.26) In addition, rhythmic ostinatos and pedal tones which are crucial constructive features of the Concerto remain functional throughout his later works.

In the Concerto's complex harmonic idiom, pedal tones and ostinatos often anchor the poles toward which the remaining voices proceed in non-tonal progressions. In Example 5.27, for instance, the open-fifth drone supports the tortuous linear polyphony and points toward the unambiguous cadence on D that concludes the section. The passage also includes the pair of punctuating five-note chords (m. 38) which continually recur at structural seams of the first movement. Usually these chords consist of one or two closely related sonorities, 5-14 and 5-24, which often reappear at the same pitch levels. Near the end of the movement (mm. 204-205), the gesture is repeated, but the sonority is a D-minor triad, related to the earlier chords by linear progressions of a minor second in almost all voices. This is only the most audible case of Weill's manipulation of non-tonal elements resulting in a large-scale reinforcement of a pole—D in this case. Yet even at the conclusion of the movement, the principal pole of D is obscured with a final G#-minor cadence—a tritone away from the movement's center of gravity. A similar passage in which a Bb-pedal provides coherence to the non-triadic harmonic idiom, dependent on five- and six-note non-diatonic sets, occurs in mm. 144-154 ("Tempo secondo"). The pedal tone substitutes for an ostinato which served an analogous function in the first occurrence of the material. (Example 5.28)

The traditional dramatic battle between the soloist and accompaniment evident in the angular first movement is relaxed in the lighthearted second movement. Each of the three sections allows melodies to soar above rhythmically animated accompaniments. The sub-movements are joined together by virtue of the fact that none ends conclusively, but instead makes transition to the next. Following a clear cadence on A, the Notturno dissolves into the Kadenza with a tonally ambiguous ostinato. (Example 5.29) A pianissimo Eb played by the trumpet acts as a bridge from the Kadenza into the Serenata, which again ends with a repeated rhythmic pattern that comes to rest on 4-14. Although the harmonic goals of individual spans of the abandoned finale are more clearly articulated than in the preceding movements, there is no simplification of musical idiom. Even the gentle tranquillity of the "Un poco meno mosso," which interrupts the tarantella-like movement, is continually threatened by the uneasy combination of the conflicting poles of A and G. (Example 5.30) The coloristic murmuring of the wood-winds centering on A major occurs over a G-pedal that is present throughout. To enhance the harmonic palette further, the oboe's alternation between B♭ and B creates additional tension in fluctuating the modal inflection of G from major to minor. Finally, the solo violin leads to a resolution in A. The frenzied conclusion to the movement is again tonally unstable, and the final cadence in F, itself unambiguous, solves none of the previous puzzles of the harmonic idiom. (Example 5.31)

The straightforward tonal conclusion of the Concerto is an artificial solution to the composer's dilemma concerning how to "end" a piece rather than to "stop" it. In a tonal work, the reaffirmation of the tonic often gives a sense of finality to the ending because it represents a large-scale resolution of earlier events. In the Violin Concerto, several different poles—B♭, D, F, E♭, F♯, for example—are equally powerful in various sections. Therefore, the final dominant-tonic cadence in F is not perceived as a large-scale resolution, but instead as a punctuation telling the listener (whose response to such a traditional gesture could be anticipated) that the composition had ended. Similar clear-cut tonal cadences subdivide the structure of *Der Protagonist*, but there they usually are directly motivated by dramatic events which demand a musical analogue. For example, the final sonority of *Der Protagonist*, a G-minor triad played by three trombones, emerges inevitably from a seven-note diatonic sonority based on G. (Example 5.32) Because the triadic conclusion had been prepared only seconds before by the intentionally hackneyed D-major fanfares for the entrance of the duke, the tonal conclusion is entirely convincing—unlike that of the Concerto.

The harmonic vocabulary of the Concerto is far more diversified than that of any of Weill's earlier compositions. To be sure, fifth-generated sonorities still occur frequently, as in the excerpt of Example 5.33. But Weill's musical language has been expanded to include bonafide atonal sets (e.g., 4-Z15)—sonorities without pan-diatonic connotations or implicit tonal function. The harmonic idiom is most easily studied in those passages where vertical constructions take precedence over confluent polyphonic lines. A straightforward excerpt from the first movement appears in Example 5.34. While vertical and linear presentations of atonal sets are utilized throughout the Concerto, there are few instances of systematic manipulation and integrated relationships which characterize atonal organization by Schoenberg, Berg, or Webern.[16] It is precisely the intuitive nature of Weill's control of his resources that poses such formidable analytic problems. Weill's compositional process was not based on a rigorous external system, but a creative and imaginative impulse that obeyed only his inner ear.

Nowhere is the acuity of that ear more apparent than in the orchestration of the Concerto. The clarity and diversity of sound he extracted from his limited instrumental forces in the Concerto are never surpassed in his later works. Although Weill himself made the piano reduction of the score—the only version published during his lifetime— the musical idiom of the Concerto cannot be condensed to the medium of violin and piano. Any study of his harmonic practice must be done from the full score, for the reduction omits not only details of orchestration but often compromises the actual notes of the composition.

Whether motivated purely by musical reasons or by the different demands of an operatic score, *Der Protagonist* represents a return to a structural organization based on directional tonal procedures. Although its harmonic vocabulary is almost identical to that of the Violin Concerto, Weill's first major theatrical success replaces polar affinities with clearly defined tonal goals. This is not to imply that the triad becomes the dominant sonority. On the contrary, the musical language is as non-triadic as that of any previous compositions, but its harmonic materials are treated in such a way that triads are articulated in conclusive cadences and serve as genuine goals of the musical flow. In every sense *Der Protagonist* is the synthesis of the experimentation of its predecessors, which Weill considered to be studies for operatic composition. It is the climax of his early development—an assimilation of the linear polyphony, non-tonal materials, pervasive chromaticism, and constructive devices that were so carefully but sometimes unsuccessfully explored in earlier works.

No other work is so characteristic of Weill's early style; yet to a listener who knows Weill only through his collaborations with Brecht, there are few superficial clues that the same composer was responsible for both. The vocal style of *Der Protagonist* has virtually nothing in common with the restricted range and modern dance idioms of the epic song style. The singers of *Der Protagonist* are expected not only to negotiate formidable vocal demands equivalent to those of Mahler and Strauss, but also to handle the equally difficult task of delineating their "real" characters from the "acted" roles in the two pantomimes, in which there are no texts to aid them. The triumphal success of the Dresden premiere can be attributed as much to that company's group of outstanding singing actors as to Weill and Kaiser. Its limited success elsewhere can be traced to the inability of other houses to find a tenor equal to the title role. That the majority of critics hailed it as a perfect blend of drama and music, rivaled only by *Wozzeck* (see Chapter 1), indicates how firmly Weill's commitment to the theatrical aspects of opera was entrenched already two years before his initial collaboration with Brecht. Indeed, if any limited group of works can be taken as representative of Weill's career in Germany, it is the three collaborations with Kaiser, not the more famous and homogeneous Brecht-Weill products. *Der Protagonist* (1924-25), *Der Zar lässt sich photographieren* (1927), and *Der Silbersee* (1932) present Weill at three critical points of his European career: the culmination of his early period, the transition to the simpler style, and the final work completed in Germany. A detailed examination and comparison of these scores, three of Weill's finest, would constitute a more profitable basis for the study of his musical style than a similar investigation of the Brecht-Weill works.

Unfortunately, in the present study a few comments about the remarkable score of *Der Protagonist* must suffice. As in the Violin Concerto, Weill's command of the orchestra cannot be overlooked. The unique placement of a wind octet on stage with the idiosyncratic orchestra (consisting of two oboes and bass clarinets, three horns and trombones, percussion, and strings) in the pit not only produced extraordinary combinations of sounds, but also imaginatively and precisely differentiated the pantomimes from the remainder of the opera. Without relying on musical depiction, Weill tapped all the resources at his command to communicate the tragedy of an artist consumed by his art. The variety in the opera's harmonic idiom, barely hinted at in Example 4.26j of the previous chapter, is extraordinary, yet the diverse elements of traditional tonal progressions, fifth-generated harmonies, non-tonal constructions, and complex polyphonic texture are united in an entirely convincing and individual synthesis. Despite his aesthetic objections to music drama, Weill had learned his lessons from Wagner well: it is the vocal line which cements all components into a logical whole. No matter how obscure the harmonic orientation of the accompaniment, the voice, acting in conjunction with the powerfully constructive bass line permeated by ostinatos and pedal tones, points toward the ultimate destination. Weill's control of his complex harmonic material manifested itself in a formal structure that obeyed only the intrinsic requirements of the music while still corresponding precisely to dramatic events. The theme-and-variations of the first pantomime is only one of many examples of Weill's uncanny sensitivity to musical organization that is itself a commentary on dramatic events. The freedom gained by his mastery of musical language allowed Weill to incorporate coloristic passages based entirely on the interval of the second without losing overall tonal coherence. (Example 5.35)

The success of *Der Protagonist* did not deter Weill from pursuing additional possibilities of extending his musical resources. Acutely aware of the isolation of the operatic composer, Weill turned to jazz and the cabaret in an attempt to communicate with a larger audience. Although some of the effects of this infusion are similar to the clarity and simplicity of *Quodlibet* and *Frauentanz*, the path of the transitional works dating from 1926 to 1927 is fundamentally a new one. Undoubtedly Weill's mature style would have been much less colorful and assured were it not for the fruitful experimentation of the Busoni-inspired compositions of 1922-1925.

Example 5.19   Recordare, mm. 139 - 140

Example 5.20   Recordare: Formal Outline

Section	Meter	Tempo	Text	Procedures	Concluding Sonority
mm. 1 - 22	4/4	Grave	v. 1	4-part free imitation	3-11 (C#)
23 - 58	4/4	Poco animato	v. 2 - 6	cantus firmus	4-23 (1,3,8,10)
59 - 61	4/4	(Poco animato)	Recordare, Domine	homophonic	4-23 (3,5,8,10)
61 - 68	4/4	(Poco animato)	v. 7	homophonic	4-14 (0,1,5,10)
69 - 81	4/4	Un poco tenuto	v. 7 - 10 Recordare, Domine	ostinato	3-11 (a)

Example 5.20 continued

82 – 101	3/4,4/4		v. 11 – 14 Recordare, Domine	recitative	3-11 (c)
102 – 108	4/4	Largo, Vivo	Recordare, Domine v. 7	homophonic	4-13 (1,2,8,11)
109 – 127	4/4	Allegro moderato	v. 15 Recordare, Domine	cantus firmus	3-11 (e^b)
128 – 138	4/4	(Allegro moderato)	v. 15 – 16 Recordare, Domine	ostinato	4-27 (3,5,8,11)
139 – 143	4/4	poco a poco allargando	v. 15 – 16 Recordare, Domine	cantus firmus in Kinderchor	5-27 (0,1,5,8,10)
143 – 151	4/4	Sostenuto	v. 16 Recordare, Domine	ostinato	3-11 (c♯)
151 – 167	4/4	Molto tranquillo	v. 1, 7, 16	2-part polyphony over homophonic acc.	5-35 (2,4,7,9,11)
168 – 184	4/4	(Molto tranquillo)	v. 7, 16 – 18 Recordare, Domine	ostinato	6-27 (2,4,5,7, 8,11)
185 – 219	3/4	Maestoso	v. 19 – 20	free imitation	3-11 (c)
220 – 233	4/4	Largo	v. 21	homophonic	6-30 (0,1,4,5 7,10)
234 – 236	4/4	(Largo)	Domine	homophonic	(F,C)
237 – 245	4/4	(Largo)	v. 22 Recordare, Domine	ostinato	3-12 (1,5,9)
246 – 252	4/4	(Largo)	Recordare, Domine	ostinato & recall of opening	3-9 (2,4,9)

Example 5.21   Motivic Family Related to "Recordare, Domine"

Example 5.22   *Recordare*, mm. 150 - 155 "Molto tranquillo"

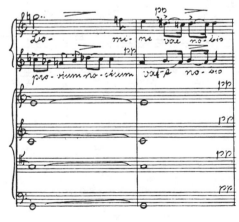

Example 5.23   Recordare, mm. 244 - 252

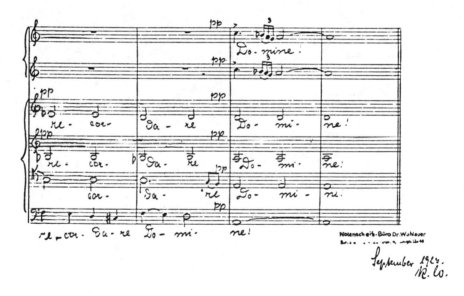

Example 5.24

a. Violin Concerto, Mvt. IIc "Serenata," mm. 1 - 4

b. Hindemith: *Kleine Kammermusik für fünf Bläser*, op. 24, no. 2, Mvt. III, mm. 1 - 3

Example 5.25

a. Violin Concerto, Mvt. I, mm. 9 - 16

Example 5.25 continued

b. *Vom Tod im Wald*, mm. 1 - 11 (trombones)

Example 5.26   Violin Concerto, Mvt. IIa, mm. 46 - 47

Example 5.27

a. Violin Concerto, Mvt. I, mm. 34 - 44

b. Punctuating Chords:

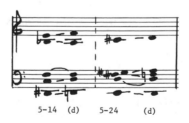

5-14 (d)   5-24   (d)

Example 5.28   Violin Concerto, Mvt. I, mm. 45 - 48

Example 5.29   Violin Concerto, Mvt. IIa, mm. 97 - 105

Example 5.30　　Violin Concerto, Mvt. III

a.　mm. 171 - 173

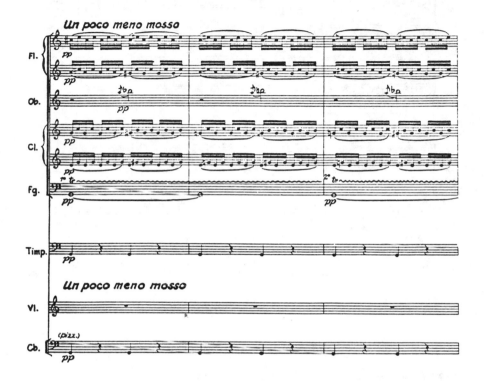

b. mm. 192 - 197

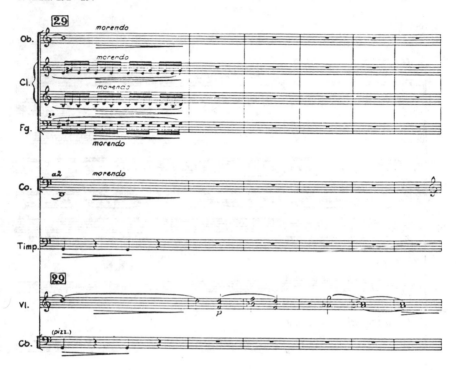

Example 5.31   Violin Concerto, Mvt. III, mm. 280 - 290

Example 5.32   *Der Protagonist*, conclusion

Example 5.33   Violin Concerto, Mvt. IIc, mm. 26 - 28

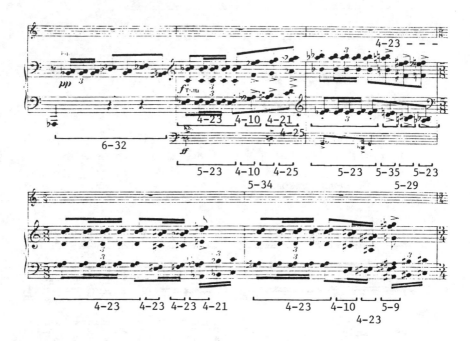

Example 5.34   Violin Concerto, Mvt. I, mm. 183 - 187

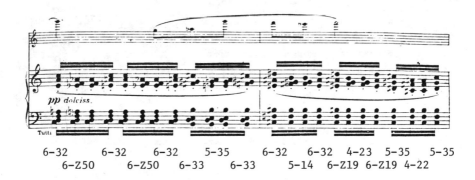

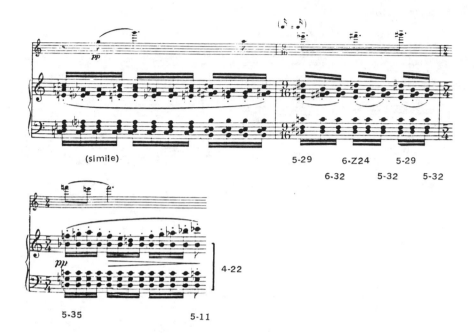

Example 5.35   *Der Protagonist*

a. (p. 65)

Example 5.35 continued

b. (p. 117)

CHAPTER 6

WEILL'S MUSIC, 1926-1933: SYNTHESIS

I have determined—something I already discovered with Der neue Orpheus—
*that I am gradually forging ahead to "me," that my music is much surer,
freer, looser, and—simpler.*[1]

— *Kurt Weill* —

I

      Weill considered *Der neue Orpheus*, composed in September 1925,
to be the first of a series of works in which he synthesized into an
assured personal style his previous experimentation, his longstanding
commitment to modern musical theater, his novel incorporation of
elements from popular dance music, and his new aesthetic goals.
Unfortunately, the compositions from this period of transition (1926-27)
have not all survived, so that a complete map of Weill's journey cannot
be reconstructed.   His intermediate junctions—incidental music for
Herzog Theodor von Gothland (1926) and his first full-length opera *Na
und?* (1926), both of which are now lost—would complement the
fragmentary account revealed in *Der neue Orpheus, Royal Palace* (1925-
26), *Der Zar lässt sich photographieren* (1927), and the *Mahagonny-
Songspiel* (1927).   Because the aesthetic and theatrical aspects of this
period in Weill's career were discussed in Chapter 3, here the focus will
be exclusively musical: the emergence of the mature style.
      The first evidence of a departure from the idiom of the Violin
Concerto and *Der Protagonist* is found in *Der neue Orpheus* and *Royal
Palace*, premiered on the same bill at the Berlin Staatsoper on Weill's
twenty-seventh birthday.   *Der neue Orpheus* represents a unique
combination of concerto, cantata, opera, and cabaret song. Isolating the
solo violin from the rest of the orchestra that includes violas, cellos,
basses, but no violins, Weill juxtaposed remarkably diverse musical
elements in his setting of Iwan Goll's free-verse surrealist poem.
Although the harmonic idiom of the cantata is no less complex than that
of *Der Protagonist*, references to popular musical material motivated by
the text are incorporated within a clear tonal structure. In setting the
text, Weill took as his starting point the vocal style of *Der Protagonist*,
which is traditionally "operatic" in its wide range, its independence from
continual doubling in the orchestra (as found later in Weill's song-style),
and its formidable technical demands on the singer. (Example 6.1)
Throughout the cantata there is a delight in virtuosity for the soprano,
violin, and orchestra alike that manifests itself more in distinct layers of
sonority than in genuine polyphony.

Constructive devices perfected in his early works are omnipresent: pedal tones, rhythmic ostinatos, fifth-generated sonorities, double-tonic diatonic configurations, non-tonal local events. All are combined in *Der neue Orpheus* with a freedom that can only be described as eclectic, because the most critical unifying mechanism of Weill's mature style—his repetition of distinctive motor-rhythms within a predominantly homophonic texture—is not yet functional. The recitative-like passage in Example 6.2 illustrates Weill's mastery of his harmonic materials and his extraordinary ability to articulate a text so that it can be easily understood. Although the tonal implications of the passage are not in doubt by virtue of the D pedal and the unambiguous vocal cadence on A, the punctuating chords (predominantly hexachords) demonstrate how far Weill's harmonic vocabulary is removed from a purely triadic basis. This excerpt centers on D, the generator of the concluding sonority, 5-35.

Such adept manipulation of non-triadic materials within a tonal framework looks backward to earlier works, but the central section of the cantata (mm. 170-293)—a set of seven variations—is entirely premonitory of the path ahead. Goll's vivid images allowed Weill to invoke popular musical idioms at the behest of the poem, which described the activities of "the new Orpheus":

Orpheus sings to men about Spring—

On Wednesday between half-past one and half-past two As a shy piano teacher liberates a girl from a mother's avarice	Variation 1: Allegretto 2/4 (quasi arpa)
Evenings in the "World-Cabaret" Between Yankeegirl and contortionist His Couplet about love for humanity is number three	Variation 2: 3/4 (waltz)
A clown at midnight In sunny golden circus Awakes the sleepers with a giant kettledrum	Variation 3: Piu animato 4/4 (circus)
Sundays for organizations of war veterans In dance halls adorned with oak foliage He is conductor of liberty songs	Variation 4: Alla marcia 4/4

Skinny organist
In quiet vestries
Playing the organ sweetly for
    Jesus-children

Variation 5:   Poco sostenuto

In all subscription concerts
    with Gustav Mahler
He drives unmercifully over hearts

Variation 6:   Vivo 3/8
               (scherzo)

In suburban movie houses on the
    "Torture-piano"
He has the Pilgrims' Chorus lament
The death of the virgin

Variation 7:   L'istesso tempo

Gramophone
Pianolas
Steamorgans
Spread Orpheus's music

On top of the Eiffel Tower
On September 11
He will give a wireless concert.

The literary images of the dance hall, circus, Mahler's subscription concerts, silent-movie pianos, and cabaret songs prompted Weill to depict each in a variation. Thus, the new stylistic impulse of musical features derived from popular models was suggested by the text and remains depictive. It does not yet serve as independent commentary on a text which has no literal association with dance idioms, as Weill's later music does. Overall, the cantata is a tentative and somewhat unsuccessful juxtaposition of old and new; undoubtedly it was the vestiges of Weill's "difficult" idiom of the Violin Concerto that moved Hugo Leichtentritt to write in his review of the premiere that "Weill has taken this cabaret number too seriously and has made of it a complicated piece of symphonic writing."[2]   Weill himself evidently recognized that the combination was by no means a satisfactory synthesis. His next work, *Royal Palace,* composed immediately after *Der neue Orpheus* and completed more than a year before the premiere of the cantata, represents a more thorough "digestion" of the simpler style based on the cabaret song and modern dance idioms.

As noted in Chapter 3, the dance idioms of *Royal Palace,* still arise from direct and literal correspondences with dramatic events, and therefore are illustrative rather than gestic in function. The fox-trot and tango are, however, incorporated into the entire structure of *Royal Palace* in such a way that they are not abrupt interpolations as they were in *Der neue Orpheus*, but logical and natural developments of preceding musical material. More important, sharply-defined propulsive rhythms are not limited to those passages involving explicit use of dance. Rhythmic ostinatos, often unrelated to any dance-derived stereotypes, are found throughout the score. The excerpt in Example 6.3 illustrates a number of features that eventually emerge as permanent characteristics of Weill's personal style. Most obvious is the repeated rhythmic pattern of the accompaniment. Just as idiosyncratic is the immediate restatement of a vocal phrase a minor third higher, often with a change in modal inflection. In the example, only one word, "Müde," is involved, but ultimately the technique is extended to encompass four- to eight-bar phrases. The B pedal provides a focus for the pervasive chromaticism and the harmonic progressions containing powerful bass movement and chromatic slides in the inner voices. Triads seldom occur in pure form, and many sonorities are fifth-generated. The ambiguity that stems from bass movement by fifth, which does not correspond in tonal function to the remainder of the harmonic context, is admirably demonstrated at the "Allegretto" of Example 6.3. Much of what can be called uniquely "Weillian" in terms of harmonic practice can be traced to the conflict between the contrasting tonal implications of bass progression and accompanying harmony.

It is unfortunate that the disastrous libretto of *Royal Palace* precluded any chance of success at its premiere and that the loss of the full score kept the opera in relative obscurity until recently. It can be seen as the genuine breakthrough into the simpler style—completed a year before Weill began his collaboration with Brecht. After this work, the first of Weill's to use saxophone, the direction of his stylistic development is set. *Zar* and the *Mahagonny-Songspiel* merely reinforce and solidify the new synthesis. To be sure, passages of Busonian polyphonic complexity and non-tonal constructions continue to appear in all three works along with the simpler style—sometimes co-existing uncomfortably, but the ultimate supremacy of tonality, simplicity of form, and clarity of texture are no longer in doubt. *Royal Palace*, as a combination of ballet, film, and opera, also suggested new avenues to Weill for enlarging the technical resources of modern opera.

Der Zar lässt sich photographieren, begun two months before the *Mahagonny-Songspiel*, is one of Weill's few attempts at comic opera—*Na und?* and *Happy End* (a play with music) were its less successful counterparts. *Zar* is the most thoroughly integrated operatic score that Weill composed. It is the last of his theatrical works to be set to music throughout; after the *Mahagonny-Songspiel* Weill preferred the number-opera format, which allowed him to work with small, closed musical forms rather than the continuous musical flow of *Zar*. In addition, in that format music was no longer responsible for conveying the plot, which could be advanced in intervening sections of dialogue. As a result of the large-scale design of *Zar*, its internal unity is unmatched by any of Weill's later operas. The most recognizable and admittedly superficial indication of this overall continuity is found in a comparison of the opening and concluding measures of the opera. (Example 6.4) The tonally ambiguous opening gesture, dominated by melodic statements of the fifth as well as fifth-generated harmonies, is "resolved" up a semitone at the conclusion of the opera. The passage ends with an E-minor triad and a cymbal "tag" that thereafter becomes a Weill mannerism.

More significant and less obvious relationships tie various segments of the score together. The most straightforward device is simple motivic repetition or transformation, functional in Weill's earliest instrumental compositions. Repetition of sizeable passages, such as the fox-trot in Example 6.5, also relates widely separated sections of the libretto. More important, such repetition itself comments on the dramatic situation in that its restatement brings to mind the theatrical events associated with earlier occurrences of the material. Note also that the musical language, although tonal, is seldom triadic; the harmony of the passage in Example 6.5 is entirely fifth-generated, while the vocal part is more dependent on triadically-based patterns. The interruption of the action by comments of the male chorus from the orchestra pit also functions structurally and formally. Often these "mysterious" interjections take place under dialogue and in the quartal-harmonic setting of Example 6.6. These comments by the uninvolved male chorus not only delineate major divisions of the score but also serve as a "distancing" agent, reminding the audience that the events on stage are to be interpreted comically. A purely musical mechanism which pervades the structure of *Zar* is the use of rhythmic and melodic ostinatos. One of the most powerful ostinato figures appears in Example 6.7. Its melodic shape, saturated with semitones, is very similar to the four-note motivic cell associated with "Where shall we go?" in the "Benares Song" of the *Mahagonny-Songspiel*. By far the most effective constructive device in *Zar* is its interrelated chain of tonal centers, usually given explicit definition in triadic cadences that conclude rather short segments and that correspond to the completion of the events on stage. Unlike *Der Protagonist*, where tonal centers are seldom audible as such, *Zar's* web of intermediate goals can be readily distinguished.

The modern dance idioms in *Zar* corroborate Weill's assertion that he did not borrow harmonic or melodic material from jazz—only its rhythmic vitality and formal clarity. For example, the "Tango Angèle," which includes the first occurrence of a "gramophone solo" in opera, has little in common with the melodic style or harmonic vocabulary of its popular model.   Weill's tango (Example 6.8) is tonally ambiguous throughout, although A minor ultimately emerges as the goal of its open-ended structure.   The harmonic idiom of *Zar* in general is an integrated combination of triadic and fifth-generated constructions, always within a tonal context.   The few genuinely atonal passages, such as the ten-note set (see Example 4.26 m-2) which occurs at the climax of the opera, are employed in direct response to the dramatic situation and do not obscure the overall tonal outlines.   For example, in Example 6.9 the C pedal in the voice gives tonal coherence to the additive fifth-generated harmonic configurations in the accompaniment (4-23, 5-35, 6-32, 7-35).   No matter how complex the harmony or how remote the progression, Weill's regard for proper voice-leading (usually by semitone in all voices except the bass) provides the necessary connections, usually non-traditional and unexpected, between successive chords related to one another by third- or fifth-movement in the bass. (Example 6.10)

Rather than the decisive stylistic change in Weill's music for which Brecht claimed credit, the *Mahagonny-Songspiel* represents only another logical step in Weill's quest for clarity and simplicity.   The three innovations introduced in the *Songspiel* are its unique orchestration (2 violins, 2 clarinets, 2 trumpets, saxophone, trombone, piano, and percussion), its new elements of vocal style borrowed from popular song, and its self-contained musical numbers.   Because the *Songspiel* had no plot and consisted of six distinct poems expressly intended as *Songs*, Weill could treat each as a separate musical entity.   The combination of the simpler vocal style that first appears in the *Mahagonny-Songspiel* with the dance idioms that were already present in *Royal Palace* and *Zar* yielded a new genre, the *Song*.   In the orchestral interludes which linked the six *Songs* into a *Songspiel*, however, Weill was not bound by any limitations inherent in the new *Song*-style and was therefore free to write in the undiluted harmonic idiom of *Zar* and *Royal Palace*.   As demonstrated in the excerpts of Example 6.11, the composer did not abandon fifth-generated harmonies, double-tonic constructions, or non-tonal sets in the *Songspiel*.   Instead, the harmonic language remains remarkably similar to that of *Zar* and *Royal Palace*, but the clarity of texture, vitality of rhythms, and unobscured tonal implications of the bass-line make the overall idiom *seem* simpler.   It is a commonly held fallacy that Weill's mature style is consistently triadic—an accurate description only of *Der Jasager* and, to a lesser extent, of *Die Bürgschaft*.

The *Mahagonny-Songspiel* is by no means an endpoint in Weill's development.   One need only compare the "Alabama Song" from the

Songspiel with the later version from *Aufstieg* to see a continuing process of simplification. Parallel passages from both settings are presented in Example 6.12. Although the melody is the same in both settings, the harmony of the second version is significantly simpler, with the continual semitone alterations occurring in a predominantly triadic rather than fifth-generated harmonic context. The tonal implications made explicit in the ubiquitous pedal tones are the same in both versions, but in the *Aufstieg* presentation Weill saw fit to simplify the texture and to excise the pungent dissonance of the fifth-generated harmonies found in the *Songspiel* setting. It is clear from Examples 6.11 and 6.12 that the *Songspiel* was neither a radical departure from earlier works nor a stylistic plateau which, once reached, remained unchanged in its successors. Instead, the *Mahagonny-Songspiel* must be seen only as a culmination, albeit a temporary one, of Weill's synthesis of his unique musical language. He discarded none of his previous harmonic innovations, but merely distilled this material down to its purest form and clothed it in a form-fitting vocal style, rhythmic texture, and instrumentation. The *Song* emerged as the most distinctive but not the only manifestation of the simpler style. Although one can speak of a "mature" style in Weill's works dating from 1928 to 1935, it should not be inferred that this represents a stabilization of compositional materials or techniques. Each of the works is a specific and individual response to the demands of intellectual content and theatrical intent. While the results share a number of identifying characteristics that stamp them as unmistakably "Weill," the mature compositions represent as wide a variety of approach and experimentation as did the earlier works.

Example 6.1   Der neue Orpheus, mm. 132 - 135

4-23

Example 6.2   *Der neue Orpheus*, mm. 83 - 90

Example 6.3   Royal Palace

Example 6.4   *Der Zar lässt sich photographieren*

a. mm. 1 - 2

b. Conclusion

Example 6.5   *Der Zar lässt sich photographieren*

Example 6.6   *Der Zar lässt sich photographieren*

Example 6.7   *Der Zar lässt sich photographieren*

Example 6.8   *Der Zar lässt sich photographieren*

Example 6.9   *Der Zar lässt sich photographieren*

Example 6.10   *Der Zar lässt sich photographieren*, 2 measures after 25

Example 6.11   *Mahagonny-Songspiel*

a. No. 1, mm. 1 - 6

b. No. 1a, Kleiner Marsch

3-9 - - - - - - - 4-23 3-9

c. No. 5a, Sostenuto (Choral)

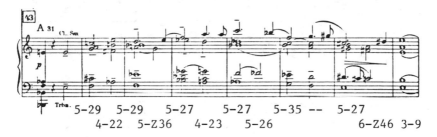

5-29   5-29   5-27   5-27   5-35 --   5-27
4-22   5-Z36   4-23   5-26   6-Z46 3-9

d. No. 5, Vivace assai

5-1

Example 6.12   "Alabama-Song"

a. *Mahagonny-Songspiel* version

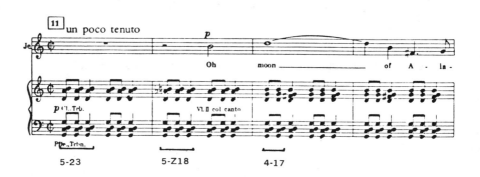

ba - - ma, we now _____ must say good

b. *Aufstieg* version

Oh show us the way to the next whis-ky bar.

For we must find the next

Oh don't ask why, oh don't ask why

b. *Aufstieg* version (continued)

*Music can only express human sentiments. I'd never write a simple measure
for purely aesthetic reasons in an effort to create a new style.*[3]

— *Kurt Weill* —

II

For anyone familiar with it, Weill's unmistakable musical style is far
easier to recognize than to describe. Throughout this study references
have been made to Weill's "mature" style, without either defining the
term or citing its identifying characteristics, although a number of
pertinent aspects were discussed in detail in Chapter 3. Naturally, when
dealing with so imaginative and prolific a composer as Weill, no group of
works is entirely homogeneous and no one composition a faithful
representative of its chronological peers. Many of the misconceptions
about Weill's output originated from the attempt to extrapolate on the
basis of the style of a few well-known works such as *Die Dreigroschenoper*; the result has been a misleading and incomplete image. Yet
unquestionably there is a "Weill-style" that imprints each of his
compositions dating from 1928 to 1935 with his own unforgeable
signature. As Ian Kemp has astutely observed, "while it is relatively easy
to devise a 4-bar *incipit* that could be mistaken for genuine Weill, any
attempt to develop it into a complete musical form, however small,
would reveal the absence of the qualities peculiar to his mastery."[4]
Although Weill's musical style defies (but certainly has not discouraged)
imitation, perhaps it is possible to isolate some of its distinguishing
components, now that their evolution in his earlier works has been
traced. Such an attempt can by no means be exhaustive, for each work
exhibits idiosyncracies unique to it alone that thwart any expectations the
listener may have accrued in his experience with Weill's other
compositions. In addition, the totality of Weill's musical style far exceeds
the sum of its individual components by virtue of the intuitive yet
supremely disciplined manner in which they are combined.

Nevertheless, selected examples from *Der Silbersee*—the last work
Weill completed in Germany and a virtual compendium of stylistic
features also found in his other works—will provide the basis here for a
summary of attributes of the mature style. *Der Silbersee*, a play in three
acts with sixteen musical numbers, incorporates the recitatives,
polyphonic choruses, heroic vocal style, and elaborate instrumentation[5]
characteristic of Weill's operas along with the simpler vocal style of the
Songs typical of his "plays with music." *Der Silbersee* could just have
easily been designated a dialogue-opera, but no government-subsidized

opera house would have been permitted to mount it in 1933.   That the Leipzig Opera's former director, Gustav Brecher, conducted one of the premieres of *Der Silbersee* is indicative of the substance and nature of the score.   The following examples illustrate a number of stylistic traits common to Weill's works from 1928 to 1935:

Example 6.13

a. *Der Silbersee*, No. 6: mm. 6 - 15

b. *Der Silbersee*, No. 10

Modern dance idioms, whether explicitly labelled as such or not, appear throughout Weill's mature scores. In Example 6.13a, Weill specifically identified the musical number as a tango. The G-pedal present throughout the passage is continually reiterated as *local* tonic—the tango ends solidly in C. The close proximity in the vocal line of B♭ and B, C♯ and C, E♭ and E keeps the modal definition in suspense. Implicit in the use of the distinctive tango-rhythm in every measure is an unchanging rhythmic pattern. Example 6.13b, although not identified as such, is a fox-trot. The regular phrasing and repeated two-bar rhythmic pattern is entirely characteristic, as is the intermixture of E♭ and c minor as a double-tonic sonority.

Example 6.14

a. *Der Silbersee*, No. 7

b. *Der Silbersee,* No. 3

Accompaniment patterns based on repeated rhythmic cells or traditional ostinatos are crucial to Weill's mature style. In Example 6.14a, the propulsive dotted rhythm of the accompaniment contrasts with the equally distinctive repeated rhythmic pattern of the melodic material. The orchestration of thematic material first for two trumpets and then for two clarinets is entirely in keeping with Weill's preference for primary solo colors set in relief against the rest of the orchestra. The bass movement in a sequence of descending fifths is also typical, as is the regular binary phrase grouping punctuated by unambiguous cadences. The harmonic progression of stepwise movement by semitone in the inner voices is fundamental to Weill's harmonic practice. Example 6.14b illustrates Weill's juxtaposition of major and minor (G), which insures modal ambiguity, over a four-note ostinato. Continual vacillation between major and minor within a chromatic harmonic and melodic context is a hallmark of his music.

Example 6.15

Der Silbersee, No. 16

Double-tonic sonorities, usually combining a major and minor triad related to one another by the interval of a third (4-20, 4-26) function in Weill's music from the Cello Sonata to the "Moritat vom Mackie Messer" to this example which concludes in G/b.

Example 6.16

a. *Der Silbersee*, No. 6a.

b. *Der Silbersee*, No. 14

b. *Der Silbersee*, No. 14 (continued)

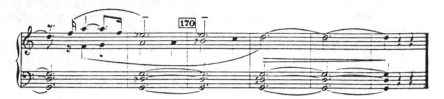

Harmonic constructions connected to one another through semitone-movement in most if not all voices account for some of the most striking progressions in Weill's music. In Example 6.16a, the dramatic juxtapositions of E minor and C minor, A minor and F minor, C# minor and C minor chords are intensified by the octave-displacement that inverts the semitone connection to a major seventh. The remote progressions are subjected to the rigorous control of the G-pedal, as well as traditional bass movement. Throughout Weill's works from this period, remote harmonic progressions, which often occur at dramatic climaxes, are usually repeated several times, either at the same pitch or in sequence, so that by sheer restatement the ear accepts the logic of their non-traditional construction. Often Weill avoids use of the third in final chords, preferring unisons, octaves, or fifths which preserve modal ambiguity. In Example 6.16b, the semitone movement from D♭ to D does not result in vacillation between major and minor forms of a triad, but between perfect fifth and tritone—an interval that Weill employed extensively (often consecutively) because its demand for resolution could be intentionally avoided or accomplished in unexpected ways. Note the gestic repetition of a rhythmic cell by percussion, another Weill trademark.

Example 6.17

Der Silbersee, No. 3

Der Silbersee, No. 3 (continued)

Often the tonal implications of Weill's bass lines, permeated by fifths and fourths that the listener tends to hear as tonic-dominant relationships, conflict with the remaining harmonic material. In Example 6.17, the bass-line is entirely traditional and carries unmistakable tonal implications. However, the alternating statements of E minor and E major in the remaining voices are "out-of-phase" with the bass progressions by two measures. The resulting peculiar ambiguity and duality accounts for the suspended tension of many passages in Weill's scores. The listener cannot easily reconcile the conflicting tonal implications which usually remain unresolved until the final cadence.

Example 6.18

Der Silbersee, No. 16

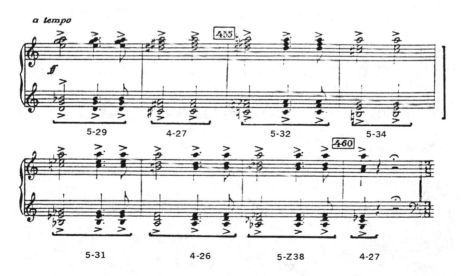

Passages containing non-tonal harmonic constructions still occur frequently in the "simpler" mature works—usually, however, within a tonal framework.   In Example 6.18, the suspended A-pedal in the upper voice acts as the tonal center and foreshadows the resolution to D major in m. 461.   But the internal logic of the progression stems from linear movement in each voice—a chromatic descent which results in a parallel chain of identical sets, 4-27, which is also the goal of the passage.   An almost identical construction can be found in Weill's Cello Sonata (1920).   [See Example 4.35.]

Example 6.19

a. *Der Silbersee*, No. 12 (p. 91)

b. *Der Silbersee*, No. 16

c. *Der Silbersee*, no. 6a

Constructions generated by the perfect fifth—the basis for much of Weill's harmonic vocabulary in his early works—are still integral to the mature style. As shown in Example 6.19a, b, fifths often account for both linear and harmonic configurations. Consecutive fifths in the bass line, related to one another by intervals of a semitone or tritone, are frequently invoked to negate the stability of the fifth by remote linear progressions. Example 6.19c indicates that Weill still utilized fifth-generated sonorities to replace triads at cadence points.

While this brief survey in no way sufficiently characterizes Weill's mature style, the examples from *Der Silbersee* demonstrate that his musical language during this period consists of a synthesis of elements found in his earlier compositions. He never completely abandoned the double-tonic sonorities, fifth-generated constructions, and contrapuntal complexity of his works dating from 1919 to 1925. Rather, the mature style is a condensation and refinement of these materials and experiments. Modern dance idioms, powerful gestic rhythms, and the *Song*-style, which first enter Weill's music during 1925-27, are totally integrated in these later scores. Clearly Weill's distinctive mature style was not a sudden shift or radical departure from that of his earlier works. It is not attributable to the influence of Brecht or anyone else, for it represents the natural culmination of a decade of experimentation—the product of one of the most imaginative musical intellects of the twentieth century.

Let us not, at this particular juncture, worry ourselves, about a precise evaluation of Weill's importance or lack of it. Too much has already been spoken and written while so much of the music is still waiting to be heard again. But without falling back on the idle excuse that time alone will tell— for time alone does not tell anything other than the appalling lateness of the hour—let us at least remember with respect a human being whose qualities are reflected in his art.[6]

— David Drew —

III

A conclusion to this study of Weill's career in Europe is in many respects an artificial terminus, for this overview represents only a beginning of the long overdue scholarly inquiry into his music. Another large and fascinating collection of compositions—his American works— awaits investigation. An accurate appraisal of Weill's legacy cannot be undertaken until this aspect of his diverse output receives critical attention. For Weill's American career, which began when he was thirty-five and at the peak of his creative power, is a continuation and culmination of his lifelong commitment to musical theater in the broadest sense. A study of the American works is perhaps more problematic than the present one, in spite of the formidable documentary issues confronted here, because the often intangible effects of a foreign cultural environment and tradition on an emigrant creative artist must be considered. Yet no fair assessment of Weill's significance can be based on the European works alone. The division of his output into two categories determined by geographical residence is itself misleading, for Weill was an international composer—not only because he wrote original works in German, French, and English, but also because his subject matter and appeal are universal. He was the foremost spokesman for the turbulent Weimar period, and at the same time the unsuspecting prophet for an entire century whose social upheavals and spiritual turmoils are powerfully and accurately reflected in his music. His compositions have survived and will continue to do so because their multi-layered duality and ambiguity transmit timeless issues of concern to all, while raising more questions than they answer.

The present study furnishes a foundation for further inquiry. Detailed analyses of individual compositions will necessarily supplement the stylistic observations cited here. The translations of Weill's major essays will enable both musical and theatrical scholars to compare his ideas with those of his contemporaries, as well as with those of Brecht.

Certainly Weill's role in the development of epic theater must be reassessed now that the extent of his contribution is known. The very form and structure of epic opera can be traced, at least in part, to Weill's adoption of historical models such as *opera seria* and his incorporation of the advances of Busoni and Stravinsky. Weill's distinctive musical style has been shown to be far less dependent on jazz and popular music than previous commentary has led us to believe. Firmly rooted in the late romantic German tradition of Mahler and Reger, his music attained new dimensions of harmonic freedom as a result of his experimentation under Busoni's tutelage. The rhythmic vitality and formal clarity gleaned from his encounter with modern dance idioms were assimilated during the period of transition, 1926 to 1927. Finally, all of these elements achieved a conclusive synthesis in the highly refined and thoroughly personal mature style.

The chronicle of Weill's European career which introduces this study indicates that contemporary critics considered him to be the foremost composer for the theater of his generation and a leader of the "new music." Before his initial association with Brecht, Weill had achieved international stature as a composer and with *Der Protagonist* had enjoyed the first sustained operatic success from the younger generation of German composers. His collaboration with Georg Kaiser, the most famous and prolific German Expressionist playwright, was resumed after the more celebrated association with Brecht had dissolved, because Weill's commitment to opera would not allow music to become subsidiary to theatrical, social, or political elements. At the time of his emigration to the United States in 1935, Weill was widely acclaimed as the greatest composer active in modern theater.

Whether Weill will regain his pre-war stature and escape his unfortunate and erroneous "threepenny" image cannot be safely foretold at this time. Many of his compositions which formed the basis for that estimable reputation have only recently been rediscovered; many others have been long out-of-print. Perhaps, as David Drew has indicated, it is neither necessary nor possible now to make a final assessment of Weill's place in the history of music, for his legacy is only just emerging from obscure war-time hiding places and the dark shadows cast by the looming figure of Brecht. But for those of us who treasure his music, Maxwell Anderson's eloquent summation of Weill's significance, delivered at his grave in 1950, still suffices:

I wish, of course, that he had been lucky enough to have a little more time for his work. I could wish the times in which he lived had been less troubled. But these things were as they were—and Kurt managed to make thousands of beautiful things during the short and troubled time he had. He made so many beautiful things that he will be remembered and loved by many not yet born. How many nobody knows, but I think many generations of men will keep his music alive. . . .

He left a great legacy in his music and in our memory of him. . . . But what he left must be saved, and we who are still here must save it for him. After a while, if we don't falter, the world's memory of him and of his work will be ours.[7]

NOTES

NOTES

INTRODUCTION

1. Sources for the above quotations are as follows: Hans Redlich, "Kurt Weill," *Music Survey* 3 (Summer 1950):5; and "Kurt Weill," *Musical Times* 109 (October 1968):930; Arnold Schoenberg, quoted by Virgil Thomson in *Virgil Thomson* (New York: Alfred A. Knopf, 1966), p. 227; Virgil Thomson, "Kurt Weill," *New York Herald Tribune*, 9 April 1951; Paul Collaer, *A History of Modern Music,* trans. Sally Abeles (Cleveland: World Publishing Co., 1955), p. 328; Clive Barnes, *New York Times*, 2 October 1972; Bertolt Brecht, quoted by Ernst Josef Aufricht in *Erzähle, damit du dein Recht erweist* (Munich: Deutsche Taschenbuch Verlag, 1969), p. 126; Herbert Fleischer, "Kurt Weill: Versuch einer einheitlichen Stilbetrachtung," *Anbruch* 14 (September 1932):135; Walter Abendroth, "Opernideale der Rassen und Völker," *Die Musik* 28 (March 1936):424, translated by David Drew in "Kurt Weill and His Critics," *Times Literary Supplement* 3839 (10 October 1975):1200.

2. Kurt Weill, as told to Edward J. Smith, "Broadway Opera," *Musical Digest* (December 1946):16.

3. Donald J. Grout, *A History of Western Music*, 2nd ed. (New York: W. W. Norton, 1973). Weill's name is mentioned as the composer of *Die Dreigroschenoper* in the chronology.

4. Arthur Cohn, *Twentieth-Century Music in Western Europe* (Philadelphia: J. B. Lippincott, 1965).

5. John F. Wharton, one of Weill's associates in the Playwrights' Producing Company, recalls how Weill's German career had been all but forgotten shortly after his death: "Even his own American publisher did not realize just how talented he was. I was counsel for his estate and asked the publisher to appraise his work. He asserted that 'September Song' and 'Down in the Valley' were of some lasting value; the value of the rest of the work was *minimal*! *Threepenny Opera* hardly came into our conversation." ["An Authentic Musical Genius," *Weill-Lenya* (New York: Goethe House, 1976), p. 26.]

6. In an obituary of Weill, Hans Redlich noted the long-term ramifications of Weill's involuntary emigration: "It is a well-known fact that most of the representative composers of this age (Schoenberg, Stravinsky, Bartók, Hindemith, Krenek, and Kurt Weill amongst them) have been driven into exile by indiscriminate forces of political factions which brutally denied them vital contact with their respective national climates. This sorry fate overtook Kurt Weill while still in his early thirties and nothing can express more poignantly the sinister implications of this enforced exodus than the simple fact that Weill's mature music, composed by the homeless artist in France, England, and ultimately in the United States, has remained a *terra incognita* even to his admirers." [*Music Survey* 3 (Summer 1950):4.]

7. Kurt Weill, "The Future of Opera in America," *Modern Music* 14 (May-June 1937):186-87.

8. Weill, "Broadway Opera," p. 16.

9. In yet another obituary written in 1950, Hans Redlich wrote: "The tragedy of our contemporary world, living as it does spiritually in water-tight compartments, is nowhere more vividly expressed than in the fact that the compositions of the mature Kurt Weill, written between his 34th and 50th year, have so far remained a closed book even to his most faithful admirers in the old world. . . . It must have been a keen disappointment to him, who had given Germany its most successful and stylistically most far reaching operatic work in this century, that the country of his origin cold-shouldered him even after the defeat of Nazidom in 1945." [*Music Review* 11 (August 1950):208.]

10. Drew, "Kurt Weill and His Critics," p. 1142.

11. Kurt Weill, quoted in the *New York Sun*, 3 February 1940.

12. Schumacher's study was published in Berlin by Rutten & Loening in 1955.

13. For detailed information concerning the most significant contributions to the Brecht-literature, see section III-A of the bibliography of this study.

14. Robert Marx, "The Operatic Brecht," *American Scholar* 44 (March 1975):287; John Willett, "Brecht: The Music" in *The Theatre of Bertolt Brecht: A Study from Eight Aspects*, 3rd ed. (New York: New Directions, 1959), p. 128.

15. Robert Marx, "Brecht, Weill, and the Birth of *The Threepenny Opera*," *New York Times*, 2 May 1976.

16. Both paperbacks were published in 1975 by Suhrkamp Verlag, Berlin. See the present author's review in *Notes* 33 (June 1977):832-835.

17. See section I-D of the bibliography of this study for specific references to these essays. Brief surveys of Weill's career by Elaine Padmore ["Kurt Weill," *Music and Musicians* 21 (October 1972):34-40] and Hans Engelmann ["Kurt Weill—heute," *Darmstädter Beiträge zur neuen Musik* 3 (1960):87-95] are useful general introductions. The unique perspective of Lotte Lenya's articles concerning her husband's career recommends them most powerfully. The brief and incomplete articles in *Groves* 5 and *MGG* are now of limited value because of recent discoveries.

18. Ph.D. dissertation in musicology, University of North Carolina at Chapel Hill, 1972. The other two dissertations, Cäcilie Tolksdorf, *John Gays "Beggar's Opera" und Bert Brechts "Dreigroschenoper"* (Rheinberg Rhl.: Sattler & Koss, 1934) and Günter Hartung, "Zur epischen Oper Brechts und Weills" (Ph.D. dissertation, Institut für Musikwissenschaft der Martin-Luther-Universität Halle-Wittenberg, 1959) both concentrate on textual and aesthetic issues.

19. Ph.D. dissertation in Germanic Languages and Literature, University of Michigan, 1974.

20. Ph.D. dissertation, University of Vienna, 1977. Two other dissertations dealing with Weill's music are in progress at the time of completion of this study (1977): Paul Bartholomäi, "Die Instrumentalmusik des Kurt Weills" (Ph.D. dissertation, Johann Wolfgang Goethe-Universität, Frankfurt), and Rudolf Franzen, "Das Musiktheater von Brecht und Weill." (Ph.D. dissertation, University of Freiberg).

21. Nadar discusses three compositions by Weill: *Die Dreigroschenoper, Aufstieg und Fall der Stadt Mahagonny,* and *Der Jasager.*

22. For example, Nadar calls A major the relative major of D minor (p. 161) and insists that the regular 16-bar phraseology of the "Moritat vom Mackie Messer" consists of 15 bars (p. 220).

23. Ernst Josef Aufricht, *Erzähle, damit du dein Recht erweist* (Munich: Deutscher Taschenbuch Verlag, 1969); Bertolt Brecht, *Bertolt Brechts Arbeitsjournal*, ed. Werner Hecht, 3 vols. (Frankfurt am Main: Suhrkamp Verlag, 1972); Hans-Jochen Irmer, *Brecht und das musikalische Theater* (Berlin: Verband der Theaterschaffenden der DDR, 1972); Sammy McLean, *The Bänkelsang and the Works of Bertolt Brecht* (The Hague: Mouton, 1972); Klaus Völker, *Brecht Chronicle*, trans. Fred Wieck (New York: Seabury Press, 1975).

24. Munich: Kinder Verlag, 1977.

25. A few notable exceptions are several essays by Drew and Ian Kemp's "Harmony in Weill: Some Observations," *Tempo* 104 (1973):11-15 and his Insert Notes to Symphony no. 2, Colouste Gulbenkian Foundation Series 6 recording (Argo ZRG 755).

26. Annotations of each essay are found in Appendix II at the conclusion of the respective translation. Specific problems that emerge from the essays are discussed there rather than in the more general treatment in Chapter 3.

27. Drew, "Kurt Weill and His Critics," p. 1200.

CHAPTER 1

1. From the eulogy that Anderson read at Weill's grave, 5 April 1950.

2. Albert Weill, *Synagogen Gesänge für Cantor und Männerchor* (Frankfurt am Main: A. J. Hofmann Verlag, 1893).

3. Ibid., "Vorwort," p. 1.

4. Although Weill came to the U.S. at Max Reinhardt's request to assist with the production of *The Eternal Road*, it did not open at the Manhattan Opera House until 4 January 1937. Meanwhile the Group Theatre had already produced *Johnny Johnson* (17 November 1936); it is Weill's first genuinely "American" composition in that, unlike *The Eternal Road*, it was entirely composed in the United States.

5. Kurt Weill, as quoted in "Protagonist of Music in the Theatre," *The American Hebrew* (8 January 1937):757.

6. Ibid. An abridged form of this article appeared in the *New York Times*, 5 December 1936. In the fall of 1934, Weill was living in Paris.

7. The production opened at the Alvin Theater in New York on 5 September 1946. Weill also published an arrangement of "Havu l'venim" ("Bring the Bricks") in a collection entitled *Folk Songs of the New Palestine* (New York: Youth Zionist Organization of America, 1938).

8. The program note for Weill's "Kiddush" read: "In Kiddush, Mr. Weill has set to music a prayer of the Sabbath. Over a goblet of wine, symbolic peace and joy, the day is sanctified in a prayer affirming the divine origin of the Sabbath and expressive of gratitude for it." Lou Harrison, writing about the first performance

in *Modern Music* 23 (Summer 1946):204, was "shocked by Kurt Weill's impudence in setting the 'Kiddush' as a low-down second act finale for a musical."

9. Weill's "Kiddush" was published in *Synagogue Music by Contemporary Composers* (New York: G. Schirmer, 1951), an anthology of thirty-eight compositions for the Sabbath Eve service by noted contemporary composers who had been commissioned to create new music for the synagogue by the cantor of the Park Avenue Synagogue, David J. Puttermann. The collection includes works by Leonard Bernstein, Paul Dessau, Lucas Foss, Darius Milhaud, Mario Castelnuovo-Tedesco, in addition to those mentioned above.

10. Rudolf Kastner, "Kurt Weill: Eine Skizze," *Anbruch* 7 (October 1925):454. Throughout this study, the journal published by Universal-Edition, entitled *Musikblätter des Anbruch* until 1929 (vols. 1-10) and thereafter *Anbruch: Monatschrift für moderne Musik*, will be referred to simply as '*Anbruch.*'

11. Robert Garland in an interview with Weill published in the *New York Journal-American*, 10 October 1948. David Drew has dated the second opera as late as 1917-21. It is unknown if either of these early operatic works was completed. An ensemble in a highly chromatic style from one of the three early operas, all of which are now lost, has survived. [See David Drew, "The History of Mahagonny," *Musical Times* 104 (January 1963):18.]

12. Kastner, p. 454. Albert Bing was a student of Hans Pfitzner. Weill dedicated his Cello Sonata and *Quodlibet*, whose premiere was conducted by Bing, to his first composition teacher.

13. Kurt Weill as quoted in the *New Yorker* (10 June 1944):16. In his "Erinnerungen um Kurt Weill," *Melos* 37 (March 1970):81-85, Hans Curjel described Weill's piano playing as "that of a well-trained, but in no way virtuoso, repetiteur."

14. Franz Willnauer, "Vom Schiffbauerdamm zum Broadway: Weg und Werk Kurt Weills," *Opern Welt* (April 1970):45.

15. The songs include "Reiterlied" (Text by Hermann Löns), "Im Volkston" (Text by Arno Holz), and "Das schöne Kind."

16. "Aktuelles Zwiegespräch über die Schuloper zwischen Kurt Weill und Dr. Hans Fischer," *Die Musikpflege* 1 (April 1930):250. A translation of the entire article appears in Appendix II. One of Weill's "Kriegs-chöre," composed when he was about fourteen, was performed at the 1975 Berliner Festwochen.

17. David Drew, ed., *Ueber Kurt Weill* (Frankfurt am Main: Suhrkamp Verlag, 1975), p. 162. Weill studied with Ernst Cassirer and Max Dessoir at the University.

18. *New Yorker* (10 June 1944):16. Humperdinck's *Spieloper*, based on a libretto by R. Misch, was premiered at the Darmstadt Landestheater on 18 March 1919 and proved to be the last opera he completed. In his essay "Kurt Weill" in the *Blätter der Staatsoper und der städtischen Oper* 9 (October 1928), Klaus Prigsheim wrote that Weill considered himself primarily a conducting student of Krasselt, the music director of the Berlin Städtische Oper from 1912 to 1923, and only secondarily a student of composition.

19. Eric Werner, "Mendelssohniana dem Andenken Wilhelm Fischers," *Die Musik-Forschung* 28 (1975):33. The rather conservative nature of the curriculum of the

Hochschule undoubtedly reflected the leadership of the school (Joachim, followed by Kretschmar) and the tendencies of the composition teachers (Humperdinck, followed by Franz Schreker).

20. David Drew, Insert Notes to Symphony No. 1, Colouste Gulbenkian Foundation Series 6 recording (Argo ZRG 755).

21. Heinrich Strobel, "Kurt Weill," *Melos* 6 (October 1927):427-28.

22. Kastner also reported that Weill conducted the Leipzig Männerchor for a period during 1919.

23. In "Kurt Weill," Prigsheim wrote that Wagner's *Der fliegende Holländer* represented the most difficult work that Weill attempted at Lüdenscheid. Several playbills from the theater have survived and indicate that Weill also conducted Mascagni's *Cavalleria rusticana* during the season. Arthur Kistenmacher served as artistic director of the Lüdenscheid Stadttheater.

24. "Protagonist of Music in the Theater," p. 757.

25. Kurt Weill, Insert notes to *Street Scene,* Columbia recording, 4139.

26. Hardt's *Ninon von Lenclos* was published as a one-act drama in 1905 by Insel Verlag, Leipzig. Ernst Hardt (1876-1947) was a German neo-romantic dramatist who adapted many of his plays from medieval legends. His most successful work was *Tantris der Narr* (1908), which won the Schiller and Volksschiller Prizes. Weill's opera was entitled *Ninon de Lenclos,* retaining the original version of the famous seventeenth-century French courtesan's name.

27. The catalogue of Weill's works in *Grove's Dictionary of Music and Musicians,* 5th edition, vol. 9:239-40 does not include either composition. The list of works in *Die Musik in Geschichte und Gegenwart* 14:388 does include the String Quartet in B minor. After their recent rediscoveries both works were performed at the 1975 Berlin Festival.

28. In Kurt Stone's essay, "Kurt Weill," *MGG* 14:388, he mentions that a performance of the String Quartet may have occurred in 1920 in Hagen, the more populous neighboring city of Lüdenscheid. I have found no evidence to confirm this assertion.

29. Since the Cello Sonata was dedicated to Rupprecht, it is quite possible that he performed the work in Dessau soon after its completion, but there is no record of such a performance. The performance by Siegfried Palm and Aloys Kontarsky at the 1975 Berlin Festival was designated the "world premiere."

30. Carl Zuckmayer, *A Part of Myself: Portrait of an Epoch,* trans. Richard and Clara Winston (London: Secker & Warburg, 1970), p. 217.

31. An understanding of the economic, political, and social setting of the Weimar Republic in the twenties is essential to any study of the music of the era. General introductions in English are: Otto Friedrich, *Before the Deluge;* Peter Gay, *Weimar Culture: The Outsider as Insider;* Erich Eyck, *A History of the Weimar Republic.* [See Bibliography for publication information.]

32. Hans Heinsheimer, *Best Regards to Aïda* (New York: Alfred A. Knopf, 1968), p. 18.

33. See Hans Heinsheimer, *Menagerie in F Sharp* (Garden City, New Jersey: Doubleday, 1947), pp. 94-97.

34. Edward J. Dent, *Ferruccio Busoni: A Biography* (London: Oxford University Press, 1933), p. 247.

35. H. H. Stuckenschmidt, *Ferruccio Busoni: Chronicle of a European,* trans. Sandra Morris (London: Calder & Boyars, 1970), p. 60.

36. David Drew, "Musical Theatre in the Weimar Republic," *Proceedings of the Royal Musical Association* 88 (1961-62):92.

37. Stuckenschmidt, pp. 60-61.   The double-bill performance of *Turandot* and *Arlecchino* occurred on 13 May 1921 at the Staatsoper with Leo Blech conducting. In January 1921 *Anbruch* sponsored three concerts of Busoni's music and devoted an issue exclusively to discussion of his career.

38. Kastner reported that Weill "learned from the newspaper that Busoni was returning to Berlin." [See "Kurt Weill: Eine Skizze," p. 454.] Note that Phillip Jarnach is not included in the class at this time. He had become a student and 'disciple' of Busoni in 1917 at the University of Zürich but did not follow him to Berlin until 1921.

39. Hans Heinsheimer, "Kurt Weill: From Berlin to Broadway," *International Musician* (March 1948):17.   Some "Kabarett-Musik" from 1921 has survived in manuscript.

40. Rosamund Ley, ed. & trans., *Ferruccio Busoni: Letters to His Wife* (London: Edward Arnold, 1938), p. 303.

41. In his article, "Phillip Jarnach," in *MGG*, Helmut Wirth stated that Jarnach undertook Weill as a private pupil from 1922 to 1925. In actuality, Weill's lessons with Jarnach lasted little more than a year. In an article written in 1926, Jarnach "maintained that Busoni was not a teacher in the narrow sense of the word; he had no vocation for teaching, besides which he lacked the necessary cool impartiality. Having himself undergone a detailed theoretical training, he did not believe in teaching systems.   What he required of an artist, was not that he should rely upon what he had learnt, but that he should allow his techniques to grow out of his original idea." [Stuckenschmidt, *Ferruccio Busoni*, p. 196.]

42. Ernst Krenek, "Busoni—Then and Now," *Modern Music* 19 (January-February 1942):88.

43. See Hans Gutman, "Young Germany, 1930," *Modern Music* 7 (February-March 1930):4.

44. Quoted and translated by Stuckenschmidt in *Ferruccio Busoni*, p. 196.

45. All of the essays appear in English translation in Appendix II.

46. Kastner, "Kurt Weill: Eine Skizze," pp. 453-54.   In "Kurt Weill," Klaus Prigsheim described Weill's relationship to Busoni as "student, friend—artistically, intellectually, humanly in his spell until the death of the rare man." Jarnach eventually was persuaded to complete *Doktor Faust*, which had been left incomplete at the time of Busoni's death.

47. Breitkopf & Härtel published the full score of the Divertimento in 1922. It is dedicated to Phillippe Gaubert. Weill's piano arrangement probably dates from the same year; it is published as B & H #5205, 1956 (c. 1922).

48. In the Preface to his edition of Symphony no. 1 (Schott, 1968), David Drew noted that Weill had mentioned the completion of a symphony in a letter to his parents dated 10 December 1920. Although there is no other documentation of such a work (it disappeared without a trace), Drew assumed that it is unrelated to Symphony no. 1 and has, therefore, labeled it Symphony no. '0.'

49. The inscription is mentioned by Strobel, "Kurt Weill," p. 428. However, he misquotes the title as "*Arbeiter, Soldaten, und Bauern.*"

50. See Lilly Becher, *Johannes R. Becher: Bild Chronik seines Lebens* (Berlin: Aufbau-Verlag, 1963), p. 71.

51. In the preface to this revised version, entitled *Arbeiter, Bauern, Soldaten: Entwurf zu einem revolutionären Kampfdrama*, Becher wrote that the earlier version had been written "in 1919 in an atmosphere of emotional Communism and a muddled, ecstatic quest for God. The place for art of this type has been radically eliminated." Both versions have been published in *Gesammelte Werke von Johannes R. Becher*. vol. 8: *Dramatische Dichtungen* (Berlin: Aufbau-Verlag, 1966-74). For the original German of the above quotation, see p. 104.

52. See *Johannes R. Becher: Leben und Werk* [hrsg. vom Kollektive für Literaturgeschichte] (Berlin: Volk und Volkseigner Verlag, 1968).

53. *Der deutsche Rundfunk* 5 (17 April 1927):1090. The same issue of the journal contains an interview with Becher by Hans Tasiemka, pp. 1084-85. David Drew dated the initial meeting of Weill and Becher as 1920 in *Ueber Kurt Weill*, p. 162.

54. See Klaus Völker, *Brecht Chronicle*, trans. Fred Wieck (New York: Seabury Press, 1975). In 1925, the best-known young German authors, including Becher, Brecht, Klabund, Tucholsky, formed "Gruppe 1925" to coordinate the interests of authors who were not represented in the literary groups and powerful dramatic circles dominated by the older generation. It is possible that Brecht and Weill became acquainted through their mutual relationship with Becher.

55. After the *Anschluss* in 1938, Nazi agents raided the offices of Universal-Edition in Vienna and confiscated many of Weill's scores. [See Drew, "The History of Mahagonny," p. 22.]

56. *New York Herald-Tribune*, 22 May 1958; and *New York World Telegram & Sun*, 24 May 1958. Both reports refer to a "Walter Fleischer," but this is probably an error, since Herbert Fleischer published an essay, "Kurt Weill: Versuch einer einheitlichen Stilbetrachtung," *Anbruch* 14 (September 1932):135-137; whose content indicates that he had access to Weill's early compositions.

57. David Drew, Preface to *Symphony no. 1* (New York: Schott Music Corp., 1968), pp. ix-x.

58. An article in the *New York World Telegram & Sun*, 24 May 1958, reported that corrections by Busoni are clearly inked in several places within the autograph. I have not been able to verify this assertion.

59. Strobel, "Kurt Weill," p. 428.

60. "Aktuelles Zwiegespräch über die Schuloper zwischen Kurt Weill und Dr. Hans Fischer," *Die Musikpflege* 1 (April 1930):50. I have been unable to locate a single reference to the premiere of the work in music journals. *Die Zaubernacht* may also have been performed in New York in 1923.

61. The excerpt from the program was quoted by Hans S. von Heister in his review of *Der Protagonist* in *Der deutsche Rundfunk* 4 (11 April 1926): 1015-16. The epigraph which introduces this section directly precedes the passage quoted above. The "Lied der Fee," the opening song of *Die Zaubernacht,* was performed at Lincoln Center, New York on 7 March 1977.

62. Strobel, "Kurt Weill," p. 431.

63. *Die Musik* 15 (August 1923):830. Also see the announcement of the premiere in *Anbruch* 5 (May 1923):162.

64. The advertisement for U-E # 8348 appeared in *Anbruch* 7 (October 1925).

65. *Quodlibet* was not a suite in the normal sense of the term, for Weill did not merely excerpt sections of *Die Zaubernacht* but recomposed it for a larger orchestra and united in *Quodlibet's* four movements various, often widely separated sections of *Die Zaubernacht* according to the considerations of an independent orchestral work.

66. "Music in Wien," *Anbruch* 9 (March 1927):143.

67. Writing about the Krefeld performance, Walter Jacobs stated that although it was elegantly composed and captivating in its dance idioms, it proved to be somewhat too long. [See "Das Tonkünstlerfest in Krefeld," *Die Musik* 19 (August 1927):807.]

68. For a commentary on these performances, see *Die Musik* 20 (February 1928):391; and *Anbruch* 11 (September-October 1929):325. Heinrich Laber conducted *Quodlibet* in the concerts of the Russian Orchestra of Gera; see *Die Musik* 20 (December 1927):235. An advertisement of "Two New Huge Successes by Kurt Weill" in *Anbruch* 9 (December 1927) featured the Violin Concerto and *Quodlibet.* It quoted a review of the latter that had appeared in the *Hannover Landeszeitung:* "Ponies and tumbler-dolls, sleeping children and a puppet doctor, a blustering bear and tin soldiers all march past in our fantasy as Weill's melodic lines, over familiar sounds and abundantly moving rhythms, are embellished with a glittering orchestration often akin to chamber music."

69. *New Yorker* (10 June 1944):16.

70. Lotte Lenya, as quoted by Jay Harrison, "Weill and Lenya—Berlin to Broadway," *New York Herald-Tribune,* 27 July 1958. An expanded account of this first contact appears in "Lotte Lenya in Conversation with Steven Paul," Insert notes to *Kurt Weill,* Deutsche Grammophon recording, 2709-064.

71. See Kastner, p. 454. Drew's "Wieder-Herstellung" of the Divertimento calls for different instrumentation for each movement: I Quasi Maestoso—Allegro deciso (solo string quartet, tutti strings, horn); II Andantino (solo string quartet); III Scherzo (solo string quartet, clarinet, bassoon, horn); IV Choral: Poco Sostenuto (tutti strings, horn, 2 trombones, 2-part male chorus). Only the final two

movements of Drew's reconstruction are conclusively based on material from the original Divertimento. The first two movements are orchestral treatments of two movements which were originally part of String Quartet no. 1, opus 8, but which were omitted from the 1924 publication of that work. There is evidence in the form of an incomplete orchestral setting of some of this material that Weill had indeed envisioned reworking the omitted quartet movements for larger forces. However, it must be noted that there is no conclusive evidence that the two quartet movements were ever included in the Divertimento. Therefore, Drew's reconstruction must be viewed as a conjecture rather than a simple reconstruction from clear-cut sources.

72. Strobel, p. 430. Busoni's Concerto, op. 39 (1906) for piano, male chorus, and orchestra consisted of five movements, the last of which utilized the chorus.

73. There may have been a private reading of the work under the auspices of 'Die Novembergruppe' before the public premiere. [See Kastner, p. 455.] Klaus Prigsheim considered this performance in the Philharmonic Concerts Weill's first genuine debut as a composer and described the work as "significant and full of expression."

74. Adolf Weissmann, "Konzerte: Berlin," *Die Musik* 15 (May 1923):625.

75. Kastner, p. 455.

76. Strobel, p. 429.

77. Note that Weill labeled op. 8 as Quartet no. 1 despite the fact that the String Quartet in B minor (1919) predates it. The Quartet was performed privately at one of Busoni's evenings during the spring of 1923. John Willett's assertion that the quartet was premiered in 1922 at Donaueschingen is incorrect.

78. Karl Holl, "Kammermusikwoche: Neue Musik," *Frankfurter Zeitung,* 27 June 1923. Also see his "Neue Musik in Frankfurt," *Die Musik* 15 (August 1923):815. The Quartet is also discussed in Paul Bekker's "Neue Musik in Frankfurt," *Anbruch* 5 (June-July 1923):188.

79. Curjel, "Erinnerungen um Kurt Weill," p. 81.

80. Ibid.

81. Igor Stravinsky, *Chronicle of My Life,* trans. from the French (London: Victor Gollancz, 1936), pp. 177-78.

82. Igor Stravinsky and Robert Craft, *Expositions and Developments* (London: Faber & Faber, 1959), p. 66. Stravinsky continued: "I also saw Weill in Hollywood during the war, and I went on stage to congratulate him after the premiere of *Lady in the Dark.*" In *Stravinsky: Chronicle of a Friendship 1948-71* (New York: Alfred A. Knopf, 1972), p. 212, Robert Craft discussed Stravinsky's reaction to the 1963 production of *Aufstieg und Fall der Stadt Mahagonny* in Hamburg: "I. S. will say no more than that 'there are good things everywhere in the score, only it is not everywhere good.'"

83. Kurt Weill, "Die neue Oper," *Die neue Weg* 55 (16 January 1926):25. There is no doubt that *The Soldier's Tale* is one of the models for epic theater as developed by Brecht and Weill.

84. The program of the concert is reproduced in Helga Kliemann, *Die Novembergruppe* (Berlin: Gebr. Mann Verlag, 1966), p. 40. Failure to differentiate between the terms "Erstaufführung" (first local performance) and "Uraufführung" (world premiere) has caused many of the numerous errors of chronology and documentation that have occurred in the literature dealing with Weill. The members of the Roth Quartet were listed as Roth, Strumfeld, Spitz, and Franke. The Paris correspondent of *Anbruch* reported that the Roth Quartet also performed Weill's op. 8 in Paris during December 1924, and "it achieved an exceptionally strong success." [See *Anbruch* 7 (January 1925):52.] Other early performances included those by the Koberger Bochröder-Quartet, whose repertoire for the 1927/28 season included Weill's Quartet, Reger's op. 94, and Hindemith's op. 22. [See *Anbruch* 10 (October 1928):314.] As late as 1931, the Quartet remained in the repertory of the Berliner Quartet. [See *Anbruch* 12 (September-October 1930):266.]

85. Kurt Weill, *Ausgewählte Schriften*, ed. David Drew (Frankfurt am Main: Suhrkamp Verlag, 1975), p. 221.

86. See Otto Friedrich, *Before the Deluge* (New York: Harper & Row, 1972), pp. 154-55.

87. H. H. Stuckenschmidt, "Musik and Musiker in der Novembergruppe," *Anbruch* 10 (October 1928):293.

88. Kliemann, p. 39.

89. Ibid., p. 76.

90. Stuckenschmidt, "Musik und Musiker in der Novembergruppe," p. 294.

91. See Weill's reference to the activities of the November Group in *Der deutsche Rundfunk* 3 (24 May 1925):1323.

92. This is a description of the published version of the Quartet. Two additional movements of the Quartet have survived in manuscript; it is unclear when they were deleted from the work. Drew used the two movements as the basis for the first two movements of his "reconstruction" of the Divertimento.

93. Kastner, p. 455; Strobel, p. 430; Fleischer, p. 135.

94. Extracts from the letter have been published in *Musikerautographen: Katalog 204* (Tutzing: Musikantiquariat Hans Schneider, 1977), item 37a. Item 37 is also a page of a letter addressed to Hertzka in reference to Alois Melichar (b. 1896), of whom Busoni wrote: "I believe this composer, like several others of his generation, is still not clear as to what is to be his own particular essence." Busoni's high praise for Weill contrasts markedly with his evaluation of Melichar, who studied with Franz Schreker from 1920 to 1923.

95. Heinsheimer, *Best Regards to Aïda*, pp. 113-14.

96. Universal-Edition announced publication of the full score (#7599) and parts (#7600) of *Frauentanz* in *Anbruch* 6 (June-July 1924). A similar announcement of the String Quartet did not appear until November-December 1924.

97. Adolf Weissmann, "Berlin: Konzerte," *Die Musik* 16 (March 1924):444. The program included Max Butting's *Kammersinfonie*. Nora Pisling-Boas (b. 1889) was a native of Holland but studied in Berlin with Anna Schoen-Rene. Her husband,

Siegmund Pisling, was music critic of the *Berliner Börsen-Zeitung* until 1926. Weill wrote of Nora's "wonderful musicality that always greatly amazes us anew" in a review in *Der deutsche Rundfunk* 4 (16 May 1926):1380.

98. Heinrich Strobel, "Erinnerungen an Kurt Weill," *Melos* 17 (May 1950):134. The first international festival of contemporary music was held in 1921 at Salzburg. At this festival the ISCM (or IGNM in Germany) was established with Edward Dent as its first president. In 1924 the main festival was in Prague, with a supplementary session in Salzburg devoted solely to chamber music. Stravinsky's *Octet*, Poulenc's Sonata for Clarinet and Bassoon, Satie's *Socrate*, and compositions by Krenek, Hindemith, Kodály, and Vaughan-Williams were performed at this series.

99. Adolf Weissmann, "Das Zweite Internationale Kammermusikfest in Salzburg," *Die Musik* 17 (October 1924):52. Lotte Leonard (b. 1884) was a frequent soloist in Berlin during the twenties. After emigrating to the United States, she taught voice at Juilliard and the Mannes School. She moved to Israel in 1968. Weill dedicated the score of *Der neue Orpheus* to her.

100. Kastner, p. 455.

101. The Viennese soprano, Ruzena Herlinger sang it in a concert of the *Revue musicale* in Paris during December 1924 with songs of Anton Webern [*Anbruch* 7 (January 1925):52]. As late as 1927, Grete Nikisch (one of the soloists in the premiere of *Cardillac*) sang it in Dresden with Weill conducting [*Anbruch* 9 (April 1927):196]. Other performances were in Karlsruhe: Tilly Blättermann, soprano; Hans Curjel, conductor [*Anbruch* 9 (April 1927):190] and in Düsseldorf: Ann Ibald, soprano; Joseph Neyes, conductor [*Anbruch* 9 (March 1927):152]. It was broadcast by the Berlin Radio in May 1927. [See *Der deutsche Rundfunk* 5 (1 May 1927):1230.]

102. See Friedrich Heinrich von der Hagen, *Minnesinger*, 5 vols. (Leipzig: Joh. Ambr. Barth Verlag, 1838-56) for the original texts of four of the seven poems: "Wir haben die winter-lange Nacht" occurs as the second strophe of XIV in vol. I, p. 101; "Dieser Stern im Dunkeln" is strophe 13 of Der von Kürenberg's poem in vol. I, p. 97; "Eines Maienmorgens schön" is II of vol. I, pp. 15-16. Movement VI of *Frauentanz*, "Ich will Trauern lassen stehn" occurs as LXXXXI in Hagen's section of poems with author unknown: vol. III, pp. 446-47. I have not been able to trace the other three texts, nor to determine a source for the modernized versions which Weill used. It is also unclear whether Weill chose the poems and ordered them in a cycle or if they appeared in that form in the source he utilized.

103. See Hanspeter Krellman, *Studien zu den Bearbeitungen Ferruccio Busonis* (Regensburg: Gustav Bosse Verlag, 1966), p. 191. A manuscript of Movement III in ink, signed "Weill-Busoni," has survived and is reproduced in facsimile in *Weill-Lenya*.

104. The only references to the work that I have found in articles written during Weill's lifetime occur in Prigsheim, "Kurt Weill," p. 3; and Fleischer, "Kurt Weill: Versuch einer einheitlichen Stilbetrachtung," p. 135. Fleischer wrote: "Weill's first vocal works, *Ricordare* [sic] and *Frauentanz*, already show his inclination to elucidate the linguistic content of the text through musical expression."

105. Fortunately Neighbour informed David Drew of his discovery and presented the manuscript to the Weill Estate. I am indebted to Mr. Drew for his account of

the history of the work. The final page of the copyist's manuscript bears the date "September 1923," the initials "K.W.," and the copyist's stamp, "Notenschreib-Büro Dr. Wohlhauer 1./2. 24." Weill's setting of a section of the Lamentations of Jeremiah predates Ernst Krenek's twelve-tone setting by almost twenty years.

106. "Aktuelles Zwiegespräch über die Schuloper zwischen Kurt Weill und Dr. Hans Fischer," *Die Musikpflege* 1 (April 1930):50.

107. David Drew, "Two Weill Scores," *Musical Times* 107 (September 1966):797.

108. Drew, Insert Notes to *Kurt Weill*, p. 19.

109. Kastner, p. 455.

110. Peter Bing, "Weill's Violinkonzert," *Anbruch* 7 (December 1925): 550-51. Stravinsky's Piano Concerto, however, calls for a much larger instrumentation. Actually the instrumentation of Weill's Concerto corresponds more closely to that of Berg's Chamber Concerto (1923-25).

111. Schoenberg's Quintet for Winds, op. 26, and Hindemith's Concerto for Orchestra, op. 38, were performed on other programs at the festival.

112. Adolf Weissmann, "Das Internationale Musikfest in Zürich," *Die Musik* 18 (August 1926):836-37. Writing in *Der deutsche Rundfunk* 4 (11 July 1926):1944-46, Rudolf Kastner shared Weissmann's opinion that the Concerto provided the strongest impression of the festival. The reviewer for *Anbruch* called the work "brilliant, full of temperament, always on the limits of tonality."

113. Alfred Einstein, "Gay German Opera," *New York Times*, 22 April 1928.

114. Aaron Copland, "Playing Safe at Zurich," *Modern Music* 4 (November-December 1926):31. *Der Protagonist* had premiered at the Dresden Staatsoper under Busch on 27 March 1926 to wide acclaim.

115. See *Anbruch* 10 (June-July 1928). The advertisement is reprinted in Appendix I. Frenkel played the Concerto in Berlin, Warsaw, New York, Dresden, Dortmund, Frankfurt, Nürnberg, Krefeld, Stuttgart, Copenhagen, and in a number of cities on his Russian tour. It was broadcast on radio in Berlin, Copenhagen, and Stuttgart. Frenkel had been a student of Karl Flesch and had served as the concertmaster of the Dresden Philharmonic.

116. Theodor W. Adorno's review of this performance appeared in *Die Musik* 22 (February 1930):379. It has been partially translated in Drew's Insert Notes to *Kurt Weill*, p. 19.

117. The full score, announced in *Anbruch* 7 (October 1925), is essential to a study of the Concerto, for the piano reduction of the Concerto is even more deceptive than most such arrangements. Weill seldom composed at the piano, and many of the features of the orchestral score of the Concerto simply cannot be adequately transcribed, especially the elaborate percussion part.

118. Note that this pre-dates Hindemith's *Marienleben* of 1923. Drew has catalogued a number of parallel aspects between Weill's and Hindemith's careers, as well as points of direct contact. He has conclusively exploded the myth that Weill's relationship to Hindemith was that of "follower." [See Drew, "Musical Theater in the Weimar Republic," pp. 95-98.]

119. *Der deutsche Rundfunk* 4 (7 November 1926):3180-81.

120. Translation: "The Book of the Monastic Life," "The Book of Pilgrimage," and "The Book of Poverty and Death." Insel-Verlag published a new edition of the work in 1922. Rilke had disowned all of his early works except *Das Stundenbuch* because he considered them "immature and inexact." For an English translation, see *The Book of Hours*, trans. A. L. Peck (London: Hogarth Press, 1961).

121. The date of the premiere is erroneously given as 14 October 1923 in *Weill-Lenya*. I have not been able to determine a more precise date than 1925, although 14 October 1925 remains a possibility.

122. See Prigsheim, p. 3; in "Kurt Weill," p. 433, Strobel wrote that "the Rilke-Lieder . . . are the most beautiful examples of the stylization of poetic content in the musical organism."

123. Apparently the two songs in manuscript were brought to the United States by Myra Mortimer, who had heard them in Berlin when she was on tour. She asked Weill for permission to sing them in Holland. There is no record of such a performance. After her death, the songs passed through several hands before being donated to the Westminster Library. See C. E. Le Massena, "Myra Mortimer: America's Lieder Singer," *Musical Observer* 26 (November 1927):36.

124. Each of the sets of parts includes six violin I, five violin II, four viola, three cello, and two double bass parts. They appear to have been utilized for a performance, since various parts contain rehearsal letters in blue ink, corrections in blue crayon, and some penciled additions to the black-ink manuscript, which is the work of several copyists. The orchestral scores contain rehearsal letters in red ink.

125. Notes to the recording of *Street Scene* (Columbia 4139).

126. For example: Hindemith's *Das Nusch-Nuschi* (1921) and *Sancta Susanna* (1922) and Krenek's *Zwingberg* (1922).

127. B. J. Kenworthy, *Georg Kaiser* (Oxford: Basil Blackwell, 1957), p. xiii.

128. Duke's version, published by Brentano (New York, 1922) was produced by Theater Guild at the Garrick Theater on 21 May 1922. Weill's review of *Von Morgens bis Mitternachts* appeared in *Der deutsche Rundfunk* 4 (7 March 1926):664; he called Kaiser "the most successful and most performed dramatist of the German stage."

129. Völker, *Brecht Chronicle*, p. 53. Völker also documented that in 1920 Brecht saw Kaiser's *Der gerettete Alkibiades* and *Gas* (which he reviewed in *Der Volkswille*), as well as *Von Morgens bis Mitternachts* in 1921. Brecht and Caspar Neher attended Kaiser's trial in Munich. In *Bertolt Brecht: His Life, His Art, and His Times* (New York: Citadel Press, 1967), p. 91, Frederic Ewen wrote that in the early twenties Georg Kaiser was the playwright whom Brecht most respected. Werner Hecht has written that "Brecht refers emphatically to Georg Kaiser as the immediate precursor of epic theater." ["The Development of Brecht's Theory of Epic Theatre 1918-1933," *Tulane Drama Review* 6 (September 1961):64.] Brecht himself wrote that Kaiser "made possible that totally new bearing of the public, that cool, searching, interested attitude of the audience in a scientific age."

130. David Drew, "Brecht Versus Opera," *The Score* 23 (July 1958):9. Most of the properties now associated with Brecht's theory of epic theater were anticipated, at least in part, in works of Stravinsky, Busoni, Wedekind, Kaiser, and Piscator.

131. Kenworthy, pp. xviii-xix.

132. Ibid., p. 154.

133. H. H. Stuckenschmidt, *Twentieth Century Composers II: Germany and Central Europe* (New York: Holt, Rinehart, Winston, 1971), p. 138. Also Fritz Busch, *Pages From A Musician's Life*, trans. Marjorie Strachey (London: Hogarth Press, 1953), p. 150. Busch succeeded Fritz Reiner as the Director of the Dresden Opera in 1922. He conducted the premieres of Strauss' *Intermezzo* (1924) and *Die ägyptische Helena* (1928), Busoni's *Doktor Faust* (1925), and Hindemith's *Cardillac* (1926).

134. Weill in the program notes for the premiere, quoted by H. S. von Heister, p. 1016.

135. H. F. Garten's translation of Kaiser's original drama, *Der Protagonist*, appeared in the *Tulane Drama Review* 5 (December 1960):133-44. It has been reprinted in *Seven Expressionist Plays: Kokoschka to Barlach* (London: Calder & Boyars, 1968).

136. Lenya, quoted by Harrison, "Weill and Lenya—Berlin to Broadway." An expanded account of the event occurs in "Lotte Lenya in Conversation with Steven Paul," p. 8.

137. See *Anbruch* 6 (November-December 1924):438; and *Anbruch* 7 (June-July 1925):343.

138. Kastner, "Kurt Weill: Eine Skizze," pp. 455-56.

139. Howard Taubman, "From Longhair to Short," *New York Times,* 23 January 1948.

140. The curtain-call-count is Lenya's.

141. Bie's review is quoted by Hans W. Heinsheimer in "Kurt Weill: From Berlin to Broadway," p. 18. The original appeared in the *Berliner Börsen-Courier*, 29 March 1926.

142. Strobel, "Kurt Weill," p. 432. In a later essay with the same title [published in *Anbruch* 10 (February 1928):57-59], Strobel wrote: "One recognizes immediately the uniqueness of this one-acter. It has a theatrical tempo like no other work that new music has produced up to now. It took by storm, it devastated. It achieved an elemental instinct for the requisites of the operatic stage and thereby stands totally apart from the course of Wagner's music drama. The best proof of Weill's spontaneous musical inclinations is that he did not permit himself to be overrun by the uncommonly theatrical poetry, that he did not subordinate himself to it, but rather forced it to conform to his own intentions. This music does not merely interpret; it does not merely embellish; it absorbs the dramatic content with a totally new intensity."

143. H. S. von Heister, pp. 1015-16. He found the psychological intellect of Busoni, the wind-writing of Stravinsky, and the delicately-veined delineation of tone color of Schoenberg intermingled in Weill's score.

144. Maurice de Abravanel, "Le Protagoniste," *La Revue musicale* 7 (July 1926):76-78.

145. In his "Erinnerung an Kurt Weill," *Melos* 17 (May 1950):134; Heinrich Strobel recalled sitting with Weill in a restaurant after the first performance of *Der Protagonist* in Erfurt. They were puzzled by the audience's surprising reaction to the opera: "This wild, expressionistic one-act opera was received simply, without applause and without whistles. The audience was silent and disconcertedly slinked away." Such a reaction to one of his own plays would have pleased even Brecht, no doubt.

146. Harrison, "Weill and Lenya."

147. Heinsheimer, *Menagerie in F. Sharp*, p. 146. Heinsheimer wrote that the String Quartet no. 1 sold only eleven copies the first year.

148. The sources of the cited essays are respectively Erik Reger in *Die Musik* 20 (February 1928):338-45 and Fritz Lauhöfer in *Neue Musikzeitung* 48 (September 1972):529-32.

149. Weill's articles appeared, respectively: *Der deutsche Rundfunk* 4 (13 June 1926):1649-50; *DdR* 5 (6 February 1927):365; *DdR* 7 (25 January 1929):98-99.

150. The broadcast of Weill's analysis of Bartók's Quartet no. 1 on 14 March 1926 included examples performed 'live' by the Roth Quartet. The lecture dealing with Busoni was broadcast on 31 March 1926.

151. Klabund was the pseudonym of the German poet, novelist, and playwright, Alfred Henschke (1890-1928). A close friend and associate of Brecht, he married Carola Neher (Polly in *Die Dreigroschenoper* and Lillian in *Happy End*). Fascinated by street ballads, hymns, Oriental poetry, and especially the works of Francois Villon, Klabund won fame for his drama *Der Kreidekreis*. Braun was director of the drama division of the Berlin Radio.

152. Roy C. Cowen, *Christian Dietrich Grabbe* (New York: Twayne Publishers, 1972), p. 18. For a plot synopsis and critical essay, see Cowen, pp. 40-53. The complete play was published in *Christian Dietrich Grabbe: Werke und Briefe*, ed. Alfred Bergmann (Emsdetten: Verlag Lechte, 1960), vol. 1, pp. 10-208. Grabbe, born in Detmold as the son of a jail warden, died from tuberculosis at age thirty-five after a turbulent life. Although his plays were rarely produced during the nineteenth century, German Expressionists were fascinated by his virulent personal life and the shocking effects, obscenities, and general contempt for bourgeois values evident in his major plays, *Die Hermannsschlacht, Napoleon oder die Hundert Tage*, and *Hannibal*. Wedekind admired Grabbe's plays; numerous novels and plays have been written about Grabbe. The most famous was Hanns Johst's *Der Einsame* (1917). Brecht saw it, thought it a wretched play, and in response wrote *Baal* on the same theme. Grabbe's influence on Brecht is far more direct, however. Grabbe believed that "a dramatic vision must give way to an epic vision attended by a concern with minute detail and mass scenes of dynamic monumentality. Logical development of plot must be supplanted by the station play, a seemingly haphazard arrangement of dramatic moments ordered more for their dynamic emotional impact than sequential consequence. The former emphasis on dramatic causality must be redirected to a dramatic collage. . . . Finally, the protagonists must appear as marionettes, grotesque and frightening in their helplessness." [Carol A. Melillo, "Grabbe," *The Readers Encyclopedia of World Drama*, ed. John Gassner and Edward Quinn (New York:

Thomas Y. Crowell, 1969), pp. 370-71.] For a more detailed discussion of Grabbe's contribution to the genesis of modern epic drama, see "Grabbe and Brecht" in Cowen, pp. 161-62. Grabbe's plays were championed by the Third Reich because of their nationalistic and anti-Semitic overtones.

153. See Felix Stiemer, "Christoph Dietrich Grabbe und sein *Herzog Theodor von Gothland*," *Der deutsche Rundfunk* 4 (29 August 1926): 2413-14; and Kurt Weill, *Ausgewählte Schriften*, ed. David Drew (Frankfurt am Main: Suhrkamp Verlag, 1975), pp. 224, 228-29. The broadcast of the play was one of a series of programs which surveyed two hundred years of German drama. Weill discussed Grabbe and Wedekind in *Der deutsche Rundfunk* 4 (29 August 1926):2419; (5 September 1926):2489; (19 September 1926):2663.

154. Although *Royal Palace* utilizes saxophones (it was completed in January 1926), it was not performed until after *Herzog Theodor von Gothland*. The reference to saxophones in Weill's score occurs in an unsigned review of Hindemith's *Cardillac* in *Der deutsche Rundfunk* 4 (21 November 1926):3326.

155. Felix Stiemer, "Die Aufführung des *Herzog Theodor von Gothland*," *Der deutsche Rundfunk* 4 (12 September 1926): 2580.

156. The erroneous and frequently encountered report that the Berlin Staatsoper commissioned *Royal Palace* as a result of the success of *Der Protagonist* in Dresden is chronologically untenable. The premiere of *Der Protagonist* occurred two months after Weill had completed *Royal Palace*. In his notes for the performance of *Royal Palace* at the 1971 Holland Festival, David Drew stated that it was originally intended as a companion piece for *Der Protagonist*, but the two were never performed as a pair.

157. Goll played a role in German Expressionism, but he was more widely known for his treatises that anticipated surrealist techniques. See K. Pollard, "Iwan Goll," *Cassell's Encyclopedia of World Literature*, 2 vols., 2nd ed. (London: Cassell, 1973), vol. I, p. 559. In a review published in *Die Volkswille* during 1920, Bertolt Brecht discussed one of Goll's farces, and called it "important for the theater." He cited its "emancipation of the stage management; simple, ghostly effects; newspaper flashes, ballad lyrics, photography; immensely alive machinery—like a placard reading: The Expressionist Courteline." [See James L. Rosenberg's translation of the review in *Tulane Drama Review* 7 (Fall 1962):181-82.] Note that Brecht looked favorably on both Kaiser and Goll, Weill's principal collaborators before his association with Brecht. One of Goll's plays has been translated into English: *Mathusalem* appears in *Seven Expressionist Plays: Kokoschka to Barlach*.

158. Drew, *Ueber Kurt Weill*, p. 168; and Stuckenschmidt, *Twentieth Century Composers II*, p. 140.

159. An advertisement in *Anbruch* 8 (June-July 1926) labeled *Der neue Orpheus* as op. 16, whereas the announcement in *Die Musik* 18 (June 1926):716, carried the designation op. 15, as did the publications themselves. However, *Der Protagonist* had been published in October 1925 as op. 15. The confusion continued as Universal advertised the cantata as op. 16 in *Anbruch* 9 (May-June 1927). Although the error still turns up today, it is clear that the proper designation for *Der neue Orpheus* is op. 16.

160. The evening also included de Falla's *Retablo de Maese Pedro*. There were no other performances of *Der neue Orpheus* during Weill's lifetime.

161. Paul Stefan, "Weill: Royal Palace," *Anbruch* 9 (March 1927):134.

162. Hugo Leichtentritt, "Berlin, too has its Jazz Opera," *Musical Courier* 94 (24 March 1927):5.

163. Strobel, "Kurt Weill," *Melos* 6 (October 1927):433. The reference to "szenische Kantate" occurs in his "Erinnerung an Kurt Weill," p. 134. Adolf Weissmann [in *Die Musik* 19 (April 1927):518] also perceived the influence of Stravinsky in the "cabaret-turned-operatic number" and mentioned the kinship of the violin solo to that of *Soldier's Tale*. Orpheus also appears briefly as a character in *Royal Palace*.

164. "Berlin Opera Mingles Auto Horn, Films, Jazz," *New York Times*, 3 March 1927. The article continued: "Herr Weill told the Associated Press: 'I didn't sit down to write jazz for its own sake, but rather opera for its own sake. In so doing I naturally found myself running into jazz as an expression of our time.'"

165. See Rudolf Kastner, "Zur Krise der neuen Oper: Von Kreneks *Jonny spielt auf* zu Kurt Weills *Royal Palace*," *Der deutsche Rundfunk* 5 (13 March 1927):728-29. Completion of the opera was announced in *Anbruch* 8 (January 1926):45.

166. Leichtentritt, p. 5.

167. Iwan Goll, "Flucht in die Oper," *Blätter der Staatsoper* 8 (February 1927):10-11.

168. *Anbruch* 9 (March 1927):133. The film scene was undoubtedly an innovation. *Royal Palace* was premiered two years before Berg began composition of *Lulu*, in which a film also depicts elapsed events of the heroine's life. Drew has sketched a possible connection between the operas in that Berg probably knew of the scene in *Royal Palace* through his relationship with Kleiber. [See "Musical Theatre in the Weimar Republic," p. 93.]

169. A three-page extract from the film-scene appeared in Elaine Padmore's "Kurt Weill," *Music and Musicians* 21 (October 1972):42-44. In "Germany's Latest Music Dramas," *Modern Music* 4 (May-June 1927):25, Adolf Weissmann wrote: "So much is presented to the eye that the spectator can hardly attend to the music which is almost relegated to the role of accompaniment for a movie."

170. In 1929, *Royal Palace* was revived for two performances in Essen. [See *Die Musik* 22 (January 1930):303.] Drew learned that Harry Graf Kessler unsuccessfully tried to interest Diaghilev in its performance as a ballet. [See *Ueber Kurt Weill*, p. 168.]

171. See Bertolt Brecht, "Ueber die Verwendung von Musik für ein episches Theater," *Schriften zum Theater* (Frankfurt am Main: Suhrkamp Verlag, 1957). The essay has been translated by John Willett as "On the use of Music in an Epic Theater," *Brecht on Theatre* (New York: Hill & Wang, 1964), p. 86. The composition of *Royal Palace* predates the first Brecht-Weill collaboration by more than a year.

172. The letter is quoted by Franz Willnauer in "Vom Schiffbauerdamm zum Broadway," p. 45.

173. This version was premiered by the San Francisco Opera in 1968.

174. Strobel, "Kurt Weill," *Anbruch* 10 (February 1928):58-59.

175. From a review of Weill's *Der Zar lässt sich photographieren* in *Frankfurter Zeitung*, 21 June 1928.

176. *Anbruch* 8 (January 1926):45.

177. *Die Musik* 18 (June 1926):711. A note with similar content appeared in *Anbruch* 8 (June-July 1926):294.

178. *Anbruch* 8 (September 1926):341.

179. *Blätter der Staatsoper* 7 (February 1927):2.

180. The advertisement appeared in *Anbruch* 8 (June-July 1926).

181. Heinsheimer, *Best Regards to Aïda*, pp. 114-18. Heinsheimer provides a colorful account of the audition episode itself, pp. 112-19.

182. Curjel, "Erinnerungen um Kurt Weill," p. 82.

183. Drew, "The History of Mahagonny," p. 18. Drew mentions that Weill had hoped that the libretto of *Na und?* would be in the Hofmannsthal tradition.

184. Both *Royal Palace* and *Na und?* may have been intended originally as companion 'pieces for *Der Protagonist*, but neither functioned in that role.

185. Discussion of the Brecht-Weill collaboration will be deferred to Chapter 2 even though the first product of their association, the *Mahagonny-Songspiel*, was premiered in July 1927, whereas *Zar* was not performed until February 1928. This slight displacement in chronology may expedite clarity of discussion.

186. See *Die Musik* 19 (July 1927):767; *Anbruch* 9 (August-September 1927):288; *Die Musik* 20 (October 1927).

187. *A Basso Porto* by Nicola Spinelli (1865-1906) is an Italian *verismo* opera that was premiered in Cologne in 1894. The cast of *Zar* included Maria Janowska, Ilse Kögel, Theodor Horand with Walter Brügmann directing. [See Alfred Baresel, "Walther Brügmann als Regisseur der neuen Oper," *Anbruch* 9 (August-September 1927):297-98.] *Der Protagonist* and *Zar* did not appear on the same bill until two months later on 22 April 1928 when Maurice Abravanel conducted them at Gera. The relationship of *Zar* and *Der Protagonist* was summarized by H. R. Gail in his review of the Altenburg production of the companion pieces: "Even if organically far separated from one another, they still remain inseparable musical mirror-images of a theatrical temperament which hastens with giant strides to the operatic arena of the future. Indeed, there are hardly two similar one-act operas so closely intertwined with one another in their specific scenic effect. For as charming as it [*Zar*] is, the stinging buffoonery is awakened in contrast to the deeply moving tragic play. Twice the playwright and composer have hit upon the infallibility of solid theatrical intention." [See *Anbruch* 10 (May 1928):179.]

188. *Die Musik* 20 (April 1928):542. A photograph of a scene from the Leipzig production appeared in *Anbruch* 10 (March-April 1928):121.

189. *Die Musik* 20 (September 1928):923-24.

190. Adolf Weissmann, "Kurt Weill's New Opera," *Christian Science Monitor*, 24 March 1928.

191. See Paul Stefan, "Antimonie der neuen Oper: Kurt Weill und Stravinsky," *Anbruch* 10 (April-March 1928):119-22; and Theodor W. Adorno's essay in *Die Musik* 20 (September 1928):923-24.   Stefan views the two works as contrasting approaches to the genre, whereas Adorno notes a "clear path from Weill to Stravinsky."

192. In comparison, during the 1928-29 season only two theaters produced *Wozzeck*, seven *Cardillac*, four *Oedipus rex*, and eight *Jonny spielt auf*.   Four of Schreker's operas combined received performances in only five opera houses.   Of Strauss' operas, only *Der Rosenkavalier* outranked *Zar*.   [See Wilhelm Altmann, "Opern Statistik 1928/29," *Anbruch* 11 (September-October 1929):309-15.]   By July 1928, Universal was advertising *Zar* as "a huge operatic success" with performances scheduled for more than thirty theaters.   [See *Anbruch* 10 (June-July 1928).]   Five performances of *Zar* in Laibach, Yugoslavia were reported in *Die Musik* 25 (November 1932):135.   The American premiere occurred a few months before Weill's death on 27 October 1949 at Juilliard, sponsored by the Metropolitan Opera Guild.   It was entitled "The Shah Has His Photograph Taken."

193. This list does not include *Jugendwerke*.

194. Note that the interest in Weill's career was not restricted to *Anbruch*, which often favored composers of Universal's family since the journal itself was published by Universal.

195. The program notes for the Berlin production of *Zar* included the following description: "The aesthetic of film, which is certainly epic in nature and works with epic tensions, appears on the operatic stage."   [See *Blätter der Staatsoper* 9 (October 1928):15.]

196. Prigsheim, "Kurt Weill," p. 1.

CHAPTER 2

1. "Zeitoper," *Melos* 7 (March 1928):107.

2. Kurt Weill, "Anmerkungen zu meiner Oper *Mahagonny*," *Die Musik* 22 (March 1930):440.   In "Lotte Lenya in Conversation with Steven Paul," Weill's widow recently stated: "As far as I can remember, we met him [Brecht] first in a very famous theater restaurant in Berlin called 'Schlichter' and we were brought together through friends.   From that point on, Kurt and Brecht visited each other quite often and started discussing what they could do together.   I think Kurt suggested at that time that he would like to set those five Mahagonny-Gesänge."

3. Martin Esslin, *Brecht: The Man and His Work* (New York: Doubleday, 1960), p. 33.   Thomas R. Nadar has discerned an echo of Chekhov's *The Three Sisters* in *Aufstieg und Fall der Stadt Mahagonny*—"The Maiden's Prayer" is utilized in both.   [See "The Music of Kurt Weill, Hanns Eisler and Paul Dessau in the Dramatic Works of Bertolt Brecht" (Ph.D. dissertation, University of Michigan, 1974), p. 160.]

4. *Der deutsche Rundfunk* 3 (24 May 1925):1323, and 4 (22 August 1926):2345.

5. *Der deutsche Rundfunk* 4 (24 October 1926):3031, and 4 (7 March 1926):664.

6. See Drew, *Ausgewählte Schriften*, p. 225.

7. *Der deutsche Rundfunk* 5 (13 March 1927):735. The first public performance in Berlin that was not associated with a radio broadcast occurred on 5 January 1928 with direction by Erich Engel and design by Caspar Neher.

8. *Der deutsche Rundfunk* 5 (27 March 1927):879.

9. Baden-Baden replaced Donaueschingen in 1927 as host for the festival of modern music which had been established in 1921. In addition to the evening of one-act operas, the 1927 festival featured compositions for mechanical instruments, the premieres of Berg's *Lyric Suite*, Bartók's *Sonata 1926*, and Eisler's *Tagebuch*, and an evening devoted to "film and music."

10. Drew, Insert Notes to *Kurt Weill* (DG 2709-064), p. 16.

11. Lotte Lenya, "August 28, 1928," Foreword to *The Threepenny Opera*, trans. Desmond Vesey and Eric Bently (New York: Grove Press, 1964), pp. vi-vii. In Brecht's "Ueber die Verwendung von Musik für ein episches Theater," published posthumously in 1957, he claimed that "on the occasion of the Baden-Baden Festival of 1927, where one-act operas were to be performed, I asked Weill simply to write new settings for half-a-dozen already existing songs." Brecht's claim must be dismissed on the basis of historical evidence. [See also Völker, *Brecht Chronicle*, p. 49.]

12. Weill, "Anmerkungen zu meiner Oper *Mahagonny*," p. 440. Weill had used the term "Songspiel" as early as 1925 in an essay in *Der deutsche Rundfunk*; thus the formal conception of the *Mahagonny-Songspiel* was most likely Weill's rather than Brecht's.

13. For an English translation, as well as the original text, Brecht's melodies, and valuable commentary by Hugo Schmidt, see Eric Bentley, ed., *Die Hauspostille: Manual of Piety* (New York: Grove Press, 1966). *Die Hauspostille* served as a source of lyrics for *Happy End, Die Dreigroschenoper, Aufstieg, Berliner Requiem, Vom Tod im Wald,* and *Legende vom toten Soldaten.*

14. Kurt Weill, "Ueber den gestischen Charakter der Musik," *Die Musik* 21 (March 1929):422.

15. Lotte Lenya, "Lotte Lenya Remembers Mahagonny," Insert notes to *Aufstieg*, Columbia recording, K31-243, p. 8. In his notes to Bentley's translation of *Die Hauspostille*, Hugo Schmidt described Brecht's English lyrics as being "in the idiom of one who has listened to American jazz singers without really knowing English" (p. 306). As a result, 'Alabama' was expected to rhyme with 'mamma' and syntax like 'Is here no telephone/There is no bar to sit us down' is not unusual.

16. Kurt Weill, "Vorwort zum Regiebuch der Oper *Aufstieg und Fall der Stadt Mahagonny*," *Anbruch* 12 (January 1930):6.

17. *New Yorker* (10 June 1944):16. Lotte Lenya recalled similar images: "All of us were of course fascinated by America, as we knew it from books, movies, popular songs, headlines—this was the America of the garish Twenties, with its Capones, Texas Guinans, Aimee Semple MacPhersons, Ponzis—the Florida boom and crash,

also a disastrous Florida hurricane—a ghastly photograph, reproduced in every German newspaper, of the murderess Ruth Snyder in the electric chair—Hollywood films about the Wild West and the Yukon—Jack London's adventure novels—Tin Pan Alley songs—I think it is not difficult to trace some of this in the make-believe America of Mahagonny." ["Lotte Lenya Remembers *Mahagonny*," p. 8.]

18. Ibid., p. 17.

19. Kurt Weill, quoted by David Drew in "Production Notes," *Mahagonny-Songspiel* (Vienna: Universal-Edition, 1963), p. 2.

20. Full score of *Aufstieg* (Vienna: Universal-Edition, 1930), p. 1.

21. Arnolt Bronnen, *Tage mit Bertolt Brecht* (Vienna: Kurt Desch Verlag, 1960), pp. 143-144. Klaus Völker quotes Brecht as describing the first mass demonstrations of storm troopers as "cavalcades of shady sons-o'-bitches." [*Brecht Chronicle*, p. 36]. See also Nadar, pp. 104-107.

22. Ibid., p. 144.

23. Michael Feingold, "The Building of Mahagonny," *Program of the Yale Repertory Theater* for *The Rise and Fall of the City of Mahagonny*, 31 January 1974.

24. Bronnen, p. 144.

25. The concluding lines of the *Mahagonny-Songspiel:* "Denn Mahagonny, das gibt es nicht,/Denn Mahagonny, das ist keine Ort,/Denn Mahagonny, das ist nur ein erfundenes Wort."

26. The original order in *Die Hauspostille* was: 1 "Auf nach Mahagonny," 2 "Wer in Mahagonny blieb," 3 "Gott in Mahagonny," 4 "Alabama Song," 5 "Benares Song." The new ordering of the *Songspiel* became: 1, 4, 2, 5, 3, Finale: "Dieses ganze Mahagonny."

27. Coincidentally, when Weill's folk opera *Down in the Valley* was premiered at Indiana University on 15 July 1948, it also shared the program with Hindemith's *There and Back*. Futhermore, the two operas were directed by Hans Busch, son of the conductor of the premiere of *Der Protagonist* in Dresden in 1926. There seems to be some confusion concerning the precise date of the premiere of the Songspiel. Drew dates it as 18 July 1927, but all other sources indicate that the performance occurred on the final day of the festival which concluded on 17 July 1927.

28. Ernst Wolff coached the singers, who included Lenya, Eden, Erik Wirl, Georg Ripperger, Karl Giebel, and Gerhard Pechner.

29. Neher's contribution to the theoretical and practical aspects of epic theater in general and the Brecht-Weill works in particular has not been sufficiently recognized. Neher and Brecht were childhood friends, classmates at the Augsburg Realgymnasium in 1911. Already in November of that year, Brecht at the age of thirteen, had nominated Neher his "brother *in arte*." They remained lifelong friends as Neher designed the productions for all of the Brecht-Weill theatrical works. [See Völker's *Brecht Chronicle* for a summary of Neher's relationship with Brecht.] The boxing ring was one of Brecht's favorite scenic devices; he had used it for a production of *Die Hochzeit* at the Frankfurt Schauspielhaus in December

1926. In addition to its symbolic representation of the brutal and combative nature of a capitalist society, the boxing ring signified Brecht's passion for sports in general and boxing in particular. [See Brecht's "Mehr guten Sport," *Berliner Börsen-Courier*, 6 February 1926; trans. in Willett, *Brecht on Theatre*, pp. 6-8.] Use of the boxing ring on stage was not original with Brecht, however; Piscator had used it in his *Revue Roter Rummel* (1924). It served as a topical feature because boxing was a middle-class obsession at the time.

30. The American bar was not original either—Cocteau and Milhaud had introduced a similar setting in *Boeuf sur le toit* (1919).

31. Ernst Wolff, the coach for the first performance of the *Mahagonny-Songspiel*, recalls that the controversy which surrounded the premiere began already during rehearsals when Brecht insisted that the two females in the cast appear in the nude. Although Brecht threatened to withdraw the work if his wishes were thwarted, the city council of Baden-Baden intervened, and Lotte Lenya and Irene Eden appeared clothed in evening dresses.

32. Strobel, "Erinnerung an Kurt Weill," p. 134.

33. Hans W. Heinsheimer, *Fanfare for Two Pigeons* (Garden City, N. J.: Doubleday, 1952), pp. 174-75. Of course, such demonstrations were not exceptional; often they were encouraged or incited for their beneficial free publicity. In the case of *Mahagonny*, Brecht had anticipated the mixed reaction. Describing the situation from her viewpoint on stage, Lenya recalled: "Brecht had thoughtfully provided us with whistles of our own, little *Trillerpfeifen*, so we stood there whistling defiantly back. Later, I walked into the lobby of the fashionable hotel where most of the audience went for drinks after the performance, and found a frenzied discussion in progress. Suddenly I felt a slap on the back, accompanied by a booming laugh: 'Is here no telephone?' It was Otto Klemperer. With that the whole room was singing the Benares-Song and I knew that the battle was won." ("Lenya Remembers Mahagonny," p. 8.)

34. Olin Downes, "Mahagonny," *New York Times*, 14 August 1927. It should be noted that Downes never mentions the name of Bertolt Brecht in his review, and he credits Weill with the "ideas which are not for the drawing room." Curjel recently corroborated Downes' impression (which is the opposite of the current standing of Brecht in criticism of the Brecht-Weill collaboration): "it was entirely Weill's hour." [See "Kurt Weill: Die grossen Berliner Jahre," *Neue Zeitschrift für Musik* 133 (August 1972):504.] The "offensive and insurrectionary placards" seem quite innocuous by today's standards: "Für die Sterblichkeit der Seele!" "Gegen die Civilis!" "Für vidischen Lohn," "Für die natürliche Unzucht," "Für Weill!"

35. Universal-Edition published excerpts from their reviews in an advertisement for *Mahagonny* in *Anbruch* 9 (August-September 1927).

36. Strobel, "Kurt Weill," *Melos* 6 (October 1927):433.

37. John Willett listed performances of the *Songspiel* in Hamburg during 1932 and broadcasts over the Stuttgart and Frankfurt radio stations in 1927. [*The Theatre of Bertolt Brecht: A Study from Eight Aspects* (Norfolk, Conn.: New Directions, 1959), p. 29; also see "Die Baden-Badener Kammeropern im Rundfunk," *Der deutsche Rundfunk* 5 (7 August 1927):2195.] In contrast, Drew, in his essay, "The History of Mahagonny," wrote that the score was temporarily withdrawn after the

Baden-Baden Festival but in fact was not performed in that version again until after Weill's death. A "Paris version" of *Mahagonny*, which consisted of the *Songspiel* augmented by those sections of *Aufstieg* which required only a small instrumental accompaniment was performed in Paris during December 1932, as well as in London, Rome, Venice, and Turin. The contents of the "Paris version" are inventoried in Roberto Leydi, "Precisazioni su 'Mahagonny' e altre questioni a proposito di Kurt Weill," *La Rassegna Musicale* 32 (1962):209. This composite version, originally made by Hans Curjel with Weill's reluctant consent (in 1932 he could not obtain a production of the full opera because of economic and political conditions), resurfaced in the first post-World War II performances and further confused the identities of the various versions of the work. Weill viewed the conflation of the *Songspiel* and the opera with some distaste: "The thing that I wish to prevent above all else is that the piece should simply be cut down to the basis of Songs or song-like pieces. In principle, I would much prefer that here and there a song is dropped than that the more exacting passages be cut." [Drew, "The History of Mahagonny," p. 22.] Because the *Songspiel* had been withdrawn, *Aufstieg* was often referred to as *Mahagonny* in the literature without ambiguity. To avoid confusion here, the works will be differentiated as *Mahagonny-Songspiel*, *Aufstieg*, and "Paris version."

38. See *Anbruch* 9 (August-September 1927) and *Anbruch* 10 (February 1928). Universal published Drew's edition of the *Songspiel* in 1963.

39. Weill, "Anmerkungen zu meiner Oper *Mahagonny*," p. 440. In his "Notiz zum *Berliner Requiem*" [*Der deutsche Rundfunk* 7 (17 May 1929):613], Weill referred to the *Songspiel* as a "sketch" for the opera.

40. Drew, "The History of Mahagonny," p. 18.

41. Kurt Weill, "Zeitoper," *Melos* 7 (March 1928):107.

42. Curjel, "Erinnerungen um Kurt Weill," p. 82. The production at the Krolloper scheduled for the 1929/30 season never materialized because of the delay in the opera's completion, its controversial nature (reportedly even Klemperer considered the libretto 'immoral'), and the instability of the Krolloper itself.

43. For a more complete discussion of the complex evolution of *Aufstieg* and a detailed description of the various versions and revisions, see Drew, "The History of Mahagonny," pp. 18-24; Peter Bransombe, "Brecht, Weill and Mahagonny," *Musical Times* 102 (August 1961):483-86; and David Drew, "Preface to the 1969 Edition," *Aufstieg und Fall der Stadt Mahagonny* (Vienna: Universal-Edition, 1969).

44. Universal-Edition #9851: "Klavierauszug von Norbert Gingold."

45. For a collection of critical literature dealing with *Aufstieg*, see Ernst Schumacher, *Die Dramatischen Versuche Bertolt Brechts 1918-1933* (Berlin: Rutten & Loening, 1955), pp. 263-78; and Hans Christoph Worbs, *Welterfolge der modernen Oper* (Berlin: Rembrandt Verlag, 1967), pp. 68-71. Excerpts from reviews of the productions in Leipzig, Kassel, and Braunschweig were published in *Anbruch* 12 (March 1930):112-15.

46. Caspar Neher designed the production, and the cast included Paul Beinert as Jim, Mali Trummer as Jenny, and Marga Dannenberg as Begbick. The same theater had produced the premiere of Krenek's *Jonny spielt auf* three years earlier.

47. Geraldine de Courcy, "Opera Satire on Modern Life Creates Uproar," *Musical America* 50 (10 April 1930):5. She also observed that all actors in the Leipzig production wore short white masks.

48. Stuckenschmidt's review appeared in *Die Scene* 20 (March 1930):75-77. The quotation above is an excerpt from a translation published in *Opera* 14 (February 1963):88-89.

49. Following the Kassel performance Weill commented: "Altogether everything has finally convinced me that the path which I have hacked out for myself is the right one, and that it is absolutely out of the question for me to renounce this path simply because its beginnings accidentally became involved with the direst cultural reaction and because, like all challenging innovations, it was powerfully resisted." [Drew, "The History of Mahagonny," p. 20.]

50. Drew was in error when he wrote that "all seems to have gone well, . . . the production passed without untoward incidents." ["The History of Mahagonny," p. 20.] In reviewing the Festival, Adorno wrote that he knew of no other work that was more in keeping with the concept of the avante-garde than *Aufstieg* and that "despite and because of its primitive facade, it must be considered one of the most difficult works that exists today." ["Die Opernfestspiele in Frankfurt am Main," *Die Musik* 23 (December 1930):198-200.]

51. For an account of the disturbance, see the *Frankfurter Zeitung*, 21 October 1930; and Heinsheimer, *Best Regards to Aïda*, pp. 130-33. Performances at Altenburg in October 1930 suffered similar disruptions by Nazi agents. [See Walter S. Rubsamen, "Political and Ideological Censorship of Opera," *Proceedings of the Music Teachers National Association 1941*, pp. 127-28.]

52. Heinrich Strobel, "Situation der Oper: Gespräch mit Kurt Weill," *Melos* 10 (February 1931):43.

53. When *Aufstieg* finally was produced in a Berlin theater, Herbert F. Peyser wrote: "Wherever it may have turned up, *Mahagonny* has more or less disturbed the peace. Such disturbances may mean little or much. More insidiously influential has been the fact that the work has nowhere maintained itself. And so if the Berlin opera houses might at a pinch have countenanced a rumpus or two, they were not yearning for something that might damage the furniture without profiting the box office." [See "Berlin Hears *Mahagonny*," *New York Times*, 10 January 1932.]

54. *Die Musik* 22 (May 1930):646.

55. It must be stressed that even with the revisions for the Berlin production (deletion of the "Crane Duet" and "Benares Song," for example), *Aufstieg* is not in any sense a play with incidental music. While heroic operatic voices may not be required or even desirable for certain roles, the demands of the score preclude a performance by actors who "try to sing." Indeed, Weill's singing actors were precisely that; they were extremely versatile performers who could both sing and act, although they were not necessarily operatically trained. Of the cast for the Berlin production, only Lenya was vocally untrained. Paulsen was described by Weill as a "beloved operetta-tenor"; Trude Hesterberg, Franz Forrow, Albert Peters, the eight 'men of Mahagonny' and the five 'girls of Mahagonny' were all carefully chosen singers. Surprisingly, this Berlin production in a theater rather than an opera house may have been the most musically skilled and polished

performance that the opera received before the war. [See Adorno's review in *Anbruch* 14 (February-March 1932):53.] Casting the roles of Jim, Jenny, Begbick, Fatty, or Moses with actors who cannot negotiate the musical demands of the score has led to disastrous results in several recent productions in the United States.

56. Aufricht has provided a vivid account of the circumstances surrounding the production in his *Erzähle, damit du dein Recht erweist* (Munich: Deutscher Taschenbuch Verlag, 1969), pp. 108-12. He recalled that Weill rejected his suggestion that Theo Mackeben be engaged as conductor for the production; Weill insisted upon Zemlinsky, who conducted an orchestra of thirty-five musicians (reduced from the larger forces, including a twenty-one piece stage orchestra, that were originally called for). Adorno wrote that Zemlinsky finally rescued the music of *Aufstieg* from misconceptions and demonstrated its smoldering vividness. [*Anbruch* 14 (February-March 1932):53.] Coincidentally, in 1931 Mackeben was serving as musical director of a production of Molnar's *Liliom*, which later was adapted as *Carousel* by Rodgers and Hammerstein. After his arrival in the United States, Weill himself attempted to secure the rights to adapt *Liliom* as a musical. A news item in the *New York Times* recorded the following account: "Mr. Weill has also been keen to score a musical version of *Liliom* and, so far as he knew last week, everything was settled between himself and the Theater Guild. He had done a good deal of preliminary work on it, along the lines of *The Threepenny Opera*. But the unhappy news is that Ferenc Molnar does not want his play set to music and that is that."

57. Aufricht, *Erzähle*, pp. 110-11. The nature and causes of conflict between Brecht and Weill will be explored in greater detail in Chapter 3.

58. See Brecht, *Die Hauspostille: Manual of Piety*, ed. Eric Bentley, pp. 134-37, for the text and a translation of the poem.

59. *Anbruch* 9 (December 1927):444. Bass soloist was Heinrich Hermanns. The concert included Bartók's *Dance Suite* and "songs with orchestral accompaniment" by Schoenberg, sung by soprano Ruzena Herlinger. An advertisement for the concert appeared in the *Berliner Tageblatt*, 20 November 1927.

60. Weill, "Notiz zum *Berliner Requiem*," p. 613.

61. David Drew, "Vorwort" to *Das Berliner Requiem* (Vienna: Universal-Edition, 1967), pp. v-vi.

62. The production opened at the Königgrätzer Theater on 27 October 1927. Fritz Engel reviewed it in the *Berliner Tageblatt*, 28 October 1927. The score was never published. Strindberg (1849-1912) wrote *Gustav III* in 1902, but it was not produced until 1916. Set in eighteenth-century Sweden, this drama of intrigue centers on the mercurial monarch who brought the Enlightenment to Sweden. "Bastille-Music" from Weill's score was revived at the 1975 Berlin Festival.

63. Kenneth Tynan summarized Piscator's contribution to the evolution of epic theater as follows: "Epic theater is a phrase which Brecht borrowed from Piscator in the Twenties and went on defining until the end of his life." [See Maria Ley-Piscator, *The Piscator Experiment* (New York: James H. Heineman, 1967).]

64. In addition to several plays, Lania wrote a number of novels, as well as *Hemingway: A Pictorial Biography*. He was one of Brecht's collaborators for the

screenplay of the film version of *Die Dreigroschenoper* produced by the Nero-Film Gesellschaft in 1930. For a description of *Konjunktur*, see Erwin Piscator, *Das Politische Theater*, new edition by Felix Gasbarra (Hamburg: Rowohlt Verlag, 1963), pp. 196-205.

65.   The song was published for voice and piano in Weill's *Song-Album* (Vienna: Universal-Edition, 1929). It is the only section of the score that has been published. A few other fragments of the score have survived, including a nocturne which Weill reused in *Street Scene* and an "Arbeiterlied."

66.   Alfred Kerr, "Konjunktur," *Berliner Tageblatt*, 11 April 1928; and Herbert Jhering, "Konjunktur," *Berliner Börsen-Courier*, 11 April 1928.

67.   Leo Lania, *Today We Are Brothers: The Biography of a Generation*, trans. Ralph Marlowe (Boston: Riverside Press, 1942), p. 278.

68.   More detailed and complex parallels can be drawn by comparing Weill's "Vorwort zum Regiebuch der Oper *Aufstieg und Fall der Stadt Mahagonny*," *Anbruch* 12 (January 1930):5-7 with Lania's description of *Konjunktur* in *Today We Are Brothers*, pp. 277-78.

69.   The production was mounted at the Staatliches Schauspielhaus on 20 April 1928. Arnolt Bronnen, the son of an Austrian-Jewish dramatist, had lived with the Brecht family for a short time after Brecht's mother died in 1920; they were associates thereafter. [See Völker, *Brecht Chronicle*, pp. 30-38.] In 1933 Bronnen managed to pass himself off as the illegitimate son of an Aryan and remained in Germany. [See Edwin Klinger, *Arnolt Bronnen: Werk und Wirkung* (Hildesheim: H. A. Gerstenberg, 1974). *Katalaunische Schlacht* had been published in 1924 by E. Rowohlt, Berlin.]

70.   Kerr wrote in the *Berliner Tageblatt*, 27 April 1928; Jhering in the *Berliner Börsen-Courier*, 26 April 1928.

71.   *Die Musik* 21(December 1928):222.

72.   Lotte Lenya, "That Was a Time," *Theater Arts*, May 1956. Reprinted as "August 28, 1928," Foreword to *The Threepenny Opera*, trans. Eric Bentley and Desmond I. Vesey (New York: Grove Press, 1964), pp. v-xiv; and Ernst Aufricht, *Erzähle*, pp. 55-69.

73.   Kurt Weill, "Korrespondenz über *Dreigroschenoper*," *Anbruch* 11 (January 1929):25.

74.   Hauptmann and Brecht were not alone in their interest in Gay's ballad opera. In the May 1928 issue of *Anbruch*, Schott advertised its publication of a German translation of *Die Bettler-Oper* by Dr. Otto Ehrhard and Dr. Kurt Elwenspoek. A production of this version was announced for the 1928/29 season at Darmstadt. As early as 1925, Ludwig Strecker had suggested to Hindemith a modernized version of *Beggar's Opera*. [See Geoffrey Skelton, *Paul Hindemith: The Man Behind the Music* (London: Victor Gollancz, 1975), p. 81.]

75.   Aufricht, *Erzähle*, p. 56. Erich Engel and Brecht were long-time friends and associates. Engel had directed the world premiere of *Im Dickicht der Städte* (Munich, May 1923) and its subsequent production in Berlin (October 1924), as well as *Mann ist Mann* at the Volksbühne (Berlin, January 1928). As artistic director of Reinhardt's Deutsches Theater in 1923, Engel had employed Brecht

and Zuckmayer as dramaturgists. Brecht considered Engel's production of Fritz Kortner's *Coriolanus* to be a decisive attempt at epic theater. [See Völker, *Brecht Chronicle*, p. 41.]

76. Aufricht recalled that when Brecht mentioned Weill's name to him, he went to see *Der Protagonist* and *Der Zar lässt sich photographieren* at the Charlottenburger Oper (Berlin Städtische Oper) and found his music "too atonal for a theater piece." [See Aufricht, *Erzähle*, pp. 56-57.] However, Weill's operas were not produced in Berlin until 14 October 1928—after *Die Dreigroschenoper* had already opened. Perhaps Aufricht saw a performance in another city (possibly Leipzig or Frankfurt) or merely acted on his knowledge of Weill's reputation.

77. Although the "Morgenchorale" is no longer the first musical number of the score because a prologue, "Ballad vom Mackie Messer," was added during rehearsals, it was originally the first vocal number in Brecht's and Weill's conception. Note that Gay's first air is entitled "An Old Woman Cloathed in Gray"—perhaps the inspiration of the "Lady in Gray" in *Happy End*.

78. The haste and seclusion of the collaborators accounts for the fact that no mention of *Die Dreigroschenoper* can be found in *Anbruch* or *Die Musik*, both of which chronicled Weill's projects very carefully, until the reviews of the premiere appeared. Weill's publishers had not seen the score or libretto before the premiere.

79. Weill's use of Hawaiian guitar in the score of *Die Dreigroschenoper* coincided with Hans Nevermann's "Hawaii-Musik" in *Die Musik* 20 (August 1928):818-821. The Hawaiian guitar had reached its peak of popularity at that time.

80. Most of the cast were well-known to Berlin audiences. Of the principals, only Lenya was relatively unknown as an actress. Aufricht described his first hearing of Weill's score and his first meeting with Lenya in *Erzähle*, p. 59. He described Carola Neher as the best interpreter of Weill's and Brecht's works other than Lenya.

81. See Aufricht, *Erzähle*, p. 62.

82. Kurt Weill, "Anmerkung zu der 'Unterdrückten Arie der Lucy,'" *Die Musik* 25 (November 1932):128. The aria was first published in the same issue. It also appears as an appendix to the full score published by Universal (#14901). [See also Aufricht, *Erzähle*, p. 58.]

83. Weill's score, dated "23.8.1928," confirms this conjecture. Weill seldom worked in that manner, however; even in the United States, he usually orchestrated his Broadway shows before casting and rehearsals had begun—unlike almost all other Broadway composers who shifted keys for performers up to opening night and usually "sublet" orchestration of their music to specialists.

84. Lenya, "August 28, 1928," p. xii; and Aufricht, *Erzähle*, pp. 62-63. On opening night the hand organ did not work, so the first two strophes of the "Moritat" were sung without accompaniment. It should be noted that the reprise of the "Moritat" at the end of the play which has become ingrained in performance tradition is not authentic. It does not appear in the original script, nor does Weill call for it in the score. Brecht wrote the three verses of the reprise for the film version; they appear in his *Versuche* as "Die Schlussstrophen des Dreigroschenfilms," along with two optional verses for the "Moritat" itself. The film omits all three "Dreigroschenfinales" (along with a good deal of other music)

and thus a reprise of the "Moritat" is a logical conclusion to the film. To append such a reprise to the play after the third finale clearly undercuts the intent to conclude with a straightforward operatic finale. Weill wrote: "The last 'Dreigroschenfinale' is by no means a parody; rather here the concept of 'opera' is applied directly to the resolution of conflict; that is, as an action-structuring element, and therefore had to be molded in its purest, most fundamental form." [Weill, "Korrespondenz über Dreigroschenoper," p. 25.] The symmetrical structure of the opera is destroyed by an attempt to send the audience out humming the "Moritat." Weill clearly marked the final chord of "III. Dreigroschenfinale" as "Ende der Oper." His directions should be followed.

85. Lenya's "August 28, 1928" apparently refers to the date of the premiere, but newspaper advertisements, programs, reviews, and Aufricht all date the opening as 31 August 1928.

86. Anbruch 11 (January 1929). Only the British seemed entirely unimpressed by Die Dreigroschenoper. It is as if Weill and Brecht could not be forgiven for their mutilation of Beggar's Opera. Most critics assumed in advance that Weill was merely attempting to "re-arrange" the material of the original (as Britten later did). Eric Blom's colorful, entertaining, and entirely wrong-headed essay, "Three-Groats Opera," is indicative of the general critical reception for the work in England: "The distressing fact is that the Dreigroschenoper is not the Beggar's Opera at all. The piece is described as 'after John Gay.' It is—a long way after. Satire has yielded to coarse invective, pointed dialogue to blunt twaddle, polished verse to lamentable doggerel. . . . Foulness and silliness alternate where they do not happen to combine. . . . It must be confessed that both words and music of the Dreigroschenoper look suspiciously as if they had been written for cretins. . . . One thinks of the moonlit tenement backyards in the slums of Berlin, where a consumptive cornet player, trying to snatch some fresh air, practices among the dustbins, while a lovelorn saxophonist utters his puling notes from an upper window." [The Sackbut 11 (March 1931):211-15.] A review of a concert version of the work, presented in London at Broadcasting House on 8 February 1935, dismissed Weill and Brecht as "lacking our touchstone and our sensitiveness." [Musical Times 76 (March 1935):260.]

87. Songs from Die Dreigroschenoper were recorded by Columbia, Grammola, Homocord-Electro, Odeon, Orchestrola-Vocalion, Parlophon, and Polyfar.

88. A roll of Dreigroschen-wallpaper has been preserved in the Theater Museum of Cologne.

89. George Antheil, "Wanted—Opera by and for Americans," Modern Music 7 (June-July 1930):12.

90. Heinsheimer, Best Regards to Aïda, pp. 122-27.

91. The "Ballade von der sexuellen Hörigkeit" was included in Weill's Song-Album (U-E #9787) of 1929. The "Salomon Song," although omitted from the first performance, did appear in the piano-vocal score. It was also published in Die Music 21 (March 1929). Kiepenheuer Verlag also published a number of songs from Die Dreigroschenoper in the spring of 1929.

92. In the Berliner Tageblatt, 3 May 1929, Kerr accused Brecht of plagiarism in that he had failed to credit translations of four ballads by Francois Villon to K. L.

Ammer in the published libretto. Brecht's reply appeared in the *Berlin Börsen-Courier*, 6 May 1929. Eventually Ammer's publisher sued Brecht, who had to pay royalties to Ammer.

93. The hearings of the case occurred on 17 and 20 October 1930. Brecht did receive a settlement and did not appeal the case. The cast of the film included Rudolf Forster, Carola Neher, Fritz Rasp, Valeska Gert, Reinhold Scheunzel, Ernst Busch, and Lotte Lenya. Although Weill supervised the music, the screenplay, which differs significantly from the stage version, omitted more than half of the original score. Weill was not adverse to the changes. Hans Heinsheimer reported: "He [Weill] has taken the standpoint that the sound-film has its own artistic principle of form which is not to be interpreted by engineers or theatre conductors, that the laws of the sound-film are not subordinate to the film director, but that here there is a new realm for the creative musician, to which he alone possesses the key. Trespassing is to be punished. There has been up till now scarcely a single instance of a musical film constructed according to the fundamental principles of new form. On this account Kurt Weill's lawsuit will have an historical significance." [Hans Heinsheimer, "Film Opera—Screen vs. Stage," *Modern Music* 8 (March-April 1931):14.]

94. All of Brecht's works that relate to the *Dreigroschen*-material may be found in Siegfried Unseld, ed., *Brechts Dreigroschenbuch* (Frankfurt am Main: Suhrkamp Verlag, 1960).

95. *Kleine Dreigroschenmusik* should not be confused with the "Suite from *Die Dreigroschenoper*" for orchestra with voice *ad libitum*, arranged and orchestrated by Max Schoenherr.

96. Weill excludes oboes from the score. It appears that the oboe was his least favorite wind instrument. He omits it entirely from *Der Jasager, Divertimento, Die Dreigroschenoper, Happy End, Mahagonny-Songspiel, Frauentanz, Vom Tod im Wald, Der Lindberghflug*, and *Berliner Requiem. Der Silbersee, Aufstieg, Die sieben Todsünden*, Symphony no. 1, and the Violin Concerto utilize just one oboe.

97. *Anbruch* 11 (March 1929):143, 185.

98. The advertisement appeared in *Anbruch* 13 (January 1931). Universal published the score in 1929. [See Theodor W. Adorno's review of the publication in *Anbruch* 11 (September-October 1929):316-17.]

99. Therese Langfield danced Juno and Charlotte Bidmead, Minerva in the original production. The London Ballet presented *Judgment of Paris* on 5 December 1938, the Ballet Rambert on 1 October 1940, and the New York Ballet Theatre on 23 January 1940.

100. *New York Herald-Tribune*, 24 January 1940.

101. The instrumentation of *Judgment of Paris:* flute (piccolo), oboe, clarinet (tenor saxophone), alto saxophone (2nd clarinet), bassoon, horn, two trumpets, two trombones, percussion, piano, and strings.

102. David Drew, Insert Notes to *Die Dreigroschenoper*, Columbia recording, 02S 201. The request did not dissuade Francesco von Mendelssohn from opening his production of *The Threepenny Opera* at the Empire Theater in New York on 13 April 1933. It closed after twelve performances.

103. Strobel, "Erinnerung an Kurt Weill," p. 133.

104. Quoted in *Weill-Lenya*, p. 42.

105. Compositions were also commissioned from four other composers, including Weill's former associates in the November Group, Max Butting (1888-1976) and Heinz Tiessen (1887-1971). The *Illustrierte Wochenschrift des Berliners Tageblatts* published Butting's "Berlin im Licht Blues" and Otto Stransky's "Berlin im Licht Marschlied" after the festival.

106. For a more detailed account of the event, see the *Berliner Tageblatt*, 13-16 October 1928. For specific references to Weill's "Berlin im Licht-Song," see *Anbruch* 10 (October 1928):304; and *Melos* 7 (October 1928):503. Weill himself mentions the festival in *Der deutsche Rundfunk* 6 (26 October 1928):2964.

107. David Drew, Program Notes to Four Concerts by the London Sinfonietta, March 1977.

108. Universal-Edition #8862 (1928) and VCJ No. 104 (1929).

109. *Die Musik* 21 (November 1928):155.

110. *Melos* 8 (January 1929):37.

111. See Felix Stiemer, "Geschichte eines Requiems," *Der deutsche Rundfunk* 7 (31 May 1929):731: and David Drew, Preface to *Das Berliner Requiem* (Vienna: Universal-Edition, 1967), p. v.

112. "Vom ertrunkenen Mädchen" also had appeared in *Baal* (1922) and was first published in *Die Weltbühne* in November 1922. In his insert notes to *Kurt Weill*, Drew discusses the commemorative features of the cantata: the tenth anniversary of the conclusion of World War I and the murder of Rosa Luxemburg, whose body was recovered from a canal in Berlin—a real "ertrunkenes Mädchen."

113. *Anbruch* 11 (February 1929):97.

114. Weill, "Notiz zum *Berliner Requiem*," p. 613. This was Weill's final contribution to *Der deutsche Rundfunk*.

115. Ibid. The quotation has not been translated because it consists primarily of the titles of the various movements.

116. For a more complete account of the various versions and revisions of the cantata, see Drew's preface, p. vi. He labeled the version that Weill described as Version A, which was never performed. Version B is that of the premiere.

117. The cantata is scored for 2 clarinets, 2 alto saxophones (2nd doubling on tenor saxophone), 2 bassoons, 2 trumpets, 2 horns, 2 trombones, (tuba *ad lib.*), tympani/percussion, guitar/banjo, and piano/harmonium. If a male chorus is not available, the *Requiem* may be performed by three solo voices.

118. Stiemer, p. 731. "Können einem toten Mann nicht helfen" is the title of a movement from the version of *Das Berliner Requiem* that was broadcast on 22 May 1929. Eventually that chorus was deleted from the *Requiem* because it had become the finale of *Aufstieg*.

119. See Karl Westermeyer, "Musik für Arbeiter," *Die Musik* 22 (January 1930):299. "Die Legende vom toten Soldaten" was intended for performance by amateur

groups. Its declamation is entirely syllabic and the musical texture is homophonic throughout. It was never published, but a manuscript copy is in the possession of the Library of Congress.

120. An excerpt from "Bericht über das Unerreichbare," No. 15 of *Der Lindberghflug*, translated by Lawrence Gilman in "A Musical Picture of Lindbergh's Great Flight," *Music and Youth* 11 (June 1931):122.

121. Hindemith and Weill composed alternate sections of the cantata. Hindemith's movements were never published; the manuscript is now in the Hindemith-Archive. Hindemith's setting of Brecht's *Das Badener Lehrstück vom Einverständnis* was premiered at the same festival.

122. *Christian Science Monitor*, 24 August 1929. [See also Eberhard Preussner, "Gemeinschaftsmusik 1929 in Baden-Baden," *Die Musik* 21 (September 1929):900-901.] Brecht described the Baden-Baden performance in some detail: "On the left of the platform the radio orchestra was placed with its apparatus and singers, on the right the listener, who performed the Flier's part, i.e. the paedagogical part, with a score in front of him. He read the sections to be spoken without identifying his own feelings with those contained in the text, pausing at the end of each line; in other words, in the spirit of an *exercise*." ["An Example of Paedagogics," *Brecht on Theater*, p. 32.]

123. Weill, "Notiz zum *Berliner Requiem*," p. 613. It should be noted that in this essay Weill referred to the *Mahagonny-Songspiel*, *Das Berliner Requiem*, and *Der Lindberghflug* as "studies to some extent for the now completed opera *Aufstieg*."

124. In an advertisement for *Der Lindberghflug* in *Anbruch* 12 (January 1930), Weill is quoted: "I consider it necessary to designate a practical purpose for vocal music beyond its use in the concert hall. Here Brecht's poem, 'Der Lindberghflug,' is presented in a musical setting which is intended for performance in schools."

125. Alfred Einstein, "Lindbergh Cantata," *New York Times*, 2 February 1930.

126. Respectively U-E #9938 and #8838. The full score included Antheil's English translation of the text. A note in Weill's orchestral score states that the soprano and alto parts of the chorus should be executed by boys if possible.

127. The autographed vocal score that Weill sent Lindbergh is now part of the Lindbergh Collection of the Missouri Historical Society, St. Louis. For a more complete discussion of *Der Lindberghflug*, see the present author's "*Der Lindberghflug*: Kurt Weill's Musical Tribute to Lindbergh," *Missouri Historical Society Bulletin* 23 (April 1977):193-96.

128. Willett, *The Theater of Bertolt Brecht*, p. 34. The new title is not original; Arno Schirokauer wrote a radio play with the same title in 1928. [See *Der deutsche Rundfunk* 6 (5 April 1928):967.]

129. *Gesammelte Werke*, 3 vols. (Hamburg: Rowohlt Verlag, 1960), 2:126. Translated in Ewen, *Bertolt Brecht: His Life, His Art, and His Times*, p. 178.

130. Advertisements and reviews of *Happy End* identified the story as "Under the Mistletoe," published in the *J. L. Weekly* (St. Louis). [See C. Hooper Trask, "Down, But Not Out, On the Berlin Stage," *New York Times*, 27 October 1929; and Esslin, *Brecht: The Man and His Work*, p. 42.] I have not been able to

verify the existence of such a story or of the journal itself. Recent scholarship points to the possibility that the story in question actually appeared in the *Saturday Evening Post;* the obscure title and the fictitious journal were merely an invention to avoid copyright squabbles. [See Völker, *Brecht Chronicle,* p. 55; and Michael Feingold, "The Unhappy Beginnings of *Happy End,*" Program Notes to the Yale Repertory Theater production, 1974.]

131. The cast included Carola Neher, Helene Weigel, Kurt Gerron, Peter Lorre, Theo Lingen, and Oskar Homolka. Lotte Lenya was unavailable because she was appearing as Marion in Max Reinhardt's production of *Danton's Death.* Opening night of *Happy End* was originally planned for 31 August 1929 to coincide with the first anniversary of the premiere of *Die Dreigroschenoper,* but the premiere was delayed until 2 September.

132. Aufricht, *Erzähle,* p. 88.

133. Ibid.

134. Feingold, "The Unhappy Beginnings of *Happy End,*" p. 2. For an eyewitness description of the tumultuous premiere, see Alfred Kerr's review in the *Berliner Tageblatt,* 3 September 1929; and Herbert Jhering's in the *Berliner Börsen-Courier,* 3 September 1929.

135. Universal-Edition nos. 9892, 9893, and VCJ nos. 114 and 115. The original instrumentation of *Happy End* is, of course, virtually identical to that of *Die Dreigroschenoper,* since the same personnel were involved.

136. Universal-Edition #11685.

137. *Die Petroleuminseln* was first published in 1927. It is included in Lion Feuchtwanger, *Gesammelte Werke,* vol. 2: *Stücke in Prosa* (Amsterdam: Querido Verlag, 1936). A review of the premiere on 31 October 1927 at the Deutsches Schauspielhaus in Hamburg appeared in the *London Times,* 2 November 1927. Although in that review, the critic mentions that Piscator planned to stage the work in Berlin, this production evidently did not materialize until 1929. For a brief discussion of the play, see Lothar Kahn, *Insight and Action: The Life and Work of Lion Feuchtwanger* (London: Associated University Presses, 1975), pp. 128-29. Only the one published song of Weill's incidental music is known to have survived.

138. Kurt Weill, "Ueber meine Schuloper *Der Jasager,*" *Die Scene* 20 (August 1930):232-33. He lists the three possibilities of *Schuloper* as training for composers, training for operatic production, and training for students in schools.

139. "Aktuelles Zwiegespräch über die Schuloper zwischen Kurt Weill und Dr. Hans Fischer," *Die Musikpflege* 1 (April 1930):48-49.

140. Hauptmann's translation of Waley's version was publihed in *Der Scheinwerfer* 3 (1929/30):7-14. Brecht's first published version, which follows Hauptmann's translation very closely, appeared in *Die Musikpflege* 1 (April 1930):53-58, following "Aktuelles Zwiegespräch über die Schuloper zwischen Kurt Weill und Dr. Hans Fischer." For a comparison of this first version with Brecht's later revisions, see Michael Feingold, "The Difficulty of *Einverstaendnis:* A Note on

Der Jasager and Brecht's Didactic Plays," *Yale/Theatre* 6 (Winter 1975):32-34. Feingold's translation of the text follows on pp. 35-43.

141. Weill, "Ueber meine Schuloper *Der Jasager*," p. 233. Note that Brecht had treated the topic of *Einverständnis* in the *Badener Lehrstück vom Einverständnis* which was composed by Hindemith and premiered at the Baden-Baden Festival in July 1929.

142. See David Drew, "Weill's School Opera," *Musical Times* 106 (December 1965):934. Drew gives a more complete account of the genesis of *Der Jasager* than is presented here.

143. See Völker, *Brecht Chronicle*, pp. 56-57; and Ewen, *Bertolt Brecht: His Life, His Art, and His Times*, p. 251. The similarity in content of many of Brecht's didactic works is accentuated by the fact that when Brecht submitted the sketch for *Die Massnahme* to the festival committee, it bore the title "Der Jasager (Musik von Hanns Eisler)." [See Nadar, p. 206.]

144. Kurt Weill, "Musikfest oder Musikstudio?", *Melos* 9 (May-June 1930):230-32.

145. Although the music had been rehearsed by Professor Heinrich Martens, Weill insisted that a student, Kurt Drabek, conduct the performance. [See Drew, "Weill's School Opera," p. 934.] The Zentralinstitut für Erziehung and Unterricht published the monthly journal *Die Musikpflege*, in which Weill's discussion with Fischer and Brecht's text for *Der Jasager* were published.

146. Perhaps the most appropriate criticism, in the eyes of Weill and Brecht, was written by the pupils of the Elisabeth Gymnasium (Breslau) who performed the work and then discussed their reactions to it. Their views appeared in *Anbruch* 13 (February-March 1931):52-54.

147. Drew has noted that Kestenberg's "department adopted *Der Jasager* as, so to speak, a set piece, and it was performed in almost every major state school in Germany—one of the achievements for which Kestenberg was savagely attacked, and finally hounded from his post." ["Musical Theater in the Weimar Republic," p. 105. See also Josef Rufer, "Leo Kestenberg: Zu seinem Ausschieden aus dem Preussischen Kultusministerium und zu seinem 50. Geburtstag," *Anbruch* 14 (December 1932):212.]

148. Weill, "Ueber meine Schuloper *Der Jasager*," p. 232.

149. "Aktuelles Zwiegespräch über die Schuloper zwischen Kurt Weill und Dr. Hans Fischer," p. 51.

150. Völker, *Brecht Chronicle*, pp. 57-58.

151. In the revised version, the town suffers from a plague of which the mother is just one victim. In *Der Neinsager*, the boy refuses to acquiesce to the old custom that he must be thrown into the valley. Instead he states the need for the new custom of thinking afresh in each new situation. For a brief synopsis, see Esslin, *Brecht: The Man and His Work*, p. 290. A useful compendium of documents which relate to all versions of *Der Jasager* is Peter Szondi, ed., *Bertolt Brechts Der Jasager und Der Neinsager: Vorlagen, Fassungen, Materialen* (Frankfurt am Main: Suhrkamp Verlag, 1966). It includes Waley's adaptations, the transcript of Brecht's discussion with students of the Karl Marx Schule, and numerous reviews. The

most detailed discussion of the work itself occurs in Horst Braun, *Untersuchungen zur Typologie der zeitgenössischen Schul- und Jugendoper* (Regensburg: Gustav Bosse Verlag, 1963), pp. 100-122. [See also Nadar, pp. 166-77.]

152. There is no record of a performance of both *Der Jasager* and *Der Neinsager* according to Brecht's instruction.

153. *Die Musik* 25 (September 1932):74. *Der Jasager* was also performed in Amsterdam and Vienna.

154. Actually this was a production of the "Paris version" of *Mahagonny*. [See *Anbruch* 14 (December 1932):220.]

155. Curjel, "Erinnerungen um Kurt Weill," pp. 83-84. Reviews of the performance: A. Machabey in *Le Menestrel* 30 (December 1932):534; Henri Prunières in *La Revue musicale* 13 (January 1933):45-47. Universal advertised the concerts as "a sensational success by Kurt Weill in Paris" in *Anbruch* 15 (January 1933).

156. Maurice Abravanel, "Kurt Weill, Symphonist," *Program Notes* to a performance of Symphony no. 2 at Wolf Trap Farm Park for the Performing Arts, 1972. Cocteau also considered collaborating with Weill on an opera, but the project was not completed.

157. A. Lehman Engel conducted, Sanford Meisner directed. The opera had been translated into English by Alice Mattulath. The cast included F. W. Britton, Alan MacMurray, and Gertrude Black. [See the *New York Times*, 26 April 1933; the *New York Herald-Tribune*, 26 April 1933; and the *Musical Courier*, 6 May 1933.]

158. *Anbruch* 16 (January-February 1934):35.

159. *New York World Telegram*, 21 December 1935.

160. "Aktuelles Zwiegespräch über die Schuloper zwischen Kurt Weill und Dr. Hans Fischer," p. 51.

161. An announcement that *Schwejk* was to be the basis for Weill's next opera appeared in *Die Musik* 22 (July 1930):796. In the United States Aufricht managed to bring Brecht and Weill together for a proposed *Schwejk* again in 1943, but negotiations were unsuccessful. [See Bertolt Brecht, *Bertolt Brechts Arbeitsjournal*, ed. Werner Hecht, 3 vols. (Frankfurt am Main: Suhrkamp Verlag, 1972), 2:568, 579; and Völker, *Brecht Chronicle*, pp. 120-24.]

162. The production at the Staatliches Schauspielhaus, in which Peter Lorre played Galy Gay, was directed by Brecht himself, who put the actors on stilts and in masks.

163. See Gunther Rühle, ed., *Theater für die Republik 1917-1933 im Spiegel der Kritik* (Frankfurt am Main: S. Fischer Verlag, 1967):1071-72.

164. "More Americans and Kurt Weill in Berlin," *Modern Music* 9 (May-June 1932):187.

165. During the month of December 1927 there were 202 operettas performed in fifty theaters in Germany. During the same month three years later, the number of performances of operettas in the same theaters had more than doubled. [See Hans W. Heinsheimer, "Die Umgestaltung des Operntheaters," *Anbruch* 15 (August-September 1933):107-113.] The increase in the production of operettas in German theaters from 1930 to 1931 was more than 400 percent. A fascinating

progressive account of the deterioration of the artistic institutions in Germany from 1931 to 1933 as a result of the economic crisis and the rise of the National Socialists to power has been supplied in the "annual reports" concerning the situation by Hans Heinsheimer: "A New Patron for Music," *Modern Music* 8 (January-February):14-19; "German Music on the Breadline," *Modern Music* 9 (March-April 1932):115-20; "Nightmare in Germany," *Modern Music* 10 (January-February 1933):115-17.

166. See Alfred Einstein, "German Opera, Past and Present," *Modern Music* 11 (January-February 1934):67.

167. Kurt Weill, "Wirklich eine Opernkrise?", *Deutsche allgemeine Zeitung*, 8 July 1932; "Das Formproblem der modernen Oper," *Der Scheinwerfer 5* (February 1932):3-6; and Heinrich Strobel, "Situation der Oper: Gespräch mit Kurt Weill," *Melos* 10 (February 1931):43-45.

168. Weill, "Wirklich eine Opernkrise?"

169. Herder's parable appears as a preface to the piano-vocal score of *Die Bürgschaft* (Vienna: Universal Edition, 1932), no. 1525.   In her review of the opera, Geraldine de Courcy summarized Herder's tale as follows: "A judge in darkest Africa is called upon to decide the ownership of a bag of money found in a sack of chaff.   The man who buys the chaff returns the money to the miller, but the latter refuses to accept it on the grounds of having sold the sack with its entire contents.   The judge therefore orders the two children of the disputants to marry and gives them the money as dowry.   Whereupon Alexander of Macedonia, who witnesses the incident, is moved to reflect that in the civilized world, of which he is the head and ornament, the State would have promptly settled the matter by beheading the litigants and confiscating the money." [*Musical America* 52 (10 April 1932):5.]

170. Herbert F. Peyser, "Weill's *Die Bürgschaft*," *New York Times*, 27 March 1932.

171. The cast included Wilhelm Rode, Hans Reinmar, Josef Burgwinkel, Charlotte Müller, Irene Eisinger, and Ruth Berglund.   Carl Ebert had directed the production of Brecht's *Im Dickicht der Städte* in Darmstadt during December 1927.

172. Although Hindenburg outpolled Hitler by seven million votes, a runoff was required since neither candidate had received a majority of the total votes cast. Hindenburg won the second election, and at the age of 84 served as the titular head of government while a succession of chancellors (Brüning, von Papen, Schleicher) attempted to patch together coalitions in the Reichstag.   In 1932 the National Socialists became the largest party in the Reichstag.

173. de Courcy, review in *Musical America* 52 (10 April 1932):5.

174. Peyser, "Weill's *Die Bürgschaft*."

175. Ernst Bloch, "Fragen in Weill's *Bürgschaft*," *Anbruch* 1 (December 1932):207-9. Herbert Fleischer also considered *Oedipus rex* to be the historical and intellectual background of *Die Bürgschaft*. ["Kurt Weill: Versuch einer einheitlichen Stilbetrachtung," p. 137.]

176. Between 1925 and 1930 Handel's *Rodalinda, Radamisto, Guilio Cesare, Joshua, Belshazzar, Ottone, Saul, Samson* were all revived in Germany.   There was a

Handel-festival in Göttingen in 1927.   Egon Wellesz has noted that "it is significant that from the moment when new operas inspired by this spirit began to be written, Handelian operas gradually disappeared from the stage," and that "the performances of Handel unquestionably prepared the way for the Verdi-renaissance." [*Essays on Opera*, trans. Patricia Kean (London: Dennis Dobson, 1950), p. 130.] Verdi was one of Weill's favorite composers, and Handel's operatic style had already served as the model for the third "Dreigroschenfinale."

177.   Geraldine de Courcy noted: "From his first opera, *The Protagonists* [*sic*], down through the *Dreigroschenoper, Mahagonny* and *Jasager* to the present work, [Weill's] line of development has been straight and consistent."

178.   Fleischer, p. 137.   Herbert Connor, who considered *Die Bürgschaft* Weill's "most interesting, most disunited, and most significant (for the future of opera) work," also noted that "in this opera, Weill the musician triumphs over Weill the theoretician and intellectual." ["Kurt Weill und die Zeitoper," *Die Musik* 25 (November 1932):102-3.]

179.   Kurt Weill, "Kurt Weill antwortet," *Melos* 11 (October 1932):337.

180.   Drew, *Ueber Kurt Weill*, p. xxviii.   The productions in Wiesbaden (Karl Rankl, conductor; Paul Bekker, director) and Düsseldorf (Jascha Horenstein, conductor; W. B. Iltz, director) did take place.   Drew noted that *Die Bürgschaft* was the last progressive opera to be staged in a state-subsidized opera house before Hitler assumed power.

181.   Einstein, "German Opera, Past and Present," p. 67.

182.   Steinthal was music critic of the *Zwölf Uhr Mittagsblatt*.

183.   Supposedly Weill and Neher decided on the cuts and revisions when they were working on *Die sieben Todsünden* in Paris.   [See Ross Parmenter, "Carl Ebert to Revive a Weill Opera He Produced in pre-Hitler Berlin," *New York Times*, 16 June 1957.]

184.   From a letter to *Life* magazine dating from 1947.   Quoted in *Weill-Lenya*.

185.   The announcement of *Der Silbersee* (*The Silver Lake: A Winter's Tale*) appeared in *Anbruch* 14 (September 1932):149.

186.   One still encounters considerable confusion about the premiere of *Der Silbersee*. In his biography of Kaiser, B. J. Kenworthy reported that the work premiered simultaneously in ten cities in Germany.   H. W. Heinsheimer, numerous reference books, and interviewers quoting Weill and Lenya assert a simultaneous premiere in eleven theaters.   I have been able to authenticate only the three productions in Leipzig, Magdeburg, and Erfurt, which were announced in *Anbruch* 15 (January 1933).   I have not ascertained whether the other alleged productions were initially planned and then scrapped or if they are merely the embellishment of hazy memories.

187.   F. P. Hauptmann, "*Der Silbersee*," *Völkischer Beobachter*, 24 February 1933. Reprinted in Drew, *Ueber Kurt Weill*, pp. 110-11.   The above excerpt is quoted by Kotschenreuther in *Kurt Weill*, p. 70.   The review ended with a direct attack on Brecher, who was forced to seek refuge in the Netherlands.

188.   *Berliner Tageblatt*, 20 February 1930.

189. The first post-War revival of *Der Silbersee* occurred in Berlin during 1955.

190. Respectively U-E #10464 and #10471.

191. Taubman, "From Long Hair to Short."

192. Brecht later changed the title to *Die sieben Todsünden der Kleinbürger*. In France it was entitled *Le Sept Péchés Capitaux*, in England *Anna-Anna*, and in the United States *The Seven Deadly Sins*.

193. Virgil Thomson, "Paris News," *Modern Music* 11 (November-December 1933):45.

194. In *Die sieben Todsünden* a tuba replaced the second trombone of *Der Silbersee*, and a banjo-guitar part was added.

195. Each city leads to an encounter with one of the deadly sins: sloth enroute from Louisiana, pride in Memphis, anger in Los Angeles, gluttony in Philadelphia, lust in Boston, covetousness in Baltimore, and envy in San Francisco.

196. Thomson, "Paris News," pp. 42-45. [See also Paul Bertrand's review in *Le Menestrel* 95 (16 June 1933):244.]

197. Letter of 10 June 1933, quoted by Völker, *Brecht Chronicle*, pp. 64-65.

198. Völker, *Brecht Chronicle*, p. 78. Marc Blitzstein attempted to mount a production of *Anna-Anna* in 1936, as the following excerpt from an unpublished letter to Weill, dated 22 June 1936, indicates: "I should like to consider the possibility of performing your *Anna-Anna* next season in a small series of chamber-operas. Would such a performance interest you? And do you have the score here? I should greatly appreciate the opportunity of examining the score; I have heard of the work only through reviews, and your own comment; and the idea seems to me very attractive." The performance did not take place.

199. The piano-vocal score, edited by Wilhelm Brückner-Rüggeberg, was published in 1955 by Hullenhagen & Griel in Hamburg and B. Schotts Söhne in Mainz.

200. Other works which were commissioned or sponsored by the Princess, who was born in the United States as Winaretta Singer (of the sewing machine family), include: de Falla's *El retablo da maese Pedro*, Fauré's Suite from *Pelléas et Mélisande*, Ravel's *Pavane pour une infante défunte*, Satie's *Socrate*, and Stravinsky's *Renard*. [See K. H. Ruppel, "Die Prinzessin Edmond de Polignac," *Melos* 34 (June 1967):198-203.]

201. *Die Musik* 26 (February 1934):394. The reference to a musical comedy is probably to *A Kingdom for a Cow*. Note that the symphony is labeled as Weill's First Symphony.

202. David Drew, Preface to *Symphony no. 2* (Mainz: B. Schotts Söhne, 1966).

203. The letter has been reprinted and translated in the Notes to the Calouste Gulbenkian Foundation Series 6 recording, Argo ZRG 755.

204. Herbert Antcliffe, "Holland," *Musical Times* 75 (November 1934):1035. Note that Weill is the mere "musical editor" of *Die Dreigroschenoper* and that the writer's definition of a proper sonata form is thematically based.

205. The program on 13 and 14 December included Handel's Concerto in D Major for Orchestra and Organ, Mozart's "Haffner" Symphony, K. 385, and Beethoven's Violin Concerto.

206. Lawrence Gilman in the Program of the Philharmonic Society of New York, 13-14 December 1934.

207. *New York Herald-Tribune*, 14 December 1934.

208. *Modern Music* 12 (January-February 1935):90.

209. *New York Times*, 14 December 1934.

210. The program notes of the Philharmonic Concert erroneously stated that the symphony had been published in 1934.

211. Weill, as quoted by "R.C.B." in the *New York World Telegram*, 21 December 1935.

212. Program Notes of the Philharmonic Society of New York, 13-14 December 1934.

213. Virgil Thomson, "Most Melodious Tears," *Modern Music* 11 (November-December 1933):13-17.

214. The production was conducted by Edmond Mahieux, and the directorial staff included André Lefaur and H. Henriot.

215. Marc Blitzstein, "Theatre-Music in Paris," *Modern Music* 12 (March-April 1935):132-33. *Marie galante* was scheduled for production in New York, but its failure in Paris precluded that possibility. "The Road to Promise" ultimately was renamed *The Eternal Road*.

216. Published by Edition Coda in 1934: E.C. 191, 233.

217. The first description is by Walter Abendroth, "Opernideale der Rassen und Völker," *Die Musik* 28 (March 1936):424. Schmitt's outburst is quoted by Blitzstein in "Theater-Music in Paris," p. 128. Florent Schmitt had publicly protested performances of Weill's music already in 1933 when Maurice Abravanel conducted three songs from *Der Silbersee* with Madeleine Grey as soloist in a concert of the Orchestre Symphonique de Paris on 26 November. Abravanel described the ugly incident: "Georg Kaiser's lyrics were translated by Madeleine Milhaud, and Madeleine Gray was the soloist. When the storm of applause was ebbing I was shocked to hear a shout of 'Vive Hitler!' We were backstage, the 'Vive Hitler!' ringing in my ears, and I thought then how right Kurt had been. But Madeleine Grey had heard only the shouts of 'Bis!' and naturally wanted to encore the last song; I wanted only that the earth would open and swallow me, but back we went. She sang. Again thunderous applause, and then again the vicious shouts of 'Vive Hitler!'—which actually came from Florent Schmitt and several other composers. Kurt came to me backstage after the concert, his eyes even larger than usual, not even reproachful but infinitely sad: 'Did I need that?' The next day all the papers had banner headlines about the incident, of course." [Abravanel, "Kurt Weill, Symphonist," p. 10.]

218. Curjel, "Erinnerungen um Kurt Weill," p. 84. [Also see *Die Musik* 16 (March 1934):16.]

219. I am indebted to Professor Ernst Wolff, the musical assistant to Ernst Mehlich for the *Mahagonny-Songspiel*, to William Steinberg for *Aufstieg* and to Weill himself

for *The Eternal Road* and *A Kingdom for a Cow*, for the information about the premiere of the last work. The original director, Felix Weissberger, was replaced by Matray Ernst, who was unable to salvage the production.

220. See "Weill Works Are Given," *New York Times*, 18 December 1935.

221. *A Part of Myself*, p. 217.

CHAPTER 3

1. Kurt Weill, "Kritik am zeitgenössischen Schaffen," *Melos* 8 (March 1929):109.

2. For a more complete account of the history of Funk-Stunde Berlin AG, see Drew, *Ausgewählte Schriften*, pp. 215-216.

3. See Drew, *Ausgewählte Schriften*, pp. 207-8.   After Weill became Berlin correspondent, Wiener continued to contribute to the journal as "K.W.", the Stuttgart correspondent.

4. During July 1926, Felix Stiemer ("Sti.") wrote at least one of the regular features usually assigned to Weill.

5. A second radio station in Berlin was not established until January 1926.

6. An index of Weill's signed articles that appeared in *Der deutsche Rundfunk* appears in Appendix IIA.

7. Kurt Weill, "Verschiebungen in der musikalischen Produktion," *Berliner Tageblatt*, 1 October 1927.

8. Kurt Weill, "Bekenntnis zur Oper," *25 Jahre neue Musik* (Vienna: Universal-Edition, 1925), p. 226.

9. Weill's case for a renewal of the formal bases of opera is presented in "Bekenntnis zur Oper," "Die neue Oper," and "Busonis *Faust* und die Erneuerung der Opernform."

10. It should not be inferred that Weill disliked all of Wagner's works.   On the contrary, in several reviews in *Der deutsche Rundfunk* Weill wrote appreciatively of individual operas.   His anti-Wagnerian aesthetic position stemmed from a belief that the path of music drama that originated in Wagner's examples had led to a dead end.   Weill's distaste for music drama was directed more toward the products of Wagner's imitators than toward those of the master himself.

11. Kurt Weill, "Die neue Oper," *Die neue Weg* 55 (16 January 1926):24.

12. Weill, "Bekenntnis zur Oper," p. 226.

13. Ibid., p. 227.

14. Ibid., p. 228.

15. Kurt Weill, "Busoni und die neue Musik," *Die neue Weg* 54 (16 October 1925):283.

16. Weill cited *Wozzeck* and *Docktor Faust* as the most significant representatives of musical theater of the era.   Whereas, in his estimation, Busoni's opera was a

starting point for a new development, *Wozzeck*, which he considered a masterpiece of the greatest power, signified the climax of music drama. [See "Die neue Oper," p. 25.]

17. Kurt Weill, "Busonis *Faust* und die Erneuerung der Opernform," *Jahrbuch Oper* (Vienna: Universal-Edition, 1926), p. 53. It is noteworthy that Wagner had voiced an almost identical view, but the methods of realizing this concept in Weill's and Wagner's music are certainly very different.

18. Weill's use of a four-part male quartet in *Die sieben Todsünden* is not unique in his career. A similar quartet, composed of lumberjacks (who, like Anna, spent seven years in hardship to earn money), is found in *Aufstieg*. In using a four-part male ensemble, Weill was able to exploit various styles associated with such a sonority: *Singverein* idiom, barbershop "close harmony," chorale texture, and beer-hall boisterousness. Recordings of American dance music, especially fox-trots, often used a vocal group of four men singing in close harmony; for example, "Sunny Disposish" from Philip Charig's and Ira Gershwin's *Americana* (1926) received wide circulation in such a format.

19. Weill's works for the American musical stage also display a similar imaginative approach to formal problems. The most striking example is *Lady in the Dark*, in which, with just one exception, music is heard only during the dream sequences. Again the music reflects the subject matter in that it provides the material for Liza Elliot's psychoanalysis. Weill described each of the musical segments of *Lady in the Dark* as self-contained one-act operas.

20. One can trace similar ideas in Busoni's writings: "The composition of opera leads us back to purer and more absolute music because by means of the suggested future and banishment of everything illustrative, only those elements which are organically suitable to music attain their own rights." [Busoni, *The Essence of Music and Other Papers*, trans. Ley, p. 6.]

   "The principal thing for me to do was to mould musically independent forms which at the same time suited the words and the scenic events and which also had a separate and sensible existence detached from the words and the situation." [Ibid., p. 73.]

21. Kurt Weill, "Zeitoper," *Melos* 7 (March 1928):107.

22. Weill's belief that the action on stage should function as an optical extension of musical events finds it direct precedent in Wagner's writings. Objecting to the label "Musikdrama" for his works, Wagner suggested that "dramma per musica" would be a more accurate description. Since that was an Italian phrase, he coined the analogous German expression "ersichtlich gewordene Taten der Musik" (deeds of music made visible).

23. Kurt Weill, "Tanzmusik," *Der deutsche Rundfunk* 4 (14 March 1926):732.

24. Ibid.

25. Kurt Weill, quoted by "R.C.B." in *New York World Telegram*, 21 December 1935.

26. Kurt Weill, "Notiz zum Jazz," *Anbruch* 11 (March 1929):138. Stravinsky expressed a similar reaction to his encounter with jazz: "At my request, a whole pile of music was sent to me, enchanting me by its popular appeal, its freshness, and the

novel rhythm which so distinctly revealed its negro origin. These impressions suggested the idea of creating a composite portrait of this new dance music, giving the importance of a concert piece, as, in the past, composers of their periods had done for the minuet, the waltz, the mazurka, etc." [*Chronicle of My Life*, pp. 130-31.]

27. Weill, quoted by "R.C.B." in *New York World Telegram*, 21 December 1935.

28. Weill, "Notiz zum Jazz," p. 138.

29. Aaron Copland, "The Jazz Interlude," *The New Music 1900-1960*, revised ed. (New York: W.W. Norton, 1968), p. 62.

30. For example, the Tango-Finale of *Royal Palace* occupies seventeen pages of the 83-page vocal score.

31. Weill, "Verschiebungen in der musikalischen Produktion."

32. Ibid.

33. Ibid.

34. Ibid.

35. Ibid.

36. Weill's first usage of the term "epic" in respect to his own works occurs in 1927 in "Verschiebungen in der musikalischen Produktion." Brecht first used the term "epic theatre" in 1926 in an interview published in *Die literarische Welt.*

37. Kurt Weill, "Korrespondenz über Dreigroschenoper," *Anbruch* 11 (January 1929):24-25. Note how this contrasts with Busoni, who wrote: "Above all, the opera should not be identified with the spoken drama. More than this, they should be distinguished from one another like man and wife." [Busoni, *The Essence of Music and Other Papers*, trans. Ley, p. 7.]

38. Kurt Weill, "Gebrauchsmusik und ihre Grenzen," *Berliner Tageblatt*, 31 October 1929.

39. Ibid.

40. Kurt Weill, "Musikfest oder Musikstudio?" *Melos* 9 (May-June 1930):231.

41. Such categorization with composers of *Gebrauchsmusik* has usually been the result of attempts to relate Weill's quest for simplicity and clarity to similar aesthetic goals of other composers. However, one must remember that Weill composed primarily for the theater, and he believed that music must be especially understandable and lucid if it is to be successful in the theatrical domain.

42. Kurt Weill, "Aktuelles Theater," *Melos* 8 (December 1929):524.

43. Weill, "Zeitoper," p. 106.

44. Weill, "Aktuelles Theater," p. 525.

45. Weill, "Verschiebungen in der musikalische Produktion."

46. Weill, "Zeitoper," p. 107.

47. The *Mahagonny-Songspiel* is a pivotal work in Weill's German career because it includes not only the new song-style and "loose" structure characteristic of his

later epic operas, but also the most sophisticated rhythmic and harmonic procedures which had been worked out in earlier works. In the *Songspiel*, the simple ballad style is juxtaposed with highly dissonant and complex instrumental interludes which reflect Weill's expansion of musical resources. Even the religious allusions of his early music are preserved in the *Mahagonny-Songspiel:* for example, the chimes, recitation tones, and the chorale of "Gott in Mahagonny" are transformed in meaning by the satirical context in which they are presented.

48.   Weill, "Zeitoper," pp. 107-8. *Aufstieg* and *Die Bürgschaft* must be regarded as Weill's most complete formulations of epic opera; however, all of his works for the theater from 1927 to 1933 display various attempts to incorporate aspects of epic style. Certainly *Happy End* is radically different from *Aufstieg*, but for the purposes of this discussion the author has chosen to treat Weill's mature theatrical works as a group, in which Weill sought varied ways to apply epic principles to musical theater. It should be noted that Weill even considered such non-theatrical works as *Das Berliner Requiem* and *Der Lindberghflug* as studies within the epic mold.

49.   Weill considered *Die Zauberflöte* and *Der Freischütz* to be the most exemplary models of dialogue-opera.

50.   Weill, "Korrespondenz über *Dreigroschenoper*," p. 25.

51.   Kurt Weill, "Entwicklungstendenzen der Oper," *Berliner Tageblatt*, 31 October 1929.

52.   Donald Jay Grout, *A Short History of Opera*, 2nd ed. (New York: Columbia University Press, 1965), p. 182.

53.   Ibid., p. 200. Brecht might have taken issue with such an analogy because *opera seria* was still more "culinary" than didactic in intent.

54.   Both Weill and Brecht stated that the "Third Threepenny Finale" was to be a straightforward operatic presentation. Weill wrote: "The last 'Dreigroschenfinale' is by no means a parody; rather, here the concept of 'opera' was applied directly to the resolution of conflict, that is, as an action-structuring element. Therefore, it had to be constructed in its purest, most fundamental form." ["Korrespondenz über *Dreigroschenoper*," p. 25.] Brecht warned that "the third finale must be played with complete seriousness and extreme dignity." ["Notes to the *Threepenny Opera*," trans. by Desmond Vesey in *The Threepenny Opera* (New York: Grove Press, 1964), p. 110.]

55.   Grout, p. 190.

56.   *Aufstieg* presents an even more convincing case: the opera's structure permitted Weill to rearrange and alter the score for each production according to the capabilities of the cast and theater.

57.   Grout, p. 193.

58.   Ibid., p. 186.

59.   Brecht, "Notes to the *Threepenny Opera*," p. 106.

60.   Ibid.

61.   Ibid. Of course, the types of departures from the melodic line in epic opera are entirely different in vocal technique from those of *opera seria*. Weill probably

concurred with Brecht's instructions to the performers; in "Notiz zum Jazz," p. 138, Weill wrote: "The manner of performance of jazz is finally breaking through the rigid system of musical practice in our concerts and theaters and this is more important than its influence on musical composition. . . . A good jazz musician . . . cultivates a free, unrestrained style of playing in which the interpreter achieves to the highest degree a productive performance. The extent to which all this can be applied to art music naturally depends primarily on the musical product itself, which certainly does not always allow such freedom of interpretation."

62. The "valse Boston" or simply "Boston" is a term widely used in Germany after World War I to describe the hesitation waltz, characterized by frequent suppression of single beats or entire measures.

63. Although *Gestus* is a German noun and therefore should be capitalized, I have adhered to the practice found in most literature dealing with Brecht where the term appears italicized and in the lower case.

64. Manfred F. Bukofzer, *Music in the Baroque Era* (New York: W. W. Norton, 1947), p. 388.

65. Claude V. Palisca, *Baroque Music* (Englewood Cliffs, N. J.: Prentice-Hall, 1968), pp. 3-5.

66. Esslin, *Brecht: The Man and His Work*, p. 134.

67. Bertolt Brecht, "A Short Organum for the Theatre," trans. by John Willett, *Brecht on Theatre*, p. 198.

68. Kurt Weill, "Wirklich eine Opernkrise?" *Deutsche Allgemeine Zeitung*, 8 July 1932.

69. For a description of Lessing's use of the term, see Willett, *Brecht on Theatre*, p. 42.

70. Kurt Weill, "Ueber den gestischen Charakter der Musik," *Die Musik* 21 (March 1929):419. In "Beethoven und die Jungen," *Sozialistische Monatshefte* 33 (1927):193, Weill was even more explicit: "We are withdrawing from the nineteenth century and seem to be instinctively approaching the views of the early Classic and pre-Classic composers." Also in "Das Formproblem der modernen Oper," *Der Scheinwerfer* 5 (February 1932):5, he wrote that a series of new stylistic elements of modern opera represent a "return to the pure operatic forms of earlier times."

71. Weill, "Ueber den gestischen Charakter der Musik," p. 421.

72. Ibid.

73. Johann Mattheson, *Der vollkommene Capellmeister*, trans. by Hanns Lenneberg in "Johann Mattheson on Affect and Rhetoric in Music II," *Journal of Music Theory* 2 (November 1958):202.

74. Numerals in the diagram denote lengths of phrase structures. Letters represent primary harmonic areas.

75. In both songs the introduction of the bandoneon (an Argentine variety of accordion) in the instrumentation reinforces the exotic quality of the tango.

76. In discussing *Der Jasager*, Weill stated: "Certainly I do not renounce rhythmic effects in the new didactic opera, but they are no longer avowed dance rhythms; rather these rhythms are transformed and 'digested'." ["Aktuelles Zwiegespräch über die Schuloper zwischen Kurt Weill und Dr. Hans Fischer," *Die Musikpflege* 1(April 1930):50.]

77. The sub-categories often serve a more specific gestic function than is implicit in the parent category. For example, Weill does not label the "Liebeslied" (No. 8 of *Die Dreigroschenoper*) of Macheath and Polly as a waltz, but as a "Boston," because the stilted awkward stylization of the slower Boston was more appropriate to the dramatic situation than a simple waltz. Similarly, the shimmy, a special type of fox-trot which evolved into a virtuosic solo-dance, was more suited to Macheath's carefree "Ballade von Angenehmen Leben" than a straight fox-trot would have been. Note that when Weill published the song as an instrumental movement in *Kleine Dreigroschenmusik*, where it is no longer tied to a gestic function, the "Ballade von Angenehmen Leben" is designated as a fox-trot.

78. It is often possible to determine a proper performance tempo for those musical numbers without metronome indications by consulting relatives in the same gestic family that have precise tempo specified.

79. Because of the Ländler-like tempo and pattern of accompaniment, this family could easily be considered a representative of an explicit dance idiom.

80. Macheath's "Ruf aus der Gruft" presents one of the clearest examples of gestic music. The entire preceding dramatic scene is accompanied by the bass drum with the rhythmic 'gest' of the situation: |¾ ♪♪ ♩ ⅜|. When Macheath sings "Ruf aus der Gruft" the rhythm which captured the urgent agitation of the dialogue continues as the basis of Weill's music. Here the means of establishing the *gestus* of a scene in music are presented in primitive and additive format.

81. David Drew has expressed this feature eloquently: "Ambiguities of structure and expression, together with apparent anomalies of tone and idiom, are now exploited with such merciless accuracy that no formal or emotional expectations are secure." ["Kurt Weill and His Critics," p. 1144.]

82. Kurt Weill, "Ferruccio Busoni: Zu seinem 60. Geburtstag," *Der deutsche Rundfunk* 4 (28 March 1926):872.

83. Kurt Weill, "Anmerkungen zu meiner Oper *Mahagonny*," *Die Musik* 22 (March 1930):440.

84. Kurt Weill, quoted by "R.C.B." in *New York World Telegram*, 21 December 1935. Weill probably intended 'verse' to mean stanza (as opposed to refrain) rather than its literal meaning of 'a line of poetry.'

85. Brecht had entitled two of the "Mahagonny-Gesänge" of *Die Hauspostille* as "Alabama Song" and "Benares Song." As early as 1925 Weill had already extended the term *Song* to *Songspiel.*

86. For example, "Hochzeits Lied" of *Die Dreigroschenoper* is hardly an art-song in Weill's deliberately vulgar and trite musical setting. In the scene in which the number appears, however, Macheath had called for a "*Lied*" (a song suitable for

the occasion of his wedding), and therefore Weill's setting is admirably suited to the irony of the dramatic situation.

87. Kurt Weill, "Vorwort zum Regiebuch der Oper *Aufstieg und Fall der Stadt Mahagonny*," *Anbruch* 12 (January 1930):6.

88. All musical numbers of *Die Bürgschaft* (Neher) and *Der Silbersee* (Kaiser) are identified only by number in the scores.

89. Of course, "pure" strophic structure may only exist in notation, because in almost all instances the performers of folk songs, hymns, ballads, and other strophic forms were expected to vary the performances of successive stanzas to reflect the meaning of the text.

90. The non-strophic "Arie der Lucy" was dropped from *Die Dreigroschenoper* in the rehearsal period and therefore is not included in this count.

91. The four musical numbers of *Happy End* that consist of only one stanza each could be considered the first strophe of an incomplete strophic form.

92. Only one stanza was printed in the piano-vocal score, but in its revised version the duet consists of two stanzas.

93. "Moritat vom Mackie Messer" is a special type of *Ballade* modelled on those sung by streetsingers listing the crimes of notorious criminals. For a discussion of the etymology of the term "*Moritat*," see Sammy McLean, *The Bänkelsang and the Works of Bertolt Brecht* (The Hague: Mouton, 1972):55-56.

94. Because of the various editions and versions of *Aufstieg* there is some discrepancy in the numbering of musical numbers. To avoid confusion, the author refers to the final "Largo" of Act II before 93 as No. 21 because Weill specifically mentions in several essays "twenty-one closed musical numbers."

95. The most primitive and economical use of repetition as a large-scale formal device occurs in *Der Jasager* where the "Einverständnis" chorus opens both acts and concludes the opera.

96. Elaine Padmore, "Kurt Weill," *Music and Musicians* 21 (October 1972):38-39.

97. When Weill does use a key signature, one should not be misled into assuming that it is a conclusive clue to the tonic. "Die Ballade von der Höllenlili" (No. 12 of *Happy End*) carries a four-sharp signature. One might expect E major or c# minor to function as tonic, but, in fact, neither is so treated. Instead, the tonal scheme is as ambiguous as the subject of the *Ballade*: "What tomorrow brings: Who knows, Who cares." Nor are final cadences a conclusive guide to the tonality of Weill's music, for he often began solidly in one key and then side-stepped to a seemingly unrelated key to conclude with powerful dramatic effect. Such is the case with the "Anstatt-dass-Song" in which the refrain points to Bb minor, but through a characteristic slide by semitone, the final two measures are disconcertingly jerked to A minor to capture the emotional turmoil of the Peachums. Needless to say, it is misleading to consider A minor as the "key" of the *Song*.

98. A more complete discussion of the theoretical basis of this "double-tonic" sonority appears in Chapter 4.

99. Parentheses indicate introductions or codas added to the central structural unit of the number in order to facilitate movement to the next musical number.

100. I am indebted to Robert Bailey for his formulation of the terminology "expressive use of tonality," "directional tonality," and "paired tonality."

101. Weill, "Busonis Faust und die Erneuerung der Opernform," p. 53.

102. David Drew, "Kurt Weill and His Critics," *Times Literary Supplement* 3838 (3 October 1975):1144.

103. Ibid., p. 1143.

104. Translated by John Willett, *Brecht on Theatre,* p. 86.

105. Bertolt Brecht, *Bertolt Brechts Arbeitsjournal,* ed. Werner Hecht, 3 vols. (Frankfurt am Main: Suhrkamp Verlag, 1972), 1:188. "COURAGE" refers to *Mutter Courage und ihre Kinder,* written in 1939. Weill never studied with Schreker, although at one time he considered doing so.

106. Hecht's study was published in Berlin by Henschelverlag in 1962. Part of it had appeared in English as "The Development of Brecht's Theory of the Epic Theatre 1918-1933," *Tulane Drama Review* 6 (September 1961):40-97. Weill's name does not appear in the latter.

107. Esslin, *Brecht: The Man and His Work,* p. 34.

108. Susan Clydette Harden, "The Music for the Stage Collaborations of Weill and Brecht," Ph.D. Dissertation, University of North Carolina at Chapel Hill, 1972.

109. That in his "Anmerkungen zur Oper *Aufstieg und Fall der Stadt Mahagonny"* Brecht borrowed Weill's perennial operatic models, *Die Zauberflöte, Figaro* and *Fidelio,* to serve as examples indicates how deeply the interaction had penetrated. Brecht's "Anmerkungen" has been translated in Willett, *Brecht on Theatre,* pp. 33-42.

110. John Willett dates Brecht's first use of the term as 1936.

111. Weill, in discussing Busoni's music which provided "commentary for the incidents of the stage," used the term *"Geste"* in 1926, but his comprehensive treatment of gestic music did not appear until 1929.

112. The quotation is from one of the most blatant expositions of this wrong-headed notion: Robert Marx, "Brecht, Weill, and the Birth of *The Threepenny Opera,"* *New York Times,* 2 May 1976.

113. Zuckmayer, *A Part of Myself: Portrait of an Epoch,* p. 267.

114. Lenya, "August 28, 1929," p. ix.

115. Weill, "Ueber den gestischen Charakter der Musik," p. 422.

116. David Drew is one of the few scholars to have penetrated the essence of the Brecht-Weill relationship: "When Eisler remarked that the 'highly gifted' Weill never grasped what Brecht was aiming for, he should have added that the reverse was equally true." ["Kurt Weill and His Critics," p. 1144.]

117. Weill, "Zeitoper," p. 107.

118. Weill's essays were written independently of Brecht; likewise, Weill was not consulted for Brecht's "Anmerkungen."

119. Aufricht, *Erzähle, damit du dein Recht erweist,* p. 126. "Während wir *Mahagonny* probierten, stritt Brecht für Priorität des Wortes, Weill für die Musik. Anwälte kamen ins Theater, sie drohten mit einstweiligen Verfügungen. Brecht schlug einem Pressefotografen die Kamera aus der Hand, er hatte ihn mit Weill zusammen aufgenommen. 'Den falschen Richard Strauss werfe ich in voller Kriegsbemalung die Treppe hinunter!' schrie Brecht hinter Weill her."

120. Weill, "Ueber den gestischen Charakter der Musik," p. 420.

121. Lotte Lenya, "Kurt Weill's Universal Appeal," *Music Journal* 17 (January 1959):48.

122. Drew, "Kurt Weill and His Critics," p. 1144.

123. Unpublished letter dated 23 March 1939 now in the possession of the Weill-estate.

124. Brecht, *Arbeitsjournal,* 1:414. Dated 15.4.42.

125. Ibid., 2:568. Brecht wrote "Kinderkreuzzug" in 1941. Benjamin Britten completed his musical setting, intended for performance by members of a school or children's music group, in January 1969.

126. Ibid., 2:579. Dated 28. 6. 43. Others shared Brecht's respect for Weill's dramatic instincts; Maxwell Anderson wrote: "Kurt Weill's voice has been added to our councils, and we have discovered that there is no better theater man extant, not only in the field of music but in the realm of scripts and managerial decisions." "The Playwrights' Birthday," *New York Times,* 10 October 1948.

127. Kurt Weill, "Gesellschaftsbildende Oper," *Berliner Börsen-Courier,* 19 February 1929.

128. Kurt Weill, "Bekenntnis zu Bach," *Die Musik* 22 (January 1930):267.

129. Weill, "Die neue Oper," p. 24.

130. Kurt Weill, "Carl Maria von Weber—Zum 100. Todestag des Komponisten am 5 Juni," *Der deutsche Rundfunk* 4 (30 May 1926):1518.

131. Ibid. Weill continued by praising Weber's economical and transparent treatment of the orchestra.

132. It has been widely observed that *Aufstieg* contains rather explicit musical references (but not direct quotation!) to the duet of the armored men from the Finale of *Die Zauberflöte* and to the Bridesmaids' Chorus of *Der Freischütz.* No doubt Weill intended to pay explicit homage to two of the works he most admired.

133. Weill, "Carl Maria von Weber," p. 1518.

134. Kurt Weill, "Bekenntnisse zu Beethoven," *Magdeburgische Zeitung,* 13 March 1927.

135. Kurt Weill, "Beethoven und die Jungen," *Sozialistische Monatshefte* 33 (1927):194. Partially reprinted in *Die Musik* 19 (May 1927):593.

136. Kurt Weill, "Beethoven im Urteil der jungen Musiker," *Die literarische Welt* 3 (25 March 1927):3-4. A more extensive version of this essay appeared as "Beethoven und die Jungen," where Weill singled out the Grosse Fuge (op. 133), *Missa*

solemnis, and the last string quartets as works whose formal freedom transcended the limitations of the material and which have never been surpassed in this respect.

137. Kurt Weill, "Schubert-Feiern," *Der deutsche Rundfunk* 6 (16 November 1928):3176.

138. In "Beethoven und die Jungen," p. 193, Weill wrote: "Both Wagner and Brahms convincingly traced the fundamentals of their works back to the composer of the *Eroica*, and the entirely different results that these two composers achieved demonstrates the powerful scope of Beethoven's sphere of influence. At the beginning of the twentieth century the revolutionary formal advances of late Beethoven constituted the bases of a musical movement whose most significant product was certainly Schoenberg's Quartet in D minor."

139. Kurt Weill in *Der deutsche Rundfunk* 3 (5 July 1925):1697. Excerpts from the essay have been reprinted in *Ausgewählte Schriften*, pp. 147-48. In "Bekenntnis zur Oper," Weill wrote that "we can understand why Wagner had to create for himself the form of music drama: for how could the string quartet, symphony, or opera satisfy him, since his art reflects only the feelings of larger-than-life figures—of gods, kings, and heroes?"

140. Kurt Weill, "Musikalisches Theater," *Aufbau*, 16 January 1942. Excerpt reprinted in *Ausgewählte Schriften*, p. 90.

141. Kurt Weill in *Der deutsche Rundfunk* 3 (27 December 1925):3422. Reprinted in *Ausgewählte Schriften*, pp. 153-54.

142. Weill, "Die neue Oper," p. 24.

143. Kurt Weill in *Der deutsche Rundfunk* 3 (1925), quoted and translated by David Drew in his Insert Notes to Symphony no. 1, Angel recording S-36506.

144. Kurt Weill, "Gustav Mahler: 9. Symphonie," *Der deutsche Rundfunk* 4 (20 June 1926):1723.

145. Kurt Weill in *Der deutsche Rundfunk* 5 (29 May 1927):1511.

146. Weill, "Die neue Oper," p. 25.

147. Kurt Weill, quoted in an interview published in the *New York Sun*, 3 February 1940.

148. Kurt Weill in *Der deutsche Rundfunk* 3 (1925), quoted and translated by David Drew in his Insert Notes to Symphony no. 1.

149. Kurt Weill in *Der deutsche Rundfunk* 4 (28 February 1926):582.

150. Kurt Weill in *Der deutsche Rundfunk* 4 (27 June 1926):1796.

151. Arnold Schoenberg, quoted by Virgil Thomson in *Virgil Thomson* (New York: Alfred A. Knopf, 1966), p. 227. Thomson's recollection is corroborated by Marc Blitzstein: "I came upon *Mahagonny* late: it was not one of the works which influenced my youth, as had *Dreigroschenoper*. (I practically went to school to the latter. I can remember vividly its effect on me, and my scandalizing my fellow-students at Arnold Schoenberg's master-class at the Berlin Hochschule, when I sat at the piano and croaked in execrable German and a composer's squeal the *Mack the Knife* and *Jealousy Duet* songs, just as Schoenberg himself was entering the room. To the twelve-tone-row boys the whole of Kurt Weill was treated as so much craftsmanlike trash.)" [Marc Blitzstein, "On *Mahagonny*," *The Score* 23

(July 1958):11.] One must remember, however, that Schoenberg was probably familiar with a very limited number of Weill's compositions and that the reported evaluation of Weill's music was issued in response to two intentionally primitive and banal songs.

152. Kurt Weill in *Der deutsche Rundfunk* 6 (16 November 1928):3177.

153. These have been summarized by David Drew in "Musical Theater in the Weimar Republic," *Proceedings of the Royal Musical Association* 88 (1961-62):95-97.

154. Weill, "Busonis *Faust* und die Erneuerung der Opernform," p. 56.

155. Weill, "Ferruccio Busoni: Zu seinem 60. Geburtstag," p. 872.

CHAPTER 4

1. Arnold Schoenberg, *Structural Functions of Harmony* (London: Williams & Norgate, 1954), p. 113.

2. Musical examples for this chapter are found at the end of each section.

3. "Sonata-form" is used here in its twentieth-century conceptualization in which genuine ternary organization has replaced the binary form of its eighteenth and early nineteenth-century counterparts.

4. Schoenberg, *Structural Functions of Harmony*, p. 102. David Neumeyer has convincingly demonstrated a tangible connection between Hindemith's and Reger's musical style. [See David Neumeyer, "Counterpoint and Pitch Structure in the Early Music of Hindemith," Ph.D. Dissertation, Yale University, 1976.] I would argue that Reger exerted an equally powerful influence on Weill.

5. Ibid., p. 51. Neumeyer observed that Hindemith also "places little value on unequivocal presentation of specific modes. He mixes them together and, despite his preference for diatonicism, for the most part employs all twelve tones of the chromatic scale in a relatively short space." ["Counterpoint and Pitch Structure in the Early Music of Hindemith," p. 161.]

6. Arnold Schoenberg, *Harmonielehre* (Leipzig, Vienna: Universal-Edition, 1911), pp. 431-34: "Die chromatische Skala als Grundlage der Tonalität." In citing Schoenberg's theoretical writings in this chapter, I do not wish to imply that Weill "studied" from them; rather Schoenberg presents one of the few (and certainly one of the most complete) contemporary treatments of the harmonic resources of post-Wagnerian music.

7. In *Structural Functions of Harmony* Schoenberg noted that the tonic minor, minor and major mediant and submediant are close relatives of a given major tonic. [p. 51.]

8. Robert Bailey, "The Genesis of *Tristan und Isolde* and a Study of Wagner's Sketches and Drafts for the First Act" (Ph.D. Dissertation, Princeton University, 1969), p. 239.

9. Schoenberg, *Structural Functions of Harmony*, p. 67.

10. David Drew, "First Symphony," Notes to Symphony no. 1, Colouste Gulbenkian Foundation Series 6 recording (Argo ZRG 755).

11. Ferruccio Busoni, "Sketch of a New Esthetic of Music," in *Three Classics in the Aesthetic of Music* (New York: Dover, 1962), p. 91.

12. Henry Cowell, "New Terms for New Music," *Modern Music* 5 (May-June 1928):21.

13. Bailey, "The Genesis of *Tristan und Isolde*," p. 149.

14. Robert Bailey is working on such a theoretical exegesis at the present time; I am indebted to him for sharing his preliminary findings with me.

15. Schoenberg, *Structural Functions of Harmony*, p. 110.

16. Ibid., p. 111. The reference in *Harmonielehre* occurs on p. 430 under the heading "Ueber schwebende und aufgehobene Tonalität": "Two very significant cases of suspended tonality in my compositions are the orchestral song "Voll jener Süsse," opus 8, number 5, which fluctuates mainly between D♭ and B major and opus 6, number 7 ("Lockung") which expresses E♭ major without introducing in the course of the piece a single time an E♭ major triad that one could regard as pure tonic." The opening of Schoenberg's *Gurrelieder* (1900) is entirely based on a sonority comprising the pitches of an E♭-major triad and a C-minor triad.

17. The terminology was coined by Robert Bailey.

18. Willi Apel, "Added Sixth," *Harvard Dictionary of Music*, 2nd ed. (Cambridge, Mass.: Harvard University Press, 1969), pp. 12-13.

19. Allen Forte, *The Structure of Atonal Music*, 2nd ed. (New Haven: Yale University Press, 1977).

20. Abstract set terminology is particularly useful to describe non-triadic configurations. Set labels do not carry connotations of function and are, therefore, adaptable to almost any musical structure. In a sense, such nomenclature is only an expansion of traditional labels such as major triad, augmented triad, diminished-seventh, etc. Because all twelve transpositions of C—E—G are reducible to a single chord-type, it was convenient to apply the term "major triad" to any one of the twelve. In the terminology of pitch-class sets, the major triad is assigned the name 3-11, since it is the eleventh trichord on the list of twelve trichords. The diminished-seventh chord is assigned the name 4-28. Each of the 220 possible pitch-class sets is assigned a fixed name, a name that is always associated with the set, regardless of its mode of occurrence or function within a particular musical composition. In the present study, the reader will find musical configurations labeled with set names. For a comprehensive discussion of set terminology, see Allen Forte, *The Structure of Atonal Music*.

21. An alternative and equivalent method of generation by perfect fourths is possible, but the actual occurrences of such harmonic units in Weill's music and historical perspective argue in favor of derivation by fifths. Simple inversion yields sonorities based on the perfect fourth.

22. A more comprehensive theoretical discussion of the properties of diatonic pitch-class sets in general is given by Neumeyer in "Counterpoint and Pitch Structure in the Early Music of Hindemith," pp. 43-54.

23. Berg noted the general objection to non-triadic harmony: "I tell you, this whole hue and cry for tonality comes not so much from a yearning for a keynote relationship as from a yearning for familiar concords—let us say it frankly, for the common triads. And I believe it is fair to state that no music, provided only it contains enough of these triads, will ever arouse opposition even if it breaks all the holy commandments of tonality." ["Was ist atonal?" trans. M. D. Herter Norton in *Music Since 1900*, p. 677.]

24. Otto Beer, "Die Funktionswerte der Quartenharmonien," *Die Musik* 22 (November 1929):91.

25. John C. G. Waterhouse, "Weill's Debt to Busoni," *Musical Times* 105 (December 1964):897.

26. Ibid., p. 898.

27. This passage has survived as an autograph fragment and was appended as an introduction to the first movement of David Drew's reconstruction of the Divertimento without conclusive evidence that this was its original function.

28. Alma Mahler, ed., *Gustav Mahler, Briefe 1897-1911* (Berlin: P. Zsolnay, 1925), p. 187.

29. David Drew, Notes to Symphony no. 1 (Argo ZRG 755).

30. In his edition of Symphony no. 1, Drew recommends doubling the horn parts. This would tend to distort the balance within the brass choir, however, and therefore seems inadvisable.

31. Strobel, "Kurt Weill," p. 428.

32. Anton Webern, quoted by Luigi Dallapiccola in "Incontro con Anton Webern (1883-1945), Pagine di diario," *Il Mondo*, 3 November 1945. The passage was translated by John C. G. Waterhouse in *Tempo* 99 (1972):5. Dallapiccola recalled: "The name of Kurt Weill is mentioned incidentally. And Webern, who up to this moment has always spoken in a subdued voice, suddenly explodes. Red in the face, he points his index finger towards me, but it wasn't I who uttered the name of a composer so repugnant to him! . . . My opinion of Weill is somewhat different from Webern's. In my diary of 21 March 1936, published under the title 'Meeting with Gustav Mahler,' I wrote: 'I see at last, and with the utmost clarity, that the admirable third movement of Mahler's First Symphony is where part of the world of Alban Berg develops from, and that it contains, in embryo, the 'ribald' side of Kurt Weill.'"

CHAPTER 5

1. Kurt Weill, quoted by "R.C.B." in *New York World Telegram*, 21 December 1935.

2. The chorale was one of Brecht's favorite satirical forms; he admitted that the Bible was the most powerful literary influence on his work. The change in function of the chorale within Weill's music is at least partially due to its role in Brecht's librettos.

3. In certain instances, lengthy examples from unpublished works have been included here in order to give the reader a sense of the work.

4. Busoni, "A New Esthetic of Music," p. 92.

5. Drew, "The History of Mahagonny," p. 18.

6. For example, only the inner voices of the chorale undergo changes in the Quartet, where the decision to include a full A♭-triad in m. 8 necessitated alterations in the tenor and alto parts in preceding measures.

7. Kurt Weill, quoted by "R. C. B." in *New York World Telegram,* 21 December 1935.

8. "Aktuelles Zwiegespräch über die Schuloper zwischen Kurt Weill und Dr. Hans Fischer," p. 50.

9. Ibid., p. 48.

10. *Frauentanz* was also published in a piano-vocal score, but the composer specified that this version was restricted to study purposes and should not be performed.

11. In No. V, however, the textual refrain, "Har-ba-lo-ri-fa," does receive similar musical treatment in its recurrences.

12. Kurt Weill, quoted by "R. C. B." in *New York World Telegram,* 21 December 1935.

13. "Aktuelles Zwiegespräch über die Schuloper zwischen Kurt Weill und Dr. Hans Fischer," p. 50.

14. Second strophe of Movement VI of the *Rilke-Lieder,* "Vielleicht, dass ich durch schwere Berge gehe," translated by A. L. Peck in *The Book of Hours* (London: Hogarth Press, 1961), p. 117.

15. Igor Stravinsky, *Poetics of Music,* trans. Arthur Knodel and Ingolf Dahl (Cambridge: Harvard University Press, 1947), pp. 35-37.

16. Weill's non-tonal constructions have more in common with those of Stravinsky, Hindemith, and Busoni than with those of Schoenberg, Berg, or Webern.

CHAPTER 6

1. Kurt Weill, from a letter to his parents, quoted by Franz Willnauer in "Vom Schiffbauerdamm zum Broadway," p. 45.

2. Hugo Leichtentritt, "Berlin, too has its Jazz Opera," p. 5.

3. Kurt Weill, quoted in *Weill-Lenya,* p. 41.

4. Ian Kemp, "Harmony in Weill," p. 15.

5. The score calls for two flutes, oboe, two clarinets, bassoon, two trumpets, two trombones, tympani, percussion, piano, harp, and a full complement of strings.

6. David Drew, Introduction to *Kurt Weill,* Deutsche Grammophon recording 2709-064, p. 16.

7. From Maxwell Anderson's eulogy read at Weill's grave on 5 April 1950, cited from a copy in the archives of the Weill-Estate, included in the exhibition, "Weill-Lenya," at the New York Public Library and Museum of the Performing Arts, September 1976-March 1977.

APPENDIX I

CATALOGUE OF WEILL'S COMPOSITIONS, 1900-1935

CATALOGUE OF WEILL'S COMPOSITIONS, 1900-1935

Because no catalogue of Weill's compositions dating from 1900 to 1935 has been published, Appendix I summarizes relevant information concerning these works. Wherever possible, the following data has been included:

Title
Date and place of composition
Publication information
Dedication
Instrumentation
Cast
Duration
First performance
American premiere
Arrangements and excerpts
Present availability of scores
Contemporary reviews consulted by this author[1]
Plot synopsis

NOTES

1. Such a list is not intended to be exhaustive. Those reviews which have been reprinted (at least in part) in David Drew, ed., *Ueber Kurt Weill* (Frankfurt am Main: Suhrkamp Verlag, 1975), are denoted by an asterisk (*). Readers are also urged to consult Siegfried Unseld, ed., *Bertolt Brechts Dreigroschenbuch* (Frankfurt am Main: Suhrkamp Verlag, 1960) and Ernst Schumacher, *Die dramatischen Versuche Bertolt Brechts 1918-1933* (Berlin: Rutten & Loening, 1955) for additional reviews of the Brecht-Weill works.

WORKS COMPOSED BEFORE 1919

Surviving:

    a) Songs: "Reiterlied" (Herman Löns)
             "Im Volkston" (Arno Holz)
             "Das schöne Kind"

    b) Kriegs-Chöre (c. 1914)

    c) Choral setting of Psalm 8 (date of composition unknown)

Lost:

    a) One-act opera based on a play by Karl Theodor Körner

    b) One-act opera based on Hermann Sudermann's *Das Hohe lied*

    c) *Ninon de Lenclos*, one-act opera. Libretto by Ernst Hardt. 1919.

    d) "Schilflieder"

    e) "Maikäferlied"

    f) "Sulamith" (Choral Fantasy)

    g) Symphonic Poem based on Rilke's *Die Weise von Liebe und Tod des Cornets Christoph Rilke*. Composed in Berlin during 1918. Performed by the Berlin Hochschule Orchestra during 1919.

    h) Miscellaneous piano compositions

String Quartet in B Minor

    I   Mässig.
    II   Allegro ma non troppo. In heimlich erzählenden Ton.
   III Langsam und innig.
   IV Lustig und wild.

Composed in Dessau during Autumn 1919.

Unpublished.

Duration: 22 minutes

First Performance: 1975 Berliner Festwochen
                            Akademie der Künste, Berlin
                            9 September 1975
                            Melos-Quartette

Sonate für Violoncello und Klavier

    I   Allegro ma non troppo

    II   Andante expressivo

    III   Allegro assai. Wild bewegt grotesk vorzutragen.

Composed in Berlin during 1920.

Dedication: "Für Fritz Rupprecht und Albert Bing"

Unpublished. Copyist's manuscript in Weill-Estate.

Duration: 24 minutes

First Performance: 1975 Berliner Festwochen
                        Akademie der Künste, Berlin
                        9 September 1975
                        Siegfried Palm, cellist
                        Aloys Kontarsky, Pianist

Symphony No. 1 ("Berliner Sinfonie"; "Sinfonie in einem Satz")

Title page bears an inscription from Johannes R. Becher's *Festspiel, Arbeiter, Bauern, Soldaten—Der Aufbruch eines Volkes zu Gott* (Leipzig: Insel Verlag, 1921).

Composed in Berlin, April-June 1921.

Full score published by B. Schotts Söhne, Mainz & New York, 1968; edited by David Drew.   Parts available on rental basis.

Instrumentation: 2 flutes (2nd also piccolo)
                    oboe
                    2 clarinets (2nd also bass clarinet)
                    2 bassoons
                    2 horns
                    trumpet
                    trombone
                    tympani
                    percussion
                    strings

Duration: 25 minutes

First Performance: Hamburg, NDR Symphony Orchestra
                     1957
                     Wilhelm Schüchter, conductor

American Premiere: 21 October 1978
                     Greenwich Philharmonia Orchestra
                     David Gilbert, conductor

Autograph *Partitur* and incomplete 4-hand piano arrangement in Weill-Estate.

Divertimento für kleines Orchester mit Männerchor

Composed in Berlin during 1922.

Unpublished.   Originally comprised six movements.   Two movements were reconstructed from manuscript sources by David Drew in 1971, and two additional movements based on material omitted from the published version of String Quartet no. 1, op. 8, were added to comprise a four-movement "Wiederherstellung" of the *Divertimento*.

First Performance: November Group Concert
                       Berlin, 1923.

Instrumentation of Drew's reconstruction:

    I   Quasi Maestoso - Allegro deciso
        solo string quartet
        tutti strings
        horn

    II   Andantino
        solo string quartet

    III   Scherzo
        solo string quartet
        clarinet
        horn
        bassoon

    IV   Choral: Poco Sostenuto
        tutti strings
        horn
        2 trombones
        male chorus

Duration: 25 minutes

First Performances of Reconstruction: 1971 Baden-Baden Festival
                                        1971 Holland Festival
                                        Ernst Beur, conductor

Sinfonia sacra: Fantasie, Passacaglia und Hymnus für Orchester, op. 6

Composed in Berlin during 1922.

Unpublished. Only fragments have been preserved.

First Performance: Berlin Philharmonic Concert
                       April 1923
                       Alexander Selo, conductor

Review:

Weissmann, Adolf. *Die Musik* 15 (May 1923):625.

Die Zaubernacht

Ballet-Pantomime. Scenario by Vladimir Boritsch.

Commissioned by Russische Kindertheater. Composed in Berlin during
 1922.

Unpublished. Incomplete piano-vocal manuscript score in possession of
 the   Weill-Estate.

Instrumentation/Cast: soprano
                        2 dancers
                        9 instrumentalists
                        a number of children

Duration: 75 minutes

First Performance: Theater am Kurfürstendamm, Berlin
                        18 November 1922
                        Directed by Franz-Ludwig Hörth

American Premiere: "Lied der Fee" from *Die Zaubernacht*
                        revived in a concert at Lincoln Center, New York on
                        7 March 1977

String Quartet No. 1, op. 8

Introduktion, Scherzo, Choralphantasie (Played as one)

Composed in Berlin during 1923.

Published by Universal-Edition (Vienna, 1924):   #7699 Score
                                                   7700 Parts

Two Movements originally part of the Quartet but deleted before the premiere survive in manuscript. The "Andantino" and "Allegro deciso" were incorporated in David Drew's *Wiederherstellung* of the *Divertimento*. These "Two Movements for String Quartet" were first performed as such at Lincoln Center, New York on 7 March 1977.

Dedication: "Meinem Vater gewidmet"

Duration: 20 minutes

First Performance: Frankfurt Kammermusikwoche
                      24 June 1923
                      Hindemith-Amar Quartet

Other Early Performances: Berlin, 22 January 1924
                             Roth-Quartet

                             Paris, December 1924
                             Roth-Quartet

American Premiere: Yale University
                     13 May 1971
                     Debut String Quartet

Reviews:

   Bekker, Paul. *Anbruch* 5 (June-July 1923):188.

   Holl, Karl. *Frankfurter Zeitung*, 27 June 1923.

   _____. *Die Musik* 15 (August 1923):815.

   Weissmann, Adolf. *Die Musik* 16 (March 1924):444.

Quodlibet (*Eine Unterhaltungsmusik*), op. 9

"Orchestersuite aus dem Pantomime *Zaubernacht*"

I	Andante non troppo—Allegro molto—Andante
II	Molto vivace—Allegretto-Molto vivace—Allegro non troppo
III	Un poco sostenuto—Alla marcia funebre
IV	Molto agitato—Tempo di marcia—Molto vivo

Composed in Berlin during 1923.

Published by Universal-Edition (Vienna, 1926): #8348 Full score.

Dedication: "An Albert Bing"

Instrumentation:
2 flutes	2 trumpets
2 oboes	2 trombones
2 clarinets	tympani
2 bassoons	percussion
2 horns	strings

Duration: 26 minutes

First Performance: Friedrich-Theater, Dessau
15 June 1923
Albert Bing, conductor
(as "Orchestersuite aus dem Pantomime
Zaubernacht")

Coburg
6 February 1926
Albert Bing, conductor
(as *Quodlibet*)

American Premiere: Town Hall, New York
24 February 1963
Friends of Live Music
Eric Simon, conductor

Reviews:

Hamann, Ernst. *Die Musik* 15 (August 1923):830.

Hernried, Robert. *Neue Musik-Zeitung* 48 (July 1927):449.

Jacobs, Walter. *Die Musik* 19 (August 1927):807.

R.S.H. *Anbruch* 9 (March 1927):143.

Advertisement for *Quodlibet*, op. 9.
Anbruch 9 (December 1927).

Frauentanz, Sieben Gedichte des Mittelalters, op. 10

Composed in Heide during July 1923.

Published by Universal-Edition: #7599 Full score (Vienna, 1924)
                                  7600 Parts (Vienna, 1924)
                                  7748 Piano-vocal score (Vienna, 1925)

Instrumentation: soprano
                  flute
                  viola
                  clarinet
                  horn
                  bassoon

Duration: 8 minutes

First Performance: Akademie der Künste, Berlin
                         February 1924
                         Nora Pisling-Boas, soprano
                         Fritz Stiedry, conductor

Other Early Performances: IGNM Kammermusikfest-Salzburg
                         6 August 1924
                         Lotte Leonard, soprano
                         Phillip Jarnach, conductor

                         Vienna, December 1924
                         Ruzena Herlinger, soprano

                         Paris, January 1925
                         Ruzena Herlinger, soprano

                         Dresden, March 1927
                         Grete Nikisch, soprano
                         Kurt Weill, conductor

American Premiere: Mannes College, New York
                         11 May 1953
                         Lotte Leonard, soprano

Reviews:

Stiemer, Felix. *Der deutsche Rundfunk* 5 (1 May 1927):1230.

Weissmann, Adolf. *Die Musik* 16 (March 1924):444.

_____. *Die Musik* 17 (October 1924):52.

Chronicle of Performances: *Anbruch* 6 (March 1924):130.
6 (June-July 1924):265.
7 (January 1925):52.
7 (February 1925):98.
9 (March 1927):151, 152.
9 (April 1927):190, 195, 196.
9 (December 1927):446.
Die Musik 17 (December 1924):540.

Translation of Texts by Eric Simon:

FRAUENTANZ

1. We greeted the winter-long night with much pleasure, a well-countenanced knight and I—his will prevailed. As we both had envisioned, so it was accomplished with much joy and love. He is as my heart desires.
— Dietmar von Aiste —

2. When two lovers go dancing their eyes gleam bright as they exchange glances. Their eyes gleam bright, caring not who sees them. They are thinking in their hearts, oh, could I but lie near you.
— Anonymous —

3. Oh, were my love a cool fountain springing from a rock, and were I the green forest I would drink it in and would never stop. I would take it all in, yesterday and today, and on and on into blissful eternity.
— Anonymous —

4. See how this star shrouds itself in darkness. Fair Lady, do likewise when you catch sight of me. Let your eyes fall onto another man, so no one may ever know what has passed between us.
— Der von Kürenberg —

5.   One bright morning I arose early, I wanted to play in a beautiful orchard. There I found three maidens. One began to sing, the other chimed in: harbalorifa, harba harbalorifa. When I saw the lovely shoots in the orchard, and heard the sound of lovely maidens, my heart was refreshed; I had to join their song: harbalorifa, harbalorifa. I greeted the fairest among them, my arm encircled her, and straight I tried to kiss her lips. She said: Let be, let be, harba, harbalorifa.

                    — Duke John of Brabant —

6.   I shall leave all sorrow behind me, let us go out into the heath, my dear friends, where we see the flowers glow. To you I say, dear companion come with me. Sweet love, you shall be mine. Wind me a garland, that shall be worn by a proud man who is true in the service of ladies. To you I say, dear companion come with me.

                    — Anonymous —

7.   I sleep, I wake, I walk, I stand—and yet I can't forget you. I seem to see you all the time, you have bewitched my heart. How graceful is your bearing; through you I have no more peace on earth or in this world.

                    — Anonymous —

Recordare: Klagelieder Jeremiae V. Kapitel, op. 11

4-part mixed chorus and 2-part boys' chorus, *a cappella.*

Composed in Berlin during September 1923.

Unpublished. Copyist's manuscript in Weill-Estate.

Dedication: "Meinem Bruder Hanns Weill."

Duration: 24 minutes

First Performance: Utrecht, 1971 Holland Festival
                      NCRV Radio Vocal Ensemble
                      Marinis Voorberg, conductor

British Premiere: London, 17 November 1975
                    BBC Singers
                    John Poole, conductor

Konzert für Violine und Blasorchester, op. 12

I   Andante con moto
II   a) Notturno
      b) Cadenza
      c) Serenata
III   Allegro molto un poco agitato

Composed in Berlin, April-May 1924.

Weill's own reduction for violin and piano was published by Universal-
   Edition in 1925 (#8339). A full score was not published until 1965
   (#8340).

Instrumentation: solo violin
                   2 flutes (2nd also piccolo)
                   oboe
                   2 clarinets
                   2 bassoons
                   2 horns
                   trumpet
                   tympani
                   percussion
                   double bass (4)

Duration: 33 minutes

First Performance: Paris, 11 June 1925
                       Marcel Darrieux, violinist
                       Walter Straram, conductor

Other Early Performances: ISCM Festival in Zürich
                           23 June 1926
                           Stefan Frenkel, violinist
                           Fritz Busch, conductor

                           Friedrichstheater, Dessau (German Premiere)
                           October 1975
                           Stefan Frenkel, violinist
                           Franz von Hoesslin, conductor

Reviews:

Adorno, Theodor W. *Die Musik* 22 (February 1930):379.

Bing, Peter. *Anbruch* 7 (December 1925):550-51.

Copland, Aaron. *Modern Music* 4 (November-December 1926):31.

Kastner, Rudolf. *Der deutsche Rundfunk* 4 (11 July 1926):1944-46.

Weissmann, Adolf. *Die Musik* 18 (August 1926):836-37.

Advertisement for Weill's Violin Concerto, op. 12.
Anbruch 10 (June-July 1928).

Das Stundenbuch: Orchesterlieder nach Texten von Rilke, op. 13, 14

2 sets of three songs each.   Texts from Rainer Maria Rilke's *Das Stundenbuch*, first published in 1905.

Composed in Berlin during 1922 - 1925.

The songs were never published.   Only two of the six have survived: I "Vielleicht, dass ich durch schwere Berge gehe" and VI "In diesem Dorfe steht das letzte Haus."   Copyists' manuscripts of piano-vocal reductions, full scores, and sets of parts for the two songs are held by the Westminster Choir College Library, Princeton, New Jersey.

Instrumentation:	I:	3 flutes	2 trombones
		2 oboes	tympani
		2 clarinets	percussion
		2 bassoons	voice
		4 horns	strings
		2 trumpets	
	VI:	2 flutes	2 trumpets
		2 oboes	3 trombones
		2 clarinets	tympani
		2 bassoons	voice
		2 horns	strings

First Performance: Philharmonic Hall, Berlin
                       1925

Der Protagonist, op. 15*

One-act opera by Georg Kaiser.

Play written in 1920. First performed at Lobettheater, Breslau on 16
March 1922. Published in 1921 by Gustav Kiepenheuer, Potsdam.
English translation by H. F. Garten in *Tulane Drama Review* 5
(December 1960):133-44; and in *Seven Expressionist Plays:
Kokoschka to Barlach* (London: Calder & Boyers, 1968).

Opera composed in Grünheide and Berlin: January 1924 - April 1925.

Published by Universal-Edition (Vienna, 1926): #8388 Libretto
                                                 8387 Piano-vocal score

Dedication: "Für Lotte Lenja"

Instrumentation: In the Pit: 2 oboes   On stage: 2 flutes
                             2 bass clarinets   2 clarinets
                             3 horns   2 bassoons
                             3 trombones   2 trumpets
                             percussion
                             strings

Characters: Protagonist   Tenor
             Schwester   Soprano
             Der junge Herr   Baritone
             Der Hausmeister des Herzogs   Tenor
             Der Wirt   Bass
             1. Schauspieler   Bass
             2. Schauspieler   Baritone
             3. Schauspieler   Alto
             The Eight Musicians of the Duke

Duration: 1 hour and 15 minutes

First Performance: Dresden Staatsoper
                      27 March 1926
                      Fritz Busch, conductor
                      Joseph Gielen, director

*(Both *Der Protagonist* and *Der neue Orpheus* were published as opus 15.)

Adolf Mahnke, designer
Kurt Taucher, Protagonist
Elisa Stünzer, Schwester

Piano-vocal score out of print.
Available at New York Public Library and Library of Congress.

Reviews:

*Abravanel, Maurice. *La Revue musicale* 7 (July 1926):76-78.

*Adorno, Theodor W. *Die Musik* 20 (September 1928):923-24.

*Bie, Oskar. *Berliner Börsen-Courier*, 29 March 1926.

Einstein, Alfred. *Berliner Tageblatt*, 15 October 1928.

Hartmann, Albert. *Die Musik* 21 (May 1929):618.

Heister, Hans S. von. *Der deutsche Rundfunk* 4 (11 April 1926): 1015-16.

Holl, Karl. *Frankfurter Zeitung*, 21 June 1928.

Horenstein, Jascha. *Anbruch* 8 (May 1926):225-26.

Jhering, Herbert. *Berliner Börsen-Courier*, 17 April 1926.

Matthes, Wilhelm. *Anbruch* 9 (May-June 1927):255-56.

Rhode, Erich. *Neue Musik-Zeitung* 48 (July 1927):454.

Schmitz, Eugen. *Die Musik* 18 (May 1926):618.

Schrenk, Walter. *Blätter des Staatsoper* 7 (February 1927):8-9.

Strobel, Heinrich. *Anbruch* 9 (March 1927):140.

Weissmann, Adolf. *Die Musik* 21 (December 1928):216.

Plot Synopsis:

"The action takes place in the England of Shakespeare's time, in an inn where a troupe of actors is rehearsing a performance which they are to present in the evening before the Duke and his guests; as some of these are foreigners with no knowledge of the language, the little play has to be given in mime, so that the rehearsal is entirely a dumb-show. Immediately before it begins, we learn that the leading player relies upon his sister, who travels with the troupe, to recall him from his vicarious existence to the reality of his life: she is, for him, the symbol of this reality at its most pure. The protagonist's sister has one secret which her brother does not share—she has a lover, whom she wishes to present to him, so that they can marry with his consent and approval. Knowing the need her brother has of her, and how jealously he regards her, she determines to bring the young man to him after the rehearsal: for he is playing a comedy, which will leave him in high spirits and disposed to receive her lover favourably. And so, having told her brother the secret after the rehearsal, she goes out to find him.

While she is gone, however, a messenger from the Duke brings instructions that, out of deference to a bishop who has just arrived, a more serious piece than the one already rehearsed must be performed. The whole scene is at once re-cast and a new rehearsal begins, the protagonist now playing the part of a deceived husband. As he is about to stab his rival, his sister, unaware of the change, returns to announce the coming of her lover. All the players at once stop acting, the musicians interrupt their accompaniment—but the protagonist cannot distinguish so rapidly between the imaginary world to which his acting transports him and the real world represented by his sister. Her confession becomes for him an element in the world of the play, in which he had discovered the deception practised upon him by an unfaithful wife; the reality of his sister's confession that she had hidden her love from him merges into the jealousy that possesses him as an actor; the dream of passion ceases to be a fiction. Instead of stabbing his rival on the stage, he actually stabs his sister—who, in her death, brings him back for the last time to the real world."

[From B. J. Kenworthy, *Georg Kaiser* (Oxford: Basil Blackwell, 1957), pp. 154-56.]

Advertisement for *Der Protagonist*.
Anbruch 8 (May 1926).

Der neue Orpheus, op. 16*

Cantata for Soprano, Violin, and Orchestra. Text by Iwan Goll.

Composed in Berlin during September 1925.

Published by Universal-Edition (Vienna, 1926):   #8471 Full score
8472 Edition for Piano,
Violin, Voice by
Arthur Willner

Dedication: "Für Lotte Leonard"

Instrumentation: 2 flutes   percussion
2 oboes   harp
2 clarinets   solo violin
2 bassoons   violas
2 trumpets   cellos
2 trombones   basses

Duration: 18 minutes

First Performance: Berlin Staatsoper (Kroll)
2 March 1927
Erich Kleiber, conductor
Delia Reinhardt, soprano
Rudolf Deman, violinist

Unofficial American Premiere: New Haven: Woolsey Hall
5 October 1972
Yale Collegium Orchestra
Gustav Meier, conductor
Emelia Simone, soprano
Daniel Stepner, violinist

*(*Der neue Orpheus,* op. 16, was incorrectly labeled as opus 15 in U-E #8472.
This is clearly an error, because *Der Protagonist,* the proper opus 15, pre-dates *Der neue Orpheus* in both publication and composition. Furthermore, *Der neue Orpheus* was advertised as opus 16 in *Anbruch* 8 (June-July 1926) and *Anbruch* 9 (May-June 1927). It immediately pre-dates *Royal Palace,* opus 17, in composition and was premiered on the same program. The confusion has been compounded in that *Vom Tod im Wald,* opus 23, frequently has been labeled erroneously as opus 16.)

American Professional Premiere: New Haven: Woolsey Hall
                                      13 January 1976
                                      New Haven Symphony Orchestra
                                      Erich Kunzel, conductor
                                      Phyllis Curtin, soprano
                                      Ruggiero Ricci, violinist

Reviews:

Leichtentritt, Hugo. *Musical Courier* 94 (24 March 1927):5.

Stefan, Paul. *Anbruch* 9 (March 1927):134.

Weissmann, Adolf. *Die Musik* 19 (April 1927):518.

Westermeyer, Karl. *Berliner Tageblatt*, 3 March 1927.

Royal Palace, op. 17

One-act opera by Iwan Goll.

Composed in Berlin, October 1925 - January 1926.

Published by Universal-Edition (Vienna, 1926):   # 8690 Piano-vocal score
8691 Libretto

Dedication: "Für Georg Kaiser"

Instrumentation:	2 flutes	4 horns
	piccolo	2 trumpets
	2 oboes	2 trombones
	2 clarinets	bass tuba, tympani
	alto saxophone	percussion
	2 bassoons	piano
	contrabassoon	harp
		strings

On stage: percussion, glockenspiel, 5 bells, celeste.

Characters:	Dejanira	Soprano
	Der Ehemann	Bass
	Der Geliebte von gestern	Baritone
	Der Verliebte von morgen	Tenor
	Der junge Fischer	Tenor
	Der alte Fischer	Bass

Soprano solo and women's chorus off-stage.

Duration: 50 minutes

First Performance: Berlin Staatsoper (Kroll)
2 March 1927 (7 performances)
Erich Kleiber, conductor
Franz-Ludwig Hörth, director
Max Terpis, choreographer
Cast: Delia Reinhardt, Carl Jöken, Leo
Schützendorf, Leonhard Kern

The only other production (2 performances) during Weill's lifetime occurred in Essen in 1929; Erich Hezel, director.

The libretto is available at the New York Public Library; the piano-vocal score at the Library of Congress. The full score and orchestral parts were lost after the production in Essen and have not been recovered. Because of the unusually detailed piano-vocal score, which includes instrumental cues, Gunther Schuller and Noam Sheriff reconstructed an orchestral score. This version was premiered as a "dance drama with singing" at the San Francisco Opera, 5 October 1968.

Reviews:

Baresel, Alfred. *Neue Musik-Zeitung* 48 (April 1927):316-17.

Kastner, Rudolf. *Der deutsche Rundfunk* 5 (13 March 1927):728-29.

Leichtentritt, Hugo. *Musical Courier* 94 (24 March 1927):5.

Stefan, Paul. *Anbruch* 9 (March 1927):133-34.

Weissmann, Adolf. *Die Musik* 19 (April 1927):518.

Westermeyer, Karl. *Berliner Tageblatt*, 3 March 1927.

Plot Synopsis:

"A fashionable young woman, surrounded by three men, is seen in the Royal Palace Hotel on the shores of an Italian lake. She is thoroughly bored by her vulgar, rich husband, her shallow lover of yesterday and her romantic lover of tomorrow. They vie with one another to amuse her. Her husband starts by ordering a luxurious supper, during which the hotel director, waiters and bus boys dance to burlesque jazz music, and after which he sends her on a trip, by aero-express, through Europe. A real aeroplane descends in Berlin, Paris, London, etc., which are seen via cinema. But Dejanira, the fair lady, remains bored. The first lover then gives her the Heavens of Our Nights, a fantastic ballet of the moon and stars, in luxurious style. The second lover's present is Fantasy, a spectacular, cubistic, expressionistic, symbolical play of engines, wheels, angles, all jumping and whirling in the most fantastic shapes and colors. Dejanira laughs at the stupidity of her adorers and drowns herself in the lake."

[From Hugo Leichtentritt, "Berlin, Too Has Its Jazz Opera," *Musical Courier* 94 (24 March 1927):5.]

Incidental Music for *Herzog Theodor von Gothland*

Commissioned by the Berliner Rundfunk for Klabund's and Alfred
   Braun's adaptation of Christian Dietrich Grabbe's five-act tragedy that
   was broadcast as a radio play.   Composed in Berlin during July-
   August 1926.

Unpublished. Manuscript lost. The work was scored for large orchestra,
   including saxophone, and chorus.

First Performance: Berliner Rundfunk
                        1 September 1926
                        Bruno Seidler-Winkler, conductor
                        Cast: Theodor Loos (Olaf); Werner Krauss
                               (Theodor); Lothar Müthel (Friedrich);
                               Johanna Hofer (Cäcilia)

See *Der deutsche Rundfunk* 4 (29 August 1926):2413-14; 4 (September
   1926):2580; 4(21 November 1926):3326.

Na und?

Comic opera in 2 acts. Libretto by Felix Joachimson.

Composed in Berlin during 1926.

Unpublished. Unperformed. Only an incomplete folder of sketches has survived.

Advertisement for Weill's compositions, including *Na und?*, a publication which never
materialized.
Anbruch 8 (June-July 1926).

KURT WEILL

Mahagonny-Songspiel (*Das kleine Mahagonny*)

Text by Bertolt Brecht.

Composed in Berlin and Charlottenburg, May 1927.

Unpublished during Weill's lifetime. Original version restored and edited by David Drew and published by Universal-Edition (Vienna, 1963): #12889 Piano-vocal score.

Instrumentation: 2 violins
                       2 clarinets (one doubles on bass clarinet)
                       2 trumpets
                       alto saxophone
                       trombone
                       piano
                       percussion

Characters:	Charlie	Tenor
	Billy	Tenor
	Bobby	Bass
	Jimmy	Bass
	Jessie	Soubrette
	Bessie	Soubrette

Duration: 35 minutes

First Performance: Baden-Baden, Deutsche Kammermusikfest 1927
                          17 July 1927
                          Ernst Mehlich, conductor
                          Walter Brügmann, director
                          Caspar Neher, designer
                          Cast: Lotte Lenya, Irene Eden, Erik Wirl, Georg
                                        Ripperger, Karl Giebel, Gerhard Pechner

American Premiere: New Haven, Yale Repertory Theater
                          23 May 1971
                          Gustav Meier, conductor
                          Michael Posnick, director
                          English translation by Michael Feingold

Reviews:

Copland, Aaron. *Modern Music* 5 (November-December 1927):31-34.

Downes, Olin. *New York Times*, 14 August 1927.

Ennslin, Hermann. *Neue Musik-Zeitung* 48 (August 1927):492-93.

Mersmann, Hans. *Melos* 6 (August-September 1927):374-75.

Preussner, Eberhard. *Die Musik* 19 (September 1927):886-89.

R. Z. *Der deutsche Rundfunk* 5 (7 August 1972):2195.

Stefan, Paul. *Anbruch* 9 (August-September 1927):271-72.

Stiemer, Felix. *Der deutsche Rundfunk* 5 (17 July 1927):1981-82.

Advertisement for *Mahagonny: Ein Songspiel*.
Anbruch 9 (August-September 1927).

Der Zar lässt sich photographieren, op. 21

"Opera buffa" in one act by Georg Kaiser.

Composed in Berlin, March-August 1927.

Published by Universal-Edition (Vienna, 1927):   # 8964 Piano-vocal score
                                                                                edited by Erwin Stein
                                                                      8965 Libretto
                                                                      9465 Full score

Instrumentation: 2 flutes
                             2 oboes   tympani
                             2 clarinets   percussion
                             2 bassoons   piano
                             3 horns   strings
                             2 trumpets
                             2 trombones

Characters: Ein Zar von   Baritone
                     Angèle   Soprano
                     Der Gehilfe   Tenor
                     Der Boy   Alto
                     Die falsche Angèle   Soprano
                     Der falsche Boy   Alto
                     Der Anführer   Tenor
                     Der Begleiter des Zaren   Bass
                     Erster Kriminalbeamter
                     Zweiter Kriminalbeamter
                     Verschwörer, Offiziere, Polizisten
                     (Male chorus in orchestra pit)

Duration: 50 minutes

First Performance: Leipzig Neues Theater
                                18 February 1928
                                Gustav Brecher, conductor
                                Walther Brügmann, director
                                Cast: Ilse Kögel, Maria Janowska, Theodor Horand

Other Early Performances: Düsseldorf, 18 March 1928
Hugo Balzer, conductor
Dr. Friedrich Schramms, director

Altenburg, 25 March 1928
Maurice Abravanel, conductor
Rudolf Otto Hartmann, director

Frankfurt, 19 June 1928
Klaus Nettstraeter, conductor
Hans Mutzenbecher, director

Berlin Städtische Oper, 14 October 1928
Robert Denzler, conductor
Walter Brügmann, director

American Premiere: *The Shah Has His Photograph Taken*
Metropolitan Opera Guild
Juilliard School, New York
27 October 1949
Dino Yannopoulos, director

Both piano-vocal score and full score are out of print. Piano-vocal score available at the Library of Congress, New York Public Library, and Columbia University Library; full score at the Library of Congress. U.S. agent: Theodore Presser. The "Tango-Angèle" was published separately for piano solo.

Reviews:

Aber, Adolf. *Die Musik* 20 (October 1927):542.

Adorno, Theodor W. *Die Musik* 20 (September 1928):923-24.

Baresel, Alfred. *Neue Musik-Zeitung* 49 (1928):383-84.

Einstein, Alfred. *Berliner Tageblatt*, 15 October 1928.

_____. *New York Times*, 22 April 1928.

Eisenmann, Alexander. *Die Musik* 21 (February 1929):380.

Epstein, Peter. *Anbruch* 10 (June-July 1928):218.

Gail, H. R. *Anbruch* 10 (May 1928):179.

Gärtner, H. M. *Die Musik* 20 (September 1928):924.

Hamann, Ernst. *Die Musik* 20 (June 1928):690.

Heinzen, Carl. *Die Musik* 20 (May 1928):613.

Heister, Hans S. von. *Der deutsche Rundfunk* 6 (2 March 1929): 614-15.

Holl, Karl. *Frankfurter Zeitung*, 21 June 1928.

Kürschner, Arthur. *Das Theater* 9 (November 1928):480.

Lessing, Theodor. *Anbruch* 11 (April 1929):168.

Rau, Walter. *Anbruch* 10 (October 1928):299.

Schab, Günter. *Anbruch* 10 (October 1928):300.

*Stefan, Paul. *Anbruch* 10 (April-May 1928):119-22.

Strobel, Heinrich. *Melos* 7 (December 1928):557.

Weissmann, Adolf. *Christian Science Monitor*, 29 March 1928.

Plot Synopsis:

A czar who is visiting Paris appears at the studio of the beautiful Madame Angèle to have his photograph taken. Before he arrives, conspirators substitute a "false" Angèle for the authentic photographer and place in the camera a pistol that will fire when the picture is taken. The Czar arrives. Taken by the beauty of the false Angèle, he laments his responsibilities as Czar and wishes that he were merely a private citizen, so that he would be less unapproachable and more appealing to Angèle. They chat, become affectionate, but do not get the picture taken. Finally the false Angèle gets to the point of counting "One - Two -", but the Czar interrupts the whole procedure. Then he decides they should exchange roles; he will take a picture of his charming photographer, who finds herself in front of the dangerous camera. The action continues back and forth until the policemen arrive and announce that the trail of an attempted assassination plot leads right to this studio. But the Czar, preoccupied with his interest in Angèle, is unconcerned. The false Angèle disappears, and the bewildered Czar hardly notices that it is the real Angèle who eventually takes his photograph.

Advertisement for *Der Zar lässt sich photographieren.*
Anbruch 10 (March-April 1928).

„Eine der köstlichsten Buffo - Opern der neuen Zeit"
(Alfred Baresel)

DER ZAR LÄSST SICH PHOTOGRAPHIEREN

Opera buffa in einem Akt
Text von Georg Kaiser

MUSIK VON

KURT WEILL

**Uraufführung unter Leitung von Gustav Brecher und Walter
Brügmann am Neuen Theater in Leipzig am 18. Februar 1928**

AUS DER PRESSE:

„Weill wird mit dem Zaren sein Glück machen . . . nach Kreneks
‚Jonny' ein neues Erfolgstück der modernen Oper."
(Berliner Tageblatt, Karl Westermeyer)

„Ein geschlossener musikalischer Organismus."
(Berliner Börsen-Courier, Heinrich Strobel)

„Allerbester Komödienstil in dieser Partitur."
(Deutsche Allgemeine Zeitung, Walter Schrenk)

„Ein köstlicher Groteskstoff."   (Berliner Morgenpost, Rudolf Kastner)

„Ein überaus wirkungsvolles, witziges und unterhaltendes Stück."
(Leipziger Neueste Nachrichten, Adolf Aber)

„Tango Angèle: Künstlerisch geformter Zeitgeist. Die populäre Wirkung des Stückes ist nicht abzusehen. Jeder wird sich diese Platte
kaufen."   (Thüringer Allgemeine Zeitung)

DIE ERSTEN ANNAHMEN:
**Altenburg, Braunschweig, Chemnitz, Dessau, Dortmund,
Düsseldorf, Frankfurt a. M., Gera, Mainz, Stettin**

Erschienene Ausgaben:
U. E. Nr. 8964 Klavierauszug mit Text . . . . . Mk. 10·--
U. E. Nr. 8965 Textbuch . . . . Mk. —·50

In Vorbereitung:
TANGO ANGÈLE, FÜR KLAVIER
Die Grammophonplatte ›Tango Angèle‹ ist von der Firma
Parlophon-Beka hergestellt und im Handel erschienen

Ausführliche illustrierte Pressestimmen gratis von der
UNIVERSAL-EDITION A. G., WIEN—LEIPZIG

Vom Tod im Wald, op. 23

Ballade für Bass Stimme und 10 Bläsern.

Poem by Bertolt Brecht, written in 1918.   First published in *Der Erzähler*, March 1918.   Appeared as "Chroniken 3" of *Die Hauspostille* (Berlin: Propyläen-Verlag, 1927).

Composed in Berlin during 1927.   Originally included in *Das Berliner Requiem*, but never performed in that context.

Unpublished. Manuscript copy in the Library of Congress.

Instrumentation: 2 clarinets   2 trumpets
                      bassoon   tenor trombone
                      contrabassoon   bass trombone
                      2 horns   bass voice

Duration: 10 minutes

First Performance: Berlin Philharmonic Concert
                      23 November 1927
                      Eugen Lang, conductor
                      Heinrich Hermanns, Bass
                      Only known performance during Weill's lifetime.

American Premiere: Lincoln Center, New York
                      Alan Titus, Baritone
                      Curtis Chamber Ensemble
                      7 March 1977.

Review:

   Anbruch 9 (December 1927):444.

Incidental Music 1927-1931

Gustav III. Play by August Strindberg (1902). Composed in October 1927 for Victor Barnowsky's production at the Koniggrätzer Theater, 27 October 1927. Scored for a twelve-piece orchestra consisting of 2 piccolos, 2 clarinets, 2 trumpets, 2 horns, trombone, percussion, violin, harmonium/piano. First performance conducted by Walter Goehr. Originally consisted of fifteen short pieces, of which about half have survived in manuscript. David Drew constructed a suite from the surviving material; it was first performed at Aberdeen University (England) during 1971.

Konjunktur. Play by Leo Lania in collaboration with Bertolt Brecht. Composed in March 1928 for Piscator's production at the Theater am Nollendorfplatz (Berlin) on 10 April 1928. Originally scored for flute, clarinet (doubling on alto saxophone), 2 trumpets, trombone, violin, and piano. A fragmentary manuscript is in the Weill-Estate. David Drew arranged the surviving material as "Oil Music," which was premiered at the 1975 Berlin Festival. Universal-Edition published one song from the score, "Die Muschel von Margate: Petroleum Song," as part of Weill's *Song Album* (#9787) in 1929.

Katalaunische Schlacht. Play by Arnolt Bronnen (1924). Composed in Berlin during March-April 1928 for a production at the Staatliches Schauspielhaus (Berlin) on 25 April 1928. Unpublished. Score presumed lost.

Die Petroleuminseln. Play by Lion Feuchtwanger (1923). Score composed in Berlin during 1929 for a production at the Staatliches Schauspielhaus. "Das Lied von den braunen Inseln" was published in Weill's *Song-Album* (#9787). The remainder of the score has not survived.

Lied von Hoboken. Weill's music was composed during 1929 for a production at the Berlin Volksbühne.

Mann ist Mann. Play by Bertolt Brecht (1924-25). Composed in Berlin during 1930-31 for a production at the Staatliches Schauspielhaus on 6 February 1931. Score is presumed lost.

Die Dreigroschenoper

Ein Stück mit Musik in einem Vorspiel und acht Bildern nach John Gay's "The Beggar's Opera." Uebersetzt von Elisabeth Hauptmann. Deutsche Bearbeitung von Bertolt Brecht.

Composed in Le Lavandou, France and Berlin during Summer 1928.

Published by Universal-Edition: #8851 Piano-vocal score by Norbert Gingold (Vienna, 1928)
8843 Libretto (Vienna, 1928)
14901 Philharmonia Partitur No. 400 (Vienna, 1972)

Instrumentation: alto saxophone (also flute, clarinet, baritone saxophone)
tenor saxophone (also soprano saxophone, bassoon, bass clarinet)
2 trumpets
trombone (also double bass)
banjo (also guitar, cello, Hawaiian guitar, mandolin, bandoneon)
tympani and percussion
harmonium, celeste, piano

Characters: Macheath, genannt Mackie Messer
Jonathan Jeremiah Peachum
Celia Peachum
Polly Peachum
Brown, oberster Polizeichef von London
Lucy, seine Tochter
Die Spelunken-Jenny
Smith
Pastor Kimball
Filch
Ein Ausrufer
Die Platte
Bettler
Hüren
Konstabler

Duration: about 3 hours

First Performance: Theater am Schiffbauerdamm, Berlin
                       31 August 1928
                       Erich Engel, director
                       Caspar Neher, designer
                       Theo Mackeben, musical director
                       Ernst Aufricht, producer
                       The Lewis Ruth Band
                       Cast: Erich Ponto, Rosa Valetti, Roma Bahn, Harald
                             Paulsen, Kurt Gerron, Kate Kühl, Lotte Lenya

American Premiere: Empire Theater, New York
                       13 April 1933
                       Translation by Gifford Cochran and Jerold Krimsky
                       Francesco von Mendelssohn, director
                       (12 performances)

Other Important Productions: Théâtre de l'Etoile, Paris
                                28 September 1937
                                Ernst Aufricht, producer
                                Francesco von Mendelssohn, director

                                Theater de Lys, New York
                                10 March 1954
                                English adaptation by Marc Blitzstein
                                Carmen Capalbo, director
                                Samuel Matlowsky, musical director
                                (2,611 performances)

Agent for Blitzstein version: Tams-Witmark. (Note that this version does not use the original instrumentation.)

Copyist's manuscript of the full score, dated 23 August 1928, is in the Library of Congress.

Excerpts and Arrangements:

"Arie der Lucy," omitted from the original production, published in *Die Musik* 25 (November 1932):128.

"Salomon-Song" published in *Die Musik* 21 (March 1929):432.

"Ballade von der sexuellen Hörigkeit," omitted from U-E #8851, published in Weill's *Song-Album*, U-E #9787.

Universal-Edition published the following for voice and piano (Vienna, 1929):

"Kanonensong"	#8847
"Barbarasong"	9594
"Liebeslied"	9596
"Moritat"	9772
"Tango-Ballade"	8848
"Seeräuberjenny"	9652
"Ballade von angenehmen Leben"	9595

In 1929, Universal-Edition published the following for jazz orchestra:

"Kanonensong" and "Tango-Ballade"	VCJ No. 102/103
"Blues-Potpourri"	VCJ No. 110
"Foxtrot-Potpourri"	VCJ No. 111

"Moritat vom Mackie Messer." Spezialarrangement für Jazz- und Salonorchester von Isko Thaler.

Universal-Edition also published:

"Tango-Ballade" für Klavier, #8848
Dreigroschenoper-Potpourri für Klavier, #12663
Sieben Stücke nach der *Dreigroschenoper* für Violine und Klavier, arranged by Stephan Frenkel, #9969 and 9969b (Simplified). (1930)
"Alle 17 Songs aus der *Dreigroschenoper*," #13832 (Voice and Piano)

Suite from *The Threepenny Opera* for full orchestra, with voice *ad libitum*, orchestrated by Max Schoenherr, is available on rental.

Judgment of Paris, an unpublished one-act ballet for which Weill arranged music from *Die Dreigroschenoper* in 1938, is available at the Library of Congress. Premiere: London Ballet, Westminster Theater, 15 June 1938; Book and Costumes by Hugh Laing, Choreography by Antony Tudor. Cast: Agnes de Mille, Therese Langfield, Charlotte Bidmead.

Songs from *Die Dreigroschenoper* were also published by Kiepenheuer Verlag (Berlin) in 1929 and Lied der Zeit Verlag (Berlin) in 1969.

Reviews:

*Adorno, Theodor W. *Die Musik* 21 (December 1928):221-22.

*_____. *Die Musik* 21 (March 1929):424-28.

Baresel, Alfred. *Neue Leipziger Zeitung*, 25 January 1930.

*Bie, Oskar. *Anbruch* 10 (August-September 1928):260-61.

*Bloch, Ernst. *Anbruch* 11 (January 1929):125-27.

Blom, Eric. *The Sackbut* (March 1931):211-15.

Heister, Hans S. von.   *Der deutsche Rundfunk* 6 (14 September 1928):2551-52.

Hijman, Julius. *Caecilia en de Musiek* 87 (December 1929):43-46.

Jacobs, Monty. *Vossische Zeitung* (Berlin), 1 September 1928.

Jemnitz, Alexander. *Melos* 7 (October 1928):498.

Jhering, Herbert. *Anbruch* 10 (August-September 1928):259-60.

_____. *Berliner Börsen-Courier*, 1 September 1928.

A. W. K. *Musical America* 53 (25 April 1933):27.

Kerr, Walter. *Berliner Tageblatt*, 1 September 1928.

Kürschner, Arthur. *Das Theater* (Berlin) 9 (September 1928):400.

Lamey, Bernhard. *Das Theater* (Berlin) 11 (February 1930):40.

McN., W. *The Musical Times* 76 (March 1935):260.

Mersmann, Hans and Strobel, Heinrich.   *Melos* 8 (January 1929): 15-17.

Preussner, Eberhard. *Die Musik* 21 (March 1929):464.

Servaes, Franz. *Berliner Lokal-Anzeiger*, 1 September 1928.

Strobel, Heinrich. *Melos* 7 (October 1928):498.

Trask, C. Hooper. *New York Times*, 2 December 1928.

Wiegler, Paul. *B. Z. am Mittag*, 1 September 1928.

Program from the original production of *Die Dreigroschenoper*.

Theater am Schiffbauerdamm

Direktion: Ernst Josef Aufricht

Die Dreigroschenoper

(The Beggars Opera)

Ein Stück mit Musik in einem Vorspiel und 8 Bildern nach dem
Englischen des John Gay.
(Eingelegte Balladen von François Villon und Rudyard Kipling)

Übersetzung: Elisabeth Hauptmann
Bearbeitung: Brecht
Musik: Kurt Weill
Regie: Erich Engel
Bühnenbild: Caspar Neher
Musikalische Leitung: Theo Makeben
Kapelle: Lewis Ruth Band.

Personen:

Jonathan Peachum, Chef einer Bettlerplatte	Erich Ponto
Frau Peachum	Rosa Valetti
Polly, ihre Tochter	Roma Bahn
Macheath, Chef einer Platte von Straßen-banditen	Harald Paulsen
Brown, Polizeichef von London	Kurt Gerron
Lucy, seine Tochter	Kate Kühl
Trauerweidenwalter	Ernst Rotmund
Münzmatthias	Karl Hannemann
Hakenfingerjakob	Manfred Fürst
Sägerobert	Josef Bunzel
Jimmie	Werner Maschmeyer
Ede	Albert Venohr

Advertisement for *Die Dreigroschenoper*.
Anbruch 11 (February 1929).

Kleine Dreigroschenmusik für Blasorchester

Composed in Berlin during Autumn 1928

Published by Universal-Edition (Vienna, 1929): #9712 Full score.

Instrumentation: 2 flutes (1st also piccolo)
                      2 clarinets
                      alto saxophone
                      tenor saxophone (also soprano saxophone)
                      2 bassoons
                      2 trumpets
                      trombone
                      tuba
                      banjo (also guitar, bandoneon)
                      tympani
                      percussion

Duration: 22 minutes

First Performance: Berlin Staatsoper Orchestra Concert
                        7 February 1929
                        Otto Klemperer, conductor

Reviews:

*Adorno, Theodor W. *Anbruch* 11 (September-October 1929):316-17.

Einstein, Alfred. *Berliner Tageblatt*, 8 February 1929.

Epstein, Peter. *Pult und Taktstock* 6 (March-April 1929):36-37.

Oppenheimer, Ernest. *Rheinische Musik- und Theater-Zeitung* 31 (26 April 1930):148-50.

Strobel, Heinrich. *Berliner Börsen-Courier*, 8 February 1929.

"Berlin im Licht-Song" (Slow-Fox)

Text by Kurt Weill

Commissioned by the "Berlin im Licht" Festival, October 1928. Composed in Berlin during 1928.

Published for voice and piano by Universal-Edition (Vienna, 1928): #8862. Arrangement for jazz orchestra published in 1929: V.C.J. #104.

First Performances: "Berlin im Licht" Festival
                        15 October 1928
                        Promenade Concert (Voice and Piano)
                        Military Band Concert (Wind Ensemble)
                        Wittenberg Platz
                        Hermann Scherchen, conductor

The edition for voice and piano is available at the New York Public Library.

Das Berliner Requiem

Cantata for Tenor, Baritone, Male Chorus, and Wind Ensemble

Text by Bertolt Brecht

Composed in Berlin, November-December 1928. Commissioned by the Reichs-Rundfunk-Gesellschaft.

Piano-vocal score published by Universal-Edition (Vienna, 1967): #9786. Piano reduction by Karl Heinz Füssl; edited by David Drew.

Dedication: "Dem Frankfurter Sender gewidmet"

Instrumentation: 2 clarinets
                    2 alto saxophones (2nd also tenor saxophone)
                    2 bassoons
                    2 trumpets
                    2 horns
                    2 trombones
                    tuba *ad lib.*
                    tympani
                    banjo/guitar
                    piano/harmonium

Duration: 21 minutes

First Performance: Frankfurt Radio
                      22 May 1929
                      Ludwig Rottenburg, conductor
                      Hans Grahl, tenor; Johannes Willy, baritone;
                      Jean Stern, bass

American Premiere: Cincinnati Symphony Orchestra
                      May 1970
                      Erich Kunzel, conductor

"Materl" published in Weill's *Song-Album* (U-E #9787).

Reviews:

   Stiemer, Felix. *Der deutsche Rundfunk* 7 (21 May 1929):731.

Zu Potsdam unter den Eichen (Langsamer Marsch)

Text by Bertolt Brecht.

Composed in Berlin during 1929.

Originally "Zu Potsdam unter den Eichen" served as the concluding movement of the version of *Das Berliner Requiem* that was broadcast in 1929. However, this version of "Zu Potsdam. . . ," undoubtedly scored for chorus and orchestra, has not survived. Weill later detached it from the *Requiem* and arranged it for four-part *a cappella* male chorus (U-E #9983, 1930) and for solo voice with piano accompaniment (included in *Song-Album*, U-E #9787).

Duration: 3 minutes

First Performance: See *Das Berliner Requiem.*

First Performance of *a cappella* version: Berliner Schubertchor
                                             Karl Rankl, conductor
                                             December 1929

The versions for solo voice and male chorus are available at the Library of Congress.

Review:

   Westermeyer, Karl. *Die Musik* 22 (January 1930):299.

Die Legende vom toten Soldaten

A cappella mixed chorus.

Text by Bertolt Brecht (1918).

Composed in Berlin during 1929.

Unpublished. Manuscript copy in the Library of Congress.

Duration: 5 minutes.

First Performance: Berliner Schubertchor
                       Karl Rankl, conductor
                       December 1929

Review:

     Westermeyer, Karl. *Die Musik* 22 (January 1930):299.

Der Lindberghflug

Cantata for soloists, chorus, and orchestra by Bertolt Brecht.

Text revised by Brecht in 1930, "Der Flug des Lindberghs."   Title
    changed by Brecht in 1950 to "Der Ozeanflug."

Version I: Weill and Hindemith composed alternate numbers.
              Berlin, Spring 1929. Unpublished.

Version II: Weill set the entire text himself. Berlin, Autumn 1929
               Published by Universal-Edition (Vienna, 1930):
                   #9938 Piano-vocal score
                    8838 Full score, with an English translation by George
                    Antheil.

Instrumentation: 2 flutes   piano
    (Version II)   2 clarinets   strings
                    2 bassoons
                    2 trumpets   Lindbergh. . . . Tenor
                    2 trombones   Baritone Solo
                    tympani   Bass Solo
                    percussion   Mixed Chorus

Duration: 40 minutes

First Performance: Version I—   Deutsche Kammermusikfest, Baden-
                                     Baden
                                     28 July 1929
                                     Hermann Scherchen, conductor
                      Version II—   Berlin Staatsoper Orchestra Concert
                                     5 December 1929
                                     Otto Klemperer, conductor
                                     Erik Wirl, Lindbergh
                                     Fritz Krenn & Martin Abendroth,
                                     soloists

American Premiere: Philadelphia Academy of Music
                      Philadelphia Orchestra
                      4 April 1931
                      Leopold Stokowski, conductor

First Performance in the U. S. as *Der Ozeanflug*:   17 May 1974
Avery Fisher Hall, New
York
New York Choral
Society

British Premiere: Summer 1970, The Proms
20 January 1971, Festival Hall
Colin Davis, conductor
Robert Tear, Lindbergh

Piano-vocal score and *Partitur* are both out of print.   The former is available at the New York Public Library and the Library of Congress. The latter only at New York Public Library.

"Vorstellung des Fliegers Lindbergh" was published in Weill's *Song-Album* U-E #9787 (1929).

Reviews:

Einstein, Alfred. *Berliner Tageblatt,* 6 December 1929.

_____. *Die Musik* 22 (January 1930):296.

_____. *New York Times,* 2 February 1930.

Gilman, Lawrence. *Music and Youth* 11 (June 1931):121-22.

Preussner, Eberhard. *Die Musik* 21 (September 1929):900-901.

Strobel, Heinrich. *Der deutsche Rundfunk* 7 (9 August 1929):1015-16.

_____. *Berliner Börsen-Courier,* 6 December 1929.

_____. *Melos* 8 (August-September 1929):395-97.

Advertisement for *Der Lindberghflug.*
Anbruch 12 (January 1930).

Ein neues Werk von

KURT WEILL

DER LINDBERGHFLUG
Für Soli, Chor und Orchester
Dichtung von **BERT BRECHT**

„Ich halte es für nötig, bei einer Vokalmusik auch außerhalb
ihrer Verwertung im Konzertsaal den praktischen Zweck zu
bezeichnen, für den sie geschrieben ist. Die Dichtung „Der
Lindberghflug' von Brecht liegt hier in einer musikalischen
Fassung vor, die in ihrem Endzweck für Aufführungen in
Schulen gedacht ist"
                                        Kurt Weill

Uraufführung in Berlin unter Otto Klemperer
am 5. Dezember 1929

„Auch die Musik, die nun dem Werke dient, hat es irgendwie in
sich . . . es schwingt in ihrer Totalität **ein Echtes, ein Etwas, das
zu sich hin zwingt, das erregt . . .**"
                                (Max Marschalk, Vossische Zeitung)

„Die Musik Weills folgt mit lebhaften inneren Impulsen dem Schick-
sal des Fliegers, seinem Kampf mit dem Nebel, dem Schneesturm
und dem Schlaf, und sie wird hochromantisch im Gespräch Lindberghs
mit seinem Motor . . . **Kurt Weill hat in dieser Partitur einige
ganz bezaubernde Einfälle** . . . **Das Orchester ist mit einem
außerordentlichen Klangsinn behandelt** und die Solisten haben
ebenso wie der Chor dankbare **Aufgaben** . . . **Der Erfolg war sehr
herzlich.**"   (Walter Schrenk, Deutsche Allgem. Zeitung)

„Weill ist diesmal wieder viel eingefallen. In Fortbildung des Stils
der Dreigroschenoper ist er jetzt zu einer ganz einfachen Ausdrucks-
weise gekommen, die ihrer Wirkung sicher sein kann . . . es ist ein
durch und durch modernes Werk . . . **es faßt wirklich Zeitatmo-
sphäre** . . . es befreit von dem peinlichen Gefühl, daß wir vor
lauter Kompliziertheit unserer Instrumente das Nächstliegende
nicht bewältigen können. Lebhafter Applaus für das neue Werk
und die Ausführenden."
                                (Viktor Zuckerkandl, Tempo)

„**Das Werk birgt viele Schönheiten** . . . die ganze Idee der Ver-
teilung der Stimmungen ist im besten Sinn wirksam und wirklichkeits-
nah. Ein starkes Stück, begeistert aufgenommen." (8-Uhr-Blatt)

„Die musikalische Anlage ist bewußt einfach gehalten . . . **Volks-
tümlich** in ihrer sangbaren Melodik und ihrem treibenden Jazz-
rhythmus ist sie stilistisch der „Dreigroschenoper' nahe verwandt
Die Musik, stets bedacht auf letzte Verständlichkeit des Textwortes,
wandelt die gleichfalls gewollt primitive Sprache in rhythmische Be-
wegung. Kurt Weill weist mit dieser Komposition neue Wege
künstlerischer und formaler Gestaltung . . . mußte der Komponist
wiederholt auf dem Podium erscheinen."
                                (Dr. Arno Huth, Breslauer Zeitung)

Klavierauszug in Vorbereitung

UNIVERSAL-EDITION A. G., WIEN — LEIPZIG

Happy End

Comedy with music in 3 acts by "Dorothy Lane."
Lyrics by Bertolt Brecht.

Composed in Berlin, May-August 1929.

Piano-vocal score published by Universal-Edition (Vienna, 1958): #11685.

Instrumentation: alto saxophone (also flute, clarinet)
                   tenor saxophone (also clarinet, bass saxophone)
                   2 trumpets
                   trombone
                   banjo (also Hawaiian guitar or mandolin, bass guitar,
                       bandoneon or Fisarmonica)
                   piano/harmonium
                   percussion

Characters: Bill Cracker
              Sam Worlitzer
              Dr. Nakamura
              Jimmy Dexter
              Bob Merker
              Johnny Flint
              Captain of the Salvation Army
              Hanibal Jackson
              Lilian Holiday
              The Lady in Gray (The Fly)
              Miriam
              Jane & Mary (Salvation Army Girls)
              Two strangers, Salvation Army soldiers, Policemen

First Performance: Theater am Schiffbauerdamm, Berlin
                     2 September 1929 (3 performances)
                     Erich Engel, director
                     Caspar Neher, designer
                     Theo Mackeben, musical director
                     Ernst Aufricht, producer
                     The Lewis Ruth Band
                     Cast: Carola Neher, Peter Lorre, Oscar Homolka,
                         Kurt Gerron, Theo Lingen, Helene Weigel

American Premiere: Yale Repertory Theater, New Haven
                     6 April 1972
                     American Adaptation by Michael Feingold
                     Michael Posnick, director
                     Thomas Fay, musical director

Although Universal-Edition did not publish the score during Weill's lifetime, it did publish the following individually:

U-E #9892 Bilbao-Song
9893 Matrosen-Song   Voice and piano
9862 Surabaya-Jonny

V.C.J. No. 114 Bilbao-Song for Jazz Orchestra
          115 Matrosen-Tango for Jazz Orchestra

Reviews:

Das Theater Berlin 10 (October 1929):243-44.

Jhering, Herbert. *Berliner Börsen-Courier*, 3 September 1929.

Kerr, Alfred. *Berliner Tageblatt*, 3 September 1929.

Marschalk, Max. *Vossische Zeitung*, 3 September 1929.

Trask, C. Hooper. *New York Times*, 27 October 1929.

Plot Synopsis:

"The action is laid in the toughest district of Chicago. Bill's Dance Hall,
a rowdy bar, is the hang-out of a gang headed by the Lady in Gray and
Bill Cracker. When this engagingly venomous creature asks one of her
co-workers for a light for her cigarette, it is a sign that she no longer is
satisfied with his efforts and that he will be done in within the hour. At
the beginning of the act a crook nicknamed The Governor has received
this unsympathetic notice. A Salvation Army troupe, headed by
Hallelujah Lillian, makes its appearance and Lillian delivers a redhot
tirade to the gang, with a special emphasis on their leader, Bill. Left
alone with the gangster, she kisses him in a moment of religious
enthusiasm, just as a shot from the next room tells us that The Governor
has crossed the Tennysonian bar. The rest of the gang returns and,

under the convivial influence of a couple of whiskies, Lillian sings a highly peppered seaman's song with which she hopes to convert Bill. Her Salvation Army buddies overhear the dubious ditty and go off to report her fall from grace. In the Salvation Army shelter she is turned out by the sanctimonious Major and she goes back to Bill in the dance hall. Here she uses her influence to keep him from taking part in a robbery and the Lady in Gray asks him quietly for a light. To a Christmas celebration in the shelter comes Bill, who is trying to escape from the gang. They follow him in and, when a detective appears, try to pin the murder of The Governor on their former leader, but are unsuccessful because Lillian admits that she was with him when the shot was fired in the next room. And for the "happy end," The Governor makes his appearance—he has merely been stunned by the shot. To bring the cup of happiness to overflowing, the Lady in Gray discovers in the Salvation Army Major her long-lost husband. At the exhortation of Lillian, the whole crew joins the Army and as stained glass windows with Ford, Rockefeller and Morgan as saints light up, a paean of praise is sung."

[From C. Hooper Trask, "Down, But Not Out, On the Berlin Stage," *New York Times*, 27 October 1929.]

Aufstieg und Fall der Stadt Mahagonny

Opera in 3 acts by Bertolt Brecht.

Composed in Berlin, May 1927–November 1929. Revised until December 1931.

Published by Universal-Edition: # 9851 Piano-vocal score by Norbert Gingold (Vienna, 1929)
9851 Piano-vocal score revised by David Drew (Vienna, 1969)
9852 Libretto

Instrumentation: 2 flutes
oboe
clarinet
alto saxophone (also soprano saxophone)
tenor saxophone
2 bassoons (2nd also contrabassoon)
2 horns
3 trumpets
2 trombones
tuba
tympani
percussion
piano (harmonium *ad lib.*)
banjo (bass guitar, bandoneon)
6 violins
3 violas
2 cellos
2 double basses

On Stage: 2 piccolos   2 trombones
2 clarinets   tuba
3 saxophones   percussion
2 bassoons   piano
2 horns   zither or xylophone
2 trumpets   banjo
bandoneon

Characters: Leocadia Begbick   Alto (Mezzosoprano)
                Fatty   Tenor
                Trinity Moses   Baritone
                Jenny Hill   Soprano
                Jim Mahoney   Tenor
                Jack O'Brien   Tenor
                Bill   Baritone
                Alaska Wolf Joe   Bass
                Tobby Higgins   Tenor
                6 Girls of Mahagonny
                Men of Mahagonny

Duration: about 3 hours

First Performance: Neues Theater, Leipzig (5 performances)
                      9 March 1930
                      Gustav Brecher, conductor
                      Walter Brügmann, director
                      Caspar Neher, designer
                      Cast: Marga Dannenberg, Mali Trummer, Paul
                              Bennert, Walter Zimmer, Theodor Horand.

Other Performances: Kassel Staatstheater (7 performances)
                      March 1930
                      Maurice Abravanel, conductor
                      Jacob Geis, director
                      Cast: Laurenz Hofer, Viktor Mossi, Barbara Klema,
                              Annelis Jolowiecz, Hans Oswald

                      Braunschwieg Landestheater (2 performances)
                      March 1930
                      Klaus Nettstraeter, conductor
                      Heinrich Voigt, director
                      Cast: Else Ludke, Trüde Weber, Valentin Haller

                      Deutsches Landestheater, Prague (2 performances)
                      15 July 1930
                      Georg Szell, conductor
                      Max Liebl, director
                      Cast: Margret Melan, Willy Trenk-Trebitsch

Frankfurt Staatsoper (12 performances)
16 October 1930
Wilhelm Steinberg, conductor
Herbert Graf, director
L. Sievert, designer
Cast: Else Gentner-Fischer, Wilhelm Wörle, Magda
           Spiegel, Jean Stern, Paul Reinecke

Theater am Kurfürstendamm, Berlin (50
    performances)
21 December 1931
Alexander von Zemlinsky, conductor
Caspar Neher, director and designer
Ernst Aufricht, producer
Cast: Harold Paulsen, Trude Hesterberg, Lotte
           Lenya, Franz Forrow, Albert Peters

Raimund Theater, Vienna (11 performances)
26 April 1932
Gottfried Kassowitz, conductor
Hans Heinsheimer, director
Cast included Lotte Lenya as Jenny

Darmstadt Landestheater, November 1957
First post-World War II performance of the
    authentic version

Sadler's Wells, Stratford, England
9 January 1963
English version by David Drew and Michael Geliot
Colin Davis, conductor
Michael Geliot, director

Shakespeare Festival, Stratford, Canada
2 July 1967 (North American Premiere)
Louis Applebaum, conductor
Jean Gascon, director

U.S. Performances: Concert Version
                      New York, 23 February 1952

Staged Premiere
New York, 20 February 1970

Opera Society of Washington, Kennedy Center
15 December 1972
Gunther Schuller, conductor
Ian Strasfogel, director

Yale Repertory Theater, New Haven
31 January 1974
Translation by Michael Feingold
Otto Werner-Mueller, conductor
Alvin Epstein, director
Cast: Grace Keagy, Gilbert Price, Stephanie
        Cotsorilos

Excerpts and arrangements published by Universal-Edition:

Alabama Song #8900 (Vienna, 1929). Voice and piano.

Vier Songs aus "Mahagonny"

Suite aus der Oper "Mahagonny," arranged by Brückner-
Rüggeberg.   #13542

The original piano-vocal score (Gingold) is available at the New York
Public Library, the Library of Congress, and Columbia University
Library. A full score is held by the Library of Congress.

Reviews:

Aber, Adolph. *Die Musik* 22 (April 1930):521-22.

*Adorno, Theodor W. *Die Musik* 23 (December 1930):198-200.

_____. *Anbruch* 14 (February-March 1932):53.

*_____. *Der Scheinwerfer* 3 (April 1930):111-115. Reprinted in
    Moments musicaux, pp. 131-40.

de Courcy, Geraldine. *Musical America* 50 (10 April 1930):5.

Einstein, Alfred. *Berliner Tageblatt*, 10 March 1930.

_____. *Berliner Tageblatt*, 22 December 1931.

Gutman, Hans. *Modern Music* 7 (June-July 1930):32-36.

Heuss, Alfred. *Zeitschrift für Musik* 97 (May 1930):392-95.

Holl, Karl. *Frankfurter Zeitung*, 17 October 1930.

Kralik, Heinrich. *Die Musik* 24 (July 1932):768.

*Latzko, Ernst. *Rheinische Musik- und Theater-Zeitung* 6 (22 March 1930):81-82.

Leichtentritt, Hugo. *Die Musik* 24 (February 1932):360-62.

Machabey, A. *La Revue musicale* 111 (January 1931):177-78.

Malipiero, Anna and Francesco, G. *Musical America* 51 (25 January 1931):7.

Mersmann, Hans; Schultze-Ritter, Hans; and Strobel, Heinrich. *Melos* 9 (April 1930):172-74.

Peyser, Herbert F. *New York Times*, 10 January 1932.

Prigsheim, Klaus. *Die Weltbühne*, 28 January 1930.

Ramler, Alfred. *Die Musik* 23 (October 1930):49.

Rubhardt, Paul. *Signale* 88 (19 March 1930):329-31.

Schrenk, Walter. *Christian Science Monitor*, 19 April 1930.

Stefan, Paul. *Anbruch* 12 (March 1930):521-22.

_____. *Anbruch* 14 (April-May 1932):83.

Stier, Ernst. *Die Musik* 22 (July 1930):765.

Strobel, Heinrich. *Melos* 11 (January 1932):28.

Stuckenschmidt, H. H. *Die Scene* 20 (March 1930):75-77.

Unger, Max. *Deutsche Musiker-Zeitung* 61 (29 March 1930):81-82.

Plot Synopsis:

"Two men and a woman, in flight from the authorities, break down in a
desolate region.   They decide to found a city, where men who pass
through from the Gold Coast would be able to fulfill their needs. In this
"Paradise City" that arises here, people lead a contemplative, idyllic life.
But in the long run that cannot satisfy the men from the Gold Coast.
Discontent reigns. Prices drop. During the night of the typhoon that is
moving toward the city, Jim Mahoney discovers the new law of the city:
"You can do anything."   The typhoon curves away.   People live on
according to the new law. The city flourishes. Needs increase—and
prices with them. For people are permitted everything—but only if they
can pay for it. When his money runs out, Jim Mahoney is condemned
to death.   His execution is the occasion for a gigantic demonstration
against the high cost of living, which announces the end of the city.
That is the history of the city Mahagonny. . . . It arises from the needs of
men, and the needs of men are what cause its rise and fall. But we
present the particular phases in the history of the city merely in their
repercussions on man.   For just as the wants of men influence the
development of the city, so again the development of the city alters the
conduct of men."

[From Kurt Weill, "Vorwort zum Regiebuch der Oper *Aufstieg und
Fall der Stadt Mahagonny*," *Anbruch* 12 (January 1930):5-7.]

Advertisement for *Aufstieg und Fall der Stadt Mahagonny.*
Anbruch 14 (April-May 1932).

Der Jasager

Schuloper in 2 acts. Text adapted by Bertolt Brecht from the Japanese Noh-drama *Taniko*, translated into German by Elisabeth Hauptmann from Arthur Waley's English version. .

Composed in Berlin, January-May 1930.

Published by Universal-Edition (Vienna, 1930):   #8206 Piano-vocal score
                                                                                  8225 Full score

Instrumentation: flute (*ad lib.*)
                                clarinet (*ad lib.*)
                                alto saxophone (*ad lib.*)
                                2 pianos
                                harmonium
                                percussion (*ad lib.*)
                                plucked instruments (*ad lib.*)
                                Violin I
                                Violin II
                                Cello
                                Bass

Characters: Boy
                          Mother
                          Teacher
                          First Student
                          Second Student
                          Third Student
                          Chorus

Duration: 35 minutes

First Performance: Zentralinstitut für Erziehung und Unterricht, Berlin
                                    23 June 1930
                                    Musical preparation by Heinrich Martens
                                    Conducted by Kurt Drabek, a student
                                    Directed by Weill and Brecht
                                    Designed by Caspar Neher

American Premiere: Grand Street Playhouse, New York
                         Music School of the Henry Street Settlement
                         25 April 1933
                         Translation by Alice Mattulath
                         Sanford Meisner, director
                         Lehman Engel, conductor

Reviews:

Einstein, Alfred. *Berliner Tageblatt*, 24 June 1930.

"F.D.P." *New York Herald-Tribune*, 26 April 1933.

Günther, Siegfried. *Die Musik* 23 April 1933.

"H.H." *New York Times*, 26 April 1933.

Heuss, Alfred. *Zeitschrift für Musik* 97 (June 1930):449-54.

Hirschberg, Walther. *Signale* 88 (2 July 1930):846-47.

Leichtentritt, Hugo. *Die Musik* 22 (August 1930):834-35.

Machabey, A. *La Revue musicale* 12 (February 1931):178.

_____. *Le Menestrel* 30 (December 1932):534.

*Martens, Günther. *Anbruch* 12 (September-October 1930):244.

*Preussner, Eberhard. *Anbruch* 12 (September-October 1930):243-44.

Prunières, Henri. *La Revue musicale* 13 (January 1933):45-47.

R.M.K. *Musical Courier* 106 (6 May 1933):11.

Strobel, Heinrich; Mersmann, Hans; and Schultze-Ritter, Hans. *Melos* 9 (July 1930):305-307.

Students and Teacher of the Elisabeth-Gymnasium, Breslau. *Anbruch* 13 (February-March 1931):52-54.

*Vuillermoz, Emile. *Anbruch* 15 (January 1933):31.

Westphal, Kurt. *Anbruch* (September-October 1930):245-46.

Plot Synopsis:

"The boy wishes to go with the teacher on a journey to the city in order to get medicine for his sick mother. The trip is dangerous; therefore, the mother does not want the boy to go. The teacher also advises against it. The boy goes, however, in order to help his mother. On the way when they come to the most dangerous place, the boy becomes tired, thereby endangering the whole traveling party. The decision is put to him: should they turn back or should they follow the old custom, which dictates that the sick be thrown into the valley? The boy decides to be tossed into the valley. 'He has said Yes,' sings the chorus."

[From "Aktuelles Zwiegespräch über die Schuloper zwischen Kurt Weill und Dr. Hans Fischer," *Die Musikpflege* 1 (April 1930):48-52.]

Advertisement for *Der Jasager*
Anbruch 12 (September-October 1930).

KURT WEILL
BERT BRECHT
DER JA-SAGER
EINE SCHULOPER

Sensationeller Erfolg der Uraufführung
durch Schüler der staatlichen Akademie für
Kirchen- und Schulmusik, Berlin

Die ersten Aufführungen:

Realgymnasium Kassel (Studienrat Lehmann) /
Schülergruppe Frankfurt (Rudolf Buchdahl) Rundfunk
Frankfurt (Schüler Prof. Gambke) / Reform-Real-
gymnasium Breslau (Wilh. Sträußler) Holtschneider
Konservatorium, Dortmund / Gymnasium Höchst
a. M. (Georg Heyland) / Stadtgymnasium Stettin /
Wöhler Gymnasium, Frankfurt / Walter-Rathenau-
Schule, Neukölln / Opernschule, Aachen (Anton
Ludwig) / Pädagogische Akademie, Altona (Dr. Hoff-
mann) / Realgymnasium, Quedlinburg (Fritz Reich) /
Deutsches Land-Erziehungsheim, Haubinda (Thürin-
gen) / Freie Bühne, Rendsburg / Pädagogische Aka-
demie, Breslau (Prof. Brieger) Gesellschaft für neue
Musik, Köln / Lichtwarckschule Hamburg / Folkwang-
schulen Essen / Gymnasium Dortmund (C. Dahlke)
Berner Singbuben, Bern (Aufführung im Stadttheater) /
Landestheater Oldenburg (Aufführung mit Schülern) /
Schauspielhaus Remscheid (Dr. Oberborbeck) / Städti-
sches Oberlyzeum Bottrop (B. Martin).

Orchestermaterial und Aufführungsbedingungen nach Ver-
einbarung

U. E. Nr. 8206 Klavierauszug mit Text . Mk. 4·50
U. E. Nr. 8225 Partitur . . . . Mk. 30·—
U. E. Nr. 8207 a d Chorstimmen . . . . à Mk. —·50

Durch jede Musikalienhandlung zu beziehen

UNIVERSAL-EDITION A. G., WIEN — LEIPZIG

Die Bürgschaft

Opera in 3 acts.   Text by Caspar Neher.   Based on Herder's "Der afrikanische Rechtspruch."

Composed in Berlin, August-October 1931.

Published by Universal-Edition (Vienna, 1931):   #1525 Piano-vocal score, edited by Erwin Stein.

Dedication: "Walter Steinthal gewidmet."

Instrumentation: 2 flutes   tuba
                   2 oboes   tympani
                   2 clarinets   percussion
                   2 bassoons   2 pianos
                   3 trumpets   strings
                   2 trombones

Characters: Johann Matthes   high baritone
              Anna, seine Frau   mezzo soprano
              Luise, seine Tochter   soprano (young)
              David Orth   high bass
              Jakob, sein Sohn   tenor (young)
              Der Richter von Urb   tenor
              Ellis, der Kommissar   tenor
              Sein Adjutant   tenor
                          Gläubiger
                          Wegelagerer   tenor
              Die drei   Erpresser   baritone
                          Häscher   bass
                          Agenten
              Der Mann, der seinen Acker
                 verkaufen will   tenor
              Der Schreiber des Richters   (1 actor)
              Ein Ausrufer
              Male chorus on the stage
              Small mixed chorus in orchestra pit

Duration: about 3-1/2 hours

First Performance: Berlin Städtische Oper
           10 March 1932
           Fritz Stiedry, conductor
           Carl Ebert, director
           Caspar Neher, designer
           Hermann Lüddecke, choral director
           Cast: Wilhelm Rode, Hans Reinmar, Josef
               Burgwinkel, Charlotte Müller, Irene Eisinger,
               Ruth Berglund

First Post-World War II Performance: Berlin Städtische Oper
                 Autumn 1957
                 Artur Rother, conductor
                 Carl Ebert, director
                 Caspar Neher, designer
                 New version by Neher & Ebert

Reviews:

Bekker, Paul. *Die Musik* 25 (October 1932):7-11.

*Bie, Oskar. *Anbruch* 14 (February-March 1932):49-51.

*Bloch, Ernst. *Anbruch* 14 (April-May 1932):89.

_____. *Anbruch* 14 (November-December 1932):207-209.

Connor, Herbert. *Die Musik* 25 (November 1932):101-104.

de Courcy, Geraldine. *Musical America* 52 (10 April 1932):5.

Einstein, Alfred. *Berliner Tageblatt*, 11 March 1932.

_____. *Modern Music* 11 (January-February 1934):71-72.

Fitelberg, Jerzy. *Modern Music* 9 (May-June 1932):186-87.

Leichtentritt, Hugo. *Die Musik* 24 (April 1932):516-17.

Peyser, Herbert F. *New York Times*, 27 March 1932.

Stuckenschmidt, H. H. *Anbruch* 14 (November-December 1932):217.

Trantow, Herbert. *Melos* 11 (August-September 1932):276-77.

_____. *Sozialistische Monatshefte* 38 (October 1932):877-79.

Plot Synopsis:

"The scene is laid in the small backward land of Urb, in which old, humane customs and laws still persist; the story concerns the physical, moral and ethical deterioration of the citizens resulting from the occupation of the little country by "the great powers." Totalitarianism and industrialization are major ingredients of the unnamed forces of evil that destroy men's characters and personalities."

[From Everett Helm, "Berlin Festival," *The Music Review* 19 (1958):55.]

"The plot concerns Johann Matthes who finds gold hidden in two sacks of straw, and brings the money back to the seller who refuses to accept it. The judge decides that Matthes' son should marry the daughter of Orth the seller and the money be given them as a dowry. But a powerful commissar decides otherwise and arrests the two friends, confiscating the money. During the war Matthes and Orth become profiteers, and their friendship is destroyed by greed. When Matthes, hounded by the mob, seeks refuge with Orth the latter betrays him and turns him over to the vengeance of the people."

[From Jerzy Fitelberg, "More Americans and Kurt Weill in Berlin," *Modern Music* 9 (May-June 1932):186.]

[For a more detailed summary, see David Drew, "Topicality and the Universal: The Strange Case of Weill's *Die Bürgschaft*," *Music and Letters* 39 (July 1958):242-55.]

Advertisement for *Die Bürgschaft*.
Anbruch 14 (February-March 1932).

Der Silbersee: Ein Wintermärchen

A play with music in 3 acts.

Text by Georg Kaiser. Play published by Kiepenheuer Verlag (Berlin, 1930).

Composed in Berlin, July-October 1932.

Published by Universal-Edition (Vienna, 1933): #10464 Piano-vocal score.

Instrumentation:	2 flutes	tympani
	oboe	percussion
	2 clarinets	piano
	bassoon	harp
	2 trumpets	strings
	2 trombones	

Characters: Olim, der Landjäger
Severin
Frau von Luber
Fennimore
Baron Laur
Der dicke Landjäger
Alter Arzt
Junger Arzt
Krankenschwester
Erste Verkäuferin
Zweite Verkäuferin
Vier Burschen
Ein Diener, zwei Mädchen, Leute

First Performances: 18 February 1933 in Leipzig, Erfurt and Magdeburg

Alte Theater, Leipzig	Stadtstheater, Magdeburg
Detlef Sierck, director	Helmut Götze, director
Gustav Brecher, conductor	Georg Winkler, conductor
Caspar Neher, designer	Ernst Rufer, designer

The piano-vocal score is out of print; it is available at the Library of Congress.

Universal-Edition published "Sechs Stücke aus *Der Silbersee*" for voice and piano (U-E #10471). Karel Solomon has arranged a "Suite aus *Der Silbersee*" for 2 flutes, 2 oboes, 2 clarinets, 2 bassoons, 2 trumpets, 2 horns, 2 trombones, percussion, piano, harp (*ad lib.*), strings.

Reviews:

*Aber, Adolf. *Leipziger Neueste Nachrichten*, 19 February 1933.

*Burger, Erich. *Berliner Tageblatt*, 20 February 1933.

**Chemnitzer Tageblatt*, 20 February 1933.

*"F.Z." *Völkischer Beobachter*, 24 February 1933.

*Hauptmann, F. A. *Völkischer Beobachter*, 24 February 1933.

*"L.St." *Berliner Tageblatt*, 20 February 1933.

Reindl, L. E. *Die Musik* 25 (April 1933):521.

Stuckenschmidt, H. H. *Modern Music* 10 (March-April 1933):163-67.

**Vossische Zeitung*, 22 February 1933.

Plot Synopsis:

"Olim, a gendarme, shoots and injures Severin, one of a band of starving unemployed who are escaping after stealing food from a provisions shop: food which is left over from the previous day, and which the shopgirls are forbidden to distribute to the hungry. While he is writing his report of the shooting, Olim becomes aware that his sympathy lies with his victim, whom he had shot only as a matter of duty and without any personal animus. Now his conscience prompts him to devote himself to Severin and to atone for the injury he had done to a body already weakened by hunger. Olim wins the first prize in a lottery. He resigns from the police force, secures the release of Severin and buys a large house, in which he may tend him until he has recovered. But Severin's recuperation is slow: his mind is poisoned by an uncontrollable desire to be revenged upon the man who had shot him. At last he learns that Olim, his benefactor, had been responsible for his misfortune. He is on the very point of attacking Olim, when suddenly his conscience asserts itself triumphantly over his rage: even as he chases Olim, he knows that his violent passion must be restrained, even though he cannot control it himself. The two men, both changed in their attitude to each other and to their fellow men as a result of the accident that had brought about their association, are reconciled. But Olim is tricked out of his home and his fortune by two impoverished and unscrupulous aristocrats, Frau von Luber, his housekeeper, and her friend Baron Laur. So they are left homeless, penniless and hopeless; when they rest in a ditch the police move them on. Finally they decide to go to the Silbersee and to make an end of their present wretchedness by throwing themselves into the lake. A heavy snowstorm begins as they approach the lake, and when they come to it, the water is covered by a sheet of ice. Olim and Severin have discovered, as individuals, a new relationship—and they are not utterly disillusioned. They still owe a duty to each other and to life."

[From B. J. Kenworthy, *Georg Kaiser* (Oxford: Basil Blackwell, 1957), pp. 87-88.]

Advertisement.
Anbruch 15 (January 1933).

Die sieben Todsünden

Ballet with singing; text by Bertolt Brecht, who later changed the title to *Die sieben Todsünden der Kleinbürger*.

Composed in Paris, April-May 1933. Commissioned by "Les Ballets 1933."

Piano-vocal score, edited by Wilhelm Brückner-Rüggeberg, published in 1955 by Hullenhagen & Griehl, Hamburg. B. Schotts Söhne, Mainz, published the same reduction in 1955 (#5078) and an edition which included an English translation by W. H. Auden and Chester Kallman as well as an appendix with the version for low-voice (#6005, 196?).

Instrumentation:	2 flutes (2nd also piccolo)	tuba
	oboe	tympani
	2 clarinets	percussion
	bassoon	harp
	2 horns	piano
	2 trumpets	banjo/guitar
	trombone	strings

Characters:	Anna I	Soprano
	Anna II	Dancer
	Family	Tenor I, Tenor II, Baritone, Bass (Mother)

Duration: 40 minutes

First Performance: Théâtre des Champs Elysées, Paris
7 June 1933
Les Ballets 1933; Orchestre Symphonique de Paris
Georges Balanchine, choreographer
Caspar Neher, designer
Maurice Abravanel, conductor
Lotte Lenya, Anna I. Tilly Losch, Anna II.

Same production performed in London at the Savoy Theatre, 1-15 July 1933 as *Anna-Anna*.

American Premiere: City Center, New York
                      4 December 1958
                      New York City Ballet
                      George Balanchine, choreographer
                      Rouben Ter-Artunian, designer
                      Lotte Lenya, Anna I. Allegra Kent, Anna II.
                      Translation by Auden & Kallman.

German Premiere: Städtische Bühne, Frankfurt, 1960
                      Wolfgang Rennert, conductor
                      Tatiana Gsovsky, director
                      Lotte Lenya, Anna I. Karoline von Aroldingen,
                      Anna II.

Reviews:

Bertrand, Paul. *Le Menestrel* 95 (16 June 1933):244.

Mehring, Walter. *Das neue Tagebuch* 1 (July 1933):24-26.

Thomson, Virgil. *Modern Music* 11 (November-December 1933):
    42-46.

Plot Synopsis:

"Two sisters (actually two facets of one person) Anna I and Anna II, one
representing the self-repression and self-denial necessary for success in
modern society; the other representing the natural instincts and healthy
needs and responses, set out to earn money to enable their family in
Louisiana to build a house. Anna II is tempted to give way to sins, that
is, her natural desires: sloth (she likes to sleep); wrath (she resents
injustice); gluttony (she doesn't like to starve herself); pride (she doesn't
want to strip-tease); and lust (she falls in love). As an 'entertainer' she
does succeed in overcoming her natural impulses, and her venture is
crowned with monetary rewards."

[From Fredric Ewen, *Bertolt Brecht: His Life, His Art and His
Times* (New York: The Citadel Press, 1967), p. 303.]

The seven deadly sins (sloth, pride, anger, gluttony, lust, covetousness,
envy) are confronted as the Annas travel from Louisiana to Memphis,
Los Angeles, Philadelphia, Boston, Baltimore, and San Francisco.

Symphony No. 2

At various times entitled "Fantasie für Orchester," "First Symphony," "Nocturne Symphonique," "Symphonische Fantasie," and "Three Night Scenes."

Composition begun in Berlin, January-February 1933. Completed in Paris, Summer 1933-February 1934. Commissioned by and dedicated to Madame la Princesse Edmond de Polignac. Autograph owned by the heirs of the Princess.

David Drew's edition of the orchestral score was published by B. Schotts Söhne (Mainz) and Heugel et Cie (Paris) in 1966.

Instrumentation: 2 flutes (2nd also piccolo)
                        2 oboes
                        2 clarinets
                        2 bassoons
                        2 horns
                        2 trumpets
                        2 trombones
                        tympani
                        strings

Duration: 28 minutes

First Performance: Concertgebouw Orchestra, Amsterdam
                        11 October 1934
                        Bruno Walter, conductor

American Premiere: Carnegie Hall, New York
                        New York Philharmonic Orchestra
                        13 December 1934

Reviews:

Antcliffe, Herbert. *Musical Times* 75 (November 1934):1035.

Downes, Olin. *New York Times*, 14 December 1934.

Gilman, Lawrence. *New York Herald-Tribune*, 14 December 1934.

Saminsky, Lazar. *Modern Music* 12 (January-February 1935):90.

Marie galante

Piece en 2 Actes et 10 Tableaux de Jacques Deval.

Composed in Paris, 1934.

Seven songs published for voice and piano in 1934 by Heugel et Cie (H. 30,916). This edition is available at the New York Public Library.

First Performance: Théâtre de Paris
                      22 December 1934
                      André Lefaur, Mise en scène
                      H. Henriot, Direct<u>r</u> de la scène
                      Pazzi-Préval, Regisseur général
                      Edmond Mahieux, Chef d'Orchestre

Revived by the Canadian Broadcasting Corporation, 28 November 1962.

A Kingdom for a Cow

Operetta in 2 acts by Robert Vambery.

Composed in Paris and London, January-July 1934.

Unpublished. Manuscript score in Weill-Estate.

First Performance: Savoy Theatre, London
28 June 1935
Muir Matheson, conductor
Felix Weissberger, director (Replaced by Matray
Ernst)

APPENDIX II

ANNOTATED TRANSLATIONS OF ESSAYS BY KURT WEILL

EDITORIAL POLICY

Appendix II comprises twenty-seven of Weill's more substantial essays, all of which were originally published in German. Only one has been previously printed in English translation in its entirety. I have attempted to remain as close to the original text as possible within the context of readable English. Whenever feasible, the integrity of Weill's sentence and paragraph structure has been honored. The original title and source of the essay, as well as reprint information, have been included at the beginning of each essay. The essays have been arranged in chronological order according to date of initial publication. The following conventions have been adhered to in editing the English translations:

1. All double quotation marks (" ") are Weill's own punctuation. Single marks (' ') are editorial, inserted to indicate the translator's use of idiomatic or figurative English equivalents.

2. All footnotes denoted by an asterisk (*) are Weill's own; they are found at the beginning of the notes section for each essay.

3. Footnotes denoted numerically are the translator's insertions. The notes appear at the end of each essay under the caption, "NOTES."

4. Passages that appeared in italics in the original text have been preserved in that format.

5. All foreign words that occur in the translations have been underlined.

6. When an English equivalent has been deemed insufficient for the original text, the German follows the English phrase in question in brackets [ ].

7. Parentheses in the translation parallel those in the original text.

1925

Bekenntnis zur Oper
Busoni und die neue Musik

1926

Die neue Oper
Busonis *Faust* und die Erneuerung der Opernform
Tanzmusik
Ferruccio Busoni: Zu seinem 60. Geburtstag

1927

Verschiebungen in der musikalischen Produktion

1928

Zeitoper

1929

Korrespondenz über *Dreigroschenoper*
Gesellschaftsbildende Oper
Ueber den gestischen Charakter der Musik
Notiz zum Jazz
Kritik am zeitgenössischen Schaffen
Notiz zum *Berliner Requiem*
Die Oper—Wohin?
    "Gebrauchsmusik" und ihre Grenzen
    Entwicklungstendenzen der Oper
Aktuelles Theater

1930

Vorwort zum Regiebuch der Oper *Aufstieg und Fall der Stadt Mahagonny*
Anmerkungen zu meiner Oper *Mahagonny*
Zur Uraufführung der Oper *Mahagonny*
Aktuelles Zwiegespräch über die Schuloper zwischen Kurt Weill und Dr.
    Hans Fischer
Musikfest oder Musikstudio?
Ueber meine Schuloper *Der Jasager*

1931

Situation der Oper: Gespräch mit Kurt Weill

1932

Vom Wesen der Musikzeitschrift—Diskussion über *Melos*
Kurt Weill antwortet
Das Formproblem der modernen Oper
Wirklich eine Opernkrise?

"Bekenntnis zur Oper," *25 Jahre neue Musik* (Jahrbuch 1925 der Universal-Edition, Vienna), pp. 226-28. Reprinted in *Ausgewählte Schriften*, pp. 29-31.

COMMITMENT TO OPERA

We cannot approach opera with the snobbism of indifferent renunciation. We cannot write operas and at the same time lament the shortcomings of this genre. We cannot view operatic composition as the fulfillment of a purely superficial obligation while we expend our true substance in other forms. We must understand that our formal ideal is fulfilled in the actualities of the stage; we must be convinced that a theatrical work is capable of reproducing the significant elements of our music; without reservation, we must commit ourselves to opera.[1]

The conviction that nothing more could be drawn from or added to the genre of music drama made us fanatics for absolute music. We have been burdened by a literary wrapper, by a materialistic orientation of art. Music was again to be the solitary goal of our creative endeavors. An intensification of musical experience could arise from the occupation with Bach and the pre-Classics and from the cultivation of chamber music. And yet it was not possible to decide to disregard the operatic stage altogether. Some were attracted by the possibility of a broader consequence, others by opposition to their own sentiment. Some wrote ballets—that is, enriched the effect of concert music with an optical impression. But dance also was constructed according to the precepts of music, and the pacing of the stage was still missing. And through disdain for this theatrical pacing, many believe the justification for their music-only posture [*Nur-Musikertums*] to have been established.

It is important to understand that we should not approach a theatrical work with a change in musical attitude. We must compose music in opera with the same unrestrained development of imagination as in chamber music. But, therefore, it cannot be a matter of transferring the elements of absolute music into opera; that would be the path that leads to the cantata and oratorio. Rather the reverse: the dramatic impetus that opera requires can be a very essential component of any musical product. Mozart taught me that. He is no different in opera than in the symphony or string quartet. He always possesses the pacing of the stage; therefore, he can remain an absolute musician even when he permits the infernal noise to cave in over *Don Giovanni*. Therefore, we can have a stage-like presentation even in the 'Brio' movements of his symphonies. With Mozart this reaches the point where with the addition of a text one can convert any movement from his chamber music or orchestral works into a dramatically-animated operatic aria or even to a finale which advances the plot.[2] On the other hand, it is also possible for a concert-like performance of the conversation between Sarastro and Pamina to transmit a theatrical experience. Mozart certainly does not achieve this by extra-musical means; on the contrary, it is achieved by the most fundamental expression of music. For ultimately what moves us in the theater is the same as what affects us in all art: the heightened experience—the refined expression of an emotion—the human condition.

When what we all feel is expressed in exponential form and with affecting eloquence, it is always of direct dramatic effect—be it the recitative of the *St. Matthew Passion*, the dungeon aria of Florestan, or the final duet of Carmen-Don José. This clarity of expression is found in all the masters who stem from Mozart: Weber, Berlioz, Bizet, Strauss, Busoni; in a different sense also in the great Italians from Pergolesi to Puccini. It had to vanish with the Romantics; for here the spiritual experience became so complicated or so externalized that the simplest, most mortal, ancient and yet always new, emotional stirrings were forgotten. But these are precisely what touch us. In this connection, we also understand why Wagner had to create for himself the form of music drama: for how could the string quartet, symphony, or opera satisfy him, since his art reflects only the feelings of larger-than-life figures—of gods, kings, and heroes? But we also understand the success of verismo: its brutal, erotic, and criminalistic production does not exactly express the most noble human sentiments of pre-War man but, nonetheless, common ones.

The crystalline clarity and the inner tension of musical diction can be based only on the transparency of our emotional substance, and then our music can again possess the typical operatic elements: sharp accentuation, precision of dynamics, speech-like agitation of melody.[3] Thus, opera again can be the most precious vessel, absorbing all forms and types of music.

NOTES

1. The title of Weill's essay, "Bekenntnis zur Oper," was later borrowed as the caption for the issue of *Anbruch* devoted to contemporary opera [*Anbruch* 8 (May 1926)]. In his introductory essay to that issue (pp. 203-4), Paul Stefan credited Weill with the phrase, which had appeared in Weill's notes for a performance of *Der Protagonist*, and listed Weill with Berg, Krenek, and Wellesz as composers who signified a new course for opera.

2. In his "Ueber die Partitur des *Doktor Faust*" (Leipzig: Breitkopf and Härtel, 1926), Busoni adds a text to an excerpt from one of Mozart's piano concertos in order to illustrate a similar idea. That Weill's Mozartean model for his operas

was actually perceived is evident from numerous contemporary reviews; see especially Heinz Jolles, "Paraphrase über Kurt Weill," *Neue Musik-Zeitung* 49 (May 1928):541-44, where Weill's operas are compared with those of Mozart and Verdi.

3. The demand of opera for sharper accents and more powerful diction than suffices for other music is central to Busoni's argument in "Ueber die Möglichkeiten der Oper" (Leipzig: Breitkopf and Härtel, 1926).

"Busoni und die neue Musik," *Die neue Weg* 54 (16 October 1925):282-83.
Reprinted in *Ausgewählte Schriften,* pp. 19-21.

BUSONI AND MODERN MUSIC

There are some major productive artistic figures whose names survive only in their works and whose own lives and creative processes disappear entirely behind their creations. Then there are others who, already within their lifetimes, exert such an influence through the charisma of their personalities that the memory of the vividness of their appearance remains as precisely awake as their artistic legacy itself. Ferruccio Busoni's life fulfilled itself in the light of a spirit that attempted to embrace all attainable domains—a conviction whose sincerity alone already placed him above his contemporaries. The blessed harmony of this artistic nature necessarily induced happy sentiments not only in the people of his closest company, but also those standing at a distance, experiencing the imperceptible influence of a figure whose serene goodness shattered any malice and baseness. It was seldom recognized, but everyone experienced it: Busoni had become the invisible leader of European musical life; everyone suspected that he was one before whose righteousness only a true and great art could exist. The powerful consequence of such a life is not terminated by death; it meshes so strongly into the events of its time that its traces continue to be preserved in the most recent generations. And if Busoni had not left us his compositions and writings, his Bach edition, and the memory of his unforgettable piano-playing, then his personal influence alone would be a bequest to future generations.

Many know Busoni as the greatest pianist of his era. They know only a small part of this figure; they cannot comprehend the influence of this man, since they do not know that creative genius was united to an unusual degree with the highest reproductive ability. Busoni's piano evenings were not entertainment sessions; he was also productive as a transcriber; he always had to say the special, the new, the surprising. Every expression of this intellect, from the interpretation of a virtuoso piece to the most emotionally-expressive phrase of *Doktor Faust,* was of direct effect on the artistic development of his time. He had a presentiment of every new stylistic tendency in music; he stimulated and guided it until he perceived that it was obsolete. But then he also had the courage to turn back for renewal. Like Bizet, Berlioz, Mendelssohn, and Weber, he was among those composers who consciously acknowledge Mozart as their master. That is already shown by his youthful works,

whose maturity and ease made him a member of the Academy of
Bologna at age fifteen.[1] He did not succumb to Brahms's strong sphere
of influence.   His early world-wide fame, his numerous triumphs
throughout the Old and New Worlds never permitted the slightest superficiality to encroach and never prevented him from keeping a manifest
introspection, a striving for the essential, in sight as a unique purpose.

He did not experiment indiscriminately; he sought new paths; he
found them effortlessly and followed them only if they seemed promising
to him.   In his orchestral concerts he was the first who ventured to bring
Impressionism to Germany.   Here Debussy, Delius, and Sibelius were
heard in Berlin for the first time.[2]   The response was disdain and
ridicule—but ten years later Debussy was the great rage.   Busoni was the
first who interceded almost fanatically for Schoenberg: in his house
Pierrot Lunaire underwent one of its first performances; a piano piece of
Schoenberg toured throughout the world in Busoni's version.[3]   It also
encountered deep-seated lack of understanding—but today Schoenberg is
his successor to the highest musical professorship that Germany has to
offer.   Numerous ideas, which appear self-evident to today's musicians,
are expressed for the first time in his *Entwurf einer neuen Aesthetik der
Tonkunst*:   the renunciation of music drama, the movement forward to a
thorough relaxation of tonality, even the thought of the 1/3 - tone, which
is discussed so much today.   Then Pfitzner answered him in his
Futuristengefahr with a challenge seething with hatred.[4]   But the most
significant turning point for Busoni was accomplished during the War.
After the outbreak of war in autumn 1914, he first went to America and
then moved to Zürich, where he waited for five years—yearning for a
return to Berlin.

After the revolution in Germany we young musicians also were
filled with new ideals, swollen with new hopes.   But we could not shape
the new that we longed for; we could not find the form for our content.
We burst the fetters, but we could not begin anything with the acquired
freedom.   We stepped upon new shores and forgot to look back.   Thus,
through the years of seclusion from the outside we underwent a spasm of
excess which lay on the breast like a nightmare and yet which we loved
because it had made us free.   Then Busoni came to Berlin.   We praised
him because we believed him to have achieved the goal that we were
striving for.   But he had become a different person.   He recognized no
impediments.   Through the agility of his clear-sighted intellect and
through the transcending vastness of his creative genius, he was able to
display a synthesis of all stylistic types of recent decades, a new
restrained, sediment-free art, a *"junge Klassizität."*[5]   In this sense, he had
an effect in the last years of his life: on the few whom he had chosen

for students; on the musicians of the world to whom he appeared as the symbol of the purest, highest artistic comprehension; on the future through his theatrical work, *Doktor Faust*, that most consummate work with regard to form, that most moving musical work of art of our day. And today the creative musicians of all situations stand in the spell of the models which the dying Busoni had prophesied for them.

NOTES

1. In March 1882 Busoni gave five concerts in Bologna, after which the Accademia Filharmonia awarded him its diploma in composition and piano performance. No composer since Mozart had been admitted to membership at so youthful an age. [See Edward J. Dent, *Ferruccio Busoni: A Biography* (London: Oxford University Press, 1933), pp. 41-42.]

2. The repertoire of Busoni's twelve orchestral concerts in Berlin from 1902 to 1909 is listed in appendix III of Dent, *Ferruccio Busoni*, pp. 332-336.

3. In a review of *Pierrot Lunaire* in *Der deutsche Rundfunk* 5 (11 November 1927):3168, Weill wrote that "this work has created a new epoch in music history." Busoni's "concerto version" of Schoenberg's op. 11, no. 2 is described by H. H. Stuckenschmidt in *Ferruccio Busoni: Chronicle of a European*, trans. Sandra Morris (London: Calder and Boyars, 1970), pp. 87-88. Schoenberg succeeded Busoni as Professor of Composition at the Prussian Academy of Arts in 1925. Schoenberg and Busoni were acquainted as early as 1903, when Busoni requested Schoenberg to orchestrate Heinrich Schenker's *Syrische Tänze* for one of Busoni's concerts in November 1903.

4. Busoni's *Entwurf einer neuen Aesthetik der Tonkunst* was published in 1907 by Schmidl (Trieste). Pfitzner's *Futuristengefahr* appeared in the *Süddeutsche Monatshefte* during 1917. Busoni responded with an open letter to Pfitzner which appeared in the *Vossische Zeitung*; it has been translated by Rosamond Ley in *The Essence of Music and Other Papers* (New York: Philosophical Library, 1957), pp. 17-19.

5. In an essay published in the *Frankfurter Zeitung*, 7 February 1920, Busoni wrote: "By 'young classicism' I mean the mastery, the sifting and the turning to account of all the gains of previous experiments and their inclusion in strong and beautiful forms." The essay was reprinted in *Anbruch* 3 (January 1921):25-27 (the entire issue was devoted to Busoni) and was translated by Ley in *The Essence of Music and Other Papers*, pp. 19-22.

"Die neue Oper," *Die neue Weg* 55 (16 January 1926):24-25. Reprinted in *Chemnitz Opera Program Book*, 17 June 1927; also in Hans Curjel, *Experiment Krolloper 1927-31* (Munich: Prestel-Verlag, 1975), pp. 190-92.

NEW OPERA

If we examine the development of opera in recent years, we must state that a fundamental change has been carried out in the position of creative artists concerning the problems of musical theater. The musical development of recent years had led initially to the realization that people must withdraw as much as possible from the sphere of influence of Richard Wagner.[1] People attempted that in different ways in various countries. In France the Expressionists believed that they could escape from the world of gods and heroes by emphasizing natural impressions; but the most significant theatrical work of this tendency, Debussy's *Pelléas et Mélisande*, again falls completely into the Wagnerian orbit. In southern countries people attempted to liberate themselves from the larger-than-life figures that appear on the stage of the nineteenth century with the representation of realistic events with an erotic or criminal infusion—but the musical means still show the unmistakable influence of Wagner. In Germany the decisive step emanated from Richard Strauss. The purely background, plot-supporting character of the music in *Elektra* and the attempt in *Ariadne auf Naxos* to conform to an eighteenth-century perception of an opera for the sake of music-making (*Musizieroper*) are probably the most important events in the realm of opera in the pre-war (World War I) era.

But the general musical development of the young generation followed a course that temporarily led away from opera. An energetic purification process initially eliminated all extra-musical influences, especially the literary points of congruence. Absolute music became the goal of young composers. Complete renunciation of any external or inner "program," intentional avoidance of large orchestral forces, limitation of the means of expression in favor of an intensification of the inner powers of expression, instinctive ties to the style of the masters of *a cappella* music and the pre-classicists, finally a nearly fanatical preference for chamber music—these were the characteristics of this development. People looked on opera somewhat scornfully as an inferior genre, for they thought only of music drama, from which they wanted to escape. But soon they noticed that absolute music was directly in a position to pave the way for genuine opera. For the musical elements of opera are no different from those of absolute music. In both it is only a question of the musical ideas unfolding in a form that corresponds with the emotional content. The tempo of the stage, which always demands an exceptional response from the operatic composer, is by no means a special, new component of opera, but must be clearly recognizable in our chamber and orchestral music before we approach opera. There are composers whose music always possesses dramatic impetus to the highest degree, and there are others with whom an operatic admixture would annoy us immediately. To the latter belong Schumann, Brahms, Bruckner.

In contrast, Mozart is the operatic composer *par excellence*. His music is always filled with the passionate breath of the theater whether he writes a piano piece, a quartet movement, or an operatic finale, but it also always exhibits that straightforwardness of expression that constitutes the most essential characteristic of operatic music. Now it is certainly one of the most significant achievements of the musical development of the last ten years that this clarity has again been attained or at least issued as the highest challenge: that our music no longer wishes to express floating atmosphere or nervously exaggerated sentiments, but the powerful emotional complexes of our era. In the transparent clarity of our emotional life lie the possibilities for the creation of new opera; for precisely from this clarity arises the simplicity of musical language that opera demands.

Naturally all of us are participating too actively in this development to be able to judge at what rate we ourselves approach the objective. Perhaps a later era will term what we are creating only an intermediary genre. Ballet, in particular, strongly favored by composers today, must be seen as a provisional result. Of course, ballet is of powerful educational effect, for dance is another form of music; it requires an accompaniment, which is shaped only according to the rules of music; dance requires clarity of form and rhythm; most of all, it also requires that vacillating [*beschwingte*] theatrical pacing absolutely necessary for opera. However, one can label neither ballet nor the genre compounded from ballet and opera as an ultimate result. What Stravinsky attempted in his *Soldier's Tale* undoubtedly can be appraised as the intermediary genre with the most certain future. Standing on the boundary between play, pantomime, and opera, this piece still displays such a strong predominance of operatic elements that it perhaps can become the foundation for a certain course of new opera.

Two works for the musical theater of our era—the most significant and typical representatives of contrasting views—can already be appraised as results: Alban Berg's *Wozzeck* is the grandiose conclusion to a development which, based throughout on Wagner and leading beyond French Impressionism and the naturalistic background of *Elektra* to

Schoenberg's tone-color melody [*Klangfarbenmelodie*], here arrives at its zenith in a masterpiece of the strongest power. On the other side is Busoni's *Doktor Faust*, which can become the starting point for the formation of a new golden age of "opera" (in contrast to "music drama"): for this *Faust* is theater in the purest and most beautiful sense. It presents great thought-uniting humanity in vital form—but at the same time, to the most significant degree, it is a musical work unique in our time, which in its unlimited abundance of sheer musical beauty possesses enduring value for music history beyond that of the operatic stage.

Naturally the subsequent development of opera depends upon whether it goes hand-in-hand with a modification of operatic performance. Our opera singers are able to cope with the new problems vocally and musically. But in purely theatrical matters, in the play of expression, gesture, and bodily movement, operatic performance often still lags far behind what is accomplished today in spoken drama. Particularly often the naturalness and the matter-of-factness of the play are lacking. However, positive examples—like *Intermezzo* in Dresden and *Wozzeck* in Berlin—have shown that this is purely a question of ensemble-training.[2] And the attempts of the Russian opera troupes under Dantchenko have proven that musical theater can even surpass drama in this point, because it can fill every minute area of the stage with musical activity through the inherent mobility of opera.[3] Boundless possibilities are still implicit here.

The remarks of a creative artist about his art can have informative character only retrospectively. We can sift the material to see where we stand. We know very little of what tomorrow will bring.

NOTES

1. A note in *Musical Times* 70 (March 1929):224, quotes an excerpt from an essay by Weill published in the *Berliner Tageblatt* in which Weill responded to an inquiry of how he would address an audience of school children on the subject of his own music. Weill wrote: "I have just played to you music by Wagner and by his followers. You have seen that this music consists of so many notes, that I was unable to play them all. You would have liked now and then to join in singing the tune, but this proved impossible. You also noticed that the music made you feel sleepy, and drunk, as alcohol or an intoxicating drug might have done. You do not wish to go to sleep. You wish to hear music that can be understood without explanation. You probably wonder why your parents attend concerts. It is, with them, a mere matter of habit: nowadays, there are matters of greater interest to all, and if music cannot serve the interests of all, its existence is no longer justified."

2. Strauss' *Intermezzo* premiered in Dresden on 4 November 1924 with Fritz Busch conducting. Berg's *Wozzeck* was first performed at the Berlin Staatsoper on 14 December 1925 under Erich Kleiber, who demanded and received an unprecedented 127 rehearsals.

3. Vladimir Ivanovich Nemirovitch-Dantchenko (1858-1943) headed the Soviet Art Studio and wrote the libretto for Rachmaninoff's one-act opera, *Aleko* (1893).

"Busonis *Faust* und die Erneuerung der Opernform," *Jahrbuch Oper* (Jahrbuch 1926 der Universal-Edition, Vienna), pp. 53-56. Reprinted as "Das Problem der neuen Oper," *Vossische Zeitung*, 22 January 1927. Also reprinted in *Ausgewählte Schriften*, pp. 31-36.

BUSONI'S *FAUST* AND THE RENEWAL OF OPERATIC FORM

The path toward a restoration of opera could proceed only from a renewal of the formal bases of this genre, from which the musical stage works of the late nineteenth century had departed so widely that the concept of opera had to undergo a complete derangement and misunderstanding. For opera has much less in common with literary stage works than the music drama of the last decades would have us believe. It by no means proposes to limit itself to the declamation of a dramatic event fixed in expression, in tempo, in pitch and dynamics; but instead it represents, far beyond that, a purely musical art work, whose ebb and flow are intimately associated with those of the stage by means of an intrinsic connection. For that reason, it is not a matter of appending a theatrical gesture to the musical event or a dramatic action to a musical illustration. The reciprocal effect involving the action, which presents an optical animation of the musical proceedings, and the music, which furnishes only a commentary for the incidents of the stage, still does not constitute opera.[1] Only the absolute blending of all expressive means of the stage with the expressive means of music produces that type of most intensified theater that we call opera.

Above all, it is the renunciation of a purely musical shaping that has caused the development of opera to deviate so far from its intrinsic goals. Musical form is more than a mere collection of individual segments; it is one of the only effective powers of expression completely appropriate to music. Its abandonment or mere subordination means a substantial curtailment of the expressive potential of music. Now the formal idea—just as the melodic or harmonic—is subject to no other laws than that of the total idea, that of the intellectual material. This material creates the stimulus for formal construction in the first place. The symphonic idea must find itself completely fulfilled in the form of the symphony. Similarly, both the tangible and concealed content of an operatic scene must be in absolute agreement with its musical form. Indeed, we see that the rigid forms of the eighteenth century, which grew out of a certain constriction of the symphonic idea, make room in opera for a free form that obeys only the precepts of the respective materials of the stage. But in every type of music there are specific situations in which the form approaches the intellectual content more closely. Such situations, in which the musical element is detached from purely formal thought, are found in all cadenzas of soloistic instrumental works, but, above all, also in the development sections of most symphonic movements from Beethoven to Mahler. Similarly with musical stage works—under the corresponding changing influx of materials—the operatic stage elements can step more forcefully into the foreground—not in the sense of a purely theatrical effect, but as an important component of the musical form. With the orchestral recitatives in *Die Zauberflöte*, with the Wolf's Glen scene in *Der Freischütz*, with the storm music in *Rigoletto*, the stimuli toward formal renovation arise from a complete identification of the dramatic and musical events.[2]

It is largely to Busoni's credit that these perceptions are no longer theory for us; we can recognize them retrospectively in his work and in our own efforts as the basis of recent operatic creations.[3] The fusion of musical and theatrical impulses as the basis of operatic form is already reached to the highest degree in *Doktor Faust*. We discover from the score that this fusion is once again capable of intensification; that a more powerful dramatic result is generated not by piling up theatrical effects, but by intensification of this union of stage and music. This alternating interpolation of more forceful and weaker theatricality and the resulting balancing of musical form from the stage (which we find already in *Elektra* and in *Der Rosenkavalier*, by the way) is the strongest characteristic of Latin operatic composers. It is this unerring indication of that instinct for accent and theatrical pacing that is innate to the Latin people. The total image of *Doktor Faust* clearly exhibits an ideal union of idea and form. Busoni knows that only with difficulty is theater susceptible to a rigorous polyphony, and he has deviated perhaps further in *Die Brautwahl* and in *Turandot* from the style of *Contrappuntistica* than in any of his other works.[4] But for him, opera, on account of its unlimited developmental possibilities, appeared as the most significant genre of musical production, and it must have stimulated him to write a stage work in the style that was closest to his nature. Also in this sense the work is confessional: the "Faustian obsession" of the composer aspires to the shaping of his own particular subject by his own particular means. Thus, the polyphony in Busoni's Faust-opera is not an end in itself; it is the only musically-feasible constructive form for the Faustian subject matter. It is the milieu of this opera, like the Turkish color in *Die Entführung aus dem Serail* and the Spanish rhythm in *Carmen*. Its sole function exists in accompanying the main figure of the work through the whole range of emotions which have found musical expression.

Actually Busoni's music moves into pure polyphony with dreamlike sureness exactly at the point where Faustian thought pushes into the foreground: in the powerful struggles [*Ringen*] of the second prologue, in the entire closing scene, and even in the student scene of the second tableau, which presents a unique discussion of the Faustian struggle between body and spirit.[5] But a possibility of intensification also results here: in the entire Faust-music, commencing with the two orchestral studies which were made at the outset, the struggle occurs throughout between the sensual and the spiritual impulses, between harmonic accompaniment of melody and contrapuntal interweaving of voices.[6] Only in the Credo of the second prologue, where the final triumph of the divine in Faust shines through by intimation, does the polyphony intensify to attain its purest, most powerful "church-like" form.[7]

The purely musical shaping of form through the medium of the stage is also revealed in the characterization of the figures. Richard Wagner's intention to announce each idea and every character through a motif necessarily brought with it a literary influence upon the fashioning of musical form—one that certainly has acquired deep significance for music drama. But the closed musical periods of opera form themselves unconsciously from abstract material, and the inclusion in musical form of characterization by means of motifs (as, moreover, already attained in *Tristan*) belongs just as much to compositional inspiration as does melodic invention or instrumentation. Carmen, too, has her leitmotif; but it only circumscribes, emphasizing the contradiction of her outward appearance and the tragic side of her character. Therefore, it appears only at places which signify high points not only for the action, but also for the musical structure. Similarly, Busoni has provided the Duchess with a melody and Mephistopheles with a series of dissonant chords, which emerge with the greatest economy only at critical points and always with new formal variation.

Busoni has amply expressed himself concerning the architecture of the work.[8] What in *Arlecchino* was still a musically-determined arrangement of separate numbers with linking dialogue is in *Doktor Faust* now an arrangement of compact forms of greatly expanded format, generated from the plot, whereby the recitatives are drawn into the musical progression either as contrast or as transition. It would be just as superfluous to establish thematic elaboration through literary-symbolic associations as, for example, to furnish programmatic commentary for a Beethoven symphony. The extent to which the formation of an opera occurs below the surface of consciousness is shown, for example, in the boldness with which Busoni anticipates the rhythm of the "Sarabande" with the knocking of the creditors; the effect of this idea would be diminished if one wished to credit it with a "deeper significance." Another example of musical form deriving from the stage occurs at the end when Faust once more confronts the most important personages encountered along his path—the Duchess and the girl's brother. Now with the dying recognition of a man who is finished, the earlier musical events appear in compressed form (the organ sound is transferred to the orchestra, Valentin's prayer to the male chorus). The transformation of naturalistic effects into the expressive sphere of absolute music is decisive for the development of the genre. When Mephisto kills the creditors in front of the door, the music leaves the description of the crass incident to the imagination of the listeners and contents itself with a delicately detached, liberating gesture. A similar effect of contrast is attained in the scene in the cathedral; here the organ is not treated as an atmospheric stimulus. By no means does it propose to inspire the impression of a church service; rather, it gives the emotional content of the scene in an instrumentation appropriate to the setting of the action. Here, too, a new musical form results from the change from peacefully prayerful and passionately moving organ tones to military music, struggle, murder, and a total return to churchly stillness. This reciprocal impregnation of musical and theatrical imagination is demonstrated on every page of the score.

As the consequence of the encounter of a personality with his subject matter, wrestled with over a lifetime, Busoni's *Faust* is something unique—like *Die Zauberflöte* and *Missa Solemnis*. The consequence of such testimonial works tends to leap over generations, and to determine the lasting influence of a work scarcely premiered cannot be the task of the artist who is also creating. For him a stylistic observation can have significance only as a clear backward glance and as a view of the material. But all new operatic endeavors of our day are based on the aesthetic foundation of this type, in the resurrection of which Busoni's *Faust* has the lion's share.[9]

> It is obvious, after all, that the librettist, with respect to the arrangement and management of the whole, must be guided by the rule of drama derived from the nature of the problem; at the same time he actually does need to make a special effort to arrange the scenes in such a way that the story unfolds clearly and plainly before the beholder's eyes. Almost without understanding a word, the beholder must be in a position to form an idea of the plot from what he sees happening. No dramatic poem needs this to such an extreme degree as does opera, for as I said, subject matter, action, and situation, not showy language, must inspire the composer, and, aside from the so-called poetic images, each and every reflection is for him a real mortification.[10]
>
> E. T. A. Hoffman (*Die Serapionsbrüder*)

NOTES

1. Weill's use of the phrase *theatralische Geste* and his assertion that music must furnish a commentary for the incidents of the stage, which present only an optical realization of the musical proceedings, is a rudimentary postulation of the concept of *Gestus* which he later defined more clearly.

2. That the models cited by Weill are by Mozart, Weber, and Verdi is not a unique occurrence in his writings; throughout his career Weill mentioned them as his operatic ideals.

3. Many of the ideas which Weill expresses in this essay can also be traced in Busoni's own "Ueber die Partitur des *Doktor Faust*" and "Ueber die Möglichkeiten der Oper." Both essays have been translated by Ley in *The Essence of Music and Other Essays.*

4. *Fantasia Contrappuntistica*, Busoni's attempt in 1910 to complete "Bach's last unfinished work," appeared in four different versions. Busoni authorized an orchestration of it by Frederick Stock of Chicago and also published the work in his own edition for two pianos.

5. In the second prologue, Faust summons six spirits, dismisses five of them because they are not powerful enough, and finally accepts the sixth, Mephistopheles, as his servant and ultimate master. Weill's use of the word "Ringen" refers to the struggles between good and evil which occur within the magic circle of the second prologue. In the "student scene of the second tableau" (pp. 220-24 of the piano-vocal score), a philosophical discussion erupts into a musical "battle" between Protestant and Catholic students; "Ein' feste Burg" and the "Te Deum" are combined polyphonically.

6. The "orchestral studies" are the *Nocturne Symphonique*, op. 43 (sketch for the Symphonia of *Doktor Faust*) and the Second Sonatina (a sketch for the first prologue).

7. The Credo (p. 83 of the piano-vocal score) is characterized by alternation of homophonic and polyphonic texture.

8. See Busoni's "Ueber die Partitur des *Doktor Faust*," translated by Ley in *The Essence of Music and Other Essays*, pp. 70-76.

9. Weill wrote another essay concerning *Doktor Faust* (a preview to the broadcast on Berlin Radio on 2 November 1927) which has not been included here: "Busonis Faust-Oper," *Der deutsche Rundfunk* 5 (28 October 1927):3028-29.

10. The translation of Weill's excerpt from E. T. A. Hoffmann's *Die Serapionsbrüder* is that of Oliver Strunk in *Source Readings in Music History* (New York: W. W. Norton, 1950), pp. 794-95.

"Tanzmusik," *Der deutsche Rundfunk* 4 (14 March 1926):732-33. Reprinted in *Ausgewählte Schriften*, pp. 132-34.

DANCE MUSIC

A branch of musical programing which is a part of the existing institutions in all radio broadcasting stations of the entire world has never before been appreciated in its full significance here. Like all large European broadcasting stations, the Berlin Radio Station also broadcasts dance music every evening after the conclusion of its evening programs.[1] For metropolitan people of our time dance is one of those few things that can lift them up above daily routine; naturally, dance music achieves a significance that it did not possess in earlier times.[2] On the one hand, this has led to an artistically alienating industrialization of the light-music business: the carefree gypsy life of dance musicians of earlier times has yielded to blatant commercialization. But on the other hand, a certain branch of dance music so completely expresses the spirit of our times that it has even been able to achieve a temporary influence over a certain part of serious art music. The rhythm of our time is jazz.

The Americanization of our whole external life, which is happening slowly but surely, finds its most peculiar outcome here. Unlike art music, dance music does not reflect the sense of towering personalities who stand above time, but rather it reflects the instinct of the masses. And a glance into the dance halls of all continents demonstrates that jazz is just as precisely the outward expression of our time as the waltz was of the outgoing nineteenth century. Even inveterate opponents of this "spirit of the time" must concede that in an institution which broadcasts dance music every evening the shimmy must occupy by far the predominant part. But jazz music is not created by merely playing a syncopated 2/2 bar. Negro music, which constitutes the source of the jazz band, is full of complexity of rhythm, harmonic precision, auditory and modulatory richness, which our dance bands simply cannot achieve. Every night for a week now we have heard an actual jazz band on the radio: the jazz-symphonists of Erno Rapée.[3] If one measures it against the splendid jazz bands of the Negro revue, this ensemble is also lacking in subtle balance. But it already exhibits that stomping confusion of saxophones, jazz drums, and muted trumpets, that liberated rhythm and improvised humor which make the jazz band uniquely tolerable.

Everything else of dance music that the radio offers us is merely a substitute. Franz von Szpanowsky's dance band does not have the instrumental means at its disposal to imitate Rapée, which it lately aspires to do; the wind orchestra of Woitschach plays commonplace polka rhythms. If even the "Band of the Third Intelligence Department" grinds out one of the most beautiful Warren shimmies in the style of a military march, then the degree of what can be tolerated has been far exceeded. Every evening London offers jazz music from the Hotel Savoy, Rome from the Hotel di Russia—no large radio station renounces jazz bands of the most modern type. The Berlin Radio too must incorporate the performance of first-rate dance music as a permanent institution in its programs. For a wide circle of the Berlin public, the dance music of Rapée's jazz symphonists has been the most powerful point of attraction for the radio programs. In addition to Rapée, a number of excellent bands are available (Julian Fuchs, Etté, Marek Weber, etc.).[4] And if they cannot appear in the broadcasting studio, let the microphone be sent to them.

Now for the events of the coming week. In the entertainment music of Sunday morning the Hungarian musician, Dr. v. Szilagyi will take part among others. Some time ago he offered us a selection of his interesting collection of old folksongs from his homeland. The following "Hour of the Living" is likewise devoted to a Hungarian musican who lives in Budapest, 45-year-old Béla Bartók, one of the most distinguished representatives of today's music.[5] The writer of these lines will make the attempt to facilitate understanding of a modern piece of music by wider circles of radio listeners with a formal analysis preceding the performance. The more or less loud rejection that modern music occasionally finds is mostly due to the fact that it is simply impossible to judge a work after a single hearing. On this occasion this will be remedied, in that Bartók's String Quartet No. 1 will be dissected first in terms of the accurate course of its musical development before it is presented in that context. It is good that, to begin with, a work was chosen for this purpose that does not belong to the very latest tendencies, but rather one that can be seen as a cornerstone for today's development.

NOTES

1. In *Der deutsche Rundfunk* 5 (31 July 1927):2124, Weill discussed the "generation gap" between the dance music of the older generation (waltzes, mazurkas) and that of the younger generation (foxtrot, blues, tango, Charleston).

2. The radio industry journal, *Der deutsche Rundfunk*, often carried articles on popular dance, especially "how to" diagrams for the tango, Charleston, and foxtrot. For example, see "Wie tanzt man Tango?" *Der deutsche Rundfunk* 6 (3 February 1928):347-49.

3. Erno Rapée (1891-1945) began his career as an assistant conductor of the Dresden Opera. After conducting operas in Magdeburg and Kattowitz, in 1917 he became

the conductor for the Rialto Theatre in New York.   From 1932 to 1945 he was musical director at Radio City Music Hall.

4. Marek Weber also had a successful career in the United States as a radio and recording artist who specialized in Viennese waltzes.

5. "Die Stunde der Lebenden" was a weekly feature of the Berlin Radio, hosted by critic Adolf Weissmann. The broadcast of Weill's lecture occurred on 14 March 1926.

"Ferruccio Busoni: Zu seinem 60. Geburtstag," *Der deutsche Rundfunk* 4 (28 March 1926):872. Reprinted in *Ausgewählte Schriften*, pp. 21-23.

FERRUCCIO BUSONI: FOR HIS SIXTIETH BIRTHDAY

When Busoni closed his eyes a year and a half ago, the musical world realized that it had lost one of its greatest assets. We mourned for the loss of the "greatest pianist of all time," the ingenious creative musician, the great theorist and author, the teacher and stimulator, the splendid man. This man's unlimited fruitful activity in each of these areas could fill volumes—but Busoni was one of those figures who, beyond the fruitfulness of their immediate lifework, bequeathe to posterity yet something else that finally makes their names immortal. It was the purity of conviction which gave such a splendor to this figure and made any encounter with this man a fortunate experience.

The pianist Busoni, who captivated the world in his childhood but who then developed from the sphere of virtuosity to the highest degree of interpretive art, is still remembered by all of us. His unforgettable farewell from the concert hall, those three evenings when he made nine piano concertos of Mozart radiate in new light, still echoes in us long after.[1] Busoni's productive activity encompassed all areas of musical creativity. His youthful works already show accomplished mastery. If he had continued along this path—like most of his successful contemporaries—he surely would have found the appreciation of those who again and again thrust themselves against the new, and who also brought against him an animosity and a misunderstanding unlike any other artist of his time.

Busoni sought the extraordinary; his music had to free itself from the narrow limits of classical forms and from the narrow scope of tonal constraint. He steadily led the way on the painful path which musical production traveled in the first two decades of this century. In work and deed, as composer and interpreter, he was the prophet of Impressionism as well as of the ensuing complete disengagement until he finally arrived at his ultimate goal in the "new classicism" which he developed—a synthesis of all new achievements with the useful material of earlier generations.

Busoni's love belonged entirely to opera. His first stage work, *Die Brautwahl*, performed this season at the Berlin Stadtsoper, is an homage by the master to his favorite city, Berlin. *Turandot* (after Gozzi) is an arrangement of the frequently-performed incidental music for Reinhardt's production of *Turandot*. *Arlecchino* is the ingeniously cheerful, *Doktor*

Faust the serious confessional work of Busoni.[2]   This *Faust*, which unfortunately was not entirely finished, represents the most complete expression of all the master's views of life and art; in every respect it can be considered the basis for a further development of musical stage works. For us Germans, this work gains an elevated significance because in it a man who always stood above nations makes the symbol-laden German national legend the outlet for his essential spiritual expression.   Busoni was the Faustian man of the twentieth century.   His life was a struggle, and his victory is his work which survives and is the love of thousands whom he made happy.

NOTES

1.   The concerts to which Weill referred occurred in Berlin during 1921.

2.   *Die Brautwahl,* a three-act opera based on E. T. A. Hoffmann's story, was composed during 1908-11 and premiered in Hamburg on 12 April 1912.   It is dedicated to Gustav Brecher.   The two-act *Turandot,* dedicated to Toscanini, was composed in 1917 and first performed on 17 May of that year in Zürich. *Arlecchino,* composed during 1914-16 and dedicated to Arthur Bodansky, was also premiered in Zürich, a week before *Turandot,* on 11 May 1917.   *Doktor Faust,* left unfinished at Busoni's death and completed by his student Phillip Jarnach, was premiered in Dresden on 21 May 1925.

"Verschiebungen in der musikalischen Produktion," *Berliner Tageblatt,* 1 October 1927. Partially reprinted in *Die Musik* 20 (December 1927):206.

SHIFTS IN MUSICAL COMPOSITION

The young composer, whose opera *Royal Palace* was performed last spring in the Staatsoper, has just completed a new opera, *Der Zar lässt sich . . .* , with a text by Georg Kaiser. [The Editor.][1]

If I am to reply to the question regarding the current musical situation from the standpoint of a creative musician, I must restrict myself to reflection upon the situation from the position of the development of my own production.

Recently the development of music has been predominantly an aesthetic one: liberation from the nineteenth century; struggle against extra-musical influences (program music, symbolism, realism); return to absolute music; achievement of a new means of expression (enrichment of harmony, production of a new linearity) or extension of the old—those were the ideas that claimed the attention of the musician. Today we are a step further. A clear separation is reaching its completion between those musicians who, filled with disdain for the audience, continue to work toward the solution of aesthetic problems as if behind closed doors and those who take up an association with any audience whatsoever, who classify their creations in some larger movement because they realize that, beyond the artistic, there is a general human consciousness that springs from a social feeling of some kind and that this must determine the formation of an art work.

It is clear that this *departure from individualistic artistic principles* which can be observed everywhere stands out nowhere with so much eruptive power as in *Germany,* where quite certainly the preceding development (the influence of the nineteenth century and the powerful liberation from it) also had been much more intense. While with us this search for community is in no way to be confused with submission to the taste of any audience, a great number of musicians of *Latin countries* are engaged with a very cultivated type of *Gebrauchsmusik* (Rieti, Poulenc, Auric, etc.). Earnestly seeking a new means of expression, these musicians obviously have been even more isolated there and less regarded by the public than is the case with us. But it seems that in an advancing musical generation, especially in *Paris,* a renewal of Catholicism arising from literature is leading toward a new sense of community. An inclination toward the cultic, which is unusual for French art and which expresses itself in the preference for ancient subject matter, is also characteristic of the situation (Stravinsky's *Oedipus Rex*, Milhaud's *Opéras minutes*). On the other hand, the Russian musicians, as far as they are known to us, appear to take a rather hostile position toward the formation of a communal art, contrary to what one would expect from them more than from anyone else. A noticeable dependence on Scriabin by many Russian musicians precludes a "revolutionary" bearing.

Thus, in Germany it is most clearly shown that musical production must win a new justification for existence. *An unmistakable regrouping of the public* is also to be observed here. The socially-exclusive arts [*gesellschaftlichen*], originating from a different era and from a different artistic attitude, are losing more and more ground.[2] Today new orchestral and chamber music, for which a regular public demand prevailed earlier, is almost exclusively directed toward musical societies and organizations devoted to the cultivation of new music, whose sphere of listeners is composed primarily of musicians. Therefore, music seeks an approach to the sphere of interest of a broader audience, since only thus can it maintain its viability. To begin with, it does so by utilizing the recently-won facility and joy in performance to create a worthwhile "*Gebrauchsmusik.*" The whole area of *mechanical music and film music* should no longer remain abandoned as a cheap daily commodity; instead, a young musical generation is endeavoring to work out and to develop these branches of musical practice in which the vast audience is interested. Today it rests only on the determination of the relevant "industry" to obtain for itself the most worthwhile talents among the younger musicians and thereby to give them the basis for a new development that would in no sense include any superficiality.

Moreover, we find attempts to draw an audience directly for the appreciation and encouragement of new music. The activity of a whole series of musicians in the milieu of the "musicians' guild" [*Musik-antengilde*] (Hindemith, Ludwig Weber) possesses decided symptomatic significance in this connection, although it remains to be seen whether this youthful movement is not restricted too much to certain circles of people to create the actual basis for a renewal of musical appreciation or even for the formation of a people's art.[3] That today a large number of musicians whose quality is beyond doubt again consider the possibility of direct effect on a broader public seems to be more important than those endeavors. For so much is certain: the clarity of language, precision of expression, and simplicity of feeling, which new music has regained following a rectilinear development, form the reliable aesthetic bases for a broader ramification of this art.

The present constellation is shown most distinctly in the area of musical theater. For *opera today no longer represents a closed musical genre* (as in the nineteenth century); rather, it is again classified (roughly since Busoni's *Doktor Faust*) as an equal to the whole complex of absolute music. Beyond this, it will represent the most significant factors in the development that no longer confers on music the role of a socially-exclusive [*gesellschaftlichen*] art, but that of a community-engendering [*gemeinschaftsbildenden*] or community-advancing art. Therefore, it can exhaust itself neither in an aesthetic Renaissance movement, which allows musical stylistic principles alone to be determinant, nor in representation of superficial items of current interest which possess value only for the narrowest sphere of time in which they originated. Above all, I believe that musicians must first overcome the anxious awe of truly equal collaborators. It has been proven that it is very possible to enter into closer collaboration with equal representatives of other arts for the creation of a musical stage work that can give a non-topical, unique and conclusive representation of our time. I am also convinced that on the basis of a newly acquired inner and outer simplicity of content and means of expression, a branch of opera is evolving into a new epic form, as I employ it with Brecht in the *Mahagonny-Songspiel*. Although this form of musical stage work pre-supposes theatrical music from the outset, it nonetheless ultimately makes it possible to give to opera an absolute-musical, even *concertante* form.

In this and other areas of new opera, it is clearly evident that its musical development achieves a new fertilization from *theater-film*.[4]

NOTES

1. *Der Zar lässt sich photographieren* was initially entitled "Photographie und Liebe" and later "Der Zar lässt sich. . . ." before it received its final formulation. A short essay by Weill, "Ueber die zeitgemässe Weiterentwicklung der Oper," appeared in the *Blätter der Staatsoper* 8 (October 1927):18-19. It is too similar in content to "Shifts in Musical Production" to warrant inclusion of a translation here. It has been reprinted in *Ausgewählte Schriften*, p. 36.

2. Weill uses the term "*gesellschaftlichen*" to describe an aristocratic art limited in its appeal to a small group of connoisseurs. He prefers a "*gemeinschaftsbildenden*" art which strives for a more democratic basis in a broader community of listeners.

3. Ludwig Weber (1891-1947) composed for and was instrumental in the organization of youth-movement musical groups. His *Chorgemeinschaften* called for the audience to sing along with the performers, and his *Hymnen* were specifically intended for the youth movement.

4. The genre "theater-film" refers to films of plays that were originally intended for the theater. The opera libretto corresponds to the screenplay in that sense. Weill's *Royal Palace* utilized an extended film sequence. An essay by Weill entitled, "Tonfilm, Opernfilm, Filmoper" [*Frankfurter Zeitung*, 24 May 1930], has been reprinted in Drew, *Ausgewählte Schriften*, pp. 181-85.

"Zeitoper," *Melos* 7 (March 1928):106-108.   Reprinted in an abridged version in *Melos* 25 (January 1958):9-10.   Also reprinted in *Ausgewählte Schriften*, pp. 37-40.

ZEITOPER*

Most Respected Professor:

You ask me to take a position concerning the concept of "*Zeitoper*"[1] from the standpoint of the opera composer, and I am able to respond to this invitation because you added that you find this concept embodied "most thoroughly" in my most recent works. For only thus does the clear "one-sidedness" of my point of view excuse itself.

This word "*Zeitoper*" has also had to suffer the unfortunate transformation from concept to slogan. It was just as hastily coined as it was incorrectly employed. This hasty, premature, incorrect utilization of a concept is not absolutely detrimental; it is perhaps necessary because it might allow a subsequent application to appear with the kind of naturalness that creates the correct conditions for its public acceptance. The "*Zeitstück*,"[2] as we have come to know it in recent years, moved superficial manifestations of life in our time onto center stage. People took the "tempo of the twentieth century," combined it with the much-praised "rhythm of our time" and, for the rest, limited themselves to the representation of sentiments of past generations. The powerful stimuli which transplanting accompanying phenomena of daily life to the stage conceals in the process should not be underestimated. But they are stimuli, nothing more. Man in our time looks different, and what drives him outwardly and motivates him inwardly should not be so portrayed for the mere purpose of being current at any price or in the interest of topicality which holds validity only for the narrowest time span of its creation.

In recent years the task of "*Zeittheater*," with which most of us have been concerned in one form or another, has been to technicalize the stage conclusively and to broaden theater in its form, process, and sentiments. This task has been realized, and the means have quickly been made into an end in themselves. Only now, after the hitherto existing *Zeittheater* has freed the material, have we reached the unintentionality, the self-evident level where we can represent the world view that we see—each perhaps in his own way—no longer as a photograph, but as a mirror reflection. In most cases it will be a concave or convex mirror, which reproduces life in a magnification or reduction proportionate to how it appears in reality.

You will ask whether this definition of "*Zeitoper*" in terms of "*Zeitspiegel*" [mirror of the times] does not bring with it a limitation in choice of subjects. But note that the intellectual [*geistigen*] and emotional [*seelischen*] matrices which music can depict are quite narrowly restricted already and have remained fundamentally the same for centuries.[3] Only the object and the methods of application have changed. The human quality that music can articulate has remained the same. But man has changed: he reacts differently to external influences, events, and emotions.

The new type of man emerging on all fronts today does not accept much of what appeared significant to preceding generations as presupposition. Therefore, the proportions between man and the things within and around him must also appear to shift in art that aims at a presentation of this type. However, this new type of man whom we see results in the possibility of again basing opera upon great, comprehensive, generally valid themes which no longer deal with private ideas and emotions but with larger relationships. In that context the intellectual and human fundamentals of the new type of man may make use of any really major theme. Stravinsky's *Oedipus rex* is no less a mirror of our time than, for example, Chaplin's *The Gold Rush.*[4] But I am convinced that our era can also deliver major themes if one views it from the standpoint of a certain attitude. Yet the pure theater of opinion can find its application for opera (likewise for drama) only if it does not appear as proclamation of a trend, but if it instead gives the reflection of a world-picture from the viewpoint of an encompassing, enduring idea. Without a doubt, this treatment in opera of great ideas of our time can result initially only from the collaboration of a musician with one of the representatives of literature who is at least equivalent in standard. The repeatedly-expressed apprehension that such a collaboration with worthy literary figures could bring music into a dependent, subservient, or only equal relationship to the text is completely unfounded. For the more powerful the writer, the more he is able to adapt himself to music, and so much the more is he stimulated to create genuine poetry for music. (May I inform you that I have found in my present close collaboration with Brecht the feasibility of constructing a libretto whose total plan and scenario has been worked out together in all details, word for word, according to musical considerations.) In other respects, I believe that the collective conception that is entering the theater today, especially in opera, in which it always played a role, will become more prominent again.[5]

In opera great subjects demand a great form for their representation. The broader and more significant the occasions for making music become, the greater the possibilities for the development of music in opera. The new operatic theater that is being generated today has epic character. It does not propose to describe, but to report. It no longer proposes to form its plot according to moments of suspenseful tension, but to tell about man, his actions and what impels him to commit them. Music in the new operatic theater renounces pumping up the action from within, glazing over the transitions, supplying the background for events, and stirring up passions. It goes its own vast, peaceful way; it begins only at the static moments of the plot, and it can therefore preserve its absolute *concertante* character (if it hits upon the right subject matter). Since the narrative form never permits the spectator to be in suspense or uncertainty over the stage events, music can reserve for itself its own independent, purely musical effect. The sole prerequisite for such an uninhibited musical realization in opera is that music must naturally be "theater music" (in the Mozartean sense) in its innermost essence in order to be able to achieve a complete liberation from the stresses of the stage.

As we have seen, this altered fundamental attitude can lead to a junction with the form of the oratorio. It can also fundamentally recreate the genre of opera. But then it must fall in line with that development evident in all artistic areas which today proclaims the end of the socially-exclusive, "aristocratic" art. And if through our work we ourselves thoroughly project the form of our audience, then we see the simple, naive, unassuming and traditionless listeners, who, trained by work, sport, and technical skill, bring along their healthy sense of fun and seriousness, good and bad, old and new.

Yours truly,

Kurt Weill

NOTES

*The author, invited to formulate the concept of "Zeitoper" with reference to his epic operatic play "Mahagonny" (Baden-Baden 1927), expressed himself in an open letter to the editors.

1. Because the term *Zeitoper* has gained wide usage and is not easily translated into concise English, it will be left in the original German. Perhaps the closest English equivalent is "topical opera." The term *Zeitoper* was first linked with Weill's name in reviews of his one-act opera *Royal Palace*, which was premiered at the Berlin Staatsoper on Weill's twenty-seventh birthday, 2 March 1927. It appears that at first he accepted the label, but later, when it had been applied indiscriminately to any opera with topical references, Weill resented the appellation. Even after the premiere of *Die Bürgschaft* (1932), critics insisted on

classifying Weill's output under the umbrella of *Zeitoper*. [See Herbert Connor, "Kurt Weill und die Zeitoper," *Die Musik* 25 (November 1932):101-4.]

2. *Zeitstück* refers to the whole realm of topical theater, including *Zeitoper*.

3. The adjectives *geistigen* and *seelischen* occur frequently in Weill's description of the subject matter proper for opera. Although the terms have been translated here as "intellectual" and "emotional" respectively, the reader is advised that the German carries broader connotations than these English equivalents. The unwieldy phrase "intellectual/spiritual" might be a more inclusive translation of *geistigen* and "emotional/spiritual" of *seelischen*; both affinity and contrast are embodied in Weill's usage of the terms.

4. *Oedipus rex*, with a libretto by Jean Cocteau (translated into Latin by J. Daniélou) was premiered in Paris on 30 May 1927. Chaplin's silent feature *The Gold Rush* dates from 1925.

5. In 1928 Weill was still an active member of Piscator's collective, which included Georg Grosz, Hanns Eisler, Leo Lania, Felix Gasbarra, as well as Brecht.

"Korrespondenz über *Dreigroschenoper*," *Anbruch* 11 (January 1929):24-25. Published as "Breifwechsel über *Dreigroschenoper*," *Die Scene* 19 (February 1929):63-65. Reprinted in *Ausgewählte Schriften*, pp. 53-56, and in *Bertolt Brechts Dreigroschenbuch*, pp. 219-220.

CORRESPONDENCE ABOUT *DIE DREIGROSCHENOPER*

Dear Mr. Weill:

The sensational success of *Die Dreigroschenoper*, which allows a work of totally novel style that points to the future to become suddenly a box-office hit, confirms most gratifyingly the prophecies that were repeatedly expressed in these pages. The new popular opera-operetta, which draws the proper inference from the artistic and social assumptions of the present, has succeeded in this beautiful, exemplary model. May we ask you, since you have the advantage of unequivocal legitimization of practical result and demonstrated success over our sociological and aesthetic derivations, to comment now in these pages theoretically about the course that has been traveled. [The Editor.]

Dear *Anbruch*:

Thank you for your letter and I confess to you that it is not entirely easy for me to provide a theoretical basis for what I have done in *Die Dreigroschenoper*. But I will gladly say something about the path that we, Brecht and I, followed in this work and along which we contemplate continuing.

In your letter you allude to the sociological significance of *Die Dreigroschenoper*. Indeed, the success of our play proves that the creation and success of this new genre came not only at the correct moment for the artistic situation, but also that the public seemed almost to be waiting for a renewal of a privileged theatrical genre. I do not know if our genre will now replace operetta. Since even Goethe has now appeared on earth again through the medium of an operetta-tenor, why should not a still further succession of historical or at least princely personalities utter their tragic outcry at the conclusion of the second act?[1] That is easily settled: I do not believe at all that this is an opening that is worth filling. More important for all of us is the fact that here a breakthrough into a consumer industry, which until now had been reserved for a completely different type of composer or writer, has been accomplished for the first time. With *Die Dreigroschenoper* we addressed a public that either did not know us at all or denied us the capability of interesting a circle of listeners that far exceeded the boundaries of the musical and operatic audience.

Seen from this standpoint, *Die Dreigroschenoper* appears to join a movement which today touches almost every young musician.   The problem of the art-for-art's-sake standpoint, the renunciation of individualistic artistic principles, the film-music ideas, the connection with the youth music movement, all those that stand together for the simplification of the means of musical expression—those are all steps along the same path.

Only opera remains in its "splendid isolation."   The operatic audience still represents a closed group of people who seemingly stand apart from the larger theatrical audience.   "Opera" and "theater" are still treated as two entirely distinct concepts.   In new operas a dramatic technique is still employed, a language is spoken, and subjects are treated that would be completely unthinkable in the contemporary theater. Again and again, one must hear: "Maybe that is possible in theater, but not in opera!"   Opera was established as an aristocratic genre, and everything called the "tradition of opera" emphasizes that basic socially-exclusive nature of this genre. But even today in the whole world there is no artistic form of a more pronounced socially-exclusive bearing. The theater in particular has decisively turned in a direction that one can characterize accurately as socially-creative [*gesellschaftsbildend*].   If the frame of opera does not bear an approximation of that kind to the contemporary theater, quite certainly that framework must be exploded.[2]

Only in this way can one understand that the fundamental character of almost all genuinely worthwhile operatic endeavors of recent years has been purely destructive.   A reconstruction was possible in *Die Dreigroschenoper* since the possibility existed to start totally afresh here. What we wished to make was the prototype of opera.   The question emerges anew with each musical stage work: how is music, above all how is song possible in the theater at all?   This question was resolved here in the most primitive manner.   I had a realistic plot.   Therefore, I had to set the music against it, since I reject the notion that music has any possibility of realistic effect. Thus, either the action was interrupted in order to make music, or it was led deliberately to a certain point where it simply had to be sung.   Moreover, this piece offered us the opportunity to posit the concept of "opera" as the theme of a theatrical evening.   Right at the beginning of the play this was made clear to the audience: "This evening you will see an opera for beggars. Because this opera was conceived so splendidly, as only beggars would imagine it, and because it still had to be so cheap that beggars could afford it, it is called *The Threepenny Opera*."   Therefore, the last "Dreigroschenfinale" is by no means a parody; rather, here the concept of "opera" was applied directly to the resolution of conflict, that is, as an action-structuring element. Therefore, it had to be constructed in its purest, most fundamental form.

This reversion to a primitive operatic form brought with it a far-reaching simplification of musical language. It was a question of writing music that could be sung by actors, that is, by musical amateurs. But what appeared initially to be a limitation proved to be a huge enrichment in the course of the work. Only the realization of a comprehensible, palpable melodic structure made possible what was achieved in *Die Dreigroschenoper*, the creation of a new genre of musical theater.

Yours truly,

Kurt Weill.

NOTES

1. Weill's reference is to Franz Lehár's *Friederike*, which opened at the Metropol Theater in Berlin on 4 October 1928. The libretto by Ludwig Herzer and Fritz Lohner was based on an episode from Goethe's youth—the conflict between his career and his love for Friederike. Goethe was played by the most famous operetta-tenor of the time, Richard Tauber, and Friederike by Kathe Dorsch. A performance of the operetta was broadcast by the Berlin Radio on 30 January 1929. Weill's brief preview of the broadcast appeared in *Der deutsche Rundfunk* 7 (25 January 1929):105. In Heinrich Strobel's review of *Die Dreigroschenoper* that appeared in *Melos* 7 (October 1928):498, he contrasts the "most distinctive occurrence of the season," namely *Die Dreigroschenoper*, with the "sentimental Kitsch" of *Friederike*.

2. An alternative translation of the preceding paragraph appeared in Eric Blom's "Three-Groats Opera," *The Sackbut* 11 (March 1931):212-13.

"Gesellschaftsbildende Oper," *Berliner Börsen-Courier*, 19 February 1929. Reprinted in Hans Curjel, *Experiment Krolloper 1927-31* (Munich: Brestel-Verlag, 1975):361-62.[1]

SOCIALLY-CREATIVE OPERA

Today a process of regrouping that is concerned with the elimination of the "socially-exclusive" [*gesellschaftlichen*] character of art and that stresses the *socially-creative* [*gesellschaftsbildenden*] *power of art* is being accomplished in all artistic domains. The struggle of the old against the new, which always is connected with such a decisive change in course, will be fought out in the musical sphere with particular vehemence, because here the concepts of tradition, piety, and sanctity, which have always been detrimental to the development of art, are thrown about more than in other artistic areas. The agitation against Klemperer is one of the last power-struggles of the aged musical water-lilies [*Mummelgreise*] who wish to retard a development which already has passed over them today.[2] For Klemperer's appearance represents one of the most significant forces in this process of regrouping. Since no criticism can be leveled against the quality of his performances, it is aimed at the ultimate objective of his work.

Klemperer is to be aligned as a unique practical musician in the production-network of the most valuable forces of modern theater. Klemperer's production of *Oedipus rex* can be discussed only in the context of the greatest international theatrical events. The rescue of opera from the state of solemn seclusion—that is his sole point of view, from which he approaches the selection of new works and the production of classic operas. His *Fidelio, Don Giovanni,* and *Der fliegende Holländer* have demonstrated that there is no tradition at all for presentation of worthwhile classic operas and that fundamental renewal of scenic and material aspects of classic opera is possible when an equally fundamental musical renewal is carried out with that intensity which characterizes all of Klemperer's performances.

In the short time of his activity in Berlin, Klemperer has arrived at the point where opera once more finds its circle of interested people, who until now had scarcely known anything about the existence of such an institution. In his performances, even his concerts, he gathers together intellectual Berlin. And what is most embarrassing for his opponents is that he is successful. In his performances one experiences storms of applause of an aggressive vigor, as is not be attained in that museum-like temple where art is celebrated.

NOTES

1. Weill's essay was just one of a group of articles which appeared under the general heading, "Für die Erneuerung der Oper." The other contributors were Walter Gropius, Paul Hindemith, Heinrich Erbprinz Reuss, Ernst Toller, Harry Graf Kessler, and Kurt von Muzenbecher.

2. See Weill's later essay "Rettet die Kroll-Oper," *Das Tagebuch* 11 (15 November 1930):1854. It is reprinted in *Ausgewählte Schriften*, p. 72.

"Ueber den gestischen Charakter der Musik," *Die Musik* 21 (March 1929):419-23. Reprinted in *Ausgewählte Schriften*, pp. 40-45.

CONCERNING THE GESTIC CHARACTER OF MUSIC[1]

In this essay composer Kurt Weill, who has created typical *Gebrauchsmusik* for our time, discusses the constructive principles of his operatic works. [The Editor.]

In my attempts to arrive at a prototype for works of musical theater, I have made a few observations which at first seemed to me to be completely new perceptions, but which with closer consideration can be classified as being thoroughly within the historical continuum. While working on my own compositions, I continually forced myself to consider the question: "What are the occasions for music on the stage?" In retrospective consideration of my own or others' operatic works another question emerged: "How is music for the theater constructed, and are there definite characteristics that identify it as theatrical music?" It has been confirmed often that a number of significant composers either have not been involved with the theater at all or have attempted in vain to conquer the stage. Therefore, there must be specific features that permit music to seem appropriate for the theater, and I believe that these qualities can be summarized under the concept that I am inclined to call the gestic character of music.[2]

In so doing I take as a given that form of theater which seems to me to offer the only possible basis for opera in our time. The theater of the preceding era was written for its sensual palatability [*Geniessende*]. It sought to titillate, excite, stimulate, and upset the spectator. It pushed the material aspects into the foreground, and for the presentation of the material it enlisted every theatrical device from authentic grass to conveyor belts. And what it offered to its spectators could not be denied to its creator: when he wrote his work, he was an epicurean [*Geniessender*] too; he experienced the "intoxication of the creative moment," the "ecstasy of the creative impulse of the artist," and other pleasurable emotions. The other form of theater, which is beginning to be successful today, counts on a spectator who follows the proceedings with the quiet composure of a thinking man and who, since he really wants to think, perceives any demand on his pleasure centers [*Genussnerven*] as an annoyance. This theater seeks to show what man does. It is interested in material aspects only up to the point where they provide the framework or pretext for human relations. Therefore, this theater puts greater value on actors than on stage apparatus, and it denies its creator the epicurean posture that its audience renounces.[3] To the highest degree, this theater is unromantic; for "romanticism" in art precludes thinking, it involves narcotic properties, it shows mankind in an exceptional state, and in its golden age (Wagner) it generally relinquished any representation of mankind.

If both forms of theater are employed in opera, it becomes evident that today's composer may no longer approach his text with the attitude of the epicurean. In the opera of the nineteenth and incipient twentieth century the task of music consisted of manufacturing atmosphere, supplying the background for situations, and emphasizing the dramatic accents. Even that form of musical theater which only utilized the text as an occasion for free, uninhibited music-making is ultimately only a final consequence of the romantic ideal of opera, since here music participated in development of the dramatic idea even less than in music drama.

The form of opera is an absurdity if it does not succeed in granting music a predominant position in its overall structure and in execution of even the most particular details. The music of an opera cannot abandon the whole task of the drama and its idea to the text and the stage setting; it must take an active role in the presentation of the proceedings.

And since the primary goal of today's theater is the representation of human beings, the music must also be related solely to mankind. Now, as is well-known, music lacks all capacity for psychological or characterizing effect. Instead, music possesses one capability which is of decisive significance for the representation of man in the theater: it can reproduce the *gestus*, which elucidates the events on stage. It can even create a type of fundamental *gestus* which prescribes a definite attitude for the actor and eliminates any doubt or misunderstanding about the respective incident. In the ideal case, it can fix this *gestus* so powerfully that a false representation of the relevant action is no longer possible. Every observant theater-goer knows how often the simplest and most natural human occurrences are presented on stage by counterfeit sounds and untruthful movements. Music has the potential to define the basic tone and fundamental *gestus* of an event to the extent that at least an incorrect interpretation will be avoided, while it still allows the actor abundant opportunity for deployment of his own individuality of style. *Naturally, gestic music is in no way bound to a text,* and if, in general, we perceive Mozart's music, even the non-operatic compositions, as "dramatic," we do so because it never abandons its gestic character.

Generally we find gestic music wherever an incident relating men to one another is presented musically in a naive manner. The most striking examples are in the recitatives of Bach's Passions, in Mozart's operas, in *Fidelio* ("Nur hurtig fort, nur frisch gegraben"), and in the compositions of Offenbach and Bizet.[4] In "Dies' Bildnis ist bezaubernd schön" the attitude of a man who is gazing upon a picture is fixed by the music alone.[5] He can hold the picture in either his right or left hand; he can raise or lower it; he can be illuminated by a spotlight or he can stand in the dark—his basic *gestus* is correct because it is correctly dictated by the music.

What are the gestic means of music? First of all, the *gestus* is expressed in a rhythmic fixing of the text. Music has the capacity to notate the accents of language, the distribution of short and long syllables, and above all, pauses. Thereby, the sources of the most serious errors in the treatment of the text are eliminated from the stage. Furthermore, one can interpret rhythmically one phrase in the most diverse ways, and the same *gestus* may be expressed in various rhythms; the critical factor is only whether the proper *gestus* is found. This rhythmic fixing which is obtained from the text in this way forms only the basis for gestic music. The specific creative work of the composer occurs when he utilizes the remaining means of musical expression to establish contact between the text and what it is trying to express. Even the melody is stamped by the *gestus* of the action that is to be represented, but, since the stage action is already absorbed rhythmically, much wider latitude exists for the essential means of musical expression—the formal, melodic and harmonic construction—than in purely descriptive music or in music which parallels the action under constant danger of being concealed. Thus, the rhythmic restriction imposed by the text is no more severe a fetter for the operatic composer than, for example, the formal schemes of the fugue, sonata, or rondo were for the classic master. Within the framework of such rhythmically predetermined music, all methods of melodic elaboration and of harmonic and rhythmic differentiation are possible, if only the musical spans of accent conform to the gestic proceeding. Thus, a coloratura-type dwelling on a single syllable may be completely suitable if it is based on a gestic lingering at the same spot.

I will give an example from my own practice. Brecht, out of the necessity of making the *gestus* clear, had earlier sketched tunes for a few of his poems. Here a basic *gestus* has been defined rhythmically in the most primitive form, while the melody adheres to the totally personal and inimitable manner of singing with which Brecht performed his songs. In this version, the "Alabama-Song" appears as follows:[6]

One sees that this is nothing more than an inventory of the speech-rhythm and cannot be used as music at all. In my composition of this text the same basic *gestus* has been established, only here it has actually been "composed" for the first time with the much freer means of the musician.[7] In my case the song has a much broader basis, extends much farther afield melodically, and even has a totally different rhythmic foundation as a result of the pattern of the accompaniment—but the gestic character has been preserved, although it occurs in a completely different outward form:

It is still necessary to say that by no means can all texts be set in a gestic manner. The new (or renewed) form of theater which I take as a basis for my exposition concerns only a very few poets nowadays, and only this form permits and makes feasible a gestic language. Therefore, the problem raised here is to an equal extent a problem of modern drama. But for the theatrical form that aims at saying something about mankind, music is indispensable because of its capacity for fixing the gestus and elucidating the action. *And only a form of drama for which music is indispensable can adapt itself fully to the needs of that purely musical work of art that we call opera.*

Lotte Reiniger:
Kanonensong aus der Dreigroschenoper von Kurt Weill

NOTES

1. Also translated by Erich Albrecht as "*Gestus* in Music," *Tulane Drama Review* 6 (September 1961):28-32. This is Weill's only essay in German to have been published previously in English translation in anything approaching complete form. I include my own translation here because Albrecht's version, for the most part accurate and readable, omits portions of the original and obscures some of Weill's terminology.

2. Neither Weill nor Brecht defined the term "*Gestus*" in any concise formulation. John Willett wrote that it means "both gist and gesture; an attitude or a single aspect of an attitude expressible in words or actions." [Willett, *Brecht on Theatre*, p. 42.] Martin Esslin called it "the clear and stylized expression of the social

behavior of human beings toward each other." [*Brecht: The Man and His Work*, p. 141.] The most extensive discussion of Brecht's use of the term occurs in Nadar, "The Music of Kurt Weill, Hanns Eisler and Paul Dessau in the Dramatic Works of Bertolt Brecht," pp. 90-94. Nadar asserts, without any supporting evidence, that the concept of gestic music was Brecht's not Weill's. It is not clear and really unimportant which of them used the term first, since Lessing differentiated between *Gestus* and *Geste* as early as 1767. If indeed Brecht employed the term before Weill (in "Aus der Musiklehre," 1926-28?), there are immediate precedents for his usage. Frederick Ewen observed that Vsevohold Meyerhold, an associate of Stanislavski, had earlier advocated the "principle of bio-mechanics, that is, translating dramatic emotion into typical '*gestus*'; the abolition of individual characterization and the emphasis on the 'class-kernel' of the dramatic presentation." [Ewen, *Bertolt Brecht: His Life, His Art, and His Times*, p. 146.] Weill's "Ueber den gestischen Charakter der Musik" predates Brecht's discussion of *Gestus* in "Anmerkungen zur Oper *Aufstieg und Fall der Stadt Mahagonny*" by a year.

Whoever used the term first, the renunciation of individual characterization and the psychological function of music in favor of a more "social" presentation appears in Weill's music as early as 1924 in *Der Protagonist*. Furthermore, Weill's discussion of the dramatic characteristics of Mozart's music in essays dating from 1926 would indicate a mutual affinity between Weill and Brecht for the qualities of gestic music rather than the successive influence of Weill upon Brecht or *vice versa*. The definitions of *Gestus* by both Weill and Brecht were written after the concept had been tested in several of their works for the theater. However, as early as July 1927, the adjective "*gestisch*" was applied to Weill's *Quodlibet* in a review of its performance at the Krefeld Tonkünstlerfest. [See *Neue Musik-Zeitung* 48 (July 1927):449.]

3. Lest it be incorrectly assumed that Brecht was the originator of the aesthetic distance advocated by Weill here, see Busoni's *Ueber die Möglichkeiten der Oper und über die Partitur des Doktor Faust* in which he wrote: "if an artist wishes to move others, he must not allow himself to be moved."

4. "Nur hurtig fort, nur frisch gegraben" is Rocco's and Leonora's duet—Number 12 of Act II of *Fidelio*. The accompaniment maintains a triplet rhythmic figure that is present throughout the composition.

5. "Dies' Bildnis ist bezaubernd schön" is Number 3 of Act I of Mozart's *Die Zauberflöte*. Tamino sees a picture of Pamina for the first time.

6. Brecht's melodies for the Mahagonny-Gesänge appeared as an appendix to *Die Hauspostille* (Berlin: Propyläen-Verlag, 1927).

7. Weill's "Alabama-Song" is that of the *Mahagonny-Songspiel* rather than that of *Aufstieg*.

"Notiz zum Jazz," *Anbruch* 11 (March 1929):138.   Reprinted in *Ausgewählte Schriften*, pp. 197-98.

A NOTE CONCERNING JAZZ

Undoubtedly today we stand at the end of the epoch in which one can speak of an influence of jazz on art music.   The most essential elements of jazz have been taken up by art music.   In the case of composers who have not manifestly fought against this influence, the most essential elements of jazz form firm components of musical structure that cannot be wished away; yet they no longer appear in the form of jazz, as dance music, but in transformation.   Modern music has been reproached because its composers allowed themselves to be influenced more strongly by jazz through its dance forms than by art music of earlier times.   In so doing, one forgets that jazz, being more than a social dance, includes elements which vastly exceed the influential capabilities of the waltz.   In the midst of a time of heightened artistry jazz appeared as a piece of nature—as the healthiest, most vigorous expression of art, which arose immediately from its popular origin to an international folk music of the broadest consequence.   Why should art music barricade itself against such an influence?   It depended on the strengths of the individual talents who allowed themselves to embrace jazz whether or not they could resist that influence.   For the serious European musician the question of wanting to imitate American dance music or even of wanting to ennoble it could never arise.   But it is obvious that jazz has played a significant role in the rhythmic, harmonic, and formal relaxation that we have now attained and, above all, in the constantly increasing simplicity and comprehensibility of our music.

Today it appears to me that the manner of performance of jazz is finally breaking through the rigid system of musical practice in our concerts and theaters and that this is more important than its influence on musical composition.   Anyone who has ever worked with a good jazz band has been pleasantly surprised by an eagerness, a devotion, a desire for work that one seeks in vain in many concert and theater orchestras.   A good jazz musician completely masters three or four instruments; he plays from memory; he is accustomed to the art of ensemble playing, in which each player contributes individually to the collective sound.   But, above all, he can improvise; he cultivates a free, unrestrained style of playing in which the interpreter achieves to the highest degree a productive performance.   The extent to which all this can be applied to art music naturally depends primarily on the musical product itself, which certainly does not always allow such freedom of interpretation. Also, economic questions play a role here: the jazz musician is not a civil servant; he is allowed competition; his artistic ambition is greater, since better performance results in increased pay. But it is quite possible that from here on we will experience an artistic and economic reorganization in the domain of the interpreter.[1]

NOTES

1. Because most artistic institutions were subsidized by various levels of government, orchestra members and most other employees of theaters and opera houses were officially employees of municipal or state governments. As "civil servants" they were not subject to dismissal nor to reduction of salary, which was based on their rank in the civil service.

"Kritik am zeitgenössischen Schaffen," *Melos* 8 (March 1929):109-111. Reprinted as "Ueber Musikkritik," *Melos: Zeitschrift für neue Musik* 17 (May 1950):129-33; "Kritik und zeitgenössische Musik" in *Die Stimme der Komponisten* (Rodenkirchen am Rhine: P. J. Tonger Verlag, 1958), pp. 122-26; *Ausgewählte Schriften*, pp. 185-89.

CRITICISM OF CONTEMPORARY CREATIVE WORKS

The duties of criticism of contemporary creative works are first to inform the newspaper-reading public of the value and significance of a new composition and to acquaint the public with the related events in the total production of our time, and secondly to give the creative musician himself an opinion concerning his work either from the standpoint of the public or from that of the technical consultant. In most cases the present situation of criticism destroys these two possibilities in their effect. For example, it is impossible for an opera or concert visitor to form an opinion himself concerning a newly performed work when he compiles all the critiques that were published about it. After reading all these critiques, he has no idea whether the piece is good or bad, old or new, significant or insignificant. Since the "tasters" are so different, he could still comprehend that he might find absolutely appreciative next to completely deprecatory opinions. But it totally perplexes him that each critic applies a different standard to the work, that the views diverge much too far for them to be understood as still pertaining to the same subject. He lacks any basis for a common method of consideration, if only an approximate one. He recognizes that only in the rarest cases is a single attitude advanced with consistency or another rejected. He sees a confusion of standards which often renders worthless even valuable opinions of a particular critic.

It is incorrect to shove the blame for this situation onto the critic. The critic does what his editorial staff demands of him; they engaged him, they pay him, and they always stand behind him "fully and totally." The emergence of the critic fits logically and consistently into the overall picture of the contemporary press, which has been established much too rigidly and powerfully for it to allow any doubt of its accuracy and its necessity to arise. Whether or not this system can be changed—that is a political question. But it is certain that even within this system, the overall picture of the press itself will change. Along with a young generation of musicians, a young generation of critics is growing, and already today a more distinct division between an old and a new generation is beginning to be marked off. Their mutual struggle is all the more violent because the disappearing generation feels threatened in its existence by the upcoming one, and because a struggle for existence is waged with more intense means than a struggle for intellectual ideas. Therefore, it is not a question of lamenting this situation, but at most of outlining the situation of present-day criticism as it presents itself to the creative musician.

Criticism As Reportage

One could also label it (to use an expression of Brecht) "Criticism as Entertainment Advertiser" ["*Kritik als Vergnügungsanzeiger*"]. The newspaper naturally wants to recommend to its readers that which it can assume would have pleased them on their own. For the number of subscribers is increased if the reader finds the opinion of the newspaper corroborated by his own impression. While he has his readers before his eyes, the critic then reports the outward accompanying circumstances of the performance: the success, the "disposition" of the audience, and the background, earlier achievements, family situation of the composer. Some also say something about the work itself, without committing themselves. Without doubt, this manner of reportage-criticism is indispensable for all parties: for the newspaper, the reader, the composer, and the performers. In western countries music and theater criticism is clearly limited to this reporting function.

Of course, since it is executed by experts, with us such reportage is frequently colored by the personal opinion of the critic—which has no justification within a reportage. In this way numerous false reports about the attitude of the audience at a premiere originate. Every creating and performing musician knows a song to sing about these total falsifications of success. Demonstrations of approbation are either withheld or termed "pleasantly polite success." If the success cannot be denied, then it is a matter of "strange to say, it appeared to please the audience," or the testimony is given that the applause "naturally" applied only to the performance. It would be worthwhile if, to begin with, reasonable information about the title and content of the work, about the performance and reception of the audience, would appear detached from the criticism, and if only then the critic followed with a detailed, technically-grounded, genuinely productive appraisal. (See below.)

Criticism as Politics

One is involuntarily inclined to bring a newspaper's musical and theatrical criticism into association with its political attitude. Actually it is conceivable that even in this way a clear and unequivocal situation could be attained. Then, of course, a newspaper oriented toward the right would employ a right-oriented critic and *vice versa*. Especially in a time when even art receives an evermore distinct political coloring through the advancing politicization of daily life, such an orderly inclusion of criticism within the overall character of the newspaper could eliminate much uncertainty. What should one say when a large leftist, democratic newspaper has a critic of stiffly conservative, fanatically reactionary attitude, while other critics, whose papers stand further right of the first paper, stand up with courage and conviction for everything new in the area of music. The fact that one cannot know from a review what transpires on the editorial page creates special difficulties for that part of critical activity which nowadays is moving evermore forcefully into the foreground: the politics of art.[1]

Indeed, today it is among the most important duties of the critic to follow attentively the events of public musical life and consistently and persistently to pledge that in the administration of large concert, theatrical and educational institutions, in the distribution of appointments, in the drawing up of programs, in the support or opposition of controversial personalities, guarantees be given for advancement of those artistic tendencies that he considers valuable or essential. Naturally such artistic politics can attain the intended effect only if the attitude of the critic is supported by the overall stance of the publication. Accordingly, it should not be possible to employ within a progressively-disposed feuilleton a music critic who continually works against the artistic-political tendency of his paper through his fundamentally deprecating attitude toward everything new.

Criticism as Appraisal

Certainly there are a number of people in German musical criticism who practice their vocation with genuine seriousness, supported by scrupulous musical preparation and unprejudiced by interfering signs of old-age. These critics almost completely renounce reportage. (Furthermore, this appears to be easier for large provincial newspapers than for Berlin papers.) They do not work with traditional phrases, with hackneyed catchwords. They do not want to reproduce the "smell," the atmospheric impression of a performance. They do not attempt to embellish their commentary by incidental personal observations. Also, they do not take that ambiguous posture which always asserts in the second sentence the opposite of the first—they give a factual, theoretically-based evaluation of the art work. They can judge, beyond the momentary impression of a performance dependent upon accidents, how a piece was invented and how it was fashioned, what significance it has within the production of its creator and within modern music in general.   They are acquainted with larger relationships and seek to classify each phenomenon and each work in a movement, about whose values and dangers they have been accurately informed.   In this manner they accomplish genuinely productive work.

The inescapable condition of such appraising criticism is a discernibly singular attitude.   If a critic delivers three totally contradictory opinions in three newspapers concerning one and the same work after one and the same performance, if he attempts to conceal his own uncertainty behind witty glimpses, then he cannot expect people to ascribe any significance to his opinion.   Today the productive critic himself has recognized two dangers of his profession: personal vanity, which treats composers with patronizing shoulder-patting in order to increase the critic's own stature, and the exploitation of some trend, by which the critic seeks to gain for himself a share of the fame of a performing or creative musician.

SMALL APPENDIX

Criticism as Voice of the Beyond

A curious phenomenon that frequently still occurs in the most varied regions of Germany.   In our time there are actually men living, out of whom speaks the voice of the good old days when we still had our Kaiser and generally such a thing was not possible.   They represent views which no longer appeared credible even to the preceding generation.   No one can convince them that the total transformation of the world-picture that has been accomplished in recent years might also possibly have brought about some change in questions of art.   With respect to these phenomena the admiringly quiet attitude that one accords any marvel is to be recommended.

NOTES

1.   Weill's text in German: "Diese Tatsache, dass man oft 'unter dem Strich' nicht weiss, was 'über dem Strich' vorgeht, ist besonders erschwerend für jenen Teil der Kritiker-Tätigkeit, der heute immer starker in den Vordergrund rückt, für die Kunstpolitik."   The idiomatic "below the line" refers to the feuilleton section of the newspaper (usually at the bottom of the page, separated from actual news items by a line), devoted to light literature, fiction, or criticism.   In translating Weill's essay, I have attempted to convert the terminology to parallel present-day American journalistic practice.

"Notiz zum Berliner Requiem," *Der deutsche Rundfunk* 7 (17 May 1929):613.
Partially reprinted in *Ausgewählte Schriften*, pp. 139-41.

A NOTE CONCERNING *DAS BERLINER REQUIEM*

The cantata *Das Berliner Requiem*, which is dedicated to the Frankfurt Broadcasting Station, belongs to the domain of a series of works within my output that to some extent are meant as studies for the now completed opera *Aufstieg und Fall der Stadt Mahagonny*.[1] The works which grew out of this domain represent a specific type of vocal composition with small orchestra. Here it is a question of a genre which can be performed in the concert hall in the form of a cantata, but which can also be performed just as well in the theater through the gestic fixing of content and through the attempted vividness of musical language. It could not be very difficult to enlarge for the requirements of radio such a form that encompasses both concert and theatrical possibilities. For the bases of radio art are present: a strong musical construction whose theoretical conformity must be adjusted to the intellectual content of the work, and the musical definition of a fundamental *gestus* that can be represented scenically, but which, without the aid of the stage, must be communicated powerfully enough purely as music so that the listener can imagine the picture of mankind that addresses itself to him. Here, it is not a question of lyrics nor of portrayal of a situation, but of representation of a process.

I have written three smaller compositions of this type: the *Mahagonny-Songspiel*, which was performed two years ago in Baden-Baden and represents a sketch for the opera just mentioned; the cantata *Das Berliner Requiem*; and the musical composition for radio, *Der Lindberghflug*. All three pieces were written with texts by Bert Brecht; the latter two are expressly intended for the use of radio broadcasting stations.[2] Concerning this task of writing music for the radio, the obvious prerequisite for me was knowledge of the acoustic restrictions of the broadcasting studio, the orchestral and instrumental capabilities of microphones, the distribution of vocal registers and harmonic limitations that are fixed for a radio composition.[3] Several years of observations when listening to radio music and some of my own efforts have convinced me that this medium is not so much dependent on a particularly crafty technique of instrumentation as on the clarity and transparency of phrasing and texture. So for me the main task was to try out an art form which actually had to conform in its content and means of expression to what the radio uses today.

In that light, the foremost consideration is that the radio audience is composed of all classes of people. Consequently, it is impossible to apply the assumptions of the concert hall to radio music. For in its conception, concert music was meant for a definite and limited circle of listeners of cultured and affluent classes. For the first time radio poses for the serious musician of the present the task of creating works which can be taken up by as large a circle of listeners as possible. The content and form of these radio compositions must also be capable of interesting a large number of people of all classes; and the means of musical expression also must not cause any difficulty for the untrained listener.

The content of *Das Berliner Requiem* unquestionably corresponds to the sentiments and perceptions of the broadest levels of the population. We attempted to express what urban man of our era has to say about the phenomenon of death. Some especially stringent censors of the radio have found it necessary to question this.[4] That attitude gives evidence of an alarming ignorance of the artistic requirements of those classes which, in terms of the radio audience, occupy the broadest scope.

Perhaps later something will still be said about the peculiar events behind the scenes of this performance.[5] The overall impression of the performance must show if we were correct in our statement that we are dealing here with a serious, non-ironic work, a type of secular Requiem, an expression about death in the form of memorial tablets, epitaphs, and funeral dirges.

The individual parts of the piece are as follows: a ballad "Vom Tod im Wald" for bass and ten wind instruments; a song "Können einem toten Mann nicht helfen," which has been adopted as the finale of the opera *Mahagonny*; a song "Vom ertrunkenen Mädchen" and a "Matterl" for the tombstone of this girl; two songs about the unknown soldier under the triumphal arch, the first for vocal ensemble and orchestra, the second for baritone and organ; and at the conclusion, a chorale of thanksgiving for male chorus and orchestra.[6]

NOTES

1. In fact, *Aufstieg* continued to undergo revision until 1931. The "Crane Duet," for example, was composed in October 1929.

2. After the unfortunate circumstances surrounding the broadcast of *Das Berliner Requiem* and after the premiere of *Der Lindberghflug* (the version by Weill in association with Hindemith) on 28 July 1929 at Baden-Baden, Weill composed his own version of *Der Lindberghflug*. Reflecting his dissatisfaction with the radio medium, he redesignated the work as a "didactic cantata," intended for performance in schools.

3. In "A New Patron for Music" [*Modern Music* 8 (January-February 1931):14-19], Hans Heinsheimer described the role of contemporary music in German radio programing. "Along with the theatres the German radio is maintained and supported as a great cultural institution responsible to public control. Nine German broadcasting stations (with several subsidiaries) are united in the National Radio Company and are advised by a committee of intellectuals—a Cultural Advisory Council. . . . Contemporary music is energetically fostered. There are laboratories and research units for the new sound requirements of the microphone; special works are commissioned from composers of all tendencies. Thus an individual radio literature has arisen in Germany. Music that meets the special technical requirements of the microphone and whose spirit and form take into account the peculiar, diversified audiences of radio listeners. There are no private broadcasters here and no radio advertising. It is obvious, therefore, that beside the life of the theatre, the radio in Germany is creating a special place for publisher and composer."

4. Censors delayed the initial broadcast of *Das Berliner Requiem*, originally scheduled for 22 February 1929, until 22 May 1929, when its transmission was restricted to the Southwest and West German broadcasting groups.

5. This essay was the last which Weill contributed to the journal of the German radio industry, *Der deutsche Rundfunk*. With the success of *Die Dreigroschenoper*, Weill could comfortably afford to protest the handling of *Das Berliner Requiem* in this manner.

6. The version of the work listed here was never performed. Before the premiere, Weill deleted *Vom Tod im Wald*, added "Zu Potsdam unter den Eichen," and rearranged the order of the cantata.

"Die Oper—Wohin?" *Berliner Tageblatt*, 31 October 1929. Partially reprinted in *Die Musik* 22 (January 1930):322.

OPERA—WHERE TO?

The following works by Kurt Weill, the composer of *Die Dreigroschenoper*, will be premiered: a Worker's Chorus at the end of November, the cantata *Der Lindberghflug* under Klemperer on December 5, and the opera *Aufstieg und Fall der Stadt Mahagonny* in the spring of next year. [The Editor.]

"GEBRAUCHSMUSIK" AND ITS BOUNDARIES

Today, the idea of *"Gebrauchsmusik"* has permeated all those camps of modern music for whom it is at all within reach.   We have forced back our aesthetic verdicts.   We have come to understand that we must again create for our output its natural fertile ground; that music in its significance as the simplest human need can also be offered with heightened artistic means of expression; that the boundaries between "art music" and "music for use" must be brought closer and gradually eliminated.

For that reason, we have attempted to create music that is capable of satisfying the musical needs of broader levels of the population without giving up artistic substance.   Therefore, we have not contented ourselves with simplifying our means of expression a little.   We have, in fact, put aside aesthetic appraisal.   In our music we want to allow men of our time to speak, and they ought to speak to many.   The first question for us: is what we do useful to a general public?   It is only a secondary question if what we create is art, for that is determined only by the quality of our work.[1]

This attitude, expressed by a representative of "serious music," would have been inconceivable a few years ago.   People would have rejected such a claim on the grounds that such a conversion of "art music" would be tied to the needs of the masses with severe concessions to the so-called public taste.   The accuracy of this claim could only be tested through application.   Today that has occurred.*   But in no case is it the purpose of all these efforts to enter into combat with the composer of "hit-tunes," but rather merely to bring our music to the masses.   That can be attained only if our music is capable of expressing simple human emotions and actions, only if it reproduces the natural condition of man.

With the attempt to advance this genre and to employ it in different areas, we also naturally recognize the dangers of this overall course.   If we attempt gradually to eliminate the boundaries between art music and music for use, under no circumstances should the impression be created that we want to renounce the intellectual bearing of the serious musician in order to be able to compete fully with producers of lighter market wares. The superficial or hostile observer sees (or wants to see) only that simplification of the means of musical expression has been carried out to a high degree here; that the question "tonal or atonal?" is no longer discussed; that the question of originality no longer stands in first place; that fear of banality is finally overcome (which Busoni already had demanded ten years ago); above all, that here, with the use of elements of jazz, simple, easily-comprehensible melodies originate which superficially produce a more or less strong resemblance to the melodies of "light" music. In the process the observer all too often overlooks that the effect of this music is not catchy, but instead rousing; that the intellectual bearing of this music is thoroughly serious, bitter, accusing, and, in the most pleasant cases still ironic; that neither the poetry of this music nor the form of the music itself would be conceivable without the vast background of an ethical or social nature on which it is based. Also, one must not forget that the songs of *Die Dreigroschenoper* discovered or created a totally different attitude on the part of the public, and that this public expects something different from the continuance of this genre than from the older forms of 'music for use.' [*Verbrauchsmusik*] Here lie the dangers and at the same time the boundaries of our genre; we must not imitate the "hit" (and it has been proven often that we are not really able to do that). We may change our music only to the extent that we can carry on our intellectual tasks, the duties of the artist in his time, in an entirely perceptible, entirely understandable language.

THE DEVELOPMENTAL TRENDS OF OPERA

Seen in this way, this musical movement seems especially adapted to influence the development of opera. The situation of opera approximately corresponds to the general situation of music, as I have attempted to sketch it previously. On the one hand, one reckons that today a clearly delimited typical operatic audience still exists. This audience, which is not too large numerically, expects in the opera house quite specific impressions, which are not allowed to proceed beyond the traditional concept of opera. Thus, one adjusts for this circle of listeners; in the choice of librettos [*Textbuchen*] and in the plan of the music one allows for the demands and the receptive capability of this operatic audience.

On the other hand, the attempt is also made not to adjust exclusively for a relatively narrowly defined circle of special-interest groups, but rather to bring opera closer to the theater of the present. At the outset, this is a daring undertaking, for a genre in which more is supposed to be spoken than sung must always occupy an exceptional position.   But the modern theater comes to meet these endeavors forcefully, for its most important representatives have realized that certain stylistic elements of the new drama can only be accomplished musically. Since this new theater is aimed at the representation of man, of what he says and what he does, it approaches our musical endeavors, because we, too, seek new expressive possibilities for simple human events and relationships.

If we succeed in finding a musical language which is just as natural as the language of the people in modern theater, it is also possible to deal with the monumental themes of our time with purely musical means in the form of opera. (This would have a great advantage in comparison to the spoken drama in that we could determine musically the expression, the *gestus* of the presentation, and in this way could prevent the serious performance errors from which the modern theater has too often suffered.)   These endeavors toward an approach by opera to spoken drama seem, on the other hand, to be deemed of considerable interest by the leaders of spoken drama.   Today it is already possible to mount in a private theater in Berlin an opera with a libretto of literary merit and limited technical demands.[2]   A well-known theatrical director in Berlin has already adapted one of his theaters primarily for musical works. Another concern has even expressed the intention of erecting a permanent musical stage.   In an inquiry to directors, the most famous representatives of this specialty have stated that a large musical stage work would attract them most of all.[3]

If opera wishes once again to find a connection to "great theater," it must adopt the loose form that probably represents the most valuable achievement of new theater. The loosest form of operatic theater until now has been the dialogue-opera, in which the plot is advanced in the spoken dialogue, while the music enters only at static moments of the plot. The principle of number-opera has been taken up again in many musical stage works of recent years as a reaction to music drama. But it has been accomplished for purely musical-formal reasons. The music has been arranged in numbers, to be sure, but it has in addition been given the ungrateful duty of supplying the background for the incidents of the stage, of sustaining the plot.

In *Die Dreigroschenoper*, which we designated from the beginning as the prototype of opera, the music again assumes its irrational role: it interrupts the plot when the action has arrived at a situation that permits music and song to appear. In the opera, *Aufstieg und Fall der Stadt Mahagonny*, this principle could be pushed still further. Here the plot is nothing more than the history of a city. Every musical number is a complete musical scene and short intervening texts create the possibility for the entry of new music in every case.

NOTES

*To this belongs also the musical *Volksstück* as it is manifested in my *Die Dreigroschenoper* and *Happy End*.

1. The preceding paragraph provides the proper context for one of Weill's most often quoted and misinterpreted statements: "Through my work for the theater, I have arrived at the conclusion that the distinction between 'serious' and 'light' music is one of the misconceptions of the Wagnerian period of music. The only distinction we should make is the one between good music and bad music." [*New York Sun*, 3 February 1940.]

2. Weill's reference may be to *Die Dreigroschenoper*, mounted in the Theater am Schiffbauerdamm, rented by Ernst Joseph Aufricht, an independent producer.

3. Weill had already collaborated with Piscator, Jessner, and Brecht. Reinhardt planned a production of *Aufstieg* in 1930, but Weill's first collaboration with Reinhardt as director was *The Eternal Road* (New York, 1937).

"Aktuelles Theater," *Melos* 8 (December 1929):524-527. Also published in
Die Scene 20 (January 1930):4-7. Reprinted in *Melos* 37 (July-August
1970):276-77 and in *Ausgewählte Schriften*, pp. 45-49.

TOPICAL THEATER

Topicality, at all times an important functional component of
theater, today is made into an incorrectly understood slogan, in that it is
pushed into the foreground as the main task of modern theater.[1]   As
such, the situation of German theater completely corresponds to the
political situation in Germany, in that a concept which could represent a
positive value within a healthy progressive movement gradually becomes
a reactionary danger (in the process of coalition politics that levels
everything).   No other factor of modern theater has been snatched up so
hastily by representatives of conservative commercial theater and
assimilated in the most superficial manner than the call for topicality.
And since the same concept of topicality also served many representatives
of the young generation as a bridge to the audience and to success—
without cautioning against its incorrect employment—today a state of
mutual misconceptions has resulted.   Concerning a general camaraderie
under the password of topicality, people forget only all too easily that a
new form of theater, recognizable in productions of the most diverse
tendencies, is appearing today, for which quality and intention are more
decisive than the stimulus of topicality.

The influence of contemporary events on dramatic productions was
clearly noticeable in all theater epochs.   To be sure, almost everywhere
great ideas of the period, intellectual or political currents, were treated in
the theater, often in a transformed manner.   Rarely were the incidents of
plot drawn from events of reality, yet there are even examples of that.
There are *Zeitstücke* (*Figaro, Fidelio*) even in operatic theater.   But it was
always a matter of presenting ideas or themes that could claim to be
treated in a more enduring, more significant form than the newspaper
would probably be capable of offering.   And with regard to the
characteristics that kept those works alive, their artistic form stands at
least equal to the subject matter.

I am convinced that great art of all periods was topical in the sense
that it was intended not for eternity, but for the time in which it
originated, or at least for the near future, to whose formation it was
intended to contribute.[2]   That is valid for us also.   In a time of violent
social upheaval, we have enough to do in demonstrating the utility of our
work and its justification for existence.   We can do that only if we give

those ideas of our time, which we ourselves acknowledge, an undeniably artistic form. If art is to be just as useful as science, journalism, and politics, it must have perfect control over its own resources. *But it must be as "topical" in its means of expression as in its subject matter.* We cannot express ideas of this period with the same language, the same music, the same theatrical form as for the imperialist era of fifty years ago, not only because we speak to a different audience, but also because we expect a different influence on our audience.

Of the two forms of topical theater which have come into fashion in recent years and are still utilized today, the first is totally misleading, while the second possesses great significance as a transitional phenomenon in a period of growing reactionary danger. One could classify the first of these two species of topical theater as *Metropolis-*topicality, because it expressed itself most clearly in the film of that name.[3] It borrows from the life of this era a few superficial requisites, among which it allows people of the previous century to act. It holds meticulously to ideologies of past eras and attempts to dress them up with vague, verbose presentations of social problems. Any taking of a stand is avoided. Everything that we have experienced in recent years of the "rhythm of machines," the "tempo of the large city," the "melody of the skyscraper," and similar phrases belong to this category. It was obvious that this cheap topicality was also snatched up by representatives of the conservative theater; it changed nothing of the established form of theater, it did not shake the fundamental point of view of theatrical patrons, and such a small move toward the left made its profitable mark at the evening box-office. Basically this whole tendency is still strongly imprisoned in the Wagnerian circle of ideas. It is still theater of supermen, theater of climax, theater of heavy viscous form.

The other of the two forms of topical theater employed to date has attempted a much wider and more important thrust. It is that form of modern theater which takes its *subject matter* from the events of the present. One of the prototypes of this genre was the literary topical revue, which originated in western Berlin. But it already succumbed to the danger that topical occurrences were indeed mentioned, but without taking a position, except with that knowing wink and that half-irony, which even permit a friendlier interpretation than most topical events allow. This danger also exists in the strongest degree for that form of topical play which is in fashion today. Well-known events from public life, law suits, and scandalous affairs of our time or the most recent past are manufactured into dramas. This "supply of subject matter" from the present has the advantage that authors are forced to depict people of today, people who differ fundamentally in their feelings and actions from those of the pre-war period. But up to now most "topical plays" have failed in one point: they show events of our time, but they do not show larger relationships; they do not depict people of today in their true form; they propose to photograph the period instead of holding a mirror up to it so that it can see itself. Thence another danger of this genre results: the relapse into naturalism. The representative style of these topical plays scarcely differs from that of the turn of the century—topical subject matter in an antiquated theatrical form.

But all these hazards seem to be alleviated when the topical play develops in the direction of political theater. For a political subject can be represented only in its *large relationship*, and a "dramatized lead-article," after all, is already a step further than an earth-shaking drama of the "twilight of humanity."[4] For that reason, the attempts of Piscator (even where they are only half-successful) represent the boldest thrust from the area of topical theater. They do not restrict themselves to representation of specific questions of the day that are already forgotten a year later, but instead treat great political themes of the era: war, capitalism, inflation, revolution. And this also results in the immediate necessity to reach *a new large form of theater*. It is this same theatrical form that Brecht, from a different direction, has sought for a long time and which also is continued in our collaborations since *Die Dreigroschenoper*. On the one hand, this theatrical form enables great subject matter of the time to be transmitted to that plane where art alone is possible, where once more elevated speech, pure music, and independent paintings can be employed. On the other hand, it also allows for a new make-up of audience that seeks in theater more than gratification of its entertainment requirements.

This modern form of theater, in which the chorus also again assumes a decisive role, produces new and powerful provisions for music in the theater. Since this theater is aimed primarily toward the *gestus* of the presentation, it leaves ample room for music that is expected neither to illustrate nor to advance the action, but rather only to capture and to realize the gestic character of a succession of situations. *Here unquestionably lies a possibility to lead opera out of its isolation into the region of valuable relevant theater.* Of course, we are certainly so far behind in the domain of opera that the necessity of such an approach for opera to contemporary theater is still denied today. Opera is supposed to be the theater of "singing people"; it is supposed to be fixed in traditional paths through this limitation; it is supposed to have originated as an aristocratic art and it must remain that even today. If this assertion is correct, then opera would be nothing other than a museum-piece; then all those who have recognized the genuine duties of theater at this time would have to abandon opera in full flight. But we know and we have previously demonstrated that especially in modern theater there can again be singing, that today's theater allows music enough room for play and allows the formation of a new, musically well-founded operatic form to become possible. Of course, what before was demanded of topical theater is valid in increased measure here. It no longer suffices to install a few requisite items or figures from modern life in the existing form of music drama; a playful occupation with the formal problems of musical theater no longer suffices either. An accommodation of contemporary subject matter must be found for the appropriate form of topical musical theater.

NOTES

1.   Note the similarity of Weill's usage of and attitude toward the terms *Zeitoper* and *Aktuelles Theater*. In both cases, he refers to them as incorrectly employed slogans.

2.   In an interview printed in the *New York Sun*, 3 February 1940, Weill stated: "I am convinced that many composers have a feeling of superiority toward their audiences. Schoenberg, for example, has said he is writing for a time fifty years after his death. But the great 'classic' composers wrote for their contemporary audiences. They wanted those who heard their music to understand it and they did. As for myself, I write for today. I don't give a damn about writing for posterity."

3.   *Metropolis*, Fritz Lang's film of 1926, deals with the dehumanizing aspects of industrial society and its inherent class distinctions. Weill objected to its topicality because the melodramatic plot was in his opinion a camouflaged romantic treatment of contemporary social problems.

4.   Weill's Wagnerian parallel between "*dramatisierter Leitartikel*" and "*Menschheitsdämmerung*" is partially lost in translation.

"Vorwort zum Regiebuch der Oper *Aufstieg und Fall der Stadt Mahagonny*," *Anbruch* 12 (January 1930):5-7. Reprinted in *Ausgewählte Schriften*, pp. 57-60.

FOREWORD TO THE PRODUCTION BOOK OF THE OPERA *AUFSTIEG UND FALL DER STADT MAHAGONNY*

Kurt Weill, together with Caspar Neher and Bert Brecht, worked on a "production book" for the opera *Mahagonny*. It contains precise suggestions for the scenic representation of the work, and it is provided to theaters along with material for the musical performance and Neher's slides. Here we present the principal statements of the Foreword. [The Editor.][1]

In *Die Dreigroschenoper*, an attempt was made to renew the original form of musical theater. There music is no longer plot-advancing, but rather the actual entrance of music is synonymous with an interruption of plot. The epic form of theater is a stepwise *sequence of situations*. Therefore, it is the ideal form of musical theater, for only such situations can be set to music in closed forms, and a sequence of situations arranged according to musical considerations results in the heightened form of musical theater: opera.

In *Die Dreigroschenoper*, the action had to be carried on between the musical pieces; therefore, approximately the form of "dialogue-opera," a mixed genre of play and opera, was produced here.

The subject matter of the opera *Aufstieg und Fall der Stadt Mahagonny* made possible an *organization according to purely musical precepts*. For the form of the chronicle, which could be chosen here, is nothing other than a sequence of situations. Therefore, a new situation in the history of Mahagonny is introduced each time by an inscription, which sets up in narrative form passage into the new scene.

Two men and a woman, in flight from the authorities, break down in a desolate region. They decide to found a city where men who pass through from the Gold Coast would be able to fulfill their needs. In the "Paradise City" that arises here, people lead a contemplative idyllic life. But in the long run, that cannot satisfy the men from the Gold Coast. Discontent reigns. Prices drop. During the night when a typhoon moves toward the city, Jim Mahoney discovers the new law of the city. The law states: "You can do anything." The typhoon curves away. People live on according to the new law. The city flourishes. Needs increase—and prices with them. For people are permitted everything—but only if they can pay for it. When his money runs out, Jim Mahoney himself is condemned to death. His execution is the occasion for a gigantic demonstration against the high cost of living, which announces the end of the city.

That is the history of the city Mahagonny. It is presented in the loose form of a sequence of *"morality-pictures of the twentieth century."* It is an allegory of contemporary life. The main figure of the play is the city. It arises from the needs of men, and the needs of men are what cause its rise and fall. But we present the particular phases in the history of the city merely in their repercussions on man. For just as the wants of men influence the development of the city, so again the development of the city alters the conduct of men. Therefore, all the songs of this opera are an expression of the masses, even where they are performed by the individual as spokesman of the masses. In the beginning, the group of founders stands in contrast to the group of arrivals. At the end of the first act the group of supporters of the new law struggles against the group of opponents. The fate of the individual is depicted in passing only where it exemplifies the fate of the city.

To seek psychological or topical associations beyond these fundamental thoughts would be spurious. The name "Mahagonny" denotes only the concept of a city. It was chosen on the basis of its sound (phonetic basis). The geographic location of the city is unimportant.

We stress that it is not advisable to shift presentation of the work to the side of the ironic or grotesque. Since the incidents are not symbolic but typical, economy in the scenic means and in the expression of the individual actor commends itself most strongly. The dramatic conduct of the singers, the movement of the chorus, as well as the entire performance style of this opera, are principally defined by the style of the music. At no time is this music illustrative. It endeavors to concretize the behavior of people in the various situations that the rise and fall of the city bring about. This behavior of people is already so determined in the music that a simple, natural interpretation of the music indicates the style of performance. Therefore, the performer can also restrict himself to the simplest and most natural gestures.

In staging the opera, it must be continually taken into consideration that *closed musical forms* are present here. Therefore, an essential task is to guarantee the purely musical flow and to group the performers so that an almost *concertante* musical presentation is possible. The style of the work is neither naturalistic nor symbolic. Rather, it can be labeled as "real," for it shows life as it is represented in the sphere of art. Any exaggeration toward the pathetic or toward dance-like stylization is to be avoided.

Caspar Neher's projection plates form a component of the production material. (Therefore, they should be sent to theaters along with the production notes.) These slides independently illustrate the scenic events with the means of the painter. They furnish illustrative material for the history of the city; the slides are projected successively on the screen during or between individual scenes. The performers play their scenes in front of this screen, and it suffices completely if only the most necessary requirements of the performers for the elucidation of their acting are employed here. In this opera it is not necessary to utilize complicated stage-machinery. More important are a few good projectors as well as skillful arrangement of the projection surfaces, making it possible for the pictures as well as the explanatory inscriptions to be recognized clearly from all seats. The stage construction should be so simple that it can be transplanted just as well from the theater to any platform. The soloistic scenes should be played as near as possible to the spectators. Therefore, it is advisable not to deepen the orchestra pit, but to place the orchestra at the level of the first row of seats and to construct a platform from the stage into the Orchestra area so that some scenes can be played in the midst of the Orchestra.

NOTES

1. Actually the "Foreword" reflects Weill's and Neher's ideas far more than Brecht's. Weill published his three essays concerning *Aufstieg* independently of Brecht, just as Brecht and Suhrkamp issued their "*Anmerkungen zur Oper Aufstieg und Fall der Stadt Mahagonny*" in 1930 without consulting Weill. Comparison of the essays reveals Weill's and Brecht's fundamentally opposed views of opera, which eventually led to the dissolution of their association.

"Anmerkungen zu meiner Oper *Mahagonny*," *Die Musik* 22 (March 1930):440-41.   Reprinted in *Ausgewählte Schriften*, pp. 56-57.

NOTES TO MY OPERA *MAHAGONNY*

To our request for some introductory statement about his new opera to be performed on six German stages in the second week of March, the composer responded with the following remarks.   [The Editor.][1]

As early as my first meeting with Brecht in Spring 1927, the word "Mahagonny" emerged in a conversation concerning the possibilities of opera and with it the conception of a "Paradise City."   In order to pursue further this idea, which had seized me immediately, and in order to test the musical style that I envisioned for it, I first composed the five Mahagonny-Songs from Brecht's *Die Hauspostille* (*Manual of Piety*) and linked them into a small dramatic form, a "Songspiel," which was performed in Baden-Baden during the summer of 1927.   This Baden-Baden *Mahagonny* is thus nothing more than a stylistic study for the opera, which, once begun, was continued only after the style had been tested.   For almost a year Brecht and I worked together on the libretto for the opera. The score was completed in November 1929.

The genre of "*Song*" which originated in the Baden-Baden piece and was further developed in later works (*Die Dreigroschenoper, Das Berliner Requiem, Happy End*) was naturally unable to support a full-length opera by itself.   Other larger forms had to be added.   But the simple ballad-like style always had to be preserved.

The subject of this opera is the history of a city, its formation, its first crises, then the decisive turning point in its development, its time of glory, its decline.   It is a set of "morality-pictures of our time" projected on an exaggerated level.   Corresponding to this subject, the purest form of epic theater, which is also the purest form of musical theater, could be selected.   It is a series of twenty-one separate musical forms.   Each of these forms is a closed scene, and each is introduced by an inscription in narrative form.   The music here is no longer a plot-advancing element; it enters at the point where certain conditions are reached.   Therefore, from the beginning the libretto is planned so that it presents a series of conditions yielding a dramatic form only in its musically-determined dynamic course.

NOTES

1. The six theaters which scheduled productions of *Aufstieg* for March 1930 were reduced to three (Leipzig, Kassel, and Braunschweig) after the riotous premiere in Leipzig.

"Zur Uraufführung der Oper *Mahagonny*," *Leipziger Neueste Nachrichten*, 8 March 1930. Reprinted in *Ausgewählte Schriften*, pp. 60-61.

CONCERNING THE PREMIERE OF THE OPERA *MAHAGONNY*

The catchwords "theater of the times" ["*Zeittheater*"], "jazz opera," etc., as they are understood today, are difficult to apply to this work. The idea of topical theater, of tremendous significance for the development of modern theater, can find application for musical theater only if a grand form and an elevated language are found for contemporary events. The subject of an opera can be topical in somewhat the same way as the biblical stories of the prodigal son, the banquet, and the adulterous woman are.[1] Therefore, from the start we endeavored to present the history of a city, in that sense a "biblical" event already, only in those stages which allow for a serious, elevated representation. Since we depicted the history of the city in its repercussions on the relationships of men to one another, we ourselves came upon great concepts of the social life of men as they are pictured in art in all times and places: friendship and betrayal, poverty and prosperity, acquiescence and revolt, fear and courage. A form of operatic theater that might be labeled a "musical picture-sheet" originated from these human events embedded in the narrative of the rise and fall of the city Mahagonny.

NOTES

1.   Weill's biblical references are probably the following: Luke 15:11-32; John 2:1-10 or Matthew 22:2-14; John 4:6-26.

"Aktuelles Zwiegespräch über die Schuloper zwischen Kurt Weill und Dr. Hans Fischer," *Die Musikpflege* 1 (April 1930):48-52.   Reprinted in *Ausgewählte Schriften*, pp. 63-70.[1]

TOPICAL DIALOGUE ABOUT *SCHULOPER* BETWEEN KURT WEILL AND DR. HANS FISCHER

Dr. Fischer: I hear that your didactic opera [*Schuloper*] will be premiered during this year's music festival, "Neue Musik Berlin 1930."[2] I recall that *Der Lindberghflug* was already a piece intended primarily for elementary schools.[3]   In order to introduce our conversation on the theme "new music and didactic music," I wish to ask you, Mr. Weill, how you came to the style of simple popular music?

Kurt Weill: I share the attempt to write simple popular music with many of today's composers. For us music should not remain a private or parlor affair: rather, we strive for broader, newer possibilities of influence. I already aspired to this intention in *Die Dreigroschenoper* and accomplished it there to a quite marked degree.

Dr. Fischer: *Die Dreigroschenoper* has in fact penetrated the public. When we speak of new music in the schools, students speak best of *Die Dreigroschenoper*. And they not only speak of it, but they also sing and play it. Students are, I believe, your most enthusiastic audience.

Kurt Weill: I'm happy about what you say of *Die Dreigroschenoper* because I aim precisely at youth as the audience of the future. I desire that initially the children who are my special audience should experience and possess what I want to express in my music. When the present generation of school children has grown up, *the* audience I'm counting on will exist.

Dr. Fischer: If you aim in your music at youth as your audience, how do you deal with, let us say in musical-psychological terms, the receptivity of children and how does your accommodation for children affect the style of your compositions?

Kurt Weill: When I write for students, I submit myself above all to an intensified self-control.   That is, I must reach the utmost degree of simplicity if I want to write for students and wish to be comprehensible to them.   But despite all such simplicity, I must give my best and highest. To be sure, in the theater I can also write in a simple style, but I can still count on the support of more ingenious and complicated means. In the theater I can still display "artistic" simplicity to a certain extent, but with children I must remain totally stringent in my simplicity.

Dr. Fischer: This appears to me to be the salient point. For heaven's sake, no "childish music for children," written by adults for children, somewhat as an adult imagines a song for the little ones. . . . Such music that condescends to children is not wanted by children at all. Music should be simple but not intentionally primitive.

Kurt Weill: You are right.   Simplicity must not be construed as primitiveness. Instead it works this way: either I possess this simplicity or I do not. Simple music can only be written by the simple musician. The simple style is no problem for him; simple works are not minor works but major works.

Dr. Fischer: Unfortunately there are not yet enough such major works of simple style that are suitable for schools.

Kurt Weill: Yes, and not only for schools but also for other groups. For me, there are different directions in which simpler music may have wider influence—which does not need to preclude "depth." One course is the movement of *workers' choruses* [*Arbeiterchöre*].   There I find genuine amateurs for whom it is rewarding to write simple music. I would not consider it a disgrace for a composer to count on singers who can't read a note of music. Simple music should be understandable even to musical illiterates. The *theater* offers a further possibility, although here it becomes more and more difficult to move forward in a clear direction. Perhaps at some point the *sound-film*, not yet an artistic possibility, will be part of this tendency.[4] However, that can't be foreseen at this point. But what can be very well foreseen is that the *school* will enable the composer to have broader influence.

Dr. Fischer: But one objection is to be made with schools. Ordinarily outsiders consider schools as a tight, self-contained community. Today schools are not yet homogeneous institutions. Schools are split into groups that attack each other vehemently. Thus one can't count on a uniform audience for music in schools today either, only on an utterly divided one.

Kurt Weill: But I do not fear this split at all—I like to regard it as an advantage. I even consider it an advantage that things are *discussed* in schools.

Dr. Fischer: If I understood correctly, you desire to make music more accessible through the discussion of students with one another.

Kurt Weill: Yes, music should be a *topic of conversation*, under no circumstances a petrified formal structure, but something alive, so that excitement is justified. Precisely because the school is composed of diverse elements, circles, and talents which are forced to interact with one another, it has the greatest advantage. It is difficult but very worthwhile to meet with such a diversity of gradually maturing ideas and views at their point of intersection and while they're still developing. That is why, when I enumerated the various possibilities for the expansion of music, I did *not* speak of the radio. For the radio audience consists of an anonymous community of adults from the most diverse circles with whom little can be done. One can offer nothing to these adults because their ideas diverge much too far. There is no longer a point of inter-section present, and no more development is possible. Even observation about diversity of views is fruitless here, and no one ever seriously attempts it.[5] Children can still have a dispute; adults can only conceal it or proclaim its permanence.

Dr. Fischer: You speak so vividly about this that I assume you have just related your own school memories. In that case, what was the nature of your musical activity in school?

Kurt Weill: Even though the singing instruction was bad, the director of my Dessau Gymnasium and the professor of the upper classes showed the greatest interest in music. At that time already they vigorously encouraged me. I composed for the school orchestra and even wrote—amazingly enough, considering who I am today—war choruses.

Dr. Fischer: Except for the content, were your compositions already conceived from simple and popular material at that time?

Kurt Weill: Yes, they were simple, but still quite immature, without stylistic impulse. The first work in which the simple style can be recognized was probably the ballet *Die Zaubernacht*. At that time I studied with Busoni. I wrote this work, which was my first commission, for a children's theater. (I later used it in the Suite *Quodlibet*.)[6] In the following years, artistic experiments, characterized by struggles for new harmonic and melodic means of expression, overpowered my work. In *Mahagonny*, which was performed in Baden-Baden, the new simple style had its breakthrough; in *Die Dreigroschenoper* it probably found its first valid expression. In *Der Lindberghflug* Bert Brecht and I thought for the first time directly in terms of the schools. In my latest piece, the *Lehrstück vom Ja-Sager*, a didactic opera, I intend to continue along this path.

Dr. Fischer: Then how has your latest work, the *Lehrstück vom Ja-Sager*, been constructed formally? Does it contain closed forms?

Kurt Weill: It is good that you mentioned that. In the *Lehrstück vom Ja-Sager* I propose to present closed musical forms rather than any more definite songs. Thereby, I want to include everything that I have recognized to be right until now; for example, what I once termed the *gestus* in music.[7] The *gestus* should already be expressed unequivocally through melody. Clarity, not unintelligibility, should govern what the composer proposes to express. And, as stated, this didactic piece should be a fully valid work of art, not a minor piece.

Dr. Fischer: I must once again mention *Die Dreigroschenoper*. There it is rhythm that makes such a strong impression on the students. The musical experience of the young is essentially based on the motor-rhythmic element [*Motorischen*].

Kurt Weill: I certainly do not renounce rhythmic effects in the new didactic opera, but they are no longer avowed dance rhythms; rather these rhythms are transformed and "digested."

Dr Fischer: You emphasize that you will write a didactic opera that should be taken absolutely seriously. But it was precisely the parodistic element that achieved great success with the young. I would like to discuss still further the parodistic expression. I do not mean parody in the sense of a joke, but as a mixture of seriousness and jest.

Kurt Weill: Perhaps we might say that it is a serious-ironic style. Because the irony in *Die Dreigroschenoper* is meant seriously too, it is incorrect for most people to have interpreted *Die Dreigroschenoper* only parodistically as fun. Modern composers are not at all as parodistically focused as the public and critics would tend to believe. For us, *Die Dreigroschenoper* is serious in subject matter and music. Children have the correct understanding of this also. They believe in seriousness during play. It might be that not all the texts of *Die Dreigroschenoper* are suitable for children.

Dr. Fischer: But children do not really perceive that. Even if they did know something about that, it means nothing to them.

Kurt Weill: Yes, that is true and marvelous. But if one said that, no one would believe it. One could certainly go much further in the subject of a student play, but at the moment this is probably impossible to carry out.

Dr. Fischer: What is the text of your new didactic opera?

Kurt Weill: I have deliberately chosen a serious subject as the text of the first didactic opera. (A comedy will follow as the second.) We came upon the text of the *Lehrstück vom Ja-Sager* in an old Japanese fable, "The Valley-Hurling."[8] The main character is a boy. That already gave me the idea to have this play performed by students also. Briefly, the content is: the boy wishes to go with the teacher on a journey to the city in order to get medicine for his sick mother. The trip is dangerous; therefore, the mother does not want the boy to go. The teacher also advises against it. The boy goes, however, in order to help his mother. On the way, when they come to the most dangerous place, the boy becomes tired, thereby endangering the whole traveling party. The decision is put to him: should they turn back or should they follow the old custom, which dictates that the sick be thrown into the valley? The boy decides to be hurled into the valley. "He has said Yes," sings the chorus. Brecht has given some of the text a motivation different from that of the original Japanese play. Above all, we thought that students should also learn something from a didactic play. Therefore, we have introduced the concept of acquiescence [*Einverständnis*], namely: "It is important to learn acquiescence." That is what students should learn. They should know that a community which one joins demands that one actually bear the consequences. The boy goes the way of the community to the end when he says yes to being tossed into the valley.

Dr. Fischer: I like the text very much from its pedagogical aspects too. The allegiance demanded of students must be repeatedly emphasized. In the text this is accomplished very effectively. The portrayal of the relationship between student and teacher seems to me just as valuable pedagogically. A third beautiful motif in the text is the characterization of the love of the son for his mother.

Kurt Weill: By the way, the motivation that the boy wishes to get medicine for his sick mother in order to save her life was first introduced into the play by Brecht. I am especially glad that you have just now also stressed the importance of allegiance. Through this development of "agreement" the didactic play works in a higher sense politically, but obviously not factionally.

Dr. Fischer: How do you visualize the scenic construction?

Kurt Weill: Simple. It can be played in the school auditorium. The stage is in front on the podium. The chorus sits on or in front of the podium. A circle is drawn in the middle of the podium; in the middle of the circle is a door (The Mother's Room). In the second act, the door is removed; to represent the mountain, a platform with a staircase is placed over to one side of the circle. Simplicity, you see, is the principle of this didactic opera in the musical part too. The orchestral and vocal parts are performed by students. For the make-up of the orchestra I envision violins (*no* violas!), cellos, two pianos, plucked instruments (lute, mandolin), and contrabass *ad libitum.* In addition, winds (flutes, saxophones), perhaps trumpets too. Of course, all wind parts can also be performed by the harmonium. Do you consider such an instrumentation feasible?

Dr. Fischer: It is feasible. There are saxophone players and flutists in many schools; many schools even have their own wind ensembles. But clarinetists and oboe players are more difficult to find. It is good that you decided to do without them. But it seems more important to me that freedom of instrumentation be observed. Performance practice must be changed according to local conditions. As it was earlier in school music, so it must be again. For example, there are many students who play contrabass in southern Germany; in northern Germany they are the exception. Moreover, it will increase the teacher's appreciation for the play if one gives him a choice of performing forces. How did you arrange the vocal parts?

Kurt Weill: All occurring vocal parts must be sung by students. I think the boy should be sung by a 10-12 year-old, the teacher by a 16-18 year-old, the mother by a 14-16 year-old girl. Similarly, the three Students who participate in the journey should be sung by students. And finally the entire school chorus should also participate. Carrying the melody is simple. The vocal parts are supported by the accompaniment in all exposed passages. (Kurt Weill plays the first act of his didactic opera.)

Dr. Fischer: Having just listened to the excerpts from the first act of your didactic opera, I am convinced that the music is simple and indeed can be performed by students. Didactic music, which awaits a truly performable work of New Music, will gladly assimilate didactic opera as a splendid new form of didactic music. Perhaps we will soon again experience a rise of didactic opera, which had a rich golden age in the sixteenth and seventeenth centuries in the Latin schools of Germany. The first performance of the *Lehrstück vom Ja-Sager* in Berlin in June of this year will make it clear whether this is the correct path. I hope that school musicians and creators can work together on the improvement of didactic music more than they have in the past. Perhaps our dialogue can have a clarifying effect in this direction.

NOTES

1. *Der Jasager* was first published at the end of this article, pp. 53-58. It was entitled "Lehrstück vom Jasager: Schuloper von Kurt Weill nach einem japanischen Märchen von Bert Brecht."

2. Weill and Brecht withdrew *Der Jasager* from the "Neue Musik Berlin 1930" festival because of the rejection of Brecht's and Eisler's *Die Massnahme. Schuloper* is best translated as 'didactic opera' because Weill considered 'school opera' only one of the functions of *Schuloper*. [See his essay, "About My Didactic Opera *Der Jasager*."]

3. If, indeed, Weill's didactic cantata was intended for schools, students were to be the audience, not the performers.

4. A year later, *Die Dreigroschenoper* was transformed into a "sound-film" by the Nero-Film Gesellschaft.

5. Note the contrast of Weill's present evaluation of the radio medium with that revealed in previous essays. Yet when *Der Jasager* was premiered by the students of the Staatliche Akademie für Kirchen- und Schulmusik, it was in a radio broadcast, with a public performance the following day.

6. *Die Zaubernacht* premiered at the Theater am Kurfürstendamm in Berlin on 18 November 1922. *Quodlibet: Eine Unterhaltungsmusik*, then entitled "Orchestersuite aus dem Pantomime *Zaubernacht*," premiered at Dessau's Friedrichstheater on 15 June 1923 with Weill's former teacher, Albert Bing, conducting.

7. Note that Weill seems to have abandoned the term *Gestus* already at this point, not as Nadar asserts, after the collaboration with Brecht had dissolved. [See Nadar, p. 101.]

8. "The Valley-Hurling" [*Taniko* by Zenchiku (1405-1468)] was one of four classical Japanese Noh-plays adapted into English by Arthur Waley. Elisabeth Hauptmann translated Waley's adaptation into German. Both of these documents are included in Peter Szondi, ed., *Bertolt Brechts Der Jasager and Der Neinsager: Vorlagen, Fassungen, Materialen* (Frankfurt am Main: Suhrkamp Verlag, 1966).

"Musikfest oder Musikstudio?" *Melos* 9 (May-June 1930):230-32. Reprinted in *Ausgewählte Schriften*, pp. 191-94.

MUSIC FESTIVAL OR MUSIC STUDIO?

Differences have arisen between the leadership of "Neue Musik Berlin 1930" on the one hand and the composers Weill and Eisler, as well as the poet Brecht, on the other. Through an exchange of letters that have been published in several places, these differences have found public reverberation. The pieces by Weill and Eisler, originally planned for the week, are produced in a special context. We have invited Kurt Weill to make a fundamental formulation of his standpoint for us. [The Editor.][1]

As is well known, difficulties no one had anticipated concerning compilation of the program for "Neue Musik 1930" have set in recently. Although in this case they primarily concern only a specific work, the difficulties have gained fundamental significance in their consequences. From the events which have taken place, I have the impression that it is a question of a distinct secessionist movement, based not only on the contested organization of "Neue Musik 1930," but also in a general movement in the most diverse areas of modern art.

The attempts at stabilization undertaken in artistic production today (just as in the most diverse areas of public life) involve a grave danger: the danger of superficiality. It is not possible to stabilize art on the basis of given actualities. It is not possible to create "*Gebrauchskunst*," whereby one merely hones the expressive means for use at broader levels. Especially in an art designed for use, the concept of quality must again be emphasized more strongly, since otherwise the danger of confusion with that utilitarian art always present as "daily merchandise" emerges again and again. But quality in art is not purely an aesthetic question. Great art of all eras achieved quality in that it relied on great far-reaching ideas of its time. What stands behind a work of art determines its qualities; for the shaping of a work of art receives its value insofar as the means of expression are constantly measured against the magnitude, purity, and power of the idea. A work of art that consciously renounces any intellectual background or whose backgrounds are reactionary remains reactionary even if its means of expression are loosened or technically expanded. Progress announces itself only at the point where technical innovations give shape to those ideas which only then make the technical innovations appear for valid reasons.

This realization gains increased significance with those organizations called into existence expressly for the purpose of demonstrating and promoting progress in musical areas. In the years after the war, when new music was fulfilling its purely aesthetic process of liberation, modern music festivals were a necessity. New talents to whom the public music industry was still closed could succeed there; new forms were tried and outmoded forms were tested for their suitability to our time. Today much of this has changed. There is a whole series of public concert and theatrical institutions which give preference to mounting new productions. The radio alone has such a demand for music that composers of all tendencies can make themselves heard there effortlessly. In addition, there are the great music festivals of societies (A.D.M.V., I.G.N.M.) established expressly for the promotion of younger talents.[2] In any event, an additional place could still be imagined where new types of music, generated today through the activation of the listener and the opening of new consumer strata, are tried out. Such an organization could fulfill functions of two kinds: it could assume the role of an exhibition, in which consumers orient themselves toward the utility of the product intended for them; but then one would have to be in the position to take into account all classes of consumers without exception. Or genuine experiments in which a new technique is employed as a means of expression for new content could be exhibited; then no limitation should be imposed from the standpoint of either technique or content.

The prerequisite condition of any artistic institution is *complete independence.* The government cannot finance an experimental music festival; for among the subjects we can treat is politics, which intervenes daily in our lives—and the government can have no interest in financing the formation of an artistic course in which either political or economic relationships are discussed. Likewise, tomorrow some city government that would certainly not be offended by political pieces might come forward as financier but in return would forbid the "Lehrstück von der Korruption," for example.

Above all, it is questionable whether a qualitative utilitarian art, as we intend it, can experiment within the scope of a music festival, which cannot be staged without strong financial and technical resources. In many cases it will be possible to introduce the works written for a definite use directly to their consumers without the detour involved in a public exhibition. But in addition, we must attempt to organize a place of experimentation, linked neither to a financier nor to particular dates, but which presents something only when something worth presenting exists. Such experimental presentations would be purely studio events intended principally for the internal use of musicians, interested parties, and consumers. Therefore, any external advertisements and any pretenses could be avoided. It need not be difficult for these "interested party performances" to take up alliance with the studio division of a progressively-oriented private theater that would place its auditorium and its studio organization at their disposal. So far as one requires technical resources, one would have to turn directly to the industry that had the strongest interest in new possibilities for using the apparatus. Perhaps in this way a music studio can be established as a permanent institution giving a loosely-allied working group the opportunity to test new genres, in which music is no longer introduced as mere enjoyment, but as an active application. In the choice of experiments, those works whose technical innovations are sufficiently based on content must be favored. The most essential advantage of such a music studio, as opposed to a music festival, would be that one limits oneself in external means instead of subjecting oneself to a dependence which, from the outset, precludes a whole series of very important experiments.

NOTES

1. The festival committee included Paul Hindemith, Heinrich Burkhard, and Georg Schünemann; they rejected the preliminary sketch of *Die Massnahme*, which Brecht and Eisler had submitted under the title "Der Jasager," on the basis of its "artistic mediocrity." The open letters appeared in various newspapers and journals during May 1930. Eventually Brecht and Eisler withdrew *Die Massnahme* (premiered on 10 December 1930 in Berlin by the Greater Berlin Workers' Chorus), and Weill withdrew *Der Jasager* in protest.

2. "A. D. M. V." is an abbreviation for the Allgemeiner deutscher Musikverein, founded by Franz Liszt and Franz Brendel in 1861. Each year until 1932, it sponsored a *Tonkünstlerfest* in a different city in Germany. Alexander von Zemlinsky conducted Weill's *Quodlibet* at the Krefelder *Tonkünstlerfest* in July 1927. The "I. G. N. M." or International Society for Contemporary Music was founded in 1921 with Edward J. Dent as its first president. Annual festivals (often more than one) were held in various European cities; the society is still very much in existence.

"Ueber meine Schuloper *Der Jasager*," *Die Scene* 20 (August 1930):232-33. Reprinted in *Ausgewählte Schriften*, pp. 61-63.

ABOUT MY DIDACTIC OPERA *DER JASAGER*

The intention to write a didactic opera [*Schuloper*] occurred to me about a year ago.   From the beginning the word "Schuloper" encompassed for me several possibilities of combining the concept of "training" ["*Schulung*"] with the concept of "opera."   First of all, an opera can be training for composers or for a generation of composers. At precisely this time, when it is a matter of positing new foundations for the genre of "opera" and of redefining the boundaries of this genre, an important task is to create prototypes of this genre, in which the formal and thematic problems of a primarily musical form of theater are examined afresh on the basis of new hypotheses.   In this sense, one could also label Busoni's *Arlecchino*, Hindemith's *Hin und Züruck*, Milhaud's *Le pauvre matelot* and *Die Dreigroschenoper* as didactic operas, for each of these works seeks to establish a prototype of opera.

An opera can also be training for operatic production.   When we succeed in fashioning the entire musical design of a stage work so simply and naturally that we can designate children as the ideal interpreters of these works, then such a work would also be suitable to force opera singers (or those who wish to become opera singers) to achieve that simplicity and naturalness in singing and in presentation that we still so often miss in opera houses.   In this sense, the didactic opera can serve somewhat like an "etude" for operatic training and undertakings (to be performed once daily before the start of rehearsal).

The third interpretation of the word "Schuloper" is one that contains the first two: opera that is intended for use in schools.   It is to be classified among the attempts to create a musical production in which music is not an end in itself, but serves those institutions that need music and for which a new musical production represents something of value. Now principally two new market outlets have emerged next to the old (concert, theater, radio):   the workers' choral movement and the schools. Therein, a rewarding task exists for us: to create for these new areas works of greater scope, which are nonetheless restricted in the external means to such a degree that the possibility of performance in the intended places is not hindered.   Therefore, I have arranged *Der Jasager* in such a way that it can be performed by students in all parts (chorus, orchestra, and soloists), and I can even envision students designing the scenery and costumes for this play.   The score has been arranged appropriately for the instrumentational possibilities of a student orchestra: a basic orchestra of strings (without violas) and two pianos, with three woodwinds (flute, clarinet, saxophone), percussion, and plucked instruments added *ad libitum*. But I do not believe that one should reduce the level of difficulty of the music for a didactic opera too far or that one should write particularly "child-like," easily singable [*nachsingbare*] music for this purpose.[1]

The music of a didactic opera must absolutely be calculated for careful, even lengthy study. For *the practical value of didactic opera consists precisely in the study*, and as far as the performers are concerned, the performance of such a work is far less important than the training that is linked to it. At first this training is purely musical, but it should be at least as much intellectual. For the pedagogical effect of the music can arise in the course of intensive musical study because the student in the process of study occupies himself with a specific idea, which presents itself to him more plastically through the music and which establishes itself in him more strongly than if he had to learn it from a book. *It is absolutely worth every effort, therefore, to see that a didactic piece offers the students the opportunity of learning something in addition to the joy of making music.*

While the old Japanese play that we (Brecht and I) selected as the textual basis for the first didactic opera seemed to us suitable in its basic character for immediate use in schools, the events still lacked that foundation which allows a pedagogical utilization to appear justified. Therefore, we added the concept of "acquiescence" [*Einverständnis*] and changed the play accordingly: now the boy is no longer (as in the old play) involuntarily thrown into the valley. Rather, he is questioned beforehand and proves through the declaration of his "acquiescence" that he has learned to take upon himself all the consequences for the sake of a community or for an idea to which he had attached himself.

NOTES

1. The term "*nachsingbare*" is derived from "*nachsingen*," which literally means to sing the melody after someone else has sung it once.

"Situation der Oper. Gespräch mit Kurt Weill," *Melos* 10 (February 1931):43-45. Reprinted in *Ausgewählte Schriften*, pp. 73-76.

THE SITUATION OF OPERA: A CONVERSATION WITH KURT WEILL BY HEINRICH STROBEL

Question: What is characteristic of the operatic situation this season?

Weill: Characteristic for the present situation of musical theater is the remarkably sharp decline of all pieces that come to terms with the formal and thematic problems of opera in any new or unobscured manner.[1] If one considers the repertoire of large opera houses and provincial theaters, if one speaks with the leaders of large theaters or other leading personalities of musical life, one observes how strong the attempts are everywhere to stamp the operatic theater as a museum-like undertaking. As always in such cases, a theoretical rationalization is quickly enlisted for this movement. Although the movement originates purely from a consideration of specific external circumstances, the attempt aims to present it as an inner necessity, as an inevitable consequence of a process. The concept of opera is supposed to become so unilaterally stabilized, in the museum-like sense, that every productive discussion, every attempt at undoing this concept is denied from the start or is labeled as belonging to another category.

Question: How do you explain the decline of modern works in the repertoire of this season?

Weill: The decline of modern operas is first to be classified in the general cultural reaction. Like all manifestations of this movement, it is above all a consequence of the senseless anxiety-psychosis of those in authority, whose duty it is to guide production for consumers.[2]

My experience with *Mahagonny* has proven the accuracy of this assertion from both the positive and negative sides. The Frankfurt city officials did not permit themselves to be shoved into a corner by a horde of illiterates (led by a long-pursued railroad thief apprehended on this occasion) who demonstrated against the epic opera. Since the second performance, which was disrupted, ten additional performances have taken place without disturbance. However, other theaters tried to hide their anxiety behind all kinds of excuses. They voluntarily submitted to a censorship which in reality does not yet exist and which, if it should really come, will be attributable primarily to this anxiety in a time of transition like the present.[3]

Question: Do you believe that the decline of modern operas with respect to the repertoire can be attributed to a reduction in their composition?

Weill: No; first, I am convinced that there exist a number of pieces which would be enough to supply a consciously goal-oriented theater with the necessary modern works for two years. And it might be added that artistic production also follows the law of supply and demand.

Question: Isn't the artistic situation perhaps related to the economic situation of theaters?

Weill: It can be proven numerically that successes can also be achieved with new operas guaranteed the same number of performances in a season as most revivals [*Neueinstudierung*] of older works, as far as these are not decided public box-office successes. Moreover, modern opera (like modern theater in general) demands with respect to its overall theatrical format a much smaller expenditure for costumes, etc. than, for example, a revival of works in the genre of "splendor-and-show operas."

I also cannot imagine that the royalty question should play a role in the decline of modern works in the repertoire of opera houses. Nevertheless, that is the impression. One hears that the large German operatic theaters receive instructions from their boards of directors to limit themselves to royalty-free works as much as possible. Also, the well-known move of the theatrical union, which aims for a reduction of the author's share, can be mentioned in this connection. But as I have learned from a statistic, the totals that are paid to the authors constitute perhaps 2% of the total budget of a theater. It is hardly possible that the economic crisis of German theater depends upon this 2%, which is solely and uniquely the financial basis for the valuable further development of operatic composition.[4]

One cannot quite make production accountable for the fact that the German operatic theater today has arrived at a state of reorganization and new organization and that this regrouping is not being accomplished without struggle. The consolidation of several operatic theaters that lie near one another geographically, which, as the Rhineland shows, becomes ever more palpable, is also worthwhile for composers. At first glance such an adjustment of performance figures for new works appears to be a detrimental influence. However, through consolidation of scattered forces into a central place, an improved standard of performance certainly would be achieved, which definitely also benefits the effect of modern productions. And this is even more beneficial because, in the case of a success, the performances in cities that lie in geographical proximity are no longer hindered by the competitive jealousy of various theatrical producers.

Question: Since the economic difficulties do not appear insurmountable to you, what do you perceive as the basis for the present restraints?

Weill: Modern opera is evolving into its own particular type. The previous phases of this evolution have developed certain stylistic elements that alone do not yet determine the concept of new opera but rather signify only a part of a complete development. Such stylistic elements are: epic unfolding of events, renunciation of the illustrative force of music, removal of illusion from the scene, elimination of false pathos, dramatic utilization of absolute musical form, etc. It is characteristic of the present confused situation that these elements of a new theatrical style are selected and then employed either already debased in themselves or misleadingly mixed with other traditional stylistic forms. Especially dangerous are those attempts that one can label as modernistic, where certain stylistic elements of modern theater are merely used to dress up productions of classical opera as new. There are those who preach a resolution toward the theatrical side and thereby accomplish no more than those older operatic directors who, out of antipathy against the music, destroyed musical form through a directorial point or an excess of "directorial ideas." Others attempt to employ the form of statuesque theater for older works, whose dramatic impulse they kill in this manner. But these endeavors are only evasions. Some believe they comply with the practice of modern theater if they employ its formal elements in works whose production in other respects is not connected with risks of any sort. But it must be stated that these elements of modern theater can be convincingly realized in their totality only in works of new theater.

Question: Therefore, how do you estimate the prospects of opera?

Weill: To begin with, I assert that there is still public interest in opera, because it offers more precise execution than a play and because at least a portion of the audience has an expert understanding of musical and vocal accomplishment. I have always argued that opera must keep pace with contemporary theater. That was difficult when modern theater aimed at a true-to-life presentation of topical events. For this form of actualized theater offered opera only slim chances.   Today, when a grand form of theater is once again emerging, a form which seeks with elevated language and in heightened reality to incorporate ideas of the present with timeless ones, opera must then also find its sociological sphere. What is more, it can be assumed that this form of theater can by no means do without the gestic effect and stylizing power of music. Of course, that requires music which does not intoxicate the listener, but rather motivates him to reflect consciously—music, therefore, which is itself self-consciously reflective and which, with utilization of the formal powers of music, determines for itself the dramaturgy of the work in order to renounce its absolute effect.

NOTES

1. The number of productions of new operas in German theaters declined from a peak of sixty during the 1927-28 season to only sixteen during the 1931-32 season.

2. In an essay that was published in the United States a year after Weill's had been written, Hans Heinsheimer described the situation to which Weill referred: "An alarming development is the growing fear inspired by the political parties on whom theatres depend for the means of their existence. Outstanding is the terror spread by the Hitlerites, which has already penetrated deep into the theatre. Recently one of our most prominent theatre directors was forced out of his position because he did not follow the popular spirit strongly enough to suit the National Socialist minister who ruled Braunschweig. The grotesque threat of the Hitlerites to every modern theatre art and every modern production can be deduced from these first definite occurrences in Braunschweig and also in Weimar. In the writings and newspaper articles they reveal a program that far outdistances present evils. We can hope that these insane demands and ideas will remain mere theories." ["German Music on the Breadline," *Modern Music* 9 (March-April 1932):118.] .

3. Weill's *Aufstieg* was produced in October 1930 as the concluding event of the fiftieth anniversary jubilee of the Frankfurt Opera. Hundreds of Nazi agitators disrupted the second performance when they forced their way into the theater. The city council voted to allow the performances to continue, however. Managers of other theaters tried to avoid such confrontations and cancelled plans to produce *Aufstieg*. No Berlin opera house would risk a production of the work.

4. Again Heinsheimer discussed the fiscal crisis that Weill mentions: "After the war . . . municipal and state theatres were not expected to make a profit. It was not their aim to show a balance at the end of the year, to operate on a successful commercial basis. They were completely subsidized activities, like museums, hospitals or other public enterprises, and this situation determined their efforts. . . . Then the subsidies for the theatres were curtailed, slowly in the beginning, then more and more rapidly with the new economic policies that the German governments and cities were forced to adopt about 1929 when the industrial crisis began. The first emergency decree came in December 1930; for the first time the current payrolls were affected by law, salaries of all employees of the public

theatres being reduced six percent. But by the summer of 1931 this slight cut had been far outdistanced and subsidies were mercilessly restricted. Generally speaking they were allowed half the salaries that had been paid two years before." ["German Music on the Breadline," pp. 115-16.]

"Vom Wesen der Musikzeitschrift—Diskussion über *Melos*," *Melos* 11
(January 1932):2-3. Reprinted in *Melos: Zeitschrift für neue Musik* 17
(May 1950):132-33 and in *Ausgewählte Schriften*, pp. 190-91.

THE PATHS OF MUSIC JOURNALISM—DISCUSSION ABOUT *MELOS*

In my opinion, there are only two possibilities nowadays for defining the domain of a music journal so that it does not take a position on all questions of music and musical life in a general way, but rather confines itself to a previously ascertained and always recognizable sphere of purpose and assists the breakthrough of a useful and advantageous form of musical consideration.

One possibility is to create a periodical for the specialist. Here, taking the available musicological materials as a base, inquiries would be undertaken as to what relationships exist between the stylistic forms of music of one epoch and the social-economic conditions of the same period. People would no longer investigate how music and musical practice appeared in different eras but why they did so. While until now musical views based on the "experience" of music frequently attempted to explain retrospectively the musical laws which permitted this experience to occur, people should now examine whether the experiential capacity of music is not merely the demand of an era which wants even music to provide the individual with an experience that it denies to others. An application of this point of view to our era would yield that aesthetic value and functional value are equivalent concepts of musical inquiry and that a value judgment concerning today's music is possible only if one recognizes as equally existent the completely different levels on which music is made today.

The other possibility, a musical journal for a larger public, is conceivable for me only in the form of a purely polemical tool. Here at once the question emerges: how is it possible to build a front in a time of general disorder, in this confusion of views, catchwords, and cliques? A few years ago it still sufficed to issue the "Struggle for the New" as a password. In the subsequent time of transition to the present situation, one could push the struggle for quality into the foreground. Today other decisions are required. I believe that the great struggle that is now occurring is concentrated on a certain point in each of the areas of politics, economics, science and art: that in every one of these sectors a stronghold is to be defended or reconquered, which some, in resignation, have considered lost already. In music the immediate task is to continue the struggle against those forms of expression of the nineteenth century which we already considered to have been overcome: verbosity, deluge, unnaturalness, and false pathos. Perhaps here, too, a provisional "united front" might be constructed, which possibly develops from the struggle against the common enemy into a struggle for a common goal.

"Kurt Weill antwortet," *Melos* 11 (October 1932):336-37.   Reprinted in *Ausgewählte Schriften*, pp. 70-71.

KURT WEILL RESPONDS

Dear Professor Mersmann:

In the last volume of *Melos* you published a series of questions directed to me concerning *Die Bürgschaft*.[1] I have attempted to answer these questions. But that is hardly possible because these questions represent only a different form of *subjective criticism*. When the views that form the basis and obvious hypothesis of an art work are questioned or denied from the standpoint of subjective criticism, then assertion directly confronts assertion.

I assert the proposition that we formulated concerning the conditions which change the conduct of men is correct and that it has been formulated incorrectly by Trantow, since we do not want to show any heroes or supermen here, but rather types of people whose "intellectual perceptions and internal experiences" are less important than their conduct. Obviously there are "conditions" in our make-up which determine our conduct. Perhaps it would help the questioner if he could perceive the "economic conditions," as we mean them, as a concrete image of what the ancients called "fate."

I assert that the ending of *Die Bürgschaft* is tragic as well as "instructive." Although the tragedy lies less in the death of Matthes than in the explanation which Orth gives in his closing words, the "instruction" which the spectators can take home lies in the despair of this realization.

With this we come to the "main point of the indictment":   the accusation of negativity. Here the interrogator evidently forgets that at all times art critical of society endeavored to show things as they are, often to the point of excessive clarity, and to suggest to the spectator the condemnation of what has been shown him only by the means of representation. Art that is critical of society is satisfied to dismiss the spectators with the awareness that existing conditions must be changed, and it seeks to achieve that by showing the state of things in their most crass form and without varnish. This path was also traversed by *Die Bürgschaft*, intended from the very outset as a tragic opera. Naturally it would be nice to fashion something positive and affirmative on the same ideological background, and I would be the first to grab the opportunity if it presented itself.   I consider it very dangerous to seek this opportunity in the area of a "pure humanity," since I believe that it is the task of opera today to forge ahead beyond the private, individual fate to common validity.

Finally, another statement that still seems important to me: *Die Bürgschaft* is not a didactic play but an opera. It was written for the theater. Its purpose is not to demonstrate doctrines, but rather, corresponding to the function of theater, to fashion *human* events against the background of a timeless idea.

And something else: in a time when some occupy themselves with artistic games, while others prefer to produce nothing so as not to give offense to anyone, *Die Bürgschaft* attempts to take a position on things which concern all of us. Of course, such an attempt must bring about discussion; that is part of its function. For a discussion, however, it would be necessary for the opposing viewpoint to be analyzed scrupulously and carefully. The questions you published are at most useful to add still new misconceptions to the existing ones.

With best wishes
Yours,

Kurt Weill

NOTES

1. Weill's letter was written in response to Herbert Trantow's "Fragen an Kurt Weill, seine *Bürgschaft* betreffend," *Melos* 11 (August-September 1932):276-77. *Die Bürgschaft* had been premiered at the Berlin Städtische Oper on 10 March 1932.

"Das Formproblem der modernen Oper," *Der Scheinwerfer* 5 (February 1932):3-6. Reprinted in *Ausgewählte Schriften*, pp. 49-51.

THE PROBLEM OF FORM IN MODERN OPERA

It cannot be denied that people in theatrical circles today are attempting to revise their views concerning the function of theater and, as it turns out, in the same way as they have already done with film. Film producers, who have been forced to the greatest prudence by enormous financial risks, nowadays make no secret whatsoever of their view that film is a business and that art is therefore allowable only insofar as it is capable of benefiting the business or at least of not interfering with the business (which often fails to turn a profit even without art). If we have not yet reached this crass form of industrialization in the theater, it is essentially due to the fact that most theaters work with subsidies from public resources and therefore must still stress the cultural purposes of theater. Nevertheless, today the view is heard remarkably frequently that in such difficult crisis-ridden times the audience looks to the theater merely for an evening's pleasant entertainment, whose most essential effect is to make the spectators forget their "everyday worries." This view is only another veiled form of that timid, fearful attitude which we have been able to observe more and more distinctly in recent theatrical life. People are afraid of clear resolute theatrical politics; they attempt to find a pleasant middle-of-the-road solution, and thereby they assume as self-evident that what has been recognized as being without risk is the same as what the public desires.

On the other hand, the notion that such an underestimation of the audience is not permissible is now beginning to permeate ever larger circles. In all times, even during epochs of general prosperity in which a more carefree view of life could be accomplished, a large sector of the public has sought more in theater than mere entertainment. It is not clear why, in such an agitated time as today, when the interest of individuals for general all-encompassing questions is increased to a maximum, the public should avoid those theatrical evenings which take a position on great questions of the day. Naturally the form of this position plays a decisive role, for the fear of the theatrical administrator is in part a reaction to that misunderstood topicality which sees the function of modern theater as dramatization of semi-important subsidiary problems of daily life. But today we are on the way to a theatrical form that projects the great, enduring contemporary ideas in simple typical events and which thereby leads back again to the original purpose of theater: representation of types of human behavior.[1]

The realization that the great form of theater is more than possible and necessary today gives us the justification to believe also in the future of opera, the most elevated form of theater. In the nineteenth century opera evolved into a form of theater that exerts an intoxicating, exciting effect on the audience. If now we again wish to stimulate the operatic audience to reflect and to think ahead, then here we must succeed in presenting simplified, typical, basic situations even more than in spoken drama. The prevailing phases of development have already evolved a series of new stylistic elements which in part return to the pure operatic forms of earlier times. We can count among these stylistic elements perhaps the renunciation of the illustrative function of music, the elimination of false pathos, the division of action into closed musical numbers, and the dramatic utilization of absolute musical form. To be sure, recent modernistic endeavors in the domain of opera have appeared in which certain elements of this operatic style are selected and then either debased or brought to miscalculated effect through mixture with other contrasting stylistic forms. Especially characteristic are those cases in which the formal and expressive means of a new type of opera are superimposed on operatic works of earlier epochs, for here it becomes evident that new form without new content is not possible. That holds not only for the scenic form of theater but also for the music, for the bearing of the music is part of the fundamental intellectual posture of an epoch.

NOTES

1. The preceding paragraph was reproduced verbatim in Weill's "Wirklich eine Opernkrise?" *Deutsche Allgemeine Zeitung*, 8 July 1932.

"Wirklich eine Opernkrise?" *Deutsche Allgemeine Zeitung*, 8 July 1932. Reprinted in *Ausgewählte Schriften*, 77-78.

ACTUALLY AN OPERATIC CRISIS?

There is a crisis in opera which befalls operatic theaters and naturally also operatic producers correlatively to a considerable degree. The crisis of operatic theater consists of the problem that works which can draw a specialized operatic audience (Wagner, Strauss) demand an extraordinarily large production, but on the other hand this specialized audience is not numerous or lucrative enough to be able to cover the costs of production. Therefore, constant subsidies are necessary, which in today's crisis exceed the resources of the financial backer in most cases. In order to eliminate the economic crisis of opera, it would be necessary to reach a wider public that is not limited to the specialized operatic audience. Here we surely come into the proximity of that crisis which in no way confounds operatic theater alone, but theater in general.

I am not inclined to blame the public for this general theatrical crisis. I believe that in almost all cities there is an audience possessing sufficient interest for worthwhile theatrical productions. *The point is to genuinely interest the public.* Naturally it is easiest—as today numerous theaters in the country do—to attract an audience with *Im Weissen Rössl.* [White Horse Inn][1] I am enough of an optimist to assume that we in Germany today have not yet come to so barbaric a cultural situation that replaces opera—always a significant component of German culture—with the most superficial type of theater.[2]

Rather, I believe that full responsibility for this situation falls on those whose constant pressure nowadays makes German theatrical administrators into timid, overly-cautious businessmen. Naturally in this connection the question emerges whether there exists an operatic output which makes balancing a budget possible for the theater manager with the very highest artistic aspirations. *It is my strong conviction that this output is available*, or at least would be immediately available if it were stimulated by a courageous, determined agreement of theater managers and if numerous managers would not repeatedly submit to an invisible censorship which in reality does not exist.

In all times, even during epochs of general prosperity in which a more carefree view of life could be accomplished, a large sector of the public has sought more in the theater than mere entertainment. It is not clear why, in such an agitated time as today, when the interest of individuals for general all-encompassing questions is increased to a maximum, the public should avoid those theatrical evenings which take a position on great questions of the day. Naturally the form of this position plays a decisive role, for the fear of the theatrical administrator is in part a reaction to *that misunderstood topicality which sees the function of modern theater as the dramatization of semi-important subsidiary problems of daily life.* But today we are on the way to a theatrical form that projects great, enduring contemporary ideas in simple typical events and which thereby leads back again to the original purpose of theater: representation of types of human behavior.

Obviously theater managers can justly demand that operatic production abandon its excessively stressed art-for-art's-sake standpoint and in the choice of its themes, as well as in form and musical language, reach an artistic form that concerns everyone and is suitable to generate broader interest. Also opera can no longer bring to the stage any old private love-affairs, paroxysms from the time of the Renaissance, or family conflicts. Our era conceals within itself an abundance of great ideas and human or generally valid subjects. If one resolves to free opera from the sphere of naturalistic theater and to see in it that heightened form of theater best suited to translate great ideas of the time into a timeless humanistic form, then a new belief in the future of opera is produced quite by itself.

NOTES

1. *Im Weissen Rössl*, composed by Ralph Benatzky (1884-1957) with additional songs by Robert Stolz (1880-1975), received its premiere in Berlin on 8 November 1930 at the Grosse Schauspielhaus. A *"Singspiel"* in three acts with a libretto by Hans Müller, *Im Weissen Rössl* was evocatively set in 1914 with a background of the Wolfgangsee and the Bavarian Alps. It achieved a colossal popular success although its intellectual appeal was negligible.

2. Heinsheimer was not as confident as Weill: "Formerly an occasional operetta was smuggled into the programs of the subsidized theaters but not without the shame-faced feeling that accompanies an unworthy action. Now, after the short lapse of two years, the most important theatres of the Reich, like those of Leipzig, Köln, and Frankfurt, have plunged into the field of modern operetta. These stages are gradually yielding to the performance of modern revues. Anything to attract the public. A revue like the farce *Im Weissen Rössl* is the hit of the winter. *Im Weissen Rössl* appears four and five times a week in repertory at the most important theatres which two years ago would scornfully have laughed down the suggestion that such a work enter their precincts so rich in the tradition of art. . . . It means the crass triumph of commercial principles in our theaters and is a fundamental change of the greatest significance." ["German Music on the Breadline," pp. 117-18.]

APPENDIX II-A

INDEX TO WEILL'S SIGNED ARTICLES IN *DER DEUTSCHE RUNDFUNK*

Vol.	No.	Date	Pages	Comments on Content[1]
III	15	12 April 1925	933-36	Offenbach: *Orpheus in der Unterwelt*
	16	19 April 1925	1003-6	*Don Giovanni*
	17	26 April 1925	1066-70	Haydn: *The Creation*; Lortzing
	18	30 April 1925	1131-34	*Fidelio*
	19	10 May 1925	1193-96	*Der Freischütz*
	20	17 May 1925	1259-62	*Der fliegende Holländer*
	21	24 May 1925	1321-25	*Die Novembergruppe*
	22	31 May 1925	1385-89	*Rigoletto*
	23	7 June 1925	1450-53	
	24	14 June 1925	1515-18	
	25	21 June 1925	1573-76	
	26	28 June 1925	1625-28	Möglichkeiten absoluter Radiokunst
			1631-34	

The issues dating from July through December 1925 are missing from the set of *Der deutsche Rundfunk* in the New York Public Library, which holds the only copies of the journal that are known in the United States.

IV	1	3 January 1926	7-10	Halevy: *Die Jüdin*
	2	10 January 1926	81-85	Unsigned
	3	17 January 1926	151-54	Szenisches im Berliner Sender
	4	24 January 1926	224-27	Second essay unsigned
	5	31 January 1926	297-300	Eine neue Lösung des Sendespiel-problems
	6	7 February 1926	369-70	Hans Pfitzner als Sendespiel-dirigent
	7	14 February 1926	439-441	Berliner Opernabende
	8	21 February 1926	511-14	
	9	28 February 1926	581-84	Schoenberg
	10	7 March 1926	662-65	Kaiser: *Von Morgens bis Mitternachts*
	11	14 March 1926	732-35	Tanzmusik; Bartók: String Quartet no. 1
	12	21 March 1926	803-6	
	13	28 March 1926	872, 875-78	Ferruccio Busoni
	14	4 April 1926	947-51	von Suppé
	15	11 April 1926	1019-21	
	16	18 April 1926	1093-95	
	17	25 April 1926	1163-65	Max Trapp: Violin Concerto; Siegfried Wagner
	18	30 April 1926	1235-38	
	19	9 May 1926	1307-9	
	20	16 May 1926	1379-82	

21	23 May 1926	1447-50	
22	30 May 1926	1517-18	Weber: Zum 100. Todestage
		1520-22	
23	6 June 1926	1587-89	
24	13 June 1926	1649-50	Der Rundfunk und die Umschichtung
		1655-58	des Musiklebens
25	20 June 1926	1723-27	Mahler: Symphony no. 9
26	27 June 1926	1795-98	Schoenberg; Shakespeare: *Midsummer Night's Dream*
27	4 July 1926		no article; Felix Stiemer substitutes for Weill
28	11 July 1926	1933-35	
29	18 July 1926	2001-2	
30	25 July 1926	2069-70	
31	31 July 1926	2135-38	
32	8 August 1926	2207-10	Shaw
33	15 August 1926	2275-78	
34	22 August 1926	2343-45	Second article unsigned
35	29 August 1926	2417-20	Grabbe: *Herzog Theodor von Gothland*
36	5 September 1926	2489-92	Wedekind
37	12 September 1926	2577-80	Stravinsky: *Soldier's Tale*
38	19 September 1926	2661-64	Wedekind: *König Nicolo* (Rosa Valetti)
39	26 September 1926	2735-39	Hindemith
40	30 September 1926	2807-11	*Die Zauberflöte*
41	10 October 1926	2883-86	Bruckner
42	17 October 1926	2955-58	Lortzing: Zu seinem 125. Geburtstag
43	24 October 1926	3031-34	Kaiser
44	31 October 1926	3103-6	
45	7 November 1926	3179-83	Rilke
46	14 November 1926	3251-55	Walt Whitman; Zur Psychologie der funkischen Programmbildung; Bellini: *Norma*
47	21 November 1926	3326-27	Obituary of Joseph Schwarz
		3329-32	Offenbach: *Die Grossherzogin von Gerolstein*
48	28 November 1926	3403-6	Loewe
49	5 December 1926	3479-83	*Carmen*
50	12 December 1926	3559-62	
51	19 December 1926	3639-43	
52	26 December 1926	3723-26	

(From this point on, Weill was writing three articles.)

V	1	2 January 1927	7-12	
	2	9 January 1927	83-88	
	3	16 January 1927	158-61	Allgemeine Sendesbericht
	4	23 January 1927	227, 229-32	*Otello*
	5	30 January 1927	301-4	Honegger: *Pacific 231*

6	6 February 1927	365, 372 374-77	Ueber die Möglichkeiten einer Rundfunkversuchsstelle
7	13 February 1927	443, 445-48	Büchner: *Danton's Tod*
8	20 February 1927	515-20	
9	27 February 1927	587-93	
10	6 March 1927	660, 662-64	Puccini: *Turandot*
11	13 March 1927	734-36	Schreker; Brecht: *Mann ist Mann*
12	20 March 1927	797 804, 806-9	Beethoven in unserer Zeit— unsigned
13	27 March 1927	876, 878-80	Busoni; Brecht: *Mann ist Mann*
14	3 April 1927	948, 950-53	Schoenberg
15	10 April 1927	1022-24	
16	17 April 1927	1083-84 1087-92	Die Berliner "Ring"-Aufführungen Schoenberg: *Pelleas und Melisande*
17	24 April 1927	1159-64	Vom Strindberg zu Bronnen
18	1 May 1927	1229-32	Frauentanz; Frenkel
19	8 May 1927	1300-5	
20	15 May 1927	1373-75	
21	22 May 1927	1442-44	Stravinsky
22	29 May 1927	1510-12	Reger: String Quartet, op. 109
23	5 June 1927	1578-81	Moderne Opern und Dramen im Berliner Sender
24	12 June 1927	1644 1646-49	*Geschichten vom braven Soldaten Schwejk; Bettelstudent*
25	19 June 1927	1714-17	
26	26 June 1927	1782-85	*The Barber of Seville*; Schreker: *Der Schatzgräber*
27	3 July 1927	1850-53	
28	10 July 1927	1916, 1918-20	
29	17 July 1927	1986-88	
30	24 July 1927	no essays	
31	31 July 1927	2121-25	
32	7 August 1927	2191-94	
33	14 August 1927	2253	Die Salzburger Festspiele
34	21 August 1927	no essays	
35	28 August 1927	no essays	
36	4 September 1927	no essays	Ascoltante's essays appear for the first time
37	11 September 1927	no essays	
38	18 September 1927	2616-17	Rhythmus Amerika
39	25 September 1927	2687-88	Weill writes only "Die Sender"
40	30 September 1927	2755-57	
41	7 October 1927	no essays	
42	14 October 1927	2885-90	Heinrich von Kleist; *Jonny spielt auf*
43	21 October 1927	2963-65	Boxing match on radio
44	28 October 1927	3028-29 3031-32	Busonis Faust-Oper
45	4 November 1927	3099-101	Dvořák, Tschaikowsky, Macdowell
46	11 November 1927	3167-68	Schoenberg: *Pierrot Lunaire*
47	18 November 1927	, 3236-37	
48	25 November 1927	3303-4	

	49	2 December 1927	3371-72	Moderne Oper in Berlin
	50	9 December 1927	3439-40	
	51	16 December 1927	3511-12	
	52	23 December 1927	3583-84	Unsigned
VI	1	30 December 1927	7-8	
	2	6 January 1928	75-76	
	3	13 January 1928	143-44	
	4	20 January 1928	211-12	
	5	27 January 1928	279-80	Paul Whiteman
	6	3 February 1928	347-49	
	7	10 February 1928	415-16	
	8	17 February 1928	483-84	
	9	24 February 1928	551-52	Mahler
	10	2 March 1928	619-20	
	11	9 March 1928	691-92	
	12	16 March 1928	759-60	Ibsen
	13	23 March 1928	827-28	Gorki
	14	30 March 1928	896-97	
	15	5 April 1928	963-64	Feuchtwanger
	16	13 April 1928	1031-32	
	17	20 April 1928	1099-101	Eduard Steuermann
	18	27 April 1928	1166-68	
	19	4 May 1928	1236-38	Scherchen
	20	11 May 1928	1304-6	
	21	18 May 1928	no entry	
	22	25 May 1928	no entry	(Brecht & Weill on French Riviera
	23	1 June 1928	no entry	working on *Die Dreigroschenoper*)
	24	8 June 1928	no entry	
	25	15 June 1928	1643-44	
	26	22 June 1928	no entry	
	27	29 June 1928	1779-81	
	28	6 July 1928	1848-50, 1852	*Rhapsody in Blue*
	29	13 July 1928	1916-18, 1920	Baden-Baden
	30	20 July 1928	1985-87, 1989	
	31	27 July 1928	2050-52, 2054	
	32	3 August 1928	2119-21	
	33	10 August 1928	2187-89, 2191	Signed "K. Wll."
	34	17 August 1928	2255-57, 2259	
	35	24 August 1928	2324-25, 2328	Trudi Hesterberg
	36	31 August 1928	2394-95	
	37	7 September 1928	2477-78 2481	Erwin Weill; Reines Unterhaltungs- programm in Berlin; Janáček
	38	14 September 1928	2545-56 2554-56	Was wir von der neuen Berliner Sendesaison erwarten
	39	21 September 1928	2619-21 2624	
	40	28 September 1928	2687-88 2691	
	41	5 October 1928	2755-57 2760, 2767	Kerr und Kisch; Robert Blum

	42	12 October 1928	2824-26, 2828	
	43	29 October 1928	2891-92, 2895	Kommunisten—"Attentat"
	44	26 October 1928	2960-61, 2964	Josephine Baker
	45	2 November 1928	3031-33 3035	Feier zur Wiederkehr des Revolutionstages; Kleist
	46	9 November 1928	3103-5 3107	
	47	16 November 1928	3176-78 3180	Schubert: 100. Todestag; Stravinsky: *Oedipus rex*
	48	23 November 1928	3244, 3247-49 3251	Kaiser
	49	30 November 1928	3319-21, 3323	
	50	7 December 1928	3391-92, 3395	
	51	14 December 1928	3463-64, 3467	
	52	21 December 1928	3535-36, 3539	
	53	28 December 1928	3611-12, 3615	
VII	1	4 January 1929	7-8	*Mann ist Mann*
	2	11 January 1929	39-40, 43	Poulenc, Antheil
	3	18 January 1929	71-72, 75	
	4	25 January 1929	98-99 103-4, 107	Der Rundfunk und die neue Musik
	5	1 February 1929	135-36, 139	Vogel
	6	8 February 1929	167-68	Schumann: Scenes aus Goethes *Faust*
	7	15 February 1929	196 199-200, 204	Zum Theme "Musikalisches Hörspiel"
	8	22 February 1929	231-32, 236	
	9	1 March 1929	263-64, 267-68	Jazz-Klasse
	10	8 March 1929	297-98, 302	
	11	15 March 1929	no entry	
	12	22 March 1929	361-62, 366	
	13	29 March 1929	393-94	
	14	5 April 1929	419-20 425-26, 430	Wo liegt der Fehler? (Hörspielproduktion)
	15	12 April 1929	457-58, 462	
	16	19 April 1929	490-41, 495	Moderne Musik in Berlin
	17	26 April 1929	523-24, 527-28	
	18	3 May 1929	553-54, 557-58	
	19	10 May 1929	586-87 590-91	*Rhapsody in Blue*
	20	17 May 1929	613 618-19, 622-23	Notiz zum *Berliner Requiem* Brecher

NOTES

1. My comments concerning the contents are seldom identical with the title of the article, which was usually a variation of "Sendesbericht" or "Rundschau." Where no contents are specified in the list, no one topic received particular treatment in the essay.

BIBLIOGRAPHY

BIBLIOGRAPHY

The following bibliography of works *about* Kurt Weill and related topics is organized according to this outline:

A list of Weill's musical compositions is *not* included in the following bibliography; publication information concerning these works is found in Appendix I. Weill's literary works are not catalogued here either, since they appear with pertinent bibliographic data in Appendix II. Reviews of the first performances of Weill's compositions (1900-1935) are entered under the respective work in Appendix I. No reviews of performances which occurred after Weill's death have been included in the following bibliography unless the essay involved an extensive discussion of the composition itself.

I. Weill: General

A. Books

Drew, David, ed. *Ueber Kurt Weill.* Frankfurt am Main: Suhrkamp Verlag, 1975.
Kotschenreuther, Hellmut. *Kurt Weill.* Berlin: Max Hesse Verlag, 1962.
Marx, Henry, ed. *Weill-Lenya.* New York: Goethe House, 1976.
Weill, Kurt. *Ausgewählte Schriften.* Edited by David Drew. Frankfurt am Main: Suhrkamp Verlag, 1975.

B. Dissertations

Harden, Susan Clydette. "The Music for the Stage Collaborations of Weill and Brecht." Ph.D. Dissertation [Musicology], University of North Carolina at Chapel Hill, 1972.
Luxner, Michael D. "The Early Instrumental Style of Kurt Weill." Master's Thesis, Eastman School of Music, 1972.
Nadar, Thomas Raymond. "The Music of Kurt Weill, Hans Eisler and Paul Dessau in the Dramatic Works of Bertolt Brecht." Ph.D. Dissertation [Germanic Languages and Literatures], University of Michigan, 1974.
Wagner, Gottfried. "Die musikalische Verfremdung in den Bühnenwerken von Kurt Weill und Bertolt Brecht." Ph.D. Dissertation, University of Vienna, 1977. Published as *Weill und Brecht: Das musikalische Zeittheater* (Munich: Kindler Verlag, 1977).

C. Essays: 1900 - 1935

(The * denotes essays which have been reprinted or partially reprinted in David Drew's *Ueber Kurt Weill.*)

*Bekker, Paul. "An Kurt Weill." *Briefe an zeitgenössische Musiker.* Berlin: Max Hesse Verlag, 1932.
Connor, Herbert. "Kurt Weill und die Zeitoper." *Die Musik* 25 (November 1932):101-4.
Fitelberg, Jerzy. "More Americans and Kurt Weill in Berlin." *Modern Music* 9 (May-June 1932):184-87.
*Fleischer, Herbert. "Kurt Weill: Versuch einer einheitlichen Stilbetrachtung." *Anbruch* 14 (September 1932):135-37.
Jolles, Heinz. "Paraphrase über Kurt Weill." *Neue Musik-Zeitung* 49 (May 1928):541-44.
*Kastner, Rudolf. "Kurt Weill: Eine Skizze." *Anbruch* 7 (October 1925):453-56.

Machabey, A. "Schreker, Kurt Weill, Hindemith." *Le Menestrel* 92 (10 October 1930): 417-19.

_____. "Kurt Weill et le Théatre Musical Allemand Contemporain." *Revue d'Allemagne* 5 (15 April 1931):317-33.

_____. "Kurt Weill et le Drame Lyrique Allemand." *Revue d'Allemagne* 7 (15 July 1933):632-38.

Nataletti, Giorgio. "Kurt Weill." *Musica d'oggi* 16 (January 1934):9-13.

Noth, Ernst-Erich. "Le compositeur Kurt Weill." *Cahiers du sud* 22 (June 1935):451-61.

Prigsheim, Klaus. "Kurt Weill." *Blätter der Staatsoper und der Städtischen Oper* 9 (October 1928):1-4.

Prunières, Henri. "Oeuvres de Kurt Weill." *La Revue musicale* 13 (January 1933):45-47.

*Strobel, Heinrich. "Kurt Weill." *Melos* 6 (October 1927):427-33.

_____. "Kurt Weill." *Anbruch* 10 (February 1928):57-59.

_____. "Situation der Oper: Gespräch mit Kurt Weill." *Melos* 10 (February 1931):43-45.

D. Essays: 1936 - 1977

Curjel, Hans. "Weills Come-Back." *Melos* 26 (September 1959):249-52.

_____. "Erinnerungen um Kurt Weill." *Melos* 37 (March 1970):81-85.

_____. "Kurt Weill: Die Anfänge." *Neue Zeitschrift für Musik* 133 (August 1972): 432-35.

_____. "Kurt Weill: Die grossen Berliner Jahre." *Neue Zeitschrift für Musik* 133 (September 1972):503-7.

_____. "Kurt Weill: Nach 1933." *Neue Zeitschrift für Musik* 133 (October 1972):576-79.

Downes, Olin. "Memorial to Weill." *New York Times*, 9 July 1950.

Drew, David. "Kurt Weill and His Critics." *Times Literary Supplement* 3838 (3 October 1975):1142-44; and 3839 (10 October 1975):1198-1200.

_____. "Gespräch über Kurt Weill." *25. Berliner Festwochen Magazin* (September 1975):11.

Engelmann, Hans Ulrich. "Kurt Weill—heute." *Darmstädter Beiträge zur neuen Musik* 3 (1960):87-95.

Fiechtner, Helmut A. "Die Bühnenwerke von Kurt Weill." *Oesterreichische Musikzeitschr[fi* 16 (May 1961):213-17.

Fleischer, Herbert. "Kurt Weill." *Il Diapason* 1 (April 1950):7-9.

Harrison, Jay S. "Weill and Lenya—Berlin to Broadway." *New York Herald-Tribune*, 27 July 1958.

Hartung, Günter. "Zur epischen Oper Brechts und Weills." *Wissenschaftliche Zeitschrift des Martin-Luther-Universität Halle-Wittenberg, Geschaft-Sprachwissenschaft* 8 (June 1959):659-74.

Heinsheimer, Hans W. *Fanfare for 2 Pigeons*. Garden-City, New York: Doubleday & Co., 1952.

_____. "Kurt Weill: From Berlin to Broadway." *International Musician* (March 1948):17-21.

Heyworth, Peter. "Putting Weill in His Place." *The Observer* (London), 23 January 1972.

_____. "Music-Dramas for the People." *Times Literary Supplement* 3899 (3 December 1976):1523.

*Kemp, Ian. "Harmony in Weill: Some Observations." *Tempo* 104 (1973):11-15.

Kotschenreuther, Hellmut. "Um den ganzen Weill bittend." *25. Berliner Festwochen Magazin* (September 1975):12-13.

Kowalke, Kim H. Review of *Kurt Weill: Ausgewählte Schriften* and *Ueber Kurt Weill*, edited by David Drew. *Notes* 33 (June 1977):832-35.

_____. "Kurt Weill's European Legacy." *High Fidelity* 28 (July 1978):62-69.

_____. Review of three recordings of Weill's music in *Musical Quarterly* 63 (July 1977):441-46.

Lenya, Lotte. "Lotte Lenya in Conversation with Steven Paul." (Interview of 22 October 1975). Insert Notes to *Kurt Weill*, Deutsche Grammophon recording, 2709-064, pp. 8-10.

_____. "That Was a Time!" *Theater Arts* (May 1956). Reprinted as "August 28, 1928," Foreword to *The Threepenny Opera*. Translated by Eric Bentley and Desmond I. Vesey.   New York: Grove Press, 1964.

_____. "Kurt Weill's Universal Appeal." *Music Journal* 17 (January 1959):48.

Merkling, Frank. "The Saga of Jenny." *Opera News* 23 (December 1958):32-33.

Padmore, Elaine. "Kurt Weill." *Music and Musicians* 21 (October 1972):34-40.

"Protagonist of Music in the Theater." *The American Hebrew* (8 January 1937):756-60.

Redlich, Hans. "Kurt Weill." *Music Review* 11 (August 1950):208.

Rognoni, Luigi. "Kurt Weill e la 'Gebrauchsmusik'." *Il Diapason* 1 (April 1950):10-14.

Sabin, Robert. "Kurt Weill: Theatre Man of His Time." *Musical America* 70 (April 1950):7, 49.

Stern, Guy. "Woman with a Mission: Lotte Lenya Stands Guard Over Kurt Weill's Music." *The Theatre: A Magazine of Drama-Comedy-Music* 1 (July 1959):12-13, 44-45.

*Strobel, Heinrich. "Erinnerung an Kurt Weill." *Melos* 17 (May 1950):133-36.

Taubman, Howard. "From Long-Hair to Short." *New York Times*, 23 January 1948.

"The Story of Kurt Weill." *Music Journal* 13 (March 1955):27-30.

Thomson, Virgil. "Kurt Weill." *New York Herald-Tribune*, 9 April 1950.

_____. "Memorial to Weill." *New York Herald-Tribune*, 5 February 1951.

Vogel, Johann Peter.   "Kurt Weill auf den Festwochen." *Musica* 29 (November-December   1975):498-99.

Weinraub, Bernard. "Lenya on Weill: The Memory Lingers On." *New York Times*, 25 October 1964.

Whitwell, David.   "Hindemith, Blacher, Weill, and Busoni—Their Music for Winds." *The Instrumentalist* 23   (February   1969):39-40.

Willnauer, Franz.   "Vom Schiffbauerdamm zum Broadway—Weg und Werk Kurt Weills." *Opern Welt* (April 1970):44-48.

Wilson, J. S. "Weill—Period Spokesman." *New York Times*, 2 August 1964.

E.   Articles in Music Dictionaries and Encyclopedias

Baker's Biographical Dictionary of Musicians, 5th ed. S.v. "Weill, Kurt."

Redlich, Hans F.   "Kurt Weill." *Grove's Dictionary of Music and Musicians.*   5th ed. Vol. 9:238-40.

Stone, Kurt. "Kurt Weill." *Die Musik in Geschichte und Gegenwart* 14:386-89.

II.   Criticism of Individual Compositions

A. *Aufstieg und Fall der Stadt Mahagonny* and *Mahagonny-Songspiel*

"Background to *Mahagonny*." *Opera* 14 (February 1963):84-89.

Blitzstein, Marc. "On 'Mahagonny'." *The Score: A Music Magazine* 23 (July 1958):11-13.

Branscombe, Peter.   "Brecht, Weill and 'Mahagonny'." *Musical Times* 102 (August 1961):483-84.

Braunmuller, A. R.   Introduction to *The Rise and Fall of the City of Mahagonny*. Translated by W. H. Auden and Chester Kallman.   Boston: David R. Godine, 1976.

Drew, David. "The History of Mahagonny." *Musical Times* 104 (January 1963):18-24.
Joachim. H. "Parodie macht noch keine Zeitoper; Brecht/Weill's 'Mahagonny' nach drei Jahrzehnten." *Neue Zeitschrift für Musik* 123 (November 1962):510-11.
Leydi, Roberto. "Precisazioni su 'Mahagonny' e altre questioni a proposito di Kurt Weill." *La Rassegna Musicale* 32 (1962):195-209.
Lenya, Lotte. "Lotte Lenya Remembers *Mahagonny*." Insert Notes to *Aufstieg und Fall der Stadt Mahagonny*, Columbia recording, KL-5271 (K3L-243).
Stuckenschmidt, H. H. "City of Nets." Insert Notes to *Aufstieg und Fall der Stadt Mahagonny*, Columbia recording KL-5271 (K3L-243).

B. Die Dreigroschenoper

Aufricht, Ernst Joseph. "Die Moritat vom Mackie Messer." *Melos* 33 (November 1966):359-63.
*Bloch, Ernst. "Lied der Seeräuber-Jenny in der *Dreigroschenoper*." *Anbruch* 11 (January 1929):125-27.
Drew, David. "Weill und *Die Dreigroschenoper*." Insert Notes to *Die Dreigroschenoper*, Columbia recording, 02S 201.
Heinsheimer, Hans W. "Film Opera—Screen vs. Stage." *Modern Music* 8 (March-April 1931):10-14.
Keller, Hans. "The Threepenny Opera." *Music Review* 17 (May 1956):153-54.
Koegler, Horst. "Rebirth and Homecoming." Insert Notes to *Die Dreigroschenoper*, Columbia recording, 02S 201.
Mersmann, Hans; Schultze-Ritter, Hans; and Strobel, Heinrich. "Zur Soziologie der Musik: *Die Dreigroschenoper* von Brecht-Weill." *Melos* 8 (January 1929):15-17.
Mitchell, Donald. "Kurt Weill's 'Dreigroschenoper' and German Cabaret Opera in the 1920's." *The Chesterian* 25 (July 1950):1-6.
Tolksdorf, Cäcilie. *John Gays "Beggar's Opera" und Bert Brechts "Dreigroschenoper."* Rheinberg Rhl: Sattler & Koss, 1934.
Unseld, Siegfried, ed. *Bertolt Brechts Dreigroschenbuch.* Frankfurt am Main: Suhrkamp Verlag, 1960.

C. Der Jasager

Braun, Horst. *Untersuchungen zur Typologie der zeitgenössischen Schul- und Jugendoper.* Regensburg: Gustav Bosse Verlag, 1963.
Bridgewater, Patrick. "Arthur Waley and Brecht." *German Life and Letters* 17 (April 1964):216-32.
Drew, David. "Weill's School Opera." *Musical Times* 106 (December 1965):934-37.
Feingold, Michael. "The Difficulty of Einverständnis: A Note on *Der Jasager* and Brecht's Didactic Plays." *Yale/Theatre* 6 (Winter 1975):32-43.
Günther, Siegfried. "Lehrstück und Schuloper." *Melos* 10 (December 1931):411.
Heuss, Alfred. "Bert Brechts Schulstück vom Jasager." *Zeitschrift für Musik* 97 (June 1930):449-54.
Reinhardt, Klaus. "Eine musikalische Fassung des *Neinsagers* von Brecht im Anschluss an Weill's Schuloper *Der Jasager*." *Munterricht* 59 (October 1968):352-54.
Szondi, Peter, ed. *Bertolt Brechts Der Jasager und Der Neinsager: Vorlagen, Fassungen, Materialen.* Frankfurt am Main: Suhrkamp Verlag, 1966.
Westphal, Kurt. "Schulopern." *Schweizerische Musikzeitung* 72 (February 1932):84-87.

D. Miscellaneous

Abravanel, Maurice. "Kurt Weill, Symphonist." *Program Notes* to a Concert at Wolf Trap Farm Park, 1972.

Danuser, Hermann. "25. Berliner Festwochen." *Schweizerische Musikzeitung* 116 (January-February 1976):28-29.

Drew, David. Introduction and Notes to *Kurt Weill*, Deutsche Grammophon recording, 2709-064; pp. 16-19.

_____. "Topicality and the Universal: The Strange Case of Weill's *Die Bürgschaft*." *Music & Letters* 39 (July 1958):242-55.

_____. "Two Weill Scores." [Violin Concerto] *Musical Times* 107 (September 1966): 797-98.

_____. Program Notes to "Four Concerts by the London Sinfonietta," March 1977.

_____. Insert Notes to *Happy End*, Columbia recording, OL 5630 (COS 2032).

_____. Insert Notes to Symphony no. 1, Colouste Gulbenkian Foundation Series 6 recording (Argo ZRG 755).

Goodman, Randolph. "The Seven Deadly Sins of the Lower Middle Class." *From Script to Stage: Eight Modern Plays*. San Francisco: Rinehart Press, 1971. pp. 487-537.

Kemp, Ian. Insert Notes to Symphony no. 2, Colouste Gulbenkian Foundation Series 6 recording (Argo ZRG 755).

Kowalke, Kim H. "*Der Lindberghflug*: Kurt Weill's Musical Tribute to Lindbergh." *Missouri Historical Society Bulletin* 33 (April 1977):193-96.

Vogel, Johann Peter. "Kurt Weill auf den Festwochen." *Musica* 29 (November-December 1975):498-99.

Wagner, Klaus. "Weills 1. Sinfonie nach einem halben Jahrhundert in Hamburg." *Melos* 38 (May 1971):204-5.

III.   Weill and His Collaborators

A.   Bertolt Brecht

1.   Brecht's Own Works

Brecht, Bertolt. *Bertolt Brechts Arbeitsjournal.* Edited by Werner Hecht. 3 vols. Frankfurt am Main: Suhrkamp Verlag, 1972.

_____. *Die Hauspostille: Manual of Piety.* Edited and translated by Eric Bentley. New York: Grove Press, 1966.

_____. *Gesammelte Werke.* Edited by Elisabeth Hauptmann and Werner Hecht. 20 vols. Frankfurt am Main: Suhrkamp Verlag, 1967.

_____. *Brecht on Theatre: The Development of an Aesthetic.* Edited and translated by John Willett. New York: Hill and Wang, 1964.

2.   Books

Bronnen, Arnolt. *Tage mit Bertolt Brecht.* Vienna: Kurt Desch Verlag, 1960.

Demetz, Peter, ed. *Brecht: A Collection of Critical Essays.* Englewood Cliffs, New Jersey: Prentice-Hall, 1962.

Esslin, Martin. *Brecht: The Man and His Work.* Garden City, New York: Doubleday & Co., 1961.

Ewen, Frederic. *Bertolt Brecht: His Life, His Art, and His Times.* New York: Citadel Press, 1969.

Fassmann, Kurt. *Brecht: Eine Bildbiographie.* Munich: Kindler Verlag, 1958.

Grimm, Reinhold. *Bertolt Brecht.* 3rd. ed. Stuttgart: J. B. Metzlersche Verlagsbuchhandlung, 1971.

_____. *Episches Theater.* Berlin: Kiepenheuer und Witsch, 1966.

Hecht, Werner; Bunge, Hans-Joachim; and Rülicke-Weiler, Käthe. *Bertolt Brecht, sein Leben und Werk.* Berlin: Volk und Wissin Volkseigener Verlag, 1969.

Hecht, Werner. *Brechts Weg zum epischen Theater: Beitrag zur Entwicklung des epischen Theaters 1918-1933.* Berlin: Henschelverlag, 1962.

Irmer, Hans-Jochen. *Brecht und das musikalische Theater.* Berlin: Verband der Theaterschaffenden der DDR, 1972.

Klotz, Volker. *Bertolt Brecht: Versuch über das Werk.* Darmstadt: Hermann Gentner Verlag, 1957.

Marsch, Edgar. *Brecht Kommentar zum lyrischen Werk.* Munich: Winkler Verlag, 1974.

McLean, Sammy. *The Bänkelsang and the Works of Bertolt Brecht.* The Hague: Mouton, 1972.

Schumacher, Ernst. *Die Dramatischen Versuche Bertolt Brechts 1918-1933.* Berlin: Rutten & Loening, 1955.

Völker, Klaus. *Brecht Chronicle.* Translated by Fred Wieck. New York: Seabury Press, 1975.

Willett, John. *The Theatre of Bertolt Brecht: A Study from Eight Aspects.* New York: New Directions, 1959.

3. Essays in Periodicals

Dneprow, W. "Die revolutionäre Moral Brechts." *Kunst und Literatur* 19 (February 1971):172-88.

Drew, David. "Brecht versus Opera: Some Comments." *The Score: A Music Magazine* 23 (July 1958):7-10.

Hecht, Werner. "The Development of Brecht's Theory of the Epic Theatre 1918-1933." *Tulane Drama Review* 6 (September 1961):40-97.

Marx, Robert. "The Operatic Brecht." *American Scholar* 44 (March 1975):283-90.

Pischner, H. "Brecht und die gesellschaftliche Funktion der Musik." *Musik und Gesellschaft* 18 (February 1968):75-86.

Reinhardt, Martin. "Brecht und das musikalische Theater." *Melos* 34 (December 1967): 441-44.

B. Georg Kaiser

Kaiser, Georg. *The Protagonist.* Translated by H. F. Garten. *Tulane Drama Review* 5 (December 1960):133-44.

Kenworthy, B. J. *Georg Kaiser.* Oxford: Basil Blackwell, 1957.

Koenigsgarten, Hugo F. "Georg Kaiser, The Leading Playwright of Expressionism." *German Life and Letters* 3 (1938-39):195-205.

Paulsen, Wolfgang. *Georg Kaiser: Die Perspektiven seines Werkes.* Tübingen: Max Niemeyer Verlag, 1960.

Shürer, Ernst. *Georg Kaiser und Bertolt Brecht: Ueber Leben und Werk.* Frankfurt am Main: Athenäum Verlag, 1971.

C. Other Collaborators

Anderson, Maxwell. "The Playwrights' Birthday." *New York Times*, 10 October 1948.

Aufricht, Ernst Josef. *Erzähle, damit du dein Recht erweist.* Munich: Deutscher Taschenbuch Verlag, 1969.

Becher, Johannes R. *Gesammelte Werke von Johannes R. Becher.* Vol. 7: *Dramatische Dichtungen.* Berlin: Aufbau Verlag, 1966-74.

Becher, Lilly. *Johannes R. Becher: Bild Chronik seines Lebens.* Berlin: Aufbau Verlag, 1963.

Bronnen, Arnolt. *Katalaunische Schlacht.* Berlin: E. Rowohlt, 1924.

Cowen, Roy C. *Christian Dietrich Grabbe.* New York: Twayne Publishers, 1972.

Feuchtwanger, Lion. *Gesammelte Werke.* Vol. 2: *Stücke in Prosa.* Amsterdam: Querido Verlag, 1936.

*Goll, Iwan. "Flucht in die Oper." *Blätter der Staatsoper* 8 (February 1927):10-11.

Grabbe, Christian Dietrich. *Werke und Brief: Historisch-kritische Gesamtausgabe.* Edited by the Academie der Wissenschaften in Göttingen. Emsdetten: Verlag Lechte, 1960.

Lania, Leo (Lazar Herrmann). *Today We Are Brothers: The Biography of a Generation.* Translated by Ralph Marlowe. Boston: Riverside Press, 1942.

Ley-Piscator, Maria. *The Piscator Experiment.* New York: James H. Heineman, 1967.

Piscator, Erwin. *Das Politische Theater.* Edited by Felix Gasbarra. Hamburg: Rowohlt Verlag, 1963.

Rilke, Rainer Maria. *The Book of Hours.* Translated by A. L. Peck. London: Hogarth Press, 1961.

IV. Musical Context

A. Weill and Busoni

Busoni, Ferruccio. "Sketch of a New Esthetic of Music." *Three Classics in the Aesthetic of Music.* Translated by Dr. Th. Baker. New York: Dover Publications, 1962.

_____. *The Essence of Music and Other Papers.* Translated by Rosamund Ley. New York: Philosophical Library, 1957.

_____. *Ueber die Möglichkeiten der Oper und Ueber die Partitur des "Doktor Faust."* Leipzig: Breitkopf & Härtel, 1926.

Dent, Edward J. *Ferruccio Busoni: A Biography.* London: Oxford University Press, 1933.

Krellman, Hanspeter. *Studien zu den Bearbeitungen Ferruccio Busonis.* Regensburg: Gustav Bosse Verlag, 1966.

Krenek, Ernst. "Busoni—Then and Now." *Modern Music* 19 (January-February 1942):88-91.

Stuckenschmidt, H. H. *Ferruccio Busoni: Chronicle of a European.* Translated by Sandra Morris. London: Calder & Boyars, 1970.

Waterhouse, John C. G. "Weill's Debt to Busoni." *Musical Times* 105 (December 1964):897-99.

B. Die Novembergruppe

Kliemann, Helga. *Die Novembergruppe.* Berlin: Gebr. Mann Verlag, 1969.

Stuckenschmidt, H. H. "Musik und Musiker in der Novembergruppe." *Anbruch* 10 (October 1928):293-95.

C. Music Festivals

Burkard, Heinrich. "Die Musikfeststädte Donaueschingen—Baden-Baden." *Anbruch* 9 (May-June 1927):221-24.

Copland, Aaron. "Baden-Baden, 1927." *Modern Music* 5 (November-December 1927):31-34.

Gutman, Hans. "The Festivals as Music Barometers." *Modern Music* 8 (November-December 1930):27-32.

Laux, Karl. "Skandal in Baden-Baden." *Hindemith-Jahrbuch II.* Mainz: B. Schotts Söhne, 1972.

Preussner, Eberhard. "Deutsche Kammermusik: Baden-Baden 1927." *Die Musik* 19 (September 1927):884-92.

D. Music in Germany

Gutman, Hans. "Berlin and Modern Works." *Modern Music* 6 (November-December 1928):40-42.

_____. "Französische Musik in Deutschland." *Anbruch* 12 (April-May 1930):163-65.

_____. "Young Germany, 1930." *Modern Music* 7 (February-March 1930):3-10.

Heinsheimer, Hans. "A New Patron for Music." *Modern Music* 8 (January-February 1931):14-19.

_____. *Best Regards to Aïda.* New York: Alfred A. Knopf, 1968.

_____. "German Music on the Breadline." *Modern Music* 9 (March-April 1932):115-20.

_____. *Menagerie in F Sharp.* Garden City, New Jersey: Doubleday, 1947.

_____. "Nightmare in Germany." *Modern Music* 10 (January-February 1933):115-17.

Preussner, Eberhard. "Germany's New Music Literature." *Modern Music* 7 (February-March 1930):38-41.

Redlich, Hans. "Die Kompositorische Situation von 1930." *Anbruch* 12 (June 1930):187-90.

Reger, Erik. "Die Musikalische Welt im Maschinenzeitalter." *Die Musik* 20 (February 1928):338-45.

Sachs, Joel. "Some Aspects of Musical Politics in Pre-Nazi Germany." *Perspectives of New Music* 9 (Fall-Winter 1970):74-95.

Schrenk, Oswald. *Berlin und die Musik: Zweihundert Jahre Musikleben einer Stadt, 1740-1940.* Berlin: Ed. Bote & G. Bock, 1940.

Weissmann, Adolf. "Berliner Musik." *Anbruch* 6 (March 1924):100-105.

E. The New Music

Bekker, Paul. "Was ist 'neue' Musik?" *Die Musik* 20 (December 1927):161-74.

_____. "Zeitwende." *Die Musik* 15 (October 1922):1-10.

Butting, Max. "Music of and for the Radio." *Modern Music* 8 (March-April 1931):15-19.

Closson, Hermann. "The Case Against 'Gebrauchsmusik'." *Modern Music* 7 (February-March 1930):15-19.

Cowell, Henry. "New Terms for New Music." *Modern Music* 5 (May-June 1928):21-27.

Einstein, Alfred. "The Newer Counterpoint." *Modern Music* 6 (November-December 1928):29-34.

Hammond, Richard. "Music and the Dance Theatre." *Modern Music* 7 (February-March 1930):20-23.

Heinsheimer, Hans, and Stefan, Paul, eds. *25 Jahre neue Musik.* Vienna: Universal-Edition, 1925.

Katz, Eric. "Vokalmusik im Schaffen der Gegenwart: Moderne Liederkomponisten." *Anbruch* 10 (November-December 1928):399-408.

Lourie, Arthur. "Neogothic and Neoclassic." *Modern Music* 5 (March-April 1928):3-8.

Mauck, E. "Die Musik im Kabarett." *Berliner Tageblatt*, 22 February 1925.

Peyser, Herbert F. "Some Fallacies of Modern Anti-Wagnerism." *Musical Quarterly* 12 (April 1926):175-89.

Preussner, Eberhard. "Der Wendepunkt in der Modernen Musik oder Die Einfachheit der neuen Musik." *Die Musik* 21 (March 1929):415-18.

Sabaneyev, Leonide. "To Conquer New Tonal Regions." *Modern Music* 4 (May-June 1927):15-19.

Seeger, Charles Louis. "On Dissonant Counterpoint." *Modern Music* 7 (June-July 1930):25-31.

Steinhard, Erich. "Bemerkungen zum Expressionismus." *Die Musik* 15 (October 1922):49-50.

Tiessen, Heinz. *Zur Geschichte der Jungsten Musik (1913-28): Probleme und Entwicklungen.* Mainz: Der Melos Verlag, 1929.

Wellesz, Egon. "Probleme der Modernen Musik." *Anbruch* 6 (November-December 1924):392-402.

F. Jazz, Dance Music, Popular Music and European Art Music

Belaiev, Victor. "Stravinsky, Weill, and Jazz." *Christian Science Monitor*, 18 May 1929.

Blitzstein, Marc. "Popular Music—An Invasion." *Modern Music* 10 (January-February 1933):96-102.

Copland, Aaron. "Jazz Structure and Influence." *Modern Music* 4 (January-February 1927):9-14.

Holl, Karl. "Jazz am Konservatorium." *Frankfurter Zeitung*, 25 November 1927.

Krug, Walter. "Ueber das Wesen des Rhythmus in der 'zeitgemassen' Musik, gesehen am
Beispiel von Brechts und Weills 'Mahagonny'." *Kölnische Zeitung*, 19 December 1927.

Melichar, Alois. "Walzer und Jazz." *Die Musik* 20 (February 1928):345-49.

Osgood, Henry O. "The Blues." *Modern Music* 4 (November-December 1926):25-28.

Schildberger, Hermann. "Jazz-Musik." *Die Musik* 17 (September 1925):914-23.

Seldes, Gilbert. "Jazz Opera or Ballet?" *Modern Music* 3 (January-February 1926):10-16.

Stefan, Paul. "Rhythmus der Generation." *Anbruch* 10 (February 1928):39-56.

Stuckenschmidt, H. H. "Jazz auf der Opernbühne." *Vossische Zeitung*, 8 October 1927.

_____. "Hellenic Jazz." *Modern Music* 7 (April-May 1930):22-25.

G. Collections of Criticism

Adorno, Theodor W. *Philosophie der neuen Musik.* 3rd Edition. Frankfurt am Main: Europaische Verlags-Anstalt, 1966.

_____. *Moments musicaux; neu gedruckte Aufsätze 1928-62.* Frankfurt am Main: Suhrkamp Verlag, 1964.

Copland, Aaron. *The New Music: 1900-1960.* Revised Edition. New York: Norton & Co., 1968.

_____. *Copland On Music.* Garden City, New Jersey: Doubleday, 1960.

Demuth, Norman. *Musical Trends in the Twentieth Century.* London: Rockliff, 1952.

Rosenfeld, Paul. *Discoveries of a Music Critic.* New York: Harcourt, Brace and Co., 1936.

Thomson, Virgil. *The State of Music.* New York: W. Morrow, 1939.

V. Operatic Context

A. Essays: 1920 - 1935

Altmann, Wilhelm. "Ur- und Erstaufführungen von Opernwerken auf deutschen Bühnen in den letzten Spielzeiten 1899/1900 bis 1924/25." *Jahrbuch der Universal-Edition.* Vienna: Universal-Edition, 1926.

Antheil, George. "Wanted—Opera by and for Americans." *Modern Music* 7 (June-July 1930):11-16.

Bekker, Paul. "Von der *Rose* bis zur *Bürgschaft.*" *Die Musik* 25 (October 1932):7-11.

_____. "Die neue Oper." *Anbruch* 7 (January 1925):8-13.

_____. "The Opera Walks New Paths." Translated by Arthur Mendel. *Musical Quarterly* 21 (July 1935):266-78.

Bennett, Howard G. "Opera in Modern Germany." *Proceedings of the Music Teachers National Association* 29 (1934):65-73.

Bie, Oskar. "Stand der Oper." *Die neue Rundschau* 43 (July-December 1932):124-31.

Einstein, Alfred. "German Opera, Past and Present." *Modern Music* 11 (January-February 1934):65-72.

Günther, Siegfried. "Gegenwartsoper." *Die Musik* 20 (July 1928):718-26.

Heinsheimer, H. W. "Die Umgestaltung des Operntheaters in Deutschland." *Anbruch* 15 (August-September 1933):107-13.

Mersmann, Hans. "Unser Verhältnis zur neuen Oper." *Melos* 8 (October 1929):418-23.

Strobel, Heinrich. "Neues Operntheater." *Die Scene* 20 (March 1930):73-75.

Stuckenschmidt, H. H. "Short Operas." *Anbruch* 10 (June-July 1928):204-7.

_____. "Opera in Germany Today." *Modern Music* 13 (November-December 1935):32-37.

Weissmann, Adolph. "Germany's Latest Music Dramas." *Modern Music* 4 (May-June 1927):20-26.

B. Essays: 1935 - 1977

Drew, David. "Musical Theatre in the Weimar Republic." *Proceedings of the Royal Musical Association* 88 (1961-62):89-108.

Henning, Roslyn Brogue. "Expressionist Opera." *American-German Revue* 32 (August-September 1966):19-22.

Krenek, Ernst. "Opera between the Wars." *Modern Music* 20 (January-February 1943): 102-11.

Padmore, Elaine. "German Expressionist Opera 1910-35." *Proceedings of the Royal Musical Association* 95 (1969):41-53.

Rubsamen, Walter. "Political and Ideological Censorship of Opera." *Papers of the American Musicological Society's Annual Meeting, 1941*:30-42.

C. Books

Bekker, Paul. *Wandlungen der Oper.* Zürich and Leipzig: Orell Füssli, 1934.

Brandl, Willy. *Der Weg der Oper.* Stuttgart: Curt E. Schwab, 1949.

Brockway, Wallace, and Weinstock, Herbert. *The Opera: A History of Its Creation and Performance, 1600-1941.* 2nd ed. New York: Pantheon Books, 1962.

Burian, K. V. *Die Oper: Ihre Geschichte in Wort und Bild.* Prague: Artia, 1961.

Curjel, Hans. *Experiment Krolloper 1927-1931.* Munich: Prestel-Verlag, 1975.

Dieter, Carlin. *Operas of the Twentieth Century.* Wiesbaden: Otto Harrassowitz, 1966.

Gilman, Lawrence. *Aspects of Modern Opera.* New York: Dodd & Mead, 1924.

Grout, Donald J. *A Short History of Opera.* 2nd ed. New York: Columbia University Press, 1965.

Kapp, Julius. *Die Staatsoper Berlin 1919 bis 1925.* Stuttgart: Deutsche Verlags-Anstalt, 1925.

Loewenberg, Alfred. *Annals of Opera.* 2nd ed. 2 vols. Geneva: Societas Bibliographica, 1955.

Mohr, Albert Richard. *Die Frankfurter Oper 1924-1944.* Frankfurt am Main: Waldemar Kramer, 1971.

Panofsky, Walter. *Protest in der Oper: Das provokative Musiktheater der zwanziger Jahre.* Munich: Laokoon-Verlag, 1966.

Siegfried, Boris. *Oper im XX. Jahrhundert.* 2 vols. Wolfenbüttel: Möseler, 1962 & 1973.

Smith, Patrick J. *The Tenth Muse: A Historical Study of the Opera Libretto.* New York: Schirmer Books, 1970.

Snyder, Richard Dale. "The Use of the Comic Idea in Selected Works of Contemporary Opera." Ph.D. Dissertation [Musicology], Indiana University, 1968.

Stuckenschmidt, H. H. *Oper in dieser Zeit.* Hannover: Friedrich Verlag, 1964.

Thomas, Ernst, ed. *Die Oper im XX. Jahrhundert; Kongressbericht, Internationaler Kongress Zeitgenössisches Musiktheater Hamburg 1964.* Hamburg: Deutscher Musikrat, 1966.

Wellesz, Egon. *Essays on Opera.* Translated by Patricia Kean. London: Dennis Dobson, 1950.

Worbs, Hans Christoph. *Welterfolge der modernen Oper.* Berlin: Rembrandt Verlag, 1967.

VI. Theatrical Context

Brustein, Robert. *The Theatre of Revolt.* Boston: Little, Brown, & Co., 1962.

Garten, H. F. *Modern German Drama.* Fairlawn, New Jersey: Essential Books, 1959.

Jhering, Herbert. "Zeittheater." *Melos* 7 (November 1928):522-24.

_____. *Vom Reinhardt bis Brecht: Vier Jahrzehnte Theater und Film.* 3 vols. Berlin: Aufbau-Verlag, 1959.

Kerr, Alfred. *Die Welt im Drama.* Edited by Gerhard F. Hering. Cologne: Kiepenheuer & Witsch, 1954.

Rühle, Günther. *Theater für die Republik 1917-1933: Im Spiegel der Kritik.* Frankfurt am Main: S. Fischer, 1967.

VII. Political, Social, Economic and Cultural Context

Appelbaum, Stanley, ed. *Simplicissimus: 180 Satirical Drawings from the Famous German Weekly.* New York: Dover Publications, 1975.

Eyck, Erich. *A History of the Weimar Republic.* Translated by Harlan P. Hanson and G. L. Waite. 2 vols. Cambridge, Mass.: Harvard University Press, 1962-63.

Friedrich, Otto. *Before the Deluge: A Portrait of Berlin in the 1920's.* New York: Harper & Row, 1972.

Gay, Peter. *Weimar Culture: The Outsider as Insider.* New York: Harper & Row, 1968.

Heinsheimer, Hans W. "The Berlin of *Threepenny Opera.*" Insert Notes for *Die Dreigroschenoper,* Columbia recording, 02S 201.

Nelson, Walter Henry. *The Berliners: Their Saga and Their City.* New York: D. McKay, 1969.

Solbrig, Ingeborg H. "Cultural and Political Perspectives of the Weimar Republic."
Hindemith-Jahrbuch IV. Mainz: B. Schotts Söhne, 1975.

Vermeil, Edmond. *Germany in the Twentieth Century: A Political and Cultural History of the Weimar Republic and the Third Reich.* New York: Praeger, 1956.

Zuckmayer, Carl. *A Part of Myself: Portrait of an Epoch.* Translated by Richard & Clara Winston. London: Secker & Warburg, 1970.

VIII. Theoretical and Historical References

Austin, William W. *Music in the Twentieth Century from Debussy through Stravinsky.* New York: W. W. Norton, 1966.

Bailey, Robert. "The Genesis of *Tristan und Isolde* and a Study of Wagner's Sketches and Drafts for the First Act." Ph.D. Dissertation, Princeton University, 1969.

Chrisman, Richard A. "A Theory of Axis-Tonality for Twentieth-Century Music." Ph.D. Dissertation [Music Theory], Yale University, 1969.

Ewen, David. *American Composers Today: A Biographical and Critical Guide.* New York: H. W. Wilson, 1949.

Forte, Allen. *The Structure of Atonal Music.* New Haven: Yale University Press, 1973.

Graf, Max. *Geschichte und Geist der modernen Musik.* Stuttgart: Humboldt-Verlag, 1953.

Greer, Thomas H. "Music and Its Relation to Futurism, Cubism, Dadaism, and Surrealism: 1905-50." Ph.D. Dissertation, North Texas State University, 1969.

Grohmann, Will. *Zwischen den beiden Kriegen.* Berlin: Suhrkamp Verlag, 1953.

Hartog, Howard, ed. *European Music in the Twentieth Century.* New York: Frederick A. Proeger, 1957.

Nestler, Gerhard. *Der Stil in der Neuen Musik.* Freiburg: Atlantis Verlag, 1958.

Neumeyer, David. "Counterpoint and Pitch Structure in the Early Music of Hindemith." Ph.D. Dissertation [Music Theory], Yale University, 1976.

Oehlmann, Werner. *Die Musik des 20. Jahrhunderts.* Berlin: W. DeGruyter, 1961.

Prieberg, Frederick K. *Lexikon der Neuen Musik.* Munich: K. Alber, 1958.

Schoenberg, Arnold. *Harmonielehre.* Leipzig, Vienna: Universal-Edition, 1911.

_____. *Structural Functions of Harmony.* London: Williams & Norgate, 1954.

Schuh, Will. *Von neuer Musik.* Zürich: Atlantis Verlag, 1955.

Slonimsky, Nicolas. *Music Since 1900.* 4th ed. New York: C. Scribner's Sons, 1971.

Sternfeld, F. W., ed. *A History of Western Music.* Vol. 5: *Music in the Modern Age.* London: Weidenfeld & Nicolson, 1973.

Stuckenschmidt, H. H. *Twentieth Century Composers II: Germany and Central Europe.* London: Weidenfeld & Nicolson, 1971.

_____. *Neue Musik.* Berlin: Suhrkamp Verlag, 1951.

Vinton, John, ed. *Dictionary of Contemporary Music.* New York: E. P. Dutton, 1971.

INDEX

INDEX